SELECTIONS FROM *ṢUBḤ AL-A'SHĀ* BY AL-QALQASHANDĪ, CLERK OF THE MAMLUK COURT

Ṣubḥ al-A'shā by al-Qalqashandī is a manual for chancery clerks completed in 1412 and a vital source of information on Fatimid and Mamluk Egypt which, for the first time, has been translated into English.

The text provides valuable insight into the Mamluk and earlier Muslim eras. The selections presented in this volume describe Cairo, Fustat and the Cairo Citadel and give a detailed picture of the Fatimid (AD 969–1172), Ayyubid (AD 1172–1250) and Mamluk (AD 1250–1412) court customs, rituals and protocols, and depict how the Mamluk Sultanate was ruled. It also contains a wealth of details covering the geography, history and state administration systems of medieval Egypt. An introduction preceding the translation contextualizes al-Qalqashandī's role and manuscript, as well as introducing the man himself, while detailed notes accompany the translation to explain and elaborate on the content of the material. The volume concludes with an extensive glossary of terms which forms a mini-encyclopaedia of the Fatimid and Mamluk periods.

This translation will be a valuable resource for any student of medieval Islamic history.

Heba El-Toudy is an independent researcher and translator.

Tarek Galal Abdelhamid is an assistant professor of architecture at MSA University, Egypt. His previous publications include *The Mamluk Army* (2013), *War In the Mamluk Period* (2013), *A Concise History of North Syria in the Mamluk Period* (2013) and *Lectures on Computer Applications in Archaeology* (2014, 2015).

ROUTLEDGE MEDIEVAL TRANSLATIONS

In the same series:

Guta Law and Guta Saga edited by *Christine I. Peel*

The Danish Medieval Laws edited by *Ditlev Tamm and Helle Vogt*

Selections from *Ṣubḥ al-A'shā by al-Qalqashandī, Clerk of the Mamluk Court* translated and edited by Heba El-Toudy, revised and edited by Tarek Galal Abdelhamid.

SELECTIONS FROM *ṢUBḤ AL-A'SHĀ* BY AL-QALQASHANDĪ, CLERK OF THE MAMLUK COURT

Egypt: "Seats of Government" and "Regulations of the Kingdom", From Early Islam to the Mamluks

Edited by Heba El-Toudy and Tarek Galal Abdelhamid

Routledge
Taylor & Francis Group
LONDON AND NEW YORK

First published 2017
by Routledge
2 Park Square, Milton Park, Abingdon, Oxon OX14 4RN

and by Routledge
711 Third Avenue, New York, NY 10017

Routledge is an imprint of the Taylor & Francis Group, an informa business

British Library Cataloguing-in-Publication Data
A catalogue record for this book is available from the British Library

Library of Congress Cataloging-in-Publication Data
A catalog record for this book has been requested

ISBN: 978-1-138-66993-2 (hbk)
ISBN: 978-1-315-40526-1 (ebk)

Typeset in Times New Roman
by Swales & Willis Ltd, Exeter, Devon, UK

MIX
Paper from responsible sources
FSC
www.fsc.org
FSC® C013056

Printed and bound in Great Britain by
TJ International Ltd, Padstow, Cornwall

CONTENTS

List of Maps vii

Introduction **1**
Ṣubḥ al-A'shā, **On the Egyptian Lands**

PART I
The Twelfth Purpose: The Established Seats of Government **27**

The First Seat of Government: Fustat **29**
The Neighbourhoods of Fustat 33
The Houses of Fustat 35
The House of the Amir 38
The Expansion and Decline of Fustat 41
Al-Rawḍa Island 44
The Establishment of al-Mahrānī 45
Al-Ḥabash Pond 46
The Mosques of Fustat 48
The Madrasas of Fustat 57
The Khanqas and Ribats of Fustat 59
The Hospital 60

The Second Seat of Government: Cairo **61**
The Fatimid Palaces 64
The Gates and Walls of Cairo 71
The Neighbourhoods of Cairo 78
The Mosques of Cairo 96
The Madrasas of Cairo 100
The Khanqas and Ribats of Cairo 103
The Five-Prayer Mosques 104

The Hospital 104
Construction and Description of Cairo 106

The Third Seat of Government: The Citadel **108**
The Cemetery 120

PART II
The Third Purpose: The Regulation of the Kingdom **123**

The First Status: Rulers Appointed by the Caliphate until the end of the Ikshidid Dynasty **125**

The Second Status: Status of the Egyptian Lands under the Fatimids **126**
The First Clause: Royal Instruments 126
The Second Clause: The Caliph's Warehouses 134
The Third Clause: The Armies 143
The Fourth Clause: The Holders of Offices 148
The Fifth Clause: The Appearance of the Caliph 183
The Sixth Clause: The Fleets, Ruling Subjects and Persuading Opponents 222
The Seventh Clause: The Salaries, Grants and Banquets 226
The Eighth End: The Vizier's Audiences for Grievances 234

The Third Status: The Ayyubids and Mamluks **235**
The First Purpose: The Protocols and Instruments of Royalty 237
The Second Purpose: The Sultan's Warehouses 241
The Third Purpose: The Kingdom's Dignitaries and Holders of Posts 249
The Fourth Purpose: The Attire of the Kingdom's Dignitaries 288
The Fifth Purpose: The Sultan's Appearance in Royal Protocol 294
The Sixth Purpose: The Salaries 301
The Seventh Purpose: The Special Territories 310
The Eighth Purpose: How News Reaches the Sultan 313
The Ninth Purpose: The Appearance and Regulation of Amirs 315
The Tenth Purpose: The Governors, Men of the Sword 319

Glossary 332
Bibliography 451
Index 462

MAPS

INTRODUCTION

Ṣubḥ al-A'shā (*Morning of the Nightblind*), *Kitab Ṣubḥ al-A'shā* (*Book of the Morning of the Nightblind*) *Ṣubḥ al-A'shā fī Ṣinā'at al-Inshā* (*Morning of the Nightblind on the Craft of Composition*), *Ṣubḥ al-A'shā fī Kitābat al-Inshā* (*Morning of the Nightblind on the Writing of Compositions*) are among the variant names of this colossal fifteenth-century work by a renowned Egyptian clerk of the Mamluk court, al-Qalqashandī. The book is a manual for chancery clerks, or official scribes, providing them with the various composition formulae required for their work, covering numerous topics on the principles, needs, skills and necessary knowledge for proper composition. Although the linguistic, literary and calligraphic aspects of writing take up a considerable proportion of the work; necessarily, and luckily for all medieval scholars, it also contains a wealth of information covering the geography, history and state administration systems of Egypt, Syria and other Muslim lands. This information was deemed part of the basic knowledge necessary for those working in the Chancery Bureau (*dīwān al-inshā'*). This translation specifically selects several segments related to Egypt which give us a wealth of information especially on the Mamluk period, the era which the author witnessed. The selected segments also contain information that covers earlier historical eras dating back to the Islamic conquest of Egypt, with elaborate details especially of the Fatimid period.

The importance of this book comes from the fact that it is written by al-Qalqashandī (AH 756–820/AD 1355–1418), an experienced and esteemed official scribe in the Chancery Bureau, the official bureau for all state correspondence in the court of the Mamluk sultans al- Ẓahir Barquq and his son al-Naṣir Farag. Due to his position and long appointment to the chancery, al-Qalqashandī had great experience and knowledge of the workings of government, protocol, treaties and the other intricacies of the Mamluk state. He was a scholar, educated to the highest standards of jurisprudence in his time. He was once a judge with an untarnished reputation, so we may expect his account and information to be unbiased and truthful. He was also a creative author and poet, with great mastery of the Arabic language, and was appointed to the job partly because of a mandatory requirement for the post: eloquence. With the documents he composed, he was the official voice of the Mamluk state, the official voice of the sultan and, through his scribes, he saw and recorded all decrees, treaties, monetary transactions, bequests, gifts and whatever documents were produced or passed through formal government. His reputation as a pious and honourable man adds great credibility to his testimony. His account is that of an actual eyewitness and active participant at all levels of government, which should be of the highest value due to its accuracy by one of the most honourable, educated, eloquent and learned men of his time.

What is *al-Inshā'*?

Al-inshā, al-inshā' ("literary composition") or *kitabat al-inshā'* ("writing texts or writing literary compositions") is a term used to refer to all tasks of construction or composition of documents in prose for the workings of the state,[1] that is composition of letters, state-related documents and correspondence.[2] All types of documents created in prose fall under this heading. The task of writing was considered by al-Qalqashandī to be of two main types: composition of texts (*kitābat al-inshā'*) and accounting (*kitābat al-amwāl*). He gave greater importance to the task of composition, or prose, than to accounting or even poetry and considered that those who are assigned to that task, the scribes, had to be necessarily more educated and eloquent than others to be able to fulfil their tasks.[3] The term was also used to designate a type of literature which is basically manuals for scribes on how to do their tasks, with sample letters and documents that can be used as models for their work.

During the fifteenth century, the task of writing official texts in Egypt was referred to by two terms, *kitabat al-inshā'* and *tawqi'* ("signature"). *Kitabat al-inshā'* was the term used by those who worked in the actual Chancery Bureau, while the common people used the term *tawqi'*, which refers to the directives written and signed on the different petitions brought before the ruler or his deputy: thus the signatory could be the caliph, the sultan, the wazir (first minister) or even scribes delegated to do the work. The written directive was a phrase or two summarizing the decision of what should be done with that petition, which was then officially signed and stamped for execution of that decision.[4]

Under the different Islamic dynasties, the *dīwān al-inshā'* referred to the bureau or office (*dīwān*, pl. *dawawīn*) where official documents originating from the presiding ruler were produced, signed, stamped, copied, recorded and kept:[5] that is,

1 Al-Qalqashandī, *Ṣubḥ*, Vol. 1, 54. *Al-insha'* has been also defined as "the art of expressing what is intended by choosing the appropriate expressions and arranging them accordingly" (Gully, "Epistles for Grammarians", 147).

2 See "Inshā'", *Encyclopedia of Islam*, 1242–3.

3 Al-Qalqashandī, *Ṣubḥ*, Vol. 1, 55–61.

4 Ibid. Vol. 1, 52.

5 "Chancery, in a pre-1500 Islamic administrative context, denotes an office where official documents were produced and recorded, copies of which were generally preserved in archives." Storage of documents, or the archives, was a separate process and function with its own officers and attendants, but directly related to the chancery. See Van Berkel "Archives and Chanceries".

the state archives department. This function was directly linked to the highest ruling authority in office at the time, whether he was a caliph or sultan, with close connections to his other aids, especially his viceroy or wazir, if either position existed at the time. The *dīwān* was the source from which all official decrees and correspondence originated and other correspondence received. In essence it is the official secretaryship of the ruler.[6]

The chief scribe or secretary, the overseer or chief officer responsible for the chancery, was known by many titles throughout the medieval period, depending on the dynasty and region in the Muslim lands, with the titles reflecting his main task, that of being the ruler's secretary and scribe. He was known as *kātib al-sirr* (the "Scribe of the Secret"), what we might call a "confidential secretary" or "confidential scribe", but usually, he was named according to how the *dīwān* was known at the time: if the *dīwān* was known as *dīwān al-rasā'il*, then he was known as *ṣāḥib dīwān al-rasā'il* or *mutawalli dīwān al-rasā'il*; if the *dīwān* was known as *dīwān al-mukatabāt*, then he was known as *ṣaḥib dīwān al-mukatabāt* or *mutawalli dīwān al-mukatabāt*; if the *dīwān* was known as *al-inshā'*, then he was known as *ṣaḥib dīwān al-inshā'* ("Master of the Chancery Bureau"), also known as *naẓir dīwān al-inshā'* ("Supervisor of the Chancery Bureau")[7] and other titles.[8]

The position of a scribe, and specifically the chief scribe, was obviously not one for anybody. Al-Qalqashandī gave two groups of traits that a scribe should posses. The first group are what he considers to be the basic traits: Islamic faith,[9] masculinity, freedom, adulthood, justice, eloquence, sound mind and opinion, knowledge of jurisprudence and literary arts, strong will and efficiency.[10] The second group of traits are those that scribes were traditionally expected to posses, which vary from general good and gentle manners to how the scribe handled himself with others, his appearance, attire, personal hygiene, length of beard, intelligence and many other traits.[11] Al-Qalqashandī also adds the need for an impeccable reputation,[12] proper manners and demeanour, giving ten different necessary attributes the scribe should posses that cover almost all cases to which the scribe might be exposed when dealing with his sovereign, the sultan, or with others of lower rank or with the general populace.[13]

6 The term is used by several scholars (see Bosworth, "A 'Maqāma' on Secretaryship").

7 For a summary of the term and *diwan*, see al-Maqrīzī, *Al-Mawā'iẓ* (ed. Sayyid); see also al-Qalqashandī, *Ṣubḥ*, Vol. 1, 104.

8 For example, in Morocco he was called *sahib al-qalam al-a'ala* ("Master of the Supreme Pen") (see al- Maqrīzī, *al-Mawā'iẓ* (ed. Sayyid), Vol. 3, 732).

9 This was not always followed. We have records of numerous scribes for caliphs, sultans and Mamluk amirs who were not Muslims, especially Copts in Egypt.

10 Al-Qalqashandī, *Ṣubḥ*, Vol. 1, 61–7.

11 Ibid. 67–9.

12 Ibid. 69–73.

13 Ibid. 73–89.

History of the Chancery Bureau

The art of writing for a sovereign is "probably as old as writing itself".[14] The function of the *kātib al-sirr* for a sovereign in Islam is considered to date back to the time of the Prophet Muḥammad (PBUH), with the first *kātib al-sirr* considered to be Zaid b. Thābit,[15] who was trusted by the Prophet to read correspondence that he received but that he did not want to be read by "everyone".[16] The Prophet also had numerous other scribes who were needed for different tasks and for recording the Qur'an as it was revealed to him.[17] Subsequently, each Muslim ruler had his own *kātib al-sirr* who was entrusted with all correspondence and decrees, confidential and public. Such a position entailed a close connection between the ruler and his secretary and, depending on the dynasty and era, gave its holder varying degrees of influence and control, sometimes culminating in ultimate control of the state second only to the sultan or caliph, since the importance of the post was derived from the duties of kingship. The position was sometimes closely related to that of the position of the wazir, which underwent changes in degree of importance depending on the dynasty.

The basic function of writing official documents was performed during the Prophet's time in Medina. As mentioned above, the production of official documents was handled by different scribes, with probably the first official document being the Treaty of Yathrib that outlined the relationship between the different factions in Medina. We have records of other correspondence sent by the Prophet, such as his letters to the rulers of Egypt and Byzantium, the Treaty of Ḥudaibiyya and other documents that were necessary for the new Islamic state. The Prophet had specific scribes for the specific tasks that were performed by the Chancery Bureau, so we may consider that this means the first *dīwān* should be dated to this early stage, older than the first known *dīwān*, the Army Bureau (*dīwānal-jaish*), created by Caliph ʿUmar b. al-Khattāb.[18] Subsequently, during the times of the caliphs, other offices necessary for the administration of the countries conquered by the Arabs were created, in continuity with the existing systems in the pre-Islamic languages (Greek, Coptic and Persian). Arabic was gradually introduced, sometimes with bi-lingual documents being used in the provinces with some Islamic additions, as was the use of the same legal formulae and epistolary conventions throughout the Islamic lands.

Under the Umayyads, offices for handling state-issued documents were established in both the capital, Damascus, and in the provinces, with a *dīwān* for seals

14 Gully, "Epistles for Grammarians", 147; for a detailed history of the chancery, see al-Qalqashandī, *Ṣubḥ*, Vol. 1, 89–100.

15 Zaid was entrusted by Caliph Abu Bakr to organize the first collection of the Qur'an in one book.

16 Al-Maqrīzī, *Al-Mawā'iẓ* (ed. Sayyid), Vol. 3, 730–31; see also al-Qalqashandī, *Ṣubḥ*, Vol. 1, 89–100.

17 Al-Qalqashandī gives the names of more than 30 scribes for the Prophet, with Moʿaiwiyah b. Abi Sufyan and Zaid b. Thabet being the ones with the longest history in that task (*Ṣubḥ*, Vol. 1, 92).

18 See ibid. Vol. 1, 91–2.

(*dīwān al-akhtām*) and subsequently an archive, or a *dīwān* for copying and filing copies of the formal letters and other documents.[19] A clear centralized and uniform system for those offices emerged in the reign of Caliph ʿAbdal-Malik b. Marawān (r. AH 65–86 / AD 685–705) with Arabic established as the one official language throughout the Islamic state, at least in the capital Damascus, where a chancery was firmly established, while the provinces continued with bi-lingual use for a while longer.[20] Eventually, high standard literary texts were produced in the chancery, and its head was known as *ṣaḥib dīwān al-rasāʾil* ("Master of the Office of Letters"). The head of the *dīwān* under the Umayyad caliph Marwān b. Muḥammad (r. AH 127–32 / AD 744–50) was the well-known scribe ʿAbd al-Ḥamīd b. Yaḥyā (d. AH 132 /AD 750) known as ʿAbd al-Ḥamīd al-Katib ("the Scribe"), whose letters became model texts for future chancery scribes. Continuity and tradition were established with members of the *dīwān* being recruited from secretarial families.[21]

The tradition and expertise of the Chancery Bureau continued into the Abbasid period, with an increase in the production of a large and varied number of documents throughout the Islamic state.[22] From the first Abbasid caliph, Al-Saffaḥ, till the time of Harun al-Rashid, the caliphs ruled while directly overseeing the daily duties themselves. The *tawqiʿ* was an important process and one of the actions reserved by the sovereign, maintaining his authority and confirming his power, for what he decreed in his handwriting and signed with his name was an uncontested order that was to be followed by all.[23] Harun al-Rashid delegated his authority to his wazir, Jaʿafar al-Barmaky, who was the first of the Abbasid wazirs to be given the authority to act and sign decrees in his own hand instead of the sultan. With this authority, the wazir signed all decrees, bestowments, rulings for remedying injustices, monetary compensations, stipends and salaries. This gave the wazirs great power, status and political control, second only to the caliph. The wazir became responsible for the chancery, which also became known as *al-dīwān al-ʿazīz* (the "treasured office") and became the formal entity and recipient of all correspondence addressed to the caliphs, even from other kings. The chancery was sometimes supervised by individuals who did not have the same powers as the wazir, but reported directly to him, and they were called *saḥib dīwān al-inshāʾ* and sometimes *kātib al-sirr*. The many scribes employed in the *dīwān* were called *kuttab al-inshāʾ* ("chancery clerks" or "chancery scribes").[24]

Thus a model and tradition was established that was followed by subsequent ruling dynasties from Andalusia to Iran, based on the traditions of the late

19 Van Berkel, "Archives and Chanceries".

20 Ibid.

21 Ibid.; see also al-Qalqashandī, *Ṣubḥ*, Vol. 1, 93.

22 Van Berkel, "Archives and Chanceries".

23 Al-Qalqashandī, *Ṣubḥ*, Vol. 1, 110–11.

24 Al-Maqrīzī, *Al-Mawāʿiẓ* (ed. Sayyid), Vol. 3, 732; see also al-Qalqashandī, *Ṣubḥ*, Vol. 1, 93.

Umayyad and the Abbasid system of chancery, using similar terms, functions and routines in operation, with some variations depending on the dynasty.[25]

In Egypt,[26] when it was ruled by governors under the Umayyad or Abbasid dynasties, there was a Mail Bureau (*dīwān al-barid*) and its supervisor was known as *saḥib al-barid* ("Master of the Mail"). He was responsible for all mail arriving from the caliphal capitals (Madina, Kufa and Damascus) and he sent reports on the state of affairs of the country. The governors had their own scribes for the necessary correspondence, including that being sent to the caliph.[27]

Jawhar al-Ṣaqalli, the commander of the army who conquered Egypt in the name of the Fatimid caliph, personally signed his correspondence and decrees until the caliph, al-Muʿizz, arrived and signed them for himself. Under the Fatimid caliphs several wazirs were appointed who were Men of the Pen, and their influence and control varied, with Caliph al-ʿAziz Bi-Allah appointing Yaʿqūb. Killis as his wazir, delegating all authority to him, so that he could sign in place of the caliph, exerting influence and control similar to the wazirs of the Abbasid caliphs. Yaʿqūb is considered the first of the wazirs to have such control in Egypt during the Fatimid dynasty. Caliph al-Muṣtanṣir removed his wazir to the chancery, which he directed for a long time, until the time of Badr al-Jamali, the first Fatimid military wazir of the "Men of the Sword" who had complete control over all state issues. He was followed by his son al-Afḍal Shāhinshāh, who held the same position and power. From that time onwards there was a separation between the two positions, that of the wazir who had full political control and that of the chancery, with the chancery being supervised by only the most respectable and knowledgeable of men, an arrangement which was carried over to the Ayyubid and Mamluk periods.[28] The Supervisor of the Chancery in the Fatimid period was also responsible for the correspondence (*mukatabāt*), thus he was called *ṣahib dīwān al-inshāa'wa-l-mukatabāt* ("Master of the Chancery and Correspondence") and was addressed as *al-ajall* or the "most esteemed" or "most dignified"[29] and *kātib al-dast al-sharīf* ("Scribe of the Honourable Pedestal"), the pedestal being that on which the caliph sat.[30] During the Fatimid period the chancery had two more important tasks that were below the Master of the Chancery: "signing the grievances with the fine script" (*al-tawqīʿ bi-l-qalam al-daqīq fī al-maẓālim*) and

25 Van Berkel, "Archives and Chanceries". For example, during the Seljuk dynasty, the chancery was called *dīwan al-tughraa*. The *tughra* being a round emblem with the phrase *bism allah al-raḥmān al-raḥim* ("In the name of God, the merciful, the compassionate") over which the sultan's name and titles were written in a thick pen. This was used in place of the signature of the sultan on all decrees and formal documents (see al-Maqrīzī, *Al-Mawāʿiẓ* (ed. Sayyid), Vol. 3, 732).

26 Al-Qalqashandī divides the history of the chancery in Egypt into five eras, giving the names of each chief scribe under the different dynasties (see *Ṣubḥ*, Vol. 1, 93–100).

27 Al-Maqrīzī, *Al-Mawāʿiẓ* (ed. Sayyid), Vol. 3, 732–3.

28 Ibid., Vol. 3, 733. See also below and glossary.

29 See below and glossary; see also al-Baqli, *Al-Taʿrīf*, 15; A. Sayyid, *Nuzha*, 48°.

30 See below and glossary; al-Qalqashadni, *Ṣubḥ*, Vol. 1, 137.

"signing with the dignified script" (*al-tawqī' bi-l-qalam al-jalīl*). Those two tasks entailed recording the instructions of the caliph or the Head of the Chancery plus some other duties, and both entailed direct and personal contact with the caliph.[31] It is worth noting that during the Fatimid period, some caliphs had non-Muslim scribes, Egyptian Copts and Jews.[32]

Nūr al-Din Maḥmūd b. Zinkī (AH 511–69 /AD 1118–74) had his own Chancery Bureau, which was headed by a learned scribe from Isfahan, 'Imad al-Din al-Iṣfahanī[33] until Nūr al-Din's death. Al-Iṣfahanī was subsequently introduced to Salaḥ al-Dīn al-Ayyubī, founder of the Ayyubid dynasty, who appointed him first as a deputy to his wazir, Al-Qaḍī al-Faḍil, then as his own personal secretary.[34] During the reign of the Ayyubid Sultan al-Malik al-Kamil, the chancery scribes were few in number, highly honourable, reclusive and were judged with high moral standards.[35] Christian scribes were also used specifically for jobs required on Fridays, a day on which Muslim scribes did not attend the chancery.[36]

During the Bahari Mamluk period (AH 655–783 / AD 1258–1382),[37] the tradition continued. The duties of the *kātib al-sirr* entailed reading all correspondence sent to the sultan and writing responses and directives to those letters and petitions either in his own hand or by assigning lesser scribes to write the response. He was also responsible for getting the sultan's signature on those letters and, if necessary, afterwards encrypting their contents. He was further responsible for recording the sultan's decrees and sat in the audience of the sultan for review of grievances in the House of Justice (Dar al-'Adl) and read out the petitions and recorded the verdicts through the clerks. He was also responsible for the management of the council which convened to resolve important state issues in the presence of the sultan and his ruling retinue. He also mediated between the amirs and the sultan whenever there was a difference in opinion. He was responsible for all matters related to the judiciary system and scholars in the kingdom in Egypt and Syria, taking decisions on his own accord and conferring with the sultan on

31 See below on the chancery in the Fatimid period; see also al-Qalqashadni, *Ṣubḥ*, Vol. 3, 490–92.

32 For example, Abu al-Mansur b. Surdin al-Nasrani, a Copt, was the chief scribe for both al-`Aziz Bi-Allah and his son al-Hakim. A Jew by the name of Ibn Abi al-Dam al-Yahudi was one of the scribes for the caliphs al-Aamir and al-Hafiz. For a list of all scribes in the Fatimid period, see al-Qalqashadni, *Ṣubḥ*, Vol. 1, 96.

33 See al-Bundari, *Sana*, 2–6; al-Isfahani, *Al-Fatḥ al-Qissi*, 23–35.

34 'Imad al-Din al-Iṣfahanī came to be one of his most trusted aides, taking part in most of this sultan's eventful life and authoring two great works after Salaḥ al-Dīn's death: *Al-Barq al-Shami*, which is a chronicle of the life of Salah al-Din and *Al-Fatḥ al-Qissi fi al-Fatḥ al-Qudsi*, which chronicles the re-capture of Jerusalem and subsequent events. See al-Isfahani, *Al-Fatḥ al-Qissi*, 23–5.

35 To the extent that one of the scribes was dismissed from the *diwan* when it was rumoured that he was used to attending gatherings in which there was singing, a behaviour that was deemed inappropriate by the last Ayyubid sultan, al-Salih Nigm al-Din, stating that this *diwan* "does not tolerate such behaviour" (See al-Maqrīzī, *Al-Mawā'iẓ* (ed. Sayyid), Vol. 3, 733).

36 Ibid., Vol. 3, 734.

37 See al-Qalqashandī, *Ṣubḥ*, Vol. 1, 97–9.

other matters as needed. This gave the office of the *kātib al-sirr* great power, since he was needed by all other members of the ruling elite, even the viceroys.[38] The position of the wazir was annulled by al-Naṣir Muḥammad, and the function of *kātib al-sirr* or ṣa*ḥib dīwān al-inshā'* rose in prominence, together with the functions of the *dīwān*.[39] Together with the *kātib al-sirr*, a Mamluk amir was appointed with the title of *al-dawadar* ("Holder of the Inkwell"), who was responsible for the mail,[40] presenting it to the sultan and other duties, with the help of the *kātib al-sirr* who still retained his prominence and functions in the Chancery Bureau.

The two groups of scribes working in the chancery were *kuttab al-dast* ("scribes of the pedestal") and *kuttab al-darj* ("secretarial scribes"). *Kuttab al-dast* attended the audiences with the sultan, read the petitions and correspondence according to the order in which they sat, and signed the decrees with the directives reached, exactly like the *kātib al-sirr*. At the start of the Bahari Mamluk dynasty in the reign of al-Ẓahir Baibars, they were three, headed by the *kātib al-sirr*. Their number reached ten by the reign of Sultan al-Ashraf Shaʿaban. *Kuttab al-darg* recorded the directives of the *kātib al-sirr*, *kuttab al-dast*, the viceroy, the wazir or others who give rulings for petitions given. They were also called *kuttab al-inshā'*. Whenever there was an increase in *kuttab al-dast*, a similar increase was needed in *kuttab al-darg*. Other functions in the chancery were the archivist (*al-khazin*) and the controller (*al-hajib*). *Al-khazin* was responsible for storage and archiving of the documents in the chancery, while *al-hajib* was responsible for restricting entrance and exit from the *dīwān* except to those working there.[41]

In the Burji Mamluk period (AH 783–922 / AD 1382–1517), the office of *kātib al-sirr* retained its respect, prominence and functions. We have records of several learned and pious men who held the position.[42] The functions of *kātib al-sirr* and *al-dawadar* still continued as before. The prominence of the *kātib al-sirr* was still evident, which is confirmed by al-Qalqashandī's outline of his duties and the authority given to him, summarizing them in twelve basic functions: signing on behalf of the sultan, reading official correspondence directed to the sultan, drafting responses to the correspondence, enforcing proper protocol in correspondence, reading all documents issued by the chancery prior to their disbursement, handling the official mail and all matters related to the system, supervision of the carrier-pigeon system and its requirements, supervision of all matters related to the assassins for hire known as *al-fidawiyya*, supervision of spies and informants, supervision of the ambassadors and foreign embassies, supervision of the beacon towers (*al-manawir*) and the firestarters (*al-moḥriqat*), who set fires in the marches

38 This summary of the duties as outlined by al-Maqrīzī is confirmed by other references (see Al-Maqrīzī, *Al-Mawā'iẓ* (ed. Sayyid), Vol. 3, 733).

39 See al-Qalqashandī, *Ṣubḥ*, Vol. 1, 97–9.

40 Al-Maqrīzī, *Al-Mawā'iẓ* (ed. Sayyid), Vol. 3, 733. For the mail system, see Sauvaget, *La Poste*; Silverstein, "Documentary Evidence".

41 See al-Qalqashandī, *Ṣubḥ*, Vol. 1, 137–9.

42 See ibid., Vol. 1, 100–01.

and fields in case of a Mongol attack, and, finally, overseeing all general matters that benefitted the sultan and the kingdom.[43]

The numbers of the two groups of scribes working in the chancery,[44] *kuttab al-dast* and *kuttab al-darg*, gradually increased in the Burji Mamluk period. *Kuttab al-dast* reached twenty by the start of the Burji Mamluk dynasty in the reign of al-Zahir Barquq (AH 784–801 / AD 1382–99) and his son al-Nasir Farag (AH 801–15/AD 1399–1412).[45] Al-Qalqashandī recorded that in his time their number increased further till they reached 130, with their supervision becoming an unwanted job, taken only by those who were ill-suited for it. *Kuttab al-dast* became responsible for recording the important documents that were once handled by *kuttab al-darg*, who handled only minor correspondence. The position of *al-khazin* was annulled and *al-dawadar* became responsible for the archiving and other duties of *al-khazin*. The chancery also appointed helpers, each called a *mudir* (pl. *mudarā*),[46] who were responsible for taking the petitions and other documents and relaying each document down the chain of scribes, starting from *kātib al-sirr* to the different scribes below him in the chancery so that each could sign and write his directive on what needed to be done with that document.[47]

Starting from the Ayyubid period (AH 566–647 / AD 1171–1250), the chancery and its head were relatively unaffected by the violent changes in the rulers, giving *kātib al-sirr* and his staff continuity and relative security from the changes of the times. For example, Fakhr al-Din b. Luqman, *kātib al-sirr* in the reign of the last Ayyubid sultan, al-Saliḥ Nigm al-Din (d. AH 647 / AD 1250), continued into the Mamluk period serving four sultans: al-Muʿiz Aybak, al-Muẓafar Qutuz, al-Ẓahir Baibars, and al-Manṣur Qalawūn who eventually assigned him to become a chief administrator.[48] Another *kātib al-sirr*, al-Qadi Sharaf al-Din ʿAbd al-Wahab b. Faḍl-allah, served continuously under al-Ashraf Khalil b. Qalawūn, Al-Naṣir Muḥammad in his first sultanate, al-ʿAdil Katbugha, al-Manuṣr Lashin, al-Naṣir in his second sultanate, al-Muzaffar Baibars al-Jashinkir, al-Nasir Muḥammad in his third sultanate, who eventually moved him to the position of chief scribe in Damascus.[49] Usually *kātib al-sirr*'s service ended with his death and rarely due to disagreements with his patron, the sultan. This is a trend that we notice throughout the Mamluk period.[50]

43 For a detailed description of the functions see al-Qalqashandī, *Ṣubḥ*, Vol. 1, 110–30.

44 Ibid., Vol. 1, 137–9.

45 Ibid., Vol. 1, 137.

46 A term which means "the one who revolves or relays" (ibid., Vol. 1, 139). This is another meaning and different from the use of the modern term in Arabic, which means to "manage", "administer" or "direct".

47 Al-Qalqashandī, *Ṣubḥ*, Vol. 1, 139.

48 See ibid., Vol. 1, 97–8.

49 Ibid., Vol. 1, 98.

50 For other examples, see ibid., Vol. 1, 99–100.

Al-Qalqashandī

Abū al-ʿAbbās Aḥmad al-Qalqashandī is the name given on the title of his main work, *Ṣubḥ al-A'shā*. He was also known as Shihāb al-Dīn Aḥmad b. Ali b. Aḥmad al-Qalqashandī al-Shafiʿi, al-Shihab b. al-Jamal b. Abi al-Yumn al-Qalqashandī, and is also known by other names in the sources.[51] Resident of Cairo and follower of the Shāfiʿī school of interpretation and jurisprudence (AH 756–821 / AD 1355–1418), he was an excellent scholar of literature, jurisprudence and other sciences. A descendant of a tribe of Arab origins, he was born in Qalqashandah,[52] a village in the Nile delta of Egypt.[53] The name Qalqashandī was also pronounced Qarqashandī,[54] which is the modern and official pronunciation of the name of the village,[55] although that pronunciation was rarely used to refer to the author. He was well known for his humility and piety.[56] He was raised in a manner suitable for a future scholar, and was then sent to Alexandria where he lived for some time, studying with the prominent scholars of his time. In AH 777 / AD 1376, just before the age of 21, he received his diploma or certificate of eligibility (*ijāza*) in Alexandria from a well-known scholar, Ibn al-Mulaqqin, allowing him to teach and give religious scholarly rulings (*fatwā*) according to the Shāfiʿī school.[57] He became well known for his piety, honesty and knowledge and spent some time teaching jurisprudence, giving eligibility certificates to his many students.[58]

He worked as a deputy judge before he joined the Bureau of Endowments (*dīwān al-aḥbās*), where the scholars were chosen to work based on competence and piety.[59] In AH 791 / AD 1389, he joined the chancery of the sultan's court

51 The sources give several variations of his full name, including Aḥmad b. ʿAbd Allah b. Aḥmad al-Qalqashandī, Aḥmad b. ʿAbd Allah b. Aḥmad al-Qarqashandī, Aḥmad b. ʿAlī, Aḥmad b. ʿAbd Allah, Aḥmad b. ʿAbd Allah b. Muḥammad and Aḥmad b. ʿAbd Allah b. Aḥmad b. Sulaiman b. Islamʿil al-Qalqashandī also known as Ibn Abi Ghudda. Some parts of the manuscript found in Dar al-Kutub in Cairo have his name written as Aḥmad b. ʿAbd Allah b. Aḥmad b. Muhammad b. Sulaiman b. Ismaʿil. Al-Maqrīzī is the only source that uses Qarqashandī, not Qalqashandī as his last name. Al-Sakhawi specifically states that his correct name is Ibn ʿAli. See al-Samarra'i, *Al-Manhaj*, 22–3; "A Word on the Book and the Author", in *Ṣubḥ*, Vol. 14, 15 n. 1; see also al-Maqrīzī, *Kitab*, Vol. 4, sect. 1, 743–4; al-Sakhawi, *Al-Daw'*, Vol. 1, 355; Vol. 2, 8; Bauden, "Like Father, Like Son", 197.

52 See al-Maqrīzī, *Al-Suluk*, Vol. 4, sect. 1, 744.

53 In the governorate of Qalyūbiyya near the city of Tūkh.

54 See Bauden, "Like Father, Like Son", 196.

55 As can be seen on any map of Egypt and on the official list of villages in the vicinity of the city of Tūkh (see also Bauden, "Like Father, Like Son", 196).

56 "A Word on the Book and the Author", 14–15; see also Bosworth, "A 'Maqāma' on Secretaryship", 292.

57 The sources also give the name of the official scribe who recorded that eligibility certificate. See "A Word on the Book and the Author", 16.

58 Hamza, *Al-Qalqashandī*, 44–5; "A Word on the Book and the Author", 17.

59 Al-Samarra'i, *Al-Manhaj*, 3; al-Maqrīzī, *Al-Mawā'iẓ* (ed. Sayyid), Vol. 3, 734.

in Cairo, where he occupied different positions.[60] His chief was Badr al-Din b. Faḍl-Allah al-ʿUmari, who headed the chancery for Sultan al-Ẓahir Saif al-Din Barqūq (r. AH 783–801 / AD 1382–99) and had "unequalled knowledge of official procedure and protocol".[61] He had such high esteem for his master that he composed a long poetic narrative known as a *maqāma*[62] in his praise and the praise of *inshā'* in AH 791 /AD 1389.[63] His main work *Ṣubḥ al-A'shā*, was written as an elaboration on this *maqama* on the *inshā'*, written only "after careful consideration and consultation with trusty scholars".[64] He completed *Ṣubḥ al-A'shā* in AH 814 / AD 1411.[65] Al-Qalqashandī authored several other works, including *Ḍaw' al-Ṣubḥ al-Musfir wa Janyi al-Dawḥ al-Muthmir* (*The Shining Morning Light and the Reaping of Fruitful Trees*), which is an abridged version of *Ṣubḥ al-A'shā*; *al-Ghuyūth al-Hawāmi' fī Sharḥ Jāmi' al-Muḫtaṣarāt wa Muḫtaṣirāt al-Jawāmi'* (*The Flooding Rains: On the Explanation of the Collection of Summaries and the Summarizations of Compilations*), which is a book on jurisprudence according to the Shāfiʿī school;[66] *Nihāyat al-Arab fī Ma'rifat Qabā'il al-'Arab* or *Nihāyat al-Arab fī ma'rifat Ansāb al-'Arab* (*The Goal's End: On the Knowledge of Arab Tribes or On the Knowledge of the Genealogy of Arabs*), a book on the genealogy of Arab tribes, indexed alphabetically; *Qalā'id al-Jumān fī Qabā'il al-'Urbān* or *Qalā'id al-Jumān fī al-ta'rīf bi Qabā'il 'Arab al-Zamān* (*The Pearl Necklaces: On Arab Tribes or On Knowing the Arab Tribes of the Time*), another indexed work on the genealogy of Arab tribes, which he finished in AH 181 / AD 1416; *Ma'āthir al-Ināfa fī Ma'ālim al-Khilāfa* (*The Memorable Past: On Aspects of the Caliphate*), on the caliphate, its conditions, its history, and the correspondences, decrees, and other documents relevant to it, which he also finished in AH 819 / AD 1416.[67] He also authored numerous letters some of which are included in *Ṣubḥ al-A'shā*.[68]

Little is known of his private life, but his *maqāma* is almost autobiographical, justifying why he chose to work in *inshā'*, finally concluding that it is the most

60 "A Word on the Book and the Author", 17; al-Samarra'i, *Al-Manhaj*, 31.

61 Bosworth, "A 'Maqāma' on Secretaryship", 292–3.

62 A *maqāma* is a form of literary prose that uses rhyming phrases. It is a genre in Arabic literature that was known for at least a thousand years. For a definition and concise history, and translation, see Bosworth, "A 'Maqāma' on Secretaryship", 291–2. The original text can be found in al-Qalqashandī, *Ṣubḥ*, Vol. 14, 112–28.

63 Entitled *Al-Kawākib al-Durriyya fi'l-Manāqib al-Badriyya* (*The Shining Stars: Concerning the Excellences of Badr al-Din*) (see Bosworth, "A 'Maqāma' on Secretaryship", 293; see also "A Word on the Book and the Author", 17).

64 See al-Qalqashandī, *Ṣubḥ*, Vol. 1, 9.

65 See "A Word on the Book and the Author", 17.

66 This is a simplified explanation of *Jāmi' al-Muḫtṣarāt wa Muḫtaṣar Jāmi' al-Jawāmi'* (*The Collection of Summaries and the Summary of the Compilation of Collections*), which is a work on Shāfiʿī jurisprudence by Shayḫ Kamāl al-Dīn al-Nishā'ī (d. AH 757/AD 1356) (al-Samarra'i, *Al-Manhaj*, 34).

67 See "A Word on the Book and the Author", 17–19.

68 For example, see al-Qalqashandī, *Ṣubḥ*, Vol. 14, 191.

dignified and honourable of professions and the only career that a scholar should practise.[69] In his *maqāma*, he outlines the knowledge needed by the scribe:[70] traditional education in Arabic language, jurisprudence, Islamic law and history, grammar, the Qur'an, *Ḥadith*, Arabic poetry and essays, orations of eloquent persons, calligraphy and other skills. He also adds the need for knowledge of many worldly subjects like history, geography, mathematics, surveying, astronomy and numerous other crafts. He also added all knowledge needed for most functions of courts or public life, no matter how small or irrelevant.[71] From reading *Ṣubḥ al-A'shā*, it is clear that al-Qalqashandī was not exaggerating and actually did have this extensive and varied knowledge of the world around him, making him a truly universal all-round scholar of the highest calibre. One is quite impressed with the amount of information he gives and the never-ending topics he discusses. His knowledge was clearly extensive, not only of the history and geography of the Islamic lands but of most of the known lands and kingdoms surrounding Egypt, complete with the names of the rulers and the most important events in the history of those kingdoms until his own time. Clearly demonstrated throughout his book is an encyclopaedic knowledge of the intricate structure of the bureaucracy in Egypt and Syria, not only during the Mamluk sultanate but from the start of Islamic rule in Egypt. He also demonstrated his extensive knowledge of protocol and etiquette in the sultanic, official and private realms. Another point to note is his academic integrity and awareness of the limits of his knowledge, which is demonstrated in his rare admission of lack of information in the section on the organization of government before the Fatimid period. All those traits must have affected his manner and dealings with people confirming his reputation as a well mannered, honourable, polite and pious man, living up to what he wrote in his main work.

Working in the Chancery Bureau from AH 791 / AD 1389 to AH 821 / AD 1418, he must have witnessed numerous events in the history of the Jarkasi Mamluk sultanate. The two sultans who reigned in that period, al-Ẓahir Barqūq and his son al-Nasir Farag, had quite eventful careers. The times were quite turbulent for the Mamluk sultanate in Egypt and Syria, and included the sack of Syria by Tamerlane in AH 803 / AD 1400, numerous rebellions by the Mamluk viceroys in Syria throughout the reign of al-Nasir Farag with several military campaigns which continued till he was finally defeated and taken prisoner in Damascus in AH 815 / AD 1412) and killed. We can't find any mention of al-Qalqashandī's name in any of the historical accounts of that period except the record of his death in AH 811 / AD 1418. We have no record of his exact position in the chancery, and he was never appointed *kātib al-sirr*. He was quite critical of the quality of the scribes joining the chancery, lamenting the state which those who took to the honourable

69 An excellent summary is given by Bosworth, "A 'Maqāma' on Secretaryship", 295–8; see also al-Musawi, "Vindicating a Profession or a Personal Career?"

70 See Bosworth, "A 'Maqāma' on Secretaryship", 296.

71 See al-Qalqashandī, *Ṣubḥ*, Vol. 1, 145–7.

task of scribing had sunk to.[72] Obviously he was not an active participant in any of the political intrigues of that time, so, we can assume that he kept a low profile, living up to his education, upbringing and reputation: a learned, humble and pious scribe in the chancery who was obviously a master of his profession: *al-inshā'*.

Rarely does al-Qalqashandī give any first-hand eyewitness accounts of any of the events that transpired. One of the rare instances recorded in *Ṣubḥ al-A'shā* is his witnessing of the firing of a canon in the reign of al-Ashraf Sha'aban b. Hussein (AH 714–87 / AD 1363–76) in Alexandria. The exact date is uncertain, but obviously it must have been before AH 787. This rare testimony is of extreme importance since it is one of the earliest undeniable confirmations we have of the existence and use of gunpowder in canons in the Mamluk period.[73] One can consider *Ṣubḥ al-A'shā* as al-Qalqashandī's testimony and eyewitness account of his era, giving us one of the most informative, complete, detailed and useful descriptions of any Islamic era, to the best of my knowledge unequalled in Arabic literature until that time and on par or even superior to al-Maqrizi's *Khiṭaṭ*.

Al-Qalqashandī fathered at least one son we know of, named Najm al-Dīn Muḥammad (AH 797–876 / AD 1394–1471). He followed in his father's footsteps, receiving his diploma at the age of 17, becoming an official witness (*shahid 'adl*), then deputy judge, then accompanying Sultan al-Ashraf Barisbay in his campaign to Amida in AH 836 / AD 1433, then working as a scribe in the chanceries of several amirs.[74] He even authored his own manual, *Qalā'id al-Jumān fī Muṣṭalaḥ Mukātabāt al-Zamān* (*The Pearl Necklaces: Regarding the Conventions of Present-Day Epistolography*).[75] He is credited with another book entitled *Nihāyat al-Arab*, which is similar to his father's work with the same title. It is believed that he plagiarized his father's book in order to seek employment as a secretary with the amir to whom he dedicated the book.[76]

Al-Qalqashandī died on Saturday 10 Jamada AH 821 / 15 June AD 1418 at the age of 65.[77]

Inshā' Literature

Al-Qalqashandī gave a historical account of the ever-existing need all rulers have for scribes and of the importance of the task of writing or of the official scribe,

72 Al-Qalqashandī, *Ṣubḥ*, Vol. 1, 137, 139.

73 Ibid., Vol. 2, 137; see also Ayalon, *Gunpowder*, 2; see also Abdelhamid, "The Development of Pyrotechnics"; Abdelhamid, "The Impact of Firearms".

74 His full name is Najm al-dīn Abū l-Faḍl Muḥammad b. Šihāb al-dīn Aḥmad b. Jamāl al-dīn Abū l-Yumn 'Abd Allāh b. Aḥmad b. 'Abd Allāh b. Ismā'īl b. Sulaymān al-Qalqashandī al-Qāhirī al-Shāfi'ī . For his biography, see Bauden, "Like Father, Like Son", 197–200; see also al-Sakhawi, *Al-Daw'*, Vol. 1, 322–23.

75 Veselý, "Chancery Manuals"; see also Bauden, "Like Father, Like Son".

76 Bauden, "Like Father, Like Son", 201–4.

77 "A Word on the Book and the Author", 15; al-Maqrīzī, *Al-Suluk*, Vol. 4, sect. 1, 744.

claiming that writing has been always associated with a knowledgeable man. He outlined the three basic necessities for kingly rule: orders to subordinates, collection of wealth and disbursement of funds.[78] Thus those three functions needed a scribe in close connection with the sovereign to record and oversee his orders. He considered that this job was started by the "heavenly messengers of God", the prophets.[79] During the Islamic caliphate, he mentions that those who scribed for the Prophet Muḥammad like Abu-Bakr, ʿUmar b. al-Khattab, ʿUthman b. ʿAffan and Muʿawiya b. Abi Sufyan all became caliphs, so historically he considered this function to be one of the most dignified and important tasks.[80]

In the introduction to his book, al-Qalqashandī explains that many books had been written on the job of *al-inshā'*, with two that are well known. One of them was that of his teacher Ahmad b. Faḍl Allah alʿAdawi alʿUmari whose book, *al-Ta'arif bil Moṣtalah al-Sharif*, was considered to be one of the most treasured books on the subject and one of the most complete references on *al-inshā'* literature and which he used as his main reference in *Ṣubḥ al-A'shā*. Al-Qalqashandī had such high regard and esteem for al-ʿUmari that he described him as the "king of writing and its leading man, the sultan of eloquence and ruler of its reigns".[81] However, it was also al-Qalqashandī's opinion that this book, in-spite of its "completeness" ignored some necessary terms, so he had to use other books for reference. He also used Ibn Naẓir al-Jaish's *Tathqif al-ta'arif*, which followed al-ʿUmari in its methodology while adding much that which was missing. *Ṣubḥ al-A'shā* is a combination of information contained in both books, with examples and explanations of items that were missing or requiring elaboration. We have other works on the literature of *al-inshā'*: 'Abd al-Hamid al-Katib (d. AH 132 / AD 750), *Risāla 'ila al-Kuttāb*; Ibn al-Muqaffa' (d. AH 139 / AD 757), *al-Adab al-Kābir*; Ibn Qutayba (d. AH 276 / AD 889), *Adab al-Kātib*, with an informative introduction; al-Baghdadi (late third century AH / ninth century AD), *Kitāb al-Kuttāb*, which contains advice to the scribe on the tools and knowledge needed for the job; al-Shaybāni (mid-third century AH / ninth century AD), *al-Risāla al-ʿAdhra'*, probably the first handbook on the role and duties of the scribe; and al-Suli (d. AH 335/ AD 946), *Adab al-Kuttāb*.[82] The term *inshā'* was absent from those early works and that style manuals with collections of epistolary models were yet to emerge.[83]

78 "Ordering and outlining the duties of the ruler's deputies and protocol to follow, extraction of money and wealth from the different sources that are due to the ruler and finally distribution and disbursement of those funds to the different employees of government to be spent on relevant issues necessary for good government" (al-Qalqashandī, *Ṣubḥ*, Vol. 1, 39).

79 "Joseph being the scribe for the Pharaoh of Egypt, Aaron and Joshua as scribes to Moses, King Solomon to his father David and John to Jesus" (ibid.).

80 Ibid.

81 Ibid. Vol. 1, 8.

82 Gully, "Epistles for Grammarians", 148; Bosworth, "A 'Maqāma' on Secretaryship", 294–5; Veselý, "Chancery Manuals".

83 Gully, "Epistles for Grammarians", 148.

There are other works from the Ayyubid period, including Ibn Mammati, *Qawawīn al-Dawawīn*; al-Nabulsī, *Kitab Luma' al-Qawawin al-Mūḍiyya fi Dawawīn al-Diyar al-Miṣriyya*; Ibn Shith, *Ma'alim al-Kitāba*; and other works from the Mamluk period, including: Shihab al-Din b. Faḍlallah al-ʿUmari, *Masalik al-Absar*, *Ta'rīf bil-Mustalaḥ al-Sharif*, and *'Urf al-Ta'arīf*; and Qaḍi Taqiy al-Din b. Naẓir al-Jaish, *Tathqīf al-Ta'rīf*.[84]

Two other works post-date *Ṣubḥ al-A'shā*, both written in the second half of the ninth century AH / fifteenth century AD, including the one by al-Qalqashandī's son. These were the last chancery manuals in Arabic, for after the fall of the Mamluk sultanate in AH 923 / AD 1517 to the Ottomans, Turkish replaced Arabic as the official language of the state.[85] Those books are Najm al-Dīn Muḥammad b. al-Qalqashandī, *Qalāʾid al-Jumān fī Muṣṭalaḥ Mukātabāt al-Zamān*;[86] and Bahāʾ al-Dīn Muḥammad b. Luṭfallāh al-Khālidī al-ʿUmarī, *Kitāb al-Maqṣad al-Rafī' al-Manshaʾ al-Hādī ilā Ṣinā'at al-Inshāʾ*.

The Book

According to al-Qalqashandī, *Ṣubḥ al-A'shā* is the first work on *al-inshā'* to adopt its essential encyclopaedic approach.[87] It has been repeatedly cited in primary and secondary sources in Arabic due to its rich content and reliability and has been known to Western scholars since at least 1903. Completed on Friday 28 Shawwal AH 814 / 20 October AD 1411,[88] more than a century and a half into the Mamluk reign, and a century prior to its end, the book is an exceptionally valuable resource on the Mamluk and earlier Muslim eras.

Written as a handbook or manual for chancery clerks, the book is divided into chapters that guide the scribe through the different requirements for his work, with samples of actual correspondence used. Earlier works on the art of composition were insufficient, according to al-Qalqashandī, because they either solely focused on the rules of the craft of writing, its terminology and uses, or just compiled model types of writing as examples for scribes to follow.[89]

The work follows the trend of its time in being encyclopaedic and gigantic, a style that had been adopted in the Islamic world for centuries, although it particularly thrived in the fourteenth and fifteenth centuries in Egypt, with a noticeable

84 Bosworth, "A 'Maqāma' on Secretaryship", 292.

85 Vesely, "Chancery Manuals".

86 An extensive study of the unpublished manuscript can be found in Bauden, "Like Father, Like Son".

87 Al-Qalqashandī, *Ṣubḥ*, Vol. 1, 9.

88 As indicated by the author in the end of the work. The copier notes that he finished this particular copy on the 20 Safar AH 889 / 28 March AD 1484. According to the contents of the work, it appears that the author continued to add parts to it until AH 815 / AD 1413 (*Ṣubḥ*, Vol. 14, 404; al-Samarra'i, *Al-Manhaj*, 32–3).

89 Musa, *Kitāb*, 10; Van Berkel, "Archives and Chanceries".

concern for organization and focus on a single main topic.[90] Such works supplemented their principal subjects with all relevant information, and it was normal for them to include literature, history, geography, economics, religious sciences, systems of governance, biographies, arts and so on.[91]

Al-Qalqashandī's research methodology reflects his rich education and intellectual and cultural learning, typical of the scholarly figures of his time.[92] He refers to a myriad of earlier sources on different topics that cover vast geographical and historical spans, many of which are no longer extant, an aspect that adds to the value of his work.[93] Whenever he copies from a source, al-Qalqashandī cites it, even if he cannot identify the author; he copies accurately, mentioning different accounts of an issue in cases of controversy and using expressions of uncertainty as needed, then sometimes comments on the correctness or credibility of the information.[94] The care for proper citation of sources and tracing the plausibility of an account are practices inherent in Islamic religious education, particularly in reference to the study of the Prophet's traditions (Sunna).[95] In addition to books and separate articles, al-Qalqashandī is one of the few historians to rely heavily on documents, such as official decrees, agreements, correspondences, sermons, registers.[96] Documents play a vital role in historical research because they confirm or disprove questionable historical accounts.[97] The documents that al-Qalqashandī used or referred to go back as far as the time of Prophet Muḥammad, which immensely enriches his work.[98] He gives special attention to terminology and titles, their change and development over time, and their disappearance, as well as their employment over the wide geographical area he covered, many times referring to the difference between the official use of a term and its colloquial use by the people.[99]

Al-Qalqashandī divided his book into an Introduction (*muqaddimah*), ten Articles (*maqalā*, pl. *maqalāt*) and a Conclusion (*khatima*). The Introduction and the Articles are divided into chapters (*bab*, pl. *abwāb*) which are further divided into sub-chapters (*fasl*, pl. *fusūl*). The *fusūl* are sometimes divided into sections (*maqsad*, "purpose", pl. *maqāsid*). *Maqāsid* are sometimes divided into "types" (*ḍarb*), which are further sub-divided into "variations" (*wajh*), or into "statuses"

90 Al-Samarra'i, *Al-Manhaj*, 61–2; Bosworth, "A 'Maqāma' on Secretaryship", 11; Van Berkel, "Archives and Chanceries".

91 Ashour, "Kitāb Ṣubḥ al-Aʿshā", 26; Van Berkel, "Archives and Chanceries"; Gully, "Epistles for Grammarians", 147–9.

92 Al-Samarra'i, *Al-Manhaj*, 81.

93 Ibid. 81.

94 Ibid. 99, 122–3, 128–9, 132, 134.

95 Ibid. 220.

96 Ibid. 136–7.

97 Tulaymat ,"Wathā'iq al-Qalqashandī fī Ṣubḥ al-Aʿshā", 119.

98 Ibid. 121.

99 Al-Samarra'i, *Al-Manhaj*, 149–52.

(*ḥāla*), which are further sub-divided into clauses (*jumla*), which are in turn divided into "kinds" (*naw'*). Sometimes *fusul* are divided into "ends" (*taraf*), "levels" (*martaba*) and "sub-levels" (*tabaqa*) or into "ends", "sorts" (*rukn*) and "kinds". He does not use consistent divisions throughout the book, and the purpose of this inconsistency and the reasons for using different names for the various subdivisions is unclear. The number of each sub-division is clearly stated for each segment of text followed by its title and the number of its sub-divisions. A few times the numbering is in error, with the actual content slightly different than the titles. We can assume that the reason was either due to a revision that was not reflected in the title or simply just a mistake.

The following summarizes the contents of the work. The sources of the selections translated in this volume are given in bold:

Introduction: "On the Principles that Should be Established before Starting Writing Compositions" (5 chapters)

- Chapter 1: "On the Merits of Writing" (2 sub-chapters)
- Chapter 2: "On the Meaning of Chancery and its Merits" (3 sub-chapters)
- Chapter 3: "On the Traits of Scribes and their Manners" (2 sub-chapters)
- Chapter 4: "On the Origins of the Chancery and its History in Islam" (2 sub-chapters)
- Chapter 5: "On the Rules Governing the Chancery and its Structure and the Discipline of its Employees" (4 sub-chapters)

Article 1: "What Is Needed by the Scribe in the Chancery" (2 chapters)

- Chapter 1: "Scientific and Theoretical Knowledge" (3 sub-chapters)
- Chapter 2: "Practical Knowledge" (2 sub-chapters)

Article 2: "Geography and Kingdoms" (4 chapters)

- Chapter 1: "Geography of the World" (3 sub-chapters)
- Chapter 2: "The Caliphate and the Different Dynasties" (2 sub-chapters)
- Chapter 3: "On the Kingdom of the Egyptian Lands and its Additions" (3 sub-chapters)
  - **Sub-chapter 1: "On the Egyptian Lands"**
  - Sub-chapter 2: "On the Syrian Lands"
  - Sub-chapter 3: "On the Hegaz"
- Chapter 4: "On the Kingdoms and Other Countries Surrounding the Egyptian Kingdom" (4 sub-chapters)

Article 3: "On the Requirements of the Task of Writing and Types of Paper and Formats and Types of Documents Produced in the Chancery" (4 chapters)

- Chapter 1: "Names and Titles" (2 sub-chapters)
- Chapter 2: "Paper Sizes and Pens Used" (2 sub-chapters)
- Chapter 3: "Document Types, Formats and Sizes" (2 sub-chapters)

Chapter 4: “Introductory and Ending Phrases and their Formats” (2 sub-chapters)

Article 4: “General Issues Regarding Correspondence” (2 sub-chapters)

Chapter 1: “General Issues Regarding Letters and Other Types of Correspondence” (2 sub-chapters)
Chapter 2: “Terms and Titles used in Letters in the Different Historical Eras” (8 sub-chapters)

Article 5: “On the Appointment of Official Posts for Government” (3 chapters)

Chapter 1: “On the Different Ranks and Levels of the Different Posts” (3 sub-chapters)
Chapter 2: “On the Official Oaths Prior to Appointment to the Post” (2 sub-chapters)
Chapter 3: “On Vows” (2 sub-chapters)
Chapter 4: “On Official Appointments by Caliphs” (3 sub-chapters)

Article 6: “Religious Sermons, Approvals, Bequeaths and Calendar Conversions” (4 chapters)

Chapter 1: “Religious Sermons’ (2 sub-chapters)
Chapter 2: “Approvals for Exemptions from Payment and Continuation of Payments” (2 sub-chapters)
Chapter 3: “For Bequests due to Retirement from Official Service” (2 sub-chapters)
4: “Conversion of Years (Lunar and Solar Calendars)” (2 sub-chapters)

Article 7: “Fiefs [*Iqta'aat*] and Allocated Lands” (2 chapters)

Chapter 1: “Introduction to *Iqta'a*” (2 sub-chapters)
Chapter 2: “On Assignment of an *Iqta'a* and Recording that Assignment” (2 sub-chapters)

Article 8: “On Oaths” (2 chapters)

Chapter 1: “Basics that Should be Known Prior to Discussion of Oaths” (2 sub-chapters)
Chapter 2: “On Samples of Royal Oaths” (2 sub-chapters)

Article 9: “Regarding Different Contracts for Treaties and Safe Conduct and Living and Other Matters” (5 chapters)

Chapter 1: “For Safe Passage and Protection for Non-Believers”(2 sub-chapters)
Chapter 2: “On Burial” (2 sub-chapters)
Chapter 3: “On Treaties and Protection for Non-Muslims” (2 sub-chapters)

Chapter 4: "On Treaties between Muslim kings and Non-Believer Kings" (2 sub-chapters)
Chapter 5: "On Treaties between Two Muslim Kings" (2 sub-chapters)

Article 10: "On Other Types of Prose Written by Scribes and not Related to the Sultan's *Dīwāns*" (2 chapters)

Chapter 1: "On Serious Topics" (6 sub-chapters)
Chapter 2: "On Light Topics" (2 sub-chapters)

Conclusion: "On Matters Related to the Bureau of Chancery Other than Writing" (4 chapters)

Chapter 1: "The Mail" (2 sub-chapters)
Chapter 2: "The Mail-Pigeon System in Egypt and Syria" (2 sub-chapters)
Chapter 3: "The Ice Boats Arriving from the Syrian Lands to the Kings in Egypt" (2 sub-chapters)
Chapter 4: "On Lighthouses and Firestarters" (2 sub-chapters)

The translations in this book are selections from Article 2, Chapter 3, Sub-chapter 1: "On the Kingdom of the Egyptian Lands and its Additions". It is subdivided into four "purposes", the first is a general geographic description of the Egyptian lands (physical geography, flora, fauna, borders) and its established and ancient urban centres and seats of government; the second mentions the different territorial divisions of Egypt; the third discusses the rulers of Egypt from the Great Flood of Noah to al-Qalqashandī's time; the fourth discusses the monetary and economic organization of the Egyptian Lands. The fifth discusses the political and governmental structure and protocol.

Article 2, Chapter 3, Sub-chapter 1: "On the Egyptian Lands"
Purpose 1: "Its Traits and Peculiarities"
Purpose 2: "Its Wonders and Antiquities"
Purpose 3: "Its Nile"
Purpose 4: "Its Bays, which are Six"
Purpose 5: "Its Lakes, which are Four"
Purpose 6: "Its Mountains"
Purpose 7: "Its Vegetation"
Purpose 8: "Its Animals, Birds and Livestock"
Purpose 9: "Its Borders"
Purpose 10: "Its Foundation and Settlement, and Naming it Egypt"
Purpose 11: "Its Ancient Seats of Government and Remaining Great Buildings"
Purpose 12: "The Established Seats of Government"[100]

100 Al-Qalqashandī, *Ṣubḥ*, Vol. 3, 329–79.

Seat 1: "The City of Fustat"
Seat 2: "Cairo"
Seat 3: "The Citadel"

Sub-Chapter 2: "On the Regional Divisions of the Egyptian Lands"
Sub-Chapter 3: "On the Rulers of the Egyptian Lands"
Sub-Chapter 4: "The Political and Economic Organization of the Egyptian Lands"

Purpose 3: "The Regulation of the Kingdom"[101]

First Status: "Rulers Appointed by the Caliphate until the end of the Ikshidid Dynasty"
Second Status: "Status of the Egyptian Lands under the Fatimids"

Clause 1: "Royal Instruments"
Clause 2: "The Caliph's Warehouses"
Clause 3: "The Armies"
Clause 4: "The Holders of Offices"
Clause 5: "The Appearance of the Caliph"
Clause 6: "The Fleets, Ruling Subjects and Persuading Opponents"
Clause 7: "The Salaries, Grants and Related Banquets"
End[102] **8: "The Wazir's Audience for Grievances"**

Third Status: "The Ayyubids and Mamluks"[103]

Purpose 1: "The Protocols and Instruments of Royalty"
Purpose 2: "The Sultan's Warehouses"
Purpose 3: "The Kingdom's Dignitaries and Holders of Posts"
Purpose 4: "The Attire of the Kingdom's Dignitaries"
Purpose 5: "The Sultan's Appearance in Royal Protocol"
Purpose 6: "The Salaries"
Purpose 7: "The Special Territories"
Purpose 8: "How News Reaches the Sultan"
Purpose 9: "The Appearance and Regulation of Amirs"
Purpose 10: "The Governors, Men of the Sword"

Translations and Research on *Ṣubḥ al-A'shā*

No complete translation has been attempted of the full 14 volumes of *Ṣubḥ al-A'shā* by Western scholars, although the importance of the text has been recognized at

101 Ibid., Vol. 3, 471–532. This should be Sub-chapter (*fasl*) 5. There are no Purposes 1 and 2. See ibid., Vol. 3, 471, n. 1.

102 *Taraf*: the seven previous sub-divisions are titled *jumla*. See ibid., Vol. 3, 529, n. 2.

103 Ibid., Vol. 4, 6–71.

least since the 1900s.[104] Partial segments were selectively translated into French in 1903 and 1904,[105] and other studies in French exist.[106] English language studies and translations have been published with selective translations of certain segments or studies of certain issues found in *Ṣubḥ al-A'shā*, including Bosworth's studies of symbolic actions in *Ṣubḥ al-A'shā*,[107] of al-Qalqashandī's *maqāma*,[108] of Christian and Jewish appointments and titles as outlined by al-Qalqashandī,[109] and others;[110] al-Musawi's study of Qalqashandī's *maqāma* for al-'Umari;[111] Gully's translations of three specimens of letters for grammarians, one of them from *Ṣubḥ al-A'shā*;[112] Holt's analysis and translation of four treaties from *Ṣubḥ al-A'shā* and other sections describing how the treaty was drafted,[113] and his translation of a fifth treaty from *Ṣubḥ al-A'shā*, between al-Manṣur Qalawūn and Acre;[114] Lang's article on *ḥisba* based on *Ṣubḥ al-A'shā*;[115] Van Berkel's study on *Ṣubḥ al-A'shā*[116] and her article on al-Qalqashandī;[117] Khan's comparison of the petitions in *Ṣubḥ al-A'shā* with other petitions;[118] Petry's discussion of the geographic origins of *dīwān* officials in fifteenth-century Cairo;[119] Otto Spies's analysis of al-Qalqashandī's account of India;[120] and Sezgin's study of the geography and administration of Egypt according to *Ṣubḥ al-A'shā*.[121] There are also some partial German translations and studies.[122]

About this Translation

There are several editions of the original text of *Ṣubḥ al-A'shā*, all published by the Egyptian government. The first edition, by the Egyptian publisher Dar al-Kutub,

104 See Bosworth, "Some Historical Gleanings", 148.

105 Lammens, "Relations officielles"; Lammens, "Correspondances diplomatiques".

106 Sauvaire, Extraits de l'ouvrage d'el Qalqachandy; Wiet, "Les Classiques du scribe Egyptien"; Pellat, "Le 'Calendrier agricole'"; Espéronnier, Faste des costumes et insignes; Espéronnier, Les fêtes civiles; Michel, L'Organisation financière.

107 Bosworth, "Some Historical Gleanings", 148–53.

108 Bosworth, "A 'Maqāma' on Secretaryship", 291–8.

109 Bosworth, "Christian and Jewish Religious Dignitaries".

110 Bosworth, "Al-Qalqashandī", 629.

111 Al-Musawi, "Vindicating a Profession or a Personal Career?", 111–35.

112 Gully, "Epistles for Grammarians", 147–66.

113 Holt, "The Treaties of the Early Mamluk Sultans".

114 Holt, "Qalawin's Treaty with Acre".

115 Lang, "Ḥisba".

116 Van Berkel, "The Attitude towards Knowledge in Mamlūk Egypt".

117 Van Berkel, "A Well-Mannered Man of Letters".

118 Khan, "The Historical Development of the Structure of Medieval Arabic Petitions".

119 Petry, "Geographic Origins of Dīwān Officials".

120 Spies, "An Arab Account".

121 Sezgin, *Two Studies on the Geography and Administration of Egypt*.

122 Krenkow, *Arabische Berichte*; Wüstenfeld, "Calcaschandi's Geographie".

also known as Dar al-Kutub al-Khidīwiyya, was in 14 volumes in 1913, with several editions till 1922. No index was created till 1972 when al-Baqlī published his.[123] In 1984 a study of the terms of *Ṣubḥ al-A'shā* as a glossary was published also by Dar al-Kutub and edited by al-Baqlī.[124] Based on the Dar al-Kutub editions, in 2004, a new edition was published by another branch of the Egyptian government, the General Authority for Cultural Palaces,[125] with a new introduction by Fawzi Amīn and a fifteenth volume added with the glossary of the terms by al-Baqlī.[126] In 2006, Muṣṭafa Mūsa edited a short summary of the book, published in two volumes.[127]

The edition used for this translation is the 1922 edition published by Dār al-Kutub. In this current translation and editing, mistakes and blanks in the original copy on the part of the author and the copier were examined then corrected based on other sources; however, corrections were kept to the editing remarks, preserving the author's words, no matter how awkward or inaccurate.[128] It was the editors' decision to keep that awkwardness in the text as it is, to convey as much as possible the original words of al-Qalqashandī and avoid any creative interventions that may detract from his original intentions. Diacritical marks were inserted as needed,[129] with the work's linguistic anomalies explained in the footnotes.[130] The Dar al-Kutub editors' comments were incorporated into the footnotes and under the rubric "editor of *Ṣubḥ*". The chapter titles have been translated and preserved according to al-Qalqashandī's original text, so that they can be easily found in the original.

This translation is intended for scholars as well as all those interested in medieval history. It has been selectively limited to some of the parts related to Egypt in volumes 3 and 4 of the Dar al-Kutub edition. This translation started as a project to translate the whole segment describing Egypt, which is from Maqalā 2: "Geography and Kingdoms". However, we found that there was so much detail that would not be of interest to the modern scholar of Islamic medieval society that we limited the translation to only the Islamic eras, outlining the history and structure of the Islamic dynasties in Egypt. Al-Qalqashandī gives quite an exhaustive history of Egypt, starting from the Great Flood of Noah and continuing to the different Ancient Egyptian dynastic periods, with the names of each ruler and the different dynasties that ruled Egypt. It may be of interest to some scholars to compare the accuracy of his account and the names used to their Pharaonic,

123 Al-Baqli, *Fahāris kitāb.*

124 Al-Baqli, *Al-Ta'rīf.*

125 Al-Qalqashandī, Kitab Ṣubḥ al-A'shā (ed. Amin).

126 Al-Baqli, *Muṣṭalaḥāt Ṣubḥ al-A'shā.*

127 Al-Qalqashandī, *Kitāb Ṣubḥ al-A'shá* (ed. Mūsá).

128 "A Word on the Book and the Author", 19.

129 In Arabic, diacritical marks, which act as vowels and determine the pronunciation of a word, are essential to understand the correct meaning of a sentence.

130 "A Word on the Book and the Author", 20.

Persian, Greek, Roman and Byzantine equivalents, but such a job requires a separate detailed study that would be better left to other scholars who can give it due care. Other segments which we decided against including were his exhaustive description of the geography of Egypt, different territories, monetary systems, plants, crops and animals. There is an extremely important segment on the economic and monetary system of Egypt and how the government was funded, but this definitely warrants a separate study with comparison to other sources and a study of the different economic conditions of Egypt during the Mamluk period.

As can be seen from the table of contents above, the sections translated have been selected from Maqalā 2, Bab 3, Fasl 1: "On the Kingdom of the Egyptian Lands and its Additions". A small segment of Purpose 12 has been translated, together with almost all of what should have been Fasl 5, that was entitled "The Third Purpose" (*al-maqṣad al-thalith*), which covers Egypt in the Fatimid and Mamluk periods. The first part of this book is the translated text, while the second part contains a Glossary of the terms used in the text with some additions that make the glossary a separate work that can be used on its own.

The segments translated have been divided into two parts. The first is "The Established Seats of Government",[131] which discusses the urban centres from which Egypt had been governed since the advent of Islam. The centres were Fustat, Cairo, the Citadel of Cairo and the Cemetery of Cairo. Al-Qalqashandī gives a historical background and a description of each of those centres and their development, with descriptions of the most important buildings and components of each urban centre. The second part, "The Regulation of the Kingdom"[132] provides an analysis of the government of Egypt, giving a historical background of the different systems established by the Fatimid, Ayyubid and Mamluk dynasties, with a historical description of the political and bureaucratic structure, the different government positions, different caliphal or sultanic protocols and displays of power, court protocol, court customs, dress, attire, arms, monetary compensation, salaries, grants, the different governmental officers and their offices and numerous other details that give us a clear picture of how each dynasty ruled and the instruments and structure of that rule.

A Note on the Editing

This is the first translation of such magnitude of this work. More than 2,000 footnotes explain and elaborate on the content of the original text with cross references to other contemporary sources and modern studies that exceed 150 references. The Glossary summarizes a wealth of information making it a useful separate reference. This is not just a simple translation of the medieval text but, with the footnotes and the accompanying Glossary, the result is a well-researched and informative work of reference with a huge amount of information and detail

131 Al-Qalqashandī, *Ṣubḥ*, Vol. 3, 329–79.

132 Ibid., Vol. 3, 471–532; Vol. 4, 6–71.

on Egypt in the medieval period, far more information than that was contained in the original text. The editors hope that this effort will be the first of many more works that will further the study of the wealth of Islamic primary sources and serve as essential background for more in-depth and informed understanding of the Islamic medieval world.

In this translation, al-Qalqashandī's text has been cross-referenced to the sources that he cites, if available, either correcting or elaborating on his text in the footnotes. Care has been taken to elaborate and explain most of the terms used by al-Qalqashandī, making use of numerous modern studies and research on the different terms. All available relevant English-language references have been given. However, since the number of works in English on many topics covered by this translation is relatively small, the editors had to make use of the wealth of Arabic-language academic research available. The final outcome gives the English-speaking researcher an indication of the amount of research that has been covered on certain topics so that no time will be wasted researching what others have already done, and future research efforts can be concentrated elsewhere.

On the Maps

Al-Qalqashandī gives a description of the different divisions of the Egyptian kingdom. The maps included roughly outline the modern equivalents of the areas he mentions. They are not part of the original text and are entirely the work of the editors, who hope that they may be used as starting points for more detailed research on the medieval geography and urban layout of Cairo and Egypt. There are two maps. The first shows the extents of the Mamluk kingdom in the time of Qalqashandī, in the fifteenth century. The second shows Cairo and its environs round the same period.

About the Editors

Heba El-Toudy, translator and editor of this work, has an MA in Islamic Art and diverse experience in Islamic art and architecture as a lecturer, translator, editor, researcher and archivist. She has participated in and presented papers at several conferences on Islamic art history.

Tarek Galal Abdelhamid, reviewer and editor of this work, is a practising architect with a PhD in Islamic Archaeology and Architecture, an MA in Islamic Art and Architecture and an MA in Urban Design. He lectures at several universities in Egypt on the history of architecture and art, architectural design, CAD and the use of computers in archaeology. His publications include work on the history of Mamluk north Syria, *awqaf* inscriptions, history of war and weapons, the Mamluk army and Mamluk architecture.

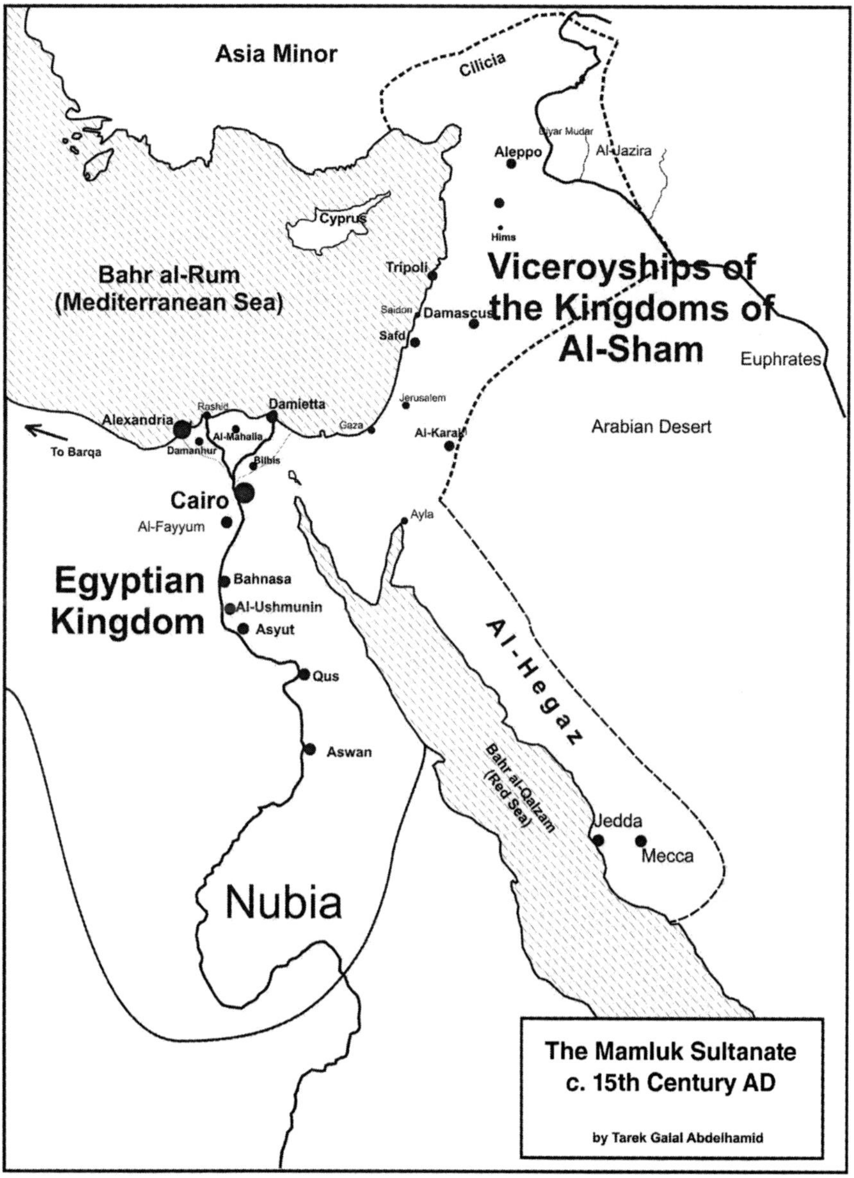

Map 1 The Mamluk Sultanate, *c.* 15th Century AD

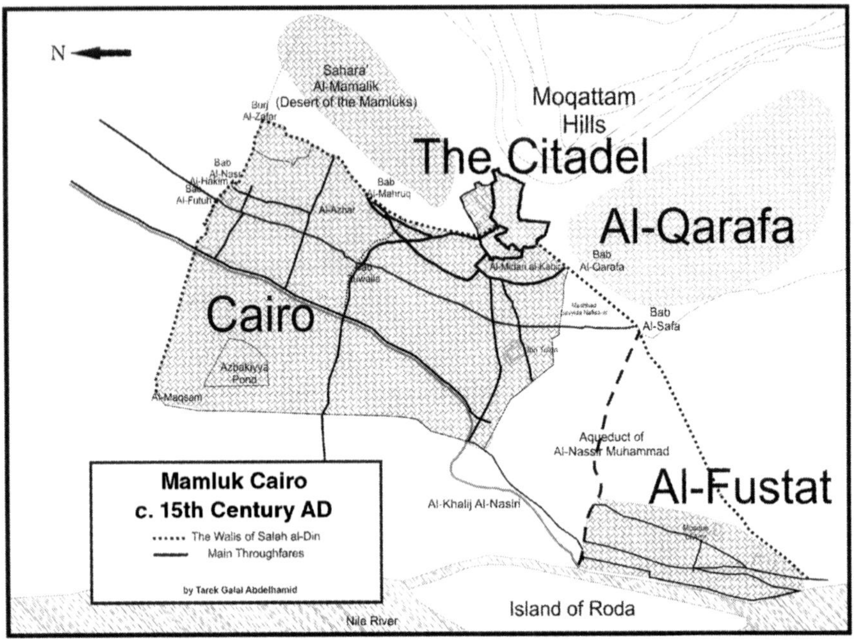

Map 2 Mamluk Cairo, *c.* 15th Century AD

Part I

THE SEATS OF GOVERNMENT

The Twelfth Purpose
On its Established Seats of Government[133]
Which are three that became proximate and combined as if one

133 "*Qawā'id*," (sing. *qā'ida*), which means "base," and denotes the seat of government of a kingdom, state or region.

THE FIRST SEAT OF GOVERNMENT

The City of Fustat

[The name] is pronounced "*fusṭāṭ*." [The city] is also called "*fustāṭ*" and "*fussāṭ*."[134]Al-Jawharī[135] said: Pronouncing the "*f*" as ["*fi*," not "*fu*"] is [acceptable] linguistically.[136] It is the city known among the commone`rs as "*Miṣr*," and

134 The author explains the pronunciation in detail, explicitly mentioning the diacritical marks for each letter. To simplify, this translation, henceforth, only transliterates such terms, rather than translating the author's description of pronunciations.

135 Abū Naṣr Ismā'īl b. Ḥammād al-Jawharī (d. 393 AH/1003 AD or 396 AH/1006 AD) was one of the most important Arabic linguists and a leading calligrapher who was born in Fārāb, learned in Iraq and died in Khurasan. His most famous work is *Al-Ṣiḥāḥ: Tāj al-Lugha wa Ṣiḥāḥ al-'Arabiyya* (*The Dictionary: The Crown of Language and Dictionary of Arabic*), which is an invaluable Arabic dictionary. It is interesting to note that al-Jawharī was one of the first men in the Islamic world to attempt manufacturing a flying machine. Unfortunately, his two wooden wings failed him and he fell to his demise. Most historians of the time report this incident claiming al-Jawharī had gone mad towards his last days. (See Ibn Aybak Al-Ṣafadī, *Al-Wāfī bi-l-Wafayāt*, ed. Ahmad al-Arna'out and Tizki Mustafa (Beirut, 2000), Vol. 9, 69).

136 "*Wa kasr al-fā' lugha fīhinn.*" (See Abū Naṣr al-Jawharī, *Muntakhab min Ṣiḥāḥ al-Jawharī* (Shamela Library, 2010), entry 3908).

its ancient name is "*bāb alyūn*" (Babylon).[137] Abū al-Sa'ādāt b. al-Athīr[138] stated "*alyūn*"[139] [as the pronunciation] in his *Nihāya*.[140]

Al-Qaḍā'ī[141] said: This is its name in the languages of the Byzantines (*Rūm*) and the Sudanese (*Sūdān*), thus, the palace in the east is known as Bāb Alyūn. It is located in the Third of the Seven Regions.[142]

The author of *Kitāb al-Aṭwāl* (The Book of Lengths)[143] said: It is 111.286 km long and 110.855 km wide.[144]

137 This was the southern part of the ancient city of Babylon, originally built by ancient Egyptians, taken up by the Greeks, and then extended by the Romans. Babylon (to the south of present day Cairo) was strategically "situated on the borders of Upper and Lower Egypt," and originally overlooked the Nile, which used to flow "further to the East." The fall of the town's fortifications into the hands of the Muslim army in 20 AH/641 AD marked the dawn of Islamic Egypt. Remains of these fortifications are still extant in the area known as Miṣr al-'Atīqa or Miṣr al-Qadīma (Old Miṣr). The Roman Fortress of Babylon was built by Emperor Trajan (98–117 AD), and is referred to in the Arabic primary sources by the names Qaṣr al-Sham'(the Palace of Wax/Candles) or Ḥiṣn al-Sham' (the Fortress of Wax/Candles). The Arabic names are probably etymological distortions that replaced *khemi* (one of the ancient names of Egypt) with *sham'*. Al-Maqrīzī, however, reports that candles were lit on the top of this fort at the beginning of each month to indicate that the sun has moved into one of the zodiac signs. (Martijn T. Houtsma, "Babylon" and "Cairo" in *E. J. Brill's First Encyclopaediaof Islam*, 1913–36 (Leiden, 1992), Vol. 2, 550 & 815–816, Ahmad Abd al-Raziq, *Tārīkh wa Āthār Miṣr al-Islāmiyya* (Cairo, 2006), 23, and Taqiy al-Dīn al-Maqrīzī, *Al-Mawā'iẓ wa-l-I'tibār bi-Dhikr al-Khiṭaṭ wa-l-Āthār*, ed. Muhammad Zeinhom and Madiha al-Sharqawi (Cairo, 1998), Vol. 1, 792).

138 Abū al-Sa'ādat Majd al-Dīn Ibn al-Athīr (d. 606 AH/1210 AD) who lived and died in Mosul of Iraq was one of the great theologists of Ḥadīth (Traditions of the Prophet). He was the brother of Ibn al-Athīr, the famous historian. "He studied, in particular, grammar and Ḥadīth, and entered the service of the Prince of Mosul." (John Haywood, *Arabic Lexicography: Its History and its Place in the General History of Lexicography* (Leiden: 1965), 107).

139 "*Bi-fatḥ al-hamza wa sukūn al-lām wa-ḍamm al-yā'*." (Majd al-Dīn Ibn al-Athīr, *Al-Nihāya fī Gharīb al-Ḥadīth wa al-Athār*, ed. Taher A. al-Zawy and Mahmoud M. al-Tanahy (Beirut, 1979), Vol. 1, 65). Al-Qalqashandī adds: "*al-muthannāt taḥt wa sukūn al-wāw wa nūn fī al-ākhir.*" (*Ṣubḥ*, Vol. 3, 329).

140 *Al-Nihāya fī Gharīb al-Ḥadīth wa al-Athār*(*The Final Study of Enigmatic Terminologies of the Prophet's Sayings and Traditions*)is an important work by Ibn al-Athīr on *'ilm gharīb al-ḥadīth* (the study of the enigmatic terminologies in the Prophet's sayings). It is a dictionary, "arranged in the modern alphabetical order." (J. Haywood, *Lexicography*, 107).

141 Abū 'Abd Allah Muḥammad Ibn Salāma b. Ja'far al-Qaḍā'ī (d. 454 AH/1062 AD) was a trusted Egyptian theologian, Ḥadīth scholar and historian. One of his important works was *al-Mukhtār fī Dhikr al-Khiṭaṭ wa al-Āthār*(*Selections on Neighbourhoods and Monuments*), which is probably the one al-Qalqashandī cites here. This manuscript is, however, no longer extant. Z. Al-Samarra'i mentions that this is one of the lost manuscripts that al-Qalqashandī refers to. (Zamya' M. al-Samarra'i. *Al-Mahnaj al-Ta'rīkhī 'inda al-Qalqashandī: Dirāsa Tah#l+liyya* (Riyadh, 2001), 75 &113).

142 Geographers such as Yāqūt al-Ḥamawī (d. 626 AH/1228 AD), author of *Mu'jam al-Buldān* (The Dictionary of Countries), define the Seven Regions as the divisions of the inhabited quarter of earth. These regions were pictured as adjacent circles of equal sizes, and were divided as follows: The First – India; The Second – Hijaz; The Third – Egypt; The Fourth – Babylon; The Fifth – The Byzantines; The Sixth – Gog, and The Seventh – China. (See Yāqūt al-Ḥamawī, *Mu'jamal-Buldān* (Beirut, 1977), Vol. 1, 25 – 32 and see fn. 383 for "Hijaz").

143 This is a manuscript that al-Qalqashandī repeatedly cites "without mentioning its author or date." (Z. al-Samarra'i, *Manhaj,* 109).

144 In text: "fifty-three degrees long and thirty degrees and ten minutes wide."

The author of *al-Qānūn* (The Canon)[145] said: It is 111.317 km long and 110.851 km wide.[146]

Ibn Sa'īd[147] said: It is 111.301 km long and 110.851 km wide.[148]

The author of *Rasm al-Ma'mūr* (The Picture of the Inhabited Countries)[149] said: It is 111.317 km long.[150]

The norm used by the people nowadays, in their employment of instruments and other means, is a length of 111.323 km long and 110.852 km wide.[151]

Different reasons are given for calling it "*al-Fusṭāṭ*" (Fustat). Ibn Qutayba[152] said: Every city is called "*al-fusṭāṭ*"; therefore *Miṣr*was called "*al-Fusṭāṭ*".[153]

Al-Zamakhsharī[154] said: "*Al-Fusṭāṭ*" is the name given to a kind of a structure that is less in size than a pavilion (*surādiq*).[155] Most [scholars] agree that it was

145 *Al-Qanūn al-Mas'ūdī* (*The Mas'ūdī Canon*), which is a compendium on astronomy and geography, by Abū al-Rayḥān al-Bayrūnī or al-Bīrūnī. Al-Bayrūnī (or al-Bīrūnī) (d. 440 AH/1048 AD) was born in Bayrūn (or Bīrūn),Khwārizm. He was a renowned geographer, astronomer, mathematician, physicist,philosopher, historian and man of literature. (See Al-Ṣafadī, *Wafayāt*, Vol. 8, 91–94).

146 In text: "fifty-four degrees and forty minutes long and twenty-nine degrees and fifty-five minutes wide." See Abū al-Rayḥān al-Bayrūnī, *Al-Qanūn al-Mas'ūdī* (Haydarabad, 1955), Vol. 2, 556.

147 Abū al-Ḥasan 'Alī b. Mūsā b. Sa'īd al-Maghribī (d. 685 AH/1286 AD) was a geographer, traveller, historian, linguist, poet and poetry anthologer. He was born in Granada to a family who claimed descent from one of the close companions of the Prophet, 'Ammār b. Yāsir, and travelled around in North Africa and the Middle East. Among his valuable accounts on the cities he visited are his descriptions of Fustat and Cairo. His famous works include: *Al-Mughrib fī Ḥulā al-Maghrib* (The Extraordinary About the Jewels of the West), *al-Mushriq fī Ḥulā al-Mashriq* (The Luminiscent About the Jewels of the East), *Nashwat al-Ṭarab fī Tārīkh Jāhiliyyat al-'Arab* (The Elation on the History of Pre-Islamic Arabs), and *al-Jughrafiya* (Geography). His visits included Morocco, Egypt, Iraq, Syria and finally Tunisia, where he died. (See Al-Ṣafadī, *Wafayāt*, Vol. 22, 157–162).

148 In text: "fifty-three degrees and fifty minutes long and twenty-nine degrees and fifty-five minutes wide". See Ibn Sa'īd al-Maghrībī, *al-Jughrāfiya*, (Shamela Library, 2010), 28.

149 Manuscript: *Rasm al-Ma'mūr min al-Bilād* or *Rasm al-Rub' al-Ma'mūr* (Book of the Picture of the Inhabited Countries), which is attributed to Abū 'Abd Allah Muḥammad ibn Mūsā al-Khawārizmī (d. 232 AH/847 AD). He was a famous mathematician and geographer of the Abbasid era. He introduced the science of Algorithm, (the English term is derived from his name), in addition to other contributions to Algebra, Trigonometry, Astronomy, and Geography. (See Z. al-Samarra'i, *Manhaj*, 110).

150 In text: "fifty-four degrees and forty minutes long."

151 In text: "fifty-five degrees and a width of thirty degrees."

152 Abū Muḥammad 'Abd Allah Ibn Muslim Ibn Qutayba (d. 276 AH/889 AD) was born in Kufa or Baghdad and died in the latter. "His studies included all branches of the traditional Arabic and Islamic knowledge of his time: religion, history, biography, philology, lexicography, literature, and some science. He left twenty works of varying lengths covering all the fields mentioned." (Paul Kunitzsch, "Ibn Qutayba," in *Encyclopaedia of the History, Science, Technology and Medicine in Non-western Cultures*, Vol. 1, ed. Helaine Selin (Berlin, 2008), 1114).

153 See Ibn Qutayba, *Gharīb al-Ḥadīth* (The Enigmatic Terms of the Prophet's Traditions), ed. Abd Allah al-Jabury, (Baghdad, 1977), Vol. 1, 318.

154 Abū al-Qāsim Muḥammad Ibn 'Umar al-Zamakhsharī (d. 538 AH/1144 AD), who was born and died in Khwarizm (Khiva), Uzbekistan, and studied in Bukhara and Baghdad, was a scholar of theology, exegesis or interpretation (*tafsīr*), lexicography and grammar. (Roy Jackson, *Fifty key figures in Islam* (Oxon, 2006), 91–92).

155 "*Ḍarb min al-abniya fī al-safar dūn al-surādiq*" (a kind of structure [used] on travel that is less [in size] to a pavilion). (Al-Zamakhsharī, *al-Fā'iq fī Gharīb al-Ḥadīth* (The Excellent on

called "*al-Fusṭāṭ*" after the tent (*fusṭāṭ*) of ʿAmr b. al-ʿĀṣ,[156] for when ʿAmr conquered and captured the fort known as "Qaṣr al-Shamʿ" in the year 21 AH/641 AD, he pitched his tent nearby. When he set off to conquer Alexandria, he ordered the dismantlement of his tent, but when a pigeon's nest with its hatchlings was surprisingly found inside the tent, ʿAmr said: "It has sought a sanctuary from us here," and commanded that his tent remains in its place and the pigeons be taken care of. He proceeded to Alexandria and conquered it, then returned back to settle in his tent, and the people settled around it. ʿAmr built his smaller house,[157] which is near the Old Mosque,[158] in place of his tent, and people started marking-out [areas of land] around him.[159] The tribes competed for locations and marking-out land, so, to administer the division of the marked-out areas (*khiṭaṭ*), ʿAmr appointed Muʿāwiya b. Ḥudayj al-Tujībī, Sharīk b. Sumayy al-Ghuṭayfī, ʿAmr b. Qaḥzam al-Khawlānī, and Ḥayūyal b. Nāshira al-Maʿāfirī.[160] They resolved the disputes among the tribes, and settled the people in their lots. So [the people] marked out the neighorhoods (*khiṭaṭ*) and built houses and mosques. Each neighborhood (*khiṭṭa*) was named after the tribe, group, or person that marked it out.

Enigmatic Terms of the Prophet's Traditions), ed. Ali al-Bajawy and Muhammad Abu al-Fadl (Beirut: Second Edition), Vol. 3, 116).

156 ʿAmr b. al-ʿĀṣ(d. 43 AH/664 AD) was one of the companions of the Prophet from the Banū Sahm branch of Quraysh tribe, the tribe to which the Prophet belongs. ʿAmr was a merchant who converted to Islam in the year 8 AH/ 629 AD, about six months before the conquest of Mecca. He was appointed as a military leader and participated in many battles and conquests under the Prophet and up to the reign of the second Caliph, ʿUmar b. Al-Khaṭṭāb, when he led a Muslim army to conquer Egypt in 20 AH/641 AD, expelling the Byzantines. Quite a controversial character in Islamic history, he was known for his intelligence and cunning, and was a shrewd politician and a wise ruler who ruled Egypt till his death and was loved by its people. He sided with and supported Muʿāwiya b. Abī Sufyān against ʿAlī b. Abī Ṭālib, in the first Muslim civil war that erupted after the murder of the third Caliph,ʿUthmān b. ʿAffān. ʿAmr was buried at the foot of the Muqattam Hills. (See Hasan I. Hasan, *Tārīkh 'Amr b. al-'Āṣ* (Cairo, 1996)).

157 Also, the "Lesser House." There were two houses attached to ʿAmr's mosque at its initial stages. One was the House of the Emirate (*dār al-imāra*), which ʿAmr built for himself to the east of the mosque. This house was called ʿAmr's Greater House (*dār 'Amr al-kubrā*). Another house was built by his son, ʿAbd Allah b. ʿAmr, and was called ʿAmr's Lesser House (*dār 'Amr al-Ṣughrā*), which was to the north of the Greater House. Qurra b. Sharīk, the Umayyad ruler of Egypt from 90 AH/709 AD to 95 AH/714 AD, incorporated both houses into the mosque during the renovations and restoration process in 91–93 AH/710–712 AD. (Khaled Azab,*Al-Fustat: 'Āṣimat Miṣr al-Islāmiyya* (Cairo, 2008), 16 & 106 and A. Abd al-Raziq, *Tārīkh*, 70).

158 Al-Jāmiʿ al-ʿAtīq, which is the Mosque of ʿAmr b. al-ʿĀṣ, to be described in detail later.

159 Could be "it," rather than "him," which would refer to either the tent or the mosque.

160 *Khiṭaṭ* (sing. *khiṭṭa*):"concession, block of land in a newly founded city." (André Raymond, *Cairo: City of History*, trans. Willard Wood (Cairo, 2007), 386). The term also means "neighbourhood"and "plan," and was used to refer to uninhabited lands or these that have no rightful owners, which were marked out with lines by new settlers to build their houses. Generally, "*khṭaṭ*" denoted unowned plots allocated by a Muslim ruler to certain groups to found neighbourhoods in new cities, such as Basra, Kufa and Baghdad. (See http://www.baheth.info/all.jsp?term=خطط). Henceforth, the term *khiṭṭa* will be translated as "neighbourhood." The *khiṭaṭ*, in written works, are the topographical descriptions of the neighbourhoods in Islamic cities (See also fn. 174).

The Neighbourhoods of Fustat

As for the neighbourhoods (*khiṭaṭ*) and houses named after the tribes and groups, [they included]:

The Neighbourhood of the People of the Banner (*Khiṭṭat Ahl al-Rāya*),[161] who were a group from [the tribes of] Quraysh, al-Anṣār, Khuzā'a, Aslam, Ghifār, Muzayna, Ashja', Juhayna, Thaqīf, Daws, 'Abs b. Baghīḍ, Jurash of Banū[162] Kināna, and Layth b. Bakr. Each of these [tribes] did not have a large enough number to be assigned a single bestowal[163] from the register (*dīwān*);[164] therefore 'Amr b. al-'Aṣ assigned them a banner that he had not ascribed to anyone. He said: You are to stand beneath it [at times of assembly], so it was like a collective ascription to them. Their register was [assigned to] it;[165] therefore, they were known as the People of the Banner (*Ahl al-Rāya*). They had their own individual neighbourhood, which was one of the grandest and widest.

The Neighbourhood of Mahra (Khiṭṭat Mahra), who are Banū Mahra b. Ḥaydān b. 'Amr b. Ilḥaf b. Quḍā'a b. Mālik b. Ḥimyar, of the tribes of Yemen.

The Neighbourhood of Tujīb (Khiṭṭat Tujīb), who are the sons of (*banū*) 'Adiy and Sa'd, themselves the sons of al-Ashras b. Shabīb b. al-Sakan b. al-Ashras b. Kinda. Tujīb was the name of their mother, after whom the tribe was known.

The Neighbourhood of Lakhm (Khiṭat Lakhm), which were three [Neighbourhood]: the first [for] Banū Lakhm b. 'Adiy b. Murra b. Udad, and those who mingled with[166] them from Judhām; the second [for] Banū 'Abd Rabbih b. 'Amrb. al-Ḥarth b. Wā'il b. Rāshida b. Lakhm, and the third [for] Banū Rāshida b. Adhabb b. Juzayla b. Lakhm.

The Neighbourhood of al-Lafīf (Khiṭat al-Lafīf),[167] which was a group of tribes who hastened to [attack] the ships of the *Rūm*as soon as the news reached

161 This was the largest and most important plot, which was allotted to the tribes to which the Companions of the Prophet who joined the conquest belonged. "In total, they comprised a little less than the quarter of the number of tribes in Fustat," which amounted to 26 tribes. (K. Azab, *Fustat*, 17)

162 "*Banū*" and "*banī*" both mean "the sons of."

163 *Da'wa*, from the verb *da'ā*, which means "call upon," as in pray or invite. The term was used to refer to the precedence of a group or tribe in receival of bestowals. (See *Al-Bāhith al-'Arabī*, http://www.baheth.info/all.jsp?term=دعوة).

164 *Dīwān* (pl. *dawāwīn*)may be translated as "register" or "bureau" and the word refers to registers, as well as administrative departments that are comparable to present day ministries. Caliph 'Umar b. al-Khaṭṭāb was the first Muslim ruler to found a system of administration based on registers, due to the vast expansion of the Islamic empire and the need for state regulation. *Dīwān* may also be used to refer to an office, office hall or court hall.

165 "Their *dīwān* was upon it," which probably means that it was assigned to it or associated with it.

166 "*Khālaṭahum*," from the verb *khālaṭa*, which may also mean "to partner with." (See *Al-Bāhith al-'Arabī*, http://www.baheth.info/all.jsp?term=خالط).

167 *Al-Lafīf* is translated as: the gathering, the crowd of various nations, the mingled crowd, and the mixed crowd. (The Quranic Arabic Corpus – Translation, http://corpus.quran.com/translation.jsp?chapter=17&verse=104).

ʿAmr that they arrived in Alexandria, at the time of its conquest. Finding them so many, ʿAmr told them: "You are just as Allah said: 'when there comes the promise of the Hereafter, We will bring you forth in [one] gathering.'"[168] Then they were called "*al-Lafīf*" (the Gathering) from that day onwards.

The Neighbourhood of Ahl al-Ẓāhir (Khiṭaṭ Ahl al-Ẓāhir),[169] who were a group of tribes that came back from Alexandria after ʿAmr's return to find that people had taken over their settlements. They sought the arbitration of Muʿawiya b. Ḥudayj, whom ʿAmr had appointed in charge of the neighbourhoods. Muʿawiya told them: I suggest that you build to the rear of those tribes and build your own houses. Their settlement was, therefore, called al-Ẓāhir (the Rear).[170]

The Neighbourhood of Ghāfiq (Khiṭat Ghāfiq), who are Banū Ghāfiq b. al-Ḥārīth b. ʿAkk b. ʿUdthān b. ʿAbd Allah b. al-Azd.

The Neighbourhood of al-Ṣadif (Khiṭat al-Ṣadif), pronounced "*ṣadif*," who are Banū Mālik b. Sahl b. ʿAmr b. Qays b. Ḥimyar, of the tribes of Yemen, also said to have been Banū Mālik b. Muraqqaʿ b. Kinda. He[171] was called al-Ṣadif because he turned his face away from (*ṣadafa*) his people when they were hit by al-ʿArim torrent.

The Neighbourhood of Khawlān (Khiṭat Khawlān), who are Banū Khawlān b. ʿAmr b. Mālik b. Zayd b. ʿArīb.

The Neighbourhood of the Persians (Khiṭat al-Fārisiyyīn), who are the remnants of the soldiers of Bādhān, the Governor of Yemen appointed by Kisrā, the King of the Persians.

The Neighbourhood of Madhḥij (Khiṭat Madhḥij), who are Banū Mālik b. Murra b. Udad b. Zayd b. Kahlān b. ʿAbd Allah.

The Neighbourhood of Yaḥṣub (Khiṭṭat Yaḥṣub), who are Banū Yaḥṣub Mālik b. Aslam b. Zayd b. Ghawth b. Ḥimyar.

The Neighbourhood of Ruʿayn (Khiṭṭat Ruʿayn), who are Banū Ruʿayn b. Zayd b. Sahl b. Yaʿfur b. Murra b. Udad.

The Neighbourhood of Banī al-Kulāʿ (Khiṭṭat Banī al-Kulāʿ), who is al-Kulāʿ b. Shuraḥbīl b. Saʿd b. Ḥimyar.

The Neighbourhood of al-Maʿāfir (Khiṭṭat al-Maʿāfir), who are Banū al-Maʿāfir b. Yaʿfur b. Murra b. Udad.

The Neighbourhood of *Saba'* (Khiṭat Saba'), who are Banū Mālik b. Zayd b. Wulayʿa b. Maʿbad b. Saba'.

The Neighbourhood of Banī Wā'il (Khiṭṭat Banī Wā'il), who is Wā'il b. Zayd b. Manat b. Afṣā b. Iyās b. Ḥarām b. Judhām b. ʿAdiy.

The Neighbourhood of al-Qabaḍ (Khiṭṭat al-Qabaḍ), who are Banu al-Qabaḍ b. Marthad.

168 Quran – Sūrat Al-Isrā' (Chapter of the Night Journey, 17:104 (in part)), Sahih International's translation (http://corpus.quran.com/translation.jsp?chapter=17&verse=104).

169 From the verb *ẓahara*, which has several meanings, including "to overcome" or "to conquer."

170 Another translation for "*taẓharū 'alā* " may mean to overcome or conquer. However, it is highly unlikely that a conflict that can be only settled by force would have been allowed by the arbitrator.

171 The great grandfather, either Mālik b. Ḥimyar or Mālik b. Kinda.

The Neighbourhood of the Reds (Khiṭṭat al-Ḥamrawāt), whichwere three. They were so called because the *Rūm*, whose colours were red, inhabited them:[172]

The First – The Nearer Ḥamrā' (al-Ḥamrā' al-Dunyā), which includes the neighbourhood of Baliy, who are Banū Baliy b. ʿAmr b. Ilḥāf b. Quḍāʿa, except those who inhabited [the neighbourhood of] the People of the Banner (Ahl al-Raya). It also includes the neighbourhood of Thurād of al-Azd, and the neighbourhood of Fahm, who are Banū Fahm b. ʿAmr b. Qays b. ʿAylān, and the neighbourhood of Banī Baḥr b. Sawāda of al-Azd.

The Second – The Middle Ḥamrā' (al-Ḥamrā' al-Wusṭā), which includes the neighbourhood of Banī Nabah, who are from the *Rūm* who were present at the conquest, and the neighbourhood of Hudhayl, who are Banū Hudhayl b. Mudrika b. Ilyās b. Muḍar, and the neighbourhood of Banī Salāmān of al-Azd.

The Third – The Farther Ḥamrā', (al-Ḥamrā' al-Quṣwā), which is the neighbourhood of Banī al-Azraq of the *Rūm*, of whom four-hundred men were present at the conquest, and the neighbourhood of Banī Yashkur b. Juzayla of Lakhm, to whom Mount Yashkur is attributed. Aḥmad b. Ṭūlūn's mosque, which will be later mentioned among the mosques of Fustat, was built upon this mountain.[173]

The Neighbourhood of Ḥaḍramawt (Khiṭaṭ Ḥaḍramawt), who are Banū Ḥaḍramawt b. ʿAmr b. Qays b. Muʿāwiya b. Ḥimyar tribe.

[All the above is] in addition to the other neighbourhoods that disappeared before there was interest in authoring works on the layouts of neighbourhoods (*khiṭaṭ*).[174]

The Houses of Fustat

And you should know that amidst these neighbourhoods, there were houses of a large group of the companions (*ṣaḥāba*)[175] of the Prophet who joined the conquest. These included the houses of: ʿAmr b. al-ʿĀṣ; al-Zubayr b. al-ʿAwwām;[176] Qays b. Saʿd b.

172 The colours referred to may be those of their hairs and complexions. K. Azab mentions another reason given to the name, which is that they used red banners. (K. Azab, *Fustat*, 76).

173 See later for the mosque and the mountain.

174 The *khiṭaṭ* were works providing topographical descriptions of the neighbourhoods in Islamic cities, with details of planning and history, such as the *Khiṭaṭ* of al-Maqrīzī and *Khiṭaṭ* of Ibn ʿAbd al-Ẓāhir. (See also fn. 160).

175 Some religious scientists defined this companionship as having met the Prophet and died a Muslim, while some others necessitate more conditions such as spending a minimum period of a year in companionship, so as to ensure that this person has indeed learned the Prophet's teachings and ethics and is worthy of the honour of being called a companion.

176 The house of al-Zubayr occupied the north-western corner of the current Mosque of ʿAmr and it was incorporated in it in the renovations of 133 AH/750 AD. (A. Abd al-Raziq, *Tārīkh*, 72).

ʿUbāda al-Anṣārī; Maslama b. Mukhallad al- Anṣārī; ʿAbd al-Raḥman b. ʿUdays al-Balawī; Wahb b. ʿUmayr b. Wahb b. Khalaf al-Jumaḥī; Nāfiʿ b. ʿAbd al-Qays b. Laqīṭ al-Fihrī; Saʿd b. Abī Waqāṣ; ʿUqba b. ʿĀmir al-Juhanī; al-Qāsim; ʿAmr b. Qays b. ʿAmr; ʿAbd Allah b. Saʿd b. Abī Sarḥ al-ʿĀmirī; Masʿūd b. al-Aswad b. ʿAbd Shams b. Ḥarām al-Balawī; al-Mustawrid b. Shaddād al-Fihrī; Ḥuyaiy b. Ḥarām al-Laythī – whose companionship is controversial –;[177] al-Ḥarth b. Mālik al-Laythī, known as Ibn al-Barṣā'; Bishr b. Arṭāt al-ʿĀmirī; Abū Thaʿlaba al-Khushanī; Iyās b. al-Bukayr al-Laythī; Maʿmar b. ʿAbd Allah b. Naḍla al-Qurashī al-ʿAdawī; Abū al-Dardāʿ al-Anṣārī; Yaʿqūb al-Qibṭī,[178] the messenger that al-Muqawqis[179] sent to the Prophet with Maria,[180] the mother of his son, and her sister, Shīrīn;[181] Muhājir, the freed slave (*mawlā*) of Umm Salamā,[182] the Prophet's wife; ʿUlba b. Zayd al-Anṣārī; Muḥammad b. Maslama al-Anṣārī; Abū al-Aswad Masrūḥ b. Sidr al-Ḥiṣnī; ʿAbd Allah b. ʿUmar b. al-Khaṭṭāb; Khārija b. Ḥudhāfa b. Ghānim al-ʿAdawī;[183] ʿUqba b. al-Ḥarth; ʿAbd Allah b. Ḥudhāfa al-Sahmī; Maḥmiyya b. Jaz' al-Zabīdī; al-Muṭṭalib b. Abī Wadāʿa al-Sahmī; Hubayb b. Maʿqil al-Ghifārī, after whom the Valley of Hubayb[184] near Alexandria is named; ʿAbd Allah b. al-Sā'ib al-Makhzūmī; Jabr

177 This expression is used to denote that the person's companionship to the Prophet is not a proven historical fact.

178 Al-Qibṭī means "the Copt," which was the term used to identify Egyptians before the Islamic conquest.

179 There is controversy about his exact name and historians give mixed accounts of his identity; however, al-Muqawqis was the ruler of Egypt and the chief of its Copts.

180 When Prophet Muḥammad sent a letter to al-Muqawqis to invite him to embrace Islam in the year 7 AH/628 AD, the latter replied with a friendly letter and some presents including two women-slaves: Maria and her sister Sīrīn. The Prophet took Maria for himself to marry and gave Sīrīn to one of his companions, Ḥassān b. Thābit. Maria gave birth to a boy with whom the Prophet was very happy and called Ibrāhīm, but the child did not survive and died of fever when he was only about a year and a half old. Maria died in the year 16 AH/ 637 AD, after living in solitary and grief for the years that followed the Prophet's death. (Muhammad A. Qutb, *Zawjāt al-Anbiyā' wa Ummahāt al-Mu'minīn* (Cairo, 2004), 182–187).

181 Other sources spell the name as Sīrīn. (M. Qutb, *Zawjāt*, 183).

182 Umm Salama (Mother of Salama), Hind bint Abī Umayya, was one of the early converters to Islam. She and her husband, ʿAbd Allah b. ʿAbd al-Asad, the Prophet's cousin, were known to have become sincere believers of the new faith. When ʿAbd Allah, a brave warrior, died of an injury in combat, the Prophet offered to marry his widow, so as to take care of her and her four children. Umm Salama had initially refused, but was later convinced. She was known to have been one of the Prophet's wise wives, to whose advice he often listened. (M. Qutb, *Zawjāt*, 148–152).

183 When ʿAmr Ibn al-ʿAṣ sent to Caliph ʿUmar Ibn al-Khaṭṭāb asking for reinforcements of three thousand horesemen during his conquest of Egypt, it is told that ʿUmar sent him only three, one of whom was Khārija. Khārija participated in the conquest of Egypt and lived there till he was killed when he was mistaken for ʿAmr Ibn al-ʿAṣ by an assassin who was one of the rebels against ʿAlī b. AbīṬālīb (known as "the *khawārij*"). These rebels had conspired to kill ʿAlī b. Abī Ṭālib, Muʿāwiya b. Abī Sufyān, and ʿAmr Ibn al-ʿAṣ, in an effort to end the chism in the Islamic caliphate at that time. (Ibn al-Athīr, *Asad al-Ghāba fī Maʿrifat al-Ṣaḥāba* (Beirut, 2012), Vol. 1, 316).

184 Wādī Hubayb, which is today's Wādī al-Naṭrūn to the south of al-Buḥayra Governorate in north-west Egypt. Al-Maqrīzī informs us that this valley was named after Hubayb when he retired

al-Qibṭī,[185] the messenger al-Muqawqis sent to the Prophet; Yazīd b. Ziyād al-Aslamī; ʿAbd Allah b. Rayyān al-Aslamī – whose companionship is controversial – ; Abū ʿUmayra Rashīd b. Mālik al-Muzanī; Sibāʿ b. ʿUrfuṭa al-Ghifārī; Naḍla b. al-Ḥarth al-Ghifārī; al-Ḥarth b. Asad al-Khuzāʿī – whose companionship is controversial – ; ʿAbd Allah b. Hishām b. Zuhara, a descendant of Tamīm b. Murra.[186]

[And] Khārija b. Ḥudhāfa b. Ghānim al-ʿAdawī,[187] who was the first to build a high chamber (*ghurfa*)[188] in Fustat. A letter was written to Caliph ʿUmar b. al-Khaṭṭāb[189] to ask him about this matter. He replied to ʿAmr b. al-ʿĀṣ saying: "Go inside Khārija's chamber, set up a seat (*sarīr*)[190] in it and have a man, who is neither tall nor short, stand on it. If he could see through its apertures,[191] then demolish it". ʿAmr did that and the man could not reach the apertures, so the chamber was approved.[192]

[The houses also included those of] Muḥammad b. Ḥāṭib al-Jumaḥī; Rifāʿa al-Dawsī; Faḍāla b. ʿUbayd al-Anṣārī; al-Muṭṭalib b. Abī Wadāʿa al-Sahmī,[193] in

there after the assassination of Caliph ʿUthmān (see Glossary: "Rightly-guided Caliphs"). The valley used to have 100 Christian monasteries, of which seven survived by the time of al-Maqrīzī. It was a source for several minerals. (Al-Maqrīzī, *Khiṭaṭ*, Vol. 1, 523–524). Today, the area includes the famous Christian monastery called Dayr Wādī al-Naṭrūn.

185 The correct name is Yaʿqūb al-Qibṭī. (See ʿAbd al-Karīm b. Muḥammad b. Manṣūr al-Samʿānī, *Al-Ansāb*, ed. Abd al-Rahman b. Yahya al-Yamani, et al (Hyderabad, 1962), Vol. 10, 330).

186 Tamīm b. Murra is the great grandfather of one of the tribes of the line of Muḍur, who descend from ʿAdnān. Arab tribes can all be traced to two major lineages: Qaḥṭān and ʿAdnān, the first is the great grandfather of the pure Arab tribes (*al-'arab al-'āriba*), while the second is the great grandfather of the Arabs of non-Arab origins (*al-'arab al-musta'riba*). The Prophet's tribe, Quraysh, is from the line of ʿAdnān. (Abd al-Hamid Hammuda, *Tārīkh al-'Arab Qabl al-Islām* (Cairo, 2006), 41–46).

187 See fn. 183.

188 The term "*ghurfa*" means a "*'ulayya*," which is a high structure. It is also used to mean a chamber or hall. We can assume that this was either a second-story structure that may expose the neighbours' single-storied houses, or it may have had high walls with windows higher than the surrounding structures.

189 Second of the Rightly-guided Caliphs (See Glossary: "Rightly-guided Caliphs"), who ruled from 13 AH/634 AD to 23 AH/ 644 AD. Egypt was conquered during the reign of ʿUmar, which is recurrently referred to in Islamic history as the role-model for just rulers.

190 Also, bed.

191 *Kuwā* (also,*kuwwāt*, sing. *kuwwa*) means the opening in a wall (see http://www.baheth.info/all.jsp?term=كوة). In architecture, the term is used to refer to any openings for ventilation or illumination, such as windows or skylights.

192 As can be understood from the passage, all the houses first built in Fustat were single-story houses, except for Khārija's, who most probably built a chamber above his house as a second floor. Privacy is most cherished in Islam and Islamic architecture provides many examples of how it can be ensured. Caliph ʿUmar's concern was that this chamber being higher than the neighbouring houses might expose the neighbours. The experiment that he ordered ʿAmr to conduct proved that such exposure was not possible, which spared this chamber from being torn down. ʿAmr was acting in his capacity as ruler and enforcer of Islamic law (*sharī'a*). Settlement of such building code issues was later relegated to the official known as the "*muḥtasib*" among his other duties to ensure privacy and apply the Islamic concept of "no harm" to others. Judges also sometimes ruled on such problems.

193 This name was already stated above.

addition to other houses that were not mentioned by the authors of the layouts of neighbourhoods (*khiṭaṭ*).

The House of the Amir (Dār al-Imāra)

I say: The rulers (amirs)[194] of Egypt, who were of the same situation as its present kings, used to reside in Fustat. Initially, the amirs did not have specific quarters; neither did they have a particular amirial residence (*dār al-imāra*).

The first amir of Egypt, ʿAmr b. al-ʿĀṣ, resided in his house near the mosque. All the amirs following ʿAmr, and up to the end of the Umayyad Dynasty,[195] resided in their own houses. [The Umayyad amir], ʿAbd al-ʿAzīz b. Marwān,[196] who ruled Egypt under the caliphate of his brother,ʿAbd al-Malik b. Marwān,[197] built a great house in Fustat in the year 67 AH/687 AD. He called this house "Dar al-Dhahab" (the House of Gold) and built it with a golden dome that when the sun came up, a beholder could not stare at in fear for his eyesight. [The house] was known as "al-Madīna" (The City) because of its spaciousness and magnificence. ʿAbd al-ʿAzīz, and his sons after him, resided in this house. When Marwān b. Muḥammad,[198] the last Umayyad Caliph, fled to Egypt, he resided in this house as well. When he was about to be caught by his pursuers,[199] he ordered it burnt down. Some descendants of ʿAbd al-ʿAzīz b. Marwān blamed him for that, so he replied: "If I stay, I will rebuild it with alternating golden and silver bricks, or else, the bigger calamity is that which harms your person, and your enemy is not to enjoy it after you are gone".

When the Abbasids defeated the Umayyads and Marwān b. Muḥammad fled to the Egyptian territories, he was followed by ʿAlī b. Ṣāliḥ b. ʿAlī al-Hāshimī,[200] until he caught up with him in Egypt and killed him. ʿAlī was established as the

194 The term *amīr* (amir), loosely "prince," means the person who has the authority to order, rule, command, and dominate. In early Islam, the term was used to denote rulers in general as well as high military leaders. Later, it came to denote the rulers of the provinces under the Islamic caliphate. During the Umayyad and Abbasid eras, it also referred to those who were next in line to become caliphs. In the Fatimid era, this title was used by the caliph's sons, and was given to some statesmen, caliph's mamluks, and provincial rulers. Members of the Ayyubid ruling family used this title. Generally, the term denoted belonging to a certain category, or was employed as a military rank, or an honourific title. By the Mamluk era, the term was used to refer to military leaders, who were categorized according to the numbers of the forces they commanded, which is later explained in this book. (Hasan al-Basha, *al-Alqābal-Islāmiyya fī al-Tārīkh wa-l-Wathā'iq wa-l-Āthār* (Cairo, 1989), 179–185 and Tarek Abdelhamid, *al-Jaysh fī al-'Aṣr al-Mamlūkī* (Cairo, 2012), 21).

195 See Glossary:"Umayyads."

196 Umayyad ruler of Egypt from 65 AH/685 AD to 86 AH/705 AD.

197 Umayyad Caliph from 65 AH/685 to 86 AH/705 AD.

198 Umayyad Caliph from 127 AH/744 AD to 132 AH/750 AD.

199 That is, the Abbasids. (See Glossary).

200 The author means Ṣāliḥ b. ʿAlī b. ʿAbd Allah b. ʿAbbās, the first Abbasid ruler of Egypt from 132 AH/750 to 133 AH/751 AD.

ruler (amīr) of Egypt under the caliphate of the first Abbasid caliph,[201] al-Saffāḥ.[202] He built himself an amirial house (*dār al-imāra*) and resided in it, and it became the residence of the amirs after him until Aḥmad b. Ṭūlūn[203] ruled over the lands of Egypt. Ibn Ṭūlūn initially resided in it until he later marked out his palace, known as "al-Maydān,"[204] in between the present Citadel of the Mountain[205] and the Shrine of al-Sayyida Nafīsa,[206] and what is beyond that, in the year 256 AH/870 AD. The palace had several doors, some near the Shrine of al-Sayyida Nafīsa and some near [Ibn Ṭūlūn's] mosque, to be accounted for later. People started marking-out lots around it, and each one cut out a segment of land (*qaṭī'a*)[207] and built on it. So, [the segments] were called: "Qaṭī'at Hārūn b. Khumārawayh" (the Segment of Hārūn b. Khumārawayh), "Qaṭī'at al-Sūdān" (the Segmentof the Sudanese), "Qaṭī'at al-Farrāshīn" (the Segmentof the Caretakers);[208]therefore, this place became known as "al-Qaṭā'i'" (the segments).[209] The construction [activities] escalated until al-Qaṭā'i' became connected to Fustat, and all became one city. Aḥmad b. Ṭūlūn resided in this palace of his, and so did his descendents after him, while the amirial house (*dār al-imāra*) that was built by 'Alī b. Ṣāliḥ was neglected. This remained the casefter Ibn Ṭūlūn, in the days of his son, Khumārawayh,[210] and his grandsons, Jaysh and Hārūn.[211] Building activities and population increased in

201 See Glossary: "Abbasids."

202 Abū al-'Abbās al-Saffāḥ, the first Abbasid Caliph who ruled from 132 AH/749 to 136 AH/754 AD.

203 See Glossary: "Tulunids."

204 *Maydān* (pl. *mayādīn*) means: field, square, arena or roundabout. Also, "field for equestrian exercises." (A. Raymond, *Cairo,* 386).

205 Qal'at al-Jabal: The citadel that Ṣalāḥ al-Dīn constructed on the Muqaṭṭam Mountain, to the east of Cairo in 579 AH/1183 AD. It became the seat of government and a military barracks that was subjected to several additions and renovations over centuries. (See later).

206 Al-Mashhad al-Nafīsī: Al-Sayyida Nafīsa (Lady Nafīsa, d. 208 AH/824 AD) was the great granddaughter of the Prophet, through his grandson, al-Ḥasan b. 'Alī. She was a learned woman who was most celebrated by the people of Egypt when she chose to come to their homeland in 193 AH/809 AD. Her shrine is still visited for blessings until today. She was buried in her house, where she dug her own grave before she died. A simple fence was built around her grave in the Abbasid era. The grave was turned into a domedshrine under the Fatimids, and has been subject to restorations and renovations ever since, turning it into a mosque-mausoleum complex. It is located in the northwest corner of the cemetery presently named after al-Sayyida Nafīsa in today's southern necropolis of Cairo. (Muhammad Abd al-Sattar Uthman, *'Imārat al-Mashāhid wa-l-Qibāb fī al-'Aṣr al-Fāṭimī* (Cairo, 2006), 122–124 and Galila ElKadi and A. Bonnamy, *Architecture for the Dead: Cairo's Medieval Necropolis* (Cairo, 2007), 23).

207 Pl. *qaṭā'i'*; also, ward.

208 The *farrāshīn* (sing. *farrāsh*) were the caretakers of the palaces. See later for further explanation.

209 Also, "the wards." This was the third Islamic capital of Egypt, which Aḥmad b. Ṭūlūn started building in 254 AH/868 AD to the northeast of the first two. The first was Fustat in 21 AH/642 AD, and the second was al-'Askar (the Soldiers) in 132 AH/750 AD.

210 Second Ṭūlūnid governor who ruled from 270 AH/884 AD to 283 AH/896 AD.

211 Third and fourth Ṭūlūnid governors who ruled in 283 AH/896 AD and from 283 AH/896 AD to 291 AH/904 AD, respectively.

al-Qaṭā'iʿ in the days of Jaysh and Hārūn, until the latter was murdered, just as were his father and brother before him. Dispatched by the Abbasid Caliph al-Mustakfī bi Allah,[212] Muḥammad b. Sulaymān al-Kātib[213] marched with the soldiers from Iraq, to arrive in Egypt in 292 AH/905 AD. The Ṭūlūnids had, at the time, established Rabīʿa b. Aḥmad b. Ṭūlūn,[214]as their ruler. He surrendered the country to [al-Kātib] who destroyed al-Qaṭā'iʿ and demolished the palace, removed its foundations, and razed its location to the ground until no trace of it remained.[215]

Badr al-Khufayfī,[216] Aḥmad b. Ṭūlūn's slave-boy (*ghulām*)[217] had built a great house in Fustat, near the old [open] prayer area (*muṣallā*).[218] It was said that Aḥmad b. Ṭūlūn bought this house for Badr before he had become displeased with him and shunned him. After Badr, Ṭāhir b. Khumārawayh resided in this house, followed by al-Ḥammāmī, Aḥmad Ibn Ṭūlūn's slave-boy. Muḥammad b. Sulaymān al-Kātib dwelled in this house after he destroyed Ibn Ṭūlūn's house in al-Qaṭā'iʿ. He was followed by the next amir of Egypt, ʿĪsā al-Nawsharī.[219] This house remained the residence of the amirs until al-Ikhshīd[220] came to rule Egypt, when he enlarged it, added to its grandeur, and provided it with a field (*maydān*) that had an iron gate, in the year 331 AH/943 AD. The house remained to be the dwelling of Egypt's amirs until the Fatimids caliphs[221] defeated the Ikhshidids, and General Jawhar[222] built

212 The Abbasid caliphwho ruled from Baghdad from 289 AH/902 to 295 AH/908 AD was al-Muktafī, rather than al-Mustakfī, who ruled from 333 AH/944 AD to 334 AH/946 AD.

213 The Abbasid general who was sent to conquer the Ṭūlūnids in 292 AH/905 AD.

214 After Jaysh b. Khumārawayh b. Ṭūlūn, the ruler of Egypt, was assassinated in 283 AH/896 AD, his young brother, Harūn was appointed ruler under the regency of Abū Jaʿfar b. Abiy. Ibn Abiy ordered Harūn's uncle, Rabīʿa b. Aḥmad b. Ṭūlūn to move to Alexandria, away from the capital, which he did. However, when some people wrote to him encouraging him to come back and claim the throne, he returned, only to be captured and killed in 283 AH/896 AD. He never made it to sovereignty and the ruler of Egypt at the advent of al-Kātib was Shaybān b. Aḥmad b. Ṭūlūn who only ruled for days in the year 292 AH/from 904 AD. (See Abū al-Maḥāsin Ibn Taghrī Birdī, *Al-Nujūm al-Zāhira fī Mulūk Miṣr wa-l-Qāhira*, Vol. 3, ed. Muhammad Husayn Shams al-Din (Beirut, 1992), 113–114 and 150–154).

215 See al-Maqrīzī's account in *Khiṭaṭ*, Vol. 1, 865–902.

216 The last name may also be pronounced "al-Khafīfī." The absence of diacritical marks in the text makes both pronunciations possible.

217 Pl.*ghilmān* and*aghlām*. A term that linguistically means "young boys" and is used to denote slave-boys or mamluks.

218 A *muṣallā* means "a place for prayers," which was a wide, open area outside city walls, mostly "uncovered and bordered by low walls," and especially used for the prayers of the two Islamic feasts: ʿĪd al-Fiṭr, on occasion of breaking the fasting of the month of Ramadan and ʿĪd al-Aḍḥā, on occasion of offering sacrifice. (Ayman Fouad Sayyid, ed., *Nuzhat al-Muqlatayn fī Akhbār al-Dawlatayn* (Beirut, 1992), 178 fn. 2).

219 Abbasid ruler of Egypt from 292 AH/905 AD to 297 AH/910 AD.

220 See Glossary: "Ikhshidids."

221 See Glossary: "Fatimids."

222 Jawhar al-Ṣaqallī was the army general that the Fatimids sent to conquer Egypt in 358 AH/969 AD. The origin of Jawhar is controversial, for he is sometimes referred to as *al-Ṣaqallī* (the Sicilian), *al-Ṣaqlabī* (the Slav), or *al-Rūmī* (the Greek). He was also termed *al-Kātib* (the Scribe, meaning:

Cairo and The Palace.[223] He then moved the door of that house[224] to Cairo, and The Palace became the residence [of the Fatimids], as will be mentioned later in the description of the layouts of the neighbourhoods (*khiṭaṭ*) of Cairo.

The Expansion and Decline of Fustat

Fustat's construction came to increase with time, until it became fully constructed and extremely beautiful with its elegant houses; standing mosques; splendid baths; magnificent caravanserais (*qayāsir*),[225] and delightful parks. People travelled to it from all countries, and set out to it from all directions. It became overpopulated, and its vast space crowded with its inhabitants, to the extent that the author of *Īqāẓ al-Mutaghaffil* (Waking the Dozy)[226] related [a story] after one of its residents; that in the year 317 AH/929 AD, during the reign of Khumārawayh b. Ṭūlūn, he went to a bath that was built by the *Rūm* to find no workers to serve him. The bath had seventy workers, the least [busy] of whom bathing three individuals [simultaneously].[227] He then went into another bath, then another, to only find someone to serve him in the fourth bath, and the man who served him had another [client at the same time].

In another part [of the book], the author related [a story] after a man he trusted, after that man's father: that the father had seen a market that ran continuously along the main axial avenue (*qaṣaba*)[228] from al-Wakra Mosque[229] in Fustat and

the Clerk), since he was the secretary to both caliphs al-Manṣūr (r. 334 AH/946 AD – 342 AH/953 AD in North Africa) and al-Mu'izz (r. 342 AH/953 AD – 362 AH/973 AD in North Africa and r. 362 AH/973 AD – 365 AH/976 AD in Egypt); and *al-qā'id* (the General) under Caliph al-Mu'izz, whose armies he led. (Farhad Daftary, *The Ismā'īlis: Their Hisotry and Doctrines* (Cambridge, 1999), 169).

223 The Great Fatimid Palace was the largest Fatimid palace in Cairo and one of its main buildings. (See later).

224 It is not clear if it is the same iron door referred to earlier.

225 Sing. *qaysāriyya*, also "covered market." The terms *qaysāriyya*, *khān* and *wikāla* (also, *wakāla*) were used to refer to caravanserais that housed merchants and their merchandise. The *qaysāriyya* originally denoted a closed or "covered market for trading luxury items." (AlSayyad, 143). The Mamluk *wikāla* comprised residential floors around a central courtyard, where the ground floor contained shops or storerooms for merchandise, as well as spaces for the beasts of burden. (Nezar AlSayyad, *Cairo: Histories of a City* (Harvard, 2011) 142–143 and A. Raymond, *Cairo*, 387).

226 *Īqāẓ al-Mutaghaffil wa-Itti'āẓ al-Muta'ammil*(Waking the Dozy and Advising the Contemplator) is a non-extant work of Judge Tāj al-Dīn Muḥammad b. 'Abd al-Wahhāb (d. 730 H/1330 AD). "This book was only referred to in the works of al-Maqrīzī and al-Qalqashandī." (Z. al-Samarra'i, *Manhaj*, 94).

227 The statement may also mean that few of the workers had at least three clients, simultaneously.

228 Al-Maqrīzī also identifies the *qas,aba* to mean the urban part of a city or its major section. Fustat's *qas,aba*, he says, was its largest market. The *qaṣaba* here is Sūq al-Qaṣaba (Al-Qaṣaba Market), which ran from al-'Askar to Ibn Ṭūlūn's mosque. It was also called Sūq al-'Askar (the Market of al-'Askar) and came to be considered as one of the markets of Fustat. (Al-Maqrīzī, *Khiṭaṭ*, Vol. 2, 580 and K. Azab, *Fustat*, 100).

229 Al-Maqrīzī gives his account citing the same source, Ibn al-Mutawwaj's *Iqaẓ al-Mutaghaffil wa-Itti'āẓ al-Muta'ammil*. Al-Qalqashandī's account seems to combine two statements made

up to Ibn Ṭūlūn's Mosque. He counted the number of stalls (*maqā'id*)[230] that sold roasted chickpeas to find that they were three-hundred and ninety in number, in addition to the shops and what they contained.

The same author also reported after a man who told him he counted the copper buckets tied to the pulleys fitted in the arches overlooking the Nile, which were used to draw water, and found them to be 16,000. He said that the daily rent of a seat (*maq'ad*)[231] near the Tulunid hospital (*bīmāristān*)[232] reached twelve dirhams.[233]

Ibn Ḥawqal[234] had mentioned that there was a house in al-Mawqif[235] of Fustat, in his time, known as Dar Ibn ʿAbd al-ʿAzīz. The residents of this house received four-hundred water leather bags[236] daily. It included five mosques, two baths, and two bakeries.[237]

I say: Fustat continued to have splendid construction and brilliant inhabitants until the Fatimid Dynasty in Egypt built Cairo, as will be mentioned later. It was then that Fustat lost its glamour and started deteriorating. People began to move out of it to Cairo and its environs, so it lost most of its inhabitants and its construction continued to dilapidate. This was until the Crusaders controlled some of

by al-Maqrīzī. The first refers to a mosque inside Khiṭṭat Masjid ʿAbd Allah, called Masjid al-Zakāt, from which ran a continuous market avenue up to the Ibn Ṭūlūn's mosque. The second statement, more directly quoted by al-Qalqashandī, refers to an account of Masjid ʿAbd Allah, from which ran the benches for selling chickpeas up to Ibn Ṭūlūn's mosque. It might be that the mosques of ʿAbd Allah and al-Zakāt were quite close, or may be were one and the same. The Arabic words "*al-zakāt*" and "*al-wakra*," in a smudged or unclear handwriting', could be mistaken one for the other.(See al-Maqrīzī, *Khiṭaṭ*, Vol. 2, 914)

230 Sing. *maq'ad*, which means seat, in this context, probably refers to a kind of stall.

231 *Maq'ad*.

232 Pl. *bīmāristānāt*; originally a Persian term.

233 One of the coin categories, the value of which fluctuated based on time and minting material. The author does not mention which type of dirham in this case. (See Glossary: "*dirham*").

234 Ibn Ḥawqal al-Nāṣibī, Abū al-Qāsim Muḥammad b. ʿAlī (d. circa367 AH/977 AD), was born in Nusaybin, Turkey. He was a merchant, traveller and geographer, known for his work *Kitāb al-Masālik wa al-Mamālik* (Book on the Routes and Kingdoms) or *Kitāb Ṣūrat al-Arḍ* (Book of the Picture of Earth). His travels included: the Maghrib, Andalusia, Egypt, Azerbaijan, Iraq, Persia, and Transoxiana, among others. (Emilia Calvo, "*Ibn Ḥawqal,*" in *Encyclopaedia of the History*(Berlin, 2008), 1103–1104).

235 The word literally means "the stop" and is used to refer to the area used for stalling horses and other rides. Al-Maqrīzī mentions that it was within the Concession of Ahl al-Ẓāhir(Khiṭṭat Ahl al-Ẓāhir). (Al-Maqrīzī, *Khiṭaṭ*, Vol. 2, 22).

236 *Rāwiyat mā'*, (pl. *rawāyamā'*).

237 In Ibn Ḥawqal's account, this was the house and residence of ʿAbd al-ʿAzīz b. Marwān, the Umayyad ruler of Egypt (65 AH/685 AD to 86 AH/705 AD). Ibn Ḥawqal appears not to mention that the house was particularly in al-Mawqif, but he says it was in Fustat. He adds that Fustat had five mosques, two baths, several bakeries (*furn*, pl. *afrān*) for baking dough for its people, as well as its two congregational mosques; the Mosque of ʿAmr and the Mosque of Ibn Ṭūlūn, built above al-Mawqif. (Ibn Ḥawqal, *Ṣūrat al-Arḍ* (Beirut, 1938) Vol. 1, 146).

the Egyptian peripheries during the reign of al-ʿĀḍid,[238] the last Fatimid Caliph, whose vizier, at the time, was Shāwir al-Saʿdī.[239] He feared for Fustat, that the Crusaders may capture it and use it for fortification, so he burnt its houses down, which led to more destruction and evacuation.

Deterioration continued until the reign of al-Ẓāhir Baybars,[240] one of the Turkish[241] kings of Egypt, when people enthusiastically destroyed [the buildings in the city's] vacated neighbourhoods, and using the debris for construction on the Nile banks of both Fustat and Cairo. The demolition of Fustat buildings increased and continues until today, to the extent that only the buildings on its Nile bank and the areas nearby have remained, up to and beyond the Old Mosque (al-Jāmiʿ al-ʿAtīq),[242] and the areas in vicinity. Most of the old neighbourhoods (*khiṭaṭ*) of Fustat disappeared, and their plans were effaced, while what was left decayed and its features changed.

If you look at the *Khiṭaṭ* of al-Kindī,[243] al-Qaḍāʿī, and al-Sharīf al-Nassāba,[244] you would know the original construction [state] of Fustat and how it has changed now. I have only mentioned some of the neighbourhoods above to preserve their names and draw attention to how they were like. Currently, however, Fustat's Nile bank and its proximity host handsome buildings, grand houses, and huge palaces that delight the viewer and please the mind.

Most of Fustat's buildings were of the strongest and firmest structures, built with scraped bricks, gypsum and lime, and its extant remnants testify to

238 The last Fatimid Caliph who ruled from 555 AH/1160 AD to 566 AH/1171 AD.

239 Shāwir was the *wālī* (governor) of Qūṣ in Upper Egypt. In 558 AH/1163 AD, he was able to imprison then kill the Fatimid vizier al-Ṣāliḥ Ṭalāʾiʿ b. Ruzayk and assume his position. Shāwir was one of the two last viziers who competed for the position during the last turbulent Fatimid years, the other being Dirghām al-Mundhirī. Shāwir was the first to call upon the help of the Sunni Zangid powerful sultan Nūr al-Dīn Maḥmūd. (Ayman F. Sayyid, *Al-Dawla al-Fāṭimiyya fī Miṣr: Tafsīr Jadīd* (Cairo, 2007), 287–288).

240 The Bahri Mamluk sultan who ruled from 658 AH/1260AD to 676 AH/1277 AD. He is famous for his participation in defeating the Mongols and the Crusaders as an amir and continuing to rule over a powerful state that subdued its enemies as a sultan. Considered the true founder of the Mamluk era, Baybars survived until modern times in the Egyptian sentiment as the only medieval sultan who had a popular epic, mixing historical fact and fiction, describing his virtues, and sung by storytellers for centuries in many parts of Egypt.

241 Al-Qalqashandī and the historians of his time usually use the term "Turkish" to refer to the Mamluk state.

242 The Mosque of ʿAmr, see later.

243 Abū ʿUmar Muḥummad b. Yūsuf al-Kindī (d. 350 AH/961 AD) was an Egyptian historian and religious scholar. He is famous for his extant works: *Tasmiyat Wulāt Miṣr* (Enumeration of the Rulers of Egypt) and*al-Quḍāt* (the Judges). (See Matthew S. Gordon, *"al-Kindī,"* in *Medieval Islamic Civilization*, Vol. 1, ed. Josef Meri and Jere Bacharach (New York, 2006), 440).

244 Al-Sharīf Muḥammad b. Asʿad al-Juwwānī al-Nassāba, author of *al-Nuqat li-Muʿjam mā Uskhil min al-Khiṭaṭ* (Points on Difficult Plans). His title, "*al-sharīf*" indicates that he was of honourable descent from the line of the Prophet. Another title, *al-nassāba*, means that he was a scientist of genealogy (*ʿilm al-ansāb*). Al-Maqrīzī mentions another work of his, which is a book on genealogy called *al-Jawhar al-Maknūn fī Dhikr al-Qabāʾil wa-l-Buṭūn* (The Jewel on Tribes). (Al-Maqrīzī, *Khiṭaṭ*, Vol. 3, 682).

that. The ruined and demolished construction of the city has formed heaps that resemble huge mountains. Most of the buildings were abandoned, while some were populated by worthless mobs, in areas which are not considered within the urban zone.

Among the famous of these heaps (*kīmān*)[245] mentioned by al-Qaḍāʿī are: Kawm al-Jāriḥ; Kawm Dīnār; Kawm al-Samaka; Kawm al-Zīna, and Kawm al-Tirmis. The author of *Īqāẓ al-Mutaghaffil* added others, namely: Kawm Banī Wā'il; Kawm Ibn Ghurāb; Kawm al-Shuqāf, and Kawm al-Mashānīq.

Al-Rawḍa Island

Opposite Fustat, in the northern direction, is Jazīrat al-Ṣināʿa (the Island of Industry), now known as al-Rawḍa.[246] The island was a site for the shipbuilding industry (*ṣināʿat al-ʿamāʾir)*, therefore was attributed to it.

Al-Kindī said: Construction started on the [island] in the year 54 AH/674 AD. It became more known as al-Rawḍa (the garden) for its beauty and bloom, for the water surrounding it, and the gardens and palaces it hosts. It is an old island that existed at the time of the *Rūm*. It used to have a fortress with walls and towers. A bridge (*jisr*)[247] formed by ships anchored in the Nile, similar to the one over the Tigris in Baghdad, extended from al-Rawḍa to Fustat. This bridge stood until al-Ma'mūn[248] came to Egypt and established a new wooden bridge, which passers-by used to come and go. After al-Ma'mūn left Egypt, a wind storm hit at night and shattered the old bridge causing its ships to collide with the new one, hence both bridges were lost. The new bridge was then rebuilt and the old one was abandoned.

Al-Qaḍāʿī mentioned that it was extant at his time, which was during the Fatimid era. Aḥmad b. Ṭūlūn, the amir of Egypt during the caliphate of al-Muʿtamid,[249] renewed the aforementioned fortress in the year 203 AH/819 AD.[250] The fortress was then destroyed due to the Nile's erosion on its towers and to the passage of time. Al-Ṣāliḥ Najm al-Dīn Ayyūb[251] built a citadel in place of

245 The *kīmān* (sing. *kawm*) were the resulting debris of the consecutive fires, famines and epidemics that Fustat faced. The major fire that started this phenomenon was in 564 AH/1169 AD and was followed by several calamities that led to the formation of such heaps of wreckage. (K. Azab, *Fustat*, 43, 49, & 58–59).

246 This is the island that bears the same name today, al-Rawḍa (the garden), and is one of the neighbouthoods to the south of Cairo's centre.

247 Pl. *jusūr*, is a bridge or an embankment.

248 Abbasid caliph from 198 AH/813 to 218AH/833 AD.

249 Al-Muʿtamid was the Abbasid caliph from 256 AH/870 to 279 AH/892 AD. The Abbasid caliph who appointed Ibn Ṭūlūn a ruler of Egypt was al-Muʿtazz (r. 252 AH/866 AD – 255 AH/869 AD).

250 In accurate date; Ibn Ṭūlūn ruled Egypt from 254 AH/868 AD to 270 AH/884 AD.

251 Ayyubid sultan from 637 AH/1240 AD to 647 AH/1249 AD. He was famous for his wars with the Crusaders and for introducing the Bahri Mamluks, his large sect of slave soldiers who resided in the Citadel of al-Rawḍa Island and from which came some of the most powerful Mamluk sultans of the Bahri era. See Glossary: "Ayyubids" and "Bahri Mamluks".

this fortress[252] in the year 638 AH/1240 AD. This citadel remained until al-Muʿizz Aybakal-Turkumānī,[253] the first of the Turkish kings, demolished it and built his school (*madrasa*),[254] al-Muʿizziyya Madrasa,[255] in Raḥbat al-Kharrūb (al-Kharrūb Plaza),[256] using the citadel's debris. People started owning [land] properties in place of the citadel and this continued until our days. Only a few towers remained from the original citadel, and those were taken up as property by people who built houses upon them. When al-Ẓāhir Baybars came to power, he set out to rebuild it, but never managed to, and it remained as it was.

The Establishment of al-Mahrānī (Munsha'at al-Mahrānī)

I say: The branch of the Nile in between al-Ṣināʿa Island and Fustat was larger and deeper than the one between the island and Jīza.[257] This was later reversed to the extent that the branch between the island and Fustat was dry except during the flood season. A place that looks like an island appears in between the end of Fustat and the island. This place is known as "Munsha'at al-Mahrānī"[258]

252 It is interesting to note that the text gives a clear distinction between a "fort" (*ḥiṣn*) and a "citadel" (*qalʿa*). It can be suggested that the difference was in size and in the presence of a residence for the ruler or his representative, as well as other residences, which would be the case in a citadel, while a fort would have been occupied only by military personnel.

253 The first male Mamluk sultan of the Bahri Mamluk era, who succeeded Shajar al-Durr, the only female sultan, his wife whom he married after the death of her first husband, Sultan al-Ṣāliḥ Najm al-Dīn Ayyūb, and who ruled for some months in 648 AH/1250 AD. Aybak ruled from 648 AH/1250 AD to 655 AH/1257 AD.

254 An Islamic higher educational institution that mainly taught religious sciences, sometimes in addition to chosen secular sciences. A *madrasa* normally included residential quarters for students and functioned as a mosque as well. The running and upkeep of this institution, as well as the similar institutions that were of a Sufi nature, depended on charitable endowments that stipulated all relevant necessary conditions in detailed deeds called a *waqfiyya*.

255 The *madrasa* of al-Muʿizz Aybak, which he built in 654 AH/1256 AD. (K. Azab, *Fustat*, 88 and see also fn. 359 for "al-Muʿizziyya").

256 Al-Maqrīzī defines the *raḥba* (plaza, pl. *riḥāb*) to be "the large space," and adds that it might become occupied by buildings while retaining its name, although its character changes, or it might lose its name and character altogether. In other cases, some building might be demolished to leave a *raḥba* in its place. K. Azab explains that the *riḥāb* were like the squares we have in our modern cities, "and the *riḥāb* of Fustat might have been the meeting points of the streets and alleys of the city." Al-Kharrūb is carob. (Al-Maqrīzī, *Khiṭaṭ*, Vol. 2, 468 and K. Azab, *Fustat*, 78).

257 Jiza is currently pronounced "Giza."

258 Munsha'at al-Mahrānī means "the establishment of al-Mahrānī," where the term establishment denotes a new neighbourhood located adjacent to a city. M. al-Shishtawy informs us that its place currently occupies "the area bordered at the west by Sayyālat al-Rawḍa, at the south by the square and park of Fumm al-Khalīj, at the east by a line from al-ʿUyūn Street southwards to al-Munīra Street northwards, and at the south by Bustān al-Fāḍil Street and its extension." The *munsha'a* was originally a huge orchard that included a mosque and some houses and supplied Cairo with grapes and other fruits during the Ayyubid era. The Nile flooded the *munsha'a* in 660 AH/1262 AD but it flourished again in 669 AH/1270 or 671 AH/1272 AD when amir Sayf al-Dīn Balbān al-Mahrānī, after whom the area became known, built a mosque and a house there. The area remained heavily

and it is located at the mouth of the Khalīj (canal)[259] of Cairo, where the dam that is opened on the occasion of the Fulfillment of the Nile (*Wafā' al-Nīl*).[260] Munsha'at al-Mahrānī was originally a heap (*kawm*) used for burning bricks and known as al-Kawm al-Aḥmar (the Red Heap), which al-Qaḍā'ī counted among the heaps of Fustat.

The author of *Īqāẓ al-Mutaghaffil* said: The first to build in this area was Balbān al-Mahrānī,[261] during the reign of al-Ẓāhir Baybars, and therefore it was named after him.

Al-Ḥabash Pond (Birkat al-Ḥabash)

A pond lies next to Fustat, to its west, is known as al-Ḥabash Pond,[262] and is a planted land.

Al-Qaḍā'ī said: It was known as the Pond of al-Ma'āfir and Ḥimyar,[263] and to its east were gardens that were named after "al-Ḥabash,"[264] therefore the pond was named after the gardens.

inhabited throughout the Mamluk era, except for occasional times of calamities, as well as during the Ottoman era. The present day Qaṣr al-'Aynī district lies within its borders. (Muhammad al-Shistawy, *Mutanazzahāt al-Qāhira fī al-'Aṣrayn al-Mamlūkī wa-l-'Uthmānī* (Cairo, 1999), 34–38).

259 The Khalīj was the canal of Fustat connecting the Nile with the Red Sea; the Ancient Egyptians were the ones who originally dug this canal. It was redug after the Islamic conquest in 23 AH/644 AD upon Caliph 'Umar b. al-Khaṭṭāb's order to 'Amr b. al-'Āṣ, providing a direct channel of transportation between the newly founded capital and the Arabian Peninsula. It then became known as Khalīj Amīr al-Mu'minīn (The Canal of the Prince of the Faithful), and later bore other names, such as, Khalīj al-Qāhira (Canal of Cairo), al-Khalīj al-Ḥākimī (al-Ḥākim's Canal), after the Fatimid Caliph al-Ḥākim, and al-Khalīj al-Miṣrī (Canal of Miṣr). (See Dorris Behrens-Abouseif, *Islamic Architecture in Cairo: An Introduction* (Cairo, 1989), 3, Muḥyi al-Dīn b. 'Abd al-Ẓāhir, *al-Rawḍa al-Bahiyya al-Zāhira fī Khiṭaṭ al-Mu'iziyya al-Qāhira*, ed. Ayman Fouad Sayyid (Cairo, 1996), 115 and Ibn al-Ṭuwayr al-Qaysarānī, *Nuzhat al-Muqlatayn fī Akhbār al-Dawlatayn*, ed. Ayman Fouad Sayyid (Beirut, 1992), 40 & 201–203).

260 *Wafā' al-Nīl*, which may also be translated asthe "faithfullness," "sufficiency" or "loyalty" of the Nile; a celebration of the Nile inundation during the flood season reaching a certain measure to provide enough water for all purposes, indicating a prosperous year. The Nile annual flood season is from August/September to October/November.

261 See fn. 258.

262 Birkat a-Ḥabash was located to the south of Fustat in between al-Muqaṭṭam Mountain and the Nile. To the south of the pond were gardens and orchards; to its east was a hill on a part of which was the village of al-Basātīn; to its north was the cemetery known as al-Qarāfa al-Kubrā, or the Northern Cemetery, with al-Raṣad Mountain (the area now known as Isṭabl 'Antar) in its north-west; and to its west was the Nile and agricultural lands. There are two opinions as to why the pond was named al-Ḥabash (the Ethiopians): either after the gardens to its south, which were attributed to Qatāda b. Qays b. Ḥabashī al-Ṣadafy, who was in the Muslim army that conquered Egypt, and whose name refers to both Ethiopian and Yemeni origins; or after the Ethiopian monks who used to own lands that included the pond. (M. al-Shishtawy, *Mutanazzahāt*, 91–94).

263 Birkat Al-Ma'āfir and Ḥimyar, where al-Ma'āfir and Ḥimyar are both names of southern Arab tribes that came to Egypt upon its conquest.

264 Al-Ḥabash Gardens.

Ibn Yūnus[265] mentions in his History that these gardens were known after Qatāda b. Qays b. Ḥabashī al-Ṣadafī, who was among those who participated in the conquest of Egypt.[266]

I say: The gardens are now an endowment (*waqf*)[267] allocated to the Honourable Descendants (*ashrāf*)[268] of ʿAlī b. Abī Ṭālib, from the children he had with Fāṭima, the daughter of the Prophet. This *waqf* was assigned to the *ashrāf* by al-Ṣāliḥ Ṭalāʾiʿ,[269] the vizier of the Fatimid caliphs al-Fāʾiz[270] and al-ʿĀḍid. South of this *waqf*, where the cemetery lies, is a place known as al-Khandaq (the trench),[271] which ʿAbd al-Raḥman b. ʿUyayna[272] dug in the year 65 AH/685 AD, when Marwān

265 Abū Saʿīd ʿAbd al-Raḥman b. Abī al-Ḥasan b. Yūnus al-Ṣadafī (d. 347 AH/958 AD) was an Egyptian historian and a scholar of the Prophet's sayings. His title, al-Ṣadafī, indicates that he is from one of the large Yemeni tribes that came to Egypt. He is not to be confused with his son, Abū al-Ḥasan ʿAlī b. Yūnus (d. 399 AH/1009 AD), one of the greatest astronomers of his time. (Ibn Khallikān, *Wafayāt al-Aʿyān wa Anbāʾ Ahl al-Zamān*, ed. Ihsan Abbas (Beirut, 1994),Vol. 3, 137–138).

266 See Abū Saʿīd al-Ṣadafī, *Tārīkh Ibn Yūnus al-Miṣrī* (The History of Ibn Yūnus, the Egyptian) (Beirut, 2001), Vol. 1, 399.

267 The *waqf* (pl. *awqāf*) "is the permanent dedication by a Muslim of any property, in such a way that the appropriator's right is extinguished, for charity or for religious objects or purposes, or for the founder of the *waqf* during his lifetime or after his death, for his descendants, and on their extinction, to a purpose defined by the founder." There are three categories of *waqf*: a charity endowment (*waqf khairī*), a family endowment (*waqf ahlī*), and a mixed endowment (*waqf mukhtalaṭ*). The family endowment supports the family and descendants of the endower, according to the stipulations of the endowment deed, while mixed endowment is used for both descendants and charity. (See Jamal J. Nasir, *The Islamic Law of Personal Status* (London, 1990), 274).

268 "The *ashrāf* (pl. of *sharīf*) – the 'nobles' – or the *sāda* (pl. of *sayyid*) – the 'masters' – are usually considered to be the descendants of the Prophet Muḥammad by the marriage of his daughter Fāṭima to ʿAlī b. Abī Ṭālib. More precisely, the *ashrāf* are descendants of ʿAlī's elder son, Ḥasan, and the *sāda*, of his younger son, Ḥusayn. During the Abbasid period, the term *ashrāf* was applied to all *ahl al-bayt* (the Prophet's family, including for example, the descendants of Muḥammad ibn al-Ḥanafiyya, ʿAlī's second wife and the Hashimites), but the Fatimid rulers of Egypt (358 AH/969 AD – 566 AH/1171 AD) restricted its use to the descendants of Ḥasan and Ḥusayn. This restriction remained in force even after the government of Egypt became Sunni again." (Michael Winter, *Egyptian Society Under Ottoman Rule, 1517–1798* (London, 2005), 179).

269 Al-Ṣāliḥ Ṭalāʾiʿ b. Ruzayk was one of the powerful Fatimid viziers of the "Great Viziers" era. (See Glossary:"Fatimids"), who was in power from 549 AH/1154 AD to 555 AH/1160 AD.

270 Fatimid caliph from 549 AH/1154 AD to 555 AH/1160 AD.

271 This trench or moat was to the east of Fustat, in its cemetery. It ran from the Nile to al-Muqaṭṭam Mountain with the mausoleum of al-Imām al-Shāfiʿī on its western edge. ʿAbd al-Raḥman b. Jaḥdam (see fn. 272) was the first to dig it in 65 AH/ 684 AD, as a defensive measure to fight the approaching Umayyad army. The digging of the trench employed Egyptian peasants from every village and took one month. The moat was redug in the Abbasid and Fatimid eras also for defensive purposes. Al-Maqrīzī (d. 845AH/1441 AD) reports that by his time, the moat had disappeared. (Al-Maqrīzī, *Khiṭaṭ*, Vol 3, 682–685).

272 Al-Qalqashandī is referring to ʿAbd al-Raḥman b. ʿUqba b. Iyās b. Jaḥdam, who was appointed a ruler of Egypt in the year 65 AH/684 AD. When ʿAbd Allah b. al-Zubayr, a companion and the son of one of the close companions of the Prophet, managed to declare an independent caliphate in Madina, separate from the Umayyads, in the year 64 AH/684 AD, many Muslim lands, including Egypt, paid homage to him. ʿAbd Allah assigned ʿAbd al-Raḥman to rule Egypt, but soon enough

Ibn al-Ḥakam[273] set out for Egypt. For that reason, the place was named after this trench.

The Mosques of Fustat

As for the mosques of Fustat, they are six:

The First:

The Old Mosque known as the Mosque of ʿAmr[274]

When ʿAmr built his smaller house in place of his tent, as mentioned earlier, he marked-out the land for this mosque inside the Neighbourhood of the People of the Banner, mentioned above.

Al-Qaḍāʿī said: According to al-Layth b. Saʿd,[275] there used to be gardens in place of the mosque. Qaysaba b. Kulthūm al-Tujībī,[276] a member of Banī Sūm[277]tribe, had earned [possession] of its location and resided there during the siege of the fortress known as Qaṣr al-Shamʿ. Qaysaba gave the land to ʿAmr upon his request when he returned from Alexandria, so that he may build a mosque on it. Qaysaba said: I give this [land] as charity or alms (*ṣadaqa*)[278] to Muslims, and

after nine months of rule, the Umayyads, who were regaining their control of the caliphate set out to Egypt to re-subdue it. The army led by Caliph Marwān was able to recapture Egypt and ʿAbd al-Raḥman was replaced by Marwān's son, ʿAbd al-ʿAzīz. (Ibn Taghrī Birdī, *Nujūm*, Vol. 1, 215–216). The last name "Ibn ʿUyayna" was not found mentioned in relevance to this personin other historical sources, and the only governor of Egypt found to bear this last name is the Abbasid Mūsā b. Kaʿb b. ʿUyayna (141 AH/758 AD – 142 AD/759 AD).

273 Umayyad Caliph from 64 AH/684 AD to 65 AH/685 AD.

274 The Ancient Mosque or the Mosque of ʿAmr, which is the mosque that ʿAmr Ibn al-ʿĀṣ built in Fustat in 20 AH/641 AD. Several additions and restorations were made at this mosque since then and much of its original plan has changed. It was the first congregational mosque to be built in Islamic Egypt, therefore, it is cherished and given the titles "The Ancient Mosque" and Tāj al-Jawāmiʿ (the Crown of Mosques). Many of the earliest mosques in Egyptian cities, towns and villages are called al-ʿAmrī mosque, most probably in reference to the first Mosque built by ʿAmr. (See "Jamiʿ ʿAmr ibn al-ʿAs," http://archnet.org/sites/1511, D. Abouseif, *Architecture*, 48–51 and A. Abd al-Raziq, *Tārīkh*, 68–75).

275 Al-Layth b. Saʿd al-Fahmī (d. 157 AH/773 AD), a famous religious scholar of his time. Al-Qalqashandī says that as well as scholarly, al-Layth was also wealthy (Z. al-Samarra'i, *Manhaj*, 210). This is a merit, for his financial prosperity would allow the independence required for an objective religious intellect.

276 Qaysaba b. Kulthūm al-Tujībī al-Sūmī al-Kindī was a companion of the Prophet who witnessed the conquest of Egypt. He was a Yemeni nobleman who was obeyed by his fellow tribesmen. (Ibn Nāṣir al-Dimashqī, *Tawḍīḥ al-Mushtabah fī Ḍabt Asmā' al-Ruwāt wa Ansābihim wa Alqābihim wa Kunāhim*, ed. Muhammad Naim al-Irqisusi (Beirut, 1993), Vol. 3, 34).

277 One of the Yemeni tribes.

278 Islam has more than one type of alms; the mandatory ones are called *zakat* and the optional ones are called *ṣadaqāt* (sing. *ṣadaqa*). Both types are further divided into several categories.

he took another Neighbourhood that he marked-out, among his people's land, in Banī Sūm's, at Tujīb's.

The mosque was built in the year 21 AH/642 AD. Its dimensions were 29 m. wide by 17 m. wide.[279] It is said that eighty men of the companions of the Prophet supervised the determination of its *qibla*[280] direction. These men included: Al-Zubyar b. al-ʿAwwām; al-Miqdād b. al-Aswad; ʿUbāda b. al-Ṣāmit; Abū al-Dardā'; Abū Dharr al-Ghifārī; Abū Baṣra al-Ghifārī, and others. At that time, the mosque did not have a recessed [prayer] niche (*miḥrāb*),[281] but had erect columns in the center of the [qibla] wall. It had two doors opposite the house of ʿAmr, two doors at its north, and two at its west. The length of the mosque, from south to north, was equal to the length of the house of ʿAmr, and between the mosque and the house was a distance of seven cubits. When ʿAmr finished the construction of the mosque, he used a pulpit (*minbar*)[282] to preach from. ʿUmar b. al-Khaṭṭāb, the Prince of the Faithful (*amīr al-mu'minīn*),[283] then sent him a letter ordering him to break this minbar, and saying: Is it not enough for you to be standing tall while Muslims sit at your feet? ʿAmr then broke the minbar, but it is said that he re-installed it at the mosque after the death of ʿUmar.

It is said that Zakariyyā b. Marqiyā,[284] the King of Nubia, gave the amir of Egypt, ʿAbd Allah b. Sarḥ al-ʿĀmirī,[285] a minbar as a gift, which he placed at the mosque of ʿAmr. Maslama b. Mukhallad al-Anṣārī,[286] the amir of Egypt under caliph Muʿāwiya b. Abī Sufyān,[287] decorated the mosque and extended it to its north. Maslama was the first to conduct funerary prayers inside this mosque. Additions and renovations continued and are still being carried out in the mosque up to our time. The first amir to arrange reciting the Quran from its manuscript at the mosque was ʿAbd al-ʿAzīz b.

279 fifty by thirty cubits. (D. Abouseif, *Architecture*, 47).

280 Henceforth: *qibla*; the direction of prayers towards the Ka'ba in Meccais called the *qibla*, which, in Egypt, is to the south-east. To establish it accurately in a mosque, geographical calculations are required.

281 Henceforth: *mihrab*; a niche or a flat carving on the wall or the columns of a mosque that indicates the direction of prayers (*qibla*), which is towards the Ka'ba in Mecca.

282 Henceforth: *minbar*; the pulpit on which the sermon deliverer stands or sits to address the congregation and be clearly heard and seen. It is normally placed next to the mihrab.

283 *Amīr al-mu'minīn* (Prince of the Faithful) was a title given to Muslim caliphs. It started being used with Caliph ʿUmar (see Glossary: "Rightly-guided Caliphs"). (H. al-Basha, *Alqāb*, 194).

284 Historians give different versions of the name: Zakariyya b. Marqanī or Maraqnī, Barqanī or Baraqnīand Marqā. (*Ṣubḥ*, Vol. 3, 341 fn. 1, al-Maqrīzī, *Khiṭaṭ*, Vol. 3, 151, Ibn Taghrī Birdī & M. Shams, *Nujūm*, Vol. 1, 87 & 87 fn. 4).

285 Ruler of Egypt from 25 AH/646 to 35 AH/656 AD, during the reign of Caliph ʿUthmān. (See Glossary: "Rightly-guided Caliphs").

286 Umayyad ruler of Egypt from 47 AH/667 AD to 62 AH/682 AD.

287 The first Umayyad caliph, who ruled from 41 AH/661 AD to 60 AH/680 AD. Muʿāwiya is a controversial character that some Muslims hate and other appreciate. He went to war againstʿAlī, the fourth Rightly-guidedCaliph, over the caliphate and was known for being a cunning politician and clever sovereign.

Marwān, during his rule, in the year 76 AH/695 AD. ʿAbd Allah b. ʿAbd al-Malik[288] raised the mosque's ceiling in the year 89 AH/708 AD, for it had been low. Qurra b. Sharīk al-ʿAbsī[289] was the one who added a concave mihrab to the mosque, following ʿUmar b. ʿAbd al-ʿAzīz,[290] who had added a similar mihrab to the Prophet's mosque in Madina.[291] Qurra also added a *maqṣūra*[292] to the mosque of ʿAmr, following Muʿawiya who had added one to the Great Mosque of Damascus.[293]

Mūsā b. Naṣr al-Lakhmī, the amir of Egypt, ordered that minbars be included in the mosques of all Egyptian villages in the year 132 AH/750 AD.[294] The first amir to hang the green tablet (*al-lawḥ al-akhḍar*)[295] in the Mosque of ʿAmr was

288 Umayyad ruler of Egypt from 86 AH/705 to 90 AH/709 AD.

289 Umayyad ruler of Egypt from 90 AH/709 to 95 AH/714 AD.

290 The Umayyad caliph who ruled from 99 AH/717 to 101 AH/720 AD. ʿUmar's great grandfather from his mother's line was ʿUmar b. al-Khaṭṭāb and he took care to follow his ancestor's foot steps in just and fair sovereignty. Although his reign was short, ʿUmar b. ʿAbd al-ʿAzīz gained himself a great reputation in the hearts of Muslims, for which he was deemed to be the fifth of the Rightly-guided Caliphs.

291 Full name is Madīnat al-Nabī (the City of the Prophet) or al-Madīna al-Munawwara (the Illuminated City), originally Yathrib, to the north of Mecca. Prophet Muḥammad was forced to immigrate from his hometown, Mecca, due to the rejection and hostility of its people towards him. His immigration (*hijra*) in 623 AD along with his closest friend and companion, and the first caliph of Muslims after him, Abū Bakr, marks the beginning of the Islamic Calendar, or the Hijri Calendar, which is a lunar calendar. He was welcomed by the people of Madina, later to be called al-Anṣār (the Supporters), then gradually joined by several of his companions (al-Muhājirūn or the immigrants). He only left his seat of rule in Medina after he was able to conquer Mecca in the eighth year of the Hijra (630 AD).

292 This was an architectural element, mostly a wooden screen, partition or enclosure, which was inserted in the qibla area of a mosque to separate the ruler and his trusted retinue from the rest of the congregation. It was introduced as a security measure after two Muslim caliphs were assassinated during their prayers in mosques, namely, ʿUmar b. al-Khaṭṭāb and ʿAlī b. Abī Ṭālib. The first ruler to use it was Caliph Muʿāwiya b. Abī Sufyān, the first Umayyad caliph, who was wounded in an assassination attempt. Some later rulers, however, used the *maqṣūra* for alientating themselves from their subjects, to boast and show their superiority. This latter development was a matter to which several religious scholars objected, for a security precaution was allowed in prayers, but not an act of discrimination. (Khaled Azab, *Aswār wa Qal'at Ṣalāḥ al-Dīn*(Cairo, 2006), 103–104).

293 See "Jami' al-Umawi al-Kabir,"http://archnet.org/sites/31.

294 Al-Lakhmī was the Abbasid ruler of Egypt from 155 AH/772 AD to 161 AH/AD 778 AD. The year 132 AH/749 AD witnessed the end of the Umayyad era and begginig of the Abbasid in Egypt, with the rule of Ṣāliḥ b. ʿAlī from 132 AH/750 AD to 133 AH/751 AD.

295 The Green Tablet or the Green Slab is mentioned in some primary sources to have existed in the Mosque of ʿAmr, although no clear description of it is provided. The term has a Shiite connotation for there was a green tablet believed to have been bestowed by Allah on Fāṭima, the daughter of the Prophet, wife of ʿAlī b. Abī Ṭālib and mother of al-Ḥasan and al-Ḥusayn, all figures revered by Shiites and respected by Sunnis. This tablet was thought to have included the names of the Prophet and Faṭima's family. Although this seems to be the only reference to a green tablet, it is unlikely that it was the one installed in the Mosque of ʿAmr. Egypt had no clear Shiite inclinations then, neither at the level of governance nor popular belief. More importantly, in his account of the Mosque of ʿAmr, al-Maqrīzī reports that in the restorations of Sultan al-Ẓāhir Baybars, the tablet was divided into pieces that were still used to adorn the northern wall of the mosque, and was replaced by another one, which was gilded and carried the sultan's name. An object of spiritual

ʿAbd Allah b. Ṭāhir,[296] in the year 212 AH/827 AD. The riwāq,[297] which included the tablet, burnt down during the reign of Khumārawayh b. Aḥmad b. Ṭūlūn, who restored it in the year 275 AH/888 AD. Al-Ẓāhir Baybars renovated the tablet in the year 666 AH/1268 AD and Burhān al-Dīn al-Maḥallī,[298] the merchant, renovated the green tablet towards the end of the reign of Sultan al-Ẓāhir Barqūq.[299]

The author of *Īqāẓ al-Mutaghaffil* described the mosque in his time, which was around the year 713 AH/1313 AD, saying: The mosque's total area was 28,000 cubits,[300] with each of its qibla and rear riwaqs comprising 8950 cubits, its courtyard (*ṣaḥn*) comprising 5000 cubits, and each of its eastern and western riwaqs comprising 2550 cubits. The mosque had 13 doors, each having its own name, and had a single door in its southern side. It had 24 riwaqs in total, seven in each of its qibla and rear riwaqs, and five in each of its eastern and western riwaqs. It contained 368 columns, some free-standing and some added to others. It had three mihrabs at the center [of its qibla wall]: the large mihrab next to the minbar, the central one,[301] and the mihrab of the five [prayers].[302] It also had five minarets

holiness would have not been treated with such disrespect. The Green Tablet was probably a decorative object of an unusual appearance that called for its particular mention in the sources. It might have had a commonly known sacred connotation at its time, quite unlikely to have been the known Shiite one. (Al-Maqrīzī, *Khiṭaṭ*, Vol. 3, 163 and Ashraf Dockrat, e-mail to H-Net Discussion Networks, September 7, 2010 http://h-net.msu.edu/cgi-bin/logbrowse.pl?trx=vx&list=H-Mideast-Medieval&month=1009&week=b&msg=OiUQG6z31eVnpXrXm0g0SQ).

296 Abbasid ruler of Egypt from 211 AH/826 AD to 212 AH/827 AD.

297 The term *riwāq* (pl. *arwiqa*, corridor, aisle, or arcade; henceforth "riwaq") has more than one meaning in Islamic architecture. It is used to refer to one of the four hypostyle halls that form a courtyard mosque plan, a corridor of columns within a hypostyle plan, and a part of a mosque where a particular class of students receive their learning, which is then named after this group.

298 Ibrāhīm b. ʿUmar b. ʿAlī, *al-tājir al-ra'īs* (Head Merchant), Burhān al-Dīn al-Maḥallī (d. 806 AH/1403 AD) descended from the line of one of the Prophet's close companions, Ṭalḥa b. ʿAbd Allah. He was the chief merchant of his time, travelled to Syria and Yemen, and was extremely fortunate and wealthy. He was also charitable and built several establishments. He restored the Mosque of ʿAmr and built a madrasa and a lavishly furnished house that overlooked the Nile. (Ibn Taghrī Birdī, *Al-Manhal al-Ṣāfī wa-l-Mustawfī Ba'd al-Wāfī*, ed. Muhammad Muhammad Amin (Cairo, 1984), Vol. 1, 130–131 and Shams al-Dīn al-Sakhāwī, *al-Ḍaw' al-Lāmi' li-Ahl al-Qarn al-Tāsi'* (Beirut, 1992), Vol. I, 112–113).

299 The first Burji Mamluk sultan, who ruled from 784 AH/1382 AD to 801 AH/1399 AD, with an interregnum in 791 AH/1389 AD. (See Glossary: "Circassian Mamluks").

300 The unit used by al-Qalqashandī is *dhirā' al-'amal* (the working arm or cubit) or *al-dhirā' al-Hāshimī* (the Hashimi Cubit), which is equivalent to 0.656 m. (Ayman Fouad Sayyid, ed., *Al-Rawḍa al-Bahiyya al-Zāhira fī Khiṭaṭal-Mu'iziyya al-Qāhira* (Cairo, 1996), 20 fn. 2 and see Glossary: "Cubit").

301 "*Al-Awṣaṭ*"can mean "the central," "the middle," or "the medium." Al-Maqrīzī states that his mihrab was built in the Umayyad era. It is possible that this miharb was of medium size as well, since, in addition to having a lage mihrab, al-Maqrīzī, citing an older source, mentions that there was a small mihrab in the mosque's western wall, whichwas known for being a place where prayers were answered. (Al-Maqrīzī, *Khiṭaṭ*, Vol. 3, 168).

302 *Miḥrāb al-khams*, used for the five daily prayers.

(*ṣawāmi'*):[303] one in its south-western corner, known as al-Ghurfa (the chamber);[304] the second in its south-eastern corner, which is al-Manāra al-Kubrā (the greatest minaret); the third in its north-eastern corner, known as al-Jadīda (the new [minaret]); the fourth in between the third and the fifth minarets, and known as al-Sa'īda (the good fortune [minaret]), and the fifth in the north-western corner, opposite the door of the roof, which is known as al-Mustajadda (the newer [minaret]).

The current mosque stands as described above, but the riwaq including the green tablet and the riwaqs inside it fell into ruins. Sultan al-Malik al-Ẓāhir[305] ordered their rebuilding, so its walls were suspended on wood, but he died before the construction started. Burhan al-Dīn al-Maḥallī, the Judge (*qāḍī*)[306] and Private [Sultanic] Merchant (*tājir al-khāṣṣ*),[307] continued this restoration and demolished the riwaq of the green tablet and all that was inside it. He renewed the tablet added by al-Ẓāhir Baybars and restored the destroyed riwaqs in the best and most precious way possible.

I say: It should be noted that, as previously mentioned, eighty men of the companions of the Prophet supervised the building of the mihrab of this mosque. The mihrab, therefore, is grouped with those of Basra and Kufa,[308] which, according to the conclusions of some of our Shāfi'ī[309] [jurist] friends, should not be subjected to further investigation so as to modify their directions, either to the right or left, as prescribed by al-Shaykh Taqiy al-Dīn al-Subkī[310]in his *Sharḥ Minhāj al-Nawawī fīal-Fiqh* (The Explanation of the Jurisprudence Methodology of al-Imām al-Nawawī).[311] However, al-Qaḍā'ī had mentioned in his *Khiṭaṭ* (Plans) that both al-Layth b. Sa'd and

303 *Ṣawma'a* (pl. *ṣawāmi'*), *manāra* (pl. *manārāt*) and *ma'dhana* (pl. *ma'ādhin*) were all terms used to mean"minaret."

304 Might have also been called 'Arafa. (D. Abouseif, *Architecture*, 49 and A. Abd al-Raziq, *Tārīkh*, 73).

305 The same al-Ẓāhir Barqūq.

306 The *qāḍī* (judge) was the authority responsible for "resolving disputes among individuals and groups according to the stipulations of the Islamic *sharī'a* (religious law)." (Hasan al-Battawi, *Ahl al-'Imāmafī Miṣr fī 'Aṣr Salāṭīn al-Mamālīk* (Cairo, 2007), 46). Al-Qalqashandī refers to Burhān al-Dīn as a *qāḍī* more than once in *Ṣubḥ*; however, this is not mentioned in the biographies of al-Sakhāwī and Ibn Taghrī Birdī.

307 *Tājir al-khāṣṣ*was the merchant who bought mamluks for the sultan. (T. Abdelhamid, *Jaysh*, 4).

308 Basra is in the south east of Iraq and Kufa is in its south.

309 Sunni Islam follows four main schools of interpretation of the Quran and the Prophet's sayings and tradition. These schools are attributed to the four pioneering religious jurists (*fuqahā'*, sing. *faqīh*): al-Imām Abū Ḥanīfa (d. 150 AH/767 AD), al-Imām Mālik (d. 179 AH/795 AD), al-Imām al-Shāfi'ī (d. 204 AH/820 AD), and al-Imām Ibn Ḥanbal (d. 241 AH/855 AD). Thus the schools are called the Ḥanafī, the Mālikī, the Shāfi'ī and the Ḥanbalī and the term "the Four Imams" is used to allude to the four scholars collectively.

310 'Alī b. 'Abd al-Kāfī Taqiy al-Dīn al-Subkī (d. 756 AH/1355 AD) was an exceptional religious scholar and jurist of the Shāfi'ī School. He studied, taught, and worked in Cairo, Alexandria and Damascus. The Mamluk Sultan al-Nāṣir Muḥammad appointed him the *qāḍī al-quḍāt* (Chief Judge, see Glossary: "*qāḍī al-quḍāt*") of Damascus in 739 AH/1339 AD. Al-Ṣafadī reports that he has composed more than 150 books. (Ibn Aybak al-Ṣafadī, *A'yān al-'Aṣr wa A'wān al-Naṣr*, ed. Ali Abu Zayd, Nabil Abu Amsha, Muhammad Maw'id, and Mahmud Salim Muhammad (Damascus, 1997), Vol. 3, 417–429).

311 Al-Imām al-Nawawī (d. 676 AH/1255 AD) was one of the famous religious jurists of his time.

Ibn Lahīʿa[312] shifted to the right when they prayed facing this mihrab, and that the mihrab's direction was too much to the east. He also mentioned that when Qurra b. Sharīk demolished and rebuilt this mihrab, he moved it slightly to the right.

Al-Shaykh Taqiy al-Dīn al-Subkī also related in his *Sharḥ al-Minhāj* that one of the scientists of timekeeping (*mīqāt*)[313] told him that the current mihrab is slightly deviated. He added that this deviation might have been caused by the building changes. I asked some scientist in this field and they told me that al-Shaykh Taqiy al-Dīn Abū Ṭāhir, the highest authority of timekeeping of our time used to say: An evidence of the correctness of our work in determining the qibla direction is its agreement with the mihrab of the Old Mosque [of ʿAmr].

The Second:

The Tulunid Mosque

Aḥmad b. Ṭūlūn built this mosque in the year 259 AH/873 AD[314] on the mountain known as Mount Yashkur.[315] Al-Qaḍāʿī said: this mountain is named after Yashkur b. Jazīla of Lakhm,[316] for it was their neighbourhood.

Ibn ʿAbd al-Ẓāhir[317] said: It is a blessed mountain known for being a place where prayers are answered.[318]

312 ʿAbd Allah b. Lahīʿa (d. 174 AH/790AD) was a scholar of the Prophet's sayings and traditions and a *qāḍī* of Egypt.

313 *ʿIlm al-mīqāt* (science of time keeping) was an established astronomical science in the medieval Islamic world. It was used to determine the times of the daily prayers, and the hours of day and night. For religious purposes, the muazzin (*muʾadhdhin*) may have confirmed the prayer times "with an astrolabe, or a professional astronomer called a *muwaqqit* could be hired.At the popular level, the hours of night could be determined by anybody who knew some astrology by looking at the lunar mansions; in daytime, by measuring the length of one's own shadow – and there were twenty or more methods of how to do this." Scholars developed "prayer-tables for each latitude," and the "muezzins were enjoined to use astronomical tables for determining prayer times and the astrolabe for finding the *qibla*." (Thomas F. Glick, "*Islamic Technology*," in *A Companion to the Philosophy of Technology*, ed. Jan Kyrre et al. (West Sussex, 2009), 34).

314 The mosque was completed in 265 AH/879 AD.

315 A hill that is to the east of the Nile, the west of the Citadel, and north-east of Fustat.

316 Lakhm is a tribe originally from Yemen.

317 Al-Qāḍī Muḥiy al-Dīn Abū al-Faḍl ʿAbd Allah Ibn ʿAbd al-Ẓāhir (d. 692 AH/1293 AD) was an important administrative state official of the early Bahri Mamluk era. In his youth, he was an exceptional scribe and prose writer. Ibn ʿAbd al-Ẓāhir held high positions that entailed direct service to the sultans, such as the confidential scribe (*kātib al-sirr*) and head of chancery bureau (*ṣāḥib dīwān al-inshāʾ*). He used to live in the heart of Fatimid Cairo, in an alley that was named after him: Darb Ibn ʿAbd al-Ẓāhir. He was buried in a mausoleum next to the mosque his son built in 683 AH/1284 AD in the Southern Cemetery. His works include: *Al-Rawḍa al-Bahiyya al-Zāhira fī Khiṭaṭ al-Muʿizziyya al-Qāhira* (*The Blooming Garden on the Description of the Neighbourhoods of Cairo*), three biographies of three of the Mamluk sultans he served: al-Ẓāhir Baybars (r. 658 AH/1260 AD – 676 AH/1277 AD), al-Manṣūr Qalāwūn (r. 678 AH/1279 AD – 689 AH/1290 AD) and al-Ashraf Khalīl (r. 689 AD/1290 AD – 692 AH/1293 AD), in addition to prose, poetry and works on other topics. (Ibn ʿAbd al-Ẓāhir, *Khiṭaṭ*,10–18°).

318 Ibn ʿAbd al-Ẓāhir, *Khiṭaṭ*, 81.

He added: And it said that Allah talked to Moses there.[319] It is also said that Ibn Ṭūlūn spent 100,000 dinars, which he had found in a treasure, to build this mosque.[320] When he finished its building, he ordered that whatever people found wrong with the building be reported to him. A man was heard saying: "Its mihrab is small," another said: "It does not have columns," and another: "It does not have an ablution area (*miḍā'a*)."[321] To that he replied: As for the mihrab, I saw the Prophetmark it out for me in a vision, and I woke up to find that ants have surrounded the same area he marked out. As for the columns, I have built this mosque using honestly acquired money (*māl ḥalāl*),[322] which is the treasure I have found, and I would not risk contaminating it with any other. Columns can only be taken from a mosque or a church, and so I kept my mosque from such [unrightful acts]. As for the ablution area, I wanted to purify the mosque from filth, so I shall now build it behind the mosque. He then ordered building the ablution area nearby.[323]

It is related that he never toyed with anything. One day he took out a sheet of white paper and extended it like a spiral. He then became aware [that he was being playful] and thought that people recognized that, so he ordered that the minaret be built in that same spiral shape. The minaret had a ship on its top, which was later imitated atop the dome of al-Īmām al-Shāfiʿī.[324] When Ibn Ṭūlūn finished building the mosque, he had a vision[325] that fire came down from the sky and burnt down the mosque, but not its surroundings. He related his vision to an interpreter [of visions] who told him: Rejoice at the glad tiding that this mosque was accepted [by Allah], for when the bygone peoples offered a sacrifice and it was accepted from them, a fire would fall down from the sky and eat it up, as in the story of Able and Cane. Ibn Ṭūlūn saw another vision, as if Allah[326] had revealed Himself to the surroundings of the mosque. An interpreter explained to him that the surroundings of the mosque will fall into ruins, but it shall be saved, as evident in Allah the Almighty's words: "But when his Lord appeared to the mountain, He rendered it level"[327].[328] This did happen, for the residence areas of the Tulunids were demolished when they were defeated, while only the mosque survived.

319 Ibn ʿAbd al-Ẓāhir, *Khiṭaṭ*, 81.

320 Ibn ʿAbd al-Ẓāhir, *Khiṭaṭ*, 76–77.

321 Ablution is a washing ritual that is done before prayers. A *miḍa'a* is the washing area in a mosque which accommodates this ritual.

322 *Māl* is money and *ḥalāl* is what is allowed or accepted by Allah, as opposed to *ḥarām*, which is what is forbidden.

323 See also the account in Ibn ʿAbd Ẓāhir, *Khiṭaṭ*, 79.

324 See fn. 309.

325 *Ru'yā* (pl. *ru'ā*); a foretelling vision seen in a dream.

326 *Al-Ḥaqq* (the Truth), one of the names of Allah.

327 Part of the verse 143 of Quran – Sūrat al-Aʿrāf (Chapter of the Heights), 7:143, Sahih International's translation (http://corpus.quran.com/translation.jsp?chapter=7&verse=143).

328 See also the account in Ibn ʿAbd Ẓāhir, *Khiṭaṭ*, 79–80.

The Third:

Mosque of Rāshida[329]

Al-Ḥākim bi-Amr Allah[330] built this mosque to the south of Fustat, near al-Raṣad.[331] He included it in his endowment (*waqf*) along with al-Azhar[332] and al-Maqs[333] mosques.

The author of *Īqāẓ al-Mutaghaffil* said: This is not really the mosque of Rāshida, but the mosque of Rāshida was near it. The original mosque was an old one built at the time of the Islamic conquest by a tribe that was called Rāshida. Therefore, when al-Ḥākim built this mosque, it was named after the old one. He said: I have seen some of its remnants and its mihrab, and it had a lot of Gum *(muql)* [334] trees.

The Fourth:

Al-Raṣad Mosque

Amir ʿIzz al-Dīn Aybak al-Afram Amir Jāndār al-Ṣāliḥī al-Najmī[335] built this mosque in the year 663 AH/1265 AD. He built the *manẓara* (belvedere)[336] known after him

329 This mosque was in the neighbourhood of Banū Rāshida, which was in al-Raṣad area to the southwest of the Mosque of ʿAmr. Banū Rāshida was among the clans of the Lakhm tribe of Qaḥṭānī origin who came to Egypt with the Islamic conquest. Caliph al-Ḥākim started builing the Mosque of Rāshida in 393 AH/1003 AD and it seems that the building was completed in 1005 AD, under the caliph's supervision. This mosque was renewed several times and was still used for Friday congregational prayers in the time of al-Maqrīzī until the year 806 AH/1403 AD. (Al-Maqrīzī, *Khiṭaṭ*, Vol. 3, 234–237 and A. Hammuda, *Tārīkh*, 41).

330 The Fatimid Caliph who ruled from 386 AH/996 AD to 412 AH/1021 AD.

331 Al-Maqrīzī reports that this was a hill to the south of Fustat, its western side overlooked the area of Rāshida, to its south was Birkat al-Ḥabash, and its eastern side could be easily reached from the Cemetery. Al-Raṣad means "the Observatory," for the hill was named after the observatory that al-Afḍal Shāhinshāh, the Fatimidvizier from 487 AH/1094 ADto516 AH/1122 AD, built upon it. (Al-Maqrīzī, *Khiṭaṭ*, Vol. 1, 356).

332 First Fatimid mosque built in Cairo in 359 AH/970 AD, which the author will discuss later in detail.

333 The no longer extant mosque that al-Ḥākim built overlooking the Nile in al-Maqs area, which was located to the west of Cairo and served as its port. The Mamluk vizier Shams al-Dīn al-Maqsī restored this mosque in 770 AH/1369 AD. (Al-Maqrīzī, *Khiṭaṭ*, Vol. 3, 237–238, and A. Raymond, *Cairo*, 77).

334 Gum guggul or Balsamodendron africanum, commonly known as African Bdellium.

335 ʿIzz al-Dīn Aybak al-Afram is the amir's name, al-Ṣāliḥī al-Najmī indicates that he was a mamluk of the Ayyubid Sultan al-Ṣāliḥ Najm al-Dīn (r. 637 AH/1240 AD to 647 AH/1259 AD). Amīr Jāndār is a royal position that entailskeeping the sultan's door as well as other graver duties that al-Qalqashandī describes in more detail later.

336 A *manẓara* is a term that originally denoted military watchtowers that were built on high areas overlooking the coasts to warn against enemy ships. The term then came to have a civil connotation during the Abbasid and Fatimid eras, when it meant a belvedere from which the royalty watched festivities and participated in them. Although the Fatimid belvederes disappeared, the

there, as well as a *ribāṭ*[337] next to the mosque, in which he stipulated [hosting] a certain number [of men] for holding Friday prayers, who stayed there, day and night.

The Fifth:

Al-Shu'aybiyya Mosque, also outside Miṣr

This mosque was built by the same Amir ʿIzz al-Dīn Aybak al-Afram in the year 693 AH/1294 AD. Al-Shaykh Shams al-Dīn b. al-Labbān,[338] the Sufi Shāfiʿī jurist, stayed in this mosque; therefore, it is currently named after him.

The Sixth

The New Mosque (Al-Jāmi' al-Jadīd)

Sultan al-Malik al-Nāṣir Muhammad b. Qalāwūn[339] built this mosque near Mawradat al-Khulafā'.[340] He began constructing it on the 9th of Muḥarram[341] of the year 710 AH (8 June 1310 AD) and it was completed on the 8th of Ṣafar[342] of the year 712 AH (15 June 1312 AD). The Chief Judge (*qāḍī al-quḍāt*),[343] Badr al-Dīn b. Jamaʿa al-Shāfiʿī,[344] delivered the sermon (*khuṭba*)[345] and led the Friday prayers in the mosque on the 9th of the same month. The judge arranged for Sufis to attend the

idea remained during the Mamluk and Ottoman eras through using the same locations for leisure and festive purposes. (M. al-Shishtawi, *Mutanazzahāt*, 227).

337 A *ribāṭ* in this context refers to one of the Sufi charitable establishments known at the time. See also below.

338 Shams al-Dīn b. al-Labbān (d. 749 AH/1348 AD) was a renowned Sufi of the Shādhilī order and a religious scholar who lived in Cairo and Alexandria. (Tāj al-Dīn b. ʿAlī al-Subkī, *Ṭabaqāt al-Shāfi'iyya al-Kubrā*, ed. Mahmud al-Tanahi and Abd al-Fattah al-Helw (Cairo, 1992), Vol. 9, 94).

339 The Bahri Mamluk Sultan who ruled from 692 AH/1293 AD to 740 AH/1341 AD with two interregnums, one from 693 AH/1294 AD to 697 AH/1298 AD and the second from 708 AH/1308 to 709 AH/1309AD. In his third reign, Al-Nāṣir Muḥammad was a very powerful sultan and a great builder who encouraged his amirs to embark on construction projects.

340 So called by al-Qalqashandī, but the correct name is Mawradat al-Ḥalfā. The *mawrada* is the place that the water reaches or the road to a water source. People used such places on the Nile and the canals to get water. The location of Mawradat al-Ḥalfa (*ḥalfa* is a plant; cortaderia selloana), rather than Mawradat al-Khulafā' (the Caliphs) currently occupies the area extending for Dayr al-Nuḥās in the south to Sūr Majrā al-ʿUyūn (the Aqueduct) in Maṣr al-Qadīma neighbourhood. During the Mamluk and Ottoman eras, the area was sometimes green and inhabited, while in other times it suffered from the Nile flood that demolished its buildings. (M. al-Shishtawi, *Mutanazzahāt*, 33–34).

341 First month of the Hijri year.

342 Second month of the Hijri year.

343 The Judge of Judges, meaning the Chief Judge. See Glossary: "*qāḍī al-quḍāt*".

344 Ibn Jamāʿa held the office of Chief Judge (*qāḍī al-quḍāt*) three times during the reign of the Mamluk Sultan al-Nāṣīr Muḥammad. (Al-Ṣafadī, *A'yān*, Vol. 5, 100).

345 Any sermon given before or after prayers. A mandatory *khuṭba*has to be preached before Friday congregational prayers.

mosque after the afternoon (*'aṣr*)[346] [prayers], as was the case in the *khāwāniq*.[347] This is one of the most beautiful mosques, which occupies a most pleasant location, especially during the flood season.

As for the mosques built for the five [daily] prayers (*masājid al-khams*),[348] they were too numerous to count, as is evident in the *Khiṭaṭ* of al-Qaḍā'ī.

I have read in some history sources that there was a fatal plague during the reign of Kāfūr al-Ikhshīdī[349] that left no poor people to receive the alms (*zakāt*). The alms were then taken to Kāfūr, who refused them and said: Build mosques and allocate endowments (*awqāf*) for them with this money, hence the large number of mosques. However, those mosques disappeared and fell to ruins with the demolition of Fustat, and only the remnants of a few of them survive.

The Madrasas of Fustat[350]

As for the madrasas, people used to sit for learning at the Old Mosque in the past. The first to build madrasas in Fustat were the Ayyubids. Sultan Ṣalāḥ al-Dīn,[351] built two madrasas: one was the Mālikiyya[352] madrasa, known as al-Qamḥiyya (the Wheat Madrasa), in Muḥarram of the year 566 AH/1170 AD. It was called al-Qamḥiyya because the rations given to teachers and students were wheat rations.

Al-'Imād al-Kātib[353] said: It was a market for selling yarn before that.

346 Afternoon, also time of the third of the five mandatory daily prayers in Islam.

347 Also, *khānqāwāt* (sing. *khānqāh*; henceforth, khanqah): A charitable establishment that housed Sufis for worship and study. See Glossary: "*khānqāh*".

348 *Masājid* (sing. *masjid*) in this context means mosques used for daily prayers, not congregational Friday prayers. A *masjid* is the more generic term applied to any place designated for prayers. Friday mosques were called *jawāmi'* (sing. *jāmi'*, also "congregational mosque"), which is an abbreviation of the terms *masājid jāmi'a* (sing. *masjid jāmi'*) and *masājid al-jum'a* (Friday Mosques). They hosted the weekly mandatory mass prayer for Muslim men, which is performed on Friday at noon instead of *ẓuhr* prayer. Listening to the Friday sermon (*khuṭba*) is an essential component of this prayer. Friday mosques may also, of course, host the congregations performing any of the other daily prayers. Conducting mandatory prayers in groupsis considered a better rewarded ritual than an individual prayer.

349 The Ikhshidid sovereign who ruled from 355 AH/966 AD to 357 AH/968 AD.

350 Schools, see fn. 254.

351 Ṣalāḥ al-Dīn Yūsuf b. Ayyūb was the first Ayyubid sultan who ruled Egypt autonomously from 569 AH/1174 AD to 589 AH/1193 AD. Ṣalāḥ al-Dīn (Saladin) is most famous in the Western world for his victories over the Crusaders.

352 Preaching the school of jurisprudence of al-Imām Mālik.

353 Abū 'Abd Allah Muḥammad b. Ḥāmid al-Iṣfahānī (d. 597 AH/1201 AD), also known as al-'Imād al-Kātib (the vizier and writer) was born in Isfahan, in present day Iran. He learned jurisprudence, excelled in the literary arts, and became the trusted secretary to Sultan al-Naṣir Ṣalāḥ al-Dīn Yūsuf b. Ayyūb, participating in most of the important events of this sultan's life, especially wars with the Crusaders, which he described in his books *al-Barq al-Shāmī* (The Syrian Lightning) and *al-Fatḥ al-Qasiy fi-l-Fatḥ al-Qudsī* (The Conquest of Jerusalem). (See Jalāl al-Dīn al-Suyūṭī, *Ḥusn al-Muḥāḍara fī Tārīkh Miṣr wa-l-Qāhira*, ed. Muhammad Abu al-Fadl Ibrahim (Cairo, 1967), Vol. 1, 564–565).

The second madrasa was the one known as Ibn Zayn al-Tujjār.[354] It had originally been a prison that Sultan Ṣalāḥ al-Dīn built into a madrasa and endowed to the Shāfiʿīs. The sultan allocated the Goldsmiths' Market (al-Ṣāgha) next to the madrasa as an endowment (*waqf*) for it.

Then Sultanal-Muẓaffar Taqiy al-Dīn ʿUmar b. Shāhinshāh b. Ayyūb[355] restored the place known as Manāzil al-ʿIzz,[356] near Bāb al-Qanṭara[357] in the south of Fustat, to be a madrasa. He allocated endowments for it, which included Jazīrat al-Ṣināʿa, known as al-Rawḍa.

Al-Muʿizz Aybak al-Turkumānī,[358] the first of the Turkish kings, then built his madrasa, al-Muʿizziyya,[359] in al-Kharrūb Plaza, in the year 654 AH/1256 AD.

Al-Ṣāḥib Sharaf al-Dīn b. al-Fā'izī[360] built his madrasa, al-Fā'iziyya, before he became a vizier, in the year 637 AH/1240 AD.

354 This school was located to the south of the Mosque of ʿAmr. Its location was originally occupied by a house then a prison in the early Islamic era. Sultan al-Nāṣir Ṣalāḥ al-Dīn tore the prison down and replaced it with the first madrasa in Egypt, which used to be called al-Nāṣiriyya, after him. It then acquired the name "Ibn Zayn al-Tujjār," (literally, son of the ornament of merchants). It was so named after a renowned Shāfiʿī scholar, Abū al-ʿAbbās Aḥmad al-Dimashqī (d. 591 AH/1195 AD), who taught there for a long time. During the time of al-Maqrīzī, it was called al-Madrasa al-Sharīfiyya, after another scholar, al-Sharīf al-Qāḍī Shams al-Dīn al-Ḥanafī. (Al-Maqrīzī, *Khiṭaṭ*, Vol. 3, 438–439).

355 The Ayyūbid Sultan who ruled Hama in Syria from 574 AH/1178 AD to 587 AH/1191 AD.

356 This was a madrasa known as Manāzil al-ʿIzz (the Houses of Prosperity). Its location was originally occupied by royal Fatimid residences for the caliphs that the mother of Caliph al-ʿAzīz (r.365 AH/976 AD– 386 AH/996 AD) built. When the Ayyubids took control of Egypt, al-Malik al-Muẓaffar ʿUmar, Ṣalāḥ al-Dīn's brother, bought this place and built several buildings in it until he left Egypt for Syria and allocated the place to Shāfiʿī jurists. (Al-Maqrīzī, *Khiṭaṭ*, Vol. 3, 440).

357 One of the gates on the western walls of the Fatimid city of Cairo. Its name means "the Bridge Gate" and was so called because General Jawhar built a bridge there to cross the canal to the west of Cairo (al-Khalīj) to al-Maqs in 360 AH/971 AD, which was a defensive act against the expected Qarmatian invasion. (Al-Maqrīzī, *Khiṭaṭ*, Vol. 2, 103, A. Raymond, *Cairo*, 37).

358 First Mamluk sultan from 648 AH/1250 ADto655 AH/1257 AD.

359 This madrasa used to overlook the Nile. Its location was taken up by the Mosque of ʿĀbidī Bek at the southern end of Miṣr al-Qadīma Street. (Ibn Taghrī Birdī & M. Shams, *al-Nujūm*, Vol. 7, 13 & 13 fn. 2).

360 Al-Maqrīzī notes that Sharaf al-Dīn built this madrasa in 636 AH/1239 AD, before he became a vizier. It was a Shāfiʿī madrasa. Sharaf al-Dīn was a convert to Islam from Christianity. He was a vizier in the early Mamluk state for Sultan al-Muʿizz Aybak. (Al-Maqrīzī, *Khiṭaṭ*, Vol. 3, 442 and Khayr al-Dīn al-Zarkalī, *Al-Aʿlām: Qāmūs Tarājim li-Ashhar al-Rijāl wa al-Nisā'min al-ʿArab wa al-Mustaʿribīn wa al-Mustashriqīn* (Beirut, 2002), Vol. 8, 72).

Al-Ṣāḥib Bahā' al-Dīn b. Ḥannā[361] built al-Ṣāḥibiyya Madrasa[362] in Zuqāq al-Qanādīl[363] after that.

The Khanqas and Ribats of Fustat[364]

As for the khanqas and the ribats, they were not known in Fustat, but al-Ṣāḥib Bahā' al-Dīn b. Ḥannā built Ribāṭ al-Āthār al-Sharīfa (Ribat of the Honourable Relics),[365] outside Fustat, to its south. He bought the honourable relics, which are a copper kohl stick (*mīl*), an iron tongs, a piece of the small spear (*'anaza*), and a

361 Ibn Ḥannā was the vizier of the Mamluk Sultan al-Ẓāhir Baybars. He managed the state without objection from the sultan due to his wisdom and ability to handle stately matters. He continued in his position under Baybars's son, Baraka Khān (r. 676 AH/1277 AD – 678 AH/1279 AD). Ibn Ḥannā died in 677 AH/1279 AD and was buried in his mausoleum in the Southern Cemetery. (Al-Maqrīzī, *Khiṭaṭ*, Vol. 3, 455–457).

362 Al-Maqrīzī reports that this madrasa was built in 654 H/1256 AD and it had a great library. He adds that it was one of the grandest schools of its time and students used to compete to join it to the extent that its residential quarters had to host two or three students in a single room. However, it deteriorated until it was demolished in 817–818 AH/1415 AD. (Al-Maqrīzī, *Khiṭaṭ*, Vol. 3, 455–458).

363 A *zuqāq* is a small street and *al-qanādīl* (sing. *qindīl*) are lanterns or lamps. This street was near the Mosque of 'Amr and it was so rich, crowded and inhabited by nobles and esteemed people. It was called the Street of Lanterns because a lamp was hung every night on every house door in it. (Al-Maqrīzī, *Khiṭaṭ*, Vol. 3, 455).

364 The *khānqāh* (khanqah), the *zāwiya* (zawiya), and the *ribāṭ* (ribat) are three types of Islamic Sufi religious, educational and residential establishments that soundly proliferated Egypt throughout the Mamluk era. The three terms were sometimes used interchangeably in the Mamluk sources, with little differentiation among their functions. These establishments were charitable, pious foundations funded by endowments documented in deeds (*waqfiyya*; pl. *waqfiyyāt*) that stipulated all the rules and conditions of running the institution and housing its residents. The *zāwiya* (Ar. corner, pl. *zawāya*) was originally a term given to any small mosque, usually with no minaret or minbar, where a man known for his piety and asceticism preached or taught. *Khānqāh* (pl. *khānqāwāt* or *khawāniq*) is a word of Persian origin. The khanqahwas a larger establishment than the zawiya, and was mostly, at least in the early Mamluk era, built by royal patrons or members of the royal entourage, while the zawiya had a wider range of patrons including the Sufi figures. The ribat (from the verb *rabaṭa*, "to tie) was originally the name given to the fortifications built for Muslim warriors on the borders or frontiers of Islamic lands (the *murābiṭūn*). It later came to also refer to establishments that sometimes hosted the poor and the needy, and some of them were dedicated solely for women; however, the ribats mostly functioned more as secluded Sufi residences. (See S. Ashour, *'Aṣr*, 443–444; S. Ashour, *Mujtama'*, 187; M. Dahman, *Mu'jam*, 85, and Emil Th. Homerin, "Saving Muslim Souls: The *Khānqāh*and the Sufi Duty in Mamluk Lands," *Mamluk Studies Review* 3 (1999): 67 & 75).

365 This *ribāṭ* was originally built by Vizier Ibn Ḥannā's grandson, also a vizier, called Tāj al-Dīn, to host the honourable relics of Prophet Muḥammad. Tāj al-Dīn died in 707 AH/1308 AD, without completing the project and another family member and a vizier too, Nāṣir al-Dīn took on the task. The building was subjected to several restorations and renovations during the Mamluk and Ottoman eras and has been replaced by a mosque. (M. al-Shistawi, *Mutanazzahāt*, 258–259).

piece of the bowl (*qaṣ'a*), with a sum of money. He authenticated these relics by *istifāḍa*[366] and placed them in the ribat to be visited.

The Hospital

As for the hospital (*bīmāristān*), the first to build one in Fustat was Aḥmad b. Ṭūlūn in the year 259 AH/873 AD, which cost him 60,000 dinars.

Al-Qaḍā'ī said: There was no hospital in Miṣr before that, and he stipulated that no soldier or mamluk be treated in it.

366 A type of testimony that is used when a case cannot be proven by a witness who has directly seen or heard what he is testifying for. It relies on common, wide-spread knowledge and may be accepted when it is difficult to prove something without it.

THE SECOND SEAT OF GOVERNMENT

Cairo (al-Qāhira)

It is pronounced "al-Qāhira"[367] and called "Cairo of al-Muʿizz" (al-Qāhira al-Muʿiziyya) because it is attributed to the Fatimid Caliph al-Muʿizz,[368] for whom it was established. It is also called "al-Muʿiziyya al-Qāhira." Cairo was so called for good omen. It is the grandest city, unparalleled under the horizons, and of which no counterpart is heard of, in any country.

General Jawhar al-Muʿizzī[369] built the city for his master, al-Muʿizz li Dīn Allah Abū Tamīm Maʿadd,[370] son of al-Manṣūr Abū al-Ṭāhir Ismāʿīl,[371] son of al-Qā'im Abū al-Qāsim Muḥammad,[372] son of al-Mahdī bi Allah Abū Muḥammad ʿUbayd Allah al-Fāṭimī (the Fatimid).[373] Jawhar, who came from the Maghrib,[374] started building the city in the year 358 AH/969 AD, after he arrived in Egypt and conquered it. Cairo is located near Fustat, to its north.

367 The name means "the Victorious" or "the Conquering" city.

368 The first Fatimid caliph of Egypt who arrived from Tunisia after his general, Jawhar al-Ṣaqallī, successfully managed to conquer Egypt. Caliph al-Muʿizz ruled Egypt from 362 AH/973 to 365 AH/976 AD.

369 One of the titles of Jawhar, "al-Muʿizzī," is in attribution to his master, Caliph al-Muʿizz.

370 Caliph al-Muʿizz (see fn. 368).

371 The Fatimid caliph who ruled over the caliphate lands in North Africa from 334 AH/946 AD to 342 AH/953 AD.

372 The Fatimid caliph who ruled over the caliphate lands in North Africa from 322 AH/934 AD to 334 AH/946 AD.

373 ʿUbayd Allah al-Mahdī, the first Fatimid caliph of the caliphate lands in North Africa who ruled from 297 AH/910 AD to 322 AH/934 AD.

374 Means "Land of Sunset" and is a term that is generally given to the region currently comprising the North African Arab countries to the west of Egypt: Libya, Tunisia, Algeria and Morocco. (Jamil M. Abun-Nasr, *A History of the Maghrib in the Islamic Period* (Cambridge, 1993), 1). The Fatimids came to Egypt from Tunisia.

The author of *al-Rawḍ al-Mi'ṭār* (The Perfumed Garden)[375] said: The distance between Fustat and Cairo is three miles.[376] He apparently meant that this was the case at the beginning of the construction of Cairo; that is the distance between the walls of Fustat and the walls of Cairo. As for now, buildings are spread and the construction is continuous, to the extent of almost connecting the two cities, or may be they are already connected.

Muḥyi al-Dīn b. ʿAbd Allah al-Ẓāhir, the judge, said in [his manuscript] "*Khiṭaṭ al-Qāhira*" (The Neighbourhoods of Cairo):[377] The settled situation is that the width of Cairo extends from the Seven Waterwheels (al-Sabʿ Saqqāyāt)[378] up to the Shrine of al-Sayyida Ruqayya.[379] Prior to that, the city's border started at [a place called] "al-Majnūna"[380].

Ibn Saʿīd said: Cairo was built in place of the Tulunid gardens that were located near the Tulunid residence areas known as al-Qaṭā'iʿ. In all cases, Cairo has the same length

375 *Al-Rawḍ al-Mi'ṭār fī Khabar al-Aqṭār* (The Perfumed Garden on the News of Countries) is a work of Muḥammad b. ʿAbd Allah b. ʿAbd al-Munʿim al-Ḥimyarī, who died some time between the years 866 AH/1462 and 900 AH/1495 AD. (Z. al-Samarra'i, *Manhaj*, 109).

376 See the account on Cairo by Ibn ʿAbd al-Munʿim al-Ḥimyarī, *Al-Rawḍ al-Mi'ṭār fī Khabar al-Aqṭār*, ed. Ihsan Abbas (Beirut, 1980), Vol. 1, 450, which states the distance as three days.

377 Abbreviation of *Al-Rawḍa al-Bahiyya al-Zāhira fī Khiṭaṭ al-Mu'izziyya al-Qāhira.*

378 Khaṭṭ al-Sabʿ Saqqāyāt (Neighbourhood of the Seven Waterwheels) was located to the east of al-Khalīj al-Miṣrī, within al-Ḥamrā'al-Dunyā neighbourhood. Khaṭṭ al-Sabʿ Saqqāyāt presently occupies the area bordered at the east by al-Sadd al-Juwwānī Street in al-Sayyida Zaynab Neighbourhood, to the north and west by Port Saʿīd Street (previously al-Khalīj al-Miṣrī Street), and to the south by Junaynat Qāmīsh area. Al-Maqrīzī informs us that the Ikhshīdid vizier, Abū al-Faḍl b. Jaʿfar b. al-Furāt (d. 391 AH/1001 AD), built those seven waterwheels as a pious endowment for all Muslims, to which water was transferred from the well he dug (Bi'r al-Waṭāwīṭ) to the east of Ibn Ṭūlūn's mosque. The seven waterwheels overlooked al-Khalīj al-Miṣrī. (Al-Maqrīzī, *Khiṭaṭ*, Vol. 1, 824 and Vol. 2, 682, Abd al-Rahman Zaki, *Mawsū'at Madīnat al-Qāhira fī Alf 'Ām* (Cairo, 1987),100, M. al-Shistawi, *Mutanazzahāt*, 187–188, and Ismāʿīl b. ʿUmar b. Kathīr al-Qurashī al-Dimashqī, *Al-Bidāya wa al-Nihāya*, ed. Abd Allah al-Turki (Riyadh, 2003), Vol. 15, 493).

379 The *mashhad* (shrine or memorial) of al-Sayyida Ruqayya, built in 527 AH/1133 AD, is located in al-Suyūfiyya Street, behind the Mosque-Shrine of al-Sayyida Zaynab. Al-Sayyida Ruqayya was the daughter of ʿAlī b. Abī Ṭālib and she never came to Egypt. This shrine is a *mashhad ru'ya*(vision) that was built in this place based on a vision that a pious man had of her visit to this location. (D. Abouseif, *Architecture*, 74, M. Uthman, *Mashāhid*, 72–73, and "Mashhad al-Sayyida Ruqayya,"http://archnet.org/sites/1541).

380 This was a small bridge that stood on an arched vault (*qanṭara*). It fed a pond known as Birkat al-Fīl (the Elephant Pond), in between Fustat and Cairo, from al-Khalīj al-Kabīr (also al-Khalīj al-Miṣrī). This bridge had partly disappeared by the time of al-Maqrīzī, leaving a single arch towards the Khalīj, which al-Amir Ṭaybars al-Manṣūrī (d. 708 AH/1308 AD) restored and established a park around. The bridge's current location is in Port Saʿīd Street (previously al-Khalīj al-Miṣrī), near Dhū al-Faqqār Bek Mosque, to its south. The bridge functioned until the end of the 19th century to feed the area and what was left of Birkat al-Fīl with water. Al-Majnūna, literally "the Mad One," is a funny name that the bridge got either from the mad speed of the water that came gushing from the canal to the much lower-leveled pond, or from al-AmirṬaybars himself, a Sufi who used to have lunatic fits and was called "al-Majnūn" or "the Mad One." (M. al-Shishtawy, *Mutanazzahāt*, 106–108 and Ibn ʿAbd al-Ẓāhir, *Khiṭaṭ*, 16).

and width as Fustat, or may be is a little wider. The story of its establishment goes back to the time when the afore-mentioned al-Muʿizz started his reign over Ifrīqiyya[381] and the rest of the Maghrib. Al-Muʿizz's covetousness of Egypt grew after the death of Kāfūr al-Ikhshīdī. At that time, Egypt, Syria[382] and Hijaz[383] were under the reign of Aḥmad b. ʿAlī b. al-Ikhshīd,[384] who was the master (*ustādh*)[385] of Kafūr. Aḥmad was a young boy who had not reached puberty and the kingdom[386] was actually ruled by his statesmen. Al-Ḥusayn b. ʿAbd Allah,[387] in Damascus,[388] was like his viceroy or partner in governance, whose name followed Aḥmad's in the prayers called out from the minbars.[389]

It was a time when Egypt's army was weak, for it had suffered from the plague and from soaring prices. Al-Muʿizz then prepared his afore-mentioned general, Jawhar, for travel.[390] Jawhar showed at the city of Raqqāda,[391] in Ifrīqiyya, in an army of more than 100,000, provided with more than 1000 boxes of money. Al-Muʿizz went out to bid Jawhar farewell and said to the shaykhs[392] who accompanied him: "By God, if this Jawhar marches on his own, he would be able to conquer Egypt! He would enter it with swords,[393] without war, settle in the ruins of Ibn Ṭūlūn, and build a city called Cairo (al-Qāhira) that would subdue the world."

381 Roughly, modern day Tunisia.

382 Greater Syria, which comprised the region occupied by the Levant countries.

383 The western region of present day Kingdom of Saudi Arabia, which comprises the cities of Jeddah, Mecca, Medina, Ta'if and Yanbuʿ.

384 The last Ikhshīdid ruler who reigned from 357 AH/968 AD to the Fatimid conquest in 358 AH/969 AD. He was indeed the master (*ustādh*) of Kāfūr, since he descended from the line of his masters. However, Kāfūr was the de facto ruler of the Ikhshīdid dynasty after the death of its founder, Muḥammad b. Ṭughj, in 334 AH/946 AD and up to his own demise in 357 AH/968 AD.

385 See later and Glossary: "*Ustādhūn*".

386 Al-Qalqashandī and the historians of the time use the term "kingdom" (*mamlaka*, pl. *mamālik*) to denote the provinces under the sovereignty of a monarch or dynasty, for example Egypt and Syria under the Mamluks, or to refer to the whole kingdom.

387 Al-Qalqashandī means Abū Muḥammad al-Ḥasan b. ʿUbayd Allah b. Ṭughj (d. 371 AH/982 AD), who was the nephew of Muḥammad b. Ṭughj al-Ikhshīd, the ruler of al-Ramla in Palestine, then the ruler of Damascusuntil 358 AH/969 AD. (See Al-Zarkalī, *A'lām*, Vol. 2, 198). Primary sources state his name with variations as those apparent between al-Qalqashandī's and al-Zarkalī's accounts.

388 Al-Sha'm (also, al-Shām), which may mean Damascus or Syria.

389 The sermons given before congregational prayers, particularly Friday prayers, normally included praying for the wellness, right guidance, and similar wishes for the ruler. This particular mention of the ruler's name was a sign of his legitimacy as a governor, and in the cases of caliphs and sultans, another major sign of such legitimacy would be minting their names on coinage.

390 *Jahhaza* (v.), which means to equip for travel or prepare with equipment (http://www.baheth.info/all.jsp?term=جهز).

391 A Tunisian city that was established by the Aghlabid dynasty in 263 AH/876 AD.Raqqāda, now in ruins and an archaeological and touristic site, is located to the south-west of the city of al-Qairawān.

392 *Shaykh* means an elderly man, and is also used to refer to religious scholars.

393 *Ardiya* (sing. *ridā'*), which means "robe," and is used to imply "sword" or "bow." (http://www.baheth.info/all.jsp?term=رداء).

Al-Muʿizz had a slave-boy (*ghulām*) in Barqa,[394] called Aflaḥ,[395] to whom he wrote to descend if Jawhar passes by him and to kiss Jawhar's hands. Aflaḥ offered to pay 100,000 dinars to be spared that, but al-Muʿizz refused so he descended from his place and kissed Jawhar's hands.[396]

Jawhar marched until he entered and conquered Egypt on the 13th of Shaʿbān, 358 AH/969 AD. At night, he resided at his settlement area [for rides] (*munākh*),[397] where he arrived from his journey, which is now the site of Cairo. He marked-out the palace's land and started building it, as well as constructing the city of Cairo, while people marked-out lands around it.

The Fatimid Palaces

As for the palace, he marked it out on the night he settled [his rides and camped], before morning. When the morning came, Jawhar saw some irregularities and skews in it that he did not like. Then he said: It was dug on a blessed night and a fortunate hour, so he kept it as is, and continued to build the palace until he finished it.

The palace used to occupy the area of length currently running from al-Ṣāliḥiyya Madrasa[398] at Bayn al-Qaṣrayn[399] to al-Aydumarī's Plaza,[400] and width running

394 In the east of today's Libya.

395 Aflaḥ al-Nāshib, amir of Barqa at the time. (Al-Maqrīzī, *Itti'āẓal-Ḥunafā' bi-Akhbār al-A'imma al-Fāṭimiyyīn al-Khulafā'*, ed. Gamal al-Din al-Shayyal and Muhammad Hilmi Ahmad (Cairo, 1996), Vol. 1, 216, 229, & 249).

396 The account shows that al-Muʿizz ordered Aflaḥ to show humility to Jawhar. The verb translated to "descend" in this paragraph is "*yatarajjal*," which means "to stand on one's feet," and is generally used to refer to dismounting one's ride. In this context, it probably refers to Aflaḥdescending from his residence to meet Jawhar, while standing on his feet, rather than mounted on a ride. (http://www.baheth.info/all.jsp?term=ترجل).

397 Settlement area for camels (see later and Glossary: "*munākh*"), which, in this context, would refer to where the army arrived and camped.

398 The madrasa-complex built by the Ayyubid Sultan al-Ṣāliḥ Najm al-Dīn Ayyūb in 641 AH/1243 AD. It was the first madrasa in Cairo to teach the four Sunni rites or schools of law: Shāfiʿī, Mālikī, Ḥanafī and Ḥanbalī. In 648 AH/1250 AD, al-Ṣāliḥ's widow and very briefly the only female sultan of Egypt, Shajarr al-Durr, attached a mausoleum to the madrasa to host the body of al-Ṣāliḥ, who died fighting the French Crusaders in the City of al-Manṣūra, in the north-east of Egypt. (D. Abouseif, *Architecture*, 87–91 and "Madrasa wa Qubbat al-Salih Najm al-Din Ayyub," http://archnet.org/sites/1539).

399 Literally, "Between the Two Palaces:" is the area inside the walls of Cairo that was originally between the western and eastern Fatimid palaces, which were demolished by the first Ayyubid sultan of Egypt, Ṣalāḥ al-Dīn. The area still goes by this name until today. (A. Raymond, *Cairo*, 32 Map 2 and A. Abd al-Raziq, *Tārīkh*, 210 Map 10).

400 Raḥbat al-Aydumarī (al-Aydymarī's Plaza) was within the bigger Raḥbat Bab Qaṣr al-Shawk (Plaza of Bab Qaṣr al-Shawk, which was one of the eastern gates of the greater eastern Fatimid Palace, see later). It was named after al-Aydumarī (d. 687 AH/1288 AD), whose house was there and who was a mamluk of ʿIzz al-Dīn Aydamur al-Ḥillī, the viceroy of Sultan al-Ẓāhir Baybars. Al-Aydumarī was promoted during the reign of Baybars until he became an amir and advanced in rank during the reign of Sultan Qalāwūn. He was buried in his mausoleum in the Southern Cemetery, near al-Imām al-Shāfiʿī's mausoleum. (Al-Maqrīzī, *Khiṭaṭ*, Vol. 2, 469).

from al-Sab' Khuwakh[401] to Bāb al-'Īd Plaza.[402] The inclusive contour of the area is as follows: If you are standing with the door of al-Ṣāliḥiyya Madrasa to your left, proceed to al-Sab' Khuwakh, then to the Shrine of al-Ḥusayn (Mashhad al-Ḥusayn),[403] to al-Aydumarī's Plaza, to al-Rukn al-Mukhallaq,[404] to Bayn al-Qaṣrayn, until you return to the door of al-Ṣāliḥiyya Madrasa from which you started. The area that was to your left throughout this tour was the location of the palace. The palace had nine gates, some of which were original, and some added to it later.

401 *Khuwakh* (sing. *khawkha* or *khūkha*) were the small doors inserted in the city gates or the gates of big buildings, which facilitated daily use instead of having to open and close the huge gates. The term was also applied to small doors in the city walls or the corners of streets and alleys. Al-Sab' Khuwakh (The Seven Khuwakh), were located in a *raḥba* (plaza) that occupied the space between Bāb al-Daylam, in the southern walls of the greater eastern Fatimid palace, and al-Azhar Mosque. To reach al-Azhar, the Fatimid caliphs exited their palace through Bāb al-Daylam then passed through al-Sab' Khuwakh. (M. al-Shishtawy, *Mutanazzahāt*, 204 fn. 1 and al-Maqrīzī, *Khiṭaṭ*, Vol. 2, 463).

402 Raḥbat Bāb al-'Īd (Plaza of the Gate of the Feast) was a vast plaza to the north-east of the greater eastern Fatimid palacethat extended from Bāb al-Rīḥ in the northern wall of the palace to Khizānat al-Bunūd (the treasury of flags and banners, which was attached to the eastern palace, in its north-eastern corner). Members of the army stood in this plaza to wait for the caliph to come out of the palace on the feast days through Bāb al-'Īd in the northern walls of the palace, and move with him on the feast processions. People started building in this plaza after 600 AH/1204 AD, and the area bore the same name at the time of al-Maqrīzī. In modern times, this area occupied the site bordered at the west by Ḥabs al-Raḥba and Bayt al-Māl streets, at the south by Qaṣr al-Shawk Street, at the east by Qaṣr al-Shawk Alley and at the north by al-Zawiya and al-Mayda alleys. (Al-Maqrīzī, *Khiṭaṭ*,Vol. 2, 196 & 468 and M. Shams, *Nujūm*, Vol. 4, 53 fn. 3).

403 Al-Ḥusayn was the Prophet's grandson who was martyred in the Battle of Karbala in Iraq in 61 AH/680 AD. He is revered by both Sunnis and Shiites, but holds a special place in the Shiite dogma. A shrine was built for his head in 549 AH/1154 AD but little or may be nothing remains of the original Fatimid structure built to host it. The current Mosque of al-Husayn, which includes his memorial or shrine (*mashhad*), is a mostly Khedieval structure from 1290 AH/1873 AD. (See also M. Uthman, *Mashāhid*, 127–131 and "Masjid al-Husayn,"http://archnet.org/sites/1543).

404 Al-Rukn al-Mukhallaq (the Perfumed Corner) is the south-western corner of al-Aqmar Mosque. Al-Maqrīzī does not specifically state that it is the corner of the mosque, although he indicates that it is in this location – to the right of the person entering the Mosque of Moses, which itself is to the right of the person coming from Bayn al-Qaṣrayn towards Raḥbat Bāb al-'Īd. Other researchers say that it was the corner where the northern and western walls of the Eastern Palace met, which was taken up in modern times by a house that stood opposite the latrines of al-Aqmar Mosque, in al-Tumbukshiyya Street. Al-Maqrīzī says that the corner was perfumed because in the year 660 AH/1262 AD a stone appeared there with a phrase engraved on it: "This is the mosque of Moses peace be upon him." He adds that "al-Mukhallaq" (the perfumed) might also refer to another meaning, which is smooth and polished, and that he was also told that some inscriptions inside the mosque referred to this corner with the name "al-Rukn al-Mukhawwaq," which means "the wide corner." (A. Abd al-Raziq, *Tārīkh*, 252, al-Maqrīzī, *Khiṭaṭ*, Vol. 2, 155–156 and Vol. 3, 563 andM. Shams, *Nujūm*, Vol. 4, 35 fn. 5).

The First: **Bāb al-Dhahab** (The Gate of Gold):[405] It is said that it was in place of the current al-Ẓāhiriyya Madrasa.[406]

The Second: **Bāb al-Baḥr** (The River Gate):[407] It is said that the current gate of the Palace of Yashbak[408] stands in its place. Ibn ʿAbd al-Ẓāhir said: It was built by al-Ḥākim.[409]

The Third: **Bāb al-Zuhūma** (Gate of Kitchen Odours):[410] It was in place of the hall (*qāʿa*)[411] of the shaykh of the Ḥanābila[412] inside al-Ṣāliḥiyya Madrasa. The [current] Goldsmiths' Market (al-Ṣāgha)[413] is in place of a palace's kitchen and Bāb al-Zuhūma was used to bring the food into the palace. The gate was, therefore, called "Bāb al-Zuhūma" for *al-zuhūma* is food cooked using fat.

The Fourth: **Bāb al-Turba** (The Burial Ground Gate):[414] It is said that it was located in between the aforementioned Bāb al-Zuhūma and the Shrine of al-Ḥusayn.

405 This gate was at the centre of the western walls of the Eastern Palace and was one of the greatest gates used for processions and by statesmen. It was opposite Qalāwūn's hospital and occupied the place later taken up by the mihrab of the Ẓāhiriyya Madrasa. (A. Raymond, *Cairo*, 32 Map 2 and M. Shams, *Nujūm*, Vol. 4, 37 fn. 1).

406 The madrasa that al-Ẓāhir Baybars built at Bayn al-Qaṣrayn in 661 AH/1263 AD. Unfortunately, most of the madrasa was demolished in 1291 AH/1874 AD and only a small part of its western corner still survives. (see "Madrasa al-Sultan al-Zahir Baybars," http://archnet.org/sites/1543).

407 *Al-Baḥr* is any body of water, be it a sea or a river. The River Nile is sometimes called Baḥr al-Nīl. This gate was one of the western gates of the Eastern Palace, used by the caliphs to access the Nile bank at al-Maqs. Its site was taken up by Bashtak's Palace's gate and is also thought to have been at the entrance of Bayt al-Qāḍī Alley in Bayn al-Qaṣrayn area. (M. Shams, *Nujūm*, Vol. 4, 36 fn. 7).

408 The Palace of Yashbak is outside Fatimid Cairo, while the palace meant to be referred to here, which al-Maqrīzī mentions in this same context, is the Palace of Bashtāk, one of the amirs of Sultan al-Nāṣir Muḥammad, who built it in 734 AH/1334 AD – 740 AH/1339 AD. (Al-Maqrīzī, *Khiṭaṭ*, Vol. 2, 516–517 and "Qasr al-Amir Bashtak,"http://archnet.org/sites/2373).

409 In his account of the palace, Ibn ʿAbd al-Ẓāhir lists Bāb al-Baḥr among the gates built by Jawhar. (See *Khiṭaṭ*, 15).

410 This gate was in the southwestern corner of the western walls of the Eastern Palace. It was taken up in modern times by the shops at the beginning of Khān al-Khalīlī Street, to one's left upon entering it from al-Qumṣānjiyya Street. (A. Raymond, *Cairo*, 32 Map 2 & 52 and M. Shams, *Nujūm*, Vol. 4, 37 fn. 2).

411 Probably means the iwan allocated to the Ḥanbalī school.

412 That is, the shaykh who teaches the Ḥanbalī school of interpretation.

413 During the Mamluk era, this market or quarter was located across the Qaṣaba, opposite Khān al-Khalīlī, to the south of Qalāwūn's Complex. The market still stands bearing the same name today. (A. Raymond, *Cairo*, 156 Map 7 and M. Shams, *Nujūm*, Vol. 4, 56 fn. 1).

414 It was in the southwestern corner of the Eastern Palace. Al-Turba (the Burial Ground), al-Turba al-Muʿizziyya (Burial Ground or Tomb of al-Muʿizz), or Turbat al-Zaʿfarān (Saffron Burial Ground) was the burial site of the Fatimid royal family, which Caliph al-Muʿizz built and where he buried the remains of his ancestors that he brought along with him from Tunisia. It was located at the site of Funduq al-Khalīlī (Khān al-Khalīlī built in 786 AH/1384 AD); in the place later taken up by the entrance of Wikālat al-Quṭn (the Cotton Caravanserai built in 917 AH/1511 AD), in Sikkat al-Bādistān Street of Khān al-Khalīlī Quarter. (Al-Maqrīzī, *Khiṭaṭ*, Vol. 2, 56 & 161–162, A. Raymond, *Cairo*, 32 Map 2 and M. Shams, *Nujūm*, Vol. 4, 37 fn. 4).

The Fifth: **Bāb al-Daylam** (The Gate of Daylam)[415]: It is the gate of the Shrine of al-Ḥusayn.

The Sixth: **Bāb Qaṣr al-Shawk** (The Thorn Palace Gate):[416] It was situated in the place known as Qaṣr al-Shawk, near al-Aydamurī's Plaza.

The Seventh: **Bāb al-ʿĪd** (The Feast Gate):[417] This is the gate of the Old Hospital (al-Bīmāristān al-ʿAtīq).[418] It was so called because the caliph used it to exit for ʿĪd prayers.[419] Bāb al-ʿĪd Plaza is named after this gate.

The Eighth: **Bāb al-Zumurrud** (The Emerald Gate):[420] It is next to the aforementioned Bāb al-ʿĪd.

415 Al-Daylam is the race and region to the southwest of the Caspian Sea. This gate was the southeastern gate of the Eastern Palace. Its location was near the Green Gate (al-Bāb al-Akhdar) of al-Ḥusayn Mosque, which still stands today. (Muhammad A. Dahman, *Mu'jam al-Alfāẓ al-Tārīkhiyya fī al-'Aṣr al-Mamlūkī* (Damascus, 1990), 78, A. Raymond, *Cairo*, 32 Map 2 and M. Shams, *Nujūm*, Vol. 4, 37 fn. 5).

416 This was the eastern gate of the Eastern Palace. Its site in modern times is taken up by the entrance to ʿAṭfat al-Qazzāzīn, off Darb al-Qazzāzīn. (A. Raymond, *Cairo*, 32 Map 2 and M. Shams, *Nujūm*, Vol. 4, 37 fn. 3).

417 This was one of the northeastern gates of the Eastern Palace. It was taken up in modern times by a part of a caravanserai (*wikāla*) in Qaṣr al-Shawk Street. (A. Raymond, *Cairo*, 32 Map 2 and M. Shams, *Nujūm*, Vol. 4, 36 fn. 5).

418 Sultan Ṣalāḥ al-Dīn built this hospital in 577 AH/1181 AD.

419 All Muslims celebrate two annual religious feasts: ʿĪd al-Fiṭr, on occasion of breaking the fasting of the month of Ramaḍān (Ramadan), the ninth month of the Hijri calendar, and ʿĪd al-Aḍḥā, the sacrificial feast that celebrates Allah's sparing of Prophet Ismaʿīl, son of Prophet Ibrāhīm (Abraham) from slaughter. ʿĪd al-Aḍḥā is celebrated on the 10th of Dhū al-Ḥijja, the twelfth and last month of the Hijri calendar, one day after the most important ritual of pilgrimage, Waqfat ʿArafa (Standing on the Mount of ʿArafa). Both feastshave their morning congregational prayers.

420 This was one of the northeastern gates of the Eastern Palace. It was in the site of the Complex of Tatar al-Ḥijāziyya (749 AH/1349 AD and 761 AH/1360 AD) in ʿAṭfat al-Qaffāṣīn, off al-Jamāliyya Street, probably in place of its mihrab. (A. Raymond, *Cairo*, 32 Map 2 and M. Shams, *Nujūm*, Vol. 4, 36 fn. 6 and see "Qubba wa-Madrasa Tatar al-Hijaziyya," http://archnet.org/sites/2228).

The Ninth: **Bāb al-Rīḥ** (The Wind Gate):[421] Ibn al-Ṭuwayr[422] mentioned that it was in the corner of the palace that faced the wall of the House of Saʿīd al-Suʿadā',[423] which is the khanqah now.[424]

Afterwards, al-Ma'mūn al-Baṭā'iḥī,[425] vizier of al-Āmir,[426] built three new belvederes (*manāẓir*)under the arch in between Bāb al-Dhahab to Bāb al-Baḥr. One belvedere (*manẓara*) was called: al-Zāhira (the Bloomy),[427] the second: al-Fākhira (the Magnificent), and the third: al-Nāḍira (the Radiant).[428]

Al-Āmir used to sit in these belvederes [to watch] the soldiers' parade on ʿĪd al-Ghadīr,[429] while the vizier stood under the arch of Bāb al-Dhahab. A chain used to be hung daily, starting noontime, extending [across the street] to an opposite point, in the current [location now known] as al-Suyūfiyyīn[430] to prevent riders

421 This was the northern gate of the Eastern Palace and was roughly in place of the gate of Wikālat Bazarʿa (11th century AH/17th century AD) in al-Tumbkshiyya Street, al-Jamāliyya Quarter. (A. Raymond, *Cairo*, 32 Map 2 and Ibn Taghrī Birdī& M. Shams, *Nujūm*, Vol. 4, 37 & 38 fn. 7 and see "Wikala Bazarʿa," http://archnet.org/sites/2434).

422 Abū Muḥammad al-Murtaḍā b. al-Ḥasan al-Qayasrānī, Ibn al-Ṭuwayr (d. 617 AH/1220 AD) was a judge who was born and lived in Egypt. He was an administrative civil servant of the Fatimid and Ayyubid states, who held high supervisory positions. He authored *Nuzhat al-Muqlatayn fī Akhbār al-Dawlatayn*, on the Fatimid and Ayyubid courts and administrations. The title of the book is, however, deceiving, for despite its reference to the two states, it gives a description of only one of them, namely, the Fatimid state. (Ibn al-Ṭuwayir, Nuzha, 9–11°).

423 Dār Saʿīd al-Suʿadā' was originally the house of a Fatimid freed slave of Caliph al-Mustanṣir (r. 427 AH/1036 AD – 487 AH/1094 AD), who was one of *al-ustādhūn al-muḥannakūn* (see Glossary: "*ustādhūn*") serving at the palace. Saʿīd al-Suʿadā' (the Happiest or the Most fortunate) was the houseowner's title. He was killed in 544 AH/1149 AD and his house became the residence of the Fatimid viziers, for it was opposite Dār al-Wizāra (the House of the Vizierate, see Glossary) and vizier al-Ṣāliḥ Ṭalā'iʿ dug a vault connecting the two buildings to facilitate his movement. When Sultan Ṣalāḥ al-Dīn came to power, he transformed this house into a khanqah for Sufis in 569 AH/1174 AD and allocated endowments to fund it. It remained a respectable Sufi foundation during the Ayyubid and Mamluk eras. (Al-Maqrīzī, *Khiṭaṭ*, Vol. 3, 570–573). The palace that al-Qalqashandī refers to here is the greater Eastern Fatimid palace.

424 Ibn al-Ṭuwayr, *Nuzha*, 183–184.

425 The Fatimid vizier from 515 AH/1121 AD to 519 AH/1125 AD. He was one of the viziers of the "Great Viziers" era (See Glossary: "Fatimids").

426 The Fatimid caliph from 495 AH/1101 AD to 524 AH/1130 AD.

427 May also be translated as "The Luminous." (See http://www.baheth.info/all.jsp?term=زاهر).

428 May also be translated as "The Bright" or "The Shining." (See http://www.baheth.info/all.jsp?term=ناضر and http://corpus.quran.com/translation.jsp?chapter=75&verse=22).

429 A Shiite feast, also called ʿĪd Ghadīr Khumm. This feast is celebrated on the occasion of the incident at Ghadīr Khumm (the Khumm Brook), which is located in between Mecca and Madina. On his way back from his last pilgrimage journey in the year 10 AH/632 AD, the Prophet stopped at this place along with his company. He gave a speech and emphasized his brotherly bond with his cousin, ʿAlī b. Abī Ṭālib, which was later interpreted by Shiite Muslims to be a declaration of ʿAlī's right to be the first caliph after the Prophet. This occasion was first celebrated in Egypt in the year 362 AH/973 AD. (A. Sayyid, *Tafsīr*, 460–461).

430 Al-Suyūfiyyīn (the Sword-makers) or Sūq al-Suyūfiyyīn (the Sword-makers Market) was the area in al-Muʿizz Street which was by the door of al-Madrasa al-Suyūfiyya, itself named after

from passing in front of the palace. This place is, therefore, known as Darb al-Silsila (the Alley of the Chain).[431]

The Shrine of al-Ḥusayn is included within the perimeter of the [non-extant] palace.

The reason the shrine (*mashhad*) was built was that the head of Imām al-Ḥusayn was [kept] at Ascalon, and al-Ṣāliḥ Ṭalā'i' b. Ruzayk feared [that it might be captured] by the Crusaders. Al-Ṣāliḥ Ṭalā'i' thus built his mosque[432] outside Bāb Zuwayla[433] and meant to transfer the head to it. [Caliph] al-Fā'iz beat him to that and ordered the establishment of this shrine, to which he transferred the head in the year 549 AH/1154 AD.

One of the strange [anecdotes] concerning the blessing of this honourable head is that which was related by Judge Muḥiy al-Dīn Ibn 'Abd al-Ẓāhir: When Sultan Ṣalāḥ al-Dīn Yūsuf b. Ayyūb took over the palace after the death of al-'Āḍid, the last Fatimid caliph of Egypt, he detained one of the palace eunuch-servants (*khuddām*),[434] shaved his head and clasped it with a bowl containing beetles, but the eunuch-servant was not affected by it. Sultan Ṣalāḥ al-Dīn then asked him about this and its secret. He related that when the honourable head was brought to the shrine, he carried it above his own head, so the Sultan released him and was good to him.[435]

There was a small palace next to the [larger] one, known as "al-Qaṣr al-Nāfi'ī,"[436] towards the direction of al-Sab' Khuwakh. This palace hosted the elderly Fatimids.[437]

the market. Sultan Ṣalāḥ al-Dīn built this madrasa (c. 573 AH/1177 AD) for the Ḥanafī school of jurisprudence and allocated endowments to sustain it. The location of the madrasa was within the site of the earlier house of the Fatimid vizier al-Ma'mūn al-Baṭā'iḥī (r. 1121–1125 AD) and is now taken up by the complex of Shaykh Muṭahhar (built in 1744 AD) at the northwest junction of al-Mu'izz and al-Muskī streets. (Al-Maqrīzī, *Khiṭaṭ*, Vol. 3, 443, Abd al-Rahman Zaki, *Mawsū'a*, 271–272, and Caroline Williams, *Islamic Monuments in Cairo* (Cairo, 2002), 161).

431 This alley was opposite Bāb al-Zuhūma (in the southwest corner of the greater eastern palace). The site of this alley was taken up in modern times by Wikālat al-Jawāhirjiyya (the Jewelers' Caravanserai) in al-Khardajiyya Street, opposite Khān al-Khalīlī Street. (Al-Maqrīzī, *Khiṭaṭ*, Vol. 2, 448 and M. Shams, *Nujūm*, Vol. 4, 56 fn. 2).

432 Mosque of al-Ṣāliḥ Ṭalā'i', see fn. 548.

433 This is one of the surviving gates of the second walls of Cairo. Bāb Zuwayla, built in 485 AH/1092 AD, was one of the southern gates, which stands today carrying on its two towers the twin handsome minarets of the Mamluk al-Mu'ayyad Shaykh's complex (built in 818 AH/1415 AD to 825 AH/1422 AD) directly inside the walls. The first Bāb Zuwayla of Jawhar's walls was located about 150 m to the north of the present day gate. (See also "Bab Zuwayla," http://archnet.org/sites/2728, M. Uthman, *al-'Imāra al-Fāṭimiyya: al-Ḥarbiyya, al-Madaniyya wa-l-Dīniyya* (Cairo, 2006), 76 & 114–125, D. Abouseif, *Islamic Architecture*, 69–72 and A. Raymond, *Cairo*, 32 Map 2).

434 *Khuddām* (sing. *khādim*) means "servants" and denotes eunuchs who were normally responsible for the palaces or the households.

435 See Ibn 'Abd al-Ẓāhir's account in *Khiṭaṭ*, 30–31.

436 This was one of the smaller palaces in the vicinity of the Eastern Palace and it was located in the area to the south of al-Ḥusayn Mosque. (Al-Maqrīzī, *Khiṭaṭ*, Vol 2, 162–163 and M. Shams, *Nujūm*, Vol. 4, 51 fn. 3).

437 See Ibn 'Abd al-Ẓāhir's account in *Khiṭaṭ*, 34.

I say: This [larger] palace remained the residence of the Fatimid caliphs, from al-Mu'izz, their first caliph in Egypt, and up to the final days of al-'Āḍid, their last. The viziers used to reside in the House of the Vizierate (Dār al-Wizāra)[438] that Badr al-Jamālī,[439] the Amir of the Armies (Amir al-Juyūsh),[440] built inside [Cairo walls, within the enclosure of], Bāb al-Naṣr (Gate of Victory),[441] in place of the current al-Rukniyya Khanqah.[442] When Sultan Ṣalāḥ al-Dīn Yūsuf b. Ayyūb was assigned the vizierate of Caliph al-'Āḍid, following his uncle Asad al-Dīn Shīrkūh,[443] he resided in the aforementioned House of the Vizierate until the death of al-'Āḍid, when Ṣalāḥ al-Dīn moved to the palace. After [the death of] Ṣalāḥ al-Dīn, his brother al-'Ādil Abū Bakr[444] resided in the palace as well. When al-Kāmil Muḥammad b. al-'Ādil Abū Bakr[445] became sultan, he moved from the palace to the Citadel, as will be mentioned later in the description of the Citadel. The House of the Vizierate then became a residence for the ambassadors arriving from [other] kingdoms until Sultan al-Malik al-Muẓaffar Baybars al-Jāshankīr[446] built the khanqah named after him in its place. Since that time, no one resided in the palace, which was neglected and therefore fell to ruins.

Judge Muḥyi al-Dīn b. 'Abd al-Ẓāhir said: In the year 630 AH/1233 AD, Murhaf, a gatekeeper of Bāb al-Zuhūma, told me: I had spent a long time guarding this door without seeing firewood going in through it, or dust thrown out of it. He said: One of the reasons for the palace's dilapidation was the burning of its wood and the piling of its dust.[447] After that, people started owning and ground-renting[448] it, and houses

438 See Glossary: "Dār al-Wizāra."*Dār* (house) is a word that is used to mean "place, home or office." It was also employed in honourific titles of caliphs or royal women. (Muhammad al-Baqli, *Al-Ta'rīf bi-Muṣṭalaḥāt Ṣubḥ al-A'shā* (Cairo, 1984), 127).

439 Badr al-Jamālī was the commander and ruler of Acre whom Caliph al-Mustanṣir called upon to come to Egypt to control the extreme chaos that hit it due to the calamities of famine and riots. Badr, who was of Armenian origin, was known for his extreme firmness and strength. He completely enforced order in Egypt and started the era of the "Great Viziers." (See Glossary: "Fatimids"). Badr remained in power from 466 AH/1073 AD to 487 AH/1094 AD and executed the project of the new fortified stone walls of Cairo.

440 Caliph al-Mustanṣir bestowed this title on Badr al-Jamālī after he appointed him vizier. (M. Uthman, *'Imāra*, 83).

441 This is one of the surviving northern gates of the stone wall fortifications of Cairo built by Badr al-Jamālī from 480 AH/1087 AD to 485 AH/1092 AD). (See also "Bab al-Nasr," http://archnet.org/sites/2727, M. Uthman, *'Imāra*, 90–100 and D. Abouseif, *Architecture*, 68).

442 This is the khanqah built by the Mamluk Sultan Rukn al-Dīn Baybars al-Jāshankīr in al-Jamāliyya area in 706 AH/1307 AD – 709 AH/1310 AD. (See also "Funerary Complex of Baybars al-Jashankir," http://archnet.org/sites/2207, and D. Abouseif, *Architecture*, 104–107).

443 The military commander sent by Nūr al-Dīn Maḥmūd of Damascus to rescue the Fatimids. (See Glossary: "Ayyūbids").

444 Ayyubid sultan from 596 AH/1200 AD to 615 AH/1218 AD.

445 Ayyubid sultan from 615 AH/1218 AD to 635 AH/1238 AD.

446 The Mamluk amir who interrupted the rule of Sultan al-Nāṣir Muḥammad and managed to become the sultan of Egypt briefly from 708 AH/1308 to 709AH/1309 AD.

447 Ibn 'Abd al-Ẓāhir, *Khiṭaṭ*, 114.

448 Al-Qalqashandī uses the term *istiḥkār* (transforming into a *ḥikr*). A *ḥikr* is an empty land that is originally part of a *waqf* (endowment) and is allocated to a renter who pays a sum of money,

and madrasas were built inside it. Sultan al-Malik al-Ṣāliḥ Najm al-Din Ayyūb built his madrasa, al-Ṣāliḥiyya, inside it, then so did al-Ẓāhir Baybars with his madrasa, al-Ẓāhiriyya. Bashtāk, one of the amirs of the state of al-Nāṣir Muḥammad b. Qalāwūn, built his palace, which was known after him, inside it too. The Minting House[449] (Dār al-Ḍarb) was built in its middle, while none of its remains survived except the Old Hospital (al-Bimāristān al-ʿAtīq), which used to be a hall (*qāʿa*) that was built by al-ʿAzīz bi-Allah b. al-Muʿizz,[450] as will be mentioned later. Moreover, the remains included the dome in between this hospital and Bāb al-ʿĪd Plaza, and some insignificant walls that were incorporated into the properties.

The Gates and Walls of Cairo

As for the gates and walls of Cairo, when General Jawhar first planned them,[451] he built four gates: two in close proximity, and another two far apart. The two in proximity were the two Gates of Zuwayla, named after the Zuwayla tribe, one of the Berber tribes that arrived with Jawhar from the Maghrib; therefore so called by the documenters and by others.[452] One of these two gates is the arch currently standing next to the Mosque of Sām b. Nūḥ,[453] and the other was in place of the shops selling

equivalent to the land's value, as rent. This agreement entitles the renter to the ownership rights of the land, even if he is not legally the owner. The renter pays a minimal annual rental fee and may sell the lease or pass it on to his descendants. This lease is a long-term rental lease, which allows the renter to use the land, in case the owner cannot invest in it. This rental, also referred to as "*aḥkar al-buyut*" (rental of houses) is part of theannual income of the Mamluk state, known as *hilali*. See Maqrizi, Al-Mawāʿiẓ/Ayman, Vol. 1, 287, 288.

449 See Glossary: "Dār al-Ḍarb."

450 Al-ʿAzīz was the Fatimid caliph from 365 AH/976 AD to 386 AH/996 AD. The hall (*qāʿa*) referred to here is also al-Iwān al-Kabīr (the Great Iwan) which was built in 369 AH/979 AD. It was later made into the Armory Warehouses, then turned into a hospital in the early Ayyubid era. (M. Uthman, *'Imāra*, 166–167 and al-Maqrīzī, *Khiṭaṭ*, Vol. 2, 115–116 & 160).

451 Originally, when Jawhar al-Ṣaqallī started building the Fatimid capital in 358 AH/969 AD, he enclosed it inside mud brick walls. After Badr al-Jamālī, the first of the line of governing viziers, came to power, he decided to better fortify the city for protection against a Saljuq threat of invasion that never came true. The brick walls were replaced with stone ones in a project that ran between the years 480 AH/1087 AD and 485 AH/1092 AD. The walls of Badr had several gates and they expanded beyond Jawhar's walls slightly to the east and west, and considerably to the south and north, where in the last direction they incorporated the Mosque of al-Ḥākim (built from 379 AH/990 AD – 404 AH/1013 AD). (M. Uthman, *'Imāra*, 73–128 and A. Raymond, *Cairo*, 32 Map 2, 37 & 56–57).

452 The Bāb Zuwayla of Jawhar's walls was not two gates, but one with two doors or two openings for passage, and was therefore sometimes referred to as "the Two Gates of Zuwayla." (M. Uthman, *'Imāra*, 76).

453 Al-Maqrīzī reports that this was the mosque inside Bāb Zuwayla called the Mosque of Ibn al-Bannā', which had nothing to do with Sām b. Nūḥ (Sam son of Prophet Noah), but was so named by the commoners. The site was originally a Jewish synagogue called Sām b. Nūḥ, which Caliph al-Ḥākim appropriated and converted into a mosque. Muḥammad b. ʿUmar b. Jāmiʿ b. al-Bannā' (d. 591 AH/1195 AD) was a Quran reciter at this mosque. The mosque came to be known later as the Zawiya of Sām b. Nūḥ, or the Zawiya of al-ʿAqqādīn, which is on al-Manākhliyya Street. (Al-Maqrīzī, *Khiṭaṭ*, Vol. 3, 555–556 and M. Shams, *Nujūm*, Vol. 4, 38 fn. 4).

cheese to the left of this arch, which leads to al-Maḥmūdiyya.[454] The reason this gate ceased to be used and was blocked was that when al-Mu'izz arrived from the Maghrib and entered Cairo, which was built for him, he went through the arch that stands there now. People, thus, crowded [to go] through that door and avoided the other, which then acquired a reputation among people that whoever entered through it would have none of his needs fulfilled, and was, therefore, rejected and blocked. A small street (*zuqāq*) was built to its south to lead to al-Maḥmūdiyya, while another small street was built to its north to lead to al-Anmāṭiyyīn[455] and beyond it.

The two far apart gates were the arch inside Bāb al-Futūḥ (Gate of Conquests)[456] outside Ḥārat[457] Bahā' al-Dīn,[458] and another one parallel to it inside Bāb al-Naṣr,[459] near the present day Caravanserai of Qaysūn.[460] This arch was demolished then

454 Ḥārat al-Maḥmūdiyya (Al-Maḥmūdiyya Quarter) was one of the old quarters of Cairo which in modern times occupied the area around al-Ishrāqiyya Street and the east part of al-Nabawiyya Street in al-Darb al-Aḥmar Neighbourhood. It was named after a regiment of the Fatimid army, al-Maḥmūdiyya, which came to Egypt during the reign of Caliph al-'Azīz and joined his army. (M. Shams, *Nujūm*, Vol. 4, 39 fn. 1, Abd Allah Gamal al-Din, *Al-Dawla al-Fāṭimiyya: Qiyāmuhā bi-Bilād al-Maghrib wa-Intiqāluhā ilā Nihāyat al-Qarn al-Rābi'* (Cairo, 1991), 204 and A. Abd al-Raziq, *Tārīkh*, 210 Map 10).

455 Sūq al-Anmāṭiyyīn (the Rugs Market): the *anmāṭ* were rugs and covers used for making howdahs, covering saddles and the like, therefore, this market was specialized in these products. Al-Maqrīzī says this market used to be known as Sūq al-Ḥaddādīn and al-Ḥajjārīn (the Blacksmiths and Stone-makers Market), where musical instruments were sold. In modern times, the area was taken up by al-Munajjidīn Street in al-Darb al-Aḥmar Neighbourhood. (Al-Maqrīzī, *Khiṭaṭ*, Vol. 2, 83 & 98 and M. Shams, *Nujūm*, Vol. 4, 39 fn. 2).

456 The first Bāb al-Futūḥ of Jawhar's walls referred to here did not survive. It was located at the beginning of Bayn al-Sayārij Street, where it meets al-Mu'izz Street. Still standing is Bāb al-Futūḥ of Badr's walls (480 AH/1087 AD) in the northern second walls of Cairo, a little to the northeast of Jawhar's gate. (See also "Bab al-Fufuh,"http://archnet.org/sites/2180, M. Uthman, *'Imāra*, 75–76 & 100–109, D. Abouseif, *Architecture*, 69 and A. Raymond, *Cairo*, 32 Map 2).

457 A *ḥāra* (pl. *ḥārāt*) used to mean a residential quarter, unlike our present day's meaning of an alley. The *ḥāra* was originally mainly allocated for the residence of a particular group of people united by some common factor or attribute. Their houses would be grouped together in this quarter that would have its own mosques, madrasas and markets, depending on the size of the quarter. In the early Fatimid era, each *ḥāra* housed a particular army faction or regiment, which were categorized according to the tribal affiliations. (A. Gamal al-Din, *Dawla*, 197–198 and A. Raymond, *Cairo*, 385).

458 This quarter (*ḥāra*) was at the time attributed to Bahā' al-Dīn Qarāqūsh al-Asadī (d. 597 AH/1201 AD), a mamluk of Asad al-Dīn Shīrkūh and later the vizier of Ṣalāḥ al-Dīn, who used to live there. Currently, its site is roughly taken up by the area around Bayn al-Sayārij Street, which lies opposite the southwestern corner of al-Ḥākim's mosque, with Bāb al-Futūḥ Street (northern part of al-Mu'izz Street) to its east and Port Sa'īd Street to its west. (Ibn 'Abd al-Ẓāhir , *Khiṭaṭ*, 65 and 65 fn. 3 and M. Shams, *Nujūm*, Vol. 4, 40 fn. 2).

459 The first Bāb al-Naṣr of Jawhar's walls, which was located to the north of Badr's Bāb al-Naṣr. It was located about 20 m to the north of Wikālāt Qūṣūn. (M. Uthman, *'Imāra*, 76 and A. Raymond, *Cairo*, 32 Map 2).

460 Wikālat Qūṣūn: A *wikāla* is a caravanserai (see Glossary) and Qūṣūn (d. 742 AH/1342 AD), sometimes referred to as Qaysūn above, was one of the prominent amirs of Sultan al-Nāṣir Muḥammad, who was related to him by marriage. This *wikāla*, built in 724 AH/1326 AD to 741 AH/1341 AD, is located to the south of the Mosque of al-Ḥākim, in Bāb al-Naṣr Street. It was a caravanserai

the aforementioned Amir al-Juyūsh Badr al-Jamālī built a mud brick[461] wall circling around Cairo in 480 AH/1087 AD, parts of which have survived until today in the neighbourhood (*khaṭṭ*) of the Sheep Market (Sūq al-Ghanam)[462] inside Bāb al-Maḥrūq.[463] Then al-Afḍal b. Amir al-Juyūsh[464] built the presently existing Bāb Zuwayla, Bāb al-Naṣr, and Bāb al-Futūḥ, as mentioned by Judge Muḥyi al-Dīn b. ʿAbd al-Ẓāhir in his *Khiṭaṭ*. However, Ibn ʿAbd al-Ẓāhir mentions in other parts of his *Khiṭaṭ* that Bāb Zuwayla was built by al-ʿAzīz bi-Allah and completed by Badr al-Jamālī.[465] Bāb Zuwayla is one of the grandest and loftiest gates and it has no bent entrance (*bāshūra*)[466] at its doors. ʿAlī b. Muḥammad al-Nīlī[467] describes it saying:

> "My friend, if you see Bāb Zuwayla, you will appreciate its worth as a building. A gate that enveloped itself with the galaxy, wore Sirius, and wrapped Saturn around its head. Had the Pharaoh seen it, he would not have wanted an edifice, nor would he have ordered Hāmān[468] to build him one."[469]

Ibn ʿAbd al-Ẓāhir said: And [there is] Bāb Saʿāda (Saʿāda's Gate),[470] which is possibly attributed to Saʿāda b. Ḥayyān, the slave-boy (*ghulām*) of al-Muʿizz, who

for merchants who came from Syria with oils, soaps, nuts and such merchandise. It had several warehouses that Qūṣūn ordered be rented for a cheap price and instructed that no tenant should be evicted. The warehouses were therefore inherited due to these advantages. The *wikāla* remained in great prosperity until the Mongols sacked Damascus in 803 AH/1400 AD. Al-Maqrīzī reports witnessing the glorious days of this establishment, when its upper residential quarters comprised 360 units that housed almost 4000 people. (Al-Maqrīzī, *Khiṭaṭ*, Vol. 2, 576–577, C. Williams, *Monuments*, 209 and see "Khan al-Amir Qawsun," http://archnet.org/sites/4234).

461 General Jawhar built the first walls of Cairo, which were made of brick, when he established the city in 358 AH/969 AD. Al-Maqrīzī reports that Badr's walls were made of mud brick, while its gates were made of stone. (Al-Maqrīzī, *Khiṭaṭ*, Vol. 2, 96).

462 This market was located to the southeast of Bāb Zuwayla. (A. Raymond, *Cairo*, 119 Map 4).

463 This gate was originally known as Bāb al-Qarrāṭīn. It was in the southern part of the eastern side of the Badr's walls of Cairo. It earned the name of al-Bāb al-Maḥrūq (the Burnt Gate) because the mamluks of Amīr Aqṭāy burnt it down in 652 AH/1254 AD to escape from Cairo after their leader was killed by the forces of al-Muʿizz Aybak, the first Mamluk sultan, with whom Aqṭāy competed for the rule of Egypt. (Al-Maqrīzī, *Khiṭaṭ*, Vol. 2, 104–105, A. Raymond, *Cairo*, 32 Map 2, A. Abd al-Raziq, *Tārīkh*, 210 Map 10).

464 The second powerful Fatimid vizier who inherited the position from his father, Badr al-Jamālī. Al-Afḍal was vizier from 487 AH/1094 AD to 515 AH/1121 AD.

465 This is most probably inaccurate. See Uthman, *al-'Imāra al-Fāṭimiyya, 76& 114-125*; Abouseif, *Islamic Architecture*, 69–72.

466 A bent entrance, of possibly several turns, for military defense purposes.

467 A poet.

468 The vizier of the Pharaoh of Egypt at the time of Prophet Moses.

469 See also Ibn ʿAbd al-Ẓāhir's accont on the Fatimid gates of Cairo in *Khiṭaṭ*, 16–18.

470 This gate was in the southern part of the western walls of Cairo. Saʿāda b. Ḥayyān, as mentioned above, was a *ghulām* and a military commander of Caliph al-Muʿizz. The gate was located ten meters to the north of the western entance of the Appeals Court (Maḥkamat al-Isti'nāf) in Bāb al-Khalq Neighbourhood. An alley bearing the name of Saʿāda is also found behind this court today. (M. Uthman, *'Imāra*, 76–77, A. Abd al-Raziq, *Tārīkh*, 210 Map 10 and A. Raymond, *Cairo*, 32 Map 2).

came with an army sent from al-Mu'izz to Jawhar, and later became the ruler of Ramla[471].[472]

He said: And Bāb al-Qanṭara (The Bridge Gate),[473] attributed to the bridge (*qanṭara*)[474] in front of it, which General Jawhar built to cross over to al-Maqs when he feared [an invasion by] the Qarmatians[475].[476] As [for] the arch on the Great Street (al-Shāri' al-A'ẓam)[477] outside Bāb Zuwayla, at the beginning of al-Munjibiyya,[478] which is now at the Bird Sellers Market (al-Ṭuyūriyyīn),[479] it was a gate that al-Ḥākim bi-Amr Allah built outside Cairo, and it was known as "al-Bāb al-Jadīd" (the New Gate).[480]

As for Bāb al-Khawkha (Gate of the Small Door),[481] which is in the proximity of Qanṭarat al-Muskī (al-Mūskī's Bridge),[482] I think it was also built by the

471 A Palestinian city that was founded by the Umayyad Caliph Sulaymān b. 'Abd al-Malik in 97 AH/715 AD. Its location is central between Jaffa and Jerusalem, to the south-east of the former and the north-west of the latter.

472 Ibn 'Abd al-Ẓāhir adds that Sa'āda was known for being charitable. (*Khiṭaṭ*, 130).

473 This gate was in the northern part of the western walls of Cairo. Its site is at the entrance of Amīr al-Juyūsh al-Juwwāni Street in al-Jamāliyya Quarter. (M. Uthman, *'Imāra*, 76, A. Abd al-Raziq, *Tārīkh*, 210 Map 10, and A. Raymond, *Cairo*, 32 Map 2).

474 Al-Maqrīzī reports that this bridge was built in 360 AH/971 AD.(*Khiṭaṭ*, Vol. 2, 103).

475 See Glossary: "Qarmatians."

476 Ibn 'Abd al-Ẓāhir, *Khiṭaṭ*, 18.

477 A *shāri'* is a large street. Al-Shāri' al-A'ẓam literally means the Greatest Street, also known as al-Qaṣaba, was the street extending from Bāb Zuwayla in the south to Bayn al-Qaṣrayn to the north of Cairo. (Al-Maqrīzī, *Khiṭaṭ*, Vol. 2, 83).

478 Also al-Muntajibiyya, a residential quarter outside Bāb Zuwayla, which was named after a man from the Fatimid era (or state), called Muntajib al-Dawla, and was established during the era of Caliph al-Ḥākim (r. 386 AH/996 AD – 412 AH/1021 AD). (Ibn 'Abd al-Ẓāhir, *Khiṭaṭ*, 135 and al-Maqrīzī, *Khiṭaṭ*, Vol. 2, 619).

479 The Bird Sellers Market outside Bāb Zuwayla, on the extension of al-Shāri' al-A'ẓam. (Al-Maqrīzī, *Khiṭaṭ*, Vol. 2, 59 & 594).

480 According to al-Maqrīzī, Caliph al-Ḥākim built this gate outside the first Bāb Zuwayla, which marked the evolution of the extension of al-Qaṣaba (al-Shāri' al-A'ẓam) Street outside the Fatimid city walls. Al-Bāb al-Jadīd Gate (the New Gate) was on the bank of Birkat al-Fīl (the Elephant's Pond) and by al-Maqrīzī's time, only an arch remained of it, therefore, it was called Bāb al-Qaws (Gate of the Arch), a term that was also employed to describe the remnants of the arches of several other gates. The exact date of building this gate is not found in the sources. Al-Ḥākim built it to mark the limits of the lands outside Cairo that were allowed to be taken by the military regiments to settle their quarters. (Al-Maqrīzī, *Khiṭaṭ*, Vol. 2, 59, 594–595, & 619–621 and Ayman Fouad Sayyid, *Al-Taṭawwur al-'Umrānī li-Madīnat al-Qāhira Mundhu Nash'atihā wa-ḥattā al-Ān* (Cairo, 1997), 26–27). This gate is no longer extant and should not be confused with another gate by the same name in the northeastern section of the walls that the Ayyubids started building in 572 AH/1176 AD to encompass Cairo and Fustat within one fortification.

481 This was one of the southwestern gates of the Fatimid wall. In modern times, its location was identified as the beginning of Qabw al-Zīna Street (Port Sa'īd Street), from the direction of Bayn al-Nahdayn Street, opposite al-Qāḍī Yaḥyā Mosque (built in 852 AH/1448 AD to 853 AH/1449 AD). (M. al-Shistawi, *Mutanazzahāt*, 206 and A. Raymond, *Cairo*, 32 Map 2).

482 The Ayyubid Amīr 'Izz al-Dīn Mūsk (d. 584 AH/1188 AD) built this bridge, al-Mūskī Bridge, which was used to cross the Great Khalīj to the western bank. Its location is the present day

Fatimids. When Sultan Ṣalāḥ al-Dīn Yūsuf b. Ayyūb became the ruler of Egypt, he delegated Bahā' al-Dīn Qarāqūsh al-Asadī al-Rūmī,[483] the *ṭawāshī*,[484] to build the walls of Cairo and Miṣr in 569 AH/1174 AD, overseeing many Crusader war prisoners they had at the time. He started building a wall around Cairo, the Citadel, and Fustat, and the construction continued until Sultan Ṣalāḥ al-Dīn's demise.[485] This is the wall that exists now, in which he built several gates, including: Bāb al-Baḥr (The River Gate),[486] Bāb al-Sha'riyya (Gate of al-Sha'riyya),[487]Bāb al-Barqiyya (Gate of al-Barqiyya),[488] and al-Bāb al-Maḥrūq (The Burnt Gate).

intersection of Port Sa'īd and al-Mūskī streets. (Al-Maqrīzī, *Khiṭaṭ*, Vol. 2, 710 and M. al-Shishtawi, *Mutanazzahāt*, 204).

483 See fn. 458.

484 Pl. *ṭawāshiyya*: The *ṭawāshiyya* were originally "a special military formation" (D. Ayalon, 464) that was an important faction during the Ayyubid era and disintegrated by the early Mamluk era. The *ṭawāshiyya* troops of Ṣalāḥ al-Dīn's time included "both *mamluks* and freely recruited cavalrymen, each with his own horse, page or *mamluk* follower, about ten animals to carry baggage, and a salary to purchase equipment. Organized into first-rate regiments which remained close to the ruler on campaign, each *ṭawāshī* was expected to serve in the army for a certain number of months every year." (H. Nicholson, 28). Not enough information exists to know for sure whether they were mamluks, but they were amirial troops in the Mamluk era. Sometime after the Mamluks came to power, the term was used to denote eunuch servants or slaves entrusted with guarding the women-quarters, as well as bringing up the newly recruited young mamluks who resided in the barracks (*ṭibāq*); however, the trainers of the new mamluks were not always eunuchs, and many times high-ranking amirs were employed. The *ṭawāshiyya* were most respected and their chief was one of the dignitaries. Another relevant term used by historians is *khaṣiy*, "the emasculated," which al-Maqrīzī and Ibn Taghrī Birdī occasionally refer to Qarāqūsh with. (Helen Nicholson and David Nicolle, *Gods Warriors: Crusaders, Saracens and the Battle for Jerusalem*, (Oxford, 2005) 28 & 120; Hamilton A. R. Gibb, "The Armies of Saladin," in *Studies on the Civilization of Islam*. ed. S. J. Shaw and W. R. Polk (London, 1962) 76–77 & 87; T. Abdelhamid, *Jaysh*, 6; David Ayalon, "Studies on the Structure of the Mamluk Army II," *Bulletin of the School of Oriental and African Studies* 15 (1953): 464–467; Sa'id Ashour, *Al-'Aṣr al-Mamālīkī fī Miṣr wa-l-Shām* (Cairo, 1976), 455; M. Dahman, *Mu'jam*, 109, and Hany al-Jazzar, "Al-Niẓām al-'Askarī fī Dawlat al-Mamālīk -648–923 AH/1250–1517 AD" (MA Thesis, Islamic University in Gaza, 2007), 27).

485 The construction of these walls "was still in progress in (636 AH)/1238 (AD), forty-five years after (Ṣalāḥ al-Dīn's) death." (A. Raymond, *Cairo*, 91, see also K. Azab, *Citadel*, 9–25).

486 Bāb al-Baḥr was to the northwest of Cairo, in the northwest of al-Maqs. This gate should not be confused with another that bore the same name but was in the north-western walls of the Fatimid eastern palace, which al-Maqrīzī reports to have been located in between Bāb al-Dhahab in the western walls of the palace, overlooking Bayn al-Qaṣrayn, and Bāb al-Rīḥ, in the palace's north wall. (Al-Maqrīzī, *Khiṭaṭ*, Vol. 2, 214 & 218 and A. Raymond, *Cairo*, 81 Map 3).

487 Bāb al-Sha'riyya was also to the northwest of Cairo, but close to the Fatimid city, just beyond the Khalīj. Al-Maqrīzī says that it was named after three Berber tribes collectively called Banū al-Sha'riyya, but it also seems to have retained the name because of the popularity of the Sufi Shaykh al-Sha'rānī (d. 973 AH/1565 AD), who preached in the area. (Al-Maqrīzī, *Khiṭaṭ*, Vol. 2, 103 and A. Raymond, *Cairo*, 81 Map 3 and 173).

488 A gate with the same name that did not survive was in the eastern walls of Fatimid Cairo built by Jawhar, situated almost in the middle of the eastern side. Another by the same name was also built in the eastern Ayyubid walls. Al-Barqiyya is an attribution to the troops which came from Barqa (eastern Libya) along with the Fatimid Caliph al-Mu'izz and resided in a quarter (*ḥāra*) in eastern Cairo, which came to be known after them. This quarter is presently around 'Aṭfat

Qarāqūsh built two great towers, one in al-Maqs,[489] in the proximity of the Mosque of Bāb al-Baḥr,[490] which al-Ṣāḥib Shams al-Dīn al-Maqsī,[491] the vizier of al-Ashraf Sha'bān b. Ḥusayn,[492] had demolished in the beginning of the year 770 AH/1368 AD, and incorporated within the buildings of the above-mentioned mosque, when he renewed it. The second tower[493] was at Bāb al-Qanṭara (The Gate of the Bridge),[494] south of Fustat.

Judge Muḥyī al-Dīn b. 'Abd al-Ẓāhir said: The length of this wall, beginning to end, is 29,302 Hashimi Cubit.[495] This includes: 10,000 cubits[496] from Bāb al-Baḥr to the tower of al-Kawm al-Aḥmar,[497] which is at the beginning of Munsha'at al-Mahrānī previously mentioned in the [section on] the Neighbourhood of Fustat, at the mouth of the Khalīj of Cairo; 7200 cubits[498] from al-Kawm al-Aḥmar to the Citadel, from the direction of Sa'd al-Dawla

al-Darrāsa, to the southeast of al-Ḥusayn Mosque. (Ibn 'Abd al-Ẓāhir, *Khiṭaṭ*, 42, al- Maqrīzī, *Khiṭaṭ*, Vol. 2, 391, A. Raymond, *Cairo*, 37, 81 Map 3 & 91, and A. Gamal al-Dīn, *Dawla*, 201).

489 Burj al-Maqs, Qal'at al-Maqs and Qal'at Qarāqūsh are all variant names of this tower. *Burj* (tower) was a term used to describe small fortresses employed for observation and as a first line of defence. These fortresses were big enough to host a small military unit that would be responsible for defending against enemy attacks or delaying their forces until the nearby fortifications brace up for the battle. Burj al-Maqs was located at the western end of the northern Ayyubid walls. Today, its site is traceable to a location near al-Fatḥ Mosque in Ramsis Square. It was probably torn down in between 770 AH/1368 AD and 779 AH/1377 AD. (K. Azab, *Qal'a*, 13 and 13 fn. 2 & 3 and A. Raymond, *Cairo*, 81 Map 3).

490 Also Al-Maqs Mosque.

491 "Al-Ṣāḥib" was a title given to viziers, as well as denoting other offices (see Glossary). Shams al-Dīn Abū al-Faraj al-Maqsī(d. 795 AH/1393 AD) was originally a Christian administrative clerk who worked in amirial bureaus (*dawāwīn*). He converted to Islam in the year 766 AH/1365 AD and started assuming positions at the sultanic royal court. According to al-Maqrīzī, he was first appointed a vizier in 770 AH/1369 AD. Throughout his long career, he alternated between serving the state, imprisonment, and property confiscation as the sultans changed. (H. al-Basha, *Alqāb*, 367, Ibn Taghrī Birdī, *Nujūm*, Vol. 11, 24 and al-Maqrīzī, *Al-Sulūk li-Ma'rifat Duwal al-Mulūk*, ed. Muhammad Abd al-Qadir Ata (Beirut, 1997), Vol. 5, 79–133).

492 Mamluk sultan from 764 AH/1363 to 778 AH/1376 AD.

493 Al-Qalqashandī is most likely referring to Qal'at al-Kawm al-Aḥmar or Burj Yāzkūj, which was probably located on the Nile bank, at the intersection of the Ayyubid western and southern walls. It was named after Sayf al-Dīn Yāzkūj (d. 599 AH/1202 AD), a mamluk of Asad al-Dīn Shīrkūh, who was a military leader and the head of al-Asadiyya regiment of soldiers during Sultan Ṣalāḥ al-Dīn's reign. Al-Kawm al-Aḥmar was a neighbourhood to the south of Fustat. (K. Azab, *Qal'a*, 14 & 14 fn. 2 and A. Raymond, *Cairo*, 81 Map 3). In this context, al-Qalqashandī is probably referring to Bāb al-Qanṭara as an area, rather than a gate.

494 This was the gate in the southern corner of the Ayyubid walls, to the southwest of the Mosque of 'Amr b. al-'Āṣ. It should not be confused with another gate by the same name which was in the northwestern Fatimid walls of Jawhar. (A. Raymond, *Cairo*, 32 Map 2, 81 Map 3 & 119 Map 4 and M. al-Shishtawi, *Mutnazzahāt*, 205 fn. 1).

495 19,222 m. *al-dhirā' al-Hāshimī* (the Hashimi Cubit) is equivalent to 0.656 m. (See fn. 300).

496 6560 m.

497 See fn. 493.

498 4723 m.

Mosque;[499] 8392 cubits[500] from Saʿd al-Dawla Mosque to Bāb al-Baḥr, and 3110 cubits[501] surrounding the Citadel.[502] Sultan ʿImād al-Dīn,[503] the Ruler of Hama, mentioned the length of this wall in cubits in his History,[504] but without detail or referring to the extra two cubits.[505]

I say: Most of this wall perished and the features of its major part have changed due to the attachment of the properties' buildings to it, to the extent that, in most places, it is indistinguishable from the buildings. The part in between Bāb al-Baḥr and al-Kawm al-Aḥmar has fallen down, so much that none of it remains. To add, the lands of the places inside the first wall of Cairo are marshy[506] and their water is salty.

Ibn ʿAbd al-Ẓāhir said: This is why when al-Muʿizz arrived in Egypt and entered Cairo, he blamed Jawhar for not founding it in the location of al-Maqs near Bāb al-Baḥr or to the south of Fustat near al-Raṣad, so as to be close to the Nile and have fresh water in its wells.[507]

499 This mosque was in the location of the current mosque of Sultan al-Nāṣir Muḥammad at the Citadel (718 AH/1318 AD and 736 AH/1335 AD). It was probably built by the Abbasid ruler of Egypt, Ḥātim b. Hirthima (r. 194 AH/810 to 195 AH/811 AD), and might have been later restored in the Fatimid era. (K. Azab, *Qal'a*, 56–58).

500 5505 m.

501 2040 m.

502 In Ibn ʿAbd al-Ẓāhir's account, he states that the total length is 29,302 cubits, as above, including: 10,500 cubits from al-Maqs Citadel to al-Burj; 8,892 cubits from al-Maqs Citadel to Saʿd al-Dawla Mosque; 7,200 cubits from the mosque to the Burj, and 3210 cubits surrounding the Citadel from the direction of the mosque. (Ibn ʿAbd al-Ẓāhir, *Khiṭaṭ*, 20). However, the summation of these sections is 29,802 cubits.

503 Sultan ʿImād al-Dīn, al-Mu'ayyad Abū al-Fidā' Ismāʿīl, the Ayyubid ruler of Hama from 710 AH/1310 AD to 732 AH/1332 AD. He was an educated cultured man as well as a politician. He managed to restore the Ayyubid control over Hama in 710 AH/1310 AD, when he became the viceroy ruler there. In 718 AH/1318 AD, he was given the title of "sultan" by al-Nāṣir Muḥammad. He authored several works in diverse subjects; most famous were his books on history and geography: *Al-Mukhtaṣar fī Akhbār al-Bashar*, known as *Tārīkh Abī al-Fidā'* (the History of Abū al-Fidā') and *Taqwīm al-buldān*, known as *Jughrāfiyyat Abī al-Fidā'* (the Geography of Abū al-Fidā'). (See Al-Zarkalī, *A'lām*, Vol. 1, 319).

504 *Al-Mukhtaṣar fī Akhbār al-Bashar*, see fn. 503.

505 The summation of the sections mentioned above is 28,702 cubits. The total length stated by Abū al-Fidā' is 29,300 cubits, which is why al-Qalqashandī wonders about the extra two cubits, considering the total length he copies from Ibn ʿAbd al-Ẓāhir. (ʿImād al-Dīn Abū al-Fidā' Ismāʿīl, *Al-Mukhtaṣar fī Akhbār al-Bashar* (Cairo, 1907), Vol. 3, 59). The length of the walls of Cairo has been repeatedly mentioned and discussed in many Mamluk primary sources, with each writer giving a slightly different version. Modern scholars have also investigated the issue in attempt of disambiguating these descriptions. For a summarized discussion, see Tarek Abdelhamid, "Notes on Military Architecture of the Ayyubid Period" (MA Thesis, The American University in Cairo, 2005), 102–106.

506 "*Sabkha*"is the Arabic term for "salt flat." Al-Qalqashandī probably uses the term as an adjective in this context, that is "*sabikha*," which means "marshy" or "salty."

507 Ibn ʿAbd al-Ẓāhir, *Khiṭaṭ*, 20.

The Neighbourhoods of Cairo

You should know that the marked-out neighbourhoods (*khiṭaṭ*) of Cairo expanded and the construction around it increased, and what was outside its wall became multiples of what was inside. Some of the neighbourhoods are attributed to the Fatimids and some to monarchies preceding them, either because their original names disappeared and they became more known for new ones, or because the names were newly introduced, after they were nameless. Some of the names are unknown because they lost their fame with long days and passing nights. Here, only the evidently famous, well-known places will be accounted for, not others, and I will be mentioning them in order of location rather than oldness and newness.

As for its famous neighbourhoods (*khiṭaṭ*) inside the wall, they include:

- **Quarter of Bahā' al-Dīn**[508] inside Bāb al-Futūḥ, known after Bahā' al-Dīn Qarāqūsh, the *ṭawāshī*, who built the wall of Cairo mentioned above. It was known as Bayn al-Ḥaratayn (Between the Two Quarters)[509] during the Fatimid era, then it was marked out, during the same era, by people known as al-Rayḥāniyya[510] and al-ʿAzīziyya,[511] and was known after them. When Bahā' al-Dīn Qaraqūsh resided in it, it became known after him and its former names were forgotten.
- **Quarter of Barjawān,**[512] known after Barjawān al-Khādim, who was the eunuch-servant of the palaces during the reign of al-ʿAzīz bi-Allah b. al-Muʿizz, the second Fatimid Caliph of Egypt. Al-ʿAzīz appointed Barjawān a guardian over his son, al-Ḥākim, which earned him a high status, then al-Ḥākim killed him after that. It is said that he left behind, in his inheritance,

508 Ḥārat Bahā' al-Dīn (See A. Abd al-Raziq, *Tārīkh*, 210 Map 10).

509 Ibn ʿAbd al-Ẓāhir, later copied by al-Maqrīzī, says that Bayn al-Ḥaratayn was one of the quarters outside Bāb al-Futūḥ. Al-Maqrīzī also says that the old Bāb al-Futūḥ, that of Jawhar's walls (359 AH/971 AD), was by Bahā' al-Dīn's Quarter, inside the later Bāb al-Futūḥ (485 AH/1092 AD), that is of Badr's walls. Al-Qalqashandī is, therefore, referring to the latter gate here. (Ibn ʿAbd al-Ẓāhir, *Khiṭaṭ*, 122 and al-Maqrīzī, *Khiṭaṭ*, Vol. 2, 96 & 409–411).

510 A military regiment of the Fatimid army, which al-Maqrīzī notes to have been strong and feared, and which suffered a great loss in a battle with another faction, al-Juyūshiyya, in 528 AH/1134 AD. (Al-Maqrīzī, *Khiṭaṭ*, Vol. 2, 403). Al-Qalqashandī notes below, in his account of al-Ḥusayniyya, that al-Rayḥāniyya were of non-Arab origin and of different ethnicities.

511 A military regiment of the Fatimid Caliph al-ʿAzīz. (A. Sayyid, *Tafsīr*, 666).

512 Ḥārat Barjawān: Abū al-Futūḥ Barjawān al-Khādim (the eunuch-servant) al-Ṣaqlabī (the Slav) was the guardian of Caliph al-Ḥākim when he assumed power at the young age of eleven. Barjawān was able to get rid of the vizier at the time, Ibn ʿAmmār, and take over his position. He tried to monopolize all power and prevent al-Ḥākim from communicating with his statesmen. Al-Ḥākim had him assassinated in 390 AH/1000 AD. Ḥārat Barjawān occupied the area around the present day Barjawān Street and Barjawān Alley in al-Jamāliyya neighbourhood. (Muhammad Surur, *Tārīkh al-Dawla al-Fāṭimiyya* (Cairo, 1994), 85, A. Gamal al-Din, *Dawla*, 210 and A. Abd al-Raziq, *Tārīkh*, 210 Map 10).

1000 trousers with 1000 silk running bands. The house of al-Muẓaffar,[513] son of Amīr al-Juyūsh Badr al-Jamālī, was in this quarter.

- **Al-Kāfūrī Neighbourhood,**[514] which was a garden that belonged to Kāfūr al-Ikhshīdī, and was extant when Cairo was first built. The garden survived until 651 AH/1253 AD, when al-Baḥariyya[515] and al-ʿAzīziyya[516] faction[517] marked it out as stables. Its trees were removed and it remained being attributed to Kāfūr, as it was before.
- **Neighbourhood of al-Khurunshuf,**[518] which was a square (*maydān*) for the Fatimid caliphs. They used to have an underground passage that ran from the gate of the palace to this square, through which they passed mounting their rides. When al-Ṣāliḥiyya Madrasa was built, it was used as a water drain. After the year 600 AH/1204 AD, the Ghuzz[519] built stables in it using *khurunshuf* and resided in them, therefore it became so-named.[520]

513 Al-Muẓaffar Abū Muḥammad Jaʿfar (d. 515 AH/1121 AD), held a military position of command under the vizierate of his brother, al-Afḍal Shāhinshāh. This house was originally built by Badr al-Jamālī himself but he died and it became the residence of al-Muẓaffar. After al-Muẓaffar's death, this house was used as a Guest House (Dār al-Ḍiyāfa, see Glossary) until it deteriorated and was abandoned with time. In the Mamluk era, the Chief Judge of the Ḥanafī School, Shams al-Dīn b. Abī Bakr al-Ṭarabulsī renovated and resided in the house with his family from 788 AH/1386 AD, until he died in 799 AH/1397 AD. (Ibn ʿAbd al-Ẓāhir, *Khiṭaṭ*, 64 and al-Maqrīzī, *Khiṭaṭ*, Vol. 2, 480–481).

514 Khaṭṭ al-Kāfūrī: Kāfūr's gardens occupied a section of the western side of Cairo. The western Fatimid palace took up the eastern end of these gardens. The remaining part of the gardens continued to be a "resort ground" for rulers until 644 AH/1247 AD – 645 AH/1248 AD. (A. Raymond, *Cairo*, 52 & 97). The present day Bustān al-Kāfūrī Street (Kāfūr's Gardens Street) is in al-Fajjāla neighbourhood, to the north-west of Fatimid Cairo. (See also A. Abd al-Raziq, *Tārīkh*, 210 Map 10).

515 Considering the year given by the author, this would be the group of Mamluks first recruited by the Ayyubid Sultan al-Ṣāliḥ Najm al-Dīn, later to form the Bahri Mamluk dynasty (See Glossary: "Bahri Mamluks"). There was another, relevant faction by the same name, which was formed by Sultan Qalāwūn (See Glossary: "al-Baḥariyya").

516 The mamluks of the Ayyubid Sultan al-Malik al-ʿAzīz Muḥammad (d. 634 AH/1237 AD), grandson of Sultan Ṣalāḥ al-Dīn, who ruled Aleppo from 613 AH/1216 AD to 634 AH/1237 AD (613 AH/1216 AD to 629 AH/1231 AD under the regency of his guardian, Shihāb al-Dīn al-Khādim). (Ibn Taghrī Birdī, *Nujūm*, Vol. 6, 264).

517 This faction was composed of 400 men. (M. Uthman, *'Imāra*, 188).

518 Khaṭṭ al-Khurunshuf: *al-khurunshuf* (*al-khurushtuf* in al-Maqrīzī's account) is the hardened residue of the combustion process of garbage and other waste, which was used to heat water for baths. Al-Maqrīzī says that this material was used to build the stables mentioned above. Ibn ʿAbd al-Ẓāhir adds that houses were also built in this quarter using *khurunfush*. The two historians do not agree, however, on the beginning of these building activities, for while Ibn ʿAbd al-Ẓāhir states that it was al-Ghuzz who started it, al-Maqrīzī reports that it was Caliph al-Muʿizz who did. (Al-Maqrīzī, *Khiṭaṭ*, Vol. 2, 426 and Ibn ʿAbd al-Ẓāhir, *Khiṭaṭ*, 62). The street named al-Khurunfush (a distortion of the old name) today, which occupies part of original neighbourhood, is in the north-west of Fatimid Cairo. (See also A. Raymond, *Cairo*, 156 Map 7).

519 Turcoman or Turkish tribes. (M. Dahman, *Mu'jam*, 115).

520 That is, called "Khaṭṭ al-Khurunshuf."

- **Shams al-Dawla Alley,**[521] which is near Bāb al-Zuhūma and was known in the Fatimid era as Ḥārat al-Umarā' (Quarter of the Amirs).[522] It included the house of 'Abbās,[523] the vizier of al-Ẓāfir,[524] and al-Masrūriyya Madrasa,[525] built by Masrūr al-Khādim. Masrūr was one of the palace's eunuch-servants during the Fatimid era and remained in service under the Ayyubids. He was in the private service of Sultan Ṣalāḥ al-Dīn, in which he became a commander (*muqaddam*).[526] Shams al-Dawla Tūrān Shāh b. Ayyūb,[527] the brother of Sultan Ṣalāḥ al-Dīn Yūsuf, later resided in it and built an alley (*darb*), so it was known after and attributed to him.
- **Quarter of Zuwayla,**[528] which is attributed to the Zuwayla Tribe of Berbers, who arrived with General Jawhar as mentioned earlier in the part on Bāb Zuwayla. This quarter is huge and branched.
- **Al-Jawdariyya,**[529] which is known after the faction named al-Jawdariyya, from the Fatimid era that is attributed to Jawdar, the eunuch-servant (*khādim*)

521 Darb Shams al-Dawla: This alley still bears the same name today. It is located in between Jawhar al-Qā'id Street and al-Ḥamzāwī al-Ṣaghīr Street. (A. Sayyid, *Khiṭaṭ*, 57 fn. 2).

522 Al-Maqrīzī notes that it got the name from a group of *ashrāf* who resided there. (Al-Maqrīzī, *Khiṭaṭ*, Vol. 2, 398).

523 'Abbās b. Yaḥyā b. Bādīs (d. 549 AH/1154 AD), also known as 'Abbās al-Ṣinhājī, who reached the position of the vizier under the Fatimid Caliph al-Ẓāfir, and whose son killed the caliph. Al-Ṣāliḥ Ṭalā'i' b. Ruzayk (Fatimid vizier from 549 AH/1154 AD to 555 AH/1160 AD) killed 'Abbās in vengeance for the caliph's blood. (Al-Maqrīzī, *Khiṭaṭ*, Vol. 2, 486 and A. Sayyid, *Tafsīr*, 278–281).

524 Fatimid caliph from 545 AH/1150 AD to 549 AH/1154 AD.

525 The madrasa was originally Masrūr's house, which he endowed to become a school after he died. It was built after his demise. (Al-Maqrīzī, *Khiṭaṭ*, Vol. 2, 572–573 and Vol. 3, 475).

526 Al-Maqrīzī tells us that Masrūr was a *muqaddam* (commander; officer commanding a group of soldiers) of the *ḥalaqa* (see Glossary) under Ṣalāḥ al-Dīn, and remained in service until the days of Sultan al-Kāmil, when he retired at his house for secluded worship until he died. He was a charitable man, who owned and endowed several properties.He was buried near his mosque in the Cemetery. (Al-Maqrīzī, *Khiṭaṭ*, Vol. 2, 572–573 and Vol. 3, 475).

527 Al-Malik al-Mu'aẓẓm Shams al-Dawla Tūrān Shāh b. Ayyūb, Fakhr al-Dīn, who came to Egypt in 564 AH/1169 AD and governed parts of Upper Egypt for a while under the sultanate of his brother, Ṣalāḥ al-Dīn. Shams al-Dawla started the Ayyubid sovereignty of Yemen in 569 AH/1174 AD. He was later assigned to rule Damascus in 571 AH/1176 AD and other parts of Syria, until Ṣalāḥ al-Dīn summoned him back to Egypt in 574 AH/1179 AD, where he governed Alexandria until he died in 576 AH/1180 AD. His body was moved to Damascus, where he was buried in the madrasa of his sister, Sitt al-Shām bint Ayyūb. (Al-Maqrīzī, *Khiṭaṭ*, Vol. 2, 446–448 and Ibn Khallikān, *Wafayāt*, Vol. 1, 306–309).

528 Ḥārat Zuwayla: In modern times, this is the area bordered northwards by al-Khurunfush Street, westwards by Zuwayla Street and Darb al-Kitāb, southwards by al-Ṣaqāliba Street, and eastwards by Ḥārat al-Yahūd and Ḥārat Khamīs. (A. Gamal al-Din, *Dawla*, 198, M. Uthman, *'Imāra*, 188 and A. Raymond, *Cairo*, 156 Map 7).

529 This is the area taken up in modern days by al-Jawādriyya Street, its branches, Ḥārat al-Jawādriyya al-Kabīra, Ḥārat al-Jawādriyya al-Ṣaghīra, and 'Aṭfat al-Jawādriyya, in al-Darb al-Aḥmar neighbourhood. Jawdar's correct name is Jawdhar, and his biography was written by his disciple, Abū 'Alī Manṣūr al-Jawdharī. (A. Gamal al-Din, *Dawla*, 211 & 211 fn. 58, M. Uthman, *'Imāra*, 188 and A. Raymond, *Cairo*, 156 Map 7).

of ʿUbayd Allah al-Mahdī who was the father of the Fatimid caliphs. They marked it out and resided in it when Jawhar built Cairo. Later, the Jews lived in it until news reached the Fatimid al-Ḥākim that they scorned Muslims and were insolent to Islam. Al-Ḥākim then blocked their doors and burnt them down at night. After that, they resided in the Quarter of Zuwayla mentioned above.

- **Al-Wazīriyya,**[530] which is known after Abū al-Faraj Yaʿqūb b. Killis,[531] the vizier of the Fatimid al-Muʿizz bi-Allah. Ibn Killis was a Jew who served in the Ikshidid state, then escaped to al-Muʿizz, in the Maghrib, for he was in need of money. He then met the army of Jawhar and returned with them. He gained al-Muʿizz's favour until he made him his vizier. Ibn Killis's house was in the place of the madrasa of al-Ṣāḥib Ṣafiy al-Dīn b. Shukr,[532] the vizier of al-ʿĀdil Abū Bakr b. Ayyūb, which was known as al-Ṣāḥibiyya,[533] in Suwayqat al-Ṣāḥib.[534] Before that, it used to be known as Dār al-Dībāj (the House of Silk).[535]

530 This is the area bordered in modern times by al-Sikkat al-Labūdiyya and al-Wazīr al-Ṣāḥib Streets northwards, Darb Saʿāda Street westwards, the western section of Sikkat al-Nabawiyya Street and the northern section of Ḥārat al-Jawādriyya southwards, and eastwards Baybars Street. (A. Gamal al-Din, *Dawla*, 204, M. Uthman, *'Imāra*, 191 and A. Abd al-Raziq, *Tārīkh*, 210 Map 10).

531 Ibn Killis (d. 380 AH/991 AD) came to Egyptduring Kafūr's rule. He served the Ikhshīdid court faithfully and converted to Islam, which made it possible for him to become a vizier. He escaped Egypt in 357 AH/968 AD, where he met Caliph al-Muʿizz and served him. He informed the caliph of the weaknesses of the Egyptian state and came with him to Egypt in 362 AH/973 AD. During the reign of Caliph al-ʿAzīz, Ibn Killis became the indispensible statesman who successfully managed all state matters, financial, judicial, military administration, and education. Caliph al-ʿAzīz was most saddened by the death of his trusted vizier. Al-Wazīriyya were the private troops of Ibn Killis, which started with a caliphal bestowal of 500 young boys (*ghilmān*) and 1000 Maghribis, to reach 4000 when he died. The caliph continued to support these troops after the vizier's death, in his honour. (A. Gamal al-Din, *Dawla*, 205–206).

532 ʿAbd Allah b. ʿAlī b. al-Ḥusayn, Ṣafiy al-Dīn Abū Muḥammad al-Shībī Ibn Shukr, Al-Dumayrī al-Mālikī (d. 622 AH/1225 AD), was a jurist who was born and religiously educated in Egypt. He was appointed head of the bureau of the Ayyubid state's fleet by al-ʿĀdil b. Ayyūb, brother of Sultan Ṣalāḥ al-Dīn. When al-ʿĀdil became sultan, Ṣafiy al-Dīn gained more authority until he became the vizier for some years, resigned, then was called on again to serve the same position under Sultan al-Kāmil. He was known for his strong character to the extent of standing up to the sultans, as well as his efficiency. (Al-Maqrīzī, *Khiṭaṭ*, Vol. 3, 459–460).

533 Al-Ṣāḥib Ṣafiy al-Dīn b. Shukr built this madrasa and endowed it to the study of the Mālikī School. It also provided Arabic grammar lessons and contained a library. It was managed by his sons at the time of al-Maqrīzī. In the year 758 AH/1357 AD, Judge ʿAlam al-Dīn Ibrāhīm b. ʿAbd al-Laṭīf, known as Ibn al-Zubayr, who was the Nāẓir al-Dawla of the Mamluk Sultan al-Nāṣir Ḥasan, restored the madrasa and put a minbar in it for the first time, so it also served as a Friday mosque, an additional function it continued to have until al-Maqrīzī's days. (Al-Maqrīzī, *Khiṭaṭ*, Vol. 3, 458).

534 In the Fatimid era, this area used to be known as Suwayqat al-Wazīr (a *suwayqa* is a small *sūq*: market), after the vizier Yaʿqūb b. Killis, since the market was by the door of his house. Later, it became known as Suwayqat Dār al-Dībāj, then al-Sūq al-Kabīr by the Fatimid era. Suwayqat al-Ṣāḥib is a name the area gained in association with Ṣafiy al-Dīn Ibn Shukr. (Al-Maqrīzī, *Khiṭaṭ*, Vol. 2, 604–605).

535 *Dībāj* is most probably silk brocade. Dār al-Dībāj was the house of the Fatimid vizier Yaʿqūb ibn Killis. Al-Maqrīzī says that Ibn Killis's house got this name in the Fatimid era after his death, when it became used as a Dār al-Ṭirāz (see later for *ṭirāz*) that specialized in producing *dībāj*.

- **Al-Maḥmūdiyya,**[536] which Judge Muḥyī al-Dīn b. ʿAbd al-Ẓāhir said was possibly attributed to the faction known as al- Maḥmūdiyya that came to Egypt in the days of the Fatimid al-ʿAzīz bi-Allah.[537]
- **Quarter of the Rūm,**[538] which is inside the two Zuwayla gates.[539] It was marked out by the *Rūm* who arrived in the company of General Jawhar when he built Cairo. It was, therefore, known after and attributed to them until now.
- **Al-Bāṭiliyya,**[540] which Ibn ʿAbd al-Ẓāhir said was known after a group of people who approached al-Muʿizz, the builder of Cairo, after he divided the grants among people and gave them nothing. Therefore, they said: Are we untruthful (*'alā bāṭil*)?[541] So, the area was called "al-Bāṭiliyya."[542]
- **Quarter of the Daylam,**[543] which is known after the Daylam who arrived in company of Aftakīn al-Muʿizzī,[544] the slave-boy (*ghulām*) of al-Muʿizz b. Buwayh

The whole neighbourhood was for a while called: Khaṭṭ Dār al-Dībāj. (Al-Baqli, *Ta'rīf*, 129, al-Maqrīzī, *Khiṭaṭ*, Vol. 2, 604, and see Glossary).

536 See fn. 454.

537 This particular statement appears to have not been made by Ibn ʿAbd al-Ẓāhir in his *Khiṭaṭ*. He rather guessed that al-Maḥmūdiyya was either attributed to Maḥmūd, al-Ṣāliḥ Ṭalāʾiʿ's nephew or Maḥmūd b. Maṣāl al-Lakkī, a statesman in the late era of Caliph al-Mustanṣir, who was involved in the controversy of his succession. (Ibn ʿAbd al-Ẓāhir, *Khiṭaṭ*, 52, A. Sayyid, *Tafsīr*, 221 and Ibn Taghrī Birdī, *Nujūm*, Vol. 5, 140–143).

538 Ḥārat al-Rūm : Today's Ḥārat al-Rūm and ʿAṭfat al-Rūm, around which this Fatimid quarter existed, are in al-Darb al-Aḥmar Neighbourhood, near Bāb Zuwayla. Caliph al-Ḥākim demolished this quarter in 399 AH/1009 AD then it was later rebuilt. (A. Gamal al-Din, *Dawla*, 200, A. Raymond, *Cairo*, 156 Map 7 and A. Abd al-Raziq, *Tārīkh*, 210 Map 10).

539 The first Fatimid Bāb Zuwayla.

540 In modern times, it is the area around al-Bāṭiliyya (al-Bāṭiniyya) Street and Alley to the south-east of al-Azhar Mosque, in al-Darb al-Aḥmar Neighbourhood. (A. Gamal al-Din, *Dawla*, 200, M.Uthman, *'Imāra*, 190, and A. Abd al-Raziq, *Tārīkh*, 210 Map 10).

541 *Al-Bāṭil*, in Quranic context, is falsehood, untruth, or injustice, mostly mentioned opposed to *al-Ḥaqq* (the Truth, also one of the names of Allah). "*'Alā bāṭil*" means on the side of falsehood, thus being unrightful. In Ibn ʿAbd al-Ẓāhir's account, the statement is: "*ruḥnā fī al-bāṭil*," which may be translated as: "we have gained nothing" or "we have missed our chance." (Ibn ʿAbd al-Ẓāhir, *Khiṭaṭ*, 42).

542 According to both Ibn ʿAbd al-Ẓāhir and al-Maqrīzī, the offerings and bestowals were finished by the time it was these people's turn, so they exclaimed complaining of not being deserving or not getting their share. (Ibn ʿAbd al-Ẓāhir, *Khiṭaṭ*, 42 and al-Maqrīzī, *Khiṭaṭ*, Vol. 2, 383).

543 Ḥārat al-Daylam: Al-Maqrīzī tells us that the quarter known as ḥārat al-Atrāk (The Turks' Quarter) was by his time called Darb al-Atrāk, which led to ḥārat al-Daylam. Both ḥārat al-Atrāk and ḥārat al-Daylam were sometimes considered one quarter. (Al-Maqrīzī, *Khiṭaṭ*, Vol. 2, 387). "The Turks had resided in the area taken up today by al-Kaḥkiyyīn Alley, Darb al-Atrāk, and Ḥawsh Qadam Alley," in al-Darb al-Aḥmar Neighbourhood. There is a small street (*zuqāq*) in present day's Ḥawsh Qadam Alley which is known as Ḥabs al-Daylam. (M. Uthman, *'Imāra*, 189, A. Abd al-Raziq, *Tārīkh*, 210 Map 10 and A. Raymond, *Cairo*, 156 Map 7).

544 Originally, Aftakīn Abū Manṣūr al-Turkī (d. 372 AH/982AD), who, after the conflict described above held a high status in the Fatimid court, for he was Caliph al-ʿAzīz's*ḥājib*(see Glossary). Caliph al-ʿAzīz had accused his vizier, Ibn Killis, of poisoning Aftakīn, which is why he imprisoned him for a while, but then he released him and assigned him back to his office. (A. Gamal al-Din, *Dawla*, 207–208).

al-Daylamī.[545] He had seized Damascus in the days of the Fatimid al-Mu'izz, fought General Jawhar, and sought the aid of Qarmatians. Al-'Azīz bi-Allah went out to fight Aftakīn and managed to take him as a war prisoner in Ramla.[546] He brought Aftakīn back to Cairo, bestowed on him generously, and housed him and his company in this neighbourhood (*khiṭṭa*). This neighbourhood included the house of al-Ṣāliḥ Ṭalā'i' b. Ruzayk,[547] who built al-Ṣāliḥī Mosque[548] outside Bāb Zuwayla. He used to reside in this house before he became a vizier and his small door (*khawkha*) there is still known as "Khawkhat al-Ṣāliḥ"[549] until now.

- **Quarter of Kutāma**[550] near al-Azhar Mosque and next to al-Bāṭiliyya, is known after the Kutāma Berber[551] tribe that arrived accompanying Jawhar from the west.
- **Al-Ṭārima**[552] **Stable**[553] in the exterior of the Shrine of al-Ḥusayn, which was a stable for the palace. Dār al-Fiṭra,[554] [the house] which hosted the breakfast meal (*al-fiṭra*) of 'Īd al-Fiṭr, was in this neighbourhood (*khaṭṭ*). Al-Ma'mūn b. al-Baṭā'iḥī, the vizier of al-Āmir, built this house (*dār*).

545 The Buwayhid ruler of Kirman, in present day Iran, from 324 AH/936 AD to 337 AH/949 AD. (See Glossary: "Buwayhids").

546 In Muharram 368 AH/September 978. (A. Gamal al-Din, *Dawla*, 208).

547 Al-Maqrīzī relates that al-Ṣālāḥ Ṭalā'i' built this house in 547 AH/1152 AD. The mamluk amir Rukn al-Dīn 'Umar b. Qaymāz (d. 809 AH/1406 AD) then demolished the old house and built a new one in its place in 794 AH/1392 AD. (Al-Maqrīzī, *Khiṭaṭ*, Vol. 2, 511).

548 The Mosque of al-Ṣāliḥ Ṭalā'i' built in 555 AH/1160 AD (See also: D. Abouseif, *Architecture*, 76–77, M. Uthman, *'Imāra*, 358–388, A. Abd al-Raziq, *Tārīkh*, "Masjid al-Salih Tala'i'," http://archnet.org/sites/2324).

549 Al-Ṣāliḥ's *khawkha*: Al-Maqrīzī relates that this *khawkha* used to be known as Khawkhat Baḥtakīn, after the amir Jamāl a-Dawla Baḥtakīn al-Ẓāhirī. (Al-Maqrīzī, *Khiṭaṭ*, Vol. 2, 465). Baḥtakīn seems to have been an amir around the mid 5th century AH/11th century AD. His *nisba* (title of attribution) suggests that he belonged to the court of the Fatimid Caliph al-Ẓāhir (r. 412 AH/1021 AD – 427 AH/1036 AD).

550 Ḥārat Kutāma: This quarter is currently in the southeast of al-Azhar Mosque. It is taken-up by the area around Ḥārat al-Azharī, 'Aṭfat al-Dawādārī, and their surrounding alleys and lanes. (A. Gamal al-Din, *Dawla*, 201).

551 The Kutāma Berbers of the Maghrib were one of the important tribes that supported the rise of the Fatimids in the western Islamic lands. Some of them came with Jawhar and others arrived with Caliph al-Mu'izz. (A. Gamal al-Din, *Dawla*, 201, M. Uthman, *'Imāra*, 190–191, and A. Abd al-Raziq, *Tārīkh*, 210 Map 10).

552 An Arabized word that means a house made of wood or a domed, circular structure. (Ibn al-Ṭuwayir, Nuzha, 135 fn. 3).

553 The location of al-Ṭārima Stable is presently taken up by the area to the east of al-Bāb al-Akhdar, the eastern gate of al-Ḥusayn's mosque, up to Umm al-Ghulām Street. In the Fatimid era, this stable was to the south-east of the Eastern Palace, opposite Bāb al-Daylam. It was so called because it contained a *ṭārima* for the caliph to sit beneath. The stable was also to the right of al-Azhar Mosque. The stable disappeared in the 7th century AH/13th century AD, and was replaced by a big quarter called Khaṭṭ Isṭable al-Ṭārima, which included houses, a market, a bath and mosques. (Ibn al-Ṭuwayir, Nuzha, 135–136 fn. 3).

554 See Glossary: "Dār al-Fiṭra".

Before that, the breakfast meal was set at the palace gates. *Al-Fiṭra* will be described later in detail within the section on the kingdom arrangement of the Fatimid state.

- **Quarter of al-Ṣāliḥiyya,**[555] to the south of the Shrine of al-Ḥusayn, which was inhabited by a faction of the slave-boys (*ghilmān*)[556] of al-Ṣāliḥ Ṭalā'i' b. Ruzayk and was therefore known after them and attributed to him.
- **Al-Barqiyya,**[557] Ibn 'Abd al-Ẓāhir said: It was marked out by a group of people from Barqa who came with Jawhar, and so it was known after them.[558] I have seen in the margins[559] of the *Khiṭaṭ* of Ibn 'Abd al-Ẓāhir, in the handwriting of some meritorious people, that after al-Ṣāliḥ Ṭalā'i' b. Ruzayk killed 'Abbās, the vizier of al-Ẓāfir, and assumed the vizierate under al-Āmir, he appointed a group of amirs called al-Barqiyya[560] to assist him. He settled them in this neighbourhood, so it was attributed to them.
- **Qaṣr al-Shawk,**[561] near al-Aydumārī's Plaza.[562] Ibn 'Abd al-Ẓāhir said: Before Cairo was built, it was a settlement area for Banū 'Udhra[563] known as Qaṣr al-Shawk.[564]

555 Ḥārat al-Ṣāliḥiyya: Al-Maqrīzī says that this quarter was divided over two locations: al-Ṣāliḥiyya al-Kubrā (the Greater al-Ṣāliḥiyya) and al-Ṣāliḥiyya al-Ṣughrā (the Smaller al-Ṣāliḥiyya), which were located between the Shrine of al-Ḥusayn, Raḥbat al-Aydumarī and al-Barqiyya. Al- Ṣāliḥiyya al-Kubrā was located in the area bordered in modern times by al-Ja'ādiyya Street to the north; Umm al-Ghulām Street to the west; al-'Ulwa Street, al-Kafr Street and Sikkat al-Suwayqa to the east; and al-Shaykh Maḥmūd and Ruq'at al-Qamḥ streets to the south. (Al-Maqrīzī, *Khiṭaṭ*, Vol. 2, 391 and Ibn Taghrī Birdī& M. Shams, *Nujūm*, Vol. 4, 56 & 56 fn. 6).

556 Ibn Taghrī Birdī explains that this term means al-Ṣāliḥ Ṭalā'i''s mamluks. (Ibn Taghrī Birdī, *Nujūm*, Vol. 4, 56).

557 See fn. 488 A. Abd al-Raziq, *Tārīkh,* 210 Map 10.

558 In Ibn 'Abd al-Ẓāhir's account, they came with Caliph al-Mu'izz. (*Khiṭāṭ*, 42).

559 A *ḥāshiya* (pl. *ḥawāshī*, literally: fillings) are the marginal notes or remarks made by the editors or copiers of a book.

560 The ones from Barqa, in the east of present day Libya.

561 According to al-Maqrīzī's account, Raḥbat Qaṣr al-Shawk, was a huge square to the southeast of the Eastern Palace. (Al-Maqrīzī, *Khiṭaṭ*, Vol. 2, 468). The present day Qaṣr al-Shawk Alley is located to the north of al-Ḥusayn Mosque.

562 Named after al-Aydumarī (d. 687 AH/1288 AD), whose house was there. See fn. 400.

563 One of the major tribes of pure Arab Yemeni origin (*al-'Arab al-'āriba*, the descendants of Qaḥṭān), who migrated to the north of the Jazira and expanded in several Arab lands, to mix with the tribes of non-Arab origins(*al-'Arab al-musta'riba*). (A. Hammuda, *Tārīkh*, 39–41). Al-Qalqashandī is therefore referring to a group who belonged to this tribe.

564 Ibn 'Abd al-Ẓāhir, *Khiṭāṭ*, 15.

- **Khizānat al-Bunūd** (The Warehouse of Standards),[565] which was the arms warehouse of the Fatimid state. It was made a prison in the days of al-Mustanṣir[566] then was later ground-rented[567] and converted into houses.
- **Bāb al-ʿĪd Plaza,**[568] which is named after Bāb al-ʿĪd, one of the palace gates mentioned earlier.
- **Mulūkhiyya Alley,**[569] which is attributed to Mulūkhiyya, who was the equestrian escort (*ṣāḥib rikāb*)[570] of al-Ḥākim.[571] The alley included the madrasa[572] and house of al-Qāḍī al-Fāḍil,[573] the vizier of Ṣalāḥ al-Dīn Yūsuf b. Ayyūb.

565 The name of this area is missing from the manuscript, but the description fits al-Maqrīzī's account of *khizānat al-bunūd* (the Warehouse of Flags, Banners or Standards), which he refers to several times in his *Khiṭaṭ*, and lists in the section on prisons. Al-Maqrīzī says that by his time, the location of this warehouse was takenup by a small street(*zuqāq*) called Khaṭṭ Khizānat al-Bunūd, in between Raḥbat Bāb al-ʿĪd and the Shrine of al-Ḥusayn, which means that it was attached to the eastern section of the Fatimideastern palace. He agrees with al-Qalqashandī that it was first used for manufacturing arms, then turned into a prison for amirs and notables after it accidentaly burned-down in 461 AH/1068AD, and later became a residence for the high ranking crusader prisoners of war and their families during the era of Sultan al-Nāṣir Muḥammad, until the land area was ground-rented in 744 AH/1343 AD. (Al-Maqrīzī, *Khiṭaṭ*, Vol. 2, 196–200, 443, 812).

566 Fatimid caliph who ruled from 427 AH/1036 AD to 487 AH/1094 AD. His reign was rather prosperous until Egypt faced a disastrous seven-year famine from 457 AH/1065 to 464 AH/1071 AD, termed *al-shidda al-Mustanṣiriyya* (the Calamit of al-Mustanṣir's era).

567 Al-Qalqashandī uses the term *iḥtukirat* (it was transformed into a *ḥikr*).

568 Raḥbat Bāb al-ʿĪd (Plaza of the Feast Gate).

569 Darb Mulūkhiyya: Al-Marīzī says that it used to be called Ḥārat Qā'id al-Quwwād (Quarter of the Chief Commander), after Ḥūsayn b. Jawhar, son of Jawhar al-Ṣaqallī, who served caliphs al-ʿAzīz and al-Ḥākim and was a wise and reasonable man whose days were peaceful. Ḥārat Qā'id al-Quwwād was located to the east of the Fatimid eastern palace, beyond Ḥarat al-Barqiyya. Darb Mulūkhiyya is taken up today by Qaṣr al-Shawk Alley, off Qaṣr al-Shawk Street, in al-Jamāliyya Neighbourhood. (A. Gamal al-Din, *Dawla*, 210 and map of military camps, Al-Maqrīzī, *Khiṭaṭ*, Vol. 2, 396, and M. Shams, *Nujūm*, Vol. 4, 52 fn. 8).

570 Responsible for saddling and bridling the horse as well as escorting the processions.

571 Ibn ʿAbd al-Ẓāhir says that Mulūkhiyya was an amir and equestrian escort (*ṣāḥib rikāb*) of Caliph al-Ḥākim, who committed a hideous crime, so the caliph ordered him killed and personally supervised or took part in his murder. He was also known as Mulūkhiyya al-Farrāsh, for he was one of the caretakers of the palace. (Ibn ʿAbd al-Ẓāhir, *Khiṭaṭ*, 48, M. Shams, *Nujūm*, Vol. 4, 52 fn. 8, and see Glossary: "*farrāsh*").

572 Al-Madrasa al-Fāḍiliyya, which was abandoned by al-Maqrīzī's time, was built in 580 AH/1184AD. It was endowed to teach the Shāfiʿī and Mālikīschools of interpretation and had a huge library that encompassed books of diverse subjects, but was completely lost. It contained a huge Kufi Quran manuscript that was attributed to Caliph ʿUthmān b. ʿAffān. (Al-Maqrīzī, *Khiṭaṭ*, Vol. 3, 444–445).

573 ʿAbd al-Raḥīm b. ʿAlī b. al-Ḥasan, Abū ʿAlī (d. 596 AH/1199 AD), known as al-Qāḍī al-Fāḍil, was born in Ascalon and lived in Egypt. A descendant from a line of judges (*quḍāt*), al-Qāḍī al-Fāḍil (Judge al-Fāḍil) was a high administrative official of the Fatimid state and the vizier of the Ayyubid Sultan Ṣalāḥ al-Dīn, who fully trusted him and depended on him. He continued to serve Ṣalāḥ al-Dīn's son, al-ʿAzīz, and his grandson al-Manṣūr. Al-Qāḍī al-Fāḍil was an exceptional man of literature whose compositions were well-known. He was buried in the Southern Cemetry. (Ibn Khallikān, *Wafayāt*, Vol. 3, 158–163 and al-Maqrīzī, *Khiṭaṭ*, Vol. 3, 445–447).

- **Al-ʿUṭūf,**[574] the origin of its name is "al-ʿUṭūfiyya,"[575] in attribution to ʿAṭūf,[576] the eunuch-servant (*khādim*) of al-Ḥākim.
- **Al-Jawwāniyya,**[577] Ibn ʿAbd al-Ẓāhir said: [The name] is an attribute describing a withheld entity, originally being Ḥārat al-Rūm al-Jawwāniyya (the Interior Quarter of Rūm). This is because the Rūm who arrived with Jawhar marked-out the previously mentioned Quarter of Rūm, as well as this quarter. People used to say: "Ḥārat al-Rūm al-Barrāniyya" (the Exterior Quarter of Rūm) and "Ḥārat al-Rūm al-Jawwāniyya," but this became burdensome; therefore they called this one "al-Jawwāniyya" and limited the name "Ḥārat al-Rūm" to just that. He said: The transcribers (*warrāqūn*),[578] up to this time, continue to say Ḥārat al-Rūm al-Suflā (the Lower Quarter of Rūm) and Ḥārat al-Rūm al-ʿUlyā (the Upper Quarter of Rūm), known as "al-Jawwāniyya."[579] He added: It is also said that it is attributed to al-Ashrāf al-Jawwāniyyūn,[580] to whom belongs al-Sharīf al-Jawwānī al-Nassāba.[581]

As for its famous neighbourhoods (*khiṭaṭ*) outside the wall, they include:

- **Al-Ḥusayniyya,**[582] which was eight quarters outside Bāb al-Futūḥ in the Fatimid days: The first being the quarter known as the Quarter of Bahā' al-Dīn, mentioned above, which is Ḥarat Ḥamid (Ḥāmid's Quarter);[583] al-Munsha'a al-Kubrā (The

574 Also: al-ʿUṭūfiyya. The present day location of this *ḥāra* is the area around Ḥārat al-ʿUṭūf, right inside Bāb al-Naṣr. It used to be one of the finest residential areas of Fatimid Cairo. (A. Gamal al-Din, *Dawla*, 212 and A. Abd al-Raziq, *Tārīkh*, 210 Map 10).

575 A military regiment of the Fatimid army, which is attributed to ʿAṭūf. (A. Gamal al-Din, *Dawla*, 212).

576 ʿAṭūf was a black eunuch-servant (*khādim*) of al-Ḥākim's sister, Sitt al-Mulk. Al-Ḥākim killed him in 401 AH/1011 AD. (A. Gamal al-Din, *Dawla*, 212).

577 Also: al-Juwwāniyya, which means "the interior one." It occupies the area around the present day Ḥārat al-Jawwāniyya and ʿAṭfat al-Jawwāniyya off al-Jamāliyya Street, near Bābal-Naṣr. (A. Gamal al-Din, *Dawla*, 200, A. Abd al-Raziq, *Tārīkh*, 210,map 10 and A. Raymond, *Cairo*, 156, map 7).

578 Sing. *warrāq*, meaning: the papermaker. The *warrāqūn* were the transcribers (also: *nassākhūn*, sing. *nāsikh*), binders, and traders of books. They were learned men: religious scientists, linguists, men of literature, and similarly educated men, who were also fine calligraphers and who many times added their marginal editorial notes to the text. Their shops at the book markets were meeting places for cultured men to discuss and debate books and commentaries.

579 The use of "lower" and "upper" here had other insinuations than north and south, for the terms are employed for reversed directions. Al-Jawwāniyya, the upper, is in the north of Cairo, while the lower Ḥārat al-Rūm is in its south.

580 See fn. 268 for "*ashrāf*." Al-Jawwāniyyūn are the descendants of Muḥammad b. ʿUbayd Allah al-Aʿraj, great grandson of al-Ḥusayn.

581 Ibn ʿAbd al-Ẓāhir, *Khiṭaṭ*, 21.

582 This quarter still exists until today, to the northwest of Bāb al-Futūḥ. Al-Ḥusayniyya and al-Bayyūmī streets are in the heart of this area. (M. Shams, *Nujūm*, Vol. 4, 48 fn. 2).

583 Neither al-Maqrīzī nor Ibn ʿAbd al-Ẓāhir mention that Ḥārat Ḥāmid was Ḥārat Bahā' al-Dīn. (Al-Maqrīzī, *Khiṭaṭ*, Vol. 2, 411 and Ibn ʿAbd al-Ẓāhir, *Khiṭaṭ*, 122).

> Greater Establishment);[584] al-Ḥara al-Kabīra (The Great Quarter); al-Munsha'a al-Ṣaghīra (The Small Establishment);[585] Ḥarat ʿAbīd al-Shirā' (Quarter of the Bought Slaves);[586] al-Ḥara al-Wusṭā (The Middle Quarter); Sūq al-Kabīr (The Great Market) of Miṣr,[587] and al-Wazīriyya, which was the residence of the faction known as al-Wazīriyya and al-Rayḥāniyya who were Armenians, Persians and Bought Slaves.[588] Ibn ʿAbd al-Ẓāhir said: It included almost 7000 Armenians, then a group of Ḥusaynī *ashrāf* lived in it. They came from Hijaz to Egypt in the days of al-Kāmil Muḥammad b. Ayyūb b. al-ʿĀdil Abū Bakr b. Ayyūb, and resided and settled in these places, and they were named after them. After that the soldiers resided in them and built great buildings and huge houses. Ibn ʿAbd al-Ẓāhir said: It is the greatest of soldiers' quarters.[589]

I say: This was the case in his time, but it has fallen into ruins in ours. The soldiers moved to the areas near the Citadel on the Ṣalība[590] of Ibn Ṭūlūn's Mosque and its direction.

584 Al-Manshiyya al-Kabīra (The Great Establishment) in al-Maqrīzī's and Ibn ʿAbd al-Ẓāhir's accounts (Al-Maqrīzī, *Khiṭaṭ*, Vol. 2, 411 and Ibn ʿAbd al-Ẓāhir, *Khiṭaṭ*, 122).

585 Al-Manshiyya al-Ṣaghīra in Ibn ʿAbd al-Ẓāhir's account. (Ibn ʿAbd al-Ẓāhir, *Khiṭaṭ*, 122).

586 *'Abīd al-shirā'* (the Bought Slaves), were first introduced to the Fatimid army by Caliph al-Ḥākim. They multiplied in number under Caliph al-Mustanṣir, when they formed a huge brigade of 50,000 warriors. Al-Mustanṣir's mother was herself originally a black slave, which explains why she bought, and induced her son to buy, numerous black slaves to serve in the army, so as to combat the power and influence of the Turkish factions. *'Abīd al-shirā'* seem to have not been the only black forces of the Fatimid army, for the account by the Persian traveller, Nāṣirī Khusraw, who visited Cairo around 440 AH/1049 AD, specifies two black factions: the *zunūj* (the Negros), who fought with their swords only, and *'abīd al-shirā'*. (A. Gamal al-Din, *Dawla*, 190–191 and A. F. Sayyed, *Tafsīr*, 668–690).

587 In Ibn ʿAbd al-Ẓāhir's *Khiṭaṭ*: Ḥārat al-Sūq al-Kabīr (Quarter of the Great Market). (Ibn ʿAbd al-Ẓāhir, *Khiṭaṭ*, 123.)

588 Al-Qalqashandī copies Ibn ʿAbd al-Ẓāhir in suggesting that all eight quarters constituted a single bigger one. (Ibn ʿAbd al-Ẓāhir's *Khiṭaṭ*, 122–123 and M. Shams, *Nujūm*, Vol. 4, 49 fn. 1).

589 There is controversy about why this quarter was named al-Ḥusayniyya. It might be that it" owes its name to a tribal contingent quartered there." (Raymond, 55). While Ibn ʿAbd al-Ẓāhir gives the reason quoted by al-Qalqashandī above, al-Maqrīzī argues that this is inaccurate, for the quarter was named after a sect of Bought Slaves (*'abīd al-shirā'*) called al-Ḥusayniyya, during the era of Caliph al-Ḥākim. It is also believed that the quarter was named after the Chief Commander, al-Ḥusayn b. Jawhar and that it was initially the residence of a faction of the Bought Slaves, then the Armenians in the 5th century AH/11th century AD, who solely occupied the quarter upon the orders of Badr al-Jamālī, until at the time of Sultan al-Kāmil, when it became the residence of a group of Ḥusaynī *ashrāf*. (A. Raymond, *Cairo*, 55; Ibn ʿAbd al-Ẓāhir,*Khiṭaṭ*, 122–123; al-Maqrīzī, *Khiṭaṭ*, Vol. 2, 409–412; A. Sayyid,*Nuzha*, 46 fn. 1, and A. Sayyid, *Tafsīr*, 673).

590 The present day al-Ṣalība Street, or Shaykhūn Street, extends from Ibn Ṭūlūn's mosque to Maydān al-Qalʿa (the Citadel Square) below the Citadel. The area surrounding this street, which included the site of Ibn Ṭūlūn's capital, al-Qaṭā'iʿ and encompassed Birkat al-Fīl, was not much of a residential quarter before the 14th century. When Sultan al-Nāṣir Muḥammad started his project to renovate the Citadel in the 8th century AH/14th century AD, this area started being urbanized, and became the residence of amirs while housing all kinds of religious buildings, many of which still stand today. (C. Williams, *Monuments*, 46).

Bahā' al-Dīn Qaraqūsh built a caravanserai (*khān*) for the road to host passersby and wayfarers, so his quarter was known after it.

- **Al-Khandaq** (The Moat),[591] outside al-Ḥusayniyya, at the trench. It had a trench that the Fatimid al-ʿAzīz bi-Allah dug. Al-Muʿizz had settled the Maghribis there in the year 363 H/973 AD, when they had spread out in the Cemetery and Cairo, and kicked people out of their houses. He ordered a caller to call upon them every night: Any of them who spent the night in the city would deserve punishment.[592]
- **Arḍ al-Ṭabbāla** (Land of the Drummer),[593] which is attributed to a woman singer named Nashab, or may be Ṭarab,[594] who was a singer for the Fatimid al-Mustanṣir, whose name was Maʿadd. Judge Muḥyī al-Dīn b. ʿAbd al-Ẓāhir said: When the news came to al-Mustanṣir that the sermon (*khuṭba*) was given in his name in Baghdad during the rule of al-Basāsirī,[595] for almost a year, Nashab sang to him:

591 Contrary to al-Qalqashandī's account, which coincides with Ibn ʿAbd al-Ẓāhir's, General Jawhar is believed to be the one who dug this moat in front of Cairo's north wall as a defensive measure against the expected attack of the Qarmatians. Jawhar ordered his Maghribi troops to dig the moat in 360 AH/971 AD, which seems to have been a double trench, formed of two consecutive moats. It was called al-Khandaq, Khandaq al-ʿAbīd (the Trench of Slaves) and al-Ḥufra (the Hole). Later in the Fatimid era, the area became one of the greatest gardens, and remained to be so until the Mamluk era. Al-Maqrīzī reports to have seen it as a pleasant park and inhabited area with its own mosque and market, which fell into ruins in 806 AH/1403 AD, but restored some of its residents and status as a park later on. Today, the site of al-Khandaq Quarter occupies the area around Dayr al-Malāk al-Baḥarī (al-Malāk Mīkhā'īl Church) and its surroundings in Ḥadā'iq al-Qubba Neighbourhood. (Al-Maqrīzī, *Khiṭaṭ*, Vol. 2, 684–688, A. Raymond, *Cairo*, 37 and M. al-Shishtawi, *Mutanazzahāt*, 251).

592 Al-Maqrīzī relates a more detailed account where the Maghribis, whom Caliph al-Muʿizz had ordered to reside in the peripheries, rather than inside the city, had seized people's homes around the cemetery and started inhabiting the city. To solve this problem, al-Muʿizz ordered them to live in the area known as al-Khandaq and assigned them a governor (*wālī*) and a judge (*qāḍī*). Al-Maqrīzī adds that Jawhar did not allow them to reside or spend the night inside the city. (Al-Maqrīzī, *Khiṭaṭ*, Vol. 2, 688).

593 Arḍ al-Ṭabbāla was one of the best parks of Cairo that existed since the Fatimid era, continued to be partly a park and partly an agricultural land during the Mamluk and Ottoman eras, although it sometimes deteriorated and fell to ruins. Today, its site occupies the area bordered to the east by Port Said Street (previously, al-Khalīj al-Miṣrī Street); to the north by al-Ẓāhir Street and Waqf al-Kharbutlī Street and its extension; to the west by Ghamra Street, up to Ramsis Square, and to the south by al-Fajjāla and Sikkat al-Fajjāla streets. Its site, therefore, includes the present day al-Fajjāla Neighbourhood, in addition to parts of al-Ẓāhir and al-Sharābiyya neighbourhoods. (M. al-Shishtawi, *Mutanazzahāt*, 170 & 170 fn. 1).

594 Al-Maqrīzī says: Nasab or Ṭarab, who used to stand outside the palace and walk along with the processions to sing and beat her drum, with her group, on festive occasions. He adds that she built herself a tomb in the Cemetery. This tomb seems to have been a domed mausoleum that disappeared. (Al-Maqrīzī, *Khiṭaṭ*, Vol. 2, 656–657 and M. Shams, *Nujūm*, Vol. 5, 14 fn. 1).

595 Abū al-Ḥārith Arslān al-Basāsīrī, the Turk, was the powerful commander of the Turkish forces under the Abbasid Caliph al-Qā'im (r. 422 AH/1031 AD – 467 AH/1075 AD). He rebelled against the caliph and expelled him from Baghdad in favour of the Fatimid Caliph al-Mustanṣir in the last days of 450 AH/1058 AD. The Saljuqs (see Glossary) managed to kill al-Basāsīrī in 555 AH/1060 AD and restored Caliph al-Qā'im to his throne. (Ibn Khallikān, *Wafayāt*, Vol. 1, 192–193 and Ibn Taghrī Birdī, *Nujūm*, Vol. 5, 6–14).

Sons of al-ʿAbbās[596] be hindered for Maʿadd has ruled

Your kingdom was but a loan and loans are retrieved

Al-Mustanṣir then bestowed this land upon her in the year 432 AH/1041 AD,[597] and it was ground-rented and built into houses, so it became known after her. He said: It was one of the pleasures and splendours of Cairo.[598] Ibn Saʿīd al-Maghribī recited the following poetry praising it, and alliterating clover (*qurṭ*) that animals graze with earrings (*qurṭ*):[599]

May God water the land that whenever I visit whose gardens, I find the clover covering them and beautifying them with its adornment.

It has manifested like a bride, with water being its necklaces and in each region of its sides, an earring.

- **Khaṭṭ Bāb al-Qanṭara** (Neighbourhood of the Bridge Gate);[600] Ibn ʿAbd al-Ẓāhir said: ʿAlam al-Dīn b. Mamātī[601] mentioned to me that the old books of properties[602] call it "al-Murtāḥiyya"[603].[604]
- **Al-Maqs**; Al-Qaḍāʿī said in his *Khiṭaṭ*: It was an estate known as Ummu Dunayn[605] where the alms collector (*ʿāshir*),[606] who was responsible for collecting

596 Meaning the Abbasid Caliphate.

597 The correct year is most probably 450 AH/1058 AD, for this is when al-Basāsīrī seized Baghdad.

598 Ibn ʿAbd al-Ẓāhir, *Khiṭaṭ*, 119–120.

599 Clover and earrings are homonyms; both called "*qurṭ*" in Arabic.

600 This quarter was to the northwest of Fatimid Cairo, right beyond the Khalīj, near the present day area of Bāb al-Shaʿriyya. (A. Raymond, *Cairo*, 119, map 4, and 156, map 7).

601 Al-Qāḍī al-Asʿad Abū al-Makārim Asʿad b. al-Khaṭīr b. Mīnā Ibn Mamātī (d. 606 AH/1209 AD), the Egyptian, was a writer and a poet who was the Supervisor of the Bureaus (*nāẓir al-dawāwīn*) in the era of Ṣalāḥ al-Dīn. He was originally a Christian who converted to Islam when Ṣalāḥ al-Dīn came to power. Among his works were a biography of Ṣalāḥ al-Dīn and a poetry collection. (Ibn Khallikān, *Wafayāt*, Vol. 1, 210–213).

602 *Kutub al-amlāk*: the records of properties or ownership.

603 Al-Maqrīzī says that al-Murtāḥiyya were a faction (*ṭāʾifa*) of soldiers. (Al-Maqrīzī, *Khiṭaṭ*, Vol. 2, 395).

604 See Ibn ʿAbd al-Ẓāhir , *Khiṭaṭ*, 111 & 111 fn. 2.

605 Al-Maqs, al-Maks, Umm Dunayn and al-Maqsim were all names for one area, which is now bordered by ʿImād al-Dīn Street westwards, Qanṭarat al-Dikka and al-Qabīla streets southwards, al-Kanīsa al-Murqusiyya Street eastwards, and Bayn al-Ḥarāt Street up to Ramsis Square northwards. (M. al-Shishtawi, *Mutanazzahāt*, 150–151 fn. 4).

606 Is the person who collects *al-ʿushr* alms (*zakāt al-ʿushr*), which is the alms on the agricultural produce that amounts to 1/10 or 1/20 of the yield. This fraction depends on whether the land is naturally irrigated, which entails no extra cost on the cultivator, who should then hand out 10% of his yield, or requires the aid of machines, therefore more cost to receive water, whereby the cultivator gives away only 5% of the produce.

the taxes (*maks*),[607] stayed to harvest the money (*māl*).[608] It was, therefore, called al-Maks with a *kāf* (k) then the *kāf* was altered to a *qāf* (q) over the tongues.[609] Ibn ʿAbd al-Ẓāhir said: Some people called it al-Maqsim[610] because it was used for dividing the trophies of the conquests. He said: [But] I have not seen this in writing.[611] Al-Dikka,[612] one of the areas of [al-Maqs], was a garden. When the caliph rode from the Khalīj on Yawm al-Kasr (the day of breaking the dam),[613] he arrived at this garden, in his boat, coming from the west bank of the Khalīj. He entered it alone and had his horse drink there, then came out to his palace as will be mentioned later in the section on the royal arrangement of the Fatimid State.

Ibn ʿAbd al-Ẓāhir said: Al-Dikka is now [filled with] houses and quarters, and is too famous to describe. Glory be to Allah who never changes.[614]

I say: Most of these houses and quarters have now fallen into ruins that only their outlines remain on the ground, while some have survived and are inhabited by individual people.

- **Maydān al-Qamḥ** (The Wheat Square);[615] It was a sultanic garden in the old days, called al-Maqsī, to which water entered from the canal known as al-Khalīj al-Dhakar[616] that was dug by Kafūr al-Ikhshīdī. The Fatimid al-Ẓāhir

607 *Maks* (pl. *mukūs*) was a tax imposed on products and the imported and the ready to be exported commodities in ports. During the Mamluk era, these taxes were imposed on the houses; shops; *khāns* (caravanserais); baths; bakeries; mills; gardens; pastures; fisheries, and presses, as well as pilgrims; travellers; ships; fishing; sheep; buffalos; cows; weddings, etc. This tax was actually unjust and illegal, since it was not derived from any of the religious legislations (*sharī'a*); therefore, some of the Mamluk sultans abolished it, in full or in part. (Al-Baqli, *Ta'rīf*, 324–325).

608 *Māl* is generally translated to "money," means any owned belonging, such as money, goods, properties, etc. that constitute one's wealth.

609 That is, became commonly known as al-Maqs.

610 From the root *qasam* or *qassam*, to divide, and means: the division place.

611 That is, he did not find this information in written sources. This remark does not seem to be in this account by Ibn ʿAbd al-Ẓāhir. (See *Khiṭaṭ*, 125–126).

612 This area was to the southwest of al-Maqs. (A. Raymond, *Cairo*, 119, Map 4 and 150, Map 6)

613 Also, Fatḥ al-Khalīj, which was a processional celebration on occasion of the Nile rise. Al-Qalqashandī delivers a more detailed account of the occasion in later sections. (See also, Ibn al-Ṭuwayir, *Nuzha*, 195–203 and A. Sayyid, *Tafsīr*, 456–460).

614 See Ibn ʿAbd al-Ẓāhir, *Khiṭaṭ*, 125.

615 Al-Maqrīzī says this square was also sometimes referred to as Maydān al-Ghalla (Square of Grains). Presently, its site occupies the eastern half of Bāb al-Baḥr Neighbourhood. (M. al-Shishtawi, *Mutanazzahāt*, 151 fn. 6 and al-Maqrīzī, *Khiṭaṭ*, Vol. 2, 654–655).

616 This was a canal first dug by Kāfūr to irrigate al-Maqs and other gardens to the west of the Khalīj. It was originally directly connected to the Nile through its mouth, which today is the point where Qanṭarat al-Dikka Street meets ʿImād al-Dīn Street. It used to run along what is today occupied by Qanṭarat al-Dikka Street and its extension up to a point in front of al-Khurunfush area, where it met al-Khalīj. In the Fatimid era, this canal fed the pond of Baṭn al-Baqara (later to become al-Azbakiyya Pond), which Caliph al-Ẓāhir dug in the place of al-Maqs Gardens. Al-Khalīj al-Dhakar was widened and enlarged several times during the Ayyubid and Mamluk eras. (M. al-Shishtawi, *Mutanazzahāt*, 220–221).

then ordered the transfer of the garden's trees,[617] digging it and transforming it into a pond in front of al-Lu'lu'a [Belvedere].[618] He kept the mentioned canal directed at the pond, so that the water stagnates in it. When the Fatimid Caliphate weakened and its old places of scenery were abandoned in al-Lu'lu'a and elsewhere, the Sudanese known as al-Faraḥiyya Faction,[619] who resided in al-Maqs, built themselves a quarter.[620] Al-Maqs had become overcrowded for them and they built this quarter in front of al-Lu'lu'a. The quarter was called Ḥārat al-Luṣūṣ (the Quarter of Thieves) because they, along with others, attacked people there.[621] The quarter's condition continued to change, until it became the way it is now.

- **Barr Ibn al-Tabbān** (The Bank of Ibn al-Tabbān)[622] to the west of the Khalīj of Cairo. It is attributed to Ibn al-Tabbān, who was the head (*ra'īs*) of the ship (*ḥirrāqa*)[623] of the Fatimid Caliphate.[624] The Fatimid al-Āmir had commanded

617 *Anshāb*, which refers to trees or plants that are grafted, such as olive trees, palmtrees, grapes, figs, pomegranates, and others.

618 Manẓarat al-Lu'lu'a (the Pearl Belvedere): Its site is taken-up today by Saint Joseph School (the Frères des Ecoles Chrétiennes) in al-Khurunfush Neighbourhood, which overlooks Port Said Street. It was located close to Bāb al-Qanṭara, where it overlooked al-Kāfūrī Gardens to its east and the Khalīj to its west. Caliph al-ʿAzīz built this *manẓara*and Caliph al-Ḥākim destroyed it in 403 AH/1012 AD. Caliph al-Ẓāhir renovated it and it remained in use until the calamity of al-Mustanṣir's era (*al-shidda al-Mustanṣiriyya* from 457 AH/1065 AD to 464 AH/1071 AD) to be neglected again until the era of Caliph al-Āmir, who restored it again. It was reached through Bāb Murād, one of the gates of the lesser Fatimid Western Palace, which overlooked al-Kāfūrī Gardens (this means that this gate was in the western walls of the palace) and was only opened for the caliph. (A. Sayyid, *Nuzha*, 26 fn. 2).

619 One of the army factions of Bought Slaves present during the era of Caliph al-Ḥākim. Al-Maqrīzī says that Ḥārat al-Faraḥiyya was next to Ḥārat al-Murtāḥiyya, which means that it also was to the northwest of Fatimid Cairo. Ḥārat al-Faraḥiyya was adjacent to Ḥārat Barjawān, to its west. (A. Gamal al-Din, *Dawla*, 212, al-Maqrīzī, *Khiṭaṭ*, Vol. 2, 395–396 and A. Abd al-Raziq, *Tārīkh*, 210 Map 10).

620 Al-Qalqashandī is probably referring to the famine that led to what was called "the calamity years of al-Mustanṣir," which led to the abandonment of many areas around Fatimid Cairo. (A. Sayyid, *Taṭawwur*, 27–28).

621 Part of this description is copied from Ibn ʿAbd al-Ẓāhir's account, which states that the Farḥiyya, along with others, used to transgress (*ta'addī*) in this quarter, most probably meaning that they used to attack people so as to rob them. (See Ibn ʿAbd al-Ẓāhir, *Khiṭaṭ*, 112).

622 The description indicates that Barr Ibn al-Tabbān was to the southwest of Fatimid Cairo, beyond the Khalīj. The present day Zuqāq Ibn al-Tabbān, possibly around which the area used to be, is to the west of Port Said Street, north of al-Shaykh Rayḥān Street and south of Dār al-Kutub.

623 *Ḥirrāqa* (pl. *ḥarārīq* and *ḥarāriq*) – There were two types of ships referred to by this term: One was a military ship which carried fire weaponry, such as the Greek fire, and equipped to throw fireballs. The other was a non-military type which sailed the Nile carrying the amirs and the statesmen in navy parades and official celebrations. When the Mamluk Sultan, al-Ẓāhir Baybars wanted to revive the Egyptian fleet, after it had been neglected during the previous Mamluk reigns, he summoned the Men of the Fleets, whom the amirs employed in their non-military *ḥarārīq* and other ships. (Al-Baqli, *Ta'rīf*, 104 and see Glossary).

624 Ibn ʿAbd al-Ẓāhir, and al-Maqrīzī copying him, say that Ibn al-Tabbān was *ra'īs al-marākib* (Head of Ships) under the Fatimid Caliph al-Āmir. (Ibn ʿAbd al-Ẓāhir, *Khiṭaṭ*, 126 and al-Maqrīzī, *Khiṭaṭ*, Vol. 2, 629).

that construction takes place in the area opposite al-Kharq,[625] to the west of the Khalīj. The first person to build there was the mentioned Ibn al-Tabbān, who established a mosque, a garden, and a house, so the neighbourhood was known after him and continues to be until now.

- **Khaṭṭ al-Lūq** (Neighbourhood of al-Lūq),[626] which is an old, vast neighbourhood that ends at the Maydān,[627] which is set for the sultanic procession at [the time of] the Faithfulness of the Nile (Wafā' al-Nīl). It is now filled with buildings and inhabited by mobs and commoners. The place known now as Bāb al-Lūq[628] is a part of it.
- **Birkat al-Fīl** (The Elephant Pond),[629] which is a huge wide pond to the south of the wall of Cairo. It has great buildings surrounding it. Ibn ʿAbd al-Ẓāhir said: It is attributed to one of Ibn Ṭūlūn's companions, known as al-Fīl.[630] Ibn Saʿīd al-Maghribī best [described it] saying:

625 Al-Kharq was an agricultural land on the western bank of the Khalīj, after which Qanṭarat Bāb al-Kharq (Bāb al-Kharq Bridge), built by Sultan al-Ṣāliḥ Najm al-Din Ayyūb in 639 AH/1241 AD, was named. The site of this bridge *(qanṭara)* is now at the meeting point of Taḥt al-Rabʿ and Port Said streets, in Bāb al-Khalq Square (Bāb al-Khalq is a distortion of the name Bāb al-Kharq). (M. al-Shishtawi, *Mutanazzahāt*, 202 &202 fn. 5).

626 Bāb al-Lūq Neighbourhood still exists until today, indicating the location of Khaṭṭ al-Lūq, which was to the west of al-Kharq. Bāb al-Lūq is presently right to the west of ʿAbidīn Neighbourhood, and to the south west of both al-ʿAtaba and al-Muskī neighbourhoods. (A. Raymond, *Cairo*, 119 Map 4 and 150 Map 6).

627 The Maydān or al-Maydān al-Kabīr (the Grand Square) are among the variant names of al-Maydān al-Nāṣirī, which Sultan al-Nāṣir Muḥammad built to replace al-Maydān al-Ẓāhirī, established by Sultan al-Ẓāhir Baybars, in hosting festive celebrations. Al-Nāṣir converted al-Maydān al-Ẓāhirī into gardens. The site of al-Maydān al-Nāṣirī is taken up today by a section of Garden City Neighbourhood, bordered to the west by the Nile Cornice Street, to the south by ʿĀ'isha al-Taymūriyya Street, to the east by Qaṣr al-ʿAynī Street and to the north by Muḥmmad Fahmy al-Sayyid Street. As for al-Maydān al-Ẓāhirī, its site today is taken up by the area bordered at the south by al-Bustān Street, to the north by Maḥmūd Basyūnī Street, to the east by Yūsuf al-Jundī Street and to the west by Champollion Street. Al-Maqrīzī says that al-Maydān al-Ẓāhirī was at the end of Khaṭṭ al-Lūq, which means the northern end, and it seems that when al-Maydān al-Nāṣirī was established, it took up another end, the western one, for al-Qalqashandī notes more than once that the latter was within the neighbourhood (*khaṭṭ*). (Muhammad al-Shishtawi, *Mayādīn al-Qāhira fī al-ʿAṣr al-Mamlūkī* (Cairo, 1999), 73, 89, and 103, al-Maqrīzī, *Khiṭaṭ*, Vol 3, 27–28, and al-Qalqashandī, *Ṣubḥ*, Vol. 8, 333).

628 See note 626 above for Bāb al-Lūq.

629 "The Elephant Pond" was one of the oldest ponds and was located in between Cairo and Fustat, in the area opposite Aḥmad Ibn Ṭūlūn's mosque. Its area was huge during the Fatimid era, and no buildings were established around it until 600 AH/1204 AD when habitation started with the Ayyubids, then it became one of the most important residential areas during the Mamluk era. The pond's site is today taken up by the area bordered to the north by Sikkat al-Ḥabbāniyya Street, to the west by Port Said Street, Darb al-Jamāmīz Street and its extensions until it reaches ʿAbd al-Majīd al-Labbān and al-Khudairy streets, which formed the southern border. The eastern border started with Azbak Mosque Street until it reached the Mosque of Azbak, then extended further east until reaching Muhadhdhab al-Dīn al-Ḥakīm Street, all along it and up to ʿAbd al-Raḥman Bek Street, until it reaches its north-west end back at Sikkat al-Ḥabbāniyya Street. (M. al-Shishtawi, *Mutanazzahāt*, 105–106).

630 Literally, the elephant; other explanations were given for this name. One is a house that was located to the south of the pond, which hosted elephants, and may be other animals too, for leisurely activities during the Ikhshidid era. Another was a big elephant that used to be taken out to swim in this pond, and people would go watch it. (M. al-Shishtawi, *Mutanazzahāt*, 105 &105 fn. 2).

"Look at Birkat al-Fīl that is all surrounded with nice views, like the eyelashes surround the eyesight.

While the sights gaze at it, it is like planets that are rotated around the moon!"

- **Khaṭṭ al-Jāmi' al-Ṭūlūnī** (Neighbourhood of the Tulunid Mosque), from the Ṣalība and what is beyond it. It was mentioned in the earlier account of the neighbourhoods of Fustat that the settlements of Aḥmad Ibn Ṭūlūn and his army were in this land. The mountain to its northern side is known as Mount Yashkur, on which the mentioned Tulunid Mosque was built. Al-Malik al-Ṣāliḥ Najm al-Dīn Ayyūb built new palaces on it, which came out in utmost beauty and perfection,[631] and is known as al-Kabsh.[632] It continued to be inhabited by high-ranking amirs until the mobs destroyed it during the incident of the newly purchased mamluks (*jilbān*)[633] before the year 770 AH/1369 AD.[634] It remains as such until now, but people have started to ground-rent its lands for building on them now, around the year 800 AH/1398 AD.[635]
- **Khaṭṭ Ḥārat al-Maṣāmida** (Neighbourhood of the Maṣāmida Quarter),[636] which is attributed to the factionof the Berber, the Maṣāmida,[637] who came

631 Al-Maqrīzī says that this was some time in between the years 643 AH/1246 AD and 647 AH/1249 AD.(Al-Maqrīzī, *Khiṭaṭ*, Vol. 2, 676).

632 Also Manāẓir al-Kabsh, roughly the quarter known today as Qal'at al-Kabsh, within the area bordered today by 'Abd al-Majīd al-Labbān Street to the north, Ḥawsh Ayyūb area to the west, Darb al-Sāqiya and Sikkat al-Manāẓir streets to the south and Darb al-Natāyfa to the east. Al-Kabsh was an elitist residential area for a good part of the Mamluk era, amirs lived and ambassadors were hosted. (M. al-Shishtawi, *Mutanazzahāt*, 229–233).

633 The *jilbān* or *ajlāb* were the newly purchased mamluks. (T. Abdelhamid, *Jaysh*, 12 & 29 and Dahman, *Mu'jam*, 53).

634 This is the conflict that occurred in 769 AH/1367 AD between the Mamluk Sultan al-Ashraf Sha'bān and his *atābek* (see Glossary), Asandamur al-Nāṣirī, who conspired against him with a group of another amir's *jilbān*, namely Yalbughā al-'Umarī whom they had killed. The two groups met in battle and the sultan was able to defeat his rivals. He caught Asandamur then pardoned him after the high-ranking amirs interceded in his favour. Upon his release, Asandamur returned to his house in al-Kabsh only to try and conspire again against the sultan. Asandamur was defeated again, and this time sent to prison in Alexandria. The sultan then ordered the destruction of al-Kabsh, so it fell into ruins. (Ibn Taghrī Birdī, *Nujūm*, Vol. 11, 38–40 and Al-Maqrīzī, *Khiṭaṭ*, Vol 2, 678).

635 Al-Maqrīzī reports that these ground-renting and building activities started in 775 AH/1373 AD. (Al-Maqrīzī, *Khiṭaṭ*, Vol 2, 678).

636 According to Ibn 'Abd al-Ẓāhir's and al-Maqrīzī's accounts, this quarter was built during the time of vizier al-Ma'mūn al-Baṭā'iḥī (in position from 515 AH/1121 AD – 519 AH/1125 AD). Al-Baṭā'iḥī directed 'Abd Allah al-Maṣmūdī to choose a quarter for his tribal battalion. They first went to al-Yānisiyya, but when they found no space there, so the architects were sent out to choose another site. They suggested one on the bank of Birkat al-Fīl, to one's right upon exiting al-Bāb al-Jadīd, built by Caliph al-Ḥākim. The site to the left of al-Bāb al-Jadīd, however, opposite Birkat al-Fīl and overlooking the vast land up to the pond, was favoured by al-Maṣmūdī (this 'Abd Allah or may be an Abū Bakr), and this is where the quarter was built. This quarter was actually to one's right upon leaving Bāb Zuwayla, that is, to its southwest. (Ibn 'Abd al-Ẓāhir, *Khiṭaṭ*, 133, al-Maqrīzī, *Khiṭaṭ*, Vol. 2, 408, and A. Abd al-Raziq, *Tārīkh*, 210 Map 10).

637 The homeland of al-Maṣāmida was to the south of Tunisia and extended to the Atlantic Ocean. (A. Gamal al-Din, *Dawla*, 194 fn. 17).

with al-Mu'izz from the Maghrib. Their commander (*muqaddam*) was 'Abd Allah al-Maṣmūdī. Al-Ma'mūn b. al-Baṭā'iḥī, the vizier of al-Āmir, had appointed 'Abd Allah a commander and praised his name. Al-Ma'mūn entrusted al-Maṣmūdī with spending the nights guarding his doors and supplemented him with a group of his own companions.[638]

- **Al-Hilāliyya;**[639] Ibn 'Abd al-Ẓāhir said: I think that it is the quarter (*ḥāra*) built by al-Ma'mūn b. al-Baṭā'iḥī outside al-Bāb al-Jadīd (the New Gate) that al-Ḥākim built on the street, to left of a person exiting the gate, for the Maṣāmida, at the time he appointed commanders from among them and praised their name.[640] He prevented building between this quarter and Birkat al-Fīl to the extent that this quarter continued to overlook the bank of the pond up to some years into the reign of al-Ḥāfiẓ[641,642].
- **Al-Muntajibiyya;**[643] Ibn 'Abd al-Ẓāhir said: I was informed that it is attributed to a person in the Fatimid state, known as Muntajib al-Dawla[644] during the reign of al-Hakim.[645]
- **Al-Yānisiyya;**[646] Ibn 'Abd al-Ẓāhir said: I think that it is attributed to Yānis, the vizier of al-Ḥāfiẓ, who held the title of *amīr al-juyūsh sayf al-Islām* (the Commander of Armies, the Sword of Islam).[647] He was known as Yānis al-Fāṣid because he performed blood-letting on Ḥasan,[648] the son of al-Ḥāfiẓ, but left him with the cuts open until he died.[649] He said: One [of the men who worked] in the state was called Yānis al-'Azīzī. The Yānisiyya were

638 See also Ibn 'Abd al-Ẓāhir, *Khiṭaṭ*, 133 and al-Maqrīzī, *Khiṭaṭ*, Vol. 2, 408.

639 Al-Maqrīzī copies Ibn 'Abd al-Ẓāhir's account in which he says that he thinks al-Ḥilāliyya and al-Maṣāmida were the same quarter;however, he also provides a one sentence separate account of al-Ḥilāliyya: "Ibn 'Abd al-Ẓāhir mentioned that it was to one's left when leaving al-Bāb al-Jadīd of al-Ḥākim." (Al-Maqrīzī, *Khiṭaṭ*, Vol. 2, 408–409 and Ibn 'Abd al-Ẓāhir, *Khiṭaṭ*, 133).

640 "*Qaddamahum wa nawwaha bi-dhikrihim*," which, in Ibn 'Abd al-Ẓāhir's account is apparently used in reference to 'Abd Allah al-Maṣmūdī, mentioned above, who was appointed commander and praised. (Ibn 'Abd al-Ẓāhir, *Khiṭaṭ*, 133).

641 Fatimid caliph who ruled from 525 AH/1131 to 545 AH/1149 AD.

642 See Ibn 'Abd al-Ẓāhir's account of al-Maṣāmida, *Khiṭaṭ*, 133–134.

643 A residential quarter which was established during the era of Caliph al-Ḥākim. See Ibn 'Abd al-Ẓāhir, *Khiṭaṭ*, 135 and al-Maqrīzī, *Khiṭaṭ*, Vol. 2, 619.

644 See fn. 478.

645 Ibn 'Abd al-Ẓāhir, *Khiṭaṭ*, 135.

646 This quarter was outside Bāb Zuwayla, on one's left upon exiting the gate, that is to the gate's southeast. (A. Raymond, *Cairo*, 32, Map 2 and A. Abd al-Raziq, *Tārīkh*, 210 Map 10). Today, al-Yānisiyya or al-Anasiyya (possibly a later deviation of the name) Alley, to the southeast of Bāb Zuwayla, in Darb al-Aḥmar Neighbourhood, probably represents the heart of the old quarter.

647 Al-Maqrīzī says that the title was *nāṣir al-juyūsh, sayf al-Islām* (Supporter of the Armies, Sword of Islam), which he received this title from the caliph upon his appointment as a vizier. (Al-Maqrīzī, *Khiṭaṭ*, Vol 2, 402).

648 *Fāṣid*, from the verb *faṣada*, which means "to let blood."

649 Ibn 'Abd al-Ẓāhir, *Khiṭaṭ*, 135–136.

a group [that existed] at the time of al-ʿAzīz bi Allah and Yānis al-Ṣaqallī was one of them. This quarter may have been attributed to either of them.[650] Ibn ʿAbd al-Ẓāhir had listed several quarters that were [allocated] to soldiers outside Bāb Zuwayla, in addition to those he might have mentioned narratively. Some of them are famous and known ones, which are Ḥarat Ḥalab (Quarter of Aleppo)[651] and al-Ḥabbāniyya,[652] and some are not, which are al-Shawbak; al-Ma'mūniyya; al-Ḥara al-Kabīra (The Great Quarter); al-Manṣūra al-Ṣaghīra (The Small Manṣūra),[653] and Ḥarat Abū Bakr (Abū Bakr's Quarter).[654]

650 That is, either Yānis al-Fāṣid or Yānis al-ʿAzīzī. Al-Maqrīzī refutes Ibn ʿAbd al-Ẓāhir's statement explaining that the quarter was named after al-Yānisiyya, which was the military regiment of the eunuch-servant (*khādim*), Abū al-Ḥasan Yānis al-Ṣaqallī, of the Fatimid Caliph al-ʿAzīz, who continued in service under Caliph al-Ḥākim, and who was appointed the governor of Barqa in 388 AH/998 AD. Al-Maqrīzī adds that the quarter could not have been attributed to Yānis (d. 526 AH/1132 AD), the Armenian vizier of al-Ḥāfiẓ, for it existed long before him. He also disagrees with the story that Yānis killed Ḥasan by this bloodletting operation, and rather believes that someone else poisoned him. (Al-Maqrīzī, *Khiṭaṭ*, Vol 2, 400–402).

651 Ḥalab is Aleppo. Al-Maqrīzī mentions that it was outside Bāb Zuwayla, was a residence for soldiers in the old days and was called Zuqāq Ḥalab at his time. Ḥārat Ḥalab was a big quarter located to the north of Birkat al-Fīl, opposite Qūṣūn's mosque (built in 730 AH/1330 AD,the gate of which still stands overlooking al-Surūjiyya Street in al-Darb al-Aḥmar Neighbourhood). It continued to exist during the Mamluk and Ottoman eras, until a good part of it was taken up by Muḥammad ʿAlī Street, when it was inaugurated during the reign of Khedive Ismāʿīl (r. 1279 AH/1863 AD – 1296 AH/1879 AD) in 1289 AH/1872 AD. (Al-Maqrīzī, *Khiṭaṭ*, Vol 2, 415 and M. al-Shishtawi, *Mutanazzahāt*, 111–112).

652 Al-Ḥabbāniyya Gardens were to the north of Birkat al-Fīl. Al-Ḥabbāniyya was one of the Arab tribes of Banū Ṭay', one of the Qaḥṭānī branches. Sultan Ṣalāḥ al-Dīn endowed this garden to support the Khanqāh of Saʿīd al-Suʿadā'. In the Mamluk era, people built a street that separated these gardens from Birkat al-Fīl. This street is taken up today by Sikkat al-Ḥabbāniyya Street in al-Darb al-Aḥmar Neighbourhood. (M. al-Shishtawi, *Mutanazzahāt*, 106 fn. 1, al-Maqrīzī, *Khiṭaṭ*, Vol 2, 675 and A. Hammuda, *'Arab*, 41).

653 One of the quarters listed by Ibn ʿAbd al-Ẓāhir and al-Maqrīzī is al-Manṣūra (or al-Manṣūriyya), also named Ḥārat ʿAṭiyya, outside Bāb Zuwayla, to one's right upon exiting the gate and walking down the Great Street. It was mostly inhabited by the Sudanese who were responsible for the Fatimid palaces until 564 AH/1169 AD, when their leader, Mu'taman al-Dawla, conspired against Ṣalāḥ al-Dīn, who had started assuming control over the state. Consequently, Ṣalāḥ al-Dīn fought them, destroyed their quarter and later turned it into gardens. Al-Maqrīzī specifically says that al-Manṣūra quarter "was big and very wide," and in his listing of the quarters outside Bāb Zuwalya, he mentions "al-Ḥāra al-Kabīra" (the Large Quarter) and "al-Manṣūra al-Ṣaghīra" (the Small al-Manṣūra). It is possible that al-Manṣūra al-Ṣaghīra was a part of the earlier, bigger quarter, as may be understood from al-Maqrīzī's account.(Al-Maqrīzī, *Khiṭaṭ*, Vol. 2, 405–407 & 411 and Ibn ʿAbd al-Ẓāhir, *Khiṭaṭ*, 137).

654 Al-Maqrīzī lists these names, among others, as quarters outside Fatimid Cairo. (Al-Maqrīzī, *Khiṭaṭ*, Vol. 2, 411).

The Mosques of Cairo

Al-Azhar[655]

As for its mosques, the oldest of them is al-Azhar, which General Jawhar built after his master, al-Muʿizz, came to Cairo and resided in it. The mosque was completed and the first congregational Friday (Jumʿa) prayer[656] held in it in the month of Ramadan[657] of the year 361 AH/972 AD. Al-ʿAzīz, son of al-Muʿizz, renewed [some] things and built parts in it. It was the first mosque built in Cairo.

The author of *Nihāyat al-Arab* (The Ultimate Ambition)[658] said: It was renewed by al-ʿAzīz b. al-Muʿizz, and when al-Ḥākim built his mosque, he transferred the sermon (*khuṭba*) to it.[659] Al-Azhar then remained vacant until the sermon and Friday prayers were returned to it on the 8th of Rabīʿ al-Ākhir[660] in the year 665 AH/1267 AD, in the sultanate of al-Ẓāhir Baybars. Al-Azhar's situation [continued to] rise until it became the mosque of highest status in Cairo.[661]

Ibn ʿAbd al-Ẓāhir said: I heard a group saying that it had a talisman that no bird[662] could inhabit it.[663]

655 Al-Azhar is the first mosque the Fatimids started building in Cairo in 359 AH/970 AD and was added to over the years. Its name means "the Blooming" and it might have been so called in correlation with Faṭima al-Zahrā', the Prophet's daughter. It was not only established to be a mosque, but also a religious college to propagate Shiism. It remains to be the central mosque and religious institution of Egypt until today, and since the Mamluk era, its role has changed to serve Sunni Islam. The mosque is currently a composite structure of original and additional sections and restorations from the Fatimid, Ayyubid, Mamluk and Ottoman eras. (See also the more detailed account by al-Maqrīzī, *Khiṭaṭ*, Vol. 3, 213–221; D. Abouseif, *Architecture*, 58–63; M. Uthman, *'Imāra*, 275–290, A. Abd al-Raziq, *Tārīkh*, 219–237, and "Jamiʿ al-Azhar," http://archnet.org/sites/2311).

656 Weekly congregational mandatory prayers on Friday noon.

657 The ninth month of the Hijri year, when Muslims have to fast from sunrise to sunset.

658 *Nihāyat al-Arab fī Funūn al-Adab* (The Ultimate Ambition in the Arts of Erudition) by Shihāb al-Dīn Aḥmad b. ʿAbd al-Wahhāb al-Nuwayrī (d. 733 AH/1333 AD in Cairo). Al-Nuwayrī was an Egyptian statesman and researcher of several interests, born in Qūṣ, in present day Qina Governorate in Upper Egypt. He was one of the high ranking statesmen of the Mamluk Sultan al-Nāṣir Muḥammad, who served in several state administrative positions and held the office of Supervisor of the Army Bureau (*naẓar al-jaysh*, see Glossary) in Tripoli, in addition to provincial governance positions in Egypt. His major work, *Nihāyat al-Arab*, is considered an encyclopaedia of the knowledge that the Arabs had reached by his time. (Al-Zarkalī, *A'lām*, Vol. 1, 164–165).

659 The *khuṭba* is the sermon delivered with the prayers, in this case the Friday prayers. The author means that the Friday prayers were transferred to al-Ḥakim's mosque.

660 Fourth month of the Hijri year.

661 ʿAbd al-Wahhāb al-Nuwayrī, *Nihāyat al-Arab fī Funūn al-Adab*, ed. Mustafa Higazy, rev. Muhammad Mustafa Ziyada (Cairo, 2002), Vol. 30, 135–136.

662 *'Uṣfūr* specifically refers to the smaller brids, like sparrows and songbirds.

663 Ibn ʿAbd al-Ẓāhir, *Khiṭaṭ*, 85.

The Second Mosque:The Mosque of al-Ḥākim[664]

The Fatimid al-Ḥākim built this mosque near Bāb al-Futūḥ and Bāb al-Naṣr. Its building was completed in the year 396 AH/1006 AD.[665] At the time it was built, it was outside Cairo, for it was built before the presently existing Bāb al-Futūḥ and Bāb al-Naṣr were built, and it was outside the two arches that are the former Bāb al-Futūḥ and Bāb al-Naṣr.

He[666] then said: It is stated in the biography of al-ʿAzīz that he marked-out the foundation of the mosque on the 10th of Ramadan of the year 379 AH/989 AD, and in the biography of al-Ḥākim that some viziers begun [building] it and al-Ḥākim completed it. [An inscription] on the minaret near Bāb al-Futūḥ states that it was built in the reign of al-Mustanṣir, in the days of Amīr al-Juyūsh, in the year 480 AH/1087 AD,[667] then it was taken over by [someone] who possessed it. The *ziyyāda*[668] which is next to it was built by al-Ẓāhir, the son of al-Ḥākim, who did not complete it. It was proven during the reign of al-Ṣāliḥ Najm al-Dīn Ayyūb that the *ziyyāda* was part of the mosque and that it contained a mihrab. It was then seized from the person who had gotten hold of it and added to the mosque.[669] What it includes now was built in the days of al-Muʿizz Aybak al-Turkumānī,[670] and it was not roofed over.[671]

664 The mosque built between 379 AH/990 AD – 404 AH/1013 AD, with later additions and alterations. See more detailed accounts in al-Maqrīzī, *Khiṭaṭ*, Vol 3, 222–230; D. Abouseif, *Architecture*, 63-65; M. Uthman, *Imāra*, 291–321, A. Abd al-Raziq, *Tārīkh*, 237–244, and "Jami' al-Hakim," http://archnet.org/sites/2316).

665 The mosque was completed in 404 AH/1013 AD.

666 Ibn ʿAbd al-Ẓāhir.

667 The two original minarets of the mosque were stone structures built by al-Ḥākim in 393 AH/1003 AD. Al-Ḥākim ordered enveloping the lower parts of these with outer rectangular stone structures in 401 AH/1010 AD. The upper parts of the existing minarets are restorations of the Mamluk Sultan Baybars al-Jāshankīr in 702 AH/1303 AD. The inscription al-Qalqashandī is referring to is that of the construction of Bāb al-Futūḥ and the walls that incorporated the Mosque of al-Ḥākim in 480 AH/1087 AD; part of the Cairo fortification project of vizier Badr al-Jamālī, in the reign of Caliph al-Mustanṣir. (See A. Abd al-Raziq, *Athār*, 241–242, M. Uthman, *'Imāra*, 101 and D. Abouseif, *Architecture*, 64–65).

668 Also *ziyāda*: "Outer enclosure or extension of mosque common to congregational mosques in the early Islamic period." The term is derived from the Arabic root *zād*, meaning to add to or enlarge. "The best surviving examples of *ziyādas* can be found in Samarra (in Iraq) at the Great Mosque (232 AH/847 AD to 246 AH/861 AD) and the Abū Dulaf Mosque (245 AH/859 AD to 247 AH/861 AD) and also at the Mosque of Ibn Ṭūlūn in Cairo." The *ziyāda* surrounded a mosque from three sides, except for the *qibla* wall marking the direction for prayer. It normally included several doors and there are suggestions in historical sources that it might have included latrines or ablution areas. (Andrew Petersen, "Ziyāda," in Dictionary *of Islamic Architecture* (London, 1996), 318).

669 See M. Uthman, *'Imāra*, 317–321 and Bernard O'Kane, "The Ziyāda of the Mosque of al-Ḥākim and the Development of the Ziyāda in Islamic Architecture," in *L'Égypte fatimide: son art et son histoire: actes du colloque organise à Paris les 28, 29 et 30 mai 1998*, ed. Marianne Barrucand (Paris, 1999), 141–158.

670 Sultan al-Muʿizz Aybak, see above.

671 See Ibn ʿAbd al-Ẓāhir's account, which does not appear to refer to the possession of the minaret, but rather the building and demolishing of a fountain at the center of the mosque, for example. (Ibn ʿAbd al-Ẓāhir, *Khiṭaṭ*, 68–70).

The Third Mosque:Al-Aqmar Mosque[672]

It was built by the Fatimid al-Āmir, through the agency of his vizier, al-Ma'mūn b. al-Baṭā'iḥī. Its building was completed in the year 519 AH/1125 AD and it should be mentioned that it bears the names of both al-Āmir and al-Ma'mūn.

I say: The mosque did not host a sermon (*khuṭba*) until Amir Yalbughā al-Sālimī,[673] one of the amirs of al-Ẓāhir Barqūq, renovated it in the year 801 AH/1399 AD,[674] and arranged that a sermon (*khuṭba*) takes place at it.

The Fourth Mosque: The Mosque in al-Maqs at Bāb al-Baḥr,[675] which is known as al-Anwar Mosque[676]

Also built by the Fatimid al-Ḥākim in the year 393 AH/1003 AD.

The Fifth Mosque: Al-Ẓāfir Mosque, known today as al-Fakkāhīn Mosque[677]

It was built by the Fatimid al-Ẓāfir inside the two Zuwayla gates in the year 543 AH/1148 AD. It used to be a pen for rams, and the reason it was built as a mosque is that a eunuch-servant (*khādim*) was in a balcony overlooking the pen when he saw a butcher taking two rams to slaughter them. He slaughtered the first then threw

672 Al-Aqmar (the Moonlit) Mosque was built in 519 AH/1125 AD. See more detailed accounts in al-Maqrīzī, *Khiṭaṭ*, Vol. 3, 253-255; D. Abouseif, *Architecture*, 72–74; M. Uthman, *'Imāra*, 322–357, A. Abd al-Raziq, *Tārīkh*, 249–257, and "Jami' al-Aqmar," http://archnet.org/sites/2310).

673 Abū al-Ma'ālī 'Abd Allah, Amir Sayf al-Dīn al-Ḥanafī al-Ṣūfī al-Ẓāhirī, whose name was Yūsuf and who was originally a free man of Muslim descent. He was named Yalbughā upon his purchase and arrival from the east, and al-Sālimī is an attribution to the merchant who bought him, Sālim. Sultan al-Ẓāhir Barqūq appointed him amir and supervisor of two khanqas. He continued in service under Barqūq's son, Sultan Faraj (r. 801 AH/1399 AD – 815 AH/1412 AD, with an interregnum in 807 AH/1405 AD), when he went through the ups of being the *ustādār* and the vizier, and the downs of imprisonment and torture. He was killed in 811 AH/1408 AD. (Al-Maqrīzī, *Khiṭaṭ*, Vol. 3, 257–260).

674 Al-Maqrīzī reports that these restorations were made in the year 799 AH/1397 AD. (Al-Maqrīzī, *Khiṭaṭ*, Vol. 3, 253).

675 For a more detailed account of this mosque see al-Maqrīzī, *Khiṭaṭ*, Vol 3, 237–238.

676 Al-Anwar literally means "the Lit" or "the Illuminated," which is one of the titles of the Mosque of al-Ḥākim. Apparently, al-Qalqashandī got confused while copying from Ibn 'Abd al-Ẓāhir's account of the Mosque of al-Ḥākim. (Ibn al-Ṭuwayr, *Nuzha*, 219, al-Maqrīzī, *Khiṭaṭ*, Vol. 3, 222, and Ibn 'Abd al-Ẓāhir, *Khiṭaṭ*, 68).

677 Al-Fakkāhīn are the fruit sellers and the mosque was also called al-Afkhar (the Most Magnificent), al-Fākihiyyīn (also the fruit-sellers), and in modern times, al-Fakahānī, which is the singular of al-Fakkāhīn or al-Fākihiyyīn. It is located at the intersection of Khūsh Alley with al-Mu'izz Street and was restored more than once during the Mamluk and Ottoman eras, to the extent that only minimal Fatimid traces remain. In 1148 AH/1736 AD it was renewed and a caravanserai (*wikāla*) for selling fruits was built next to it, but there were most probably fruit sellers there before for the area to bear this name in the Mamluk era. (See Al-Maqrīzī, *Khiṭaṭ*, Vol. 3, 261, M. Uthman, *'Imāra*, 389–392, and A. Abd al-Raziq, *Tārīkh*, 257–259).

his knife and went to mind some business of his. The second ram then came and took the knife with his mouth and threw it in the sewer. When the butcher came back, he could not find the knife. The eunuch-servant then screamed and rescued [the ram] from the butcher. The story was reported[678] to the people of the palace, who then ordered the building of the mosque.

The Sixth Mosque: Al-Ṣāliḥī Mosque[679]

It was built by Al-Ṣāliḥ Ṭalā'iʿ b. Ruzayk, the vizier of both the Fatimid al-Fā'iz and al-ʿĀḍid, outside Bāb Zuwayla, with the intention of transferring the head of al-Ḥusayn to it from Ascalon, for fear that the Crusaders were to attack it. [However], when al-Ṣāliḥ completed the mosque, al-Fā'iz denied him that and built a shrine (*mashhad*) for the head next to the palace, which is known as "Mashhad al-Ḥusayn." He transferred the head to the shrine in the year 549 AH/1154 AD, built a cistern in it and allocated a waterwheel to it, near Bāb al-Kharq, to carry water to it from the Khalīj in the days of the Nile [rise]. This mosque did not host a sermon (*khuṭba*) and the first Friday prayer to be held in it was in the days of al-Muʿizz Aybak al-Turkumānī in the year 652 AH/1254 AD,[680] with Aṣīl al-Dīn Abū Bakr al-Isʿirdī[681] delivering the sermon.

******

The construction of mosques escalated in Cairo under the Turkish State, especially in the days of al-Nāṣir Muḥammad b. Qalāwūn, and after. [At the time], the mosques that were built in Cairo were innumerable, such as al-Māridīnī[682] and Qūṣūn's[683] mosques[684] outside Bāb Zuwayla, as well as others. Friday prayers were

678 "*Rufiʿat al-qiṣṣa*," which may also mean "the petition was submitted."

679 Built in 555 AH/1160 AD, the mosque still stands in its place today. For more detailed accounts see al-Maqrīzī, *Khiṭaṭ*, Vol. 3, 261–262; D. Abouseif, *Architecture*, 76–77; M. Uthman, *'Imāra*, 358–388, A. Abd al-Raziq, *Tārīkh*, 257–259) and "Masjid al-Salih Tala'iʿ," http://archnet.org/sites/2324).

680 Al-Maqrīzī says that this was sometime in 653 AH/1256 AD to 659 AH/1261 AD. (Al-Maqrīzī, *Khiṭaṭ*, Vol. 3, 262).

681 Muḥammad b. Ibrahīm b. ʿUmar, Abū ʿAlī Aṣīl al-Dīn al-ʿŪfī al-Isʿirdī (d. 668 AH/1270 AD), was the *khaṭīb* (preacher) at the Great Mosque of Damascus before he moved to Egypt where he became the *khaṭīb* of al-Ṣāliḥ Ṭalā'iʿ's mosque, as well as the *nā'ib al-ḥukm* (Deputy of the Chief Judge) until his demise. (Al-Ṣafadī, *Wafayāt*, Vol. 2, 5 and H. al-Battawi, *'Imāma*, 63).

682 Also al-Māridānī, Alṭinbughā al-Sāqī (the cup-bearer), was a mamluk of Sultan al-Nāṣir Muḥammad, whom he made an amir, a commander and his son-in-law. He continued to be a powerful amir and held several important posts under al-Nāṣir's sons, until his death in 744 AH/1343 AD. (Al-Maqrīzī, *Khiṭaṭ*, Vol. 3, 300).

683 The High-ranking Amir Sayf al-Dīn Qūṣūn or Qawṣūn arrived in Egypt in 720 AH/1320 AD from Central Asia as a merchant when he was about 18 years of age. Sultan al-Nāṣir Muḥammad bought him and appointed him among his cup-bearers. He advanced until he was one of the highest amirs, most trusted by the sultan. The sultan made him his son-in-law, married his sister, and appointed him guardian of his young sons after his death, that is, a regent. After the sultan's death, Qūṣūn assumed sovereignity authority through his position and ended up being killed by other amirs in 742 AH/1342 AD. (Al-Maqrīzī, *Khiṭaṭ*, Vol. 3, 298–299).

684 For Qūṣūn's mosque (built in 730 AH/1330 AD). The Mosque of al-Māridānī (built in 740 AH/1340 AD) still stands today in al-Tabbāna Neigbourhood. For accounts on both mosques

held in many of the madrasas and the small mosques scattered among the neighbourhoods due to the huge population that overflowed the congregational mosques.

The Madrasas of Cairo

As for its madrasas, during the Fatimid era and before, they were a rarity or almost nonexistent. However, there was a house near the [Fatimid] palace known as the House of Knowledge (Dār al-ʿIlm)[685] behind Khān Masrūr.[686] This house (*dār*) was where the Shiite missionary (*dā'ī*)[687] sat for his students, who studied the [religious] sciences of their doctrine, to meet with him. Al-Ḥākim had allocated part of his endowments (*awqāf*), which he had assigned to al-Azhar, al-Maqs and Rāshidamosques, to this house. Al-Afḍal b. Amīr al-Juyūsh abolished this house because people met at it and dove into discussions of doctrines, for he feared [people's] gathering over the Nizārīyya[688] doctrine. Al-Āmir resumed [the functioning of] this house, through the agency of the palace eunuch-servants (*khuddām*), and under the condition that its

see Al-Maqrīzī, *Khiṭaṭ*, Vol. 3, 297–299, D. Abouseif, *Architecture*, 113–115, and "Masjid Altinbugha al-Maridani,"http://archnet.org/sites/2329.

685 See Glossary:"Dār al-ʿIlm". Al-Maqrīzī notes that it was to the north of the western Fatimid palace. Dār al-ʿIlm was originally named Dār al-Ḥikma (House of Wisdom) and was inaugurated in 395 AH/1005 AD. It was attached to the western Fatimid palace and accessed through one of its gates, Bāb al-Tabbānīn, which faced al-Aqmar Mosque. Its name probably changed to Dār al-ʿIlm in 450 AH/1058 AD and was closed down in 513 AH/1119 AD. In 517 AH/1123 AD, it was reinaugarated, but its location was changed to a place behind Khizānat al-Daraq (The Warehouse of Shields), near Bāb Turbat al-Zaʿfarān, which was one of the southern gates of the greater easternpalace. It, therefore, stood on the eastern side of the Qaṣaba, facing the southwestern corner of the western palace. Dār al-ʿIlm disappeared after the Fatimid era and had been replaced by al-Maqrīzī's time with a large house near Darb Ibn ʿAbd al-Ẓāhir, close to Khān al-Khalīlī. (Al-Maqrīzī, *Khiṭaṭ*, Vol. 2, 274–278 and 452, Ibn al-Ṭuwayir, Nuzha, 110 fn. 1 and A. Raymond, *Cairo*, 32 Map 2).

686 Khān Masrūr (Masrūr's Caravanserai, see fn. 526) was located on the Great Street (the Qaṣaba), near its intersection with Jawhar al-Qā'id Street, to one's left upon heading to al-Azhar Street. Ibn al-Ṭuwayr indicates that it was in the place of the Fatimid Khizānat al-Daraq (The Warehouse of Shields), which was outside the western palace, opposite Bāb al-Zuhūma in the southwestern walls of the palace. (A. Sayyid, *Khiṭaṭ*, 25 fn. 1, al-Maqrīzī, *Khiṭaṭ*, Vol. 2, 572–573, and Ibn al-Ṭuwayr & A.Sayyid, *Nuzha*, 134 and 134 fn. 4). Al-Qalqashandī is, thus, referring to the second Dār al-ʿIlm inaugurated in 517 AH/1123 AD.

687 A Shiite religious position to be defined in detail later on.

688 After the death of the Fatimid Caliph al-Mustanṣir, the rightful heir to the throne, who in Ismaʿīlī Shiite thought is also the Imām; the religious leader of the community by birthright, was al-Mustanṣir's eldest son, Nizār. Vizier al-Afḍal, the most powerful figure in the state at the time, however, ignored this right of the fifty years old Nizār and instated his younger brother, al-Mustaʿlī, who was al-Afḍal's brother in law. Nizār fled to Alexandria with some of his supporters and announced himself caliph there. The army remained on its allegiance to al-Afḍal, which resulted in Nizār's failure to stand up to him. Al-Afḍal managed to capture Nizār and kill him, which led to the division of Ismaʿīlī Shiites into two sects: the majority, namely, the Mustaʿliyya, who supported the right of al-Mustaʿlī and his sons to be imams, and the minority, mostly from Persia, who supported the right of Nizār, thus were named the Nizāriyya. (A. Sayyid, *Tafsīr*, 220–223).

director (*mutawallī*)[689] would be a devout man, the missionary (*dāʿī*) would be its supervisor (*nāẓir*),[690] and [men] would be appointed responsible for reciting Quran.

Al-Misbaḥī[691] mentioned in his History that Vizier Abū al-Faraj Yaʿqūb b. Killis asked al-ʿAzīz bi-Allah [for his permission] to deliver allowances (*rizq*)[692] to a group of [religious] scholars (*ʿulamāʾ*). He granted[693] each of them a sufficient sum and built them a house (*dār*) next to al-Azhar. On Fridays, these [religious] scholars (*ʿulamāʾ*) sat in a ring[694] after prayers at the mosque to discuss jurisprudence (*fiqh*). Abū Yaʿqūb,the judge of al-Khandaq (The Trench), headed the ring and lectured the group of thirty-seven individuals until the time of *ʿaṣr* [prayers]. When the Ayyubid state came to power, it indeed patroned goodness and merit.[695] Al-Malik al-Kāmil Muḥammad b. al-ʿĀdil Abū Bakr built the Kāmiliyya House of Teaching the Prophet's Traditions (Dār al-Ḥadīth al-Kāmiliyya) in Bayn al-Qaṣrayn in the year 622 AH/1225 AD.[696] He ordered that the four Sunni schools be [taught] and the sermon (*khuṭba*) be held at it. [The area] next to Dār al-Ḥadīth remained in ruins until houses were built there in the days of Aybak al-Turkumānī in the fifties of 600 AH,[697] and an endowment (*waqf*) was endowed to the mentioned madrasa.[698] Some of the elites of the [Ayyubid] state built madrasas that did not rise up to this one, for what a great difference there is between kings and others.

When the Turkish state came to power, they reached this [level of magnificence] and excelled above it. Al-Ẓāhir Baybars built al-Ẓāhiriyya Madrasa in Bayn al-Qaṣrayn, next to al-Ṣāliḥiyya madrasa. Then al-Manṣūr Qalāwūn[699] built

689 See Glossary.

690 See Glossary.

691 ʿAbd Allah Muḥammad b. Aḥmad al-Amīr al-Mukhtār al-Ḥarrānī, ʿIzz al-Mulk (d. 420 AH/1029 AD), known as al-Misbaḥī, was a historian and scholar who lived during the era of the Fatimid Caliph al-Ḥākim and authored several works. The work al-Qalqashandī is referring to here is *al-Taʾrīkh al-Kabīr* (The Great History), which is no longer extant and is said to have been composed of thirteen-thousand folios. (Z. al-Smarra'i, *Manhaj*, 108).

692 The salaries or running payments assigned by the state or the incomes generated from endowed lands. (M. Dahman, *Muʿjam 80, and S. Ashour, ʿAsr 441* and see Glossary).

693 *Aṭlaqa*, see Glossary: "*iṭlāqāt.*"

694 *ḥalaqa*, the usual sitting arrangement of the lessons at the time.

695 "Opened the door of goodness and planted the tree of merit."

696 Dār al-Ḥadīth al-Kāmiliyya or al-Madrasa al-Kāmiliyya,built in 622 AH/1225 AD, was primarily endowed for teaching the traditions of the Prophet (*ḥadīth*), then later for the Shāfiʿī jurists. It was the most important centre for teaching the traditions of the Prophet during the 7th and 8th centuries AH/13th and 14th centuries AD, until it suffered decline after the famine of 806 AH/1403 AD. Apart from a surviving iwan, only minimal Ayyubid remains may still be found in this building today, for it was later restored, particularly by the Ottomans in 1165 AH/1752 AD. (Al-Maqrīzī, *Khiṭaṭ*, Vol. 3, 467–468, C. Williams, *Monuments*, 195 and "Madrasa al-Kamil Ayyub," http://archnet.org/sites/2242).

697 650 to 650 AH corresponds to 1252 to 1261 AD.

698 That is, Dār al-Ḥadīth.

699 Mamluk sultan who ruled from 678 AH/1279 AD to 689 AH/1290 AD.

al-Manṣūriyya Madrasa,[700] inside[701] his hospital (*bīmāristān*), which will be mentioned later, and established a splendid tomb in front of it.

After that, al-Nāṣir Muḥammad b. Qalāwūn built al-Nāṣiriyya Madrasa,[702] next to the mentioned hospital, then al-Nāṣir Ḥasan b. al-Nāṣir Muḥammad b. Qalāwūn[703] built his grandest madrasa below the Citadel,[704] which was unprecedented and its parallel unheard of in any other city. It is said that its iwan[705] is some cubits larger than the Iwan of Khusraw.[706]

Then Sultan Ḥasan's nephew, al-Ashraf Sha'bān b. Ḥusayn built al-Ashrafiyya Madrasa in al-Ṣuwwa[707] below the Citadel, but he died before completing it. Al-Nāṣir Faraj b. al-Ẓāhir Barqūq[708] then demolished it because of its imposition on the Citadel in the year 814 AH/1411 AD. He transferred its stones to use them for constructing the halls he built at the courtyard (*ḥawsh*)[709] of the Citadel. No madrasa is known to have been intentionally knocked down before this one.[710]

700 The complex built by al-Manṣūr Qalāwūn in 683 AH/1284 AD comprised a madrasa-mosque, a domed mausoleum, and a hospital. (See also "Madrasa wa Qubbat wa Bimaristan al-Sultan Qalawun,"http://archnet.org/sites/1551).

701 "*min dākhil*," which means "from inside" or "from within."

702 The madrasa complex of Sultan al-Nāṣir Muḥammad, which was begun in 694 AH/1295 AD and completed in 703 AH/1303 AD. It comprised a mosque-madrasa and a mausoleum. (see also "Madrasat wa-Qubbat al-Nasir Muhammad ibn Qalawun," http://archnet.org/sites/2227).

703 Mamluk sultan who ruled from 748 AH/1347 AD to 762 AH/1361 AD, with an interregnum from 752 AH/1351 AD to 755 AH/1354 AD.

704 Madrasa-mosque complex of Sultan Ḥasan built between 757 AH/1356 AD and 764 AH/1363 AD, which includes a four-iwan congregational mosque, four madrasas for the four Sunni rites, a domed mausoleum, as well as other architectural elements. (See "Masjid al-Sultan Hasan," http://archnet.org/sites/1549).

705 The iwan is an Islamic architectural term of Persian origin that refers to a square or rectangular room with one side opening unto a court or a roofed hall. It is always a step or more higher than the court and may be flat-roofed or vaulted.

706 Also Taq-ī Kisrā, the Sassanian iwan surviving from the palatial palace of King Anushirvan Khusraw (531–579 AD) in al-Madain, Iraq (Ctesiphon). (See "Taq-I Kisra," http://archnet.org/sites/5282).

707 One of the hills above which the Citadel was built, to its north-west.

708 Mamluk sultan who ruled from 801 AH/1399 AD to 815 AH/1412 AD, with an interregnum in 807 AH/1405 AD.

709 *Ḥawsh* means court and the full term also usually used is "al-Ḥawsh al-Sulṭānī" (the Sultanic Courtyard). Al-Nāṣir Muḥammad built this *ḥawsh* in the Citadel in 738 AH/1338 AD to host a huge number of sheep, 8000 according to Ibn Taghrī Birdī. The *ḥawsh* occupied an area of four feddans. (K. Azab, *Qal'a*, 140–141).

710 Al-Maqrīzī tells us that the site of al-Ashrafiyya Madrasa was taken up by the hospital that Sultan al-Mu'ayyad Shaykh (r. 815 AH/1412 – 824 AH/1421 AD) built in 821 AH/1418 AD to 823 AH/1420 AD and that the hospital's gate is in place of the madrasa's gate. The madrasa was not only used for Sultan Faraj's constructions at the Citadel, for some of its remaninig magnificently inlaid doors and windows, in addition to its rich library, had been bought a few years earlier for unfairly cheap prices by Amir Jamāl al-Dīn al-Ustādār for his madrasa (809 AH/1407 AD) in al-Jamāliyya quarter of Cairo. The remains of al-Mu'ayyad's hospital, including its gate, still stand in the area of Bāb al-Wazīr, and its location suggests why it was considered imposing on the Citadel. (Al-Maqrīzī, *Khiṭaṭ*, Vol. 3, 535 & 553, and see also: "Bimaristan al-Mu'ayyidi," http://archnet.org/sites/1527 and "Jami' al-Amir Jamal al-Din al-Ustadar," http://archnet.org/sites/2220).

After that, al-Ẓāhir Barqūq built al-Ẓāhiriyya Madrasa, in Bayn al-Qaṣrayn, near al-Kāmiliyya Madrasa and it came out to be of ultimate beauty and grandeur. Barqūq ordered that the sermon (*khuṭba*) [be delivered] at it; stipulated that [a number of] Sufis [reside] in it as was customary with the khanqas, as well as lessons by the imams.[711] The building was extravagantly huge and poets composed poems about it, with these verses being among what they came up with:

> "And some of his servants, at his disposal, to serve him.[712]
>
> Would call upon the stones and they would come to them, hastily."

All poets arrived at this meaning [in their praise], so, it was proposed to some of the elites that they compose verses of the sort; these included:

> "And with the aid of al-Khalīlī[713] its construction has boomed; with haste it was built, and no slowness How the whips of his wisdom have shown wonder, and how it became an example, such an outstanding example
>
> And how many stones came slowly and hastily, that you would imagine are transferred by jinn."

During this [era], the high-ranking amirs and others built madrasas that filled up and crowded the neighbourhoods.

The Khanqas and Ribats of Cairo

As for the khanqas and ribats, they were not known in Egypt before the Ayyubid state. Sultan Ṣalāḥ al-Dīn al-Ayyūbī was the one who originated [building] them, for he built al-Ṣalāḥiyya Khanqah known as Sa'īd al-Su'adā'.[714] Sa'īd al-Su'adā' was the title of a eunuch-servant (*khādim*) of the Fatimid al-Mustanṣir named Qunbur,[715] who owned this house (*dār*). The house, in the last [Fatimid] days, became the residence of al-Ṣāliḥ Ṭalā'i' b. Ruzyak, who, after assuming the vizierate, dug an underground tunnel to it from the House of the Vizierate (Dār al-Wizāra). It was also a residence for Shāwir al-Sa'dī, the vizier of al-'Āḍid, then his son, al-Kāmil. When Sultan Ṣalāḥ al-Dīn came to power, he converted it into a khanqah and allocated an endowment

711 Leaders of prayers who are also learned men, see Glossary: "imam".

712 Reference could either be to the building or the patron.

713 This is a reference to Amir Jarkas or Jahāraks al-Khalīlī, who established Khān al-Khalīlī, in the area still known by this name until today, opposite al-Ẓāhir Barqūq's madrasa, to its southeast, in 786 AH/1384 AD. Jarkas al-Khalīlī was the royal equerry (*amīr ākhūr*) of Sultan Barqūq. Al-Khalīlī's name "appears in the inauguration inscription on the façade and in the courtyard" of the madrasa, indicating that he supervised the construction process. ("Masjid al-Sultan Barquq," http://archnet.org/sites/2217).

714 See fn. 423.

715 Diacritics are absent and the vowels are assumed.

(*waqf*) to it [that comprised] the Caravanserai of Sharb (Qaysāriyyat al-Sharb)[716] inside Cairo and al-Ḥabbāniyya Garden in al-Birka Street (Zuqāq al-Birka).[717]

The Five-prayer Mosques

As for the five-prayer mosques,[718] they are innumerable and too difficult to [completely] investigate, for every neighbourhood (*khaṭṭ*) has one mosque or more, each having its own appointed imam and worshippers.

The Hospital

As for the hospital (*bimāristān*), Judge Muḥyi al-Dīn b. ʿAbd al-Ẓāhir said: It came to my knowledge that the hospital was originally in al-Qashshāshīn, meaning the place currently known as al-Kharrāṭīn,[719] near al-Azhar Mosque. the Minting House (Dār al-Ḍarb) that al-Ma'mūn b. al-Baṭā'iḥī, the vizier of al-Āmir, built, was also there, opposite the mentioned hospital. He had also ordered the building of minting houses in Alexandria, Qūṣ, Tyre and Ascalon.[720] The [Fatimid] palace comprised a hall built by al-ʿAzīz b. al-Muʿizz in 384 AH/994 AD, which existed when Ṣalāḥ al-Dīn al-Ayyūbī came to power and seized that palace. Ṣalāḥ al-Dīn transformed the hall into a hospital, which is the Old Hospital (al-Bīmāristān al-ʿAtīq) that still survives in its original form until now, inside the palace.[721] It is said that this hospital has a talisman that prevents ants from entering it, and that this was the cause for making it a hospital. Judge Muḥiy al-Dīn b. ʿAbd al-Ẓāhir said: I have asked the managers (*mubāshirūn*)[722] of the mentioned hospital about this issue in the year [6]57 AH/1259 AD[723] and they said that it is true.[724]

716 Qaysāriyyat al-Sharb or al-Sharab was located inside Cairo, according to al-Maqrīzī's description, to the northwest of al-Ẓāfir Mosque, across the Qaṣaba. *Al-Sharb* is a type of textile that was rather thin and fine, sometimes very transparent. It could have been made of linen or silk, or may be a mixture of the two, and may have been adorned with golden threads. In his account of this *qaysāriyya*, al-Maqrīzī does not describe its products, but he mentions that it had residents and was one of the busiest markets of his time. The diacritics used in other sources for the"*sharb*"referred to aboveshow that the word denotes this type of textile; however, the the editor of*Subḥ* marks it to be read "*shurb*," a pronunciation that means "drinking" and denotes "drinks" or "beverages." (See al-Maqrīzī, *Khiṭaṭ*, Vol. 2, 83–84& 558; Ibn al-Ṭuwayir, Nuzha, 129 fn. 5; A. Sayyid, *Khiṭaṭ*, 55; Al-Baqli, *Ta'rīf*, 197, M. Dahmān, *Mu'jam*, 97, and fn. 93).

717 "Small street of the pond." In al-Maqrīzī's *Khiṭaṭ*: "al-Ḥabbāniyya Garden next to Birkat al-Fīl, outside Cairo." (Al-Maqrīzī, *Khiṭaṭ*, Vol. 3, 570).

718 *Masājid al-ṣalawāt al-khams*; mosques for the five daily prayers.

719 This area currently occupies what is known today as al-Ṣanādiqiyya Street in al-Azhar Neighbourhood. (M. Shams, *Nujūm*, Vol. 4, 56 fn. 4 and al-Maqrīzī, *Khiṭaṭ*, Vol. 2, 601).

720 See Ibn ʿAbd al-Ẓāhir's account in *Khiṭaṭ*, 33–34.

721 According to al-Maqrīzī, Sultan Ṣalāḥ al-Dīnordered the inauguration of this hospital in 577 AH/1182 AD. (Al-Maqrīzī, *Khiṭaṭ*, Vol. 2, 160).

722 Sing. *mubāshir*, also "conductor" or "overseer," see Glossary.

723 The hundreds figure in this Hijri date is missing, nevertheless, it can be guessed. (*Ṣubḥ*, Vol. 3, 369 fn. 1).

724 See Ibn ʿAbd al-Ẓāhir, *Khiṭaṭ*, 60–61.

Sultan al-Malik al-Manṣūr Qalāwūn then transformed the house of Sitt al-Mulk,[725] al-Ḥākim's sister, which was known as al-Dār al-Quṭbiyya,[726] into a hospital in the year 683 AH/1284 AD,[727] under the supervision of Amir ʿAlam al-Dīn al-Shujāʿī.[728] He [built it] to comprise al-Manṣūriyya Madrasa and the tomb mentioned above, kept some of the house's features as they were, and altered others. [This hospital] is an act of great kindness that is unparalleled in the world. Its supervision[729] is a dignified rank assigned to viziers and officials of their level.

The author of *Masālik al-Abṣār* (Routes of Vision)[730] said: [It is the building] of lofty position; honourable effects; gracious altruism; great construction; plentiful endowment (*waqf*), and a variety of physicians, ophthalmologists and surgeons.[731]

******

725 Also: Sayyidat al-Mulk, both terms meaning "the Lady of Sovereignity." Sitt al-Mulk (d. 413 AH/1022 AD), Caliph al-Ḥākim's elder sister, is reported by historians to have participated in the conspiracy to assassinate her brother in 411 AH/1021 AD. It is possible that she believed this was her only way to save the caliphate and the family from her brother's actions, then considered against the Ismāʿīlī doctrine and infuriating to Sunni Muslims as well. She took the required measures to ensure the smooth transition of power to her nephew, Caliph al-Ḥākim's son, al-Ẓāhir. For almost a year, Sitt al-Mulk was the defacto ruler of the state and all decrees had to have her signature. (A. Sayyid, *Tafsīr*, 179–182).

726 This house was the residence of others after Sitt al-Mulk, the last being the Ayyubid Amir al-Malik al-Mufaḍḍal Quṭb al-Dīn Aḥmad (d. 619 AH/1222 AD), with his sisters and family. The house was therefore known as al-Dār al-Quṭbiyya. Sultan Qalāwūn traded this house with al-Mufaḍḍal's sister, Mu'nisa Khātūn, also known as al-Quṭbiyya, for another house, to build his complex in its place. Al-Maqrīzī very briefly points to a mosque at the same site which was also called Masjid al-Quṭbiyya. (Al-Maqrīzī, *Khiṭaṭ*, Vol. 3, 547 and 567, al-Nuwayrī, *Nihāya*, Vol. 29, 123 and Ibn ʿAbd al-Ẓāhir, *Khiṭaṭ*, 60–61).

727 Both al-Maqrīzī and Ibn ʿAbd al-Ẓāhir indicate that this was in the year 682 AH/1283 AD. (Al-Maqrīzī, *Khiṭaṭ*, Vol. 3, 547 and Ibn ʿAbd al-Ẓāhir, *Khiṭaṭ*, 61).

728 Amir Sanjar b. ʿAbd Allah al-Shujāʿī al-Manṣūrī (d. 693 AH/1294 AD) was one of the high-ranking amirs of Sultan Qalāwūn. He was the inspector (*shādd*, see Glossary) of Egypt's *dawāwīn* (bureaus, sing. *dīwān*), its vizier, then the Viceroy of Damascus. He had political and architectural knowledge and experience and he closely supervised the building project of Qalāwūn's Complex. After Sultan al-Ashraf Khalīl b. Qalāwūn (r. 1290–1293) was assassinated, Sanjar played an important role in ensuring passing on the throne to the rightful heir, Sultan al-Nāṣir Muḥammad. He served as a vizier for more than a month under the then child king, Sultan al-Nāṣir, but he aspired for more and ended up being killed by his rivals. (Ibn Taghrī Birdī, *Manhal*, Vol. 6, 80–83 and al-Maqrīzī, *Sulūk*, Vol. 2, 248).

729 Holding the position of its *naẓir*.

730 *Masālik al-Abṣār fī Mamālik al-Amṣār* (Routes of Vision Concerning the Kingdoms) is a geographical and historical work by Ibn Faḍl Allah al-ʿUmarī (Aḥmad b. Yaḥyā al-ʿUmarī al-Ḥanafī al-Dimashqī, d. 749 H/1348 AD). Al-ʿUmarī was a confidential scribe (*kātib sirr*) and a head of the chancery bureau (*ṣāḥib dīwān al-inshāʾ*); both state administrative positions (see Glossary), who also authored works on history, families and notables. (Z. al-Samarra'i, 93).

731 See Shihāb al-Dīn b. Faḍl Allah al-ʿUmarī, *Masālik al-Abṣār fī Mamālik al- Amṣār*, ed. Kamil Salman al-Juburi (Beirut, 2010), Vol. 3, 282 and same book ed. Hamza Ahmad Abbas (Abu Dhabi, 2002), Vol. 3, 424).

Construction and Description of Cairo

I say: Construction continued to increase in Cairo at all times, and its features kept on changing, especially after the destruction of Fustat and the movement of its residents to Cairo, as mentioned earlier. [This went on] until it became as it is in our time, [having]: grand palaces; enormous houses; vast dwellings; extended markets; [pleasant] sceneries of excursion; delightful mosques; peaceful madrasas, and splendid khanqas, of which no likes are heard of, nor are any parallels known of, in any city or country. Most of Cairo's buildings are built with brick, but its mosques, madrasas and houses of its elites are built with carved stone, having marble floors and dadoes. Most of its roofs are built with compactly fixed[732] palm and reed woods. All, or most of, its buildings are painted with bright white lime. Cairenes are most capable of elevating some of their houses, to the extent that a house would comprise from two to four floors, one above the other. Each floor would include complete apartments with their utilities and facilities, and cut roofs atop them of compact engineeringand amazing craftsmanship.[733]

The author of *Masālik al-Abṣār* said: The craftsmen of Miṣr are unparalleled in this field.[734] Outside it one finds beautiful gardens; [pleasant] sceneries of excursion; houses overlooking the Nile, and the canals branching from it and from its extension. It has enjoyable parks, especially in springtime, with brooks branching from the Nile segments, surrounded by various plants with swaying flowers that are pleasant sights to the eye and mind.

Ibn al-Athīr says in *'Ajā'ib al-Makhlūqāt* (The Marvels of Creations):[735] Travellers overland and overseas have agreed that there is no [city] that is more beautiful to see nor is there one that is more populated. All that is strange and all wondrous costumes are brought to it from all regions of the world. It has a great king with numerous armies, whose beautiful attire is unparalleled by any other king on earth. Its people live in luxury, [enjoy] delicious food and drink, and its women are most beautiful and likeable.

The author of *Masālik al-Abṣār* said: More than one person who has seen huge cities told me that he never saw a city where as many people gathered as Cairo. He added:

732 "*Al-Muḥkam al-ṣan'a*," which may mean "of compact" or "of efficient" craftsmanship. Al-Qalqashandī often uses the term to describe the fixing of roofs; therefore, it may be more plausible to assume the meaning of compactness.

733 "*Handasa muḥkama wa ṣinā'a 'ajība*"; a phrase borrowed from al-ʿUmarī. (See *Masālik* (2010), Vol. 3, 334 and fn. 600).

734 That is, architecture of multi-floored houses. (Al-ʿUmarī, *Masālik* (2010), Vol. 3, 334).

735 Al-Qalqashandī is referring to "*Tuḥfat al-'Ajā'ib wa Ṭurfat al-Gharā'b*" (The Gift of Marvels and Rarity of Oddities); a work by Ḍiyā' al-Dīn Ibn al-Athīr (d. 637 H/1230 AD), known as Ibn al-Athīr al-Kātib, a vizier of the Ayyubids. This work includes a section entitled *'Ajā'b al-Makhlūqāt wa Gharā'b al-Mawjūdāt* (The Marvels of Creations and Oddities of Things Existing) that is collected from several works.(See also Z. al-Samarra'i, 76–77).

I have asked al-Ṣadr[736] Majd al-Dīn Ismāʿīl[737] whether Baghdad and Tūrīz[738] gathered as many people as Miṣr and he replied: Miṣr has as many people as there are in all cities.[739]

He said in *al-Taʿrīf* (The Instruction)[740]: Cairo is the mother[741] of all kingdoms today. It is the capital of the country, the seat of the caliphate in our times, as well as the seat of the kingdom. It is the source of wise men and the arrival station of travels. The east and the west [lands of Muslims] follow it, except for India because it is too remote a location and too far to reach. We hear about India what we respect and what is unfamiliar to us. He added: We should have [presented] Cairo [as the center] around which all the regions circulate, but we shall confine it to [the lands] within the Egyptian borders. Then we shall [discuss] the capital of each kingdom, which is [the center] around which its region circulates. Then, all [regions] should refer to [Cairo], and all the canals should pour into its river.[742]

In *Masālik al-Abṣār*, he said: But its land is marshy, therefore its buildings deteriorate quickly.[743]

Judge Muḥyi al-Dīn b. ʿAbd al-Ẓāhir has referred to that [same issue] and said that al-Muʿizz blamed General Jawhar for building Cairo in this location, while leaving the Nile bank at al-Maqs or to the south of Fustat, where al-Raṣad is now.[744]

736 A term that literally means "chest" and indicates the person presiding over a council, sitting at its centre or occupying its most prominent position. In the early Islamic era, this title was used for religious scholars. In the Mamluk era, it was used to refer to chief merchants, the heads or masters of a certain craft, or chief officials of the sultan's entourage, such as the chief architect, or the supervisor of the warehouses. (H. al-Basha, *Alqāb*, 377–378).

737 Ismāʿīl b. Muḥammad b. Yāqūt, the *khawāja* Majd al-Dīn al-Sallāmī (d. 743 AH/1342 AD). *Khawāja* is an originally Persian word that is used to mean: "teacher, writer, merchant, shaykh or master." Ismāʿīl was the *tājir al-khāṣṣ* during the era of Sultan al-Nāṣir Muḥammad. He used to travel to the Mongol lands and come back with slaves and other merchandise. He was also an ambassador, who contributed to the accomplishment of a peace treaty between the Mamluks and the Mongols. Sultan al-Nāṣir sent him on assignments abroad, which he carried out successfully and was therefore generously compensated by the sultan. He lived a rather luxurious life and enjoyed bestowals. He was born in al-Sallāmiyya village in Mosul, Iraq and was buried in his tomb in the cemetery outside Bāb al-Naṣr. He used to live in Darb al-Sallāmī, which was named after him, in Bāb al-ʿĪd Plaza. At the time of al-Maqrīzī, this *darb* included Bāb al-ʿĪd Gate. In modern times, it was taken up by Qaṣr al-Shawk Street. (Al-Maqrīzī, *Khiṭaṭ*, Vol. 2, 459–460, Hasan al-Basha, *Alqāb*, 279–280 and M. Shams, *Nujūm*, Vol. 4, 53 fn. 3).

738 Tabriz in present day Azerbaijan.

739 Al-ʿUmarī, *Masālik*, Vol. 3, 334–335.

740 Another work by Ibn Faḍl Allah al-ʿUmarī (d. 749 H/1348 AD): *Al-Taʿrīf bi al-Muṣṭalaḥ al-Sharīf* (Instruction on the Honourable Protocol); a book on the principles of state administration and writing protocols.

741 That is, the metropolis.

742 This is the introduction made by al-ʿUmarī in *al-Taʿrīf* of his section on the regions of each Islamic kingdom and their cities and citadels. It appears that, since he found Cairo the greatest metropolis, he felt obliged to write such an introductory apology for not considering it the capital of all Islamic regions and kingdoms. His last statement about the canals pouring into one river or sea (*baḥr*) is but metaphorical. (See Shihāb al-Dīn b. Faḍl Allah al-ʿUmarī, *Al-Taʿrīf bi-l-Muṣṭalaḥ al-Sharīf* (Cairo, 1895), 172–173).

743 Al-ʿUmarī, *Masālik* (2010), Vol. 3, 334.

744 Ibn ʿAbd al-Ẓāhir, *Khiṭaṭ*, 20.

THE THIRD SEAT OF GOVERNMENT

The Citadel

Pronounced "al-Qalʿa" (The Citadel) and referred to as "Qalʿat al-Jabal" (The Citadel of the Mountain), it is the seat of the sultan and the center of his kingdom. Bahā' al-Dīn Qarāqūsh, the *ṭawāshī*, mentioned earlier, built it for Sultan al-Malik al-Nāṣir Ṣalāḥ al-Dīn Yūsuf b. Ayyūb. It is located in between the exterior of Cairo, Muqattam Mountain, and Fustat and what is beyond it – that is the cemetery, which is connected with the buildings of Cairo, and the cemetery.[745] Its length and width were mentioned earlier in the section on Fustat. The Citadel [stands] above an elevated part of Muqattam Mountain's sections,[746] where some of [its areas] are on higher locations than others.

745 Al-Qalqashandī is probably referring to the two major cemeteries of his time: al-Qarāfa al-Kubrā (the Greater Cemetery) and al-Qarāfa al-Ṣughrā (the Lesser Cemetery). The Greater Cemetery was the oldest Islamic cemetery to the east of Fustat, that is the south-west of the Citadel, while the Lesser Cemetery was a later development to the north-east of the Greater Cemetery, which clustered around the Mausoleum of al-Imām al-Shāfiʿī (built in 608 AH/1211 AD). (For more on the cemeteries and their developments see al-Maqrīzī, *Khiṭaṭ*, Vol. 3, 642–649, G. el-Kadi and A. Bonnamy, *Architecture*, and Hani Hamza, *The Northern Cemetery of Cairo* (Cairo, 2001)).

746 "*Nashaz 'āl*," (also elevated protrusion). In al-ʿUmarī's account: "a high protrusion called the Red Mountain (al-Jabal al-Aḥmar)." (Al-ʿUmarī, *Masālik*(2002), Vol. 3, 478).

Before it was constructed, the Citadel's location was taken up by mosques that the Fatimids had built, which included Rudaynī Mosque[747] that is [now] amidst the Sultanic women's quarters.[748]

Judge Muḥyi al-Dīn b. ʿAbd al-Ẓāhir said: My father told me: Al-Malik al-Kāmil offered me the position of the imam of this mosque, but I declined [the offer] because it was amidst the women's quarters.[749] Sultan Ṣalāḥ al-Dīn did not reside in the Citadel. It is said that his son, al-Malik al-ʿAzīz,[750] resided in the Citadel for a period of time, when his father was still alive, then he moved to Dār al-Wizāra.

Judge Muḥyi al-Dīn b. ʿAbd al-Ẓāhir said: My father told me: We used to climb up to the Citadel on Thursday nights, before it was inhabited, where we spent the nights watching [nature] in the same manner as we did in the pavilions (*jawāsiq*)[751] of the mountain and the Cemetery[752].[753]

747 Also "Sāriyat al-Jabal Mosque" and "The Mosque of Suleymān Pasha." This originally Fatimid mosque is located in the northeast of the Citadel. Abū Manṣūr Qasṭa, the Fatimid Governor of Alexandria built this mosque in 535 AH/1140 AD. Qasṭa was an Armenian slave-boy (*ghulām*) of al-Muẓaffar, son of Badr al-Jamālī, who was poisoned. He was a passionate reader who was most interested in histories and biographies, as well as a reasonable amir who tended to fairness. The mosque was also named after Abū al-Ḥasan ʿAlī b. Marzūq b. ʿAbd Allah al-Rudaynī (d. 540 AH/1145 AD), a religious scholar of jurisprudence, the Prophet's traditions and the interpretation of the Quran, who probably taught at the mosque and was its preacher (*khaṭīb*). When Qarāqūsh started building the Citadel, he incorporated this mosquein its walls to serve as one of the daily prayers mosque. The mosque incorporates a shrine that Qasṭa built, which includes his cenotaph and was probably dedicated to Sāriyat al-Jabal or Sīdī Sāriya, who was one of the Prophet's companions, therefore the mosque's common name. (Suad Maher, *Masājid Miṣr wa Awliyā'uhā al-Ṣāliḥūn* (Cairo, 1983), Vol. 5, 81–82, K. Azab, *Qal'a*, 175–178, D. Abouseif, *Architecture*, 158, al-Maqrīzī, *Khiṭaṭ*, Vol. 3, 38–40 and "Masjid Suleyman Pasha," http://archnet.org/sites/1548).

748 For more on the Fatimid mosques and other establishments that existed in this location before the Citadel was built, see al-Maqrīzī, *Khiṭaṭ*, Vol. 3, 34–40 and K. Azab, *Qal'a*, 55–58.

749 Ibn ʿAbd al-Ẓāhir, *Khiṭaṭ*, 132.

750 Al-ʿAzīz ʿUthmān was the son of Ṣalāḥ al-Dīn and Ayyubid ruler of Egypt from 589 AH/1193 AD to 595 AH/1198 AD. Ibn ʿAbd al-Ẓāhir makes the same remark, but says that it was al-Malik al-ʿĀdil, Ṣalāḥ al-Dīn's brother, who resided briefly in the Citadel. It is possible that both stayed for brief periods at the Citadel, however, the seat of the throne during the Ayyubid era prior to the reign of al-Kāmil was the House of the Vizierate (Dār al-Wizāra). (Ibn ʿAbd al-Ẓāhir, *Khiṭaṭ*, 131 and K. Azab, *Qal'a*, 70).

751 Pl. of the originally Persian *jawsaq*, meaning a pavilion, a small palace, or a fortress. (G. el-Kadi and A. Bonnamy, *Architecture*, 123–124 fn. 28).

752 That is the Greater Cemetery. There were eighteen of those *jawāsiq* in the Greater Cemetery during the Fatimid era. They were "usually built on high ground" to offer "a panoramic view." They were places for leisurely walks as well as meditation and prayers. Historical accounts of medieval Egypt indicate that since the Fatimid era and onwards, cemeteries were places for leisure as well as visiting the dead, places were life and death coincided. This was partly an ancient Egyptian inheritance or inspiration, where "regular extended stays in the cemetery" were customary, as well as, indeed, an old human practice in many other Muslim and non-Muslim lands. (G. el-Kadi and A. Bonnamy, *Architecture*, 14–15 & 123–124 fn. 28).

753 Ibn ʿAbd al-Ẓāhir, *Khiṭaṭ*, 131.

The first ruler to reside in the Citadel was al-Malik al-Kāmil Muḥammad b. al-ʿĀdil Abū Bakr b. Ayyūb, who moved from the Fatimid palace[754] to the Citadel in the year 604 AH/1207 AD. Since then, the Citadel has been the sultanic residence.[755]

One of the strange [anecdotes] related [about the Citadel] is that Sultan Ṣalāḥ al-Dīn once went up to it with his brother al-ʿĀdil Abū Bakr and told him: "This citadel was built for your sons." Al-ʿĀdil was saddened to hear that and Ṣalāḥ al-Dīn saw his sadness, so he said: "You did not understand what I meant. I meant to say that I am clever, so I shall not have clever children, while you are not, so your children will be clever." Al-ʿĀdil was pleased [with this explanation] and what Ṣalāḥ al-Dīn said came true, for the Citadel remained uninhabited until al-ʿĀdil became the sultan of Egypt and Syria. Then he appointed his son, al-Malik al-Kāmil Muḥammad, Viceroy of Egypt, so he resided in the Citadel.[756]

The author of *Masālik al-Abṣār* mentioned that the first to reside in the Citadel was al-ʿĀdil Abū Bakr,[757] but when the [above-]mentioned al-Kāmil resided in it, he showed concern for it, took interest in its construction, and built towers in it, such as al-Burj al-Aḥmar[758] (the Red Tower), and others.

Towards the end of the year 682 AH/1284 AD, Sultan al-Malik al-Manṣūr Qalāwūn built a great tower in the Citadel, next to Bāb al-Sirr al-Kabīr (The Great Secret Gate),[759] to which he added beautifully built rooms with balconies that had

754 Possibly meaning Dār al-Wizāra.

755 The Citadel was the seat of the throne since then and until the nineteenth century, "except for the short period when Sultan al-Ṣāliḥ Najm al-Dīn Ayyūb (r. 637 AH/ 1240 AD to 647 AH/1249 AD) resided in his own citadel on al-Rawḍa Island," which will be referred to later. (Tarek Abdelhamid, "*The Citadel of Cairo in the Ayyubid Period*," in *Creswell Photographs Re-examined: New Perspectives on Islamic Architecture*, ed. Bernard O'Kane (Cairo, 2009), 6).

756 See also Ibn ʿAbd al-Ẓāhir, *Khiṭaṭ*, 130–131.

757 Al-ʿUmarī, *Masālik* (2010), Vol. 3, 330.

758 Al-Burj al-Aḥmar (the Red Tower) was a tower near al-Bāb al-Mudarraj, one of the Citadel's gates, located along the western walls of the northern enclosure of the Citadel. The Red Tower was built by al-Kāmil and renewed by al-Ẓāhir Baybars in 659 AH/1260 AD. (K. Azab, *Qal'a*, 72–73).

759 The Great Secret Gate which "opened into the southern enclosure (of the Citadel) facing the Iwān al-Kabīr and was used only by the sultan and official guests." It was "the ceremonial entry to the palatial complex on official occasions." This gate is no longer extant, but based on historical accounts it is concluded to have stood "near the present day Burj al-Wasṭānī," built by Muhammad Ali Pasha (r. 1220 AH/1805 – 1264 AH/1848 AD), "on the northwestern side of the southern enclosure."Bāb al-Sirr is also an architectural term used in the sources to probably denote "any private door reserved for the family as opposed to a main door for visitors." (Nasser Rabbat, *The Citadel of Cairo: A New Interpretation of Royal Mamluk Architecture* (Leiden, 1995), 66–67 & 120).

festive marble and delightful ornamentation.[760] Qalāwūn resided in it in Ṣafar[761] of the year 683 AH/1284 AD.[762]

Sultan al-Malik al-Nāṣir Muḥammad b. Qalāwūn built three buildings in the Citadel, which perfected its image, and for which he deserved [to be considered] as its rightful builder, more than its founder:

The first is al-Qaṣr al-Ablaq[763] (Al-Ablaq Palace), where the sultan generally sits[764] [for audience]. It is where he receives his amirs and private retinue (*khawāṣṣ*).[765] Sultan al-Ashraf Sha'bān b. Ḥusayn introduced a sitting hall (*maq'ad*)[766] to this palace, in the side opposite the sultanic stables, which came out to be extremely delightful and beautiful.

760 This is al-Burj al-Manṣūrī (Tower of al-Manṣūr), which al-Manṣūr Qalāwūn built in 1283 AD next to Bāb al-Sirr al-Kabīr. Similar royal towers with the same *mushtarafāt* (rooms with balconies or as N. Rabbat translates it: rooms with a view) were erected in the Citadel, namely Burj al-Zāwiya by al-Ẓāhir Baybars, prior to al-Burj al-Manṣūrī, and Burj al-Rafraf by al-Ashraf Kahlīl, Qalāwūn's son. Al-Ẓāhir Baybars is reported to have built *rawāshin* (sing. *rawshan*, Persian for light, window or balcony) coming out of Burj al-Zāwiya. This is why it may be assumed that Qalāwūn was inspired to construct his tower similarly. Al-Burj al-Manṣūrī burned down in 715 AH/1315 AD. It was probably "located somewhere along the northeastern wall" of the southern royal enclosure of the Citadel. (N. Rabbat, *Citadel*, 141–143, Ibn Taghrī Birdī, *Nujūm*& M. Shams, Vol. 7, 168–169 & 169 fn. 1, and K. Azab, *Qal'a*, 91).

761 Second month of the Hijri Calendar.

762 This would mean that Qalāwūn moved from the royal residence to the tower, an event that seems only scarcely mentioned by historians and based on a single source. (N. Rabbat, *Citadel*, 142).

763 *Balaq* in Arabic is a word that refers to the combination of the white and black colours. *Ablaq* was an architectural decorative method used extensively in the Mamluk era, and inherited from the Ayyubids, which entailed the use of white and black stone or marble in an alternative arrangement. Al-Qaṣr al-Ablaq was the palace located in the western sultanic section of the Citadel, which was the constant seat of the throne during the Mamluk era, except when the sultan sat at the iwan for seeing to grievances. The palace, along with the iwan and the Mosque of al-Nāṣir Muḥammad, stood in proximity to constitute the most important royal elements of the Citadel. The facade of this palace was originally located in the court in front of the current Mosque of Muḥammad 'Alī. Sultan al-Nāṣir Muḥammad built this palace under the influence of al-Ablaq Palace of Damascus, which al-Ẓāhir Baybars built in 665 AH/1267 AD, and where al-Nāṣir stayed when he set out with his army to resist the Mongol attack in 713 AH/1313 AD. When al-Nāṣir returned to Egypt and ordered the establishment of al-Ablaq Palace in the Citadel of Cairo. Historians provide detailed descriptions of this palace and explain that it was used for the sultan's councils of governance, which were held every day of the week except for Mondays and Thursdays when he sat at the iwan for grievances. (K. Azab, *Qal'a*, 117–120).

764 *Yajlis* (to sit), in this context, for assemblies and meetings (See *majlis*).

765 These were the close, private or special elite entourage. The *khawāṣṣ* (also, *khāṣṣa*) were "the privileged class composed of caliph or sultan's kin, amirs, high officials, and wealthy merchants." *Khāṣṣa* is also used to denote "the private domains owned by caliphs, sultans or amirs." (Sato Tsugitaka, *State and Rural Society in Medieval Islam: Sultans, Muqta's, and Fallahun* (Leiden, 1997), 248).

766 The term means: the seating place or the place where one sits. "The word is usually translated as loggia, but in the Mamluk context it is a particular type of loggia with an arcaded opening." (N. Rabbat, *Citadel*, 212).

The second is al-Iwān al-Kabīr (The Great Iwan),[767] in which the sultan sits for audience on procession days for public service and establishing justice among his subjects.

The third is Jāmiʿ al-Khuṭba[768] (The Sermon Mosque), where the sultan prays the Friday Prayers (*jum'a*).

These three buildings will be described in detail later.

The Citadel has walls, towers, wide courtyards, many buildings and three entrance gates.[769]

The first gate is the one towards the cemetery and Muqattam Mountain, which is the gate least used and most difficult to reach.[770]

The second is Bāb al-Sirr[771] (The Secret Gate), which is used only by high-ranking amirs and the state's private [officials] (*khawāṣṣ*), such as the vizier, confidential scribe (*kātib al-sirr*)[772] and their likes. It is reachable via al-Ṣuwwa, which is the remaining section of the elevated part on which the Citadel is built, towards the direction of Cairo. To reach the gate, one takes the winding path by the northwestern walls of the Citadel.[773] The gate's entrance is in the direction opposite the Great Iwan, where the sultan sits for audience on procession days.

767 Al-Nāṣir Muḥammad built al-Iwān al-Kabīr, which functioned as a House of Justice (Dar al-ʿAdl), over two stages, in 715 AH/1315 AD and 735 AH/1334 AD. Sultan Qalāwūn had built his Dār al-ʿAdl in the southern enclosure of the Citadel. The first son to rule after him, al-Ashraf Khalīl, demolished his father's iwan and built his own in its place, which was used as a House of Justice. Al-Nāṣir Muḥammad then replaced this iwan when he came to power. Sources provide detailed architectural and decorative descriptions for al-Nāṣir's iwan, which was one of his royal buildings at the Citadel. (K.Azab, *Qal'a*, 107–112).

768 The Mosque of al-Nāṣir Muḥammad at the Citadel, which he built in 718 AH/1318 AD to replace the smaller original congregational mosque of the Citadel. (K. Azab, *Qal'a*, 100–107, D. Abouseif, *Architecture*, 108–110, and "Masjid al-Sultan al-Nasir Muhammad ibn Qalawun," http://archnet.org/sites/2737).

769 For the gates and walls of the Citadel see also N. Rabbat, *Citadel*, K. Azab, *Qal'a*, 55–99, D. Abouseif, *Architecture*, 78–85 and T. Abdelhamid, "Citadel," 1–41.

770 The gate referred to here is known as Bāb al-Qarāfa or Bāb al-Jabal, which was located in the eastern walls of the Northern Enclosure of the Citadel, facing the Fustat Cemetery. It was built during the era of Sultan Ṣalāḥ al-Dīn and an Ottoman gate stands bearing the same name today, which is either the same gate in a form much changed over the years, or a gate built nearby, though not at the same location. (K. Azab, *Qal'a*, 85–86 & Fig. 16, N. Rabbat, *Citadel*, 68 and T. Abdelhamid, "Citadel," 2–3 Fig. 1.1).

771 This is the Bāb al-Sirr al-Kabīr mentioned above. A gate called Bāb al-Sirr, undated and presently blocked, is located near Burj al-Ḥaddād, which is in the north-eastern corner of the Citadel. This Bāb al-Sirr may have been especially used for exit by the defence forces of the Citadel. (K. Azab, *Qal'a*, 88) However, this is not the one al-Qalqashandī is referring to here, because it does not fit the description.

772 The royal confidential scribe who headed the Chancery Bureau, see Glossary.

773 Al-Qalqashandī uses the term *baḥrī*, which, in Egypt, would normally simply mean the northern direction. Nasser Rabbat explains that since the term is used here to indicate the direction of *baḥr al-Nīl* from the Citadel, therefore the wall referred to would be the northwestern wall. (N. Rabbat, *Citadel*, 67).

This gate remains closed except when opened to admit in or see out an entitled person.

The third is the Citadel's largest gate, which is used for the entrance by the rest of the amirs[774] and all other people. It is reachable from above al-Ṣuwwa mentioned earlier. One ascends a stair of uniform steps and reaches the gate's entrance at the beginning of the eastern side of the Citadel.[775] Through this gate, one reaches a rectangular court, which leads to a lofty vestibule (*durkāh*)[776] where the amirs sit until they are permitted to enter. To the south of this vestibule are:

- **Dār al-Niyāba**[777] (the House of Viceroyship), where the Plenipotentiary Viceroy (*al-nā'ib al-kāfil*)[778] sits [for audience], if there is one;
- **Qā'at al-Ṣāḥib**[779] (the Vizier's Hall), where the vizier and the state scribes sit;
- **Dīwān al-Inshā'**[780] (the ChanceryBureau), where the confidential scribe and the scribes of his bureau sit,
- **Dīwān al-Jaysh**[781] (the Army Bureau),

as well as other sultanic bureaus.

In the centre of the main wall of this vestibule is a door called Bāb al-Qulla,[782] which leads to wide corridors.[783] A door lies to the left of the person entering

774 That is, other than high-ranking amirs.

775 This is Bāb al-Mudarraj (the Stairway Gate), which was located at the northwestern corner of the northern enclosure of the Citadel. It was the main public entrance of the Citadel from the city, which was reachable via a stairway carved in rocks. The gate was built in Sultan Ṣalāḥ al-Dīn's era (579 AH/1184 AD), renewed by Sultan al-Nāṣir Muḥammad in 710 AH/1310 AD, and restored by Burji Mamluk sultans in second half of the 8th century AH/15th century AD and in 905 AH/1500 AD. The remains of this Ayyubid gate are now included within the latter Ottoman. (N. Rabbat, *Citadel*, 28–29 & 67).

776 "Canopied entrance or vestibule." (N. Rabbat, *Citadel*, 79).

777 It was built by Sultan Baybars and renovated by Sultan Qalāwūn. "The Dār al-Niyāba was the organizational focus of the administrative area with other structures intended to house state functions." (N. Rabbat, *Citadel*, 114, & 140–141 and see Glossary).

778 See Glossary.

779 This is the residence of the vizier (same function as Dār al-Wizāra).(Al-Baqli, *Ta'rīf*, 267).

780 See Glossary.

781 See Glossary.

782 This was the gate of the keep in the south-western side of the Citadel's northern military or janissary enclosure, which served as an access between the two enclosures of the Citadel. There is no confirmed date of construction for this gate, but it may have been built by Sultan al-Ẓāhir Baybars. Bāb al-Qulla "was the sole entrance for commoners and soldiers to the sultan's southern enclosure during the day. It was closed at night to isolate the palaces from the outside, a custom that may have been copied from Fatimid practices in the Qaṣr al-Sharqī (Eastern Palace) in Cairo." Sultan al-Nāṣir Muḥammad rebuilt the gate, "enlarged its vestibule," and added a new second door inside it in 720 AH/1320 AD. The gate was renewed in the era of Muhammad Ali in 1242 AH/1827 AD. (N. Rabbat, *Citadel*, 29, 111–112, 119,188 K. Azab,*Qal'a*, 168–169 & Fig. 16 & 18).

783 Or passages: *dahālīz*, sing. *dihlīz*.

through these corridors that leads to al-Khuṭba Mosque, mentioned above, which is one of the greatest, most beautiful, festive and decorated mosques. It is huge and tall, its floor is covered with excellent marble and its ceilings are lined with gold. There is a dome in the middle of the mosque, behind which is a *maqṣūra* where the sultan prays the Friday prayers. This *maqṣūra* and the riwaqs that incorporate it are curtained by perfectly made iron windows. The mosque's court is surrounded by riwaqs, and its exterior leads to Bāb al-Sitāra (Gate of the Curtain)[784] and the women's quarters.

At the centre of the main wall of the above-mentioned corridors is a [square] platform (*maṣṭaba*)[785] upon which sits the Commander of the Mamluks (*muqaddamal-mamālīk*),[786] and at which is the entrance of Bāb al-Sirr. Next to that is a corridor leading to a yard.[787] Entering this yard, one faces the door of the Great Iwan mentioned above, which is a grand unparalleled iwan of high structures, wide courts and great columns. It has grand, perfectly made iron windows and the centre of its main wall is the throne (*sarīr al-mulk*),[788] which is an elevated marble minbaron which the sultan sits for audience on the days of great processions upon the advent of royal ambassadors and the like.

One exits this iwan to find a pleasant yard to the right, which includes the gate of al-Ablaq Palace, mentioned above. There are built, raised seats (*maṣātiab*)[789] to the sides of this yard, which are used for seating the amirs of private [sultanic] retinue (*khwāṣṣ al-umarā'*)[790] before they go inside for service (*khidma*).[791] One enters

784 This gate's name first appears in the sources towards the end of the reign of Sultan al-Ẓāhir Baybars. It marked the threshold of the private sultanic quarters, where the women resided and were "symbolically veiled behind the curtain (*sitāra*), which may or may not have existed literally." There was an actual gate in this area, which was called Bāb al-Sā'āt (Gate of the Hours). This section, along others of the Citadel, was changed over time, in the Mamluk era particularly during the reign of Sultan al-Nāṣir Muḥammad. In the era of al-Nāṣir Muḥammad, this gate was located to the east of Bāb al-Qulla, connecting al-Qaṣr al-Ablaq, from its northern side, with the women's quarters. (N. Rabbat, *Citadel*, 180 & 286 Fig. 47).

785 Pl. *maṣaṭib*, also platforms.See N. Rabbat, *Citadel*, 108 & 112.

786 Commander of the Mamluks, see Glossary.

787 Al-Qalqashandī uses the term *sāḥa*, which can be translated as "yard." Nasser Rabbat describes it as "the square in front of the Iwān al-Kabīr." (N. Rabbat, *Citadel*, 120).

788 See also Glossary: "*martaba*" and "*takht al-mulk*".

789 Plural of *maṣṭaba*.

790 See note above and Glossary for *khaṣṣa*.

791 *Khidma* means "service," and it referred to being in the caliph's or sultan's audience (the *ḥaḍra*), and therefore in his service. The term *khidma* was also used to mean saluting the caliph or sultan upon being in his presence, using a certain protocol of gestures, such as kissing the floor, kissing the sovereign's hand or feet, or bowing, or by mere salutation (*salām*). This protocol of salutation and gestures changed in specifics over time, depending on who was more favoured, since some gestures seem to have been regarded as a higher privilege than others, and apparently according to what the sovereign deemed suitable. These gestures were signs of obedience and compliance, salutation and homage, and refusing to perform them was a declaration of insubordination. Being in the *khidma* also entailed specific codes of behaviour,

the palace gate to great corridors of renowned grandeur that lead to the mentioned palace. The palace is one of great construction and high elevation. It has two iwans to the north and south, with the larger one being the northern. The iwans overlook the sultanic stables and from them, one can see the Horses' Market,[792] Cairo, Fustat and their towns, up to the Nile and what is beyond it: the villages of Giza, the mountain, and beyond. A marble pulpit, like the one in the Great Iwan, stands in the centre of the main wall of northern iwan. Sometimes the sultan sits on it at the times of service (*khidma*), which will be mentioned later.[793]

The second iwan is the southern iwan which is only used for the exit of the sultan and his private retinue (*khawāṣṣ*) from Bāb al-Sirr to the Great Iwan outside the palace, where they sit for audience on the public procession days.

The aforementioned palace, [al-Ablaq Palace], leads to three interior palaces: one of them is at the same level as the great palace, [al-Ablaq Palace], and the other two are elevated and reached by stairs. All [three] palaces have iron windows that overlook the same view that the great palace, overlooks. The interior palaces lead to the women's quarters and the sultanic Curtains' Doors (*abwāb al-sutūr*).[794]

The exteriors of all these palaces are in black and yellow stones. Their interiors are framed with marble and gold plated stone[795] that is adorned with mother of pearl and all kinds of colourants. The ceilings are lined with gold and lapis lazuli, and are pierced with apertures of coloured Cyprus glass that look like the gems with which necklaces are made. All of their floors are covered with unparalleled marble that was transported from all countries of the world.

The author of *Masālik al-Abṣār* said: As for the sultanic houses, according to the correct reports I received, they have gardens, trees and settlement areas (*munākhāt*)[796] for marvellous animals, cows, sheep, birds and poultry.[797]

such as standing at particular places according to position and status, and not talking to others to show complete attention to the sovereign. The *khidma* was not only a presence in the sovereign's court, but was also a meeting between the amirs, the men of the state, and the caliph or sultan, where they discussed the matters that needed to be presented to the him, and was therefore mainly a courtly meeting. (Sa'id Ashour, *Al-Mujtama' al-Miṣrī fī 'Aṣr Salāṭīn al-Mamālīk* (Cairo, 1992), 85–86 and Paula Sanders, *Ritual,Politics and the City in Fatimid Cairo* (Albany, 1994), 15, 18, 19, 143, 144 & 145).

792 This is the Horses Market (Sūq al-Khayl), which was first established by the Fatimids and was located in place of the present day al-Rifā'ī Mosque (1869–1912), in Ṣalāḥ al-Dīn Square, below the Citadel. (M. al-Shishtawi, *Mayādīn*, 8–9).

793 For detailed description of al-Qaṣr al-Ablaq's plan, see N. Rabbat, *Citadel*, 200–225 and and K. Azab, *Qal'a*, 117–120).

794 The Curtain Doors: *Sitāra* or curtain, was a term used to refer to royal or noble women, denoting the curtain hung on their doors to ensure their privacy. (Al-Baqli, *Ta'rīf*, 178).

795 "*Al-Faṣṣ al-mudhahhab*"; "*faṣṣ*" is a "lobe" or the "stone" or "gem" set in a ring. The term may, therefore, refer to a lobe-shaped stone.

796 Sing. *munākh*. (See Glossary).

797 Al-'Umarī, *Masālik* (2010), Vol. 3, 332.

Outside these palaces are large barracks (*ṭibāq*)[798] for the Sultanic Mamluks (*al-mamālīk al-sulṭāniyya*).[799] There are also large houses for the amirs of the private [sultanic] retinue (*khawāṣṣ al-umarā'*) from among the Commanders of Thousands (*muqaddamīn al-ulūf*),[800] and other amirs of grand status from the *ṭablakhānāh*[801] and Amirs of Tens (*umarā' al-'ashara*),[802] as well as other amirs who were no longer considered of the *khāṣṣakiyya*,[803] and [thus] came to belong to the *barrāniyyūn*.[804]

It also includes houses and residences for many people, as well as a food market, and vendors move around selling precious weapons and cloths there too.

The Citadel, although built on a mountain and being on high ground, has a flowing water well that is drilled in the rock. The aforementioned Bahā' al-Dīn Qarāqūsh was the one who drilled this well when he built the Citadel. This well is one of the most amazing wells; at its bottom are waterwheels turned by cows. These waterwheels transfer the water to the middle [level of the well], where there are other waterwheels also turned by cows that transfer the water to the upper level. There is a pathway connecting the well to the water [source] and the cows reach its water via a passage within this pathway, and all that is carved in rock and not built.

Judge Muḥyi al-Dīn b. ʿAbd al-Ẓāhir said: I heard a shaykh relating that when the well was drilled, its water was found to be non-salty, so Qarāqūsh or his deputies wanted to increase its flow. They enlarged the hole they drilled in the

798 *Ṭibāq* are floors and in this context they refer to the Sultanic Barracks, see later.

799 Mamluks that were bought and raised by the sultan, to later be set free, or ones whom he employed. (See Glossary).

800 A category of high-ranking amirs, see Glossary.

801 A category of high-ranking amirs, see Glossary.

802 A category of high-ranking amirs, see Glossary.

803 These were a group of mamluks who comprised the sultan's private mamluks, hence their name (*khāṣṣ*: private). The *Khāṣṣakiyya* were normally chosen by the sultan from the mamluks he bought at a young age, so as to make sure that they grew up in loyalty and obedience to their master, and that they are deserving of becoming his personal guards. This group of mamluks was rather privileged, for they were closest to the sultan in his seclusion and travels, entered to his presence unannounced, and were assigned with honourable missions, such as the procession and travel of the Kaʿba's covering (*maḥmil*, see Glossary). They received the most generous grants and gifts, and were known for their elegance and grace in costumes and riding. They attended the royal audience of service (*khidma*)carrying their swords and wearing their embroidered clothes. The number of mamluks in this category was not defined, and was rather a matter of the sultan's preference. (Ibn Taghrī Birdī, *Nujūm*, Vol. 7, 179–180; al-Baqli, *Ta'rīf*, 114; T. Abdelhamid, *Jaysh*, 37–41; S. Ashour, *'Aṣr*, 432–433, and M. Dahman, *Mu'jam*, 66).

804 Al-Barrāniyyūn," also "al-Barrāniyya" and "al-Kharjiyya," "the outer" or "the exterior" mamluks as opposed to al-Juwwāniyyūn or al-Juwwāniyya (the inner/insider), which was another name for the Khāṣṣakiyya. Al-Barrāniyyūn were the amirs and mamluks who did not belong to the Khāṣṣakiyya, which means that they were not close to the sultan, might not have been bought by him, and were not among his special and private retinue. (M. Shams, *Nujūm*, Vol. 11, 47 fn. 3 & 51 fn. 1 and S. Ashour, *'Aṣr*, 417).

mountain; however, a salty water spring came out of it and changed [the quality] of freshness of the water.[805]

It is also said that its ground is at the same level as the land of Birkat al-Fīl. This well is used by the Citadel's residents for all purposes except drinking. They rather drink the non-salty water carried to the Citadel from the Nile in water leather bags[806] on the backs of camels and mules, in addition to the Nile water that is run in channels to the sultanic palaces, and the houses of the high-ranking amirs that neighbour the sultan's residences. [These channels are fed] by the transporting waterwheels and the wheels[807] that are turned by cows, carrying water from one place to another until it reaches the Citadel and enters palaces and houses at a height of almost 500 cubits.[808]

Sultan al-Malik al-Ẓāhir Barqūq built a new, grand cistern in the Citadel that is filled annually at the time of the Nile [rise] with the water transported to the Citadel by the transporting waterwheels.[809] Barqūq allocated a *sabīl*[810] for supplying waterin the vestibule (*durkāh*) that includes the House of Viceroyship (Dār al-Niyāba) [to be fed from this cistern], which was a great relief for the people.

The Citadel overlooks a huge square (*maydān*) below it,[811] from [the area] beyond the sultanic palaces. This *maydān* separates the sultanic stables from the Horses' Market, is covered with green grass and is of a vast area, around which the eyes travel. It has many species of beautiful beasts to look at, and the private (*khawāṣṣ*) of the sultanic horses are tied-up at it to be used for excursions. The sultan prays the two ʿĪd prayers there, as will be described later. The sultanic horses

805 Ibn ʿAbd al-Ẓāhir, *Khiṭaṭ*, 19.

806 *Al-Rawāyā* (sing. *al-rāwiya*).

807 Most probably, the author uses the term "transporting water wheels" to refer to those carrying the water containers, while the "wheels" are the cogwheels that revolve on the axle.

808 The aqueduct built to supply water to the Citadel still stands partly today in the area of Fumm al-Khalīj in Miṣr al-Qadīma. The first aqueduct was built by Sultan Ṣalāḥ al-Dīn to the south of the one standing today, which was built by Sultan al-Nāṣir Muḥammad and later restored by Sultan Qanṣūh al-Ghūrī (r. 906 AH/1501 AD – 922 AH/1516 AD). Waterwheels were placed above the aqueduct, beasts of burden turned the waterwheels and water was raised in channels along a slight slope. The water then reached the numerous cisterns of the Citadel, "a total waterlift of more than one hundred meters." "There are remains of two other waterwheel complexes attached to the Citadel, one on the northeast side," (Sāqiyat Sāriya), "and the other on the southeast side with the name of al-Nāṣir Muḥammad carved on it." (D. Abouseif, *Architecture*, 81).

809 Both al-Maqrīzī and Ibn Taghrī Birdī also mention this cistern, where the latter states that it was opposite al-Iwān al-Kabīr. Barqūq also built a mill and a *kuttāb* in the Citadel. There were several other cisterns in the Citadel. (Al-Maqrīzī, *Sulūk*, Vol. 5, 447–448, Ibn Taghrī Birdī, *Nujūm*, Vol. 11, 238 and N. Rabbat, *Citadel*, 106, 114, 211 & 235).

810 A *sabīl* is a water reservoir that is used to distribute water for free, which is a recommended act of charity in Islam. Structurally, the *sabīl* is a building erected around an underground cistern, which is supplied with drinking water. The building overlooks the street through decoratively grilled windows and provides passersby with water using small containers or basins.

811 Maydān Taḥt al-Qalʿa (the Square Below the Citadel), presently called Ṣalāḥ al-Dīn Square. (M. Al-Shishtawi, *Mayādīn*, 7–10).

are displayed there at the Times of Grants (*awqāt al-iṭlāqāt*)[812] and at the times of arrival of bought and presented[813] [horses]. It may also be used for feeding the sultanic birds of prey. If the sultan wants to descend to it, he would exit the door of the palace iwan, ride from the stairs beyond it to the private [sultanic] horses' stable,[814] then ride down to the *maydān* with the amirs of the private [sultanic] retinue (*khawāṣṣ al-umarā'*) walking by him in his service (*khidma*). He would then return to the palace in the same manner.[815]

Judge Muḥiy al-Dīn b. ʿAbd al-Ẓāhir said in his *Khiṭaṭ*: This *maydān* and its surroundings were known before as "al-Maydān" (The Square), and it included the palace of Aḥmad b. Ṭūlūn, the house (*dār*) that he resided in and the areas known as al-Qaṭā'iʿ around it, as was mentioned earlier in the [section on the] neighbourhoods (*khiṭaṭ*) of Fustat. It remained as such until al-Malik al-Kāmil b. al-ʿĀdil b. Ayyūb built this square below the Citadel when he resided in it. Al-Kāmil made transporting waterwheels run to it from the Nile and dug three ponds by its side, which were filled up for watering it. Then thesquare ceased to be used for a while in his days, but was revived by his son, al-ʿĀdil. Later, al-Ṣāliḥ Najm al-Dīn Ayyūb showed great care for it by renewing another waterwheel for it and planting trees to its sides, which made it extremely beautiful. When al-Ṣāliḥ died, its condition gradually deteriorated until it was demolished in the year 650 or 651 AH/1252 or 1253 AD, in the days of al-Muʿizz Aybak al-Turkumānī. The waterwheels and the bridges (*qanāṭir*) were destroyed without a trace and [the situation] remained so until Sultan al-Malik al-Nāṣir Muḥammad b. Qalāwūn rebuilt it with the best construction and paved it with the most marvellous paving; and so it remains until now.[816]

812 See Glossary: "*iṭlāqāt*".

813 *Taqādum*, which although has the literal meaning of "becoming ancient or antique," in this context, it most probably stems from "*qaddama*" (to present; "*taqduma*" is "gift"), rather than "*qaduma*" (become ancient). Therefore, the term refers to the horses that were presented as gifts or offerings.

814 *Iṣṭabl al-khāṣṣ*. It should be noted that the Mamluk Sultanic Stables located near the palace at the Citadel were not mere stables. They were important establishments that along the Mamluk era included several buildings, such as: a royal loggia (*maq'ad*) which probably hosted a part of the horses' parade weekly processions, where the matters of the amirs, mamluks and *iqṭā'* were discussed; a house of military musical instruments (*ṭablakhānāh*, see Glossary); two mosques and residences for high-ranking amirs. (K. Azab, *Qal'a*, 178–182).

815 Al-Qalqashandī is referring to the two adjacent squares: Maydān al-Rumayla and Maydān Taḥt al-Qalʿa (Below the Citadel). Al-Rumayla Square was to the northwest of Taḥt al-Qalʿa Square. Al-Rumayla Square used to occupy the area bordered by the section of the Citadel's walls containing Bāb al-ʿAzab Gate (1168 AH/1754 AD) to its east; al-Rifāʿī Mosque, Sultan Ḥasan's Complex and al-Khalīfa Police Station to its west; Sikkat al-Maḥjar Street up to al-Rifāʿī Mosque to its north, and Muṣallā al-Mu'minī (built by amir Sayf al-Dīn Buktumur al-Mu'minī (d. 771 AH/1369 AD) and restored more than once until the early 10th century AH/16th century AD), along Mustafā Kāmil Museum and up to the south of Bāb al-ʿAzab Gate to its south. Taḥt al-Qalʿa Square occupied the area taken up today by Ṣalāḥ al-Dīn Square. (M. al-Shistawi, *Mayādīn*, 8–10, & 9 fn. 2).

816 See also Ibn ʿAbd al-Ẓāhir's account (*Khiṭaṭ*, 132), which al-Qalqashandī expands on above.

As for the al-Maydān al-Sulṭānī[817] (The Sultanic Square) in al-Lūq Neighbourhood, to which the sultan rides to play *kura*[818] on [the celebration of] the Faithfulness of the Nile (Wafā' al-Nīl), it was built by al-Malik al-Ṣāliḥ Najm al-Dīn Ayyūb.[819] Al-Ṣāliḥ established beautiful belvederes (*manāẓir*)[820] in it and installed [large kite-shaped] sheilds (*ṭawāriq*)[821] on its gate in the same way they

817 Also, "al-Maydān,".

818 A type of sport that was similar to polo. *Al-Kura* (the ball) was big and made of light material and the game entailed that it was thrown on the ground while the riding players, who formed two competing teams, tried to hit it, each using his *ṣawlajān* or *jūkān* (sceptre/mace or polo stick). A traveller during the Burji Mamluk era gave a description of the field, its division and how the game was played. The Arabs played this game and it was adopted by the Abbasids, who built special spacious courts for it, as well as a square (*maydān*) in Baghdad. Aḥmad b. Ṭūlūn was the first to establish a *maydān* for this sport in Islamic Egypt. The Fatimids, the Ayyubids and the Mamluks all practiced this sport, which was as much of a military training as it was a leisurely sport, for it required maximum control of the horse and excellent manoeuvring skills. The Mamluk sultans and amirs were particularly fond of this sport. Several squares around Cairo and Fustat were used for this sport, among other purposes. Historians also report that Sultan Baybars and other later Burji Mamluk sultans and amirs, played *kura* in the outskirts of Alexandria or by its sea. The sport was especially important for it had its recognized officials, tools, animals and processions. A banquet was offered following the game, usually by the defeated team if the sultan was not generous enough to offer it himself, even when he wins. The sultan also normally bestowed costumes of honour on the participants, some of their followers, and other amirs and state officials after the game. Sultans were keen on hitting the first ball, announcing the beginning of the games season, as well as indicating the end of the season themselves too. A big audience of fans and players watched the games. (Lotfi Nassar, *Wasā'il al-Tarfīhfī 'Aṣr Salāṭīn al-Mamālīk fī Miṣr* (Cairo, 1999), 243–259).

819 Al-Maydān al-Sulṭānī or al-Maydān al-Nāṣirī was built by al-Nāṣir Muḥammad b. Qalāwūn. Al-Maydān al-Ṣāliḥī, which Sultan al-Ṣāliḥ Najm al-Dīn built in 643 AH/1245AD, occupied the area bordered by Qaṣr al-Nīl Street to the north, Muḥammad Farīd Street to the east, al-Bustān Street to the south and Yūsuf al-Jundī Street to the west. When the Nile receded from its location opposite al-Maydān al-Ṣāliḥī, Sultan al-Ẓāhir Baybars established al-Maydān al-Ẓāhirī overlooking the Nile instead. Al-Maydān al-Ṣāliḥī was abandoned and its land was taken up as a *ḥikr* (that is, by ground-renting) to be used for building houses. Al-Maydān al-Ẓāhirī was located to the northeast of present day Taḥrīr Square, al-Maydān al-Ṣāliḥī was adjacent to al-Maydān al-Ẓāhirī, to its east, while al-Maydān al-Nāṣirī was to its southwest. (M. al-Shishtawi, *Mayādīn*, 87–88 & maps showing the three squares).

820 The *manāẓir* (sing. *manẓara*) of al-Maydān al-Ṣāliḥī were used as residences after the square was abandoned. A mamluk troupe resided in these *manāẓir* in 693 AH/1294 AD. (M. al-Shishtawi, *Mayādīn*, 88).

821 *Al-Ṭawāriq* "were wooden shields, originally used by the Crusaders and the Byzantines." They were of elongated forms with circular tops and single points for ends, a form that is described using the term "kite-shaped." These shields were big enough to be used for defence by the infantry and the riding horsemen. They were sometimes exceptionally decorated with gold enamel, painting with various dyes and drawing. Although some scholars define the *ṭawāriq* as other types of arms, such as swords or spears, the term most probably refers only to the shields described above. The term seems not to have appeared in Arabic primary sources before those contemporaneous with the Crusader wars. Some manuscripts show Fatimid soldiers using such shields. The etymological origin of the word is suggestive of a Latin source and Italian and French derivatives that indicate its meaning and its Arabic derivative. Putting these *ṭawāriq* on

were installed to the gates of fortresses and the like. These shields (*ṭawāriq*) remained installed on its gate until after [the year] 700 AH/1301 AD.[822] The section describing the [Mamluk] kingdom administration will explain the [protocol] of riding to this square (*maydān*) on processions.

And [as for] the Citadel of al-Rawḍa, it was described earlier in the section on the *Khiṭaṭ* of Fustat.

Al-Qarāfa (The Cemetery)

Connected to those three seats of rule,[823] and attached to them, is al-Qarāfa,[824] which is the cemetery of their dead. It is a huge burial ground extending over the foot of Muqattam and located between Muqattam, Fustat, and a part of Cairo. It extends from the Citadel, mentioned earlier, and southwards up to al-Ḥabash Pond and its surroundings. The reason for using this land as a graveyard was that related by Ibn ʿAbd al-Ḥakam,[825] that al-Layth b. Saʿd said: Al-Muqawqas asked ʿAmr b. al-ʿĀṣ to sell him the foot of Muqattam for 70,000 dinars. ʿAmr was surprised by this and wrote to the Prince of the Faithful, ʿUmar b. al-Khaṭṭāb, about the matter. ʿUmar wrote to him saying: Ask him why he made such an offer for a land that cannot be planted, from which no water can be extracted and is of no use. ʿAmr asked al-Muqawqas who replied: We find it described in books as having the plants of Paradise. ʿAmr wrote to ʿUmar b. al-Khaṭṭāb reporting that, so ʿUmar sent him saying: "I see no plants of Paradise except the believers; therefore, bury the Muslims who died ahead of you in it and do not sell it for anything." Al-Muqawqas [objected to] ʿAmr saying: This was not what you promised us. ʿAmr then allocated[826] a piece [of land] to them for Christian burials, which is [the land] near al-Ḥabash Pond. The first Muslim to be buried at the foot of Muqattam

a gate was either for actual defense or as an announcement of some of the war trophies acquired by the sultan and his army. (See Abd al-Nasir Yasin, *Al-Asliḥa 'abr al-'Uṣūr al-Islāmiyya* (Cairo, 2007), 267–268 & 276).

822 Other sources mention that the gate itself, or the door (*bāb*) remained in its place until after the year 740 AH/1340 AD. (M. al-Shistawi, *Mayādīn*, 88).

823 Fustat, Cairo and the Citadel

824 The Cemetery. The name "al-Qarāfa" originally did not denote the function of a cemetery, but the lesser and bigger cemeteries bearing this name got it from one of the clans of al-Maʿāfir tribe that was called Banū Qarāfa and had a neighbourhood (*khaṭṭ*) there. The present day connotation of the term "*qarāfa*" with any burial ground was not found in the works of al-Maqrīzī and contemporaneous historians. Words such as *maqābir* or *madāfin* were rather used to generally mean a cemetery. (H. Hamza, *Cemetery*, 20 and al-Maqrīzī, *Khiṭaṭ*, Vol. 3, 642 & 646–647).

825 ʿAbd al-Raḥman b. ʿAbd al-Ḥakam (d. 258/871) is the oldest historian of Islamic Egypt and its geographical divisions. (Z. al-Samarra'i, *Manhaj*, 108).

826 *Aqta'a*: to assign a segment of land.

was a man from al-Maʿāfir[827] [tribe] named ʿĀmir,[828] so it was said that this land became populated (*'amarat*).

It is related that Jesus and his mother passed by the foot of Muqattam during their journey, when he said: "Mother! This is the burial grounds of the people of Muḥammad, peace be upon him." [This cemetery] includes the tombs of prophets, such as the brothers of Joseph and others. It also includes the grave of Asia, the Pharaoh's[829] wife and the shrines of a group of people from the members of the House of the Prophet (*Āl al-bayt*);[830] Companions [of the Prophet] (*al-ṣaḥāba*); Followers [of the Prophet] (*al-tābi'ūn*);[831] religious scholars (*'ulamā'*);[832] ascetics,[833] and *awliyā'*.[834]

People built delightful buildings, pleasant belvederes (*manaẓir*) and marvellous palaces in this cemetery that are such pleasant sights.[835] It has congregational mosques, mosques, zawiyas, ribats and khanqahs. It is, in truth, a great city, but it has few residents.

827 A southern Arab tribe.

828 The literal meaning of the Arabic word is populous or inhabited. It is used as a name in good omen of prosperity and long life.

829 The Pharaoh of Egypt and his wife at the time of Prophet Moses, whose story is mentioned in the Quran.

830 Also, "*Ahl al-bayt*," a term used to refer to the family of the Prophet and his descendants, with different interpretations in the Sunni and Shiite doctrines. The Sunni interpretation encompasses all the Prophet's wives and descendants, sometimes extending to his clan and their descendants, while the Shiite one generally restricts the term to descendants from the line of Fāṭima and ʿAlī. (See Aliaa El Sandouby, "The Ahl al-bayt in Cairo and Damascus: The Dynamics of Making Shrines for the Family of the Prophet," (PhD Thesis, Universitiy of California, 2008), 28–39).

831 *Al-Tābi'ūn*, Muslims who have not met the Prophet, but have met, and were followers of, his companions.

832 Also, *ulama*.

833 *Zuhhād* (sing. *zāhid*), self-denying people who relinquish worldly pleasures.

834 Sing. *walī* or *waliy*, short for *waliy Allah*, Friend or Ally of God, meaning those who have attained a special spiritual closeness to Allah and are under His protection. The term is Quranic: "Behold! Verily on the friends of Allah there is no fear, nor shall they grieve." (Chapter of Yūnus, 10:62, http://corpus.quran.com/translation.jsp?chapter=10&verse=62). With the emergence of Sufism, the term came to apply to Sufi shaykhs and leaders, whose spiritual rankings are hierarchical. Various parts of the Islamic world have their own *awliyā'* and hierarchies, which may also differ along time.

835 "That invite the eyes to wander around them and please the mind with their view."

Part II

THE THIRD PURPOSE[836] ON THE REGULATION OF THE KINGDOM, OVER THREE STATUSES

836 This "Third Purpose" was not preceded by a first and a second as section titles, which could have been a mistake on part of the copiers of the manuscript. (*Ṣubḥ*, Vol. 3, 471 fn. 1).

THE FIRST STATUS

Rulers Appointed by the Caliphate until the end of the Ikshidid Dynasty

This was the status of the kingdom at the time of the rulers[837] [assigned by] the caliphs, from the [Islamic] conquest and up to the end of the Ikhshidid era. I am not well-informed of its regulation [during this era]. It appears that its viceroys and amirs at the time followed the same manner [of regulation] as the Arabs, until Aḥmad b. Ṭūlūn and his sons came to power and introduced royal regulation. However, most of Ibn Ṭūlūn's soldiers were Sudanese, to the extent that it is said that 12,000 of his soldiers were black. The Ikhshidid state followed suit until the end of its era.

837 *'ummal* (sing. *'āmil*).

THE SECOND STATUS

Status of the Egyptian Lands under the Fatimids

This is the status of the Egyptian Lands during the era of the Fatimid caliphs. The regulation of their kingdom is confined to three clauses.[838]

The First Clause

On Royal Instruments Especially [Used on] Grand Processions

They are of various kinds, including:

The Crown (al-tāj):[839] The [Fatimids] called it "The Honourable Crown" (*al-tāj al-sharīf*) and it was known as "The Wrapping of Veneration" (*shaddat al-waqār*).[840] It was a crown that the caliph rode with on the grand processions. It had a huge jewel, known as "The Matchless" (*al-yatīma*) that weighed seven dirhams[841] and was price-

838 The author ends up writing seven clauses. (*Ṣubḥ*, Vol. 3, 472 fn. 1)

839 The Fatimid crown was actually a royal turban decorated with precious stones. It was huge and had a specialized official responsible for wrapping it in a puffed and elongated shape around a *qalansuwa/qulunsuwa* (cloth or leather head cover). Historians of the early Fatimid era report various wrapping styles of the caliph's turban, depending on the material from which the turban's cloth was made, as well as the occasion. Later, the term "The Honourable Crown" (*al-tāj al-sharīf*) was used synonymously with "The Wrapping of Veneration" (*shaddat al-waqār*), which the caliph wore on grand occasions and processions. (A. Sayyid, *Tafsīr*, 388 and Ibn al-Ṭuwayr , *Nuzha*, 155–156 & 155 fn. 4).

840 P. Sanders translates "*shaddat al-waqār*" to "Winding of Majesty," which was the particular wrapping method and shape of the royal turban on grand processions and special occasions. This wrapping fashion was indeed venerated, for when the caliph wore it, flags were fluttered and people avoided talking or making any sound. (A. Sayyid, *Tafsīr*, 388, Ibn al-Ṭuwayr, *Nuzha*, 155–156 & 155 fn. 4 and P. Sanders, *Ritual*, 25).

841 The *dirham* was both a weight unit and a monetary coin. The exact measure of the *dirham* in the Mamluk era, which al-Qalqashandī would have used, was not constant. Evidence suggests that it fluctuated around the approximate value of 3 grams of weight, which was close to the

less. Around it were other less precious jewels. The caliph wore this crown instead of the turban on grand processions.

The Sovereignty Staff (qaḍīb al-mulk): This was a rod of a length of a handspan and a half, which was coverd with gold that is set with pearls and jewels. The caliph held this staff on grand processions.

The Private Sword (al-sayf al-khāṣṣ): This was the sword carried with the caliph on processions. It is said that it was made from a thunderbolt that fell and was acquired. The sword's ornament was of gold inlaid with jewels. It was put inside a gold-inscribed cover,[842] with only its hilt showing. One of the greatest amirs [was particularly assigned for] carrying this sword as the caliph rodeon procession.

The Inkwell (al-dawāt):[843] This was an inkwell made of gold and adorned with coral, which is [known for] its hardness and strength. It was wrapped in a white silk (*sharb*)[844] kerchief (*mindīl*)[845] and carried in front of the caliph during the processionby one of the Masters (*al-ustādhūn*).[846] It was placed between the caliph and his horse saddle. Later, it came to be carried by one of the esteemed equitables (*'udūl*).[847]

The Lance (al-rumḥ): This was a small lance kept in a cover that is inlaid with pearls. Its tip was enveloped with a golden ornament and it was carried by an especially assigned person.

value of the *dirham* according to Islamic Law: 2.97 grams. Al-Qalqashandī states that one *dirham* weight unit equals the weight of sixteen kernels of carob. As an officially minted coin, he describes it as mainly an alloy of two-thirds silver and one-third copper, which was produced as wholes and fractions that varied in types and value. (See *Ṣubḥ*, Vol. 3, 440 & 443).

842 *kharīṭa*, which means "leather case." The term was also used to refer to the caliphal treasury, whereby *ṣāḥib al-kharīṭa* was the same as *ṣāḥib bayt al-māl* (the Keeper of the Treasury). (al-Baqli, *Ta'rīf*, 117).

843 *Al-Dawāt* was the inkwell or the pen-box. Al-Qalqashandī lists seventeen writing tools, which were incorporated in a pen-box. Pen-boxes of al-Qalqashandī's time were made of metal, such as brass or steel or fine wood, such as ebony and sandalwood, and were adorned with inlay and ornamentation. The *miḥbara* (inkwell) was one of the main components of the *dawāt*, but it could also sometimes be carried separately. The terms *dawāt* and *miḥbara* were sometimes synonymously used to mean inkwell. In addition to the surviving Fatimid rock crystal inkwells, it seems that there were many precious pen-boxes kept in the Fatimid treasuries. (*Ṣubḥ*, Vol. 2, 430–472 and Eva Baer, *Metalwork in Medieval Islamic Art* (New York, 1983), 66–67).

844 Or linen, see Glossary.

845 See Glossary.

846 See Glossary.

847 *Al-'Udul* (sing. *'adl*: the just or equitable) were men of impeccable reputation, who held official positions. They were particularly known and deemed to be just or equitable witnesses, thus the title. (See Glossary: "*'adl*").

The Shield (al-daraqa):[848] This was a large leathern shield with golden [navel-shaped] ornaments (*kawābij*).[849] It is said that it belonged to Ḥamza,[850] the Prophet's uncle. With a silk cover on, it was carried in procession by a high, dignified amir.

The Hoof (al-ḥāfir):[851] This was a piece of red ruby that took the shape of a crescent. It weighed eleven *mithqāls*[852] and had no parallel in the world. It was elegantly sewn on a piece of silk and precious *dhubābī* emerald[853] rods formed a circle surrounding it. It was put on the face of the caliph's horse when he rode on processions.

The Parasol (al-miẓalla): It was carried above the caliph's head as he rode. It was a dome that took the shape of a tent [fixed] on a post, like the parasol that the sultan rides with nowadays. The parasol was [formed] of twelve triangular sections (*shawāzik*),[854] each one having the base-width of a handspan and a length of a three and one-third cubits. The apex of each *shawzak* was very small to allow for the tips of all twelve *shawāzik* to meet in a circle in the head of the post. The parasol's post was a lance (*qunṭāriyya*)[855] of beech wood that was coated with golden [cylindrical] tubes. In the uppermosttube, at [a length of] two-thirds of the post head, was a ring that protruded for a

848 The *daraqa* was a shield made wholly of leather. It was circular with a domed centre and was held by a handle on its inner side. (A. Yasin, *Asliḥa*, 257).

849 *Kawābij* is a plural term for a word derived from the Turkish word *göbek*, which means "navel," indicating a convex or concave ornament in the centre of the shield. In another context, *kawābij* is explained to be the plural of a term derived from another Turkish word: "*kopça*," which means a clasp, buckle, or a shoe clasp. (Ibn al-Ṭuwayir, Nuzha, 148 fn. 6 and Ahmad Iybish, *Dimashq fī 'Aṣr Salāṭīn al-Mamālīk: Mashāhid wa Aḥdāth min Nuṣūṣ Adab al-Riḥlāt al-'Arabiyya* (Damascus, 2005), 230 fn. 1).

850 Ḥamza b. 'Abd al-Muṭṭalib, uncle of the Prophet and one of the most prominent martyrs in Islam, whose conversion to the new religion was a significant support to the Prophet against the nonbelievers. Ḥamza was a nobleman and a remarkably brave warrior who earned the title "Asad Allah" or the 'Lion of Allah." He participated in the battles that the Muslim army fought before he was intentionally targeted and killed out of vengeance in the Battle of Uḥud (3 AH/625 AD).

851 It is reported that this ruby piece was originally a property of the Abbasid house that reached the Fatimids. (Ibn al-Ṭuwayir, Nuzha, 156 fn. 4).

852 The *mithqāl* was a term used synonymously with "weight," whether big or small, but was mostly applied to small weights. It was used to refer to the *dīnār* (a monetary coin), during the Umayyad era, when it was equivalent to one unit of gold (4.25 grams). (Al-Baqli, *Ta'rīf*, 297).

853 The *dhubābī* was a particular grade of emerald that was all green, without any traces of other colours, such as yellow or black. It was very glittery and was called *dhubābī* because its colour resembled that of big, green spring flies (*dhubāb*, sing. *dhubāba*). The *dhubābī* was the rarest and finest grade of emerald, which was believed to blind serpents if they looked at it, cure human eyesight defects if looked at for a long time and terminate epilepsy seizures if worn as a seal. (*Ṣubḥ*, Vol. 2, 104–105).

854 *Shawāzik* (sing. *shawzak*) is the term used by Ibn al-Ṭuwayr, al-Qalqashandī and others to refer to the triangular parts or panels forming the parasol.

855 *Qunṭāriyya* is derived from a Greek word (kontarion). It is a type of short lances made of a beech wooden body that ends in short, broad teeth, which looks like an axe. (Ibn al-Ṭuwayir, Nuzha, 151 fn. 2).

measure of the width of a thumb. This [protruding] ring pulled the tips of the *shawāzik* [together] in a golden ring and fell into the lance's head.[856] This parasol was highly respected for it was held above the head of the caliph. It was carried by one of the highest amirs.

Ibn al-Ṭuwayr said: One of the parasol's conditions was being of the same colour of the caliph's costume during the procession, and no other colour.[857]

The Flags (al-aʿlām): The most superior being the two banners known as "The Banners of Thankfulness" (*liwā'ay al-ḥamd*).[858] These were two long lances coated with golden [cylindrical] tubes up to their heads. [They carried] two banners at their tops made of white silk that is inscribed in gold. The banners were wrapped around the lances and not spread-out. These banners were brought out with the parasol to be held by two assigned amirs.

Of lesser level were two lances with solid,[859] golden crescents at their tips. Each crescent surrounded a lion made of red and yellow silk that had a ring in its mouth, into which the lance went opening them up and showing their shapes.[860] They were carried by two horsemen[861] from the Private Guards (*ṣibyān al-khāṣṣ*).[862]

856 This description of the parasol's mechanism is missing some details and includes a couple of spelling alterations that change the meaning considerably, which makes it difficult to understand. Ibn al-Ṭuwayr's explanation, which al-Qalqashandī copies, is more comprehensible. According to Ibn al-Ṭuwayr, the uppermost golden cylinder, the one that is beneath the head of the post or lance, includes a "*falaka*" (ring) that protrudes for a measure of the width of a thumb. The tips of the *shawāzik* are pulled together in a golden ring that falls, as if being hanged, into the head of the lance. The golden ring then meets the *falaka*, which prevents the parasol from collapsing down the post. Ibn al-Ṭuwayr then continues to provide a more exhaustive description of the parasol. In al-Qalqashandī's text, the word used for the ring is "*malaka*," but the editor of Subḥ notes that it could be "*falka*."Although "ring" is *falka*, rather than *falaka*, it would not be inaccurate to assume the same meaning. (*Ṣubḥ*, 473 & 473 fn. 1, Ibn al-Ṭuwayr, *Nuzha*, 157–158 and http://www.baheth.info/all.jsp?term=فلكة).

857 This tradition of unifying the colours seems to have been introduced in the 6th century AH/12th century AD, for earlier historians report that the colours of the costume and the parasol were different. (Ibn al-Ṭuwayir, Nuzha, 157 fn. 1& 177).

858 A Prophetic tradition (*ḥadith*) mentions the term *liwā' al-ḥamd* (Banner of Thankfulness) as the banner that Prophet Muḥammad holds on Resurrection Day, indicating that he is the master of all prophets and the intercessor to Allah. (Taqiy al-Dīn al-Maqrīzī, *Imtā' al-Asmā'bimā li-l-Nabiy min al-Aḥwāl wā al-Amwāl wa al-Ḥafada wa-l-Matā'*, ed. Muhammad Abd-al-Hamid al-Namisi (Beirut, 1999), 224–225).

859 *Ṣāmit*, which also means: not hollow.

860 In Ibn al-Ṭuwayr's account, wind, rather than lances, enters the rings causing the lions to inflate. (Ibn al-Ṭuwayr, *Nuzha*, 159).

861 *Fārisān* (Pl. *fawāris*, sing. *fāris*).

862 P. Sanders translates this term as "elite guards." "*Ṣibyān*" is the plural of "*ṣabiy*," which means "boy" and *al-khāṣṣ*is "the private," that is the royal; caliphal or sultanic. *Ṣibyānal-khāṣṣ* were a group of 500 who were among the special entourage of the caliph and could have been amirs or not (see Glossary). Al-Qalqashandī explains that they were like the mamluk *khāṣṣakiyya* (see Glossary). *Ṣibyānal-khāṣṣ* are also described as the sons of soldiers, amirs and servants

Behind these lances were small, coloured banners of inscribed silk that read: "Victory from Allah and an imminent conquest."[863] Each banner was two cubits long and one and a half cubits wide, had three *ṭirāz*[864] bands and was [supported by] a *qanā* lance.[865] These banners were always twenty-one in number, carried by twenty-one horsemen of the caliph's guards (*ṣibyān*); their carriers always rode mules.

The Two Fly Whisks (al-midhabbatān): These were two huge fly whisks, which bowed down like palm trees, and were carried near the head of the caliph's horse on processions.

The Arms (al-silāḥ): These were carried by the Equestrian Escorts (*rikābiyya*)[866] around the caliph. They were: polished unbending swords (*ṣamāṣim*)[867]; maces (*dabābīs*)[868] that were coated with red and black

of the state, who were hosted by the state, after their fathers died, at certain places prepared especially for them, where they were taught the arts of war and horsemanship, which is a similar definition to *ṣibyānal-ḥujar* (see Glossary). (P. Sanders, *Ritual*, 91 & 98, A. Sayyid, *Dawal*, 689, and Ibn al-Ṭuwayir, Nuzha, 158 fn. 3).

863 Sahih International's translation of part of a verse from Sūrat al-Ṣaff (Chapter of the Row), 61:13, of the Quran (http://corpus.quran.com/translation.jsp?chapter=61&verse=13).

864 *Ṭirāz* (pl. *ṭuruz*)is an Arabized word of Persian origin that in the above context refers to the inscription or decorative bands on textiles as well as on building walls. *Dūr al-Ṭirāz* (sing. *Dār al-Ṭirāz*) were the textile (*ṭirāz*) factories of the state that manufactured products for the private use of the caliph and his family (*ṭirāzal-khāṣṣa*) and for more public use to be sold in markets (*ṭirāzal-'āmma*).

865 *Qanā* (sing. *qanāt*, which also means canal) lances are defined linguistically as lances that have hollowed posts, like cylindrical tubes, ending in pointed teeth. Al-Qalqashandī, however, mentions that their bodies were made of canes or reeds, which have blocked interiors (i.e. filled, not hollow) and which grew in India, then were exported to al-Khaṭṭ in Bahrain, from where they reached the rest of the Arab world. In another instance, al-Qalqashandī refers to the *qanā*, which is a tree/plant that grows in Ethiopia, where the canes or reeds are either hollow or blocked. In this later instance, however, al-Qalqashandī makes no connection of the plant with lances. (http://www.baheth.info/all.jsp?term=قنا, A. Gamal al-Din, *Dawla*, 262, A. Sayyid, *Tafsīr*, 702 and *Ṣubḥ*, Vol. 2, 133–134 and Vol. 5, 306).

866 That is the ones who ride along with the caliph, for the *rikāb* is the stirrup. P. Sanders translates the term as "mounted escorts." Al-Qalqashandī uses the term *al-rikābiyya* in this context, while Ibn al-Ṭuwayr uses *ṣibyān al-rikāb* (Equestrian Guards), also known as *ṣibyān al-rikāb al-khāṣṣ* (Private Equestrian Guards) who were more than one-thousand or two-thousand men with twelve commanders (*muqaddamīn*). In the early Fatimid state, *ṣibyān al-rikāb* were called "*al-sa'diyya*" and were around one-hundred men responsible for joining the caliph as he rode on processions. They carried ornamented swords and at the time of Caliph al-Ḥākim, they started being responsible for executions ordered by the caliph. (P. Sanders, *Ritual*, 228 and Ibn al-Ṭuwayr , *Nuzha*, 124, 148, 148 fn. 1, & 165 fn. 1).

867 Sing. *ṣamṣām*: Strong, unbending, and possibly straight swords that cut through the bones. In another instance al-Qalqashandī explains that the word "*ṣamṣāma*" is used to describe a sword that has a blade on only one of its two sides. (http://baheth.info/all.jsp?term=صمصام, *Ṣubḥ*, Vol. 2, 133 and Ibn al-Ṭuwayir, Nuzha, 148 fn. 2).

868 Sing. *dabbūs*, which according to al-Qalqashandī was also called "*'āmūd*" (pole), was a type of mace that was made of iron and had sides (*aḍlā'*). It was used to fight warriors wearing iron headpieces. (*Ṣubḥ*, Vol. 2, 135).

leather[869] and had rounded heads, and iron axes (*lutūt*)[870] with rectangular heads,which were two-cubit long square-shaped iron poles with rounded handles.[871] Of each type [of arms], a known number [was used in the procession]. [These also included], six-hundred spears[872] with polished heads and silver joints (*julab*)[873] beneath them, as well as three-hundred leathern shields (*daraqa*) with silver navel-shaped ornaments (*kawābij*). Three-hundred black slaves carried these in the procession, each carrying two spears and one leathern shield. There were also sixty lances each seven cubits of length, with protrusions[874] at their heads, and their hiltsmade of iron. These lances were carried by a group of people called "al-Sarīriyya,"[875] who rotated them continuously with their right hands. One-hundred men marched on foot in the procession, carrying one-hundred smallleathern shields and one-hundred swords. Ten swords in red and yellow silk covers with tassels [were carried] at the end of the procession. These were called "The Swords of Blood" (*suyūf al-damm*) and were used for decapitation in case the caliph decided to kill someone.

All these items were in addition to the ones released from the Decoration Treasury (*khizānat al-tajammul*)[876] for the decoration of the vizier, the high-ranking amirs, the holders of ranks (*arbāb al-rutab*),[877] and the overseers of

869 *Kaymakht*, which is a type of tanned leather that was used for making shields. (Ibn al-Ṭuwayir, Nuzha, 148 fn. 3).

870 Sing. *lutt*: A word of Persian origin meaning the big axe. (Al-Baqli, *Ta'rīf*, 292 and Ibn al-Ṭuwayir, Nuzha, 148 fn. 4).

871 The "two-cubit long square-shaped iron poles with rounded handles" is probably a description of another instrument called "*al-mustawfiyāt*;" a term al-Qalqashandī seems to have missed copying from Ibn al-Ṭuwayr. (See Ibn al-Ṭuwayr, *Nuzha*, 148).

872 In this work, lance is used as a translation for *rumḥ*, while spear is used to translate *ḥarba*. A. Gamal al-Din remarks that the *ḥarba* was similar to a *rumḥ*, only shorter. (A. Gamal al-Din, *Dawla*, 259).

873 Sing. *julba*: a piece of silver or other material that is used to attach the head of the lance to its body. (M Shams, *Nujūm*, Vol. 4, 83 fn. 7).

874 *Tal'a*, which means a protruding part, but is too general a term to deduce the shape.

875 The correct term is "*al-sabarbariyya*," which is used by Ibn al-Ṭuwayr. *Al-Sabarbariyya* were the group which held and handled *al-sabarbarāt*; a non-Arabic term that means a type of lances of five cubits of length and broad, long heads. (Ibn al-Ṭuwayr, *Nuzha*, 151 & 151 fn. 1).

876 One of the literal meanings of *al-tajammul* is beautification. P. Sanders translates *khizānat al-tajammul* as" Treasury of Parade Equipment" and "Treasury of Parade Arms." This treasury was a part of the Treasury of Arms (*khizānat al-silāḥ*) and it included many types of arms and precious instruments used on special occasions, such as: several boxes filled with gems, jewels, gold and silver pots, golden saddles, embroidered caparisons and clothes, ornamented waist straps and other items. It had its own supervisor (*nāẓir*). (P. Sanders, *Ritual*, 177–178, Ibn al-Ṭuwayr, *Nuzha*, 135 & 149, Al-Baqli, *Ta'rīf*, 117–118, and see Glossary).

877 See Glossary.

soldiers (*azimmat al-'asākir*)[878] for the processions. These were: About four-hundred banners with inscribed borders that had silver gold-plated bosses[879] at their tops; and a number of howdahs (*'ammāriyyāt*),[880] which resembled the *kanjawāt*,[881] were covered with red, yellow and crimson silk, as well as other [cloths][882] and had silver gold-plated navel-shaped ornamets (*kawābij*). Each of the amirs entitled to carry a staff (*asḥāb al-quḍub*)[883] [rode in] one of these howdahs (*'ammāriyyāt*). Two non-spread banners on lances that were inlaid[884] with gold were particularly assigned [to each of these amirs to march] before him on processions.There are also other instruments, but they would take too long to describe and would not be easy to comprehend.

The Kettledrums (al-naqqārāt):[885] These were carried on twenty mules, each carrying three. They were like large kettledrums (*naqqārāt al-kūsāt*), but without cymbals (*kūsāt*).[886] Two by two marched in the processions, and they made a nice sound.

878 *Azimma* is the plural of *zimām* (see earlir and Glossary: "*zimām*").

879 *Ramāmīn*, pl. of *rummān*: pomegranate.

880 Sing. *'ammāriyya*, which means: a howdah. (Ibn al-Ṭuwayir, Nuzha, 149 fn. 7).

881 "*Kajāwāt*" in *Nuzha*: both words, of Persian origin, were used to refer to the same thing, which is a seated conveyance similar to the howdah. (Ibn al-Ṭuwayir, Nuzha, 149 fn. 8 and M. Shams, *Nujūm*, Vol. 4, 84 fn. 6).

882 Ibn al-Ṭuwayr mentions other types of cloths, namely, *dibāj*, *qurqūbī*, and *saqlāṭūn*.(See Glossary).

883 Al-Qalqashandī uses the term *aṣḥāb al-quḍub*, which means "holders of the staffs," while Ibn al-Ṭuwayr uses the term "*arbāb al-qaṣab*," which means "holders of *al-qaṣab*." *Al-Qaṣab* were lances "dressed with silver tubes inlaid with gold," except for an upper section that was adorned with decorated multicoloured *sharb* cloths. The heads of these lances were silver bosses (*ramāmīn*) inlaid with gold as well as hollow crescents. They had bells which rang with movement. There were around one-hundred of these lances which were taken-out of the treasury in honour of the vizier, high-ranking amirs and "the commanders of troops and of the regiments of cavalry and infantry." (P. Sanders, *Ritual*, 178 and Ibn al-Ṭuwayr, *Nuzha*, 149).

884 *Manqūsh*, from "*naqasha*," a verb that also refers to engraving and inscribing.

885 Sing. *al-naqqāra*, which was like a kettle-drum. It was particularly used in wars to announce the permission to start combat. Ibn Taghrī Birdī mentions that they were carried on fifty mules, five drums on each mule, but Ibn al-Ṭuwayr and al-Maqrīzī agree with al-Qalqashandī that they were twenty. (Ibn Taghrī Birdī & M. Shams, *Nujūm*, Vol. 4, 86 & 86 fn. 1 and Ibn al-Ṭuwayr, *Nuzha*, 151).

886 Al-Qalqashandī's description of the *kūsāt* clearly shows that they were cymbals (see later); however, they are sometimes defined as large kettledrums. The above statement is copied from Ibn al-Ṭuwayr's account, which states that these *naqqārāt* (kettledrums) were like "*naqqārāt al-kūsāt bi-ghayr kūsāt*," which may be understood to mean that they were as big as the large kettledrums (*naqqārāt al-kūsāt*), but were without cymbals (*kūsāt*). Ibn al-Ṭuwayr adds that these kettledrums were called the Drums of Aleppo (*ṭubūl Ḥalab*) and were given to their drummers who walked two by two in the procession. He also mentions that they were a sign of privilege. (Ibn al-Ṭuwayr, *Nuzha*, 151, al-Maqrīzī, *Khiṭaṭ*, Vol. 2, 248, and H. Abbas, *Masālik* (2002), Vol. 3, 64 fn. 3 & 4).

Tents and Pavilions (al-khiyām wa-l-fasāṭiṭ):[887] One of the most gigantic tents [of the Fatimids] was the one known as "*al-qātūl*" (the Killer). Its pole was seventy cubits long, and at its top was a silver "table"[888] that would accommodate a water leather bag.[889] It had a circular area of more than two feddans[890] and it was so named because a caretaker (*farrāsh*)[891] fell off its top and died.[892]

I say: I swear by my life that this is such a great memorable achievement that shows a greatness of a kingdom and a power of ability, for how would any king, of whatever dignified stature and esteemed situation, be able to own such a tent.

887 *Khiyām*, sing. *khayma* is "tent," and *fasāṭīṭ*, sing. *fusṭāṭ*, is "pavilion".

888 Al-Qalqashandī says *sufra*, which means dining table, while Ibn al-Ṭuwayr says *ṣifriyya*, which also has the meaning of a large tray or round table. The *ṣifriyya* was the term given to the round post head of huge tents. It was normally made of silver and other historical accounts than al-Qalqashandī's also measure its width by that of the leather water container (*rāwiyat mā'*), particularly the one carried by camels. (Ibn al-Ṭuwayr, *Nuzha*, 196, al-Maqrīzī, *Khiṭaṭ*, Vol. 2, 186–187, 313 & 316 and *Itti'aẓ*, Vol. 1, 242, 287).

889 *Rāwiyat mā'*.

890 Al-Qalqashandī's statement is: "*wa si'atuha mā yazīd 'alā faddānayn fī al-tadwīr,*" which can be translated as: "and its wideness is more than two feddans in roundness," and can be concluded to mean the area of the circular base of the pavilion. (See also Ibn al-Ṭuwayr, *Nuzha*, 196).

891 The *farrāsh* (pl. *farrāshūn*) was a caretaker of the caliph and his palaces in the Fatimid era. He was responsible for cleaning the palaces, interior and exterior; hanging curtains; cleaning and maintaining the belvederes (*manāẓir*), and guarding the palaces' gates after their closure at night. Each *farrāsh* received a monthly salary of ten dinars, or around. He also provided minor services in the bureau; a sort of a messenger boy.(Al-Baqli, *Ta'rīf*, 261, also see later for the position in the Mamluk era).

892 *Al-Qātūl* was the humongous tent also known as *Khaymat al-Faraj* (the Tent of Wideness/ Comfort) or *Khaymat al-Faraḥ* (the Tent of Happiness). Some historians agree that it was first made at the time of Vizier al-Afḍal, while al-Maqrīzī mentions more than once that it was made for Caliph al-'Azīz. Ibn al-Ma'mūn informs us that when al-Afḍal first made this tent, he called it *Khaymat al-Faraj*, but it later came to be known as *al-Qātūl* because two caretakers were killed while pitching it. In another instance, we are informed that whenever it was pitched, it killed one or two men. Consequently, servants and caretakers hated having to pitch it and the process was only executed in the presence of engineers. With time, only parts of it were pitched; these that formed the large hall, passageways, and a surrounding border. (Jamāl al-Dīn Ibn al-Ma'mūn, *Nuṣūṣ min Akhbār Miṣr*, ed. Ayman Fouad Sayyid (Cairo, 1983), 55–56, 55 fn. 1 & 102–103, al-Maqrīzī, *Khiṭaṭ*, Vol. 2, 186–187 and *Itti'āẓ*, Vol. 2, 287–288 and al-Nuwayrī, *Nihāya*, Vol. 28, 285).

The Second Clause On the caliph's warehouses (*ḥawāṣil*),[893] which were of five kinds[894]

The First Kind: The treasuries (*khazā'in*),[895] which were eight:

The First: The Treasury of Books (khizānat al-kutub)[896]

This was one of the most dignified and highly esteemed treasuries by [the Fatimids]. It contained a large number of honourable Quran manuscripts that were superbly handwritten in *al-mansūb*[897] scripts, as well as more than 100,000 volumes of precious books that covered a variety of sciences, which would surprise and puzzle a viewer. This treasury may have had ten or less[898] copies of a single book and it comprised scrolls[899] written in *al-mansūb* scripts,such as those of Ibn Muqla,[900] Ibn al-Bawwāb,[901] and others who followed their course.

893 Sing. *ḥāṣil*, also granary or storehouse. (See also below)

894 For more on the types of Fatimid treasuries and warehouses and their contents, see: Ibn al-Ṭuwayr, *Nuzha*; al-Maqrīzī, *Khiṭaṭ*, Vol. 2; *Aḥmad ibn al-Rashīd ibn al-Zubayr*, *Book of Gifts and Rarities* (*Kitāb al-Hadāya wa-l-Tuḥaf*), trans. by Ghadah Hijjawi Qaddumi (Harvard, 1996), and Zaki Hasan, *Kunūz al-Fāṭimiyyīn*, (Cairo, 1937).

895 Sing. *khizāna*.

896 This was a treasury and a library. For a more detailed description, see Ibn al-Ṭuwayr, *Nuzha*, 126–128 and al-Maqrīzī, *Khiṭaṭ*, Vol. 2, 163–165.

897 *Al-Khaṭṭ al-mansūb* (the proportioned script) was an Arabic calligraphic system developed by the Abbasid secretary and vizier, Ibn Muqla (d. 328 AH/940 AD). This system depended on the principles of geometric design, which were applied to letters. According to *al-mansūb* system, the sizes of letters were calculated "based on the rhombic dot formed when the nib of a reed pen is applied to the surface of the paper. Ibn Muqla calculated the height of an *alif*, the first letter of the Arabic alphabet, in terms of these dots and then calculated the size of all other letters in relation to the *alif*." *Al-mansūb* provided "a canon for each script" and "allowed a number of systematic methods or templates to be created for each of the six major scripts (*al-aqlām al-sitta*)"; members of the rounded-hand family of cursive Arabic scripts. (Jonathan Bloom, "*Calligraphy*," in *Medieval Islamic Civilization – An Encyclopedia*, ed. J. Meri (New York, 2006),Vol. 1, 134–135, Yasser Tabaa, *The Transformation of Islamic Art during the Sunni Revival* (London, 2002), 34 and Christiane J. Gruber, *The Islamic Manuscript Tradition – Ten Centuries of Book Arts in Indiana University Collections* (Bloomington, 2010), 10–11).

898 The editor of Subḥ notes that the author probably meant "or more." (*Ṣubḥ*, Vol. 3, 476 fn. 1).

899 *Durūj* (sing. *darj*), see f. 988.

900 Abū ʿAlī Muḥammad b. ʿAlī, known as Ibn Muqla, was born in Baghdad in 272 AH/885 AD. "He became a secretary in the Abbasid bureau and served as vizier three times between (316 AH) 928 (AD) and (324 AH) 936 AD." Although he was also the exceptional calligrapher of his time, his life ended tragically in prison in 328 AH/940 AD. Ibn Muqla developed the script system "*al-mansūb*," but he did not invent any new scripts, contrary to the misconception adopted by several later scholars. (Sheila Blair, *Islamic Calligraphy* (Cairo, 2006), 157–158 and Y. Tabaa, *Transformation*, 34).

901 Abū al-Ḥasan ʿAlī b. Hilāl, sometimes known as Ibn al-Sitrī, and commonly known as Ibn al-Bawwāb (d. 1022 AD in Baghdad) was a renowned, remarkable calligrapher. Ibn al-Bawwāb "(literally, son of the porter) was a man of humble origins who rose to the rank of scribe and

The Second: The Treasury of Garments (**khizānat al-kiswa**)[902]

This treasury actually incorporated two treasuries. The first was the Exterior Treasury (*al-khizāna al-ẓāhira*), which became known in our times as the Great Treasury (*al-khizāna al-kubrā*) and is currently known as the Private [Sultanic] Treasury (*khizānat al-khāṣṣ*).[903] This treasury included stores[904] of different kinds of coloured silk brocade (*dībāj*),[905] *Dabīqī* [906] *sharb* for private [caliphal use], *Saqlāṭūn*,[907] and other types of magnificent cloths that show the greatness of the kingdom. The treasury also received the products of the House of Ṭirāz (*dār al-ṭirāz*) [workshops] in Tinnīs,[908] Damietta[909] and Alexandria that were requisitioned for the private usage (*musta'malāt al-khāṣṣ*). The caliph's costumes that were made upon order, the needed robes of honour (*khila'*), costumes of honour (*tashārīf*), and other costumes, were tailored in this treasury.

librarian." One chronicler informs us that Ibn al-Bawwāb" excelled all those who had preceded him and confounded all those who came after him." Ibn al-Bawwāb "revised and refined" Ibn Muqla's method, "and vested it with elegance and splendour." (Y. Tabaa, *Transformation*, 33 and S. Blair, *Calligraphy*, 160–161).

902 For a more detailed description, see Ibn al-Ṭuwayr, *Nuzha*, 128–130 and al-Maqrīzī, *Khiṭaṭ*, Vol. 2, 165–174.

903 See Glossary.

904 *ḥawāṣil*, sing. *ḥāṣil*. The statement here is not clear. The term is used to refer to store rooms, but may also refer here to products, possibly in stacks or packs.

905 *Dībāj* is a kind of silk that is defined as both pure silk and silk brocade. The term is derived from *dabj* (carving or ornamenting, which is an Arabised, originally Persian, word). Since the term implies embroidery and the definition indicates purity, it may be understood that it is a type of pure silk, which is embroidered with silk alone. Al-Maqrīzī simply mentions that *dībāj* is "silk," while there are sources that define the term as a textile that is brocaded with silk or golden threads. (See http://www.baheth.info/all.jsp?term=ديباج; P. Sanders, *Ritual*, 47 & 244; Muḥammad b. Yazīd b. Mājah, *Sunan*, ed. Muhammad Fouad Abd al-Baqi & Mustafa Husayn Dhahabi (Cairo, 1998), Vol. 3, *ḥadīth* no. 3589; al-Maqrīzī, *Khiṭaṭ*, Vol. 2, 604, andIbn al-Ṭuwayir, Nuzha, 129 fn. 3).

906 A type of cloth that was embroidered with golden and silk threads, or embroidered silk cloth, which was attributed to Dabīq (also Dibīq and Dibqū), a no-longer extant town of present day Damietta that overlooked al-Manzala Lake. Dabīq's site is today taken up by another town called Tall Dabīq (Hill of Dabīq), to the northeast of Ṣān al-Ḥajar Village in al-Sharqiyya Governorate. (Al-Baqli, *Ta'rīf*, 133).

907 *Saqlāṭūn* was a city or town within the Byzantine Empire that was known for textile manufacture. The term "*al-saqlāṭūn*" was used to refer to a type of refined silk, or a kind of precious, cloth that is thought to have been coloured scarlet, purple, or blue, which was also manufactured in Baghdad and Tabriz. (Al-Baqli, *Ta'rīf*, 181, http://www.baheth.info/all.jsp?term=سقلاطون, and Francis J. Steingass, *A Comprehensive Persian-English Dictionary*, http://dsalsrv02.uchicago.edu/cgi-bin/philologic/search3advanced?dbname=steingass&query=saqlatun&matchtype=exact&display=utf.

908 Tinnīs was a port island and a major centre for textile manufacturing and trading to the northeast of Egypt. It was a prosperous, populated city in medieval times. Today, the remains of old Tinnīs form an archaeological site to the southwest of Port Said.

909 The coastal city in northeastern Egypt, which also overlooks the eastern branch of the Nile that carries its name. It is the capital of Damietta Governorate.

The second treasury, which is called the "*ṭisht khānāh*" (House of Basins)[910] in our times, especially served the caliph.[911] The cloths tailored for the caliph, as well as other cloths, were transferred to this second treasury from the first one.

The Third: The Treasury of Beverages (khizānat al-sharāb)[912]

This treasury is called the "*sharāb khānāh*" (The House of Beverages)[913] in our times. It exclusively included various kinds of expensive beverages and pastes, exquisite jams, numerous types of medicines and excellent perfumes. It also had precious tools and Chinaware, such as bowls, plates, pots and large jars, all only affordable by kings.

The Fourth: The Treasury of Foodstuffs (***khizānat al-ṭu'm***)[914]

This is the treasury called the "*ḥawā'ij khānāh*" (House of Assorted Needs)[915] in our times. It used to have several varieties of all kinds of fried items,[916] such as pistachio and others. It had sugar, candy, all kinds of honey, oil, wax, and others. This treasury supplied the private [caliphal] and public kitchens with their rations.[917] It also provided the Heads of Services (*arbāb al-khidam*)[918] and the Holders of Signatures (*aṣḥāb al-tawqī'āt*)[919] with rations on a monthly basis.

910 See later.

911 Called "*al-khizāna al-bāṭina*" in the Fatimid era (the Interior Treasury, as opposed to the Exterior). See more on both treasuries in Ibn al-Ṭuwayr, *Nuzha*, 128–130.

912 For more description see Ibn al-Ṭuwayr, *Nuzha*, 130–131 and al-Maqrīzī, *Khiṭaṭ*, Vol. 2, 188.

913 See later.

914 See also "*khizānat al-tawābil*" (The Treasury of Spices) in al-Maqrīzī, *Khiṭaṭ*, Vol. 2, 188–192.

915 The *ḥawā'ij khānāh* means "the House of Needs" and refers to a house of miscellaneous needs of foodstuffs and other items, such as oil for lighting. Henceforth, it will be translated as "the House of Assorted Needs." (See later).

916 *Qalawiyyāt*, which means "fried" food items.

917 *Rātib*.

918 *Arbāb al-khidam* may be translated as "Heads of Services" or "Lords of Services," which means "Providers of Services." A. Sayyid cites Ibn al-Ṭuwayr's *Nuzha* and al-Maqrīzī's *Khiṭaṭ* to show that the Collared Amirs (*al-umarā' al-muṭawwaqūn*, see later), who were Men of the Sword, were also called *arbāb al-khidam al-jalīla* (Heads of Dignified Services, meaning royal services). The reference in the primary sources may also suggest that certain category of the collared amirs was called *arbāb al-khidam al-jalīla*. P. Sanders separates the two categories, since she refers to *arbāb al-khidam* as "other high dignitaries." (Ibn al-Ṭuwayr, *Nuzha*, 208 and P. Sanders, *Ritual*,33).

919 *Aṣḥāb al-tawqī'āt* means "the Holders of the Signatures" and refers to those state officials who hold a signing authority. Al-Qalqashandī lists the state officials, from both categories: Men of the Pen and Men of the Sword, who had this authority in his time during the Mamluk era, along with a detailed description of the protocols, prologues and language of correspondence. (*Ṣubḥ*, Vol. 11, 114–133). See Glossary for the definition of *tawqī'*.

No external supplies were needed [from outside this treasury], except for meat and vegetables only.

The Fifth: The Treasury of Saddles (**khizānat al-surūj**)[920]

This is the treasury known as the "*rikāb khānāh*" (House of Stirrups) in our times. It was a large hall in the palace that contained the silver and golden[921] saddles and bridles, as well as the rest of the private caliphal horse riding equipment. Some of this equipment was almost private (*khāṣṣ*),[922] some was of medium level, assigned to theholders of high ranks,[923] and some was of lesser level, assigned for lending-out to the Heads of Services[924] on processions.

The Sixth: The Treasury of Rugs (**khizānat al-farsh**)[925]

This is the treasury known as the "*firāsh khānāh*" (House of Furnishings)[926] in our times. It was located inside the palace, near Dār al-Mulk.[927] The caliph used

920 For a more detailed description, see Ibn al-Ṭuwayr, *Nuzha*, 131–132 and al-Maqrīzī, *Khiṭaṭ*, Vol. 2, 183–184.

921 That is, ornamented or inlaid with gold and silver. (Ibn al-Ṭuwayr, *Nuzha*, 132).

922 Ibn al-Ṭuwayr explains this "near-*khāṣṣ*" or "almost-*khāṣṣ*" expression saying that the equipment belonging to this group is kept at the official's place, rather than in the treasury. The official was assigned a *shaddād* (Puller: a man or boy who ties the saddle; a groom or stable attendant) whose running wage was paid by thc caliph. (Ibn al-Ṭuwayr, *Nuzha*, 132).

923 *Arbāb al-rutab al-'āliya*, see Glossary: "*arbāb al-rutab*".

924 Ibn al-Ṭuwayr mentions that the lesser equipment was assigned for lending-out to *arbāb al-rutab wa-l-khidam* (Holders of Ranks and Heads of Services), while other elitist equipment was assigned to the *khāṣṣ* of the caliph and *arbāb al-rutab*. (Ibn al-Ṭuwayr, *Nuzha*, 132). Therefore, it is deduced that there were levels of the holders of ranks.

925 *Farsh* is the rugs, carpets or whatever furnishing that is spread out. See also Ibn al-Ṭuwayr, *Nuzha*, 133.

926 See later.

927 "The House of Sovereignty," in Ibn al-Ṭuwayr's account: Bāb al-Mulk (The Door of Sovereignty). Dār al-Mulk was originally a house of governance that the Fatimid vizier al-Afḍal built in 501 AH/1108 AD. It was located on the Nile bank of Fustat, in place of a group of buildings that today occupy the southern end of Miṣr al-Qadīma Street. Al-Afḍal moved and transferred the state administrative offices to it from Dār al-Qibāb (The House of Domes), opposite the eastern side of the eastern Fatimid Palace. Dār al-Mulk became al-Afḍal's seat of governance, where he also held banquets and bestowed gifts and endowments, all actions that served to further consolidate his power and control over state matters while diminishing all authority of Caliph al-Āmir. After al-Afḍal's death in 515 AH/1121 AD, Dār al-Mulk became one of the Fatimid belvederes (*manāẓir*) used for caliphal leisurely outdoor activities, and as a place they rode to on short processions. Al-Qalqashandī, obviously, is not referring to al-Afḍal's Dār al-Mulk in Fustat for he specifies that it was inside the palace. He is probably referring to the house of governance at the palace, possibly Dār al-Qibāb. Al-Maqrīzī lists this Treasury of Furniture among those that were in the Eastern Palace. (Al-Maqrīzī, *Khiṭaṭ*, Vol. 2, 163, 180–182 &331–334, Ibn al-Ṭuwayr, *Nuzha*, 133 and 169–170 fn. 1 and M. Shams, *Nujūm*, Vol. 4, 96–97 fn. 7).

to visit it and have a tour in it – although he did not sit there – enquire about its affairs, and give his orders to continue manufacturing what was needed and transporting it to the treasury.

The Seventh: The Treasury of Arms (**khizānat al-silāḥ**)[928]

This is the treasury known as the "*silāḥkhānāh*" (House of Arms)[929] in our times, and it had an unparalleled variety of weaponry. This included: chain-mails (*zardiyyāt*)[930] that were perfectly made, covered with silk brocade (*dībāj*) and adorned with silver; gold-plated [frontal] armour (*jawāshin*);[931] helmets (*khuwadh*)[932] that were adorned with gold and silver; Arabian and Qaljūri[933] swords; *qanā* lances and lances (*qunṭāriyyāt*)[934] that were painted and gold-plated; huge heads (*asinna*);[935] bows that were known to be attributed to the best craftsmen; crossbows of the foot and stirrups (*qisiy al-rijl wa-l-rikāb*),[936] as well

928 See also Ibn al-Ṭuwayr, *Nuzha*, 133–135 and al-Maqrīzī, *Khiṭaṭ*, Vol. 2, 182–183.

929 See later.

930 Sing. *zardiyya*, which is a chainmail: A shirt-like mail made of small iron rings that are tied or connected together in a web or linear arrangement. There were short and long chainmails of this type, where the long ones reached the ground to cover the whole body of a horseman. (A. Yasin, *Asliḥa*, 75–76).

931 Sing. *jwashan*, which is a mail or a chainmail that covers the chest only and may have been backless. The *jawshan* is described in one primary source to have been made of "small iron platelets, animal horns, or leather," and covered with cloth. Another opinion informs us that the difference between the *zardiyya/zard* and the *jawshan* is that the first is composed of one type of metal ring, while the second is made of alternating rings that are inlaid or connected together with thin tin platelets. (A. Yasin, *Asliḥa*, 51–52, al-Baqli, *Ta'rīf*, 93–94, and A. Gamal al-Din, *Dawla*, 262).

932 Sing. *khūdha*; helmets that were made of the same materials used for making armour and were worn fitting the heads beneath the cloth or leather head cover (*qalansuwa*). (A. Sayyid, *Tafsīr*, 702 and S. Ashour, *'Aṣr*, 462).

933 *Al-Suyūf al-Qaljūriyya* (Qaljūri swords) was a type of swords. Qaljūr, according to Ibn Sa'īd al-Maghribī, was a place in Africa near The Comoros, which was close to a site where an excellent metal was mined to make these swords. Al-Kindī, the famous Muslim philosopher and scientist of the ninth century, who also authored an important treatise on Islamic swords, however, says that the Qaljūri was a light sword attributed to an Andalusian city called al-Ṭurqūniyya. A. Sayyid refers to another opinion; that the word may be a derivative from the Turkish*qalj*, meaning "sword." (Ibn Sa'īd al-Maghribī, *Geography*: http://www.scribd.com/doc/3921002/الجغرافي-ابن-سعيد, 2, Abū Yūsuf Ya'qūb al-Kindī, *al-Suyūf wa Ajnāsuhā*, ed. Abd al-Rahman Zaki (Cairo, 2001) and Ibn al-Ṭuwayir, Nuzha, 134 fn. 1).

934 Sing. *qunṭāriyya*, a type of short lance. (Ibn al-Ṭuwayir, Nuzha, 151 fn. 2).

935 Sing. *sinān*, which is the spearhead, lance-head, or the like.

936 These were crossbows that were stretched by pulling with the hand and supporting with one or both feet (*rijl* is leg or foot), or with the horses' stirrups (*rikāb*). They were mostly used in fleets and coastal forts, since the standard composite bows were not suitable for humid weather, given their need for employing glue to manufacture them. (See Abd al-Mun'im Maged, *Nuẓum al-Fāṭimiyyīn wa Rusūmuhum fī Miṣr* (Cairo, 1973), Vol. 1, and *Ṣubḥ*, Vol. 2, 134–135).

as winch-spanned crossbows (*qisiy al-lawlab*),[937] which have blades that weigh five Egyptian pounds,[938] and arrows (*nabl*)[939] that are thrown from Arabian Bows that have courses for the arrows to run in.[940]

Judge Muḥyi al-Dīn b. ʿAbd al-Ẓāhir said: Annually, an amount of seventy to eighty-thousand dinars was spent on this treasury.[941]

The Eighth: The Decoration Treasury **(khizānat al-tajammul)**[942]

This is a treasury that contained various kinds of arms, which were assigned to the vizier and the amirs on processions, [such as]: banners, silver staffs, howdahs (*ʿammāriyyāt*), and others. Ibn al-Ṭuwayr said: It is affiliated to the treasuries of arms.[943]

* THE MONETARY TREASURIES (*KHAZĀʾINAL-MĀL*)[944]

As for the Monetary Treasuries, they contained innumerable amounts of money, precious jewels, great treasures, and magnificent textiles.[945]

Not to mention that when the great economic crisis[946] hit Egypt, al-Mustanṣir released a treasure from his treasury that matched its capacity in the year 462 AH/1070 AD, so as to help support the kingdom and the armies. What he spent included: 80,000 big pieces of crystal, 70,000 pieces of silk brocade (*dībāj*) and 20,000 ornamented swords. When sultan Ṣalāḥ al-Dīn Yūsuf b. Ayyūb took over the palace after the death of al-ʿĀḍid, the last Fatimid caliph, he found innumerable precious objects and rarities. Among those was the rubi hoof (*ḥāfir*) mentioned earlier. It is also said that he found an emerald staff, which was taller than a grown man, as mentioned in the earlier description of the royal jewels in

937 *Qisiy al-lawlab* (sing. *qaws al-lawlab*) were large crossbows "spanned with a windlass or winch." They had their own special arrows that were undetectable by the target until hit. (David Nicolle, *Crusader Warfare: Byzantium, Western Europe and the Struggle for the Holy Land – 1050–1300 AD* (Hambeldon, 2007) 91 & 247, A. Maged, *Nuẓum*, Vol. 1 and A. Sayyid, *Dawla*, 703).

938 Al-Qalqashandī informs us that the Egyptian "*raṭl*" (pound, pl. *arṭāl*) was a unit of weight used in the capital, that is, Fustat, Cairo and the areas in their proximity. It was equal to 144 dirhams. (*Ṣubḥ*, Vol. 3, 445).

939 The *nabl* were the arrows particularly used with Arabian bows. (*Ṣubḥ*, Vol. 2, 135).

940 Arabian Bows were wooden bows that shot several arrows in various directions simultaneously. (A. Maged, *Nuẓum*, Vol. 1 and A. Sayyid, *Tafsīr*, 702).

941 Ibn ʿAbd al-Ẓāhir, *Khiṭaṭ*, 46.

942 See Glossary.

943 "*min ḥuqūq khazāʾin al-silāḥ*." (Ibn al-Ṭuwayr, *Nuzha*, 135).

944 Plural of *khizāna*, which means treasury.

945 Ibn al-Ṭuwayr does not seem to mention these treasuries.

946 *Ghalāʾ*, which means the soaring of prices.

the first article.[947] He also found the amber pyramid that was made by al-Amīn,[948] which weighed 1000 Egyptian pounds.[949]

The Second Kind

Animal barns,[950] *called "al-Kurā'"*[951] *by the scribes of our times, which were two:*

THE FIRST: THE STABLES[952]

These were the barns for horses, mules, and their likes. Ibn al-Ṭuwayr said: The [Fatimids] had two stables, and added: The caliph hadaround 1000 animal heads in each stable, which were assigned to the private [caliphal use] (*khāṣṣ*).[953] Half of that number was assigned to the private [caliphal use] (*khāṣṣ*) and the other half was assigned to be lentout to the Holders of Ranks and other employees (*mustakhdamīn*)[954] on processions. Each three animal heads had a groom (*sā'is*)[955] and a puller (*shaddād*) for marching them. Each of the two stables had a tamer (*rā'iḍ*), like an equerry (*amīr ākhūr*).[956] Among the strange tales told about the Fatimid caliphs is that none of them ever rode a black horse[957] (*adham*) and they did not care to add such horses to the animals at their stables.

947 The First Article of *Ṣubḥ*, not translated in this work.

948 Abbasid caliph who ruled from 193 AH/809 AD to 198 AH/813 AD.

949 Ibn al-Ṭuwayr mentions this pyramid, without the reference to Caliph al-Amīn, as one of items found in the treasure and rarities left by vizier al-Afḍal after his death, which Caliph al-Āmir took possession of. (Ibn al-Ṭuwayr, *Nuzha*, 8–9). It is possible that the name "al-Āmir" was mistaken for "al-Amīn" in the manuscript of *Ṣubḥ*.

950 "Barns" is used in this section to better convey the meaning. Al-Qalqashandī uses the term "*ḥawāṣil*" (warehouses) in reference to these animal barns.

951 Literally, it means the farthest end of something, e.g. of land. In the contexts used by al-Qalqashandī, it means the provisions hoarded for war. (Al-Baqli, *Ta'rīf*, 286 and S. Ashour, *'Aṣr*, 465).

952 See also Ibn al-Ṭuwayr, *Nuzha*, 135–138.

953 The editor of Subḥ notes that the "assigned to the *khāṣṣ*" phrase in this sentence is probably an addition by the copier. The original account in *Nuzha* is in accordance with that conclusion and the further explanation proves that. (*Ṣubḥ*, Vol. 3, 478 fn. 1 and Ibn al-Ṭuwayr, *Nuzha*, 136).

954 Sing. *mustakhdam*, which is one of the terms that al-Qalqashandī uses to refer to employees. He also, apparently interchangeably, uses the term "*murtaziq*" (pl. *muratziqūn*) to mean every person employed by the state and receives a salary.

955 Also, "tender"; the tamer and trainer of horses and similar rides. (al-Baqli, *Ta'rīf*, 177).

956 Royal or amirial equerry in the Mamluk era.

957 *Adham*, which is the name given to a purely black horse, considered most valuable by Arabs.

THE SECOND: THE SETTLEMENT AREAS [FOR CAMELS] (*AL-MUNĀKHĀT*)[958]

These were the barns for camels. They had numerous camels in these barns, with all their excellent equipment.

The Third Kind

Granaries and Chopped Straw Warehouses

As for the grains, granaries were found in several places: Cairo, Fustat and al-Maqsim. These granaries provided the granted [rations] (*iṭlāqāt*)[959] assigned to those entitled to allowances (*arbāb al-rawātib*);[960] the Heads of Services; alms-deserving people (*arbāb al-ṣadaqāt*);[961] keepers of mosques and Friday mosques (*arbāb al-jawāmi' wa-l-masājid*); those entitled to running rations (*jirāyāt*); keepers of sultanic mills; the running rations (*jirayāt*) for the Men of the Fleet, and others. The grains sometimes remained in the granaries for a long period of time that they were cut into portions using shovels.

As for the Chopped Straw Warehouses, the Fustat Road[962] had two huge ones that were full of straw, packed in the manner of loading ships [that made its piles] seem like two very high mountains. These warehouses supplied the stables, the cattle affiliated to the bureau,[963] and the cows[964] [used in] the royal gardens. The tax of each sack (*shulayf*)[965] in their [Fatimid] era was 360 pounds.[966]

958 Sing. *al-munākh*: settlement area for camel and sometimes settlement area for rides in general (see Glossary).

959 See Glossary.

960 "Those entitled for allowances:" state officials, administrative and military, who receive specific allowances, as well as other officially listed recipients, for example, al-Ashrāf al-Ṭālibiyyīn. The *rātib* (allowance) was not only given in the form of money, but normally also included rations of food, clothes, fodder, etc. A relevant term is *arbāb al-rutab* (Holders of Ranks), which P. Sanders translates to "highest ranking officials." These were actually of variable ranks, for Ibn al-Ṭuwayr refers to "*arbāb al-rutab 'alā ikhtilāf al-ṭabaqāt*," "those of ranks of different levels," as well as one rank of state officials, which he terms: "*arbāb al-rutab bi-ḥaḍrat al-khalīfa*," "officials at the capital." (P. Sanders, *Ritual*, 105 & 187, Ibn al-Ṭuwayr, *Nuzha*, 75, 77, 83–85, & 113, and A. Sayyid, *Tafsīr*, 350, 363, 395, & 722–723).

961 Those deserving of or receiving *ṣadaqa*; The *ṣadaqa* is a charitable, recommended donation in Islam, which is optional but most encouraged, while the *zakāt* – alms – is mandatory and its percentage is precisely calculated, whether monetary or in kind.

962 *Ṭarīq al-Fusṭāṭ*: the road from Cairo to Fustat, overlooking the Nile, which is along the Khalīj (Ibn al-Ṭuwayr , *Nuzha*, 140 & 140 fn. 2).

963 *Al-Mawāshī al-dīwāniyya* (cattle of the bureau) in *Ṣubḥ*, while in *Nuzha*,it is "*al-awāsī*," which would mean the administrative pillars and could be understood as other administrative offices. (See Ibn al-Ṭuwayr, *Nuzha*, 140).

964 "*'Awāmil*," which are the cows used for ploughing or levelling lands. (http://www.baheth.info/all.jsp?term=عوامل).

965 In *Nuzha*: "*shinf*" (pl. *ashnāf*), which means a type of ropes used to make big sacks for transporting hay and straw. (Ibn al-Ṭuwayr , *Nuzha*, 140 &140 fn. 4).

966 For a more detailed description of these warehouses, see Ibn al-Ṭuwayr, *Nuzha*, 140–141.

The Fourth Kind

The Merchandise Warehouses (ḥawāṣil al-biḍāʿa)[967]

Ibn al-Ṭuwayr said: They included numerous [quantities of] woods; iron; Najdi mills;[968] raw mills;[969] equipment of fleets, such as flax,linen and catapults, as well as many craftsmen of every craft from the Franks and other [peoples]; all only countable in writing.[970] The [shipbuilding] industry was originally in the island known now as al-Rawḍa, which is why they used to call it Jazīrat al-Ṣināʿa (The Island of Ship Industry), as reported by al-Qaḍāʿī.

The Fifth Kind

What wassimilar to a warehouse, because it was usedfor allocation and distribution, which were: the Mills, the Kitchen and Dār al-Fiṭra.

As for the mills, they were hanging, with their axes at the bottoms and their grinders at the tops, like the waterwheels, to prevent the flour from coming near the litter of the animals running the mills, for it was the flour assigned to the caliph.

As for the kitchen, it was mentioned before in the [section on the]neighbourhoods (*khiṭaṭ*) of Cairo. Food was taken from the kitchen to the palace through Bāb al-Zuhūma, which is today in place of the Ḥanbalī Hall of the Ṣāliḥiyya Madrasa, as was described in the [section on the] neighbourhoods (*khiṭaṭ*) of Cairo. Ibn al-Ṭuwayr said: The [Faimids] did not hold public banquets (*asmiṭa*)[971] except on the two feasts[972] and in the month of Ramadan.

967 Ibn al-Ṭuwayr explains that there was a *munākh* (settlement area for camels) behind the Eastern Palace, where the wheat mills that supplied the palaces were situated. Wood, iron, and similar warehouses were also located in this *munākh*. This site is today taken up by the area behind the Khanqah of Baybars al-Jāshankīr, in Bāb al-Naṣr Street, and its extension northwards up to al-ʿUṭūfiyya Alley in al-Jamāliyya Neighbourhood. Ibn al-Ṭuwayr notes that there were many warehouses and merchandise in the Fatimid *munākhāt*. (Ibn al-Ṭuwayr , *Nuzha*, 141 & 141 fn. 2 and see Glossary: "*munākh*").

968 Najd is the plateau in the middle of the Arabian peninsula, to the east of Hijaz.

969 "*Al-Ṭawāḥīn al-ghashīma*," which may have meant that they were built of unpolished, unsmooth, or unglazed rocks or bricks, for "*ghashīma*" is a word used to refer to such rough or natural rocks.

970 "Can only be counted by a pen." (See Ibn al-Ṭuwayr, *Nuzha*, 141–142 and Glossary: "*munākh*").

971 Sing. *simāṭ*: the cloth or table spread to serve food on, and the term is used to mean "banquet."

972 ʿĪd al-Fiṭr and ʿĪd al-Aḍḥā.

The Third Clause On the armies of the Fatimid State and the ranks of the Men of the Sword, who are of three types:

The First Type: The Amirs, who are of three ranks:

The First Rank:
The rank of the Collared Amirs (*al-umarā' al-muṭawwaqūn*),[973] who were the ones bestowed upon with gold collars, [which they wore] on their necks. These were as if equivalent to the Commanders of Thousands (*muqaddamīn al-ulūf*)[974] of our times.

The Second Rank:
The rank of the Holders of the Staffs (*arbāb al-quḍub*),[975] who were the ones who rode in the processions holding the silver staffs that were released from the Decoration Treasury by the order of the caliph. These were equivalent to the Amirs of the *ṭablakhānāh* (*umarā' al-tablakhānāh*)[976] of our times.

The Third Rank:
The Lowest-ranking Amirs (*adwān al-umarā'*) who were not qualified to hold the staffs. They were equivalent to the Amirs of Tens (*umarā'al-'asharāt*)[977] and Amirs of Fives (*umarā' al-khamsāt*)[978] of our times.

973 These were high notables of the Fatimid era, and were the caliph's slave-boys or mamluks (*ghilmān*). (al-Baqli, *Ta'rīf*, 44 and Ibn al-Ṭuwayr, *Nuzha*, 187).

974 See Glossary: "Amirs of Thousands".

975 May have also been termed "*arbāb al-qaṣab*,". They were allowed to hold the staffs, whether silver or of other metal, as a privilege over the lower-ranking commanders. (Al-Baqli, *Ta'rīf*, 23–24).

976 See Glossary: "*ṭablakhānāh*".

977 See Glossary: "Amirs of Tens".

978 See Glossary: "Amirs of Fives".

The Second Type: The Caliph's Private Retinue (*khawāṣṣ*), who were of three kinds:

The First Kind: The Masters *(al-ustādhūn)*[979]

These were the ones known now as the eunuch-servants (*khuddām*)[980] and the eunuchs (*ṭawāshiyya*).[981]

They enjoyed a dignified status in the Fatimid state and the holders of privateoffices[982] [in service]of the caliph were chosen from amongst them. The most dignified among them were the *muḥannakūn*,[983] who wrapped [the tails of] their turbans under their chins as the Arabs and the Maghribis do now. Those were the closest to the caliph and the most concerned with his service. They were more than 1000 in number. Ibn al-Ṭuwayr said: Their ways entailed that whenever a master (*ustādh*) was recommended for [the level of] wearing a *ḥanak*[984] and [was initiated] by putting it on him, each of the masters who were *muḥannakūn* would bring him a whole *badla* (outfit)[985]from

979 Sing. *ustādh*. *Al-Ustādhūn* was a highly respected category of the Fatimid caliphal entourage. Some of its members had positions in the caliph's private service, which are detailed below. Abd Allah Gamal al-Din defines them as: A faction of slaves, black and white, eunuch and not, mostly of foreign origin, who served the caliph. The title of *ustādh* was one of the general titles used since the Abbasid era, when it was applied to the eunuch slave-boys (*ghilmān*). Kafūr al-Ikhshīdī, theIkhshidid ruler, carried this title before he came to power and kept it after the Abbasid Caliph, al-Muṭī', sent him his degree of investiture as ruler (*taqlīd*). The Fatimids continued to use this title, and during the Mamluk era, it was used to refer to the master who bought, broughtup, and freed mamluk soldiers; therefore termed their *ustādh* (master). The term was also used to refer to craftsmen. (Al-Baqli, *Ta'rīf*, 29, H. al-Basha, *Alqāb*, 140 and A. Gamal al-Din, *Dawla*, 220).

980 Sing. *Khadim*.

981 Sing. *ṭawāshī*.

982 *Arbāb al-waẓā'if al-khāṣṣa*, see "Holders of Positions" and "Holders of Offices" later.

983 "The *ustādhūn* who covered beneath their chins:" These were the officials who wrapped the tails of their turbans beneath their chins or mouths and back around their heads in Fatimid era, and who held great positions, some of which in the private service of the caliph. They werethe caliph's confidants, who also had the right to hold the title of amir. They received a montly salary of 100 dinars, and as Ibn al-Ṭuwayr informs us, were more than 1000 in number. It is highly unlikely that the caliph held 1000 men close enough to be exposed to all his secrets and hidden matters of the state. One can, therefore, conclude that a small group of the *muḥannakūn* was chosen and trusted by the caliph. The *muḥannakūn* appear to have worn costumes that corresponded to their ranks or levels. (Al-Baqli, *Ta'rīf*, 31–32 and A. Gamal al-Din, *Dawla*, 220–221).

984 Linguistically, the *ḥanak* has more than one meaning including: "what is under the chin," as well as "the mouth" and the "interior of the upper jaw." The act of wearing a *ḥanak* (*al-taḥannuk*) means wrapping the turban's tail under the chin, like a beard. (http://www.baheth.info/all.jsp?term=حنك and P. Sanders, *Ritual*, 89–90).

985 This was a costume for men that consisted of a number of pieces, probably ranging between three and five, and had different accessories that went with it, such as turban-cloths (*manādīl*) and sleeves. The materials from which this costume was made varied, for example, the sources mention silk and gold embroidery. This attire was worn by the caliphs, bestowed as a costume of honour, was sometimes specified as processional, and/or of a particular colour. The number of pieces, the accessories, and the material from which the costume was made, or with which it was

his wardrobe, a sword, and a horse, so that he became one of them, owning what they own.[986]

The Second Kind: The Private Guards (**ṣibyān al-khāṣṣ**)

These were a group of about 500 of the private retinue of the caliph, of whom some were amirs and some otherwise. They were equivalent to the group now known as the *khāṣṣakiyya.*[987]

The Third Kind: The Young Guards of the Barracks (**ṣibyān al-ḥujar**)[988]

This was a group of about 5000 youths who lived in separate barracks (*ḥujar*), each with its own name. They were similar to the current Mamluks of the

adorned, all determined the rank of the man allowed to wear this outfit. The processional *badla* of the Fatimid caliphs consisted of eleven pieces. (Ibn al-Ma'mūn , *Nuṣūṣ*, 41, 48–49, 50–55, & 151 fn. 1 & fn. 2, A. Gamal al-Din, *Dawla*, 221 and A. Sayyid, *Tafsīr*, 390).

986 Ibn al-Ṭuwayr, *Nuzha*, 210.

987 See Glossary.

988 *Al-Ḥujar* means "the chambers," and in this context means "the barracks." Historians give several accounts on the origins of *ṣibyān al-ḥujar* or *al-ḥujariyya*. It seems that they were introduced by Fatimid Caliph al-Mui'zz, who built seven barracks for a regiment of the Fatimid army to be composed of boys and youths who were chosen from the sons of deceased soldiers, amirs and servants of the state, and who had the required moral qualities, like courage, manliness and good manners, as well as the physical qualities of a proper body build. When they grew to become competent youths, they received full arms that they had the right to keep. The exceptional among them were promoted to amirs or military commanders. At one point in time, this regiment reached 5000 in number. The barracks of al-Mu'izz were located near Dār al-Wizāra and survived until 700 AH/1301 AD. During the era of al-Mu'izz, this regiment was under the supervision of the *ustādhūn* and each of its barracks had a certain name, such as al-Fatḥ (the Conquest), al-Manṣūra (the Triumphant), and al-Jadīda (the New). A stable was also built especially for this regiment, opposite their barracks and next to Bāb al-Futūḥ. Apparently, these barracks were abandoned and neglected after the era of al-Mu'izz, until the time of al-Afḍal who, most probably in 501 AH/1107 AD, recruited 300 sons of soldiers and reintroduced *ṣibyān al-ḥujar*, who were intended to be "a well-trained, easily mobilized regiment." Al-Afḍal divided them placing 100 in each barrack, to which he assigned a *zimām* (overseer) and a *naqīb* (captain), and appointed an amir to be responsible for the whole regiment. The men of this regiment, who were supplied with all their needs, arms and otherwise, were al-Afḍal's private guards. *Ṣibyān al-ḥujar* were housed in separate barracks near Bāb al-Naṣr and taught the arts of combat and war. They were trained to be ready at all times and to respond immediately when called for duty, for they were responsible for serving and protecting the caliph and his premises. In the era of al-Zahir, in 427 AH/1036 AD, it is reported that *ṣibyān al-ḥujar* were taught all the arts of combat, as well as other sciences. Mamluk historians equated the term "*al-ḥujar*" with the Mamluk term "*ṭibāq*," which were the barracks that housed the royal mamluks at the Citadel of Cairo. So, in a sense, this system of "*ṣibyān al-ḥujar*" may have been the direct precedent from which the Ayyubids, and consequently the Mamluks, took their system for training and upbringing of mamluks. (P. Sanders, *Ritual*, 97–98; A. Gamal al-Din, *Dawla*, 218–219; A. Sayyid, *Tafsīr*, 275 fn. 2 & 689; T. Abdelhamid, *Jaysh*, 10–11; A. Maged, *Nuẓum*, 187–189, and Ibn al-Ṭuwayr, *Nuzha*, 57–58 & 158 fn. 3).

Sultanic Barracks (*mamālīk al-ṭibāq al-sulṭāniyya*),[989] who are now called "al-Kittāniyya;"[990] however, they were fully equipped and were spared all troubles. Whenever they were called for important [service], they faced no obstacles [to fulfil their tasks]. The boys among them had a separate barrack that was the responsibility of some masters (*ustādhūn*). This barrack was isolated from the palace and situated inside Bāb al-Naṣr, in the location of the current Khanqah of Baybars al-Jāshankīr.

The Third Type: The Factions of Soldiers (*ṭawā'if al-ajnād*)

These were numerous, with each factionattributed to the remaining forces affiliated to a previous caliph, such as the Ḥāfiẓiyya and the Āmiriyya, who were affiliated to al-Ḥāfiẓ and al-Āmir, [respectively], or to past viziers, such as al-Juyūshiyya and al-Afḍaliyya, who were the remaining [forces] of Amīr al-Juyūsh Badr al-Jamālī and his son al-Afḍal. They may have also been affiliated with a contemporary vizier, such as al-Wazīriyya. [They also included] other [factions], such as the [ones from] tribes and ethnicities like: Turks; Kurds; Ghuzz; Daylam; Maṣāmida, or from [the factions] under patronage,[991] such as the Rūm, the Franks, the Slavs (Ṣaqāliba),[992]

989 See Glossary: "*al-ṭibāq al-sulṭāniyya*" and "*al-mamālīk al-sulṭāniyya*".

990 This accurate term is either al-Kitābiyya or al-Kuttābiyya. Al-Kitābiyya were the mamluks of the sultanic barracks (*al-ṭibāq* or *al-aṭbāq*), who lived in there, received military training and learned how to write (*kataba* is the Arabic verb "to write"; therefore the name). Not all mamluks were raised and educated in the barracks, for some directly joined the sultan's court and received private education and training with his sons. The *Khāṣṣakiyya* were sometimes chosen from among these mamluks who received such special treatment. Some sultans, however, like most of the amirs, sent their sons to the barracks. (Al-Baqli, *Ta'rīf*, 330 and M. Shams, *Nujūm*, Vol. 11, 220 fn. 1).

991 *Al-Mustaṣna'ūn* (also, *al-muṣṭana'ūn* and *al-muṣṭana'a*), were those under a particular system of patronage; the term is often translated as "protégés." Linguistically, the meanings of "*iṣṭinā'*" include adopting, taking up or employing, as well as is to giving bestowal or charity. In the Fatimid era, "the institution of patronage was a powerful instrument linking masters and protégés among free-born people; master to their slaves and freedmen; individuals as well as groups. The conferring of patronage on an individual or a whole group was a public act, and those on whom it was bestowed were referred to as being under patronage." (Y. Lev, 87). When used to denote "whole groups of eunuchs," the term was uncertain and Y. Lev concludes that it probably indicated that they were allowed to bear arms. (Y. Lev, 88). (Yaacov Lev, *State and Society in Fatimid Egypt* (Leiden, 1991), 87–88; P. Sanders, *Ritual*, 91 & 166; al-Maqrīzī, *Itti'āẓ*, Vol. 2, 10; al-Maqrīzī, *Khiṭaṭ*, Vol. 2, 254–255; Ibn Taghrī Birdī, *Nujūm*, Vol. 4, 94–95, and http://www.baheth.info/all.jsp?term=اصطناع).

992 Al-Ṣaqāliba (sing. *Ṣaqlabī*): This is a term used to refer to slaves of Slavic and other, mostly eastern, European origins. This faction was markedly of fair complexion and sometimes red hair. They were commonly bought by the Umayyads of Andalusia and the Fatimids of North Africa and Egypt. They managed to reach high ranks, such as personal royal guards and military leaders, and of the caliph's guards in Umayyad Spain, some were "men of letters and culture." They were also sometimes employed as eunuch-servants, which is why the term *ṣaqlabī* is occassionally synonymous with "Slavic eunuch." (Brian Catlos, "Saqaliba," in *The Historical Encyclopedia of World Slavery*, ed. Junius P. Rodriguez (California, 1997),

or from the Sudanese from [among] the Bought Slaves (*'abīd al-shirā'*), the freed slaves and other factions. Each of these factions had its chiefs (*quwwād*)[993] and its commanders (*muqaddamūn*)[994] who were in command over them.

Vol. 2, 565–566 and Harry T. Norris, *Islam in the Balkans: Religion and Society between Europe and the Arab World* (Columbia, 1993), 22–23).

993 Sing, *qā'id*, also "leader."

994 Sing. *muqaddam*, which means the one who is put in the front, foremost position, that is in leadership.

The Fourth Clause
On the Holders of Offices (*arbāb al-waẓā'if*) in the Fatimid State, who are divided into two sections

The First Section

Those in the direct presence (*ḥaḍra*) of the caliph,[995] who are of four types:

The First Type: Holders of Offices among the Men of the Sword, who are of two kinds:

THE FIRST KIND: OFFICES OF COMMON SOLDIERS (*'ĀMMAT AL-JUND*), WHICH ARE NINE OFFICES:

The First Office: The Vizierate (al-wizāra)

This was their most superior and highest-ranking office. You should know that the vizierate in the Fatimid State was sometimes assigned to a Man of the Sword, and other times to a Man of the Pen. In either case, [the nature of the office changed] from being the higher level Vizierate of Delegation (*wizārat tafwīḍ*),[996] which was similar or close to the current [authority of the] sultan, and was then called "The Vizierate" (*al-wizāra*), tothe lesser level [office of] "The Mediation" (*al-wasāṭa*).[997]

The author of *Nihāyat al-Arab* said: The first among them to be termed a vizier was Ya'qūb b. Killis, the vizier of al-'Azīz.[998] The first vizier of the great Men of the Sword was Badr al-Jamālī, the vizier of al-Mustanṣir, and the last was Ṣalāḥ al-Dīn Yūsuf b. Ayyūb, who was then able to [seize power] and become sultan, as was mentioned earlier.

The Second Office: Office of the Master of the Gate (ṣāḥib al-bāb)[999]

This is second in rank to the office of the vizierate. Ibn al-Ṭuwayr said: It was termed "the lesser vizierate." The holder of this position had a similar authority to that of the Plenipotentiary Viceroy (*al-nā'ib al-kāfil*) of our times. The Master of the Gate was responsible for looking into the grievances (*maẓālim*),[1000] if the

995 *Bi-ḥaḍrat al-khalīfa*, means "in the presence of the caliph," or in his vicinity. This term was used to refer to the caliph's capital (also *ḥaḍirat al-khalīfa* and *ḥāḍrat al-khilāfa*), besides bearing the more general connotation of any attendance in the caliph's or sultan's presence, such as serving in his main court or being in his audience.

996 See Glossary.

997 See Glossary.

998 Al-Nuwayrī, *Nihāya*, Vol. 28, 153.

999 The Keeper of the Gate/Door, the Lord of the Gate, the Master of the Gate, and the Chief Chamberlain are all translations given to this title.

1000 "Sing. *maẓlama* or *ẓalāma*, which means the violation of someone's rights, and referred to grievances or petitions. Muslim jurisprudents use the term to mean an act of injustice or corruption of the state, which cannot be ruled on by ordinary judges and has to be raised to the

vizier was not a Man of the Sword. In case the vizier was indeed a Man of the Sword, he would be the one to sit for audienceto see to the grievancesin person, while the Master of the Gate stood among those in his service (*khidma*).[1001]

The Third Office: Al-Isfihlāriyya[1002]

Ibn al-Ṭuwayr said: The holder of this office is the overseerof all overseers.[1003] He supervises and manages the soldiers. The *ḥujjāb*[1004] of all levels stood in his service (*khidma*), as well as in the service of the Master of the Gate.[1005]

The Fourth Office: Bearing the parasol in grand occasions

Such [grand occasions] included riding on the occasion of the New Year and the like. This was one of the great offices and its holder was called "The Bearer of the Parasol" (*ḥāmil al-miẓalla*). He was a dignified amir, whom they highly regarded and dignified,[1006] for he bore what was held above the caliph's head.

The Fifth Office: Bearing the caliph's sword in the processions where the parasol is borne

The holder of this office was called "The Sword Bearer" (*ḥāmil al-sayf*).

The Sixth Office: Bearing the caliph's lance in the processions where the parasol is borne

This was a small lance that was carried along the caliph on processions. The holder of this position was called "The Lance Bearer" (*ḥāmil al-rumḥ*).

The Seventh Office: Bearing the arms around the caliph in processions

The holders of this position were called "The Equestrian Escorts" (*al-rikābiyya*) and "Private Equestrian Guards" (*ṣibyān al-rikāb al-khāṣṣ*) because of their costume.

highest authority." (Al-Baqli, *Ta'rīf*, 314). The highest authority in this case means the caliph, the sultan, or who acts in their place.

1001 Ibn al-Ṭuwayr, *Nuzha*, 122.

1002 Also: *al-Isfihsalāriyya*; the holder of this office was called the "*isfihsalār*," which is a half-Persian, half-Turkish word meaning the commander of the soldiers or the army, and was also sometimes referred to as the "*sbāslār.*" The high commander of the Fatimid army, to whom the *isfihsalār* reported, during the first century of the era, remained to be the caliph, until Badr al-Jamālī's appointment as a vizier in 466 AH/1074 AD, which marked the beginning of an era of military viziers who bore the title *amīr al-juyūsh*, the prince of armies, meaning the high commander of the army. The title was also used by the Atabeks of Syria and by the Ayyubids. (See A. Gamal al-Din, *Dawla*, 223 and A. Sayyid, *Tafsīr*, 689–690).

1003 "*Zimām kul zimām*," meaning the overseer of all military men and matters. In Arabic, *al-zimām* is "the reins" and is used to denote a leader. (See *Ṣubḥ*, Vol. 5, 460 and Glossary: "*zimām*").

1004 Sing. *ḥājib*, from the verb *ḥajaba* (to veil or to conceal). The verb "*ḥajaba*" means to veil, conceal or screen; hence the *ḥājib* is the one who veils or screens the ruler from the public, and who asks permission for visitors. (See Glossary).

1005 Ibn al-Ṭuwayr, *Nuzha*, 123.

1006 "*Lahu 'indahum al-taqaddum wa-l-rif'a,*" which could also suggest that, in addition to being highly regarded and esteemed, that he was a high-ranking commander (*muqaddam*).

They are the ones called "The Holders of Arms" (*al-ṣilāḥdāriyya*) and "Holders of Battle-axes" (*al-ṭabardāriyya*) in our times. They used to be more than 2000 men, who had twelve commanders (*muqaddamūn*), and they escorted the caliph on processions.[1007] They had captains (*nuqabā'*)[1008] that they appointed themselves. The high-ranking among them were delegated for the sultanic tasks,[1009] and if they entered a provincial division (*'amal*),[1010] they were highly renowned.

The Eighth Office: The Governorship of Cairo (*wilāyat al-Qāhira*)[1011]

The holder of this office was of adignified rank and was much respected. He had his own designated place in the procession.

The Ninth Office: The Governorship of Miṣr (*wilāyat Miṣr*)[1012]

This was beneath the governorship of Cairo in rank, as it is now. However, *Miṣr* was at the time inhabited and populated, which gave it a higher status than its present day one.

The Second Kind

The offices of the caliph's private retinue (*khawāṣṣ al-khalīfa*) from the [category of] the Masters (*ustādhūn*). These comprised several offices that were [divided into] two categories.

1007 For the "The Equestrian Escorts" (*al-rikābiyya*) see (P. Sanders, *Ritual*, 228 and Ibn al-Ṭuwayr, *Nuzha*, 124, 148, 148 fn. 1, & 165 fn. 1).

1008 Sing. *naqīb*.

1009 In the Mamluk era, *al-ashghāl al-sulṭāniyya* (also *al-a'māl al-sulṭāniyya*), were the tasks of the sultan that he delegates to others. (A. Dahman, *Mu'jam*, 16). The author may have meant to refer to the same meaning, but in Fatimid context, where the ruler was a caliph, rather than a sultan.

1010 Pl. *a'māl*, which is used to give the same meaning. After the cadastral survey of 715 AH/1315 AD, in the reign of the Mamluk Sultan al-Nāṣir Muḥammad, known as *al-rawk al-Nāṣirī*, the term *a'māl* (also, *'amal*) was used to refer to provincial divisions that were equivalent to present day governorates. (Muhammad Ramzy, *Al-Qāmūs Al-Jughrāphī li-l-Bilād al-Miṣriyya min 'Ahd Qudamā' al-Miṣriyyīn ilā Sanat 1945* (Cairo, 1994), Part 2, Vol. 1, 22).

1011 The *wilāya* was the office of the governor of any of the governorates of Egypt (*wilāya* pl. *wilāyāt*: major provincial divisions which may be considered equivalent to modern day governorates). This office was sometimes promoted to the level of viceroyship in the case of Alexandria. The holder of the office was termed a "*wālī*" (pl. *wulāt*) and "the main duties of the *wulāt* were police work and keeping order." According to al-Maqrīzī, the *wilāya* was the term used to refer to what was called *shurṭa* (police) in older times. (Al-Baqli, *Ta'rīf*, 358 and al-Maqrīzī, *Khiṭaṭ*, Vol. 3, 89).

1012 Al-Fustat. See above.

The First Category: [Offices] particular to the *muḥannakūn* masters, which are nine offices:

The First: Wrapping the Crown (*shadd al-tāj*)

The holder of this office was responsible for wrapping the caliph's crown, which he wore on grand processions. This office was the same as the Wrapper (*al-laffāf*)[1013] of our current times. The holder of this office was privileged, for he touched the crown that topped the caliph's head. The special protocol of wrapping this crown was not known to everyone. It was brought in a rectangular form and wrapped using a turban-cloth (*mindīl*)[1014] of the same colour as the caliph's costume. As mentioned above, this [method and form of] wrapping was called "The Winding of Veneration" (*shaddat al-waqār*).

The Second: Office of the Master of the Audience Hall (ṣāḥib al-majlis)[1015]

The holder of this office was responsible for all that pertained to the audience hall (*majlis*) where the caliph sat for public appearance on processions. The Master of the Audience Hall would come out to the vizier and the amirs to inform them that the caliph has taken his place on the throne (*sarīr al-mulk*). He was referred to as the "Royal Trustee" (*amīn al-mulk*) and was the same as the Treasurer Amir (*amīr khazindār*)[1016] of our times.

The Third: Office of The Messenger (ṣāḥib al-risāla)[1017]

The holder of thisoffice was the one who carried the caliph's messages to the vizier and others.

The Fourth: Office of the Overseer of the Palaces (zimām al-quṣūr)[1018]

He was equivalent to the Overseer of the Houses (*zimām al-dūr*)[1019] of our times.

1013 The position of wrapping the sultan's turban during the Mamluk era.

1014 *Mindīl* (pl. *manādīl*) means"kerchief" and is used to refer to turban-cloth, handkerchief, napkin or tablecloth.The *mindīl* was a piece of the royal or elite costume and was wrapped as a turban. Vizier al-Afḍal is said to have had 100 outfits (*badla*), each having a *mindīl* of matching colour. (Ibn al-Ṭuwayir, Nuzha, 155–156 fn. 4 and G. Qaddumi, *Gifts*, 261 en. 4).

1015 Translation after P. Sanders. (P. Sanders, *Ritual*, 177).

1016 The *khāzindār* was the royal treasurer of the Mamluk state. It is not clear from this account whet her the offices of the *amīr khāzindār* and the *khāzindār* were the same. Al-Maqrīzī refers to the office of *khāzindār al-sulṭān* (the Sultan's Treasurer) in his account of the year 844 AH/1440 AD, when he mentions the death of Jawhar al-Qinqibā'ī, the *ṭawāshī*, and a Mamluk state servant under three sultans. Jawhar held two positions simultaneously during the reign of Sultan Jaqmaq (841 AH/1438 AD – 857 AH/1453 AD): the *khāzindār* and *zimām al-dūr*. (Al-Maqrīzī, *Sulūk*, Vol. 7, 480–481 and Ibn Taghrī Birdī, *Nujūm*, Vol. 15, 222–223).

1017 "The Holder of the Message" or the "Keeper of the Message."

1018 The man responsible for managing the palace servants and overseeing their work.P. Sanders translates this term as "the majordomo." (Al-Baqli, *Ta'rīf*, 173 and P. Sanders, *Ritual*, 33).

1019 See Glossary: "*zimām*".

The Fifth: Office of the Keeper of the Public Treasury (ṣāḥib bayt al-māl)[1020]

He was equivalent to the Treasurer (*khāzindār*)[1021] of our times.

The Sixth: Office of the Keeper of the Register (*ṣāḥib al-daftar*)[1022]

This was the register known as the "Register of the Council" (*daftar al-majlis*).[1023] The holder of this office supervised the bureaus (*dawāwīn*) that encompassed all the caliphate's matters.

The Seventh: Office of the Bearer of the Inkwell (*ḥāmil al-dawāt*)

This was the inkwell (*dawāt*) of the caliph that was mentioned earlier. The holder of this office situated the inkwell in front of him, on the saddle, and marched with it on processions.

The Eighth: Office of Overseeing of the Relatives (*zamm al-aqārib*)

The holder of this office controlled the *ashrāf* faction, who were the relatives of the caliph, and they had to obey his orders.

The Ninth: Overseering of Men (*zamm al-rijāl*)[1024]

The holder of this office was the one responsible for the caliph's food, like the [present day] Master of the Kitchen and Banquets (*ustādār al-ṣuḥba*).[1025]

The Second Category

The offices of those other than the *muḥannakun*, of which two are well-known:

The First: The Chieftain of the Ṭālibiyyīn (*niqābat al-ṭālibiyyīn*)[1026]

This was equivalent to the present day Chieftain of the *ashrāf* (*niqābat al-ashrāf*).[1027] The holder of this position had to be one of the most respected elderly of the Ṭālibiyyīn. He looked into their matters, prevented any imposters from joining them

1020 Sometimes also referred to as *mutawallī bayt al-māl* (Director of the Public Treasury).

1021 The *khāzindār* in the Mamluk era "was the person responsible for the sultanic, amirial, or other treasuries and their contents, such as money and grains." (Al-Baqli, *Ta'rīf*, 113).

1022 "Holder of the Register," also *ṣāḥib daftar al-majlis* (Keeper of the Council's Register).This position entailed supervising all the bureaus pertaining to caliphal matters. *Ṣāḥib al-daftar* was one of the caliph's entourage and he received a monthly salary of 100 dinars. (Al-Baqli, *Ta'rīf*, 213).

1023 This register was composed of plain papers used to record data like gifts, bestowals, *rusūm* (designated portions, pensions and other similar expenses), presents sent to other kings and several other similar royal expenses. (Ibn al-Ṭuwayr, *Nuzha*, 75, A. Sayyid, *Tafsīr*, 383, P. Sanders, *Ritual*, 66 & 84).

1024 Also, see below.

1025 Also, see later.

1026 The chieftain, deanship, or syndicate of the Ṭālibiyyīn, who are the descendants of Abū Ṭālib, the Prophet's uncle, who had four sons: Ṭālib, 'Uqayl, Ja'far, and 'Alī.

1027 The chieftain, deanship, or syndicate of the *ashrāf*.

unrightfully and [had the right], if in suspicion of anyone, to ask them to prove their lineage. He was also responsible for visiting the sick among them, walking in their funerals,[1028] seeing to their needs, and punishing the ones who transgress and prevent them from further transgression. He was not to make any decisions concerning them except with the approval of their shaykhs[1029] and the like.

The Second Office: Overseeing of Men (zamm al-rijāl)[1030]
The holder of this position supervised the factions of men and soldiers, [through tasks] such as overseeing the young guards of the barracks (*zamm ṣibyān al-ḥujar*), the Āmiriyya and the Ḥāfiẓiyya factions (*zamm al-ṭā'ifa al-Āmiriyya wa-l-ṭā'ifa al-Ḥāfiẓiyya*), the Sudanese (*zamm al-sūdān*) and others. This position is equivalent to the Commander of Mamluks (*muqaddam al-mamālīk*)[1031] of our times.

The Second Type: Holders of the offices in the caliph's presence (*ḥaḍra*)[1032] – Men of the Pen: Three Kinds

The First Kind

HOLDERS OF RELIGIOUS OFFICES, OF WHICH SIX ARE WELL-KNOWN

The First: The Chief Judge (qāḍī al-quḍāt)[1033]
This was one of their most dignified, superior and highly regarded offices. Ibn al-Ṭuwayr said: No one may precede him [in rank] or be spared his authority. He supervised [the implementation of] the religious legislative rulings (*al-aḥkām al-shar'iyya*).[1034] He also supervised the minting houses (*dūr al-ḍarb*)[1035] and regulated[1036] their calibration.[1037] The judicial authority over Egypt, Syrian cities[1038] and

1028 The Islamic funeral starts with special prayers for the dead then carrying the dead body and walking along it to its burial place.

1029 Elderly leaders.

1030 Note that this position is listed under two categories with different tasks. Al-Baqli provides a single definition for the holder of this office, which combines the above mentioned tasks under both categories. It is also possible that its holder was of either categories, and performed different tasks depending on the category he belonged to. M. Dahman notes that in the Mamluk era, the title "*al-zimām dār*" applied to military leaders, for *al-zimām al-'askarī* meant "the military leader," or "the leader of soldiers. (Al-Baqli, *Ta'rīf*, 172 and M. Dahman, *Mu'jam*, 87).

1031 See Glossary.

1032 That is, in the caliph's direct service 995.

1033 Also, see Glossary.

1034 Also, Islamic legal injunctions or canonical ordinances.

1035 Sing. *dār al-ḍarb*.

1036 *Ḍabṭ'iyārihā*, which also denotes ensuring the accuracy of the standards.

1037 See Ibn al-Ṭuwayr's account in *Nuzha*, 107–109.

1038 *Ajnād al-Shām* (*ajnād*, sing. *jund*: city).

the Maghrib might have been assigned to one judge, for whom a single diploma of investiture (*'ahd*)[1039] would be written, as will be mentioned later in the section on appointments [to official offices] (*al-wilāyāt*).[1040]

If the vizier was a Man of the Sword, he would investiture[1041] the judge in the name of the caliph.[1042] If the vizier was otherwise, the caliph would be the one to investiture him.

The judge was given a white mule from the caliph's stables, which he always rode. He was the only statesman to ride a mule of this colour. A heavy mount and a saddle with two silver rear sides were released for him from the Treasury of Saddles. On special festive occasions (*mawāsim*)[1043] he would be decorated with collars and bestowed on with golden-adornedrobes of honour (*khila'*). The terms[1044] of [the Fatimids] dictated that he would not be allowed to rule that a witness is equitable[1045] except upon the order of the caliph.[1046] He would neither attend a marriage ceremony[1047] nor a funeral except with permission. The Chief Judge would not be called by this title in the presence of a vizier, for this is one of the vizierial designations. The judge sat on the early mornings of Mondays and Thursdays at the palace to greet the caliph. On Saturdays and Tuesdays, he would sit in the *ziyyāda* of the Old Mosque in Fustat. He had his own headscarf (*ṭarḥa*),[1048] sitting rest (*masnad julūs*), and a chair (*kursī*) on which his inkwell (*dawāt*) was put.[1049]

When he presided his council (*majlis*), the witnesses were seated around him, to his right and left, in the order of ruling their equitability (*ta'dīl*). Ibn al-Ṭuwayr

1039 Also, "pledge," see later.

1040 A section not translated in this work.

1041 "*Taqlīduhu.*" *Taqlīd* (investiture), *sijill* (register), and *'ahd* (pledge) were all terms used to refer to the diplomas of investiture. (Amin Haji, "Institutions of Justice in Fatimid Egypt." in *Islamic Law: Social and Historical Contexts*, ed. Aziz Al-Azmeh (London, 2013), 201).

1042 "Substitute him," which can be understood as referring to the caliph.

1043 Sing. *mawsim,* which are recurrent festivity occasions, such as the annual feasts.

1044 "*Muṣṭalaḥ*," also "protocol."

1045 See Glossary: "*'adl*".

1046 The step of *ta'dīl al-shāhid* (ruling that a witness is just and reasonable, therefore equitable) is one of the steps of Islamic legislation and court ruling. The criteria for a witness to be deemed *'adl* (equitable) are normally five: Islam, adulthood, sanity, religious propriety, and reputability.

1047 *Imlāk* in *Ṣubḥ* and *milāk* in *Nuzha*, both meaning marriage. (*Ṣubḥ*, Vol. 3, 487 and Ibn al-Ṭuwayr, *Nuzha*, 108).

1048 A piece of cloth that was used to cover the turban, wrap around the neck and fall on one's back. It was characteristic of the office of the Chief Judge. In the Mamluk era, it was originally only worn by the holders of the office of the Shāfi'ī Chief Judge, but those occupying the same post for the Ḥanafī school were granted their request to wear it on processions and special occasions like the Shāfi'īs by the beginning of the 9th century AH/15th century AD. (H. al-Battawi, *'Imāma*, 134).

1049 "*Kursī*" is "chair." Ibn al-Ṭuwayr says that the Chief Judge had a *kursī al-dawāt* (chair of the inkwell). This silver inlaid inkwell had a special bearer who carried it from the palace treasuries to the judge. (Ibn al-Ṭuwayr, *Nuzha*, 107).

said: A young man would sit higher[1050] than an elderly man if the earlier's ruling of equitability preceded the latter's. Four signers (*muwaqqi'ūn*)[1051] were present beforehim, two facing two. At his door, five *ḥujjāb*[1052] stood: two before him, two at the door of the *maqṣūra*, and one to let in the adversaries. The judge would stand up for no one [while presiding] the Council of Judgement (*majlis al-ḥukm*).[1053]

The Second: The Chief Missionary (*dā'ī al-du'āt*)[1054]

The [Fatimids] considered the holder of this position next in rank to the Chief Judge, and he was dressed in similar costumes and other [items of attire] to the judge's. This office entailed [sitting] at a house (*dār*), known as the House of Knowledge (Dār al-'Ilm), where [learners] read[1055] the religious interpretation schools (*madhāhib*)[1056] of the Members of the House of the Prophet (*Ahl al-bayt*) before him. He was also responsible for pledging whoever decided to convert to their doctrine.[1057]

The Third: The *muḥtasib*[1058]

He was one of the respected dignitaries of the equitables. Once appointed, his diploma of investiture (*sijill*)[1059] was read on the minbar in Miṣr and Cairo.[1060] Based

1050 Higher so as to indicate superior status, possibly by sitting closer to the judge or on a higher seat.

1051 Sing. *muwaqqi'*, or signer, in this case short for *muwaqqi' al-ḥukm*: The *muwwaqi' al-ḥukm* (verdict signer) or *kātib al-qāḍī* (judge's scribe) was an assistant to the *qāḍī*. *Muwwaqi' al-ḥukm* attended the judge's council to copy the court verdicts so as to announce them to the public, record them, and execute them. He had to have an excellent knowledge of the language and be well-informed of the meanings and significances of the colloquial and classical words and terms. Knowing colloquial terminologies and expressions was essential to ensure that the signer or scribe will express the exact meanings intended by the adversaries or witnesses. In the Mamluk era, the holders of the post of verdict signer were later entitled to be promoted to the office of *nā'ib al-qāḍī* (Deputy of the Judge), then to the office of Chief Judge, if they had the required qualifications. They also contributed to other work fields, such as education and Sufism. (H. al-Battawi, *'Imāma*, 67).

1052 Sing. *ḥājib*, see Glossary.

1053 Ibn al-Ṭuwayr, *Nuzha*, 107–108.

1054 See Glossary.

1055 "*Yuqra' 'alayhi*," which was the teaching methodology of religious sciences at the time. The learner would recite a book under the supervision of the teacher, who corrected and explained as needed.

1056 Sing. *madhhab*: school of religious interpretation, rite or doctrine.

1057 The Fatimid Shiite doctrine.

1058 An office of high regulatory and executive authority.

1059 The *sijill* (pl. *sijillāt*, register) during the Fatimid era was an official document that recorded an administrative issue pertaining to the state matters or its men, such as decrees of appointment or diplomas of investiture, rulings, declarations, announcements, etc. They were written in an eloquent style, usually by the highest scribe of the Chancery Bureau (*dīwān al-inshā'*). Many examples of the Fatimid *sijillāt* are available in the primary sources. (Muhammad Z. Sallam, *Al-Adab fī al-'Aṣr al-Fāṭimī: Al-Kitāba wa-l-Kuttāb* (Alexandria, 1995), 232). In this case, the term refers to a diploma of investiture.

1060 Reading a decree on the minbar was a form of announcement. Al-Qalqashandī is probably referring to the minbars of the two main mosques of each of Cairo and Fustat.

on the rules of [his office] (*ḥisba*),[1061] he was completely authorized to command right and forbid wrong.[1062] He was not to be hampered from pursuing something he deemed of overall benefit and the chiefs (*wulāt*) were called upon to assist him in his campaigns if he needed them.[1063] He assigned his own deputies in Cairo, Miṣr and all the provincial divisions (*a'māl*), in the same way the Deputies of the Chief Judge (*nuwwāb al-ḥukm*) were appointed. He sat for public audience daily, alternating[1064] between the two congregational mosques of Cairo and Miṣr. The rest of his affairs were the same as those of the present day's *muḥtasib*.

I say: I saw in some of the [Fatimid] diplomas of investiture (*sijillāt*)[1065] that the office of the *muḥtasib* in both Miṣr and Cairo was sometimes additionally assigned to the chiefs of the police[1066] of each of them.

The Fourth: Office of the Agent of the Public Treasury (*wakālat bayt al-māl*)
This agency office was only assigned to the esteemed among the elderly equitables. The holder of this office was delegated, in the name of the caliph, to: sell what he saw [suitable] of all types of possessions that are sellable according to religious legislation; free mamluks; marry women-slaves; [ensure] that the tax farm (*ḍamān*) is applied to all [land and property] that should be subjected to it;[1067] buy what he deemed needed, and construct what he found necessary of

1061 The office of the *muḥtasib*.

1062 Or "command virtue and prevent vice"; the concept of "*al-amr bi-l-ma'rūf wa-l-nahiy 'an al-munkar*" is an Islamic behaviour practiced on the level of the authority and the individual, with several religious restrictions governing it, based on the Quranic verse: "You are the best nation produced [as an example] for mankind. You enjoin what is right and forbid what is wrong and believe in Allah." (Sahih International's translation of part of Sūrat Āl 'Imrān, Chapter of The Family of 'Imrān, 3:110 – http://corpus.quran.com/translation.jsp?chapter=3&verse=110).

1063 The *wulāt* (sing. *wālī*) mentioned here are most probably the chiefs of police. Al-Qalqashandī's sentence is unclear, and may be translated as" and the *wulāt* are called upon from him/by him." However, al-Maqrīzī's version, also after Ibn al-Ṭuwayr, is: "and the *wulāt* are called upon to assist him if he needs that," which allows the interpretation above. Ibn al-Ṭuwayr's version also suggests that the *muḥtasib*was the one who ordered the chiefs (*wulāt*) to assist him: "and the *wulāt*are called upon from him/by him if he needs that." (*Ṣubḥ*, Vol. 3, 487, al-Maqrīzī, *Khiṭaṭ*, Vol. 2, 286 and Ibn al-Ṭuwayr, *Nuzha*, 117).

1064 Al-Qalqashandī uses the expression "*yawman bi-yawm*," which means on consecutive days, but Ibn al-Ṭuwayr says "*yawman ba'd yawm*," which means "day after day," and shows that the *muḥtasib* shifted his audience between the two mosques. (*Ṣubḥ*, Vol. 3, 487 and Ibn al-Ṭuwayr, *Nuzha*, 117).

1065 Sing. *sijill*.

1066 The Chief of the Police: *Ṣāḥib al-Shurṭa* was termed "*wālī*" (also, governor) during the Mamluk era. (Al-Baqli, *Ta'rīf*, 216).

1067 "*Taḍmīn mā yaqtaḍī al-ḍamān*." The*ḍamān* (guarantee; tax farm) was a tax system that did not comply with religious legislation. This system "often involved putting up for auction of the right to collect the taxes of a given area, usually annually." (Lambton, 365). A *ḍāmin* (the tax farmer) guaranteed the annual payment of the taxes required from a village, for example, by paying them in advance to the government. In the Fatimid era, this system was apparently applied to lands, caravanserais, baths, *ribā'*, and other establishments.The actual taxes expected from the guaranteed area or establishment was normally more than the amount of money the tax farmer paid, and this is

buildings, ships and otherwise, in addition to other essential [dealings] that he carried outon behalf of the caliph.

The Fifth: The Deputy (*al-nā'ib*)

This was the deputy of the above mentioned Master of the Gate, who is called "the *mihmandār*"[1068] (the Chief of Protocol) in our present days. Ibn al-Ṭuwayr said: This office is called The Honourable Deputation (*al-niyāba al-sharīfa*). He added: It is a respected position occupied by dignified equitables and Men of the Pen. The holder of this office represented the Master of the Gate in receiving the messengers sent to the caliph at the distance [specified] for the deputies to stand for service (*khidma*). He was [responsible for] allocating a suitable residence for each messenger and supplying them with what they needed. He was not to allow anyone to meet with those messengers, was in charge of locating them[1069] and reminding the Master of the Gate of them. He was also responsible for aiding them in accomplishing their missions and introducing them to the caliph or vizier; walking ahead of them and announcing them at the doors. The messenger would enter [to the caliph's or vizier's audience] with the Master of the Gate holding his right hand and the deputy holding his left. The deputy memorized what [the messengers] said and what they were told. He made sure the messengers were sent away in the best possible manner. If he had to be absent, he assigned a deputy in his place. One of the conditions of the deputy's office was to deny being handed any gifts or rarities from a messenger unless given the permission.

Ibn al-Ṭuwayr said: The holder of this office is the one currently called "the *mihmandār*." It will be described later, in the section on the arrangement of the [Mamluk] kingdom,that the *mihmindār* is a Man of the Sword, as if to suit the state's language of communication and appearance.[1070]

how he made profit. If, however, the guaranteed area or establishment did not achieve the expected annual revenue, which was a rare occurrence, the tax farmer was not to be compensated, unless the government decided to pardon him. The Fatimids used this *ḍamān* system since the early years of their rule in Egypt, which provided a guarantee for all the state's money and ensured the availability of liquidity for paying salaries. The system also continued under the Ayyubids. The main tax farmer usually had secondary tax farmers who collected the taxes in certain areas. Most tax farmers were wealthy investors who could afford such huge commitments, and even compete for them, since in return they made enormous profits. Many times the tax farmers made outdated, therefore crooked, contracts; exploited the taxpayers by imposing higher taxes, and failed to pay the whole amounts of money he owed the government. (Ann K. S. Lambton, "*Reflections on the Iqṭā'*," in *Arabic and Islamic Studies in Honour of Hamilton A. R. Gibb*, ed. George Makdisi (Leiden, 1965), 365; A. Sayyed, *Tafsīr*, 514–516; Ibn al-Ṭuwayir, Nuzha, 80–81 fn. 1, and *Ṣubḥ*, Vol. 3, 470).

1068 In the Mamluk times, the holder of this office received the ambassadors, messengers and the Arab Bedouins who arrived to meet the sultan, hosted them at *dār al-ḍiyāfa* (House of Hospitality, that is the Guest House), and supervised all matters pertaining to them. (Al-Baqli, *Ta'rīf*, 334 and S. Ashour, *'Aṣr*, 478).

1069 "*Yatawallā iftiqādahum*," also "in charge of inspecting them" or "calling on them."

1070 See Ibn al-Ṭuwayr's account on the *niyāba* (deputation) in *Nuzha*, 118–119.

The Sixth: The Quran Reciters (al-qurrā')[1071]

The [Fatimids] had reciters who recited the Quran in the caliph's presence (*ḥaḍra*); in his audience councils (*majālis*), when he rode in processions and on other [occasions]. They were called the Reciters in Presence (*qurrā' al-ḥaḍra*)[1072] and were more than ten men. In the audience councils (*majālis*) and the processions, they used to recite Quranic verses suitable for the occasion, using even the least of analogies. They were used to this practice and it was easy for them to recall [the appropriate verses]. This used to please the caliph and the attendees, so much so that it is related that once a caliph was angry at an amir and ordered his arrest. The Reciter in Presence then recited: "Take what is given freely, enjoin what is good, and turn away from the ignorant."[1073] The caliph liked hearing this and released the amir. However, sometimes they manipulated the use of the verses to allude to a meaning that the verse did not convey. It is related that when Caliph al-Mustanṣir appointed Badr al-Jamālī as his vizier, the reciter recited: "And already had Allah given you victory at [the battle of] Badr while you were few in number."[1074] [Similarly], when Caliph al-Ḥāfiẓ appointed Riḍwān[1075] as his vizier,

1071 Sing. *al-qāri'*.

1072 Sing.Qāri' al-Ḥaḍra, which means: The Reciter in Presence; that is the presence of the caliph.

1073 Quran, Sūrat al-A'rāf (Chapter of The Heights), 7:199, Sahih International's translation (http://corpus.quran.com/translation.jsp?chapter=7&verse=199).

1074 Quran, Sūrat Āl 'Imrān (Chapter of the Family of 'Imrān), 3:123, in part, Sahih International's translation (http://corpus.quran.com/translation.jsp?chapter=3&verse=123). The preposition used with the word "Badr" in the verse, to refer to the place that witnessed the first victory of Muslims, could simultaneously mean "at" and "with" in Arabic. The play of words then becomes clear as the reciter uses the verse to associate victory with the name of the vizier, as if it can be brought on by him, while theverse had always referred to the first battle of triumph. Badr, as well as being the name of a place in between Mecca and Medina, literally means "full moon," and is used as a name, more commonly for men. See al-Maqrīzī's account of the same incident in *Itti'āẓ*, Vol. 2, 313.

1075 Riḍwān b. Walakhshī, who became the vizier of Caliph al-Ḥāfiẓ following a period of considerable turmoil. People had written to Riḍwān imploring him to relieve them of the awkward situation of having a Christian for a vizier, namely, Bahrām al-Armanī (the Armenian), especially that the Vizierate of Delegation was a most dominant position that also entailed observing religious rituals on several public occasions. Riḍwān was appointed vizier in 531 AH/1137 AD, being imposed on the caliph through power games, and was the first Sunni to hold this position in the Fatimid era. Known for his remarkable courage, he was originally one of the Equestrian Guards (*ṣibyān al-rikāb*), who was promoted to several positions until he became the governor of Qūṣ and Ikhmīm in Upper Egypt, Ascalon in Palestine, and finally al-Gharbiyya in Lower Egypt. As a vizier, Riḍwān replaced the Christian state employees with Muslims and showed much intolerance to non-Muslims. Being Sunni, he did not really recognize the authority of Caliph al-Ḥāfiẓ and tried to dethrone him, but the religious scholars (*'ualamā'*) refused to condone that. Alexandria was at the time one of the abodes of Sunni resistance against Shiite domination in Egypt; that is why Riḍwān built a madrasa for the Mālikī school there in 532 AH/1138 AD, which he, nevertheless, named al-Ḥāfiẓiyya after the caliph. Al-Ḥāfiẓ managed to arrest Riḍwān in 534 AH/1139 AD and he remained in imprisonment at the royal palace for eight years, after which he managed to escape through a hole he was able to dig. He was then able to gather some of his supporters and a group of Bedouins, but was, however, killed by the caliph's forces in 542 AH/1148 AD. (A. Sayyid, *Tafsīr*, 258–270).

the reciter recited: "Their Lord gives them good tidings of mercy from Him and approval and of gardens for them wherein is enduring pleasure (*riḍwān*);"[1076] not to mention other instances.

The Second Kind: Men of the Pen who held offices at the bureaus

THREE CATEGORIES[1077]

The First Category: The Vizierate, if the vizier was a Man of the Pen

You should know that most of the [Fatimid] viziers, since the beginning of their rule and up to the caliphate of al-Mustans (ir, were Men of the Pen who were either [assigned] the full [authority] of the office or the mediation (*wasāṭa*), which was an inferior rank to the vizierate. Ibn al-Ṭuwayr mentions several of their famous viziers who were Men of the Pen, such as:

- Ya'qūb b. Killis, vizier of Caliph al-'Azīz;
- Al-Ḥasan b. 'Abd Allah al-Yāzūrī, vizier of Caliph al-Mustanṣir;[1078]
- Abū Sa'īd al-Tustarī;[1079]

1076 Quran, Sūrat al-Tawba (The Chapter of Repentance), 9:21, in part, Sahih International's translation (http://corpus.quran.com/translation.jsp?chapter=9&verse=21). Riḍwān, the vizier's name, means "good pleasure" and "acceptance," and is the word employed in the verse. Again, the play with words is clear.

1077 The editor of Subḥ notes that four are listed, rather than three. (*Ṣubḥ*, Vol. 3, 489).

1078 Al-Ḥasan b. 'Abd Allah al-Yāzūrī was the vizier of Caliph al-Mustanṣir from 442 AH/1150 AD to 450 AH/1158 AD. He was the last of the powerful among the viziers who were Men of the Pen during the Fatimid era and the first to hold the positions of the chief judge and chief missionary, in addition to being the vizier. After he was deposed and killed, the state suffered a "serious administrative crisis" that, accompanied with rebellions, disruptions, famines, and plagues, led to the caliph's beseeching Badr al-Jamālī, Governor of Acre, to become vizier. Al-Yāzūrī was one of the most important viziers of the first century of Fatimid reign in Egypt, before Men of the Sword started assuming the position. (A. Sayyid, *Tafsīr*, 191, 321, 364, 371).

1079 The name is misspelled for he was called Ibrāhīm b. Sahl al-Tustarī, Abū Sa'd, not Abū Sa'īd. Ibrāhīm and his brother Hārūn were two Jewish brothers who held high statuses during the reign of Caliph al-Ḥākim handling several matters of royal trade. Caliph al-Ẓāhir employed Ibrāhīm as his merchant and trusted him. Ibrāhīm bought him a black woman slave who gave him a son, al-Mustanṣir. When al-Mustanṣir's mother seized control of the state, she appointed Abū Sa'd Ibrāhīm as the director of her bureau (*mutawallī al-dīwān*), which increased his power at the expense of the influence of the actual vizier at the time, Abū Manṣūr Ṣadaqa b. Yūsuf al-Falāḥī. Al-Tustarī showed much bias to the Maghribi troops, favouring them over the Turks, in alignment with al-Mustanṣir's mother's policies to undermine the power of the Turks. He also favoured Jews and assigned to them many vital positions, which infuriated Muslims. This gave the chance to al-Falāḥī, although a converted Jew himself, to play the situation to his advantage. Al-Falāḥī started showing bias to the Turks and privileging them. He incited them to kill Abū Sa'd, which they did in 439 AH/1047 AD. The Muslim regiments hated Abū Sa'd so much that when the caliph wanted to know who killed him, they all confessed to the deed and

- Al-Jarjānī;[1080]
- Ibn Abī Kudayna;[1081]
- Abū al-Ṭāhir Aḥmad b. Bābshādh, who authored *al-Muqaddima fī al-Naḥw* (An Introduction to Grammar);[1082]
- ʿAlī b. Falāḥ,[1083]the Grand Vizier (*wazīr al-wuzarā'*),[1084] and
- Al-Maghribī, the vizier of Caliph al-Mustanṣir.[1085]

the guilty ones could not be singled-out, so the caliph had to pardon all. It appears that according to some sources, Abū Sa'd at some point converted to Islam and was appointed vizier. (A. Sayyid, *Tafsīr*, 198–199 & 326).

1080 The name is misspelled for he was called Najīb al-Dawla Abū al-Qāsim ʿAlī b. Aḥmad al-Jarjarā'ī, not al-Jarjānī. He was a member of a council of three who imposed themselves on Caliph al-Ẓāhir, along with a military commander, to manage the state and spare him its troubles so he might enjoy the leisurely life he was used to and leave them to control state matters. Al-Jarjarā'ī remained a vizier under Caliph al-Mustanṣir, controlling all state political matters, for nine years until he died in 436 AH/1045 AD and his death marked the beginning of the slow internal deterioration of the Fatimid state. (A. Sayyid, *Tafsīr*, 183,188, 197).

1081 Al-Ḥasan b. Mijallī b. Asad b. Abī Kudayna, Abū Muḥammad, Khaṭīr al-Mulk, was appointed vizier and chief judge and deposed several times, seven times according to al-Maqrīzī, during the crisis years of al-Mustanṣir's reign. He was a close ally of the Turkish forces and their commanders, who enforced their control over the state at the time. He was the vizier when Badr al-Jamālī arrived in Cairo, and was arrested in Damietta and killed in 569 AH/1174 AD, as one action among many that Badr took to swiftly get rid of all potential rivals. (Al-Maqrīzī, *Itti'āẓ*, Vol. 2, 311, 313, & 333, Al-Suyūṭī, *Ḥusn*, Vol. 2, 149–150 & 203–204, and Ibn Ḥajar al-ʿAsqalānī, *Raf' al-Iṣr 'an Quḍāt Miṣr*, ed. Ali M. Umar (Cairo, 1998), 135–137).

1082 Abū al-Ḥasan Ṭāhir b. Aḥmad b. Bābshādh, al-Naḥwī (the grammarian), al-Miṣrī al-Jawharī, (d. 469 AH/1077 AD) was an employee of the Fatimid state. He worked at the ChanceryBureau as an editor of its documents; all that was written in the bureau had to pass by him before being forwarded to the concerned officials. He also studied and taught Hadith and is reported to have retired and devoted himself to worship towards the end of his life. He died after falling off the roof of the Mosque of ʿAmr b. al-ʿĀṣ where he taught literature. He was originally a jewel merchant who travelled to Baghdad for trade then stayed there to learn language from its scholars. He authored the *Muqaddima* (Introduction), as well as other works, on grammar. While referred to by some historians as a linguist and a servant of the state, Ibn al-Ṭuwayr, copied by al-Qalqashandī, lists Ibn Bābshādh among the viziers who were men of the pen. (Al-Maqrīzī, *Itti'āẓ*, Vol. 2, 318, Al-Suyūṭī, *Ḥusn*, Vol. 1, 532, Ibn Taghrī Birdī, *Nujūm*, Vol. 5, 105 and Ibn al-Ṭuwayr, *Nuzha*, 105).

1083 ʿAlī b. Ja'far, Abū al-Ḥasan, Quṭb al-Dīn b. Falāḥ, of the Kutāma Berbers tribe was appointed in the office of mediation by Caliph al-Ḥākim in 405 AH/1015 AD and was killed in 409 AH/1019 AD after a confrontation with unknown horsemen. He was appointed Governor of Damascus in 398 AH/1007 AD and commander of the Kutāma Berbers in 403 AH/1012 AD. He helped subdue some uprisings as a military commander. One source also refers to a royal document that mentioned that ʿAlī b. Falāḥ was assigned the governance of Alexandria, Damietta, and Tinnīs, as well as heading the police of both Upper and Lower Egypt, and handling the *ḥisba*, and the military protection of the country. (Al-Maqrīzī, *Itti'āẓ*, Vol. 2, 10–11, 62–64, 71, 93, 110 & 114 and A. Sayyid, *Tafsīr*, 329).

1084 *Wazīr al-wuzarā'*, which means "the Vizier of Viziers."

1085 Abū al-Faraj Muḥammab b. Ja'far al-Maghribī (d. 478 AH/1085 AD), belonged to a family that influenced the politics and literature of Iraq and Egypt in the fourth and fifth centuries of the Hijra (late twelfth to late thirteenth century AD). He was appointed vizier more than once

Al-Maghribī was their last vizier from the Men of the Pen.[1086] Badr al-Jamālī, the Amir of Armies, substituted al-Maghribī and became the vizier of al-Mustanṣir, as mentioned earlier.[1087] This earlier period [of Fatimid rule] may have witnessed some Men of the Sword occupying the position of mediation, such as Barjawān al-Khādim,al-Ḥusayn b. Jawhar who was the Commander in Chief (*qā'id al-quwwād*),[1088] and ʿAlī b. Ṣāliḥ,[1089] who was given the title: "The Most Trustworthy Man of the Sword and the Pen," (*thiqat thiqāt al-sayf wa al-qalam*).[1090]All three served in the reign of al-Ḥākim.

during the reign of al-Mustanṣir, the first appointment being in 450 AH/1058 AD. Normally, when the viziers were relieved of their posts, they were not employed elsewhere in the state. Al-Maghribī was the first to suggest the appointment of viziers as heads of some of the bureaus after being dismissed from the vizierate, and was, therefore himself appointed head of the Chancery Bureau after serving as vizier. He tried to mediate between the Turkish and black sects during the period al-Mustanṣir's mother controlled the state matters, but failed. He was the mediator between the caliph and Badr al-Jamālī, the Governor of Acre, when the caliph wrote him begging his help and demanding that he came to Egypt. (Al-Suyūṭī, *Ḥusn*, Vol. 2, 149–150 and 202–203, al-Maqrīzī, *Itti'āẓ*, Vol. 2, 322, A. Sayyid, *Tafsīr*, 200, 209–210, and Ibn al-Ṭuwayir, Nuzha, 106 fn. 2).

1086 Al-Maqrīzī and al-Suyūṭī both report that several other viziers were appointed after al-Maghribī and until the advent of Badr al-Jamālī, in the same brief assignment and quick deposition manner that marked the crisis years of al-Mustanṣir's reign. According to al-Maqrīzī's account, some men were also appointed viziers for very brief periods after the advent of Badr and before he was installed as vizier, some of whom he killed. Al-Qalqashandī copied the statement above from Ibn al-Ṭuwayr. (Al-Maqrīzī, *Itti'āẓ*, Vol. 2, 313 & 333–334, Al-Suyūṭī, *Ḥusn*, Vol. 2, 203–204 and Ibn al-Ṭuwayr, *Nuzha*, 105).

1087 This is inaccurate. See the previous note.

1088 "Commander of the Commanders"; that is, the supreme commander of the army. (Al-Baqli, *Ta'rīf*, 267).

1089 The author probably means Ṣāliḥ b. ʿAlī al-Rūzbārī, Abū al-Faḍl, who was assigned to the authority of al-Ḥasan b. Jawhar, the Commander in Chief, in 398 AH/1008 AD. It may be understood from al-Maqrīzī's account that this authority was over the administrative part of the office, which entailed signing on part of caliph al-Ḥākim, looking into petitions and implementing the caliph's orders. al-Rūzbārī was dismissed in 400 AH/1009 AD and killed in 400 AH/1010 AD. (Al-Maqrīzī, *Itti'āẓ*, Vol. 2, 72, 81, & 83).

1090 This title showed that its holder supervised both the civil and the military sectors of the state. ʿAlī b. Ṣaliḥ was given this title in 399 AH/1009 AD. (Al-Baqli, *Ta'rīf*, 80 and Al-Maqrīzī, *Itti'āẓ*, Vol. 2, 78).

Some Christians also held the position of mediation, such as: ʿĪsā b. Nasṭūris[1091] in the days of Caliph al-ʿAzīz, Manṣūr b. ʿAbdūn[1092] who held the title of "The Sufficing" (al-Kāfī), and Zurʿa b. Nasṭūris[1093] who held the title of "The Healer" (al-Shāfī); both in the days of al-Ḥākim. [The function of mediation] was sometimes a matter of consulting chivalrous men.[1094]

The costume of the viziers who were Men of the Pen included layered turban-cloths (*manādīl*),[1095] with the *aḥnāk*[1096] beneath their throats, like the equitables. Only the viziers from the Men of the Pen wore the robes (*darārīʿ*)[1097] that were open from

1091 ʿĪsā b. Nasṭūris was a Christian whom Caliph al-ʿAzīz appointed *mutawallī al-dawāwīn* (Director of the Bureaus) in 384 AH/994 AD then arrested him and confiscated a good sum of his money. People were angry at the appointment of Christians and Jews in key positions of the bureau, which caused discrimination against Muslims who were replaced by employees from the other two religions. Ibn Nasṭūris' words and actions were, in particular, subjects of such complaints. Al-ʿAzīz pardoned Ibn Nasṭūris and reappointed him after the caliph's Christian wife and his sister interceded in the vizier's favour, and on the condition that Ibn Nasṭūris employs Muslims in the bureaus. According to al-Maqrīzī, Ibn Nasṭūris remained in office of mediation under al-ʿAzīz for a year and ten months and was his last vizier. He was in post until Caliph al-Ḥākim came to power. Al-Ḥākim, however, demoted him to heading the Pirvate Caliphal Bureau (*dīwān al-khāṣṣ*), after a group from the Kutāma tribe complained again against him for favouring Christians in governmental offices and being openly hostile to Muslims. ʿĪsā b. Nasṭūris was executed in 387 AH/997 AD. (A. Sayyid, *Tafsīr*, 156 & 349, al-Maqrīzī, G. al-Shayyal & M. Ahmad, *Ittiʿāẓ*, Vol. 1, 293 & Vol. 2, 4, 4 fn. 4, 6 & 8 and M. Surur, *Tārīkh*, 82).

1092 Manṣūr Abū al-Naṣr b. ʿAbdūn was appointed in the mediation office at a time when Caliph al-Ḥākim was showing much intolerance to the People of the Book, to the extent of demolishing some churches in Cairo. Interestingly, it is reported that Ibn ʿAbdūn was the one who advised al-Ḥākim to demolish the Church of the Holy Sepulchre at Jerusalem in 400 AH/1009 AD, which inflamed the feelings of the Christian world and boosted the Crusader propaganda. In 399 AH/1008 AD, Ibn ʿAbdūn was appointed the head of the land tax (*kharāj*) bureau and in 400 AH/1009 AD, he was appointed in the mediation position. Al-Maqrīzī states that Ibn ʿAbdūn received the title of judge in the same year and was relieved of his position in 401 AH/1010 AD, even though al-Ḥākim is said to have extremely valued his service, especially his ability to collect money, because the caliph wanted to make peace with two of Ibn ʿAbdūn's adversaries, al-Ḥusayn b. Jawhar and his nephew. Nevertheless, Ibn ʿAbdūn was arrested, executed, and his money confiscated in 401 AH/1010 AD. (M. Surur, *Tārīkh*, 82–83 and al-Maqrīzī, *Ittiʿāẓ*, Vol. 2, 74–75, 76, 81, 84–85).

1093 Zurʿa b. Nasṭūris followed Manṣūr b. ʿAbdūn in the mediation office in 401 AH/1010 AD. He was the only man who Caliph al-Ḥākim appointed in this position but did not kill because he died of illness. It is reported that al-Ḥākim regretted this, because he believed Zurʿa corrupted his state and betrayed him. (A. Sayyid, *Tafsīr*, 170 & 326 and al-Maqrīzī, *Ittiʿāẓ*, Vol. 2, 86 & 93).

1094 The editor of Subḥ comments that the original text in the manuscript used a meaningless word (*al-marwādnī*) and suggests that it should be *ahlal-murūʾāt*, which is the word used by Ibn al-Ṭuwayr. *Ahl al-murūʾāt* may be translated as the "chivalrous men," and would refer to men of the best ethics and manners, in addition to good reason. (Ibn al-Ṭuwayr, *Nuzha*, 105).

1095 Ibn al-Ṭuwayr explained that the layered turban-cloths (*al-manādīl al-ṭabaqiyyāt*) meant "turbans with the *aḥnāk* (sing. *ḥanak*, see Glossary) beneath their throats, like the equitables (*ʿudūl*) do now." (Ibn al-Ṭuwayr, *Nuzha*, 106).

1096 Sing. *ḥanak*, see Glossary.

1097 Also *durrāʿāt* (sing. *durrāʿa*), same as the *jubba* or the *farjiyya* (see Glossary), which was a robe that was open from the lower neck to below the chest, with buttons and button-holes, as

the lower part of the neck to below the chest and had buttons and buttonholes, which was the sign of a vizier's costume. Some of the costumes had laced gold[1098] buttons and some had pearl ones. Customarily, a golden adorned inkwell (*dawāt*) from the caliph's treasury was released for [the use of] viziers from the Men of the Pen, and the *ḥujjāb* stood in their service.[1099] They had full authority over the Men of the Sword who were soldiers (*arbāb al-suyūf min al-ajnād*),[1100] as well as the Men of the Pen.[1101]

The Second Category: *The Chancery Bureau (dīwān al-inshā'), which in the [Fatimid] era, involved three offices*[1102]

The First: Heading the Bureauof Chancery and Correspondence (*ṣaḥābat dīwān al-inshā' wa-l-mukātabāt*)

This position was only occupied by the finest authors of rhetoric. The holder of this position was called "The Most Dignified" (*al-ajall*)[1103] and "The Scribe of the Honourable Pedestal" (*kātib al-dast al-sharīf*).[1104] He was the one to receive the

described above. It was worn by Men of the Turban (*arbāb al-'imāma*) in the later eras. It was also a term used to refer to a vest worn by girls. (Shams al-Dīn Abū 'Abd Allah Muḥammad Al-Maqdisī, *Aḥsan al-Taqāsīm fī Ma'rifat al-Aqālīm*, ed. Michael Jan de Goeje (London, 1906), 44, Ibn al-Ṭuwayir, Nuzha, 106 fn. 1, andal-Baqli, *Ta'rīf*, 133).

1098 "*Dhahab mushabbak*," which means gold that is laced and sometimes inlaid with gems.

1099 "*Bayna yadayhi*," which is an expression that literally means "between his hands." It refers to being in front of someone, before them or at their service or disposal. In the description of processions *below, it may be understood as walking directly in front of someone or preceeding t*hem. P. Sanders translates it as "immediately in front of." (See P. Sanders, *Ritual*, 89).

1100 In the Mamluk era, the regular or the rank-and-file army comprised two categories: the amirs and the soldiers (*ajnād* or *jund*, sing. *jundī*), which were divided into factions. Some of these soldiers were appointed in low-ranking official positions, lesser governorships, as commanders of small forts and in similar positions that do not require the amirial rank. (T. Abdelhamid, *Jaysh*, 18 & 44). Ibn al-Ṭuwayr, whom al-Qalqashandī copies from in the above account, may have been referring to a similar category in the Fatimid era with his use of the term "*ajnād*."

1101 See also Ibn al-Ṭuwayr's account on the vizierate in *Nuzha*, 105–106.

1102 For more on the various positions in this bureau in the Mamluk and Fatimid eras, see *Ṣubḥ*, Vol. 1, 130–140 and A. Sayyid, *Tafsīr*, 355–360.

1103 This was a most sublime title that was restricted to the Fatimid viziers and other high officials of their status. When Badr al-Jamālī, the first powerful Fatimid vizier of delegation came to power in Cairo, he terminated the use of the title *al-wazīr al-ajall* (the Most Dignified Vizier) and started the use of the new title of the viziers: *al-sayyid al-ajall* (the Most Dignified Master), which was replaced by the title "*al-malik*" (the King) with vizier al-Ṣāliḥ Ṭalā'i'. (Al-Baqli, *Ta'rīf*, 15 and Ibn al-Ṭuwayir, Nuzha, 48°).

1104 Also, "the Scribe of the Honourable Secretariat." The *dast* was the pedestal on which the sultan or caliph sat. *Kuttāb al-dast* (sing. *kātib al-dast*) were the higher category of the scribes or clerks of the Chancery Bureau, who sat in the caliph's or sultan's audience, as the subordinates of the Confidential Scribe (*kātib al-sirr*,see Glossary); the other category being the secretariat scribes (*kuttābal-darj*, see Glossary). *Kuttāb al-dast* sat in order of their seniority and participated in reading the grievances to the sultan, and writing his verdicts on them, adorned with his signature. They were the most deserving of the clerks of the Chancery Bureau of the title "signers" (*muwaqqi'ūn*), since, unlike the others, they signed in the margins of the grievances. (*Ṣubḥ*, Vol. 1, 137).

stamped correspondences addressed to the caliph and present them to him personally. He was also the one who ordered documenting[1105] them and replying to them. The caliph consulted him on most of his matters and no one could prevent him from meeting the caliph when he wanted to. He might even spend nights in the caliph's company. No one could enter his office (*dīwān*) or meet with his scribes except the caliph's private retinue (*khawāṣṣ al-khalīfa*). His *ḥājib* was one of the elderly amirs (*al-umarā' al-shuyūkh*) and he had a huge mattress (*martaba*)[1106] to sit on, with cushions and an armrest (*masnad*).[1107] His inkwell (*dawāt*) was one of the best and most special; however, it did not have a chair (*kursī*) to be put on like that of the Chief Judge. A master from the masters in the private service of the caliph (*al-ustādhūn al-mukhtaṣṣūn bi-l-khalīfa*)[1108] carried it for him when he came to see the caliph.

The Second: Signing the greivances with the fine script (*al-tawqī'bi-l-qalam al-daqīq fī al-maẓālim*)[1109]

This was a dignified rank, just beneath the rank of the Head of Chancery and Correspondence Office (*ṣāḥib dīwān al-inshā' wa-l-mukātabāt*). The holder of this office accompanied the caliph in his seclusion (*khilwa*)[1110] on most weekdays, to remind him with what he needed from the Quran and the tales of the prophets and the previous caliphs. He would read him the best biographies, remind him with honourable ethics, train him to be a better scribe, and the like. He would have a decorated inkwell (*dawāt*) with him and after his session was over, he would throw a paper cone (*kāghada*)[1111] containing ten dinars[1112] and a

1105 "*Tanzīl*," which could also mean "summarizing."

1106 Mattress, which comes from the Arabic verb *rattaba*: to arrange, order, or grade. Later in this book, al-Qalqashandī explains the emergence of the early *martaba* as a throne, from which much grander structures evolved. Linguistically, "*martaba*" means a level or a grade, which indicates that since its early use, it was elevated. According to al-Qalqashandī's descriptions, as well as other historians', the *martaba* remained to be a mattress, or a sofa-like piece of furniture, covered with embroidered or precious cloth, but was placed above the thrones and supported with cushions. As clear from the above account, the *martaba* was not only used for the caliph's throne, but also as a seat, probably above a pedestal or a platform, for the vizier and high state officials. The term was also employed to refer to a large bench or a pedestal used for sitting. In the early Fatimid era, the term was used to refer to the throne (*sarīr al-mulk*). (Ibn al-Ṭuwayir, Nuzha, 206–207 fn. 5, al-Maqrīzī, *Itti'āẓ*, Vol. 2, 4 & Vol. 3, 88).

1107 Pl. *masānid*, which could also mean backrest.

1108 The masters in the private service of the caliph refers to the *ustādhūn* who are from the caliph's private retinue (*khawāṣṣ al-khalīfa*). In Ibn al-Ṭuwayr's account: "*ustādh min khawāṣṣ al-khalīfa*," which means an *ustādh* from the caliph's private retinue. (Ibn al-Ṭuwayr, *Nuzha*, 87).

1109 *Qalam al-tawqī'* was a particular script that the caliphs and viziers used to sign the grievances. *Al-Tawqi' bi-l-qalam al-daqīq*, means signing with the fine pen, which is writing or signing in the fine or small font of the script. (See *Ṣubḥ*, Vol. 3, 104).

1110 The *khilwa* is "the place where a worshipper stays in secluded privacy for worship." (Al-Baqli, *Ta'rīf*, 122). The linguistic meaning of the word also refers to any secluded or isolated place or choice of stay.

1111 *Al-Kāghad* is an Arabised word that means a paper or a paper cone. (See *Ṣubḥ*, Vol. 2, 465 and http://baheth.info/all.jsp?term=كاغد).

1112 The ten dinars were most probably the weight of a certain incense.

paper cone (*qirṭās*)[1113] that contained three weights (*mathāqīl*)[1114] of special tripled incense (*naddmuthallath*)[1115] in the inkwell (*dawāt*), to perfume himself with their incense as he re-entered for the caliph's second session. If the vizier who was also a Man of the Sword sat for audience to look into grievances, the holder of this office would be seated next to him to write and sign the verdicts the vizier makes. He had his special place at the Bureau of Correspondence (*dīwān al-mukātabāt*) that no one unpermitted may enter. He had a messenger boy (*farrāsh*) to present him with the petitions (*qiṣaṣ*) and this is where the petitions of grievances (*qiṣaṣ al-maẓālim*) were submitted to him so as to sign them as required for each case, which is what the Confidential Scribe (*kātib al-sirr*) does now.

The Third: Signing with the dignified dcript (al-tawqīʿ bi-l-qalam al-jalīl)[1116]

This office was called the "Lesser Service" (*al-khidma al-ṣaghīra*) due to its reverence. The holder of this position had a small mattress (*ṭarrāḥa*)[1117] and an armrest(*masnad*) in his council (*majlis*), but had no *ḥājib*. This office entailed writing the instructions to execute the orders signed by the scribe of the fine script (*ṣāḥib al-qalam al-daqīq*), and expanding what he wrote.[1118] The scribe of the fine script was similar to the confidential scribe (*kātib al-sirr*) or the scribe of the pedestal (*kātib al-dast*) of our times, while the scribe of the dignified script (*ṣāḥib al-qalam al-jalīl*) was like the secretariat scribe (*kātib al-darj*).[1119] When the petitions of

1113 Al-Qalqashandī explains that the *qirṭās* is the *kāghad*, and cites an earlier scholar who mentions that the *qirṭās* was a *kāghad* made of Egyptian papyri. (*Ṣubḥ*, Vol. 2, 474).

1114 Sing. *mithqāl*.

1115 Translation of term after P. Sanders. The *nadd* was a composite paste used as perfume or incense and made by mixing several ingredients in specific proportions, using certain preparation methods. The final product came out in a variety of shapes, sometimes as necklaces or rosaries. According to al-Nuwairī (d. 733 AH/1333 AD), whom al-Qalqashandī copies, at his time, the Egyptians referred to the *nadd* as "amber," using "raw amber" to refer to the amber itself. *Al-nadd al-muthallath* (the tripled incense) was the finest and strongest type of *nadd* made in Egypt. It was composed of three kinds of amber, oud and musk. It was a soft paste that was put in pockets, used for incense, and the like. (Al-Nuwayrī, *Nihāya*, Vol. 12, 60–69, *Ṣubḥ*, Vol. 2, 119 and P. Sanders, *Ritual*, 71).

1116 *Al-Qalam al-jalīl* means the dignified pen (script) and it was considered the most supreme one used for writing documents. It was a term used to refer to a script called *qalam al-ṭūmār* (*ṭūmār* script). *Al-Ṭūmār* was a most perfectly cut type of paper and this script was attributed to it. *Al-Qalam al-jalīl* or *qalam al-ṭūmār* was an official enlarged type of the Thuluth script, one of the main cursive Arabic scripts. (*Ṣubḥ*, Vol. 3, 53–55 & 62 and Vol. 6, 194–195).

1117 Pl. *ṭarrāḥāt*, also *ṭurrāḥa*, pl. *ṭurrāḥāt*:A small, square mattress or a cushion to sit upon. (Al-Baqli, *Ta'rīf*, 229, P. Sanders, *Ritual*, 70 and Ibn al-Ṭuwayr, *Nuzha*, 82 & 88).

1118 Al-Qalqashandī uses the word *basṭuhu* (expanding it). In the first volume of this work, in his explanation of the duties of the employees of the Chancery Bureau the author shows that among the duties of the primary scribes, who had to necessarily be most articulate and fluent, was to expand a single word or meaning into a most eloquent composition. (See *Ṣubḥ*, Vol. 1, 130–133).

1119 Pl. *kuttāb al-darj*: Scribes of the *darj* – The *darj* was a large rectangular sheet of paper formed of several smaller ones, usually twenty in number, which were attached together so that the

grievances (*qiṣaṣ al-maẓālim*) were submitted, they were taken to the scribe of the fine script to issue them by writing [the verdict] that the case requires according to the orders of the caliph, the vizier, or his own orders. The petitions were then taken to the scribe of the dignified script to [eloquently] expand the instructions of the scribe of the fine script. Finally, the petitions were taken to the caliph in a leather case (*kharīṭa*) to sign them off. The case was then given to the *ḥājib* who stood at the palace gate to hand out each signed decree (*tawqī'*) to its claimer.

Concerning the caliph's hand signature (*tawqī'*) on the petitions, if the vizier was a Man of the Sword, the caliph would personally sign the petition with [the formula]: "Our vizier, the Dignified Master (*al-sayyid al-ajall*) – followed by the attribute the vizier was known by[1120] – may Allah please us with his persistence,[1121] is to proceed with so and so, Allah Almighty willing." These documents would be carried to the vizier, who, if a man of good handwriting, would write beneath the caliph's statement [a formula that read]: "I comply with the order of the Prince of the Faithful, peace be upon him." In case the vizier's handwriting was not that good, he would only write: "I comply." If the vizier was not a Man of the Sword and the caliph wanted a hasty execution of his orders, he would write: "This is to be signed"[1122] on the right side of the petition. The petition was then taken to the Head of the Council Bureau (*ṣāḥib dīwān al-majlis*)[1123] to sign it with the dignified script (*al-qalam al-jalīl*), which he did leaving the place for the mark (*'alāma*)[1124] empty. The petition was taken back to the caliph

sheet was easily folded; *kuttāb al-darj* used to write on this particular type of paper. *Kuttāb al-darj* comprised the second, lesser category of the clerks of the Chancery Bureau, the first being the secretaries of the pedestal (*kuttāb al-dast*). *Kuttāb al-darj* wrote down the documents that confidential scribe (*kātib al-sirr*) or the secretary of the pedestal (*kātib al-dast*) signed, which included decrees, announcements, orders and declarations. They were also called "*kuttāb al-inshā*'" (chancery scribes) because they wrote down the composed correspondences and other documents mentioned above; however, they were not to be called "*muwaqqi'ūn*" (signers), for *tawqī'* (signature) was a different task that entailed writing on the margins of grievances and the like. Al-Qalqashandī reports that by his time, the proficiency of *kuttāb al-darj* deteriorated and *kuttāb al-dast* were the ones who wrote the royal and other important official documents, while *kuttāb al-darj* wrote the less important documents. (*Ṣubḥ*, Vol. 1, 138 and Al-Baqli, *Ta'rīf*, 281).

1120 The attributes that were used as titles, such as al-Afḍal, al-Ma'mūn, al-Ṣāliḥ, etc.

1121 Meaning his long life in service.

1122 "*Yuwaqqa' bidhalik,*" which is an order to sign the grievance for taking the approved actions.

1123 See below: *istimāruh daftar al-majlis.*

1124 Literally: the mark, meaning: the signature. The *'alāma* was an individual, unique hand signature phrase that the caliph, the sultan and the vizier used. In the Fatimid era, some prominent women of the court like that caliphs' mothers or sisters, had to write on any document that they issued, such as letters, decrees, *tawqī'āt* (sing. *tawqī'*), etc. The *'alāma* was normally placed under the first line of the text. Ibn al-Ṭuwayr and other primary sources state that all Fatimid caliphs had the same *'alāma*: "Praise be to Allah, the Lord of the worlds." Other primary sources and surviving documents testify to the signature formulae of other rulers and statesmen. (Ibn al-Ṭuwayir, Nuzha, 89 fn. 1 and al-Baqli, *Ta'rīf*, 253 and see Glossary: "*'alāma*").

who would write one word in the place of the mark, which was "authorized";[1125] [the petition] was documented in the bureaus after that.[1126]

If he was signing [a petition] concerning a [tax] pardon (*musāmaḥa*),[1127] a permission (*taswīgh*),[1128] or an endowment (*taḥbīs*),[1129] [the caliph] would sign it, for its claimer, with [the formula]: "And we have ordered the execution of this." If he wanted to know the truth behind the petition, he would write on the side: "Let the situation (*ḥāl*) be described."[1130] It was then carried to the scribe, who would write the whole story down[1131] to be returned to the caliph to give his verdict concerning it, whether by issuing it with his signature (*tawqīʿ*) on it or by refusing it, and Allah knows best.[1132]

The Third Category: The Bureau of the Army and Allowances (*dīwān al-jaysh wa-l-rawātib*), which is divided into three sections:

The First: The Army Bureau (*dīwān al-jaysh*)

The head of this bureau could only be a Muslim. He was a man of dignified rank and sublime status. He had a *ḥājib* serving him and the soldiers escorted their horses on parades for him. The soldiers' decorations[1133] and the markings

1125 "*Yu'tamad*," which means authorized or sanctioned to be executed.

1126 Ibn al-Ṭuwayr gives a slightly more detailed description of the procedure above and mentions that the last step before the grievance was recorded in the *dawāwīn* was that the caliph put his *'alāma* on it, that being the standard one for Fatimid caliphs according to him: "Praise be to Allah, Lord of the worlds." (Ibn al-Ṭuwayr, *Nuzha*, 88–89).

1127 Misspelled as *misāḥa*. The *musāmaḥa* (pl. *musāmaḥāt*) was a term that meant pardoning the taxpayer from paying the amount remaining after the calculation of land taxes is changed from *al-hilālī* system to *al-kharājī* one. (Ibn al-Ṭuwayir, Nuzha, 90 fn. 1).

1128 Pl. *taswīghāt*, which is defined as either the permission to take the deserved compensations or payments (*istiḥqāq*) directly from a certain land or entity (*jiha*), to facilitate the process; or a form of land ownership that entails "complete immunity from taxation" (Tsugitaka, 447). (Sato Tsugitaka, "Land Tenure and Ownership, or *Iqṭā'*," in *Medieval Islamic Civilization: An Encyclopedia*, Vol. 1, ed. Josef W. Meri (New York, 2006), 447 and Ibn al-Ṭuwayir, Nuzha, 90 fn. 2).

1129 The decree to endow a piece of land or a building as a *waqf* so that its revenue is allocated for the running, maintenance and upkeeping of a religious or a social-service establishment. (Ibn al-Ṭuwayir, Nuzha, 90 fn. 3).

1130 "*Liyakhruj al-ḥāl fī dhalik*": Let the situation concerning that come out, where the *ḥāl* is a full description of the case and its circumstances.

1131 "*Wa tuḥmal ilā al-kātib fayaktub al-ḥāl*"

1132 "*Wallahu a'lam*," a prayer usually said to indicate its literal meaning for reaffirming that one might not know the whole truth about a particular issue and that knowing the whole truth is only divine.

1133 *Ḥilāhum* (or *ḥulāhum*): "their ornamentation," "decoration," or "finery"; *ḥilā* (sing. *ḥilyā*), means physical feature, appearance or attribute (see http://www.baheth.info/all.jsp?term=حلية). Al-Maqrīzī's description of the same bureaumore clearly refers to the decoration of the soldier (*fa idhā 'urida al-jundī ḥullā wa dhukirat ṣifāt farasihi*: after the soldier is presented, he is decorated and the features of his horse are mentioned). This refutes the assumption that the term *ḥilya* refers to soldiers' unique physical aspects, which were documented, just as were the horses' so as to keep track of the army members, their rides, salaries, and the grants bestowed upon them. (G. Qaddumi, *Gifts*, 86, A. Gamal al-Din, *Dawla*, 238–239 and al-Maqrīzī, *Itti'āẓ*, Vol. 3, 339).

(*shiyyāt*)[1134] of their horses were also documented for him.This bureau had to make sure that soldiers were only given good male and female horses, and no mules or horses of non-Arabian breed.[1135] The head of this bureau was not allowed to substitute any of the soldiers or change their *iqṭā'*[1136] except with a [royal] decree (*marsūm*). The amirial captains (*nuqabā' al-umarā'*)[1137] were in service of the head of this bureau to inform him of the soldiers' counts, such as mortalities, absences and the like, which is also the case in our present days.

The soldiers were allowed to barter their *iqṭā'āt*[1138] according to their interests as is the case today, based on decrees (*tawqī'āt*) signed by the Head of the Bureau (*ṣāḥib al-dīwān*), and without a [higher authorization] mark (*'alāma*).[1139] None of the amirs of [the Fatimids], even if highly esteemed, possessed a whole

1134 Sing. *shiyya*, which is any colour of a part of the horse's body that does not match its dominant colour, such as a white area on the forehead of a black horse (*adham*). Such colours, among other attributes, are indicators of the horse's grade of purity and quality of breed. (See *Ṣubḥ*, Vol. 2, 19–21, Muḥammad b. 'Alī al-Shawkānī, *Nayl al-Awṭār SharḥMuntaqā al-Akhbār*, ed. Eassam al-Din al-Sababti (Cairo, 1993), Vol. 8, 101 & 101 fn. 1).

1135 *Al-Baradhīn*: Horses brought from the Turkish or Greek lands, or ones of impure Arab breed. (*Ṣubḥ*, Vol. 2, 17 and http://baheth.info/all.jsp?term=البراذين).

1136 The *iqṭā'* was the system of allocating and exploiting lands in the Islamic world that is comparable to feudalism, although quite different. The *iqṭā'* in the Islamic world in general was not subject to rigid, formal laws, nor ownership rights or inheritance rules. There were two main types of *iqṭā'*: the first was *iqṭā' al-tamlīk* (the *iqṭā'* of ownership), which was "a concession of land designated for agricultural reclamation; in return the recipient was allowed tax reductions and the right to pass the property on to heirs." The second type was *iqṭā' al-istighlāl* (the *iqṭā'* of exploitation), which "allowed the recipient to pay a fixed rate to the treasury in return for a portion of peasants' crops that was greater in value." Al-Qalqashandī includes a section on the *iqṭā'* in *Ṣubḥ*, where he provides an account of the system's history in Islam, its legislative rules and its application in his time. He explains that the *iqṭā'* of the sultan is that which he had the right to use and allocate as he saw fit. This necessitated that the piece of land had no original rightful owner or proprietor. In the Mamluk era, the owner of the *iqṭā'* was like a sultan over his land and had the right to all its yields and income. The granted land was completely restored to the sultan's ownership as soon as the agreed upon grant period was over; the owner was dead – in cases where this was a lifetime only ownership; the owner broke one of the conditions of the grant; he fell out of favour, or at the will of the sultan. Al-Qalqashandī details the two types of *iqṭā'*, explaining that the *iqṭā'* of ownershipwas that the sultan allocated a piece of land, whether usable and inhabited or not. As for the *iqṭā'* of exploitation, he explains that it was the allocation of the due land tax revenue, such as the land tax (*kharāj*). This type was either for a specific period of time; for example, ten years, for the recipient's lifetime and his heirs after him, or for the recipient's lifetime only. He goes on to explain that in his time, the *iqṭā'āt* (lands and revenues granted as *iqṭā'*) did not follow the laws of religious legislation. (Quotes from J. Esposito, "*Iqta*," 140; *ṣubh+*, Vol. 13, 104–117, and Al-Baqli, *Ta'rīf*, 37).

1137 *Nuqabā'* (sing. *naqīb*: captain) of the amirs, which probably meant the captains of the amirs' regiments. Ibn al-Ṭuwayr also uses the term *nuqabā' al-umarā'*, while al-Maqrīzī says *nuqabā' al-ajnād* (captains of soldiers). (See Ibn al-Ṭuwayr, *Nuzha*, 83 and al-Maqrīzī, *Itti'āẓ*, Vol. 3, 339).

1138 According to Ibn al-Ṭuwayr, the soldiers were allowed this barter amongst each other (*muqāyaḍat ba'ḍihim ba'ḍan*). (Ibn al-Ṭuwayr, *Nuzha*, 83).

1139 Ibn al-Ṭuwayr's version is "*bi-l-tawqī'āt bi-ghayr 'alāma bal bitakhrīj ṣāḥib dīwān al-majlis*," which means that the highest authority needed to permit this exchange was the Head of the Council's Bureau, and no other high official's mark (*'alāma*) was required. (Ibn al-Ṭuwayr, *Nuzha*, 83).

village; save rare exceptions. This bureau was responsible for preparing the papers of those entitled to running rations (*arbāb al-jirāyāt*)[1140] and it had two treasurers responsible for the determination of land borders.

The Second: The Bureau of Allowances (*dīwān al-rawātib*)
This bureau included the names of every employee of state (*murtaziq*),[1141] as well as allallowances and running rations (*jirāyāt*). It had a fixed scribe with a small mattress (*ṭarrāḥa*) and about ten assistants (*mu'īnīn*).[1142] The bureau continually received official documents (*ta'rīfāt*)[1143] from every provincial division (*'amal*); indicating those remaining in service, the newly appointed, as well as reporting mortalities. It also documented several categories of employees[1144] that will be mentioned later in the section on Providing Running Salaries and Donations (*ijrā' al-arzāq wa al-'aṭā'*).[1145]

The Third: The Bureau of *iqṭā'* (*dīwān al-iqṭā'*)[1146]
This was the bureau concerned with whatever was bestowed [as lands or revenues][1147] to the soldiers. The managers[1148] of this bureau were not allowed to transfer[1149] the

1140 Those entitled to *jirāyāt* (sing. *jirāya*), which was the salary given in kind rather than in money. A *jirāya* could be given in bread, wheat or barley (which was called *qaḍīm* rather than *jirāya* by some historians). The portions of the *jirayāt* were standard quantities, but soldiers received different quantities since some of them were entitled to two portions, or one and a half portion, etc. A portion was called a *waẓīfa* (ration), while the number of portions per individual was called *qadr al-jirāya* (size or amount of the *jirāya*). (A. Sayyid, *Tafsīr*, 722).

1141 Pl. *murtaziqūn*.

1142 The diacritics indicated by the editor of Subḥ pronounce the word as "*mu'īnīn*" (sing. *mu'īn*), which translates to "assistants." In his Mamluk accounts, al-Qalqashandī mentions the "*ta'yyīn*" (designation or appointment) at the Chancery Bureau, where a scribe is chosen to perform a certain writing job and therefore assigned the particular kind of paper suitable for it. This scribe is referred to as "*al-kātib al-mu'ayyan*." (*Ṣubḥ*, Vol. 6, 210–212).

1143 Sing. *ta'rīfa*, apparently an official document that contained all the required recorded data, itemized, detailed, and supported by numbers. (A. Sayyid, *Tafsīr*, 534).

1144 *'Urūḍ* (sing. *'arḍ*), which, as listed in detail by Ibn al-Ṭuwayr, can be understood as the categories of employees deserving of pay. (Ibn al-Ṭuwayr, *Nuzha*, 83–85).

1145 See later.

1146 See Glossary on *iqṭā'*.

1147 *Muqṭa* or grants given as *iqṭā'*.

1148 *Mubāshirīn*, sing. *mubāshir*, which also means "conductor" or "overseer." The *mubāshirīn* were administrative employees of the Mamluk state, who like the *kuttāb* (scribes), enjoyed a better social status than the rest of the public and many of them earned money illegally from the bureaus, in addition to their salaries. They were also occasionally subjected to confiscation and humiliation in the Mamluk era. (H. al-Battawi, *'Imāma*, 31–32, M. Dahman, *Mu'jam*, 134 and S. Ashour, *'Aṣr*, 468).

1149 Term used here is (*tanzīl*). In his description of the Mamluk documents of the *iqṭā'āt*, al-Qalqashandī describes the "*nuzūl*" as a declaration document of transfer of ownership. Al-'Umarī notes that all the soldiers of the *ḥalaqa* (see Glossary) and the soldiers of the amirs are paraded or presented at the Army Bureau of the sultan, where their names, appearances and decorations (*ḥilya*) are documented. The soldiers of the amirs are not to be exchanged except if the amirs wanted and this required a *tanzīl*, which may be understood as a documented transfer. This had to be done in a way that best rewarded everyone. (Al-'Umarī, *Masālik* (2002), Vol. 3, 431, *Ṣubḥ*, Vol. 10, 401).

decoration[1150] of a soldier or the marking[1151] of his ride. The grants[1152] given to the Arab Bedouins at the peripheries of the country, and elsewhere, were called "*al-i'tidād*," which had a lower [*iqṭā'*] tax (*'abra*)[1153] than [the lands allocated to] the soldiers.

The Fourth Category: Supervision of the Bureaus *(naẓar al-dawāwīn)*[1154]
The holder of this officeheaded all the rest [of the supervisors of the bureaus] and had the authority to appoint and dismiss.[1155] He had the responsibility of presenting payroll [documents] (*arzāq*)[1156] to the caliph and the vizier at known times. He had the right to sit on the mattress (*martaba*) with the armrest (*masnad*). A *ḥājib*, who was one of the state amirs, stood in his service.[1157] An inkwell (*dawāt*) was released for him from the caliph's treasury, but without a chair. He was responsible for requesting the state's money, its collection and its accounting.[1158] No one in the state was to object to his actions. Ibn al-Ṭuwayr said: No Christian reached this position, except al-Aḥram.[1159]

1150 *ḥilya.*

1151 S*hiyya.*

1152 *Iqṭā'āt, sing. Iqṭā'.*

1153 *Al-'Abra* was the fixed monetary tax imposed on every piece of land that is allocated as an *iqṭā'*. (Ibn al-Ṭuwayir, Nuzha, 86 fn. 3).

1154 Also *dīwān al-naẓar* (The Bureau of Supervision). During the second part of the Fatimid era, roughly its second century marked by the appointment of the powerful viziers, this position was equivalent in authority and duties to the vizier's position in the first Fatimid century. The holder of this position supervised all financial bureaus. (Ibn al-Ṭuwayr , *Nuzha*, 79 & 79 fn. 2 and A. Sayyid, *Tafsīr*, 350).

1155 According to Ibn al-Ṭuwayr and al-Maqrīzī, the holder of this position had this authority over the financial bureaus. (Ibn al-Ṭuwayr, *Nuzha*, 79 and al-Maqrīzī, *Itti'āẓ*, Vol. 3, 338).

1156 In Ibn al-Ṭuwayr's and al-Maqrīzī's accounts: "*al-awrāq*" (the papers or the documents). (Ibn al-Ṭuwayr, *Nuzha*, 79 and al-Maqrīzī, *Itti'āẓ*, Vol. 3, 338).

1157 "*Bayna yadayhi*".

1158 "*Ṭalab al-amwāl wa istikhrājuhā wa al-muḥsaba 'alayhā.*" In Ibn al-Ṭuwayr's and al-Maqrīzī's accounts, the holder of this position sent delegates to collect the state's money and request its accounts. (Ibn al-Ṭuwayr, *Nuzha*, 80–81 and al-Maqrīzī, *Itti'āẓ*, Vol. 3, 338).

1159 Also, al-Akhram or al-Akram, whose name varies in the primary sources. He either held the office of the supervision of bureaus (*naẓar al-dawāwīn*) from 529 AH/1135 AD to 531 AH/1137 AD, was dismissed, then reappointed in 533 AH/1139 AD by Caliph al-Ḥāfiẓ, who had him killed shortly after; or alternated between dismissal and reappointment until 542 AH/1147 AD. (Ibn al-Ṭuwayr, *Nuzha*, 79–80 & 79–80 fn. 3).

The Second:[1160] The Bureau of Verification (*Dīwān al-Taḥqīq*)[1161]

This bureau was concerned with examining [the work of all] the bureaus.[1162] The head of this bureau had to be an experienced scribe. He was given robes of honour (*khila'*), a mattress (*martaba*) to sit on, and a *ḥājib* to serve him. This position was frequently vacant and [its duties were] added to the above mentioned Head of the Bureaus (*ra's al-dawāwīn*).[1163]

The Third: The Bureau of the Council *(dīwān al-majlis)*[1164]

Ibn al-Ṭuwayr said: This was the origin of the bureaus in the past and it contained all the knowledge[1165] of the state. It comprised several scribes, with one or two assistants (*mu'īn*). The head of this bureau was the one ruling over the *iqṭā'āt*; he was bestowed on with costumes of honour and a diploma of investiture(*sijill*) was composed for him documenting that, which was affiliated to the Bureau of Supervision. He had an inkwell (*dawāt*) that was released for him from the caliph's treasury and a *ḥājib* to serve him. The [Fatimids] used to appoint one of the state scribes, who was recommended to [later] become the Head of Bureaus, in charge of this bureau. This bureau's official record (*istīmār*)[1166] was called the "Register of the Council" (*daftar al-majlis*). The Register of the Council

1160 The editor of Subḥ notes that the Supervision of the Bureaus was probably the first, even if not so termed.

1161 Also, The Bureau of Investigation: This was the bureau responsible for revising and monitoring the state accounts through investigating all the financialbureaus. This bureaucontinued to exist throughout the Fatimid era and was mostly headed by Christians. It had a different name in the first Fatimid century, however, which is *dīwān al-tartīb* (The Bureau of Organization or The Bureau of Regulation). (Al-Baqli, *Ta'rīf*, 144, Ibn al-Ṭuwayir, Nuzha, 81 fn. 2 and A. Sayyid, *Tafsīr*, 348).

1162 "*Al-Muqābala 'alā al-dawāwīn*," which means "comparing [the work] of the bureaus," that is to investigate and audit it.

1163 That is, the Supervisor of the Bureaus (*nāẓir al-dawāwīn*).

1164 This bureau, which was one of the oldest, was called "The Bureau of Verification" (*dīwān al-taḥqīq*) during the Fatimid era. Sultan Ṣalāḥ al-Dīn abolished this bureau, but he seems to have had to keep its duties and tasks because of their necessity. The bureau was thus replaced with the Council of Bureau Heads (*majlis aṣḥābal-dawāwīn*), which included the supervisors and heads of the bureaus. (Al-Baqli, *Ta'rīf*, 148).

1165 *Ma'ālim*, which means features or marks and was probably used by the author to indicate the meaning of the word used by Ibn al- Ṭuwayr: *'ulūm* – sciences, knowledge or information. (Ibn al-Ṭuwayr, *Nuzha*, 74).

1166 The *istīmār* or *istīmāra* (pl. *istīmārāt*) is a Persian word that exists in Egypt until today to refer to the official forms used by the state administrations. The Fatimid *istīmār* was an official governmental record of budget, which comprised the allowances, wages, etc, monetary or in kind, to which the state servants were entitled, no matter what their ranks or levels were. Al-Qalqashandī summarizes Ibn al-Ṭuwayr's account on this "*istīmār*" in his description of the record of allowances (*istīmār al-rawātib*) below. Ibn al-Ṭuwayr does not specifically describe the *daftar al-majlis*as an *istīmār*; however, he lists its contents in an account that al-Qalqashandī summarizes above. Both historians apply the term "*istīmār*" generically to mean official records of budget in the bureaus. (Ibn al-Ṭuwayr , *Nuzha*, 75–79 & 76 fn. 1; Ibn al-Ma'mūn, *Nuṣūṣ*, 59 & 70–71; A. Sayyid, *Tafsīr*, 350–351, and al-Baqli, *Ta'rīf*, 30).

included the bestowals; the public[1167] designated portions (*rusūm*)[1168] that were approved at the beginning of the year; the animals allocated for sacrifice; the expenditures at Dār al-Fiṭra during ʿĪd al-Fiṭr, on the occasion of opening the Khalīj; on Ramadan banquets, and other occasions.[1169] It comprised all other [expenditures of] foods, beverages and consutmes of honour,[1170] as well as the grains released from the granaries. The register (*daftar*) also documented the allowances (*rawātib*)[1171]assigned to the caliph's sons and relatives, as well as those entitled to allowances (*arbāb al-rawātib*),[1172] recording all the levels of allowance (*murattab*).[1173] It included the presents and rarities received from kings and the complimentary gifts sent to them, the values of the grants given to messengers who arrive with written correspondences, and the shrouds released for the deceased royal women.[1174] The registeralso recorded the [annual] expenditures of the state,[1175] to know the disparity between each year and the next, in addition to other important matters. In our times, [the work] of this bureau is divided over several bureaus, such as the vizierate, Supervision of the Private [Sultanic] Bureau (*naẓar al-khāṣṣ*), Supervision of the Army (*naẓar al-jaysh*) and others.[1176]

1167 *Al-Ẓāhir*, which generally means "the exterior," but also has the meaning of "the public," which better suits this context. Ibn al-Ṭuwayr's account uses "*al-bāṭin*" (the interior, esoteric, or hidden) to describe the grants, while "*al-ẓāhir*," is used to describe the distributed designated portions. It should be noted that both "*al-bāṭin*" and "*al-ẓāhir*" are theological terms employed in the Shiite doctrine to refer to the esoteric and literal meanings of the Quran. For the Fatimids, being Ismaʿīli Shiites, the esoteric meanings were only understood by ʿAlī b. Abī Ṭālib and his descendants; the lineage of their imams. In that sense, both terms are also used to refer to the privileged or special among Shiite Muslims, in comparison to the rest. In the above context and given Ibn al-Ṭuwayr's account, "*al-ẓāhir*" refers to the public, while "*al-bāṭin*" refers to the caiph, his family, and other members of the House of the Prophet (*Āl al-Bayt*), who received designated portions and salaries from the state. (See Ibn al-Ṭuwayr, *Nuzha*, 75).

1168 P. Sanders translates *rusūm* (sing. *rasm*) "designated portions." (P. Sanders, *Ritual*, 66).

1169 The festivities of these occasions will be described in details later.

1170 *Tashrīfāt*, see also: *tashārīf*.

1171 Sing. *rātib*, also *murattab* (pl. *murattabāt*), which were allowances given in money and kind. Ibn al-Ṭuwayr's accout indicates that these were the allocated costumes: "*al-murattab min al-kuswāt*." (Ibn al-Ṭuwayr, *Nuzha*, 75).

1172 In *Nuzha*: *arbāb al-rutab* (Holders of Ranks). (Ibn al-Ṭuwayr, *Nuzha*, 75).

1173 "*'Alā ikhtilāf al-ṭabaqāt min al-murattab*"; in *Nuzha*: "*'alā iktilāf al-ṭabaqāt*," which means "for all different levels." (Ibn al-Ṭuwayr, *Nuzha*, 75).

1174 *Ḥarīm*: harem.

1175 "*Mā yunfaq min al-muhimmāt*."

1176 See later for the descriptions of these bureaus in the Mamluk era.

The Fourth: The Bureau of Garment Treasuries (*dīwān khazā'in al-kiswa*)[1177]

The [supervision of this bureau] was a grand rank among the management offices[1178] of the [Fatimids]. This bureau's warehouses were mentioned in the treasuries section above.

The Fifth: The *ṭirāz*

The notables among the employees (*mustakhdamīn*), who were Men of the Pen, were in charge of this office that especially served the caliph, rather than allother employees (*mustakhdamīn*).[1179] It was situated in Damietta, Tinnīs and other locations of [royal] requisitions (*isti'mālāt*).[1180] The requisitions (*musta'malāt*) were transported from this office to the Treasury of Garments (*khizānat al-kiswa*) mentioned before.

The Sixth: Service at the Endowments Bureau (*al-khidma fī dīwān al-aḥbās*)

Ibn al-Ṭuwayr said: This was the bureau most strictly managed.[1181] Only notable Muslim scribes from the equitable witnesses could serve in it. It had several directors[1182] on account of those deserving of allowances (*arbāb al-rawātib*).[1183] It also had two scribes and two assistants to organize the official records (*istīmārāt*).[1184] It documented in its record[1185] all that was in the *riqā'*[1186] and the allowances (*rawātib*), as well as what was collected as imposts[1187] for the bureau from Upper and Lower Egypt.[1188]

1177 Not listed by Ibn al-Ṭuwayr.

1178 "*Al-Mubāsharāt*": offices of management, see also "*al-mubāshir*" (manager or conductor).

1179 "*Dūn kāffat al-mustakhdamīn*," which may mean "without any other employees" or "prior to any other employees."

1180 Also, "manufactured items."

1181 "*Awkad al-dawāwīn mubāsharatan.*" In *Nuzha:* "*awfar*," rather than "*awkad*," which means that this bureau had the biggest number of managers. (Ibn al-Ṭuwayr, *Nuzha*, 100).

1182 *Mudarā'*, in Ibn al-Ṭuwayr: *mudabbirīn*, which can be similarly translated. (Ibn al-Ṭuwayr, *Nuzha*, 100).

1183 In Ibn al-Ṭuwayr's account, these administrators performed some tasks on behalf of the heads of service in this bureau, namely, the notable, equitable witnesses; including tasks pertaining to the Bureau of Allowances. (Ibn al-Ṭuwayr, *Nuzha*, 100–101).

1184 Sing. *istīmāra* or *istīmār*, official governmental records or forms.

1185 "*Wa yūridfī istīmārihi*," probably referring to the overall record of the office.

1186 *Riqā'* (sing. *ruq'a*) were small papers used for brief correspondences, petitions, doctors' prescriptions and similar documents.The term was also used to refer to documents written by the chiefs of *ahl al-dhimma* (non-Muslim People of the Book) to alphabetically record the names of the members of their population who were obliged to pay the annual taxes on non-Muslims (*jawālī*, see Glossary). These record lists included the names of the population in their areas, as well as travellers and those passing through. (*Ṣubḥ*, Vol. 3, 119 and al-Baqli, *Ta'rīf*, 160).

1187 *Jihāt* (sing. *jiha*), see Glossary.

1188 Ibn al-Ṭuwayr, *Nuzha*, 100–101.

The Seventh: Service at the Bureau of Allowances (*al-khidma bi-dīwān al-rawātib*)[1189]

This bureau [managed] the allowances of the vizier and all [offices] beneath him, up to the torch bearer (*ḍawwī*).[1190] Ibn al-Ṭuwayr said: In some years, it reached more than 100,000 dinars, or near 200,000, in addition to 10,000 Ardebs[1191] of wheat and barley. The Record of Allowances (*istīmār al-rawātib*) was presented annually to the caliph, who assigned allowance increases and decreases, as he saw fit. It was presented to al-Mustanṣir bi-Allah one year and he did not decrease any of the allowances. He handwrote on the back of the record (*istīmār*): "The taste of poverty is bitter, need humiliates necks,[1192] and blessings are guarded [from loss] by generating means of livelihood [to the needy]. So, let them have their decreed sums; what you have runs out, but what is with Allah remains."[1193] Then the Head of the Chancery Bureau (*kātib al-inshā'*), Waliy al-Dawla Ibn Khayrān,[1194] ordered the implementation of that.[1195]

The Eighth: Service at the Upper Egypt Bureau (*al-khidma fī dīwān al-ṣa'īd*)

This office included the southern and northern parts of Upper Egypt. It had several branch scribes (*kuttāb furū'*), who divided the financial bureau (*istīfā'*)[1196] among them. They had to prepare the memoranda (*tadhākir*)[1197]

1189 Also, compensations.

1190 May be translated as "the one who lights"; *arbāb al-ḍaw'* (masters of light) in Ibn al-Ṭuwayr's *Nuzha*, whom al-Maqrīzī explains were the torch bearers (*mashā'iliyya*). They were the ones were responsible for lighting duties, such as lighting street lanterns. (Ibn al-Ṭuwayr, *Nuzha*, 76, al-Maqrīzī, *Khiṭaṭ*, Vol. 2, 348, and M. Dahman, *Mu'jam*, 13).

1191 A unit of dry measure used in Egypt and neighboring countries, mainly for wheat, varying greatly in different localities, measuring in Egypt approximately 0.195 cubic meters. See http://www.dictionary.com/browse/ardeb.

1192 Expression that refers to humiliation, since bowing and prostrating show humiliation and submission

1193 "What you have runs out, but what is with Allah remains," is one translation of a part of the Quranic verse from Sūrat al-Naḥl (Chapter of the Bees) 16:96, which is translated in Sahih International as: "Whatever you have will end, but what Allah has is lasting." (http://corpus.quran.com/translation.jsp?chapter=16&verse=96). "What you have" or "what is with you" refer to the blessings that one has in this world, while "that which is with Allah" are one's good deeds that Allah accepts and thus become eternal. The whole Arabic text of al-Mustanṣir's words is a rhyming one.

1194 Abū Muḥammad Aḥmad b. 'Alī b. Khayrān, Waliy al-Dawla, who headed Dīwān al-Inshā' succeeding his father during the reigns of caliphs al-Ẓāhir and al-Mustanṣir starting the year 414 AH/1023 AD. He most probably died after the year 443 AH/1052 AD. (Ibn al-Ṭuwayir, Nuzha, 78 fn. 1).

1195 See Ibn al-Ṭuwayr's account in *Nuzha*, 76–79.

1196 *Al-Istīfā'* is the job perfomed by the comptroller (*mustawfī*, see Glossary).

1197 Sing. *tadhkira*: This was a memorandum issued by the sultan to his provincial deputies or viceroys, or the men he sent on particular missions, to remind them of the specific details of their assignments and provide an official proof and documentation of their missions, if requested by the authorities they were to address or deal with. The term was also used to

requesting the delayed accounts. The head of the office put these memos into words in his handwriting then presented them to the Head of the Grand Bureau (*al-dīwān al-kabīr*), who would sign them with [the order] of raising [the money] (*istirfā'*).[1198] He delegated the *ḥujjāb,* or whoever else he saw [needed], for these [money collection assignments]. The delegate had a daily wage (*muyāwma*) that he received from the employees (*mustakhdamīn*) as long as he stayed with them. He then brought copies [of the memoranda] to the principal bureaus (*al-dawāwīn al-uṣūl*).[1199]

The Ninth: Service at the Lower EgyptBureau (*al-khidma fī dīwān asfal al-arḍ*)

This office covered Lower Egypt, except for the coastal cities, and had the same system concerning the scribes and what was required for each of them as the Upper Egypt Bureau described above.[1200]

refer to a document which recorded the sums of money that a messenger travelled with, so as to serve as a reminder and an official record. (Ibn al-Ṭuwayir, Nuzha, 91 fn. 2, M. Dahman, *Mu'jam*, 43, *Ṣubḥ*, Vol. 13, 79 & al-Baqli, *Ta'rīf*, 75). Alternatively, the term is also used to refer to medical treatise and the prescriptions given by physicians. The word is a derivative of the Arabic root *dhakara*, to remember.

1198 The *istirfā'* was apparently a financial investigation and collection process of the bureaus that was usually coupled with auditing (*taftīsh*). Ibn Ḥajar mentioned the term in his narrative of an incident that happened in the late 4th century AD/10th – early 11th century AD, where a state bureau owed a sum of money to a group of people. A scribe (*kātib*) was in charge of the *istirfā'* and the auditing of the accounts of the state officials who caused this deficit by acquiring the sums of money as loans. The above description by al-Qalqashandī, copied from Ibn al-Ṭuwayr, shows that the memoranda (*tadhākir*) were probably the financial accounting and documentation part of the audit, while the *istirfā'* was the money collection part. The term *istirfā'* is probably also related to another term: *irtifā'*, which meant the return of the state revenue or its income from agriculture, sometimes specifically translated as "gross receipts" (Murphy, 101). Linguistically, *istirfā'* suggests the meaning of collection by raising the money from those legally bound to pay. (Ibn Ḥajar al-ʿAsqalānī, *Quḍāt*, 141; A. Sayyid, *Tafsīr*, 467; Ibn al-Ṭuwayr, *Nuzha*, 91, and Gladys-Franz Murphy, *The Agrarian Bureau of Egypt: From the Arabs to the Ottomans* (Cairo, 1986), 101).

1199 See Ibn al-Ṭuwayr's account in *Nuzha*, 91.

1200 Ibid.

The Tenth: Service at the Bureau of Coastal Cities (*al-khidma fī dīwān al-thughūr*)[1201]

These are: Alexandira, Damietta, Nastarūh,[1202] al-Burullus,[1203] and al-Faramā.[1204] This office had the same [system] as the Upper and Lower Egypt offices mentioned above.[1205]

The Eleventh: Service at the Bureau of the Annual Taxes on Non-Muslims and the Estates of the Heirless (*al-khidma fī al-jawālī wa al-mawārīth al-ḥashriyya*)[1206]

Ibn al-Ṭuwayr said: Heading this bureau was a job only taken up by an equitable. It had a group of scribes like the other above mentioned bureaus too.[1207]

1201 *Thughūr* (sing. *thaghr*) means cities on the borders with enemies and this includes land borders as well. Generally, it is used to mean coastal cities. (see http://www.baheth.info/all.jsp?term=ثغر).

1202 Also Nastirāwah, a non-extant island that was located between Alexandria and Damietta, to the west of al-Burullus, on the coast separating the Mediterranean Sea from al-Burullus Lake, which used to be called Nastarūh Lake in the old days. In modern times, the location of Nastarūh was taken up by a place called Kawm Mashūrah, which is in the western al-Burullus peninsula, near the Mediterranean coast, and close to Dusūq, Kafr al-Shaykh Governorate. (M. Ramzy, *Qāmūs*, Part 1, 459–460).

1203 Known as al-Burj in modern times, al-Burullus was a coastal village located between Damietta and Rosetta, to which al-Burullus Lake, originally Nastarū Lake, on the north coast of Egypt is attributed. Al-Burullus is also the name given to the coastal region or strip that is located in between the Mediterranean Sea and al-Burullus Lake. Al-Burj, or the fortress, is the name this village gained after Sultan Ṣalāḥ al-Dīn built a fortress there during the Crusader wars. (M. Ramzy, *Qāmūs*, Part 2, Vol. 2, 33–34).

1204 No longer extant, al-Faramā was one of the oldest coastal cities of Egypt that has existed since Ancient Egyptian times. It was located to the east of Suez Governorate, within present day North Sinai Governorate and between the present governorates of al-Ismā'īliyya and Port Sa'īd. The remains of this city today are called Tall al-Faramā, which is an ancient archaeological site. It used to have a fortress that remained in use until the late 18th century AD. (M. Ramzy, *Qāmūs*, Part 1, 91–92).

1205 See Ibn al-Ṭuwayr's account in *Nuzha*, 92.

1206 *Al-Jawālī* (sing. *al-jāliya*), more commonly known as the *jizya*, was one of the early terms given to the annual tax paid by non-Muslims on their person. The *jizya* was mandatory on free, adult men, while women, children, men of religion, slaves, the insane, and controversially also those without income, were exempted from it. *Al-mawārīth al-ḥashriyya* was the inheritance left when a person died and left no heir, whether through a blood relation (*qarāba*), marriage (*nikāḥ*) or having freed male slaves (*walā'*), which are the three categories entitled to inherit by Islamic law, as governed by its conditions. *Al-Mawārīth al-ḥashriyya* also included the inheritance that remained after the existing heirs had received their legitimate shares. (*Ṣubḥ*, Vol. 3, 462–464; Ibn al-Ṭuwayir, Nuzha, 92 fn. 2 & 3; M. Ahmad, *Itti'āẓ*, Vol. 3, 341 fn. 3, and see Glossary).

1207 See Ibn al-Ṭuwayr's account in *Nuzha*, 92.

The Twelfth: Service at the kharājī and the hilālī Bureaus (al-khidma fī dīwānay al-kharājī wa al-hilālī)[1208]

This was the bureau where the *ribā'*[1209] and the taxes (*mukūs*)[1210] were processed and most transfers for the employees (*murtaziqīn*) were made.[1211]

The Thirteenth: Service at the Bureau of the Beasts of Burden (*al-khidma fī dīwān al-kurā'*)

This office managed the stables and what they included, such as the private [caliphal] rides(*al-dawāb al-khāṣṣ*), other rides, mules, camels, and beasts of burden used for renovation,[1212] and allocated for shipbuilding and for serving the*ribā'*of the bureau.[1213] The office also managed the equipment and instruments required for those animals, and their fodder, to which was added the fodder of elephants, giraffes, beasts, as well as the allowances of their caretakers. This office

1208 *Al-Kharājī* or *al-māl al-kharājī* was the annual tax taken from the agricultural lands that produced grains, palm trees, grapes and fruits, as well as what was taken from peasants as gifts of kind, such as sheep, poultry, etc. *Al-Māl al-hilālī*, on the other hand, was a religiously illegal tax imposed on a monthly basis on pastures, fishing, presses and other activities. It started being imposed in Egypt after 205 AH/821 AD and was stopped by Aḥmad b. Ṭūlūn to be resumed under the Fatimids, when it became known as *al-mukūs* (sing. *al-maks*, "tax," see Glossary). Sultan Ṣalāḥ al-Dīn cancelled this tax but it was imposed again after his death. It was imposed and cancelled several times during the Ayyubid and Mamluk eras. (M. Dahman, *Mu'jam*, 67 & 153 and al-Maqrīzī, *Khiṭaṭ*, Vol. 1, 296–308).

1209 *Ribā'* (sing. *rab'*) were housing compounds containing rooms or small apartments that were rented to more than one dweller. A governmental official was appointed a guardian of the state's *ribā'*. He had to make sure they were well-protected, ensure their continuous maintenance and upkeep, and collect their monthly rents. He was responsible for delivering the rest of the money remaining from the collected rents after the maintenance expenses were met to the state treasury. (Ibn al-Ṭuwayir, Nuzha, 93 fn. 1). Since the above context couples the *ribā'* with the taxes (*mukūs*), then the author probably meant the revenue of the *ribā'* that was delivered to the state treasury.

1210 Sing *maks*, see Glossary.

1211 "*Wa 'alaihi ḥiwālāt akthar al-murtaziqīn*," which may be translated as "and most transfers of the employees were made to it." The exact meaning of the statement, which is loosely copied from Ibn al-Ṭuwayr, is unclear. (See Ibn al-Ṭuwayr, *Nuzha*, 93).

1212 *Dawāb al-maramma* (beasts of burden allocated for renovation). In Ibn al-Ṭuwayr: *ḥamīr al-maramma* (donkeys allocated for renovation). A. Sayyid gives a linguistic definition for *al-maramma*, which is the lip of hoofed animals. (Ibn al-Ṭuwayr , *Nuzha*, 94 & 94 fn. 1). It is, however, unlikely that this was the intended meaning. The word A. Sayyid is referring to is *al-miramma* rather than *al-maramma*, which means restoration, repair or renovation, a meaning that better suits the context above. (see http://www.baheth.info/all.jsp?term=مرمة).

1213 *Ribā' al-dīwān*: the more probable meaning within the above context is the *ribā'* owned by the state and managed by the state bureaus. Another probable meaning would be that of the *rabā'*, which are camels, horses and donkeys of a certain age. (http://www.baheth.info/all.jsp?term=رباع)

had two principal scribes (*kātibā aṣl*), a comptroller (*mustawfī*),[1214]and two assistants (*mu'īnān*).[1215]

The Fourteenth: Service at the Shipbuilding Bureau (*al-khidma fī dīwān al-jihād*)[1216]

This office was also called "The Shipbuilding Bureau" (*dīwān al-'amā'ir*) and it was located in al-Ṣinā'a,[1217] in Miṣr. It managed building ships for the fleet and for transporting the sultanic crops, wood, and other [commodities]. It provided the allowances for the ship captains and sailors. If its income[1218] did not suffice, it was provided with enough funding from the Public Treasury (Bayt al-Māl).[1219]

The Third Type of the Holders of Offices (*arbāb al-waẓā'if*)

Holders of the Offices of Professional Skill ***(aṣḥāb al-waẓā'if al-ṣinā'iyya)***

The greatest of those were the physicians. The caliph used to have a physician known as the Private [caliphal] Physician (*ṭabīb al-khāṣṣ*), who sat at the door of the caliph's residence each day. He sat on the benches that were in the hall called Qā'at al-Dhahab (The Hall of Gold)[1220] at the palace, along with three or

1214 One type of the holders of this title performed an administrative financial job. In this case, the *mustawfī* managed the accounts of his bureau, ensuring their accuracy, and collected the due money rightful for the state. He was also responsible for communicating what was due for collection to the head of the bureau and drawing attention to the new resources that can provide money for the benefit of the bureau. He was accountable for any delays or neglect in the collection of the due sums of money. "Due to the importance of this job, its holder was termed '*quṭb al-dīwān*' (the bureau's pole) since he managed its daily tasks as well as monitored its employees." It also seems that there were holders of this title who were not directly concerned with financial tasks.(Al-Baqli, *Ta'rīf*, 210 andS. Ashour, *'Aṣr*, 470).

1215 See Ibn al-Ṭuwayr's account in *Nuzha*, 93–94.

1216 *Al-Jihād* (jihad) may be translated as "struggling" or "fighting" and is a wide concept in Islam that ranges from fighting non-Muslim enemies to maintaining self-control. In the above context, it was given as a name to the ship building bureau.

1217 In *Nuzha*: "*ṣinā'at al-inshā'*," also *dār al-ṣinā'a* (Shipyard or Shipbuilding Factory). (Ibn al-Ṭuwayr, *Nuzha*, 94).

1218 Al-Qalqashandī uses the word "*irtifāquh*," which means "its profit" or "its advantage," while Ibn al-Ṭuwayr uses "*irtifā'uh*," which means "its income" or "its revenue." (See Ibn al-Ṭuwayr, *Nuzha*, 95 and see *istirfa'*above).

1219 See Ibn al-Ṭuwayr's account in *Nuzha*, 94–100.

1220 Also Qaṣr al-Dhahab or the Palace of Gold was a hall inside the Great Eastern Fatimid Palace. It was located inside Bāb al-Dhahab and to the west of the Great Iwan. It was a hall for public audience as well as ceremonies. Ibn al-Ṭuwayr and al-Maqrīzī report that Caliph al-'Azīz was the one who built this hall. The hall was a typical Fatimid T-shaped building, where the caliph sat at the center of the main wall (*ṣadr* or *ṣadr al-majlis*) that faced the audience coming from the longer passage (the vertical line of the "T"), and was served by the two side passages or chambers (the horizontal flanks of the "T"). The T-shaped plan

four other physicians under his supervision. The masters (*ustādhūn*) would then come out to call whoever was available of those physicians to inspect the sick from the caliph's female relatives and the private [caliphal] retinue (*khawāṣṣ*) in the palace. [The physician] then wrote prescriptions (*riqā'*) [for the patients] to obtain what they needed from The Treasury of Beverages. These prescriptions were kept by the managers (*mubāshirīn*) of the Treasury of Beverages for their recordkeeping. Each physician received a running wage and an allowance (*al-jārī wa al-rātib*) according to his level [of expertise].

The Fourth Type: The Poets

These were a large group of the people from The Chancery Bureau and others. Some of them were Sunnis and did not exaggerate their praises, but others were Shiites who did. One of the best praises said by a Sunni poet of these, called 'Umāra al-Tamīmī,[1221] was:

> "Their acts of generosity are those of Sunnis
>
> Even when they contradict me with their Shiite belief."
>
> Some of the exaggerated poetry was like these verses attributed to one of the [poets]:
>
> "This is the Prince of the Faithful, sitting in a council

that was adopted by the Tulunids and Fatimids in their houses and royal architecture was an Abbasid heritage, itself inspired by the pre-Islamic architecture of Samarra, northwest of Baghdad, Iraq. (A. Sayyid, *Tafsīr*, 377–383, Ibn al-Ṭuwayr , *Nuzha*, 88–91° & 205–220,and al-Maqrīzī, *Khiṭaṭ*, Vol. 2, 108–115).

1221 The meant poet is 'Umāra al-Yamanī, whom al-Qalqashandī mentions again later. Abū Muḥammad 'Umāra b. Abī al-Ḥasan 'Alī b. Zaydān al-Yamanī, al-Faqīh (the jurist), d. 569 AH/1174 AD, was originally from Yemen. He was of a religious upbringing and education and left Yemen a grown man and a poet. He settled in Egypt and became a renowned poet of the Fatimid court and particularly served vizier al-Ṣāliḥ Ṭalā'i', among others. Poets were in fact in service of the court during this era for they received salaries, in addition to grants and gifts, in return for their poems. As expected, the more exquisite the poem was, the more generous the grant. 'Umāra witnessed the advent of the Ayyubids, but remained faithful to the Fatimids, even though he was a Sunni, of the Shāfi'i school, just like the Ayyubids. He praised the Ayyubids, but could not conceal his lamentation over the Fatimids who were most kind to him, so much so that he composed poems in their praise after their kingdom was lost. One of his last poems, from which al-Qalqashandī mentions some chosen verses in a later section, showed his objection to the way Sultan Ṣalāḥ al-Dīn treated the Fatimids and their followers and his disapproval of the deposition of Caliph al-'Āḍid, the last of the Faimid caliphs. This poem, along with other poems in attempted praise of the Ayyubids, which in fact implied criticism and insinuated condemnation, and his conspiring against the Ayyubids to return the Fatimids to power, led to his execution. (Muhammad Z. Sallam, *Al-Adab fī al-'Aṣr al-Fāṭimī: Al-Shi'r wa-l-Shu'arā'* (Alexandria, 1988), 479–490, Ibn Khallikān, *Wafayāt*, Vol. 3, 431–436 and M. Ahmad, *Itti'āẓ*, Vol. 3, 224 fn. 3).

Where I have witnessed the revelation and the Quran

And if he appears riding in a procession

One could see Gabriel beneath his stirrups."

I say: this is an obscene exaggeration that neither a Sunni nor a Shiite should make. It is but an intrusion by abominable poets.

The Second Section

The holders of offices in the Fatimid State that are outside the capital of the caliphate (*ḥaḍrat al-khilāfa*) – Two types:

The First Type

Viceroys and Governors[1222]
It should be noted that the [Fatimid] kingdoms were [restricted][1223] to three that had their viceroys and rulers. The first was Egypt, which was established as the seat of rule of their kingdom and their destination. Egypt had four governorships (*wilāyāt*):

The First: The Governorship of Quṣ (*wilāyat* Qūṣ)[1224]
This was the greatest of the Egyptian governorships and its governor (*wālī*) ruled over all Upper Egypt. Sometimes a less-ranking [governor] was assigned to al-Ushmūnayn[1225] and its likes.

1222 *Al-Nuwwab* (sing. *al-nā'ib*: the viceroy); *al-wulāt* (sing. *al-wālī*: the governor, ruler or chief).

1223 The editor of Ṣubḥ notes that this word is missing from the original text and concluded from the context. (*Ṣubḥ*, Vol. 3, 497 fn. 1).

1224 Qūṣ is one of the oldest and most important centres of Upper Egypt, now in the Governorate of Qina, to the east of the Nile. It was a great, populous in al-Qalqashandī's time and had excellent houses, elegant *ribā'*, as well as madrasas, baths and other buildings. It had a lot of gardens and was an important centre of trade between Egypt and Yemen. (M. Ramzy, *Qāmūs*, Part 2, Vol. 3, 183 & 187–189).

1225 Also, al-Ashmūnīn: A city that has existed since Ancient Egyptian times to the west of the Nile and its location is now in the Governorate of Minya. The old city is no longer extant, but its remains are near the modern village which carries the same name. The Muslim primary sources describe it as a beautiful, inhabited, and agriculturally rich city, where a famous kind of textile was made. (M. Ramzy, *Qāmūs*, Part 2, Vol. 4, 59–60).

The Second: The Governorship of al-Sharqiyya (*wilāyat* al-Sharqiyya)[1226]
This was beneath the governorship of Qūṣ in rank and its governor (*mutawallī*) ruled over the provincial divisions (*a'māl*) of Bilbais,[1227] Qalyūb[1228] and Ushmūm.[1229]

The Third: The Governorship of al-Gharbiyya (*wilāyat* al-Gharbiyya)[1230]
This was beneath the governorship of al-Sharqiyya in rank and its governor (*mutawallī*) ruled over the provincial divisions (*a'māl*) of al-Maḥalla,[1231] Munūf[1232] and Ibyār.[1233]

The Fourth: The Governorship of Alexandria (*wilāyat* al-Iskandariyya)[1234]
This was beneath the governorship of al-Gharbiyya in rank and its governor (*mutawallī*) ruled over all the provincial division (*a'mal*) of al-Buḥayra.[1235]

1226 The modern Governorate of al-Sharqiyya (the eastern) has inherited its name from the *wilāya* that roughly occupied the same area since the Fatimid era. It was so named because it is located in the east of the Nile Delta. (M. Ramzy, *Qāmūs*, Part 2, Vol. 1, 22).

1227 Bilbais is one of the ancient cities of Egypt, which the Muslim sources describe as a medium-sized city that had mosques, madrasas, markets, gardens and caravanserais. It was the arrival point of the travel road coming from Syria. It is today in al-Sharqiyya Governorate. (M. Ramzy, *Qāmūs*, Part 2, Vol. 1, 97 & 100–101).

1228 Qalyūb, in the present day al-Qalyūbiyya Governorate, was an old city of a very rich agricultural land. It was known for its gardens and greenery. (M. Ramzy, *Qāmūs*, Part 2, Vol. 1, 57–58).

1229 The name was also pronounced Ashmūm and it became called Ashmūn al-Rummān in modern times. It is presently in al-Daqahliyya Governorate in the eastern Delta, and is located near Damietta. Muslim sources describe it as one of the main, big, famous and prosperous cities that had markets, baths and caravanserais. (M. Ramzy, *Qāmūs*, Part 2, Vol. 1, 229).

1230 Al-Gharbiyya (the western) is located in the western Delta, and although its borders have much changed over time, its name has not changed since the Fatimid era. (M. Ramzy, *Qāmūs*, Part 2, Vol. 2, 8).

1231 Al-Maḥalla is a recurrent first part of the name of many Egyptian cities and towns. The one referred to above is al-Maḥalla all-Kubrā (the Greater al-Maḥalla), which still stands today, much altered, in al-Gharbiyya Governorate. It was so named because it was the largest of the cities bearing the same first name. The Muslim sources describe it as a great city with markets and active trade. It used to have madrasas, caravanserais and gardens, as well as textilemakers (*bazzāzīn*). The present day al-Maḥalla al-Kubrā is the most important textile manufacturing centre in Egypt. (M. Ramzy, *Qāmūs*, Part 2, Vol. 2, 16–17).

1232 Munūf (also, Manūf) was one of the ancient Egyptian cities whose name still exists today as one of the major cities of al-Munūfiyya Governorate in the southwestern Delta. Muslim sources describe it as a great city with markets and baths. Its main activity was agriculture and its inhabitants were rich. (M. Ramzy, *Qāmūs*, Part 2, Vol. 2, 223–224).

1233 Ibyar is one of the old Egyptian villages, which still stands, much changed, in al-Gharbiyya Governorate. It was originally part of an island between Alexandria and Fustat. It had markets, caravanserais and baths and was famous for the Ibyarī textiles. (M. Ramzy, *Qāmūs*, Part 2, Vol. 2, 119–120).

1234 Alexandria, in northwestern Egypt.

1235 "*A'māl al-Buḥayra*" or "*'amāl al-Buḥayra*" was the name given to the provincial division of al-Buḥayra in 715 AH/1315 AD. Its borders have changed over time since the Fatimid era, but is roughly around the present day Governorate of al-Buḥayra, whose capital is the city of Damanhūr. (M. Ramzy, *Qāmūs*, Part 2, Vol. 2, 20).

Ibn al-Ṭuwayr said: Those four [governors] were bestowed on with the [gold-woven] robe (*badana*)[1236] from the Treasury of Garments; the kind that the caliph wore on the occasion of opening the Khalīj.[1237]

I say: these four governorships might have either been those of the governors under whose authorities the smaller governorships fell; or the [Fatimid] established [administrative division] by the end of their era. For I have seen many diplomas of investiture (*sijillāt*) of the rulers of Upper and Lower Egypt in the medical treatise (*tadhkira*)[1238] of Abū al-Faḍl al-Ṣūrī,[1239] one of the scribes of the chancery (*kuttāb al-inshā'*) during the days of al-Qāḍī al-Fāḍil.

1236 "A silk, golden, and inscribed robe that the Fatimid caliph wore on the procession day to open the Khalīj." It was manufactured at Tinnīs and almost all woven in golden threads so skillfully that it required no tailoring or sewing. It cost 1000 dinars. (Al-Baqli, *Ta'rīf*, 61 and Ibn al-Ṭuwayr, *Nuzha*, 124 fn. 4 & 198).

1237 Ibn al-Ṭuwayr, *Nuzha*, 124–125.

1238 In this context it means "medical treatise," see Glossary: "*tadhākir*".

1239 Abū al-Manṣūr b. Abī al-Faḍl b. ʿAlī al-Ṣūrī, Rashīd al-Dīn, (639 AH/1242 AD), was born and raised in Ṣūr (Tyre, present day Lebanon). He travelled and learned medicine, particularly pharmacy, and excelled in it. He was exceptionally informed of the types of medications, their names, characteristics and effects. He lived in Jerusalem for years until he came to Egypt with the Ayyubid Sultan al-ʿĀdil Abū Bakr and remained in service of the Ayyubid sultans in Egypt and in Syria. He stayed in Damascus and practiced pharmacy, taught students and wrote, compiled and edited a treatise on medications. (Ibn Abī Usaybiʿa, *Ṭabaqāt al-Aṭibbā'*, Vol. 2, 216–219).

The Fifth Clause of the Order of their Kingdom On the appearance of the caliph in his processions and in his palaces – Three Categories

The First Category – Sitting in audience during processions: Three sitting [occasions][1240]

The First Sitting [Occasion]

SITTING FOR PUBLIC AUDIENCE ON PROCESSIONDAYS

You should know that, until the end of the reign of Caliph al-Mustaʿlī,[1241] the caliphs used to sit for audience at The Great Iwan (al-Iwān al-Kabīr) of the palace, where the caliph sat on the throne (*sarīr al-mulk*) at the centre of the iwān's main wall. When al-Āmir, al-Mustaʿlī's son, became caliph after his father, he transferred the audience from the Great Iwan to the hall known as The Hall of Gold (Qaʿat al-Dhahab), also inside the palace. Al-Āmir started sitting on the throneat the hall's audience council,[1242] while he transformed the Great Iwan into an arms treasury (*khizānat silāḥ*). The throne was not removed from it and remained [there] until the advent of the Ayyubid state.[1243] The caliph sat for audience in this case[1244] only on Mondays and Thursdays. This was not a constant practice and was subject to decision as needed.[1245]

If the caliph decided to sit for audience in winter, silk brocade (*dībāj*) curtains were hung around the audience hall (*majlis*) and silk rugs covered its floors. If he decided to sit in summer, the hung curtain swould be *Dabīqī* and the furnishing

1240 Ibn al-Ṭuwayr's version is: "Their Appearance in Public Audience at the Royal Council," where the Royal Council or the Royal Audience is a translation of *majlis al-mulk*. Al-Qalqashandī uses the word *mawākib* (processions) to refer to the caliph's audience on ceremonial occasions (*julūsuhu fī al-mawākib* – His sitting for audience on processions). Both historians are referring to the public audiences, whether on ceremonial occasions or for weekly receptions, which were public events for all the state officials, military men and chiefs of factions to have the chance to meet the caliph and greet him. (Ibn al-Ṭuwayr, *Nuzha*, 205, *Ṣubḥ*, Vol. 3, 498 and Abd al-Munʿim Maged, *Ẓuhūr al-Khīlāfa al-Fāṭimiyya wa Suqūṭuhā fī Miṣr: Al-Tārīkh al-Siyāsī* (Cairo, 1994), 264).

1241 Fatimid caliph who ruled from 487 AH/1094 AD to 495 AH/1102 AD.

1242 "*Wa ṣār yajlis min majālisihā 'alā sarīr al-mulk bihi*," which translates to "among its sitting areas, he started sitting on the throne there."

1243 Al-Qalqashandī's use of pronouns in this account creates some confusion. Ibn al-Ṭuwayr's account conclusively shows that *sarīr al-mulk* was transferred from al-Iwān al-Kabīr to Qāʿat al-Dhahab after al-Āmir moved the audience there. (Ibn al-Ṭuwayr , *Nuzha*, 205–207, 206–207 fn. 4 & 5).

1244 Meaning in this category: Public audience or council on procession days.

1245 In *Nuzha*: "*wa laysa 'alā al-tawālī bal 'alā al-tafārīq*" (and not consecutively, but separately). In *Ṣubḥ*: "*wa laysa dhalika 'alā al-dawām, bal 'alā al-taqrīr bi-ḥasb mā yaqtaḍihi al-ḥāl*" (this was not a constant practice, but subject to decision as needed). (Ibn al-Ṭuwayr, *Nuzha*, 206 and *Ṣubḥ*, Vol. 3, 499).

[rugs] would be the excellent golden-weaved *Ṭabarī* [rugs] of Tabaristan.[1246] The mattress (*martaba*), which was arranged for him to sit on, was prepared and placed on the throne at the center of the main wall of the audience hall; the throne was covered with *Qurqūbī*.[1247] The Messenger (*ṣāḥib al-risāla*) was sent on a speedy horse moving with quickest steps, as opposed to the usual movement, to fetch the vizier from his house. The vizier would then ride in his attire with his company and the amirs in front of him.[1248] When he arrived at the door of the palace, the amirs dismounted while the vizier continued riding until the first door in the long corridors,[1249] at a corridor known as Dihlīz al-ʿAmūd (The Corridor of the Column).[1250] He walked, with the high-ranking amirs before him, to The Vizierate Section (*maqṭa' al-wizāra*)[1251] in Qaʿat al-Dhahab. When the caliph was seated, the

1246 Tabaristan was the region to the south of the Caspian Sea, now in the north of Iran. The *Ṭabarī* rugs or tapestry were originally made in this region, but were also produced in the Palestinian city of Ramla (Ramleh). The *Ṭabarī* is defined as "fabric for furnishings in the Ṭabarīstānī style. Ṭabarīstān was known for its woollen cloth and carpets," (Qaddumi, 265) which were valuable items known by the Abbasid court, and probably earlier as well. Ibn al-Ṭuwayr's account mentions two types of these rugs or furnishing cloths: *Ṭabarī* and "unparalleled golden-threaded Ṭabaristān." (G. Qaddumi, *Gifts*, 265, A. Raymond, *Cairo*, 61 and Ibn al-Ṭuwayr, *Nuzha*, 207).

1247 *Qurqūbī* is most probably an attribution to Qurqūb; a town in the southwest of present day Iran, near Ahvaz (al-Aḥwāz) in the Khuzistān region of western Iran. It was located in between Basra and Wasit, in eastern Iraq, and Ahvaz, in western Iran. Qurqūb was a centre for textile manufacture that produced embroidered silk cloth and rugs. It hosted an official royal textile manufacture workshop. Arabic dictionaries also define "*al-Qurqūbī*" (also *al-furquby* and *al-thurqubī*) as a white Egyptian linen cloth used to make robes. (Maurice Lombard, *The Golden Age of Islam* (Princeton, 2004), 186, Y. al-Ḥamawī, *Mu'jamal-Buldān*,Vol. 4, 328, and-http://www.baheth.info/all.jsp?term=قرقوب & http://www.baheth.info/all.jsp?term=فرقب).

1248 "*Bayna yadayhi*,".

1249 *Al-Dahālīz al-ṭuwāl* were described as long, narrow, vaulted and dark corridors in the Fatimid palace. "It seems that most of the gates of the Fatimid palace opened unto long, dark corridors that led either to the palace halls (*qā'āt*, sing. *qā'a*) or its various courtyards." According to al-Maqrīzī's description of one of these corridors, which he had witnessed himself, it was rather long. A. Sayyid estimates its length to have been about 32 meters and its width to have been more than six meters. (Ibn al-Ṭuwayr, *Nuzha*, 93–94°& 154 fn. 4 and al-Maqrīzī, *Khiṭaṭ*, Vol. 2, 220–221).

1250 More probably means "The Corridor of Columns" or "The Colonnade." According to Ibn al- Ṭuwayr's description, "Qāʿat al-Dhahab was preceded by a corridor of columns," which led to it. (Ibn al-Ṭuwayr, *Nuzha*, 92–93°& 206 fn. 2).

1251 P. Sanders's translation is "The Passage of the Vizierate." Researches conclude that the royal audience hall (*majlis*) was mainly composed of a central section: *al-ṣadr* (the chest), and two side halls or aisles: *al-kummān* (the two sleeves), which come together in what is termed a T-plan. The unit composed of *al-ṣadr* and *al-kummān*, with three doors that opened on the court or the rest of the hall; a central door of the *ṣadr* and two side ones in the flanking chambers or aisles (*kummān*), was sometimes referred to as the *riwāq*. Some secondary sources conclude that the *maqṭa'*(section) was the door that separated the *ṣadr* from the *kummān*. This door had carved wooden leaves or was a folded door. The description provided by Ibn al-Ṭuwayr of processional movement of the vizier and the courtly men, where the term *maqṭa'*is mentioned more than once, suggests that it was more like a vestibule than a door. Ibn al-Ṭuwayr uses the term to refer to the vizierate section (*maqṭa' al-wizāra*), as well as "the *maqṭa'* which was called *fard al-kumm*." He explains that the first was the place where the vizier waits and from which

vizier was called from the Vizierate Section to the door of the caliph's audience hall while it was shut and had a curtain drawn on it. The Overseer of the Palace (*zimām al-qaṣr*) stood to the right of the door of the audience hall while the Overseer of the Public Treasury (*zimām bayt al-māl*) stood to its left. The vizier stood in front of the door of the audience hall; surrounded by the Collared Amirs (*al-umarā' al-muṭawwaqūn*) and the Heads of Dignified Services (*arbāb al-khidamal-jalīla*). The Quran Reciters in the Caliph's Presence (*qurrā' al-ḥaḍra*) stood amidst the congregation and the Master of the Audience Hall (*ṣāḥib al-majlis*)[1252] put the ink-well (*dawāt*) at its place from[1253] the mattress (*martaba*), in front of the caliph. He then exited [from][1254] one of the [audience hall's] aisles (*akmām*),[1255] known as the Single Aisle (*fard al-kumm*),[1256] and signalled to the Overseer of the Palace and the Overseer of the Public Treasury standing by the door of the audience hall. Each of them lifted a side of the curtain and the caliph appeared seated on the throne, facing the audience. The reciters started [the proceedings] with reciting Quran and the vizier entered the audience hall then greeted the caliph and kissed his hands and feet. The vizier then retreated a distance of about three cubits and stood for an hour. A cushion is then taken out for him [and placed] to the right side of the caliph; he is ordered to lean on it.[1257] The amirs stood in their designated places. The Master of the Gate and the *isfihsalār*[1258] stood to the left and the right of the door, respectively, and next to them, outside the door and at the threshold, stood the Overseer (*zimām*) of the Āmiriyya, the Overseer of the Ḥāfiẓiyyaand the rest of the amirs according to their ranks. [This line extended] to the end of the *riwāq*,[1259] which

he enters, and the second was the aisle from which the Master of the Audience Hall (*ṣāḥib al-majlis*) exists. One may conclude that the term *maqṭa'* was applied to vestibules at the ends of aisles or near their doors. This conclusion is in accordance with P. Sander's translations of the term as "passage," "designated place," and "small structure." (Ibn al-Ṭuwayr, *Nuzha*, 89–91°, 206–208 & 206 fn. 3, A. Sayyid, *Tafsīr*, 377 and P. Sanders, *Ritual*, 23, 33 & 90).

1252 In Ibn al-Ṭuwayr's account, Amīn al-Mulk Mufliḥ ("The Royal Trustee, The Successful"). Apparently, the Master of the Audience Hall was given this composite title. (Ibn al-Ṭuwayr, *Nuzha*, 207–208 & 207 fn. 2).

1253 "*Makānihā min al-martaba*," which could also mean: upon it, at a designated place.

1254 This preposition is missing from the text, but can be deduced from the context. It is also in accordance with Ibn al-Ṭuwayr's account. (See Ibn al-Ṭuwayr, *Nuzha*, 208).

1255 Sing. "*kumm*," which means "sleeve," and in this context means "aisle."

1256 "The single sleeve," which means "the single aisle" or "the extended" sleeve or aisle. In Ibn al-Ṭuwayr's account: "and he exited from the *maqṭa'* (section) called *fard al-kumm*." (Ibn al-Ṭuwayr, *Nuzha*, 208 and P. Sanders, *Ritual*, 33).

1257 In Ibn al-Ṭuwayr's account: "He is then ordered to sit to the right side, and a cushion is put for him, to honour him." (Ibn al-Ṭuwayr, *Nuzha*, 208).

1258 See Glossary.

1259 P. Sanders translates the term to "arcade." (P. Sanders, *Ritual*, 33).

was a corridor[1260] elevated above the floor of the hall (*qā'a*).[1261] The Holders of the Staffs (*arbāb al-quḍub*) and the Riders in Howdahs (*arbāb al-'ammāriyyāt*) then stood to the left and right too, followed by the exemplary and elite soldiers (*ajnād*) who were recommended for promotion as commanders. *Nuwwāb al-bāb* (Deputies of the Doors)[1262] and the *ḥujjāb* stood leaning opposite the door of the audience hall.[1263]

When everything was in order as described, the first to salute the caliph with the service protocol (*khidma*) was the Chief Judge (*qāḍī al-quḍāt*) and the witnesses known for being in state service.[1264] The Master of the Gate allowed in the judge unaccompanied. The judge then greeted the caliph according to the caliphal protocol by raising his right hand, pointing with his forefinger[1265] and saying,in an audible voice: "Peace of Allah, His Mercy and Blessings be on the Prince of the Faithful." This [formula of] speech was especially used by the judge, rather than the rest of the greeters. Then the Honourable Relatives (*al-ashrāf al-aqārib*) were represented by their overseer (*zimām*) to greet the caliph; followed by the Honourable Ṭālibiyyīn (*al-ashrāf al-Ṭālibiyyin*), represented by their chief (*naqīb*). [These procedures] took [about] two or three hours. Then those awarded the governorship of Qūṣ, al-Sharqiyya, al-Gharbiyya, or Alexandria proceeded to greet the caliph and have the honour of kissing his threshold. If the vizier needed to talk to the caliph about something, he would stand and approach the caliph bending over his sword, which he might do once, twice or thrice. The attendees were then ordered to leave, which they did. The last to leave was the vizier, after kissing the hand and foot of the caliph. When the vizier reached the corridor where he dismounted, he rode to his house,served by those who arrived in his service. The caliph then retired to his residence along with the private retinuemasters (*khawāṣṣustādhīn*). The door of the

1260 Both al-Qalqashandī and Ibn al-Ṭuwayr describe the corridor as a "frieze (*ifrīz*) raised above the floor of the *qā'a*." (*Ṣubḥ*, Vol. 3, 500 and Ibn al-Ṭuwayr, *Nuzha*, 208).

1261 That is, Qā'at al-Dhahab.

1262 Sing. *nā'ib al-bāb*: Deputy of the Door. The holder of this office performed similar duties to those of the *ḥājib*. Ibn al-Ṭuwayr, as well as al-Qalqashadī below, mention that in one of the processions, three of *nuwwāb al-bāb* and ten of the *ḥujjāb* were delegated to accompany the judge. (Ibn al- Ṭuwayr, *Nuzha*, 220).

1263 In *Ṣubḥ*: "*yaqif mustanidan bi-l-qadr alladhī yuqābil bāb al-majlis*" (stands leaning with the degree opposite the door of the audience hall), which is an obscure meaning. Ibn al-Ṭuwayr's statement is: "*yaqif mustanidan li-l-ṣadralladhī yuqābil bāb al-majlis,*" (stands leaning at the center (*ṣadr*) that is opposite the door of the audience hall). (*Ṣubḥ*, Vol. 3, 500 and Ibn al-Ṭuwayr, *Nuzha*, 208).

1264 "*Al-Shuhūd al-ma'rūfūn bi-l-istikhdām.*" (*Ṣubḥ*, Vol. 3, 500 and Ibn al-Ṭuwayr, *Nuzha*, 209).

1265 P. Sanders translated the word into forefinger, which means that she read it: *al-musabbiḥa* (the praiser), one of the names of the forefinger. A. Sayyid uses the term "*al-masbaḥa*," which means "the rosary," in his edition of Ibn al-Ṭuwayr's text. The absence of diacritics in the original manuscript would not make it possible to decisively select one meaning over the other. (P. Sanders, *Ritual*, 33, Ibn al-Ṭuwayr, *Nuzha*, 209 and http://www.baheth.info/all.jsp?term=مسبحة).

audience hall was then closed and the curtains shut until there was a need for another audience, when the same [protocol] was repeated.

The Second Sitting[Occasion]

SITTING IN AUDIENCE FOR THE JUDGE AND THE WITNESSES ON THE FOUR NIGHTS OF LIGHTING (*LAYĀLĪ AL-WUQŪD AL-ARBA'*):[1266] THE FIRST AND FOURTEENTH[1267] NIGHTS OF RAJAB[1268] AND SHA'BĀN.[1269]

When the first half of Jumāda al-Akhira[1270] had passed, sixty candles were carried from the caliph's warehouses to the judge; each candle weighing one-sixth of an Egyptian kantar,[1271] to ride with on the procession of the first night of Rajab. On that night, the caliph sat in a high belvedere (*manẓara*) that was at Bāb al-Zumurrud, one of the gates of the palace mentioned earlier. He was surrounded by lit candles at this height, so that he was recognizable at such an elevation.[1272] The judge rode from his house after the *maghrib*[1273] prayers accompanied by the lit candles that were released for him from the caliph's warehouses; with thirty candles on each of his sides. In between the two rows of candles, the muazzins[1274] of the mosques marched, enticing the remembrance of Allah and praying for the caliph and the vizier using special ordered and memorized [formulae]. Three of the Deputies of the Door and ten of the *ḥujjāb* of the caliph rode in the judge's *ḥujba*,[1275] in addition to the five constant[1276] *ḥujjāb* of the

1266 "Also, Layālī al-Waqīd, which are the particular nights when mosques and streets are lit-up in celebration of occasions, such as *mawlid al-nabiy* (the Prophet's Birthday) or the *mawlid* (birthday) of al-Ḥusayn," etc. Such festive occasions were introduced to Egypt by the Fatimids and among them were Layālī al-Wuqūd al-Arba', which were the first and fourteenth nights of Rajab and Sha'bān months of the Hijri calendar. (Al-Baqli, *Ta'rīf*, 293).

1267 "*Laylat al-niṣf*," literally "the middle night," of a Hijri month is the fourteenth night, which dawns onto the fifteenth day.

1268 Seventh month of the Hijri calendar.

1269 Eighth month of the Hijri calendar.

1270 Sixth month of the Hujri calendar.

1271 Al-Qalqashandī informs us that the Egyptian Kantar (*qinṭār*) was equal to 100 pounds (*arṭāl*). The Egyptian Roman Kantar = 45.31 Kg, while the Cairo Kantar = 44.75 Kg.(*Ṣubḥ*, Vol. 3, 445 andhttp://uqu.edu.sa/page/ar/76218).

1272 In *Nuzha*: "with candles surrounding him, [then] he revealed himself." (Ibn al-Ṭuwayr, *Nuzha*, 221).

1273 Fourth of the five daily mandatory prayers of Islam. The *maghrib* is the sunset prayer.

1274 The muazzin (*mu'adhdhin*) is the man who chants the *adhān* (the call for prayers) five times a day to mark the time for performing the five daily prayers and summon the congregation who pray at mosques. He normally chants from the mosques' minarets, and sometimes from their rooftops. The *adhān* is a standard formula, but the Shiite formula is a little different from the Sunni one.

1275 The *ḥujba* is the job of the *ḥājib* (see Glossary). In Ibn al-Ṭuwayr's account, the deputies of the door (*nuwwāb al-bāb*)and the *ḥujjāb* are delegated for the judge's service in this procession. (Ibn al-Ṭuwayr, *Nuzha*, 220).

1276 Or settled, stable (*ḥujjāb al-ḥukm al-mustaqirrīn*).

Judgement Council (*ḥujjāb al-ḥukm*),[1277]who were dressed in amirial attire. The reciters accompanied him, while reciting the Quran, and behind him were the witnesses in order of their seating in the Judgement Council (*majlis al-ḥukm*), least senior then most senior; each surrounded by one, two or three candles. [The procession moved], in a huge crowd, to Bayn al-Qaṣrayn, until it reached Bāb al-Zumurrud,one of the palace gates. They[1278] then sat serenely and respectfully in an open space beneath the belvedere; eagerly waiting for the caliph to appear. The caliph then opened one of the apertures of the belvedere showing his face and head. Standing around him was a group of the Private Retinue Masters of the *muḥannakūn* and others. Some of the masters opened another aperture from which the caliph showed his head and right hand and saluted with his sleeve saying: "The Prince of the Faithful greets you back with peace." He first greeted the Chief Judge using his titles then similarly greeted the Master of the Gate, and finally the rest of the company collectively, without naming anyone. [Proceedings] started with the reciters'recitation of the Quran while they stood centralized with their backs against the wall of the belvedere, facing the crowd. Then the preacher (*khaṭīb*)[1279] of al-Anwar Mosque – the one at Bāb al-Baḥr -[1280] came forward and delivered a sermon in the same way he preached from the minbar (pulpit).[1281] He reminded the audience of the virtue of the month of Rajab, that this procession marked its start and ended the sermon by praying for the caliph. Then the preachers of al-Azhar and al-Ḥākim mosques,[1282] respectively, similarly came forward and preached; while the reciters recited the Quran in between these sermons. When the sermons were over, the first master put his hand outside that aperture[1283] to greet the crowd back then the two apertures were closed and the crowd left.

The judge and the witnesses then rode to the house of the vizier who sat for their audience so that they could greet him. The three preachers also delivered sermons there, only more modest than the ones given in the presence of the caliph,[1284] and prayed for the vizier. The crowd left and the judge and the witnesses then went to Miṣr. The governor (*wālī*) of Cairo accompanied the judge to be in his service

1277 Sing. *ḥājib al-ḥūkm*.

1278 In Ibn al-Ṭuwayr's account, these were the judge, the witnesses, the master of the gate, the reciters, the governor of Cairo, and the preachers (*khuṭabā'*). (Ibn al-Ṭuwayr, *Nuzha*, 221).

1279 Or "sermon-deliverer".

1280 The meant mosque is the Mosque of al-Ḥākim, which was the one given the name "al-Anwar;" a title that seems to have been confused by al-Qalqashandī. (See Ibn al-Ṭuwayr, *Nuzha*, 219).

1281 That is, at the mosque.

1282 Ibn al-Ṭuwayr's description, which is copied by al-Qalqashandī, states that the first preacher to come forward and preach was that of al-Anwar Mosque, known as the Mosque of al-Ḥākim, followed by the preachers of al-Azhar, then that of al-Aqmar. A. Sayyid concludes that this proves that al-Aqmar Mosque hosted a sermon, contrary to the statements made by both Ibn 'Abd al-Ẓāhir and al-Maqrīzī. (Ibn al-Ṭuwayr, *Nuzha*, 219 & 219 fn. 1).

1283 In Ibn al-Ṭuwayr's account: "The master put his head and his hand, which was in his sleeve, outside his aperture." (*Nuzha*, 219).

1284 "*Bi-akhaff min maqām al-khalīfa*" (more modestly than [those delivered out of respect for] the status of the caliph).

(*khidma*) until they reached Ibn Ṭūlūn's Mosque, where the latter prayed. When he came out, he found the governorof Miṣr [waiting] to receive him and move in his service. He then passed by the shrines (*mashāhid*)[1285] to receive their blessings and moved on to the Old Mosque (The Mosque of ʿAmr), which he entered from Bāb al-Ziyyāda (Door of the *ziyyāda*).[1286] The *ziyyāda* was the place where he presided.[1287] He prayed a two-*rak'a*[1288] prayer at the mosque and the silver chandelier (*tannūr*)[1289] of the mosque was lit up for him. This was a huge, beautifully structured chandelier that contained about 1500 lamps (*barrāqāt*),[1290] while its base included around 100 lanterns (*qanādīl*).[1291] The judge then left the mosque and stayed in Miṣr if he resided there. If he lived in Cairo, its governor waited at the place where he left him until he returned from Miṣr to move along in his service till he reached his house.

The judge also rode for procession on the fourteenth night of Rajab; however, after praying in the mosque of Miṣr, he headed to the Cemetery (al-Qarāfa) and prayed in its mosque. He then rode on the first and fourteenth nights of Shaʿbān as well.

1285 Sing. *mashhad*: memorial. The Fatimid memorial shrines were the funerary buildings established to commemorate the members of the family of the Prophet and his descendants, whether there was an actual burial at the place or it was built on account of a vision that was divinely revealed. A. Sayyid explains that the meant *mashāhid* in this context are the ones that were erected along the road connecting between Cairo and Fustat, al-Shāriʿ al-Aʿẓam (the Great Street), which are now on al-Ashrafiyya Street, perpendicular to al-Ṣalība Street, which the Mosque of Ibn Ṭūlūn overlooks. The term is also used to refer to another group of shrines erected for *Ahl al-Bayt* (Family of the Prophet), which are located in the area between Muqattam and al-Qarāfa. (Ibn al-Ṭuwayir, Nuzha, 168–169 fn. 2).

1286 This was the northeastern *ziyyāda* of the mosque, which had two doors, one into the mosque and one to exit. (Ibn al-Ṭuwayir, Nuzha, 107 fn. 1).

1287 The judge sat for council in this *ziyyāda* twice a week, on Tuesdays and Saturdays. (Ibn al-Ṭuwayr, *Nuzha*, 107).

1288 From the verb *raka'a,* which means to kneel down or stoop. It is the repeated act of prayers that consists of standing for Quranic recitation, bowing, then prostrating twice, with a sitting between the two prostrations, each motion having particular prayers to be uttered in association with it. Every prayer, whether mandatory or not, has a specific number of *raka'āt* (sing. *rak'a*). The above particular two-*rak'a* prayer refers to one that is optional, but encouraged, and is a salutation to the mosque after one enters it.

1289 This *tannūr* was made in 403 AH/1013 AD by the order of Caliph al-Ḥākim. It was huge and could not be taken inside the mosque until two door leaves were removed. The mosque was subject to a fire towards the end of the Fatimid era and the *tannūr* was broken and was kept at the Fatimid palace. (Ibn al-Ṭuwayr, *Nuzha*, 9 & 9 fn. 3).

1290 Sing. *barrāqa*, "that which shines," from the verb: *baraqa*; to shine. Ibn al-Ṭuwayr uses the term "*bazzāqa*," meaning snail or slug, from the verb *bazaqa*, "to spit," or "to dawn"- for the sun. The reference in both accounts is to the "glass cups" or little lamps that are installed in a metal chandelier. Ibn al-Ṭuwayr says that the *tannūr* contained sections, each section including 120 *bazzāqāt*, in addition to palm tree-shaped protrusions, each containing 300 *bazzāqāt.* (Ibn al-Ṭuwayr, *Nuzha*, 222, Eva Baer, *Metalwork in Medieval Islamic Art* (Albany, 1983), 313 and http://www.baheth.info/all.jsp?term=بزاقة).

1291 Sing. *qindīl*, "lantern." According to Ibn al-Ṭuwayr, 100 star-shaped lanterns were hung from the circular base of the chandelier. (Ibn al-Ṭuwayr, *Nuzha*, 222).

The Third Sitting [Occasion]

SITTING FOR AUDIENCE ON [OCCASION OF] THE BIRTHDAY OF THE PROPHET (*MAWLID AL-NABIY*), ON THE TWELFTH OF RABĪ' AL-AWWAL[1292]

Customarily, twenty kantars of unusual kinds of sweets were made using excellent sugar at Dār al-Fiṭra for this occasion, which put on 300 copper trays. On the night before the birthday (*mawlid*), these trays were distributed among the Men of Designated Portions (*arbāb al-rusūm*),[1293] such as the Chief Judge; the Chief Missionary; the Reciters in Presence of the Caliph; the preachers; the presiders congregational mosques[1294] at the in Cairo and Miṣr; the superintendents of shrines,[1295] and others whose names are documented in the bureau.[1296] The caliph sat in a belvedere that is near to the ground and opposite al-Dār al-Quṭbiyya, mentioned earlier – which was in place of the present day al-Manṣūrī Hospital. The judge rode after the *'aṣr* prayers, with the witnesses, and accompanied by those responsible for distributing the trays mentioned above,[1297] to al-Azhar Mosque. They sat at the mosque for the duration of the recitation of the whole Quran.[1298] The palace's street was blocked from the directions of al-Suyūfiyyīn[1299] and Suwayqat Amīr al-Juyūsh[1300]

1292 Third month of the Hijri calendar.

1293 Also, *aṣḥāb al-rusūm*, P. Sanders translates *arbāb al-rusūm* as "men of designated portions." The "*rusūm*" or "designated portions" in this context refer to the bestowals given in kind, probably food, on ceremonial occasions by the caliph to state officials, as well as those patronized by the state; for example, a visiting physician from Andalusia that al-Maqrīzī mentions in *Itti'āẓ*. Historical accounts indicate that *arbāb al-rusūm* also "sponsored their own networks of patronage." (*Ritual*, 66). The term also applied to those who received rations indirectly, since they were entitled fractions from a bestowal granted by the caliph to some dignitary. Among its meanings, "*rusūm*" was also used to refer to the pensions given to high-ranking officials. (P. Sanders, *Ritual*, 66& 84; al-Maqrīzī, *Khiṭaṭ*, Vol. 2, 115, 201 & 217; al-Maqrīzī, *Itti'aẓ*, Vol. 3, 78–80, 94, 95, 105, & 341; Ibn al-Ṭuwayr, *Nuzha*, 145, 184–185, 195 & 216).

1294 "*Al-Mutaṣaddirīn bi-l-jawāmi'*"; Al-Qalqashandī lists the *taṣdīr* among the religious offices and explains that it entailed sitting at the centres of councils or assemblies (*ṣadr al-majlis*) of mosques or similar institutions to interpret Quranic verses and provide further religious explanations. (*Ṣubḥ*, Vol. 11, 251).

1295 "*Qawamat al-mashāhid*," who, given the context, probably performed some religious role.

1296 This means those whose names were registered in the Register of the Council (*daftar al-majlis*) according to the accounts of Ibn al-Ṭuwayr and al-Maqrīzī.(Ibn al-Ṭuwayr, *Nuzha*, 145 and al-Maqrīzī, *Khiṭaṭ*, Vol. 2, 201& 217).

1297 "*Arbāb tafriqat al-ṣawānī*," those responsible for distributing the trays, that is the copper trays mentioned above.

1298 "*Al-Khatma al-karīma*" (the Honourable Completion), recitation of the whole Quran.

1299 Al-Suyūfiyyīn (the Sword-makers), or Sūq al-Suyūfiyyīn (the Sword-makers Market), "was located by the southwestern entrance of Bay al-Qaṣrayn Square." (A. Sayyid,*Nuzha*, 11 fn. 1).

1300 *Suwayqa* is a small *sūq* or market. Suwayqat Amīr al-Juyūsh by al-Maqrīzī's time, was located in between Ḥārat Barjawān and Ḥārat Bahā' al-Dīn. Al-Maqrīzī remarks his readings indicated that this market was not a *suwayqa*, but a *sūq*, which extended from the head of Ḥārat Barjawān up to the head of Suwayqat Amīr al-Juyūsh of his time. He reports that this was actually one

and the area in between was swept and sprinkled with water. The area beneath the belvedere was sprinkled with yellow sand. Both the Master of the Gate and the Governor of Cairo stood at the street heads to prevent passers by. The judge was then summoned along with his company, so they came, dismounted near the belvedere, and assembled under it waiting eagerly for the caliph to appear. He opened one of the apertures of the belvedere and showed his face from it; then one of the *muḥannakūn* masters showed his hand and signalled with his sleeve that the caliph greeted the crowd back with peace. The reciters recited the Quran and the preachers delivered sermons, like they did on the Nights of Lighting (*layālī al-wuqūd*) mentioned earlier. When the sermons were over, the master (*ustādh*) [repeated the gesture] of waving his hand to greet [the crowd] with peace, as mentioned earlier. The two apertures were then closed and the people left for their homes. The same steps were followed during the celebration of the birthday of ʿAlī b. Abī Ṭālib, which they had identified at a particular time of the year.

The Second Category

His riding on processions, which is of two kinds:

The First Kind
Riding on grand processions, which were six:

The First Procession: The New Year Procession[1301]
With the start of the last ten days of Dhū al-Ḥijja,[1302] the [Fatimids] customarily began releasing the items needed for the processions from the caliph's warehouses. The Arms Treasuries (*khazā'in al-silāḥ*) released all that was carried by the Equestrian Escorts (*rikābiyya*), and their likes, around the caliph, such as: The unbending swords (*ṣamāṣim*); the maces (*dabābīs*); the axes (*luṭūt*); the iron poles (*'umad al-ḥadīd*);[1303] the swords (*suyūf*); the leathern shields (*daraq*); the lances (*rimāḥ*); the banners (*alwiya*), and the flags (*a'lām*). The Decoration Treasury (*khizānat al-tajammul*) released the banners (*alwiya*), the staffs (*quḍub*),

of the biggest markets of Cairo, which was along one of its streets that ran from the direction of Bāb al-Futūḥ, Bayn al-Qaṣrayn and Bāb al-Naṣr to Bāb al-Qanṭara and the Nile bank. (Al-Maqrīzī, *Khiṭaṭ*, Vol.2, 595–596).

1301 Procession on the occasion of the commencement of the new Hijri year. Al-Qalqashandī combines two consecutive processions in this one. In Ibn al-Ṭuwayr's account, the first procession is called the Horses Parade Day (*yawm 'arḍ al-khayl*) on the 29th of Dhū al-Ḥijja, followed by the Beginning of the Year Procession (*yawm Istiftāḥ al-'ām*) on the next day. (Ibn al-Ṭuwayr, *Nuzha*, 153–167).

1302 Twelfth and last month of the Hijri calendar.

1303 Ibn al-Ṭuwayr mentions a type of arms or instruments called "*al-mustawfiyāt*," which were square-shaped iron poles, of two cubits length and rounded handles. These are probably the ones referred to above as "iron poles." *Al-Mustawfiyāt* is also the name that al-Qalqashandī missed in his earlier account of the royal instruments, which resulted in a combined description given for both the axes "*luṭūt*" and the "iron poles." (See Ibn al-Ṭuwayr, *Nuzha*, 148).

the howdahs (*'ammāriyyāt*), and other of the earlier-mentioned items, for the use of the vizier, the amirs and the Heads of Services (*arbāb al-khidam*). The stables released 100 trained, branded horses[1304] for the caliph's ride and his side horses[1305] during the procession.The Treasury of Saddles (*khizānat al-surūj*) released 100 saddles that were adorned with gold and silver, some of which were inlaid with jewels and had golden stirrups. The necks of the horses were decorated with golden collars and amber necklaces, while most of them wore golden and silver flattened anklets. Each horse, with its equipment, was worth 1000 dinars. Ten of these equipped horses were given to the vizier as his and his private entourage's rides. The covers of the howdahs[1306] were submitted to the settlement areas(*munākhāt*) to be carried by camels. Similarly, other processional instruments that were previously mentioned in the account of the treasuries were released. Ordinary horses were sent from the stables to the Heads of Services to ride during the procession.

On the 29th of Dhū al-Ḥijja, the caliph summoned the vizier from his house with the usual hasty protocol.[1307] When the Messenger (*ṣāḥib al-risāla*) returned from the errand of summoning the Vizier, the caliph exited his place, riding, in the palace. He descended to the *sidillā*[1308] in Dihlīz Bāb al-Mulk (The Corridor of the Royal Door),[1309] which included the Window (*shubbāk*),[1310] and had a curtain

1304 *Musawwama*, an adjective that means that these horses were trained, well bred, and branded. (See Quran, Chapter of Āl 'Imrān, 3:14 http://corpus.quran.com/translation.jsp?chapter=3&verse=14 and http://www.baheth.info/all.jsp?term=مسومة).

1305 *Al-Janā'ib* (sing. *al-junayb* or *al-janab*), which means "the side ones," were the spare horses that marched with the caliph or sultan in wars, travels, and on other occasions, in case they were needed. The term was also used to refer to the escorting guards. (Al-Baqli, *Ta'rīf*, 92, M. Dahman, *Mu'jam*, 55, and S. Ashour, *'Aṣr*, 428).

1306 *Aghshiyat al-'ammāriyyāt* (the covers of howdahs).

1307 In Ibn al-Ṭuwayr's account, the messenger is sent to fetch the vizier. He goes on this assignment assuming the haste style on a fast horse. This is to obey the caliph's order to be quick, which is unlike his usual movement. (Ibn al-Ṭuwayr, *Nuzha*, 153).

1308 The *sidillā* or *sihdillā* is an Arabised, originally Persian, term. It is described in the primary sources to have been "three houses in one," which means that it was a structure composed of a central room or iwan and two side ones. The Fatimid *sidillā* was identified as a structure with three closed sides and one open one. This fourth open side was the one that contained the *shubbāk* (window, see Glossary). According to Nāṣirī Khusraw, the Persian traveller who visited Egypt during the Fatimid era, the *sidillā* was covered with three domes. The *sidillā* was probably located at the centre of the palace, in between Bāb al-'Īd and Bāb al-Baḥr. In another non-royal, but also Fatimid context, the *sidillā* is described as a built stone pedestal (*maṣṭaba*) that is covered with rests (*masānid*) and textile sheets on one end or on two opposite ends. (Ibn al-Ṭuwayir, Nuzha, 96–98° and Ettinghausen and Grabar, *Art and Architecture*, 172).

1309 This was one of the palace's corridors that was reached through Bāb al-'Īd and contained the *sidillā* and the *shubbāk*. (Ibn al-Ṭuwayir, Nuzha, 97–98°& 154 fn. 2).

1310 The *shubbāk* was "a sort of fenced opening" or "iron-work grill" that was reached through Bāb al-'Īd (Gate of the Feast) via the long corridors and was situated roughly opposite the gate. It was located in Dihlīz Bāb al-Mulk, and there was either another *shubbāk* in the Great Iwan, or this single *shubbāk* was in between the iwan and the *sidillā*. The practice of sitting at the *shubbāk* was originally an Abbasid protocol that was adopted by the Fatimids. When

on its outer side.[1311] The Overseer of the Palace (*zimām al-qaṣr*) and the Head of the Public Treasury (*ṣāḥib bayt al-māl*) stood to the right and left [of the caliph], respectively. The Vizier rode from his house with the amirs riding in front of him. When he arrived at the palace gate, the amirs dismounted while he remained on his horse. The Vizier then entered from Bāb al-ʿĪd (Gate of the Feast) and continued to ride until the first door of the long corridors. He then dismounted and walked inside them, surrounded by his entourage and the sons and relatives that he chose.[1312] When he arrived at the Window, he found a big iron chair beneath it, on which he sat with his feet touching the floor. After he sat, the Overseer of the Palace and the Head of the Public Treasury removed the curtain, each from his side, so that the vizier saw the caliph sitting on a huge mattress (*martaba*). The vizier then stood up, saluted[1313] and gestured with his hand towards the ground thrice.[1314] He was then ordered to sit on his chair, which he did. The reciters started [the proceedings] reciting verses that were suitable for the place[1315] for half an hour. The amirs then saluted the caliph with peace and the private (*khāṣṣ*) horses[1316] mentioned before were paraded one by one, to the last one of them. After the parade ended, the reciters recited suitable verses for adjourning this audience (*majlis*). When they finished, the curtains were closed and the Vizier stood to enter to the Caliph and kiss his hands and feet. The Vizier then left the Caliph and rode again from the place where he dismounted. The amirs exited

al-Basāsīrī managed to take control over Baghdad in 450 AH/1059 AD, he sent the Abbasid *shubbāk*, among other items, to the Fatimid court. When Vizier al-Afḍal built Dār al-Wizāra (the House of the Vizierate) after 487 AH/1094 AD, he put this *shubbāk* in it "for the vizier to sit on and lean against." The *shubbāk* at Dār al-Wizāra was either golden, or according to al-Maqrīzī, made of iron. Al-Maqrīzī also reports that Baybars al-Jashankīr, the Mamluk Sultan (r. 708 AH/1308 AD – 709AH/1309 AD), acquired the *shubbāk* from the ruins of Dār al-Wizāra and embedded it in the mausoleum attached to his khānqāh, which was built in the site of the house. (Ettinghausen and Grabar, *Art and Architecture*, 172, Ibn al-Ṭuwayir, Nuzha, 97–98°, A. Raymond, *Cairo*, 53, al-Maqrīzī, *Khiṭaṭ*, Vol. 2, 231, P. Sanders, *Ritual*, 213 & for the Khānqāh of Baybars al-Jāshankīr see http://archnet.org/sites/2207).

1311 To conceal from the people. (Ibn al-Ṭuwayr, *Nuzha*, 154).

1312 In *Ṣubḥ*: "*wa man yurābuhhū*," (that he raised), while in *Nuzha*: "*wa man yarāh*," (that he chose or that he saw suitable). The second statement is more plausible. (*Ṣubḥ*, Vol. 3, 504 and In Ibn al-Ṭuwayr, *Nuzha*, 154).

1313 "*Yussalim*," means salutes with peace.

1314 P. Sanders translates this phrase, namely, "*yakhdim bi-yadihi fī al-arḍ*," to "gestures with hand toward the ground." Ibn al-Ṭuwayr, and both al-Maqrīzī and Ibn Taghrī Birdī copying him, use the preposition "*ilā*," which means "towards." Al-Qalqashandī uses "*fī*," which means "in" or "at." Al-Qalqashandī's version suggests a more dramatic gesture of possibly tapping the floor; however, the other sources concur in implying the meaning above. (P. Sanders, *Ritual*, 154, Ibn al-Ṭuwayr, *Nuzha*, 154, al-Maqrīzī, *Khiṭaṭ*, Vol. 2, 250, Ibn Taghrī Birdī, *Nujum*, Vol. 4, 88).

1315 "*Al-Makān*," which is the "place," while it is "*al-ḥāl*," in two of the manuscripts of *Nuzha*. (Ibn al-Ṭuwayr, *Nuzha*, 154).

1316 In Ibn al-Ṭuwayr's account he mentions that the "*dawāb*" (rides) were paraded. (Ibn al-Ṭuwayr, *Nuzha*, 155).

with him and moved along to his house,[1317] riding and walking depending on their statuses. After the caliph prayed *ẓuhr*,[1318] he sat for the private (*khāṣṣ*) parade of the Treasury of Garments (*khizānat al-kiswa*)[1319] so as to choose what to be worn and his attire during that procession. He chose the turban-cloth (*mindīl*) to be used to wrap the crown, an outfit (*badla*) that matched it,[1320] the precious jewel[1321] and the other jewels worn with it on the crown, as mentioned earlier. A parasol (*miẓalla*) that matched the *badla* was [then] released [from the treasury]. The parasol was wrapped in a *Dabīqī* kerchief (*mindīl*), to be uncovered only by its bearer when the caliph rode. The previously mentioned Two Banners of Thankfulness (*liwā'ay al-ḥamd*) were then also released.

On the first day of the year,[1322] the Holders of Ranks (*arbāb al-rutab*) from Men of the Sword and Men of the Pen went early, before sunrise, to wait at Bayn al-Qaṣrayn – which was then a wide open space without buildings – for the caliph to ride. The amirs went early to the Vizier's house to ride with him. The Vizier rode from his house to the palace, without being summoned,[1323] preceded by flags and banners that the Caliph had honoured him with. The amirs moved in front of him, riding and walking, and his sons and brothers moved ahead of him. All of them with the tails of their turbans lowered[1324] and not wearing a *ḥanak*. The vizier would have a majestic appearance of magnificent clothes, a turban-cloth (*mindīl*) and a *ḥanak*, and girded with the golden sword.[1325] When he arrived at the palace gate, the amirs dismounted while he entered on his horse to the place where he dismounted[1326] in the palace's corridor, known as Dihlīzal-ʿAmūd. He walked in the rest of the corridors until he reached the Vizierate Section of Qāʿat al-Dhahab,

1317 In Ibn al-Ṭuwayr's account: "up to near the place," that is, the house (*dār*). (Ibn al-Ṭuwayr, *Nuzha*, 155).

1318 The noon prayer, second of the five daily mandatory prayers.

1319 In *Nuzha*: "*khazā'in al-kuswāt al-khāṣṣa*," that is "The Private Treasuries of Garments." (Ibn al-Ṭuwayr, *Nuzha*, 155).

1320 "*Min hādhā al-naḥw'*, that is "of that kind," which probably means one that matches the *mindīl*. (See Ibn al-Ṭuwayir, Nuzha, 155–156 fn. 4).

1321 That is, *al-yatīma*.

1322 This is the beginning of the second procession detailed by Ibn al-Ṭuwayr, namely, the New Year Procession.

1323 Ibn al-Ṭuwayr mentions the reason for not summoning the vizier this time saying: "*li-annahā khidma li azimmat al-khalīfa*," which probably means that all the caliph's overseers were involved in service and no one of a proper enough rank was available to be sent to the vizier. (Ibn al-Ṭuwayr, *Nuzha*, 160).

1324 "*Irkhā' al-dhu'āba*," or "lowering the tail of the turban," was one of the aspects of costume that showed privilege, such as the *ḥanak*. Linguistically, the *dhu'āba* (also the *'adhba*) is either the tail of a turban, a hair braid, a forelock, or hairlock. (P. Sanders, *Ritual*, 90, G. al-Shayyal, *Itti'āẓ*, Vol. 1, 294 fn. 2, http://www.baheth.info/all.jsp?term=ذؤابة, andhttp://www.baheth.info/all.jsp?term=عذبة).

1325 "*Al-Sayf al-dhahab*"; in Ibn al-Ṭuwayr's account: "*al-sayf al-mudhahhab*," which is the golden inlaid or gold-plated. (See Ibn al-Ṭuwayr, *Nuzha*, 160–161).

1326 On a *maṣṭaba* (pedestal or bench) in Ibn al-Ṭuwayr's account. (Ibn al-Ṭuwayr, *Nuzha*, 161).

along with his sons, brothers and his private entourage (*khawāṣṣ*), while the amirs sat on benches prepared for them.[1327] The caliph's horse entered to the door of the audience hall (*majlis*) where he was at. By the door was a chair for him to use to mount the horse. As the horse stood properly by that chair, the parasol was taken out to its bearer, who unwrapped it and received it with the help of four [assistants],[1328] who were assigned to serve it. The bearer then fixed the parasol into an iron instrument that looked like an attached horn[1329] and was tightly fastened to the bearer's right stirrup. He held the pole with a bar above his hand.[1330] The sword was then released to its bearer, who untied the tail of his turban when he received it and did not tie it up again so long as he carried it. Then the inkwell (*dawāt*) was released to its bearer, who put it in front of him, between his body and his saddle. The Vizier left the section (*maqṭa'*) and was joined by the amirs to stand by the caliph's horse. The Master of the Audience Hall (*ṣāḥib al-majlis*) then opened the curtain and the masters (*ustādhūn*) who were in the service (*khidma*) of the Caliph came out. The Caliph came out behind them in the attire especially chosed for the day, with the Honourable Crown above his head and the Matchless (*al-yatīma*) jewel on his forehead. The Caliph would be wearing a *ḥanak*, with the tail of his turban untied and falling on his left side; girded with the Arabian[1331] sword and holding the Sovereignty Staff (*qaḍīb al-mulk*) in his hand. A group that was assigned for saluting the Vizier with peace saluted him, then the Judge and the amirs, subsequently.[1332] The amirs exited followed by the Vizier who mounted his horse and stood opposite the palace's gate. The caliph exited mounting his horse, which walked on rugs for fear of slipping over the marble floors, while the masters surrounded him. When he approached the gate and his face appeared, a man blew a small golden horn with a bent head called "*al-gharība*" (the bizarre one),[1333] which did not sound like other horns. The rest of the horns in the procession

1327 Which means furnished for them with elegant coverings suitable for the season, whether summer or winter, according to Ibn al-Ṭuwayr's account. (Ibn al-Ṭuwayr, *Nuzha*, 161).

1328 Ibn al-Ṭuwayr's account: "Four of the *Ṣaqāliba*" (Slavs) (Ibn al-Ṭuwayr, *Nuzha*, 161).

1329 "*Al-Qarn al-muṣṭaḥab*," which may be translated as "the attached horn" or "the accompanying horn"; "*al-muṣṭakhab*" (clamouring or uproaring) in Ibn al-Ṭuwayr's account; an ambigious term that researchers could not decipher. (See Ibn al-Ṭuwayr, *Nuzha*, 161 and Ibn Taghrī Birdī & M. Shams, *Nujūm*, Vol. 4, 91 & 91 fn. 5).

1330 It is not clear what this "bar" or "barrier" (*ḥājiz*) was, but Ibn al-Ṭuwayr tells us that it kept the pole firm and upright, and the parasol was never known to have fluttered in the wind. (Ibn al-Ṭuwayr, *Nuzha*, 161).

1331 In al-Maqrīzī's account: al-Maghribī (the one from the Maghrib).(Al-Maqrīzī, *Khiṭaṭ*, Vol. 2, 253).

1332 In Ibn al-Ṭuwayr's: "his relations, then the amirs." In al-Maqrīzī's and Ibn Taghrī Birdī's accounts: "the judge, his relations (*ahl*, possibly the vizier's), then the amirs." (Ibn al-Ṭuwayr, *Nuzha*, 162, al-Maqrīzī, *Khiṭaṭ*, Vol. 2, 153, and Ibn Taghrī Birdī, *Nujūm*, Vol. 4, 92).

1333 In Ibn Taghrī Birdī's account, it is called "*al-'arbāna*;" however, other historians agree on "*al-gharība*," which is the more probable name that indicates its peculiarity or uniqueness. (Ibn al-Ṭuwayir, Nuzha, 163 fn. 2 and Ibn Taghrī Birdī, *Nujūm*, Vol. 4, 92).

were then blown and the parasol was opened. The caliph exited the palace's gate and stopped for a brief moment until the *muḥannakūn* masters and others of the Holders of Ranks (*arbāb al-rutab*) who were in the service (*khidma*) inside the hall (*qā'a*)[1334] mounted their horses. The Caliph then proceeded with the Holder of the Parasol (*ṣāḥib al-miẓalla*)[1335] to his left, taking care that the Caliph was always kept in the shade. The commanders (*muqaddamūn*) of the Equestrian Guards (*ṣibyān al-rikāb*) walked surrounding the caliph: two of them holding his horse's curb bits, two on both sides of the horse's neck, and two on both his hinder sides. The right one of the last two was the one holding the riding whip (*miqra'a*) and responsible for handing it to the caliph and receiving it back.[1336] He was also responsible for announcing the caliph's orders and prohibitions on his behalf for the period of his ride.[1337] The Two Banners of Thankfulness moved on both sides of the caliph, and the Two Fly Whisks (*al-midhabbatān*) by his horse's head. The Equestrian Escorts (*rikābiyya*) to his left and right were about one thousand men, girded with their swords; their wastes wrapped with the kerchiefs (*manādīl*) and with arms.[1338] They were by the caliph's sides, like two extended wings; between them a gap for the horse's face, where no one walked. Near the horse's head, were the two Slavs (*Ṣaqāliba*) who held the Two Fly Whisks, which were raised like two palm-trees.

The procession was ordered as follows: The amirial soldiers (*ajnād al-umarā'*),[1339] their sons[1340] and the mixed groups of soldiers (*akhlāṭ al-'askar*)[1341] walked in front of the procession; followed by the lowest-ranking amirs (*adwān al-umarā'*);

1334 Qā'at al-Dhahab.

1335 Also, *ḥāmil al-miẓalla*: the Bearer of the Parasol.

1336 Which means that he handed it to the caliph as needed.

1337 This probably means that he was the one who shouted them out loudly so that the crowd heard them.

1338 "With their arms drawn in their hands." (Ibn al-Ṭuwayr, *Nuzha*, 164, al-Maqrīzī, *Khiṭaṭ*, Vol. 2, 254, and Ibn Taghrī Birdī, *Nujūm*, Vol. 4, 93).

1339 Ibn al-Ṭuwayr uses the term "*furū' al-umarā'*," which may be translated as "the branches of the amirs," or "the subordinates of the amirs." These were the independent private forces of the amirs, whom we are told, by the Mamluk era, had to be registered in the army bureau with their full names as affiliated to a particular amir. They were of a racial variety, were divided according to ranks, and answered directly to the amir. In the Mamluk era, they had their own *iqṭā'āt*, which their amirs assigned to them. (Ibn al-Ṭuwayr, *Nuzha*, 163, al-Maqrīzī, *Khiṭaṭ*, Vol. 3, 71, *Ṣubḥ*, Vol. 4, 62 and H. al-Jazzar, "Niẓām," 42–43).

1340 It is not clear whether the "sons" meant here are these of the soldiers or the amirs.

1341 "*Akhlāṭ*" means a mixed group of people. P. Sanders refers to "*akhlāṭ al-'askar*" as the "mixed groups of elite soldiers," while A. Gamal al-Din remarks that these were irregular soldiers. The term denotes that they were of various racial and tribal origins, which could mean that they were the same "Factions of Soldiers" mentioned above. In Ibn al-Ṭuwayr's account, the phrase used is "*akhlāṭ min al-'askar*," which changes the meaning to "a mixture of soldiers." In the Mamluk context, al-'Umarī uses the term "*mukhtalaṭ*" (also "mixed" or "mingled") to describe soldiers whom he goes on to mention the various races of. (P. Sanders, *Ritual*, 92; A. Gamal al-Din, *Dawla*, 270; Ibn al-Ṭuwayr, *Nuzha*, 163; al-'Umarī, *Masālik* (2002), Vol. 3, 429, and http://www.baheth.info/all.jsp?term=أخلاط).

then the amirs who held the silver staffs;[1342] the collared (*arbāb al-aṭwāq*) among the amirs; the *muḥannakūn* masters; the vizier's relatives[1343] mentioned above; the bearers of the Two Banners of Thankfulness on both sides; then the bearer of the inkwelland the bearer of the sword, both on the left side. Each one of the above-mentioned moved among ten to twenty of his company.

Then the Caliph moved among the Equestrian Escorts slowly and gently. The Governor of Cairo was among the foremost, leading soldiers, and moved back and forth to make way and urge those who stop to move. Amidst the soldiers was [the] *isfihsalār*,[1344] also moving back and forth, enticing the soldiers to move and scorning those crowding up or getting in the way. The Master of the Gate moved in the close company of the Caliph to supervise the soldiers and guard the roads that the Caliph took, also going back and forth. [As they travelled the length of the procession], the Master of the Gate met the *isfihsalār*, and the *isfihsalār* met the Governor of Cairo, each of them holding a mace (*dabbūs*). Behind the caliph was a group of Equestrian Escorts (*rikābiyya*) to protect his back. They were followed by ten men who carried ten swords that were kept inside red and yellow silk brocade (*dībāj*) covers.[1345] These swords were called The Swords of Blood (*suyūf al-damm*), and were for the execution of decapitation commands. Following them were the bearers of the small weaponry mentioned before.[1346]

The Vizier moved behind the Caliph, in magnificent appearance, followed by about 500 men that he chose from his entourage and a group of strong soldiers called "the Chainmail Guards" (*ṣibyān al-zard*).[1347] They moved on both the Vizier's sides and allowed for a decent gap in front of his horse, which was smaller than the gap preceding the Caliph. The Vizier made every effort not to lose sight of the Caliph. He was followed by numerous drums, cymbals (*ṣunūj*)[1348] and fifes (*ṣafāfīr*) that thundered and roared. Behind these was

1342 *"Arbāb al-quḍub al-fiḍḍa,"* in Ibn al-Ṭuwayr's account:"*arbāb al-qaṣab*," and *arbāb al-manāṣib* (holders of high positions) in Ibn Taghrī Birdī's account. (Ibn al-Ṭuwayr, *Nuzha*, 163 & Ibn Taghrī Birdī, *Nujūm*, Vol. 4, 93).

1343 "The vizier's relatives from the right side." (Ibn al-Ṭuwayr, *Nuzha*, 164).

1344 "The *isfihsalār*." (Ibn al-Ṭuwayr, *Nuzha*, 164, al-Maqrīzī, *Khiṭaṭ*, Vol. 2, 254 and Ibn Taghrī Birdī, *Nujūm*, Vol. 4, 93).

1345 *Kharā'iṭ*, sing. *kharīṭa*, see Glossary.

1346 "*Al-Ḥāmilūn li-l-silāḥ al-ṣaghīr*;" in Ibn al-Ṭuwayr's account: "*arbāb al-silāḥ al-ṣaghīr*," or "the Bearers of Small Arms," which refers to 300 black slaves, who each carried two spears and a shield. (Ibn al-Ṭuwayr, *Nuzha*, 148–149 & 165).

1347 *Ṣibyān al-zard* or Chainmail Guards were a group of riffraff or rabble (*awbāsh*) soldiers and commoners which al-Ḥasan, son of caliph al-Ḥāfiẓ (r. 525 AH/1131 AD – 545 AH/1149 AD), formed in 529 AH/1135 AD during his conflict with his father. Al-Ḥasan distributed shields among this group and assigned them as his private forces. According to Ibn al-Ṭuwayr, the vizier was not accompanied by two groups as shown above, but the 500 men chosen by the vizier were *ṣibyān al-zard*. Most probably a word is missing from al-Qalqashandī's account, which would equate the two groups, such as: "and they are a group . . ." (Ibn al-Ṭuwayr, *Nuzha*, 165 & 165 fn. 3).

1348 Al-Qalqashandī mentions the "*ṣunūj*" once in his description of the duff, being the small cymbals that are sometimes part of the instrument. In another instance, he mentions it among the

the Bearer of the Lance (*ḥāmil al-rumḥ*) mentioned above, and the leathern shield (*daraqa*) attributed to Ḥamza. Then there were the Men of the Fleets (*rijāl al-asāṭīl*), who were more than 500, marching on foot and carrying the Arabian bows, which were called "the crossbows of the foot and stirrups" (*qisiy al-rijl wa-l-rikāb*).[1349]

Following were the Factions of Men (*ṭawā'if al-rijāl*):[1350] the Maṣāmida; the Rayḥāniyya; the Juyūshiyya; the Furanjiyya,[1351]and the Wazīriyya. They moved consecutively and were numerous in number for they were more than 4000 men. Then [marched] the bearers of the standards (*aṣḥāb al-rāyāt*)[1352] and [the standards with] the two lions.[1353] Then [they were followed by] the factions of soldiers (*ṭawā'if al-'asākir*): the Āmiriyya; the Ḥāfiẓiyya; the Elder Guards of the Barracks (*al-ḥujariyya al-kibār*); the Young Guards of the Barracks (*al-ḥujariyya al-ṣighār*);[1354] the Afḍaliyya;[1355] the Juyūshiyya;[1356] the Turks who were under patronage (*muṣṭana'ūn*); the Daylam; the Kurds; the Ghuzz who were under patronage (*muṣṭana'a*),[1357] and others. These [factions] comprised more than 3000 horsemen.

Ibn al-Ṭuwayr said: All this is but a part of the whole [army].[1358] When the procession was organized as described above, [the caliph] moved from the palace

processional musical instruments that accompanied the sovereign, in his account of the kingdom regulation of India, which means that in this case the *ṣunūj* were big cymbals unattached to a duff. (*Ṣubḥ*, Vol. 2, 144 & Vol. 5, 97).

1349 See ealier. According to Ibn al-Ṭuwayr, they bore both hand bows (*qisiy al-yadd*) and foot crossbows (*qisiy al-rijl*). (Ibn al- Ṭuwayr, *Nuzha*, 166).

1350 "*Ṭawā'if al-rijāl*," which is also used by Ibn Taghrī Birdī, who also remarks that these were horsemen (*firsān*) and indicates that the bearers of the bows of the hands (*qisiy al-yadd*) and the bows of the foot (*qisiyy al-rijl*) marching in front of them were on foot (*mutarajjila*). In Ibn al-Ṭuwayr's and al-Maqrīzī's accounts: "*ṭawā'ifal-rājil*," which means "the infantry factions." (Ibn al-Ṭuwayr, *Nuzha*, 165, Ibn Taghrī Birdī & M. Shams, *Nujūm*, Vol. 4, 94–95 & 94 fn. 4, and al-Maqrīzī, *Khiṭaṭ*, Vol. 2, 254).

1351 Also in Ibn al-Ṭuwayr's account, which could have meant to refer to the Farḥiyya: a group of blacks or Sudanese, who marched in the processions beating the drums, or to "*arbāb al-furanjiyyāt*," which was another name given to "*arbāb al-silāḥ al-ṣaghīr*" (holders of the small arms). Another possibility is that the name was "al-Firinjiyya," which would have been the originally Crusaders or the ones from the lands of the Crusaders. (Ibn al-Ṭuwayr, *Nuzha*, 165 & 165 fn. 4, Ibn Taghrī Birdī& M. Shams, *Nujūm*, Vol. 4, 94 fn. 5, and al-Maqrīzī, *Khiṭaṭ*, Vol. 2, 254).

1352 *Al-Rāyāt* (the Standards), sing. *al-rāya*.

1353 *Al-Sabu'ayn*: the two lions. (See P. Sanders, *Ritual*, 91 & 96).

1354 In Ibn al-Ṭuwayr's and al-Maqrīzī's accounts: *al-ḥujariyya al-ṣighār al-manqūlīn* (the transferred, young *ḥujariyya*). (Ibn al-Ṭuwayr, *Nuzha*, 166 and al-Maqrīzī, *Khiṭaṭ*, Vol. 2, 254).

1355 Forces of Vizier al-Afḍal.

1356 Ibn al-Ṭuwayr also repeats al-Juyūshiyyain both categories. (Ibn al-Ṭuwayr, *Nuzha*, 165–166).

1357 In Ibn Taghrī Birdī's account: ". . . then the Kurds and the Ghuzz under patronage (*al-mṣṭana'a*), who were the navy [men] (*baḥariyya*)." (*Nujūm*, Vol. 94–95).

1358 That is, all these listed forces and factions constituted but a part of the whole Fatimid military, or according to Ibn Taghrī Birdī: the caliph's forces (*'askar al-khalīfa*). (Ibn al-Ṭuwayr, *Nuzha*, 166 and Ibn Taghrī Birdī, *Nujūm*, Vol. 4, 95).

gate where he exited at Bayn al-Qaṣrayn, proceeded with his procession until he exited Bāb al-Naṣr and arrived at a [water] basin (*ḥawḍ*)[1359] there that was known as ʿIzz al-Mulk,[1360] near Bāb al-Naṣr. The procession then turned to its left[1361] aiming for Bāb al-Futūḥ. The procession may have also turned left after exiting Bāb al-Naṣr, in alignment with the walls, until it reached Bāb al-Futūḥ and entered through it, proceeding until it stopped again at Bayn al-Qaṣrayn.[1362] Whichever [route taken], the procession entered through Bāb al-Futūḥ and moved until it stopped at Bayn al-Qaṣrayn, where the soldiers took the same positions as at the start of the procession and the amirs dismounted. When the caliph reached al-Aqmar Mosque, he stopped there among his company and the procession opened up for the Vizier to move hastily and come in front of the Caliph. When the Vizier passed by the Caliph, he saluted him with a conspicuous gesture,[1363] and the Caliph saluted him back with a slight gesture, which was the greatest honouring sign to be shown by a caliph, and was only granted a vizier who was a Man of the Sword. After the Vizier passed the Caliph, he preceded him to the palace gate and entered mounting his horse as usual, while the amirs walked in front of him until the place where he mounted in Dihlīz al-ʿAmūd, mentioned-earlier. He dismounted there and stood with the amirs waiting for the caliph. When the Caliph arrived at the palace gate, the *muḥannakūn* masters dismounted and the Caliph entered mounting his horse as they gazed at him. When the Caliph reached the Vizier, the latter walked in front of the caliph's horse up to the chair from which the Caliph mounted. The Vizier and the amirs saluted the Caliph with the service [protocol] (*khidma*), then left, and the caliph retired to his

1359 Water basin or reservoir for the animals to drink.

1360 This was a title that means "Glory of Sovereignty," which was sometimes given to certain officials. This *ḥawḍ* was attached, or was right next to, a mosque, both bearing the name of the patron: ʿIzz al-Mulk Nabā. This mosque near Bāb al-Naṣr was mentioned by Ibn al-Ṭuwayr, which was copied in the accounts of al-Qalqashandī, al-Maqrīzī, and Ibn Taghrī Birdī. It was extinct by the time of al-Qalqashandī, as is evident from his account above. (Ibn al-Ṭuwayr , *Nuzha*, 160 & 160 fn. 1, Ibn Taghrī Birdī & M. Shams, *Nujūm*, Vol. 4, 90 & 90 fn. 8, and al-Maqrīzī, *Khiṭaṭ*, Vol. 2, 251–252).

1361 The left of the basin (*ḥawḍ*), given the further explanation in the following sentences.

1362 According to Ibn al-Ṭuwayr and in accordance with al-Qalqashandī's description, there were two routes for the procession, one that reached the mosque and *ḥawḍ* of ʿIzz al-Mulk, which was the extremity of the wider or bigger route, while the smaller route moved left immediately after exiting Bab al-Naṣr. (Ibn al-Ṭuwayr, *Nuzha*, 160).

1363 "*Saka'a lahu sak'a ẓāhira*," which may be translated as: "and (he) greeted him with a visible *sak'a*." The verb *saka'a* means to be lost or confused about one's destination, or to wander. One definition given to *saka'a* in this context is to "greet someone by kissing the head." Another explanation is that the vizier "bended his legs and stood submissively on his knees." Whatever the exact gesture was, we are told that it was done noticeably or obviously, and Ibn Taghrī Birdī adds that this deliberate visibility of the gesture was particularly to show the crowd that the vizier was in the caliph's service, or to exhibit his performance of salutation protocol: "*li-yuẓhir li al-nās khidmatahu*." Conclusively, the *sak'a* was, in this case, an obvious gesture, performed closely enough to be immediately in front of the caliph (*bayna yadayhi*). (http://www.baheth.info/all.jsp?term=سكع; Ibn al-Ṭuwayr, *Nuzha*, 166 & 166 fn. 1; P. Sanders, *Ritual*, 145; M. Shams, *Nujūm*, Vol. 4, 95 fn. 1, and al-Maqrīzī, *Khiṭaṭ*, Vol. 2, 255).

residential quarters. The Vizier rode [again] at the place where he dismounted, with the amirs [walking] immediately in front of him and his relatives around him until he exited the palace gate. [At this point], those of them of riding status mounted their rides, while the others walked. All moved in the vizier's service (*khidma*) until he reached his house, which he entered mounting his horse, and dismounted it using a chair as well. His company then saluted him with the service [protocol] (*khidma*),[1364] and left.

The people will have watched the beauty of the procession, which made them joyful and pleased their minds. As the people went back to their places,[1365] they found that the caliph had sent them the *ghurra*,[1366] which was [a share of] *rubā'iyya*[1367] dinars and light round dirhams[1368] that the caliph would have ordered the minting of during the last ten days of Dhū al-Ḥijja so as to distribute on that day. The vizier, the amirs, and the Holders of Ranks (*arbāb al-marātib*)[1369] among the Men of the Sword and the Men of the Pen, each had their special allocated quantity,[1370] which they accepted as a blessing from the caliph. The perfumed letters (*mukhallaqāt*)[1371] were sent to the villages (*bilād*)[1372] and provinces (*a'māl*) bearing the good tidings of the New Year Procession (*rukūb awwal al-'ām*), like letters are sent in our present times [to inform of] the Fulfillment of the Nile (*wafā' al-Nīl*) or Riding to the Square (*rukūb al-maydān*).[1373]

The Second Procession: Riding on the First Day of the Month of Ramadan

This [celebration] for Shiites is the same as the sighting (*ru'ya*)[1374] of the crescent. The parade, costumes, instruments, and riding, as well as the procession, its organization

1364 In Ibn al-Ṭuwayr's account: "*fa yakhdimuhā al-jamā'a bi-l-wadā'*," which means that the company performed the goodbye or parting salutation protocol for him. (Ibn al-Ṭuwayr, *Nuzha*, 167).

1365 Residences or homes.

1366 "*Ghurra*" means "the beginning of," or the "forehead," or "forelock." In this case, it refers to the bestowed gift that the caliph distributed on the occasion of the beginning of the year.

1367 A coin that was especially minted for this occasion and weighed four times (*rubā'iyya*, from *arba'a*, which is four) another coin called the *qīrāṭ* (the Carat). In Ibn al-Ṭuwayr's, al-Maqrīzī's, and Ibn Taghrī Birdī's accounts, the *rubā'iyya* is listed as an independent coin, not a type of dinars as al-Qalqashandī's account implies. (Ibn al-Ṭuwayr, *Nuzha*, 167 & 167 fn. 2, al-Maqrīzī, *Khiṭaṭ*, Vol. 2, 255, and Ibn Taghrī Birdī & M. Shams, *Nujūm*, Vol. 4, 95 & 95 fn. 2).

1368 In this context, like the *rubā'iyya*, these dirhams were likely commemorative and minted for the occasion. (See Glossary: "*dirham*").

1369 See *arbāb al-rutab*.

1370 Ibn al-Ṭuwayr lists the vizier's sons and siblings among the recipients. (Ibn al-Ṭuwayr, *Nuzha*, 167).

1371 Letters perfumed with "*khalūq*," see Glossary: "*takhlīq*".

1372 Sing. *balad* or *bilda*. The meaning of the term *balad* may be "village" or "country." In plural form, *bilād* may be used to refer to a province, for example, al-Qalqashandī refers to the western oases of Egypt by the term "*bilād al-wāḥ*." (*Ṣubḥ*, Vol. 3, 393).

1373 See later.

1374 "*Al-Ru'ya*" means "the vision" or "the sighting" and in this context indicates validating the beginning of a new Hijrī month through sighting the crescent. In the case of Ramadan, the holy

and the roads it took followed the same fashion as the New Year Procession, without any deviation. It was an occasion for sending out perfumed letters (*mukhallaqāt*) bearing the good tidings, just as was done on the occasion of the New Year.

The Third Procession: Riding on the Three Fridays of Ramadan

The three Fridays were the second, third[1375] and fourth of the month. Before the Caliph rode to al-Anwar Mosque at Bāb al-Baḥr,[1376] the Head of the Public Treasury (*ṣāḥib bayt al-māl*)went to the mosque in the early morning, taking with him the caliph's special rugs carried by the high caretakers (*farrāshīn*) and wrapped in *Dabīqī*cloths (*'arāḍī*).[1377] Three small mattresses (*ṭarrāḥāt*)[1378] were used to furnish the floor of the mihrab; these were either Damascene (*shāmiyyāt*)[1379] or white *Dabīqī*, both embriodered in red, one spread above the other. Two curtains were hung to the right and left [of the mihrab]. The right curtain was embriodered in red silk with the inscriptions of Sūrat al-Fātiḥa[1380] and Sūrat al-Jumʿa.[1381] The left curtain was embriodered with Sūrat al-Fātiḥa and Sūrat al-Munafiqūn.[1382] The inscriptions on both curtains were written clearly with diacritics.[1383] The Chief Judge ascended the minbar, holding a small bamboo incense-burner that the Head of the Public Treasury brought for him. The incense-burner contained tripled incense (*nadd muthallath*) of a smell that was unmatched elsewhere. The Judge

month of fasting, this vision entails a celebration to welcome the month. Astronomical calculations are also used to determine the beginnings and ends of the months of the lunar calendar. (See Glossary: "*ru'ya*").

1375 The editor of Subḥ comments that "the third" is missing from the text, but can be concluded from the context. (*Ṣubḥ*, Vol. 3, 509 fn. 1).

1376 Al-Anwar is the Mosque of al-Ḥākim. In Ibn al-Ṭuwayr's account: "The Great al-Anwar Mosque." (See Ibn al-Ṭuwayr, *Nuzha*, 172 & 172 fn. 3).

1377 Sing. *'araḍī*, which was a term used many times by historians to refer to more than one cloth item: a piece of clothing like a scarf; a textile cover used for plates and vessels; a type of textile belt, or a kind of head cover. (Ibn al-Ṭuwayir, Nuzha, 130 fn. 1).

1378 Sing. *ṭarrāḥa*, see Glossary.

1379 Sing. *shāmiyya*, which means Damascene. The more plausible term used by Ibn al-Ṭuwayr is *sāmān*, which is a kind of precious silk cloth that was manufactured in Sāmān, one of the villages of Isfahan, in present day Iran. (Ibn al-Ṭuwayr, *Nuzha*, 173 and M. Shams, *Nujūm*, Vol. 4, 99 fn.1).

1380 The Opening Chapter, first chapter of the Holy Quran (http://corpus.quran.com/translation.jsp?chapter=1&verse=1)

1381 Friday Chapter, chapter sixty-two of the Holy Quran (http://corpus.quran.com/translation.jsp?chapter=62&verse=1)

1382 Chapter of the Hypocrites, chapter sixty-three of the Holy Quran, which Ibn al-Ṭuwayr indicates using the common practice of mentioning a part of the first verse, or sometimes the first verse, rather than the name of the chapter (Ibn al-Ṭuwayr, *Nuzha*, 173 &http://corpus.quran.com/translation.jsp?chapter=63&verse=1).

1383 "*Maḍbūṭa*," which means that the inscriptions included the vocalization and pronunciation marks. In Ibn al-Ṭuwayr's account, the word used is "*manqūṭa*," which means that the inscription was dotted; that is, dots were added to the letters that should be dotted. (Ibn al-Ṭuwayr, *Nuzha*, 173). Adding dots to some letters for clarification of proper pronunciation was a calligraphic development in the early centuries of Islam.

incensed the top of the minbar three times; upon this top was the *qanā*[1384] that looked like a dome and was for seating the Caliph to deliver speeches.

The Caliph rode in the same appearance that was described in the accounts of the beginning of the year and the beginning of Ramadan processions, with the parasol (*miẓalla*) and other instruments. His costume would be all white, without any golden threads, out of respect for prayers. He also wore the turban-cloth (*mindīl*) and the turban cover that is opened in the middle (*al-ṭaylasān al-muqawwar*).[1385]

The Quran reciters in the caliph's presence (*qurrā' al-ḥaḍra*)[1386] marched on both sides behind his ride outside the lines of the Equestrian Escorts (*rikābiyya*), reciting loudly, one after another, from the moment he started riding at the palace and until he entered Qāʿat al-Khaṭāba (the Sermon Hall).[1387] The caliph entered from Bāb al-Khaṭāba (the Sermon Door) and sat in the hall. If he needed to renew his ablution, he did. The *maqṣūra* [where he sat] was guarded from outside, from beginning to end, by the assigned Masters of the Gate (*aṣḥāb al-bāb*),[1388] the *isfihsalār* and the Private Guards (*ṣibyān al-khāṣṣ*), as well as other similar position holders. They also guarded its inside, from the door where the caliph exited to the minbar.[1389] When the Friday prayer was called for by the *adhān*,[1390] the Chief Judgeentered to the Caliph and said: "Peace, mercy and blessings of Allah be on the Prince of the Faithful, the honourable (*al-sharīf*), the judge (*qāḍī*), and the preacher (*khaṭīb*).[1391] It is time for prayer, may Allah have mercy upon you." The Caliph then exited on foot,

1384 "*Qanā* "seems meaningless here and most probably it was a mistake in copying Ibn al-Ṭuwayr's account, where he uses "*al-ghishā* "' (the cover). In Ibn al-Ṭuwayr's account: the judge" incensed the top of the minbar, upon which was the cover that looked like a dome, for seating the caliph to deliver speeches." As seen earlier, the *qanā* was a kind of lances; the word has other meanings, none of which is of relevance. (Ibn al-Ṭuwayr, *Nuzha*, 173 and http://www.baheth.info/all.jsp?term=قنا).

1385 *Al-Ṭaylasān* was a piece of cloth worn as turban veils. There were two types of *ṭaylasān*: one that waswrapped around the turban and the neck until its ends almost met,covering the cheeks or most of the face, and falling to the shoulders. The second type, namely, *al-ṭaylasān al-muqawwar* (the hollowed *ṭaylasān*), apparently had an opening at the middle to pass one's face or head through. When religious scholars wore the *ṭaylasān* in the Mamluk era, they took care that not one side was longer than the other, and used needles to attach it to the turban, to prevent it from falling down on the chest. Al-Qalqashandī mentions that *al-ṭaylasān al-muqawwar* was similar to the *ṭarḥa* of his time, which was a veil that covered the turban, was wrapped around the neck and fell on the shoulders. (Al-Battawi, *'Imāma*, 134–135 and *Ṣubḥ*, Vol. 1, 428).

1386 In Ibn al-Ṭuwayr's account, they are termed "*aṣḥāb al-rikāb al-qurrā'*," that is, the escort reciters of the procession. (Ibn al-Ṭuwayr, *Nuzha*, 173).

1387 Ibn al-Ṭuwayr more specifically says: "the sermon hall of the mosque." (Ibn al-Ṭuwayr, *Nuzha*, 173).

1388 Sing. Ṣāḥib al-Bāb.

1389 Ibn al-Ṭuwayr adds "one after the other," which probably means that each guard was responsible for a particular section. (Ibn al-Ṭuwayr, *Nuzha*, 173).

1390 The *adhān* is the call for prayers.

1391 Ibn al-Ṭuwayr's account only mentions "*al-sharīf*" and "*al-qāḍī*," not "*al-khaṭīb*." (Ibn al-Ṭuwayr, *Nuzha*, 173).

surrounded by the *muḥannakūn* Masters and followed by the Vizier, then the amirs from among the Private Guards who were holding their weapons, until he reached the minbar and ascended to its top, under the incensed dome. The Vizier stood by the door of the minbar, facing the Caliph. When the Caliph sat down, he signalled to the Vizier to ascend, which he did until he reached the Caliph. The Vizier then kissed the Caliph's hands and feet in view of the people, then buttoned [the covers] of this dome [to enclose the caliph] like a howdah.[1392] The Vizier then descended, still facing the caliph, and stood for the minbar's watch.[1393] If the Vizier was not a Man of the Sword, then buttoning the dome's covers was the responsibility of the Chief Judge and the minbar's watch was the responsibility of the Master of the Gate.

The caliph then delivered a short sermon that was sent to him in a sack[1394] from the Chancery Bureau (*dīwān al-inshā'*). The sermon included reciting a Quranic verse, praying for his father and his grandfather, the latter being Prophet Muḥammad, and praying for ʿAlī b. Abī Ṭālib. The caliph then preached the people eloquently and briefly. He mentioned [the line of] his paternal ancestors until he reached his own self, and said: "Oh Allah! I am your slave, the son of your two slaves, and I can do myself neither harm nor benefit." He pleaded to Allah with glorious prayers that suited him; prayed for the vizier, if there was one, and the armies, to be granted victory and accord; for the soldiers to be granted triumph, and that perdition and vanquish befall the infidels and disobedient. He ended his sermon with: "Remember[1395] Allah so that He remembers you,"[1396] then the person who bottoned [the minbar's dome covers] came up and unbuttoned it.[1397] This person then descended, facing the caliph. The caliph then entered the mihrab,[1398] stood as an imam upon the small mattresses (*ṭarrāḥāt*), while the vizier and the Chief Judgeformed the first line of the praying congregation behind him. Behind them, [in second line] were the *muḥannakūn* Masters, the Collared Amirsand the Holders of Ranks from the men of the sword and the pen. The muazzins stood with their

1392 Ibn al-Ṭuwayr explains that this dome could be buttoned because it was like a howdah. (Ibn al-Ṭuwayr, *Nuzha*, 174).

1393 In Ibn al-Ṭuwayr's account: "for the watch of the minbar's door." (Ibn al-Ṭuwayr, *Nuzha*, 174).

1394 *Safaṭ*, which is a basket woven of palm leaves, a casket or a chest. Historical accounts indicate that it was sometimes made of leather. The term is applied to different shapes of that may be sealed or locked.(see al-Nuwayrī & M. Higazy, *Nihāya*, Vol. 5, 105, Vol. 20, 477 fn. 3, & Vol. 22, 103; G. Qaddumi, *Gifts*, 248 en. 11, and http://www.baheth.info/all.jsp?term=سفط). The term is not mentioned in Ibn al-Ṭuwayr's account.

1395 *Udhkurū* (from the verb *dhakara*), which also means "to mention."

1396 A common prayer based on the Quranic verse from Sūrat al-Baqara (Chapter of the Cow), 2:152: "So remember Me; I will remember you. And be grateful to Me and do not deny Me." (Sahih International's translation http://corpus.quran.com/translation.jsp?chapter=2&verse=152).

1397 Ibn al-Ṭuwayr explains that this covering was because the caliph read from a written document, unlike what preachers normally do. (Ibn al-Ṭuwayr, *Nuzha*, 174).

1398 After descending the minbar, which al-Qalqashandī did not mention. (*Ṣubḥ*, Vol. 3, 511 fn. 1 and Ibn al-Ṭuwayr, *Nuzha*, 174).

backs to the wall of the *maqṣūra*,[1399] and the mosque was crowded with people praying behind the caliph. In the first *rak'a*, the caliph recited the Quranic chapters inscribed on the right curtain, and in the second he recited those inscribed on the left one.[1400]As the caliph recited, the judge repeated after him for the muazzins to hear, the so did the muazzins for the congregation to hear [the recitation clearly].[1401] When the prayers were over, people exited the mosque and rode, first ones first, and the caliph returned to the palace followed by the vizier until he reached it, while the drums and horns played back and forth.[1402]

On the third Friday of Ramadan, the caliph rode to al-Azhar Mosque too,[1403] in the same manner of the previous Friday,[1404] the only difference being the mosque.

On the fourth Friday, the Caliph rode to the the Old Mosque at Miṣr. The people of Cairo decorated [the area] from the palace's gate to the Mosque of Ibn Ṭūlūn for him and so did the people of Miṣr from the Mosque of Ibn Ṭūlūn to the Old Mosque. The two governors (*wulāt*) of both cities appointed [guards] to protect the people and the decorations. The Caliph rode from the palace's gate and marched along al-Shāri' al-A'ẓam (The Great Street) in Miṣr,[1405]moving in one street among the buildings, up to the al-Jāmi' al-'Atīq in Miṣr, where he repeated the same rituals of the previous Fridays, without deviation. When the prayers ended, the caliph returned to his palace in Cairo using the same route, and whenever he passed by a mosque, he would give a dinar to its keepers, despite the many mosques he met on his way.

1399 Ibn al-Ṭuwayr continues: "to protect him." (Ibn al-Ṭuwayr, *Nuzha*, 175).

1400 Ibn al-Ṭuwayr explains that the curtains served to make sure the caliph recited confidently, without fearing forgetfulness or stuttering. (Ibn al-Ṭuwayr, *Nuzha,* 175).

1401 It is common Islamic practice in large congregational prayers to have a man, called "*al-muballigh*" (the communicator), responsible for reciting after the imam to make sure all hear clearly, given the vast spaces.

1402 Meaning on the way to the mosque and back. (Ibn al-Ṭuwayr, *Nuzha*, 173 & 175).

1403 Ibn al-Ṭuwayr mentions that the caliph "rode to al-Azhar Mosque from al-Qashshāshīn," which later came to be known as "al-Kharrāṭīn." (Ibn al-Ṭuwayr, *Nuzha*, 175, Ibn al-Ṭuwayir, Nuzha, 175 fn.1).

1404 Al-Qalqashandī says "the first Friday," meaning the earlier one.

1405 The Greatest Street or the Main Avenue: Al-Maqrīzī tells us that the extension of the Fatimid main avenue outside Cairo started at the time of Caliph al-Ḥākim, which developed under the later Fatimid caliphs to connect Cairo to Fustat, from the Qaṣaba, longitudinally all the way to Bāb al-Ṣafā, to the south of al-Sayyida Nafīsa Mosque (modern mosque now standing in its own square, to the southwest of the Citadel). Since al- Shāri' al-A'ẓam did not lead directly to the Mosque of 'Amr, while it is specified that the caliph proceeded through al-Shāri' al-A'ẓam in Fustat, the procession must have taken a turn westwards somewhere beyond the Mosque of Ibn Ṭūlūn. Ibn al-Ṭuwayr tells us that this turn was made at the no longer extant Umayyad Mosque of 'Abd Allah b. Marwān (built between 86 AH/705 AD and 90 AH/709 AD). The location of this mosque is probably taken up today by the Mosque of Abū al-Su'ūd al-Jāriḥī, in Abū al-Su'ūd Square to the east of the Mosque of 'Amr in Miṣr al-Qadīma. (SeeAl-Maqrīzī, *Khiṭaṭ*, Vol. 2, 83& 594, Ibn al-Ṭuwayr, *Nuzha*, 168–169 fn. 2 & 175–176 & 175–176 fn. 3, and A. Raymond, *Cairo*, 81 Map 3 & 119 Map 4).

The Fourth Procession: Riding for the prayers of the two feasts: ʿĪd al-Aḍḥā and ʿĪd al-Fiṭr

The riding procession for ʿĪd al-Fiṭr was prepared for starting the last ten days of Ramadan. The processionalequipment was mobilized in the same, above-mentioned manner for the New Year [Procession] and other [processions]. There was a *muṣallā*,[1406] all built of stone, upon a hill outside Bāb al-Naṣr. A wall surrounded it and its gate was fortified. A large dome occupied its center; itself housing a mihrab at the center of its main wall. The minbar stood next to the dome, in the middle of the *muṣallā*,[1407]uncovered unto the sky with a height of 30 steps and a width of three cubits, and having a bench (*maṣṭaba*) at its top. When Ramadan ended, which the [Fatimids] counted as thirty days, no less,[1408] and it was the first day of Shawwāl,[1409] the Head of the Public Treasury (*ṣāḥib bayt al-māl*) marched to the *muṣallā* outside Bāb al-Naṣr. He spread out the small mattresses (*ṭarrāḥāt*)at the mihrab of the *muṣallā*, in the same way this was done in the mosques on Fridays as mentioned earlier, and he hung two curtains to the right and left. The right curtain was inscribed with al-Fātiḥa and Sūrat al-Aʿlā,[1410] while the left was inscribed with al-Fātiḥa and Sūrat al-Ghāshiya.[1411] Fixed at the two sides of the *muṣallā* were two banners stretched on two lances, which were dressed with silver [cylindrical] tubes. The banners were loosely spread. A small mattress (*ṭarrāḥa*) of the Damascene (*shāmiyyāt*)[1412]or *Dabīqī* kind was put at the top of the minbar.[1413] The rest of the minbar was covered with white cloth that

1406 The *muṣallā* referred to above, called Muṣallā al-ʿĪd, or the feast prayer area, was located outside Bāb al-Naṣr, to one's right upon exiting the gate. Jawhar al-Ṣaqallī built this *muṣallā* in 358 AH/969 AD and a part of it still existed by the time of al-Maqrīzī, a section of which was allocated for performing funerary prayers. We are told that this *muṣallā* was also called the Muṣallā of Cairo, for Jawhar had built another one in Fustat, allocated for its public. Caliph al-ʿAzīz renewed the Muṣallā of Cairo in 380 AH/990 AD and established several *maṣāṭib* (sing. *maṣṭaba*, bench or platform) between it and the palace. The muazzins sat on these *maṣāṭib* to recite the *takbīrāt* (special formulae prayer calls for the feasts), so that they were heard continuously from the palace to the *muṣallā*. The location of the *muṣallā* is taken up today by the burial area where Sikkat Qāitbāy Street meets Najm al-Dīn Street, in the Cemetery of Bāb al-Naṣr. (Ibn al-Ṭuwayir, Nuzha, 178 fn. 2).

1407 *Ṣadr*, which is "center," or "middle."

1408 The lunar calendar months are either 29 or 30 days. Sighting the cresent (*ru'ya*), as well as astronomical calculations, determine the beginnings and ends of these months.

1409 Tenth month of the Hijri calendar.

1410 Chapter of the Most High, chapter eighty-seven of the Holy Quran, which both Ibn al-Ṭuwayr and al-Qalqashandī refer to by the common practice of using the first verse rather than the name of the chapter. (Ibn al-Ṭuwayr, *Nuzha*, 179 &http://corpus.quran.com/translation.jsp?chapter=87&verse=1).

1411 Chapter of the Overwhelming, chapter eighty-eight of the Holy Quran, which both Ibn al-Ṭuwayr and al-Qalqashandī refer to by the common practice of using the first verse rather than the name of the chapter. (Ibn al-Ṭuwayr, *Nuzha*, 179 &http://corpus.quran.com/translation.jsp?chapter=88&verse=1).

1412 In Ibn al- Ṭuwayr's account: *sāmān*. (Ibn al-Ṭuwayr, *Nuzha*, 179)

1413 Ibn al-Ṭuwayr remarks that the *ṭarrāḥa* fit the size of the minbar's top. (Ibn al-Ṭuwayr, *Nuzha*, 179).

perfectly fit its staircase and did not shift due to the walking [steps of the climbers] or the like. At the top of the minbar, to its left and right, were two banners inscribed with gold.

The Vizier marched from his house to the caliph's palace in his usual manner as mentioned earlier. The Caliph rode in the appearance of great processions, as described earlier in the New Year [Procession], with the parasol (*miẓalla*), the crown (*tāj*), and other instruments. His costume on that day would be white clothes; ornamented (*muwashshaḥa*)[1414] and adorned with circular motifs (*mujawwama*),[1415] which was his most dignified costume; his parasol would be the same.[1416] He exited from Bāb al-ʿĪd, in the usual manner for riding on processions; however the military (*'asākir*) on that day, comprised of amirs and soldiers (*ajnād*), cavalry (*rukbān*) and infantry, were more than other [processional] days. People arranged themselves in two lines for the caliph [to pass in between] from the palace's gate to the *muṣallā*. The Caliph rode to the *muṣallā* and entered from its east side to a place where he rested for a minute, then he came out guarded by his entourage, as was described earlier in the Friday prayers, and went to the mihrab. The Vizier and the Judge followed him as mentioned earlier. He then prayed the *'īd* prayers with the *takbīrāt*[1417] that are known from the Prophet's traditions. The Caliph recited the Quranic chapters on his right side curtain in the first *rak'a* and in the second, the chapters on his left. After he ended the prayers and uttered the *salām*,[1418] he ascended the minbar to deliver the *'īd* sermon. When he reached the top of the minbar, he sat on this small mattress (*ṭarrāḥa*) for people to see him. At the foot of the minbar stood the Vizier; the Chief Judge; the Master of the Gate; the *isfihsalār*;[1419]

1414 *Al-Muwashshaḥa,* which means "the ornamented." The term bears the general meaning of ornamentation, but alsopossibly refers to adornment with two colours or with decorative bands. A *wishāḥ* is a sash or scarf and *muwashshaḥa* also has the meaning of being decorated with a sash. It is, therefore, possible that in this case, the ornamentation of the costume was with coloured bands. (See Z. Hasan, *Kunūz*, 121–122, P. Sanders, *Ritual*, 88 and http://www.baheth.info/all.jsp?term=موشح).

1415 *Jāma*, in both Arabic and Persian, means "cup" or "goblet," and was also used to refer to a kind of a pot or vessel made of ceramic, glass or silver. The term also applied to circles where it comes to decorative motifs, and was sometimes extended to other geometric motifs, such as hexagons. Commonly, the decorative bands of Fatimid textiles were composed of series of such motifs that framed floral or figural drawings (see *ṭirāz*). *Al-Mujawwama* in this context most probably refers to these bands. (See Z. Hasan, *Kunūz*, 121–122, Ibn al-Ṭuwayir, Nuzha, 190 fn. 3 and http://www.baheth.info/all.jsp?term=مجوم).

1416 The intended meaning is that his parasol (*miẓalla*)matched his costume, which was always the case as explained by Ibn al-Ṭuwayr. (Ibn al-Ṭuwayr, *Nuzha*, 177).

1417 Sing. *takbīr*: saying "Allahu Akbar" or "God is Great," which is essential in all prayers. In the regular mandatory five daily prayers, the *takbīr* marks the change of posture, from standing to bowing, etc. The number and function of the *takbīrāt* differs in the *'īd* and funerary prayers, for it they are uttered in specifics numbers, sometimes while standing without changing the posture. The *takbīrāt* of the *'īd* prayers also involve using a particular formula.

1418 *Sallama*, which means uttered: "*al-salām 'alaykum wa raḥmat Allah*" ("Peace be on you and the mercy of Allah") twice turning his head right the first time and left the second, marking the end of prayers.

1419 "*Isfihsalār al-'asākir*" in Ibn al-Ṭuwayr's account. (Ibn al-Ṭuwayr, *Nuzha*, 179).

the Holder of the Sword (*ṣāḥib al-sayf*);[1420] the Messenger; the Overseer of the Palace; the Keeper of the Council's Register (*ṣāḥib daftar al-majlis*); the Holder of the Parasol (*ṣāḥib al-miẓalla*); the Overseer of the Honourable Relatives (*zimām al-ashrāf al-aqārib*); the Head of the Public Treasury; the Lance Bearer (*ḥāmil al-rumḥ*), and the Chief of the Honourable Ṭālibiyyīn (*naqīb al-ashrāf al-Ṭalibiyyīn*). The Vizier faced towards the Caliph [who signalled to him to ascend. He ascended and stood near the Caliph until his face was at the same level as the caliph's feet], which he kissed for the people to see[1421] then rose and stood to the right of the Caliph. The Caliph then signalled to the Chief Judgeto ascend, so he did until he reached the seventh step, then looked at the Caliph waiting for what he had to say. The Caliph then signalled to him, so he took out a scroll[1422] from his sleeve. This scroll would have been brought to the Judge from the Chancery Bureau the night before, after having been shown to the Caliph and the Vizier. The Judge announced the contents of the scroll [saying]: "In the name of Allah, the Merciful and the Compassionate, it was the honour bestowed on so and so day, which is the ʿĪd al-Fiṭr of the year so and so, to ascend the minbar upon the order of the Prince of the Faithful, may Allah's prayers befall him, his pure fathers and his honourable sons, after the ascent of the Most Dignified Master (*al-sayyid al-ajall*) – then he mentioned the decreed designations of the vizier and the prayers for him." The Judge then mentioned the names of those who were honoured by the Caliph to ascend the minbar, starting with the vizier's sons,[1423] then the Judge himself, who being the announcer had to refer to himself without his designations,[1424] saying: "The mamluk so and so, son of so and so," and the like. He then went on with the names and designations of each of the men who stood by the door of the minbar, mentioned above. Whenever he mentioned one of them, he called him and the man ascended the minbar, each knowing his place on its right and left, until all stood on the minbar. The Vizier then signalled to them so that each of them took a piece of the banner to his side in his hand and they [closed them] covering themselves and the Caliph. The congregation was then ordered to listen and the Caliph delivered an eloquent sermon suitable for the occasion, which he read from the sack[1425] that was brought to him from the Chancery Bureau, [as] written,[1426] similar to what was done with the Fridays of Ramadan mentioned earlier. When

1420 Not mentioned in Ibn al-Ṭuwayr's account. (Ibn al-Ṭuwayr, *Nuzha*, 179).

1421 Between square brackets is missing from the text, as the editor of Subḥ notes, and is translated from Ibn al-Ṭuwayr's and al-Maqrīzī's accounts. (Ibn al-Ṭuwayr, *Nuzha*, 179–180, al-Maqrizī, *Khiṭaṭ*, Vol. 2, 266 and *Ṣubḥ*, Vol. 3, 513 fn. 1).

1422 *Darj* (see Glossary: "*kātib al-darj*").

1423 According to Ibn al-Ṭuwayr, mentioning the vizier's sonsand brothers was done in case the caliph decides to honour any of them with ascending the minbar. (Ibn al-Ṭuwayr, *Nuzha*, 180).

1424 That is, to showhumility.

1425 "*Safaṭ*," see Glossary.

1426 The text makes it seem as if the sermon was written on the sack itself. The sack is not mentioned by Ibn al-Ṭuwayr, who only states that the sermon was written. Most likely, a word or two were missed out while copying Ibn al-Ṭuwayr's account. (See Ibn al-Ṭuwayr, *Nuzha*, 174 & 181).

he finished the sermon, each of those holding on to the ends of the banners threw them outside the minbar uncovering themselves. The group then descended backwards, one by one, [while facing the Caliph], nearer ones then nearest. When the caliph was the only one left on the minbar, he descended and entered the place from which he came out, where he stayed for a little while and then rode in the same appearance he came in to the *muṣallā*. He took the same route back to his palace, and as he approached it, the vizier preceded him as usual. He then entered through Bāb al-ʿĪd, from where he left, and sat in the Window (*shubbāk*) of the Great Iwan. A banquet was spread out from the Window to the fountain in the centre of the iwan;its length was twenty *qaṣaba*s.[1427] It served *khushkanān*,[1428] *basnadūd*[1429] and other [delicacies] made on [occasion of] the *'īd* in quantities that seemed like a big mountain. Each piece weighed between a quarter of a kantar and one pound. People were allowed to eat and take as much as they wanted from this banquet, without any prevention or forbiddance. The Caliph then l.0eft the iwan and rode to Qaʿat al-Dhahab, where he found the throne set up, a silver table put up for him, and a banquet beneath the throne. The Caliph descended from the throne and sat to the table, called upon the Vizier to sit with him, while the amirs sat at the banquet until it was taken out by noon prayers. The Caliph left the table and the Vizier departed to his house accompanied by the amirs who marched in his service (*khidma*). The Vizier offered a banquet to the amirs at his house where they ate then left.

As for ʿĪd al-Aḍḥā, its processions were prepared from the beginning of Dhū al-Ḥijja. On the day of the *'īd*, the Caliph rode in the same appearance and arrangement as that of ʿĪd al-Fiṭr until he reached the *muṣallā*. The caliph's costume was red and ornamented (*muwashshaḥ*),[1430] and so was his parasol. He proceeded to the *muṣallā* outside Bāb al-Naṣr, delivered his sermon, and came back to the palace in the exact same fashion of the procession of ʿĪd al-Fiṭr. Then after he entered the palace, he exited from Bāb al-Faraj,[1431]

1427 *Al-Qaṣaba al-Ḥākimiyya* was one of two measurement units used to calculate agricultural land area in Egypt, the other being *al-Qaṣaba al-Sandafāwiyya*. The first and more commonly used unit was attributed to the the Fatimid Caliph al-Ḥākim, in whose reign it was introduced, while the second unit was attributed to the town of Ṣandafā, near al-Maḥalla al-Kubrā, and was only used in some of the Lower Egypt governorates. One feddan measures 400 *qaṣaba Ḥākimiyya*. (Al-Baqli, *Ta'rīf*, 274).

1428 Also: *khushkanānj*, and sometimes called *khushtanān* in Egypt,which is the originally Persian, Arabized name of a kind of pastry that is composed of two syllabi: *khushk* = crusty or dry, and *nān*=bread. It was made of fine wheat flour kneaded with sesame oil. It was formed into rectangular pieces, in the middle of each almonds and ground sugar kneaded with rosewater were put, in an almond to sugar ratio of one to two. The dough was then baked in the oven. Another description of it is that it was a kind of a puff-paste shaped like a hollow ring, with almonds or pistachio in its middle. (Ibn al-Ṭuwayir, Nuzha, 144 fn. 2 and M. Shams, *Nujūm*, Vol. 4, 100 fn. 6).

1429 A Persian dessert or delicacy made of flour and dates. (M. Shams, *Nujūm*, Vol. 4, 100 fn. 7).

1430 See Glossary: "*muwashshaḥa*".

1431 In Ibn al-Ṭuwayr's account, Bāb al-Rīḥ, which is more reasonable, since this is the gate of the palace which was in the described location, in the north walls of the greater eastern palace. Bāb

which was the palace gate oppositethe house of Saʿīd al-Suʿadā' that is now a khanqah.[1432] The Caliph would find the Vizier, mounted, by that gate. The Vizier then dismounted and walked in the Caliph's service (*khidma*) until they reached the slaughterground (*al-manḥar*),[1433] which was outside the gate and was at the time an open space devoid of buildings. There was a platform (*maṣṭaba*) there that was covered [with rugs] that the Caliph, the Vizier, the Chief Judge, the *muḥannakūn* masters and the high ranking men of the state ascended. Thirty-one little camels[1434] and female camels arrived earlier at the slaughterground for sacrifice. The Caliph held a spear while the Chief Judge held the base of its head. The animals were presented one by one to the Caliph; the Chief Judge put the head of the spear in the sacrifice's lower neck as the Caliph stabbed it at its centre.[1435] The animals fell to the ground before him until he slaughtered all of them. Then the allocated portions of sacrifice were distributed to the men of decreed, designated portions (*arbāb al-rusūm al-muqarrara*).[1436] On the second and third days, 27 and 21 heads of animals were taken, respectively, to the slaughterground, to where the Caliph rode and slaughtered them similarly.

After the slaughtering of the third day was finished, the Caliph returned to the palace and bestowed on the Vizier the red costume he wore for the *'Īd*, a turban-cloth (*mindīl*) without the Matchless (*al-yatīma*) jewel, and the necklace of precious gems. The Vizier then rode with this bestowal from the palace, through the [main] street of Cairo, to the Khalīj, which he crosses, until he enters the House of the Vizierate (*dār al-wizāra*) from Bāb al-Qanṭara. This indicated that the *'Īd* has ended.

The meat of the first slaughtered animal was cured and sent to the missionary (*dā'ī*) of Yemen to distribute it among the believers.[1437] The pieces were of weights that ranged from a quarter of a dirham to a half of a dirham. The rest of the meat was distributed among the men of designated portions (*arbāb al-rusūm*) in plates, as blessings. Most of it was given out by the Chief Judge and the Chief

al-Faraj was the south-west gate of the walls of Cairo built by Badr al-Jamālī. (See A. Raymond, *Cairo*, 32 Map 2).

1432 See Glossary.

1433 Also, sacrifice ground: "This was the location chosen by the caliphs to perform sacrificial slaughter on 'Īd al-Aḍḥā and 'Īd al-Ghadīr. This location was an empty piece of land in al-Darb al-Aṣfar that is now taken up by a group of buildings to the west of the mosque of Sa'īd al-Su'adā', between al-Darb al-Aṣfar and al-Tumbukshiyya streets of al-Jamāliyya quarter." (Baqli, 332). (P. Sanders, Ritual, 79 & 127, al-Baqli, *Ta'rīf*, 332, and Ibn al-Ṭuwayr, *Nuzha*, 183–184 fn. 2).

1434 "*Faṣīl*," which means a little camel, and more rarely, a little cow. (http://www.baheth.info/all.jsp?term=فصيل).

1435 "*Al-Labba*," the middle of the lower neck. (http://www.baheth.info/all.jsp?term=لبة).

1436 In *Ṣubḥ*: "*arbāb al-rusūm al-muqarrara*," (men of the decreed, designated portions); in *Nuzha*: "*arbāb al-rutab wa-l-rusūm*," (men of ranks and designated portions). (*Ṣubḥ*, Vol. 3, 515 and Ibn al-Ṭuwayr, *Nuzha*, 184).

1437 "*Al-Mu'taqidūn*," which in this context most probably refers Ismā'īlī Shiites.

Missionary to the students at the House of Justice (Dār al-ʿAdl) and the presiders at the congregational mosques of Cairo.

On the first day of the *'īd*, a same banquet as the one held on the first day of ʿĪd al-Fiṭr, was held at Qāʿat al-Dhahab, without a difference.

The Fifth Procession: Riding for Perfuming (*takhlīq*)[1438] the Nilometer[1439] on Occasion of the Fulfillment of the Nile (*wafā' al-Nīl*)

The earlier account of the Nile in the description of the Egypt covered the Nile rise, inundation and recession, and the calling out to people to announce the conditions of the river, as it is done now.[1440] However, at the time of these [Fatimid] caliphs, the calling out announcements were not made before the [Nile's] Fulfillment (*wafā'*). Rather, the measurement of the Nilometer's base was taken, written on a *ruq'a* and submitted to the caliph and the vizier. This measurement was then documented in the resgister[1441] assigned for it at the Bureau of Correspondence (*dīwān al-rasā'il*).[1442] This procedure was repeated daily, where by a *ruq'a* was submitted to the Chancery Bureau (*dīwān al-inshā'*) reporting the rise, to be seen by no one except the caliph

1438 *Al-khalūq* and *al-khilāq* are two words that refer to a type of perfume that might have been saffron, to which other substances were added. It was reddish and yellowish in colour. One definition of it is that it was a perfume composed majorly of musk and saffron. *Al-takhlīq* means the process of applying this perfume to something, in this case, the Nilometer. (http://baheth.info/all.jsp?term=خلوق and M. Shams, *Nujūm*, Vol. 4, 98 fn. 1).

1439 The Nilometer, which still stands at the Island of Rawḍa, was built in 247 AH/861 AD, during the reign of the Abbasid Caliph al-Mutawwakil. Egypt had for long known the establishment of similar structures, which serve to measure the rise of the Nile level during the flood season, therefore, the expected agricultural prosperity for a year. During the Islamic era, the measurement detected by the graduated octagonal column standing in the middle of the Nilometer stone pit also determined the land and agricultural taxes (*kharāj*) that may be imposed annually. (See "Miqyas" in http://archnet.org/sites/2372).

1440 A section of *Ṣubḥ* that is not translated in this work.

1441 "*Al-masīr*" is the term found in *Nuzha* and *Ṣubḥ*, which may be translated as "the path." However, one of the manuscripts of Ibn al-Ṭuwayr's *Nuzha*, and al-Maqrīzī's *Khiṭaṭ*, use another term, which is "*al-sayr*." Although *al-sayr* still has the meaning of "walking" or "journey," in this context it most probably refers to a particular register that was assigned for documenting the measurements of the Nilometer. A letter of correspondence written by the vizier Fakhr al-Dīn b. Mukānis (d. 794 AH/1392 AD) on occasion of a remarkably high flood level, mentions the "*sayr*" of the Nilometer (*sayr miqyāsihi*), which he says "encompassed [with its abundance] those absent and those present." It may, therefore, be concluded that the intended word above was "*al-sayr*," which was an administrative register, rather than "*al-masīr*," unless both terms were used synonymously. (*Ṣubḥ*, Vol. 3, 516 & Vol. 14, 275; Ibn al-Ṭuwayr, *Nuzha*, 190; al-Maqrīzī, *Khiṭaṭ*, Vol. 2, 314, andIbn Ḥajar al-ʿAsqalānī, *Al-Durar al-Kāmina fī A'yān al-Mi'a al-Thāmina*, ed. Muhammad Abd al-Muʿin Dan (Hyderabad, 1972), Vol. 3, 119–120).

1442 Also, "*dīwān al-mukātabāt*" (The Bureau of Letters or The Bureau of Correspondence): This was one of the names of *dīwān al-inshā'* (The Chancery Bureau) in the early Fatimid era. The term "*dīwān al-rasā'il*"disappeared by the 4th century AH/12th century AD to be substituted with "*dīwān al-inshā'*." Ibn Munjib al-Ṣayrafī was the head of this bureau during the reign of Caliph al-Āmir, a post that he occupied for forty years. He wrote a book called *qānūn dīwān al-rasā'il* (the Laws of *dīwān al-rasā'il*), to be used as a guide for later heads of this bureau. (Ibn al-Ṭuwayir, Nuzha, 65° and al-Baqli, *Ta'rīf*, 146).

and the vizier.[1443] The information remained confidential until only one or two fingers were left to the completion of the Fulfillment Cubit[1444] (*dhirā' al-wafā'*), which was the sixteenth cubit [of the Nilometer column]. Then the "Quran Reciters in the caliph's presence" (*qurrā' al-ḥaḍra*), the presiders at the congregational mosques of Cairo and Miṣr and their likes were ordered to spend the night at the Mosque of the Nilometer (Jāmiʿ al-Miqyās)[1445] to recite the whole Quran. They were offered a magnificent banquet and candles were lit up for them until morning.

When the morning came, and had Allah commanded the Nile level to rise to fulfillment on that night, the *ruq'a* of Ibn Abī al-Raddād[1446] was taken up to the caliph at the palace. The caliph then rode in a grand appearance of magnificent costume and great procession. He wore the crown that carried the Matchless [jewel] (*al-yatīma*), but the parasol (*miẓalla*) was not carried above his head on that day.[1447] The vizier followed him in a great crowd that marched according to processional arrangement. The caliph exited the palace, marched through Cairo, until he went through Bāb Zuwayla. He continued through the street until he passed the garden known as Bustān ʿAbbās,[1448] which as at the head of al-Ṣalība [Street], near the present day Khanqah of Shaykhū.[1449] The caliph turned towards Ibn Ṭūlūn's Mosque and crossed al-Jisr al-Aʿẓam (the Great Bridge)[1450] until he reached Miṣr. He entered through al-Ṣināʿa[1451] which was at the time full of

1443 Ibn al-Ṭuwary notes that the *ruq'a* recorded the daily rise in both the Hijri and Coptic calendars. (Ibn al-Ṭuwayr, *Nuzha*, 190).

1444 Also, "arm,"see Glossary: "*cubit*".

1445 This mosque was one of several buildings that Badr al-Jamālī established in 485 AH/1092 AD around the Nilometer. It included three construction inscriptions indicating that Badr ordered its building during the era of Caliph al-Mustanṣir. (Ibn al-Ṭuwayir, Nuzha, 191 fn. 1).

1446 Ibn Abī al-Raddād was the title given to the person responsible for measuring the Nile rise. This was originally the duty of Christian clerks, until the Abbasid Caliph al-Mutawakkil decided to replace them with Muslims in 247 AH/861 AD. Yazīd b. ʿAbd Allah al-Turkī, the ruler (*wālī*) of Egypt at the time, appointed ʿAbd Allah b. ʿAbd al-Salām b. ʿAbd Allah b. Abī al-Raddād al-Mu'addib al-ʿAjamī (d. 266 AH/880 AD), a teacher of Ḥadīth, originally from Basra, Iraq, to this job. The job remained a duty of the descendants of Ibn Abī al-Raddād until the Ottoman era, and all who held the position were, therefore, referred to with the title: Ibn Abī al-Raddād. (Ibn al-Ṭuwayir, Nuzha, 189–190 fn. 3 and Jamāl al-Dīn b. Ẓuhayra, *Al-Faḍā'il al-Bahira fī Maḥāsin Miṣr wa-l-Qāhira*, ed. Kamil al-Muhandis and Mustafa al-Sakka (Cairo, 1969), 178–179).

1447 Ibn al-Ṭuwayr notes that the caliph rode in processional attire, but without the parasol and other instruments of its status. (Ibn al-Ṭuwayr, *Nuzha*, 192).

1448 Ibn al-Ṭuwayr explains that this garden was known by his time as the Garden of Sayf al-Islām. (Ibn al-Ṭuwayr, *Nuzha*, 192).

1449 For the Khanqah of Shaykhū (756 AH/1355 AD), see "Khanqah wa Qubbat al-Amir Shaykhu," http://archnet.org/sites/2210).

1450 Literally, "the Greatest Bridge," which was a street that connected the areas of al-Kabsh and Qanāṭir al-Sibāʿ, to the east of the Mosque of Ibn Ṭūlūn, by the time of al-Maqrīzī. The bridge separated Qārūn and al-Fīl ponds to the southwest of Fatimid Cairo. (Al-Maqrīzī, *Khiṭaṭ*, Vol. 2, 758).

1451 Also, Dār al-Ṣināʿa, which was the place for building and restoration of state ships, whether military, royal, or cargo ships. The first shipbuilding site in the Islamic era was at Rawḍa Island, on its southeastern bank. M. Shams al-Din notes that al-Ṣināʿa was transferred in the Ikhshidid

buildings. It had a long corridor (*dihlīz*) with benches (*maṣāṭib*) that were covered and wrapped with[1452] ʿAbdānī[1453] rugs. He exited from its gate,[1454] through Miṣr, till he reached the belvedere (*manẓara*) known as Riwāq al-Mulk,[1455] near Bāb al-Qanṭara. The caliph entered the belvedere through the door that faced him and was accompanied by the vizier who walked up to his designated place.[1456] The private [royal] boat (*'ushārī*),[1457] now known as the *ḥirrāqa*, would be docked there on the Nile bank. The *'ushārī* carried an octagonal pavilion (*bayt*) made from ivory and ebony that was transferred to it from the palace.[1458] Each side of this pavilion measured three cubits[1459] and it was the height of a full-grown man. The pavilion was fixed on the *'ushārī* and covered with a compactly made[1460] wooden dome. The pavilion and its dome were inlaid with sheets of gold-plated silver.[1461]

era to the eastern coast of Fustat, and in the early Fatimid era to al-Maqs, then back to the eastern bank of Fustat during the reign of the Fatimid Caliph al-Āmir (r. 495 AH/1101 AD – 525 AH/1131 AD). Ibn al-Ṭuwayr's account of the above procession, however, refers to two locations called al-Ṣināʿa at the time, one in Fustat and the other in al-Maqs. According to Ibn al-Ṭuwayr, the route after reaching the Nile bank of Miṣr (*al-sāḥil*) continued through Bāb al-Ṣināʿa, which had a running corridor (or vestibule: *dihlīz*) that he exited and turned towards the other Ṣināʿa of al-Maqs. In al-Maqrīzī's account copying Ibn al-Ṭuwayr, he refers to this gate (*bāb*) as Bāb al-Ṣāgha (Gate of the Goldsmith's Market); however, he goes on to mention the "other Ṣināʿa," which indicates that "Bāb al-Ṣāgha" was probably a writing or copying error. (M. Shams, *Nujūm*, Vol. 4, 104 fn. 1, Ibn al-Ṭuwayr, *Nuzha*, 192 and al-Maqrīzī, *Khiṭaṭ*, Vol. 2, 314).

1452 Al-Qalqashandī says "*mafrūsha*" (covered) and "*mu'azzar bihā*" (wrapped with it), while al-Maqrīzī says "*basṭan wa ta'zīran*," which may be translated as "covering the top and wrapping the bottom" of the benches. (*Ṣubḥ*, Vol. 3, 517 and al-Maqrīzī, *Khiṭaṭ*, Vol. 2, 314).

1453 Rugs from ʿAbādān, on the central eastern border of present day Iran.

1454 The gate of al-Ṣināʿa. (Ibn al-Ṭuwayr, *Nuzha*, 192).

1455 Meaning: Dār al-Mulk, see Ibn al-Ṭuwayr, *Nuzha*, 192 and al-Maqrīzī, *Khiṭaṭ*, Vol. 2, 314.

1456 In Ibn al-Ṭuwayr's and al-Maqrīzī's accounts, the vizier dismounted before entering to the caliph's presence and walked to the place designated for him. (Ibn al-Ṭuwayr, *Nuzha*, 192 and al-Maqrīzī, *Khiṭaṭ*, Vol. 2, 315).

1457 Also, "*'ushāriyya*" (pl. *'ushāriyyāt*), is an Arabized term given to a type of small boats, which joined the fleets or larger ships, and were used in the Red Sea, the Mediterranean and the Nile. These boats were used frequently in the Nile for several purposes, but were mostly used by caliphs, viziers and governors. The *'ushārī* that sailed the Mediterranean employed twenty paddles and unlike ships, was able to approach the shore transporting men and cargo, like a ferry. It was also used for rescue when ships were at danger during storms. In the Fatimid era, the *'ushārīyyāt* were used along the Nile to transport travellers, as well as the state's grains and other products. Some amirs had their own *'ushāriyyāt* that they used for their leisure sails in the Nile, especially on occasion of celebrating the breaking of the Khalīj. (A. Sayyid, *Tafsīr*, 746 and al-Baqli, *Ta'rīf*, 245).

1458 Transferred on the night before. In Ibn al-Ṭuwayr's and al-Maqrīzī's accounts, the Head of the Private Royal *'Ushāriyyāt* (*ra'īs al-'ushāriyyāt al-khāṣṣ*) was the one who received the pavilion and fixed it on the boat. (Ibn al-Ṭuwayr, *Nuzha*, 192–193 and al-Maqrīzī, *Khiṭaṭ*, Vol. 2, 315).

1459 Of width. (Ibn al-Ṭuwayr, *Nuzha*, 193).

1460 "*Al-Muḥkam al-ṣan'a*,".

1461 In Ibn al-Ṭuwayr's and al-Maqrīzī's accounts, silver and gold sheets. (Ibn al-Ṭuwayr, *Nuzha*, 193 and al-Maqrīzī, *Khiṭaṭ*, Vol. 2, 315).

The caliph exited the above-mentioned Dār al-Mulk, escorted by his choice of three or four of the *muḥannakūn* masters. The caliph's private retinue (*khawāṣṣ*) ascended to the *'ushārī*, along with the vizier who was accompanied by no more than two or three of his private retinue. The vizier sat behind curtains in a *riwāq* in the exterior of the mentioned pavilion,which had turned wooden painted and gold-plated lanterns (*fawānīs*).[1462] The *'ushārī* sailed from the gate of the belvedere[1463] to the high gate of the Nilometer, the one that was on the stairs.[1464] The caliph then left the *'ushārī* and proceeded to the well[1465] where the Nilometer [column] was. The vizier and the *muḥannakūn* masters walked immediately in front of him.[1466] The caliph and the vizier each prayed two *rak'as*, separately. Saffron and musk were then brought to the caliph to mix them in a bowl[1467] with his own hands using a tool he had with him. The Head of the Public Treasury (*ṣāḥib bayt al-māl*) took the bowl and handed it to Ibn Abī al-Raddād who threw himself, with his clothes on,[1468] into the well, hung on to the column with his left hand and legs, and perfumed it with his right hand. At the same time, the Quran reciters in the caliph's presence (*qurrā' al-ḥaḍra*), on the other side, recited Quranic [verses]. The caliph left immediately in the mentioned *'ushārī* and returned to Dār al-Mulk, from where he rode back to Cairo. Sometimes he sailed down with the *'ushārī*, followed by the procession, to al-Maqs from where he moved back to Cairo. On that day, there would be about 1000 boats in the Nile, crowded with people for watching [the processions] and expressing joy.

On the second day of the perfuming [celebration] (*takhlīq*), Ibn Abī al-Raddād came to theGreat Iwanof the palace, which hosted the Window (*shubbāk*), at the palace, where he found a golden-weaved robe of honour with a turban cover that is opened in the middle (*ṭaylasān muqawwar*) and was given five pouches of money, each containing 500 dirhams that were prepared for him.[1469] He put on

1462 *Fawānīs* (sing. *fānūs*) is the term used by al-Qalqashandī, while Ibn al-Ṭuwayr and al-Maqrīzī both use "*'arānīs*" (sing. *'irnās*), which means "the post that carries the bed canopy" or "the distaff." These posts were made of turned, light wood that were attached or embedded in both sides of the door of the pavilion (*bayt*). They were painted and had fitting curtains. (Ibn al-Ṭuwayr, *Nuzha*, 193, 198 & 198 fn. 1 and al-Maqrīzī, *Khiṭaṭ*, Vol. 2, 315).

1463 In Ibn al-Ṭuwayr's and al-Maqrīzī's accounts: Bāb al-Qanṭara. (Ibn al-Ṭuwayr, *Nuzha*, 193 and al-Maqrīzī, *Khiṭaṭ*, Vol. 2, 315).

1464 The stairs that the Nile covers. (Ibn al-Ṭuwayr, *Nuzha*, 193).

1465 *Fasqiyya* (fountain). (*Ṣubḥ*, Vol. 3. 517, Ibn al-Ṭuwayr, *Nuzha*, 193 and al-Maqrīzī, *Khiṭaṭ*, Vol. 2, 315).

1466 "*Bayna yadayhi*," also means "in his service".

1467 "*Inā'*," also "vessel" or "container." In Ibn al-Ṭuwayr's and al-Maqrīzī's accounts: "*āla*" (instrument). (*Nuzha*, 193 and *Khiṭaṭ*, Vol. 2, 315).

1468 In his *ghilāla* (undershirt) and *'imāma* (turban). (Ibn al-Ṭuwayr, *Nuzha*, 193–194, al-Maqrīzī, *Khiṭaṭ*, Vol. 2, 315 and P. Sanders, *Ritual*, 113).

1469 Pouch (*kīs*). In Ibn al-Ṭuwayr's and al-Maqrīzī's accounts, four pouches carried by four employees of the Public Treasury (Bayt al-Māl), each showing the pouch in his hand, while riding a mule and marching in front of Ibn al-Raddād. (*Nuzha*, 194, *Khiṭaṭ*, Vol. 2, 316 and P. Sanders, *Ritual*, 114).

the robe of honour and exited the palace from Bāb al-ʿĪd, which was mentioned before in the account on the palace gates, where he found five mules,[1470] with jewel-decorated loads.[1471] Each mule had a rider holding one of the above-mentioned pouches in his hand, so that it was showing. Ibn Abī al-Raddād was escorted[1472] by his relatives and cousins and surrounded by his friends. [Marching] in front of him were two [rides carrying] loads [that were] sultanic kettledrums. Horns were blown in front of him, while drums followed, as [was costumary with] the amirs. He marched through Bayn al-Qaṣrayn andwhenever he passed by one of the palace gates used by the caliph to enter or exit, he dismounted and kissed it. He then exited from Bāb Zuwaylato al-Shāriʿ al-Aʿẓam (the Great Street) until he reached Miṣr and marched through its centre. He passed by the Old Mosque (the Mosque of ʿAmr), then beyond it to the Nile bank to cross over to the Nilometer with his robe of honour and money pouches. He took a certain sum from the pouches, which was decreed to him and distributed the rest among those deserving designated portions[1473] that ran since old times, such as his cousins and others.[1474]

The Sixth Procession: Riding to Break the Khalīj[1475]

This [procession] took place on the third or fourth day of the perfuming [celebration] (*takhlīq*) mentioned above, unlike our present days when the Khalīj is opened on the same day of perfuming. The preparations of the [Fatimids] for this procession started as soon as the Nile began to rise.[1476] Tables of numerous figurines of different kinds were made at the Public Treasury (*bayt al-māl*), such as gazelles, lions, elephants and giraffes. Some of these figurines were coated with amber and some with sandalwood, while their eyes and body parts were outlined with gold. Similarly, sculptures of apples, citrons and others were made. The huge tent known as "the Killer" (*al-qātūl*), which was mentioned earlier, was taken out and pitched for the caliph on the rim of the western bank of the Khalīj, by a belvedere

1470 Ibn al-Ṭuwayr states that the mules are loaded in front of him, (Ibn al-Ṭuwayr, *Nuzha*, 193).

1471 *Aḥmāl* (sing. *ḥiml*) is a term that could refer to any loads carried on mounts, including howdahs. Al-Qalqashandī uses the word either to refer to loads carried on mules in grand processions, for decoration and other uses, such as musical instruments, or loads of ice transferred on the backs of camels. Ibn al-Ṭuwayr rather mentions that if Ibn Abī al-Raddād was one of the equitable *muḥannakūn,* ten substitute rides, which were adorned with jewels, were allocated to him; five to change along the procession, and five to distribute among whomever he chose. (*Ṣubḥ*, Vol. 4, 11, Vol. 5, 97 & Vol. 14, 397, Ibn al-Ṭuwayr, *Nuzha*, 194–195 and see http://www.baheth.info/all.jsp?term=أحمال).

1472 Riding in his *ḥujba* (job of the *ḥājib*). In *Nuzha*: "in his company." (Ibn al-Ṭuwayr, *Nuzha*, 194).

1473 In *Nuzha*: *arbāb al-rusūm 'alayhi fī khila'ihi* (those deserving of portions from his bestowals). (Ibn al-Ṭuwayr, *Nuzha*, 195).

1474 Ibn al-Ṭuwayr explains that the public procession of Ibn Abī al-Raddād was meant to further announce the Fulfillment of the Nile, being one of the processional steps that people looked forward to. (Ibn al-Ṭuwayr, *Nuzha*, 194).

1475 Also, to open the khalīj. (Ibn al-Ṭuwayr, *Nuzha*, 195).

1476 When the Nile rise reached the level of the Fulfillment Cubit (*dhirā' al-wafā'*). (Ibn al-Ṭuwayr, *Nuzha*, 195).

(*manẓara*) called al-Sukkara,[1477] which was near Fumm al-Khalīj.[1478] The tent's pole was wrapped with red, white, or yellow silk brocade (*dībāj*), from top to bottom. The throne (*sarīr al-mulk*) was set up backed by the pole and covered with Qurqūbī cloth. The throne's posts[1479] were golden and exposed, and a large furnishing mattress (*martaba*) was laid down on it for the caliph. To the north of this tent, many tents of the the holders of ranks (*arbāb al-rutab*) among the amirs were pitched according to their ranks, which decided the sizes of the tents and their proximity to the caliph's pavilion.

The caliph rode as usual in grand processions, with the parasol (*miẓalla*) and what accompanied it such as the sword, the lance, the banners, the inkwell (*dawāt*), and the rest of the instruments. Forty extra horns were added to this procession: ten of gold and thirty of silver. The forty men blowing those horns were riding, while the men blowing the copper horns marched on foot. Ten of the large drums [also marched in this procession].[1480] On the procession day, the vizier came from the House of the Vizierate (*dār al-wizāra*), riding in magnificent appearance. He rode to the palace's gate where the caliph exited on his mount while the *muḥannakūn* masters walked around him. The caliph wore a robe called "*al-badana*," which he only put on for that day. It was made of silk, inscribed with gold, and the parasol matched it. Then the *muḥannakūn* masters mounted their rides and the procession marched in the same above-mentioned arrangement of the New Year Procession, along the same route the caliph took for the perfuming (*takhlīq*) until he reached the Mosque of Ibn Ṭūlūn.[1481] The chief judge-and the notable witnesses would be sitting at the gate of the mosque that was in the direction the caliph passed. The caliph paused briefly for them and saluted the judge, who approached and kissed the caliph's foot that was in his direction. The witnesses came and faced the caliph's horse, standing at a distance of four cubits then the caliph saluted them. All mounted and the procession moved until it reached the bank of the Khalīj. The procession continued until the caliph came near the tent, when the vizier preceded him as usual. The caliph dismounted at the tent's entrance[1482] and entered to sit on the mattress (*martaba*) placed upon [the

1477 One of the belvederes of the Fatimid caliphs, which was built by Caliph al-ʿAzīz bi-Allah on the western bank of the Khalīj and was especially used by the Fatimid caliphs on the Day of Breaking the Khalīj. Its location was probably taken up in modern times by an area in al-Sayyida Zaynab Neighbourhood, which bordered at its north by the extension of al-Wāfidiyya Street, at its west by Ḥilwān Street, at its south by ʿAlī Ibrāhīm Street. (Ibn al-Ṭuwayir, Nuzha, 197 fn. 1).

1478 The mouth of the Khalīj, whose site is presently taken up by a square that bears the same name: Fumm al-Khalīj, in the district of Miṣr al-Qadīma.

1479 *'Arānīs.*

1480 The drums which had silver instead of wooden parts. (Ibn al-Ṭuwayr, *Nuzha*, 197).

1481 Ibn al-Ṭuwayr comments that the same route of the perfuming (*takhlīq*) procession was followed, except that the caliph did not use the inside streets of Fustat, but rather moved outside it, along the Nile bank. (Ibn al-Ṭuwayr, *Nuzha*, 198).

1482 Ibn al-Ṭuwayr's account shows that the caliph came to find the vizier dismounted at the entrance of the tent. (Ibn al-Ṭuwayr, *Nuzha*, 199).

throne].[1483] The *muḥannakūn* masters surrounded him, followed by the collared amirs (*al-umarā' al-muṭawwaqūn*). The vizier's chair that was described earlier in the occasions [of audience] at the palace would be put for him to sit on as usual, with his feet touching the ground. The Holders of Ranks (*arbāb al-rutab*) stood in two rows on both sides of the throne up to the entrance of the tent. Quran reciters in the caliph's presence (*qurrā' al-ḥaḍra*) recited for an hour and when they finished, the Master of the Gate (*ṣāḥib al-bāb*) asked for permission to let in the poets for service (*khidma*). They were permitted and entered one by one according to their decreed levels. Each recited the poetry he composed upon the occasion, and when one finished, the next followed to recite what he composed, until all were done. The attendees criticized each poet, praising the good poetry and pointed out the weaknesses.

When this audience (*majlis*) was over, the caliph left the throne and rode to the belvedere (*manẓara*) known as al-Sukkara near the tent, with the vizier in his service.[1484] This belvedere was furnished with the furnishings designated for it. The caliph sat at his designated place, while the vizier sat separately, also inside the belvedere. The judge and the witnesses sat inside the white tent made of *Dabīqī* textile. One of the *muḥannakūn* masters looked out of the belvedere and signalled indicating permission to break the dam, which was opened using pickaxes. Drums and horns on both banks were played; meanwhile, the banquet arrived from the palace in the company of the Master of the Feast Table (*ṣāḥib al-mā'ida*),[1485] who held the same position as the present day Master of the Kitchen and Banquets (*ustādh dār al-ṣuḥba*).[1486] The banquet consisted of 100 bundles carried in wide trays (*ṭayāfīr*)[1487] inside silk covers (*qawāwīr*).[1488] All that was covered with precious cushions (*ṭarrāḥāt*)[1489] and the smell of musk and spices emanated from it. The banquette was hosted in a large tent prepared

1483 "Upon it" in text. The editor of Subḥ notes that the intended meaning is clear. (*Ṣubḥ*, Vol. 3, 519 fn. 1).

1484 "*Fī khidmatihi.*"

1485 *Al-Mā'ida* is "the table spread with food," "the feast table" or "the feast." *Ṣāḥib al-mā'ida* was one of the palace caretakers (*farrāshīn*) who directly served the caliph and was responsible for the banquets. (Ibn al-Ṭuwayr, *Nuzha*, 85, 145, 170 202, & 224 and see translations for "*al-mā'ida*"in http://corpus.quran.com/translation.jsp?chapter=5&verse=114).

1486 See later.

1487 Sing. *ṭayfūr*, which was a term employed in the Fatimid primary sources to refer to large vessels, deep plates, trays or tables that carried several vessels. Al-Maqrīzī reports that the largest *ṭayfūr* could carry three and one third kantars of delicacies and the smallest held ten pieces.(Ibn al-Ṭuwayir, Nuzha, 131 fn. 2, al-Maqrīzī, *Khiṭaṭ*, Vol. 2, 203 and P. Sanders, *Ritual*, 110).

1488 Sing. *qawwāra*, which was a textile cover for food trays that was around the bundle (*shadda*) or was used itself as the bundle. (Ibn al-Ṭuwayr , *Nuzha*, 129, 145–146 fn.1 & 170).

1489 This is the word also used by both Ibn al-Ṭuwayr and al-Maqrīzī, it is more probable that the intended word is the closely pronounced *ṭarḥa* (veil, see Glossary). In his description of the brief processions, Ibn al-Ṭuwayr uses *ṭarḥa* rather than *ṭarrāḥa* to describe the silk veils that covered the *qawwāra* (see Glossary: "*qawāwīr*"). (Ibn al-Ṭuwayr, *Nuzha*, 170 &202 and al-Maqrīzī, *Khiṭaṭ*, Vol. 2, 320).

for it, from which the usual shares of the vizier and his sons were delivered to them, then the shares of the Chief Judgeand the witnesses, then the amirs according to their ranks. The different kinds off east tables were decorated with the figurines mentioned above, except the table of the judge and the witnesses, which did not have any figurines.[1490] When the water levelled in the Khalīj, the small boats (ʿushāriyyāt) sailed through it, followed by the big ones, which were seven: The Golden, which was the caliph's private boat that he sailed in on the day of perfuming (*takhlīq*); The Silver; The Red; The Yellow; The Green; The Azure, and the Sicilian.[1491] The last one was a boat (ʿushārī) that was built by a Sicilian carpenter, following the usual establishment method, so was attributed to him.[1492] Each of these boats was dressed in coloured *Dabīqī* curtains[1493] and their prows were decorated with crescents and necklaces of amber and blue beads.[1494] The boats sailed until they docked at the bank where the caliph's belvedere (*manẓara*) was. After the caliph prayed ʿaṣr prayers, he rode wearing a different costume than the one he wore in the morning, with its matching parasol.[1495] The rest of the procession would be of the same [arrangement as above]. The procession moved on the west bank from the Khalīj, through the gardens, until it reached Bāb al-Qanṭara, where it turned right to proceed to the palace.[1496] The vizier followed the caliph according to the usual protocol (*rasm*). Then the caliph entered his palace and the vizier moved on to his house as was usual on such a day.[1497]

Judge Muhyi al-Dīn b. ʿAbd al-Ẓāhir said: When the caliph rode from the belvedere known as "al-Sukkara," he marched on the west bank of the Khalīj as

1490 Out of respect for religious law. (Ibn al-Ṭuwayr, *Nuzha*, 202).

1491 Six, missing out the green one, in Ibn al-Ṭuwayr's and al-Maqrīzī's accounts; all affiliated to the caliph's private domain (*khāṣṣ*) and allocated to service on Nile celebrations. (Ibn al-Ṭuwayr, *Nuzha*, 201–202 and al-Maqrīzī, *Khiṭaṭ*, Vol. 2, 320).

1492 Ibn al-Ṭuwayrand al-Maqrīzī say that this Sicilian carpenter, who was one of the heads of the Shipbuilding Factory (*ru'asā' al-ṣinā'a*), added to the usual shape or method of building, and therefore this *'ushārī* was named after him. (Ibn al-Ṭuwayr, *Nuzha*, 202 and al-Maqrīzī, *Khiṭaṭ*, Vol. 2, 320).

1493 According to Ibn al-Ṭuwayr and al-Maqrīzī, the coloured *Dabīqī* curtains covered each pavilion (*bayt*) on every boat (*'ushārī*). (Ibn al-Ṭuwayr, *Nuzha*, 202 and al-Maqrīzī, *Khiṭaṭ*, Vol. 2, 302).

1494 In Ibn al-Ṭuwayr and al-Maqrīzī's accounts, "on their heads and around their necks (prows) were crescents and bead-necklaces." (Ibn al-Ṭuwayr, *Nuzha*, 202 and al-Maqrīzī,*Khiṭaṭ*, Vol. 2, 320).

1495 Ibn al-Ṭuwayr and al-Maqrīzī tell us that after the caliph and his company sat at the banquets and prayed *ẓuhr*, they went on until praying *'aṣr* then the processors rode waiting for the caliph. The caliph then rode without the *badana* (robe), but in his [usual] appearance, with the matching parasol and the *yatīma* jewel. Ibn al-Ma'mūn notes that the caliph wore an all-silk *badla* (outfit). (Ibn al-Ṭuwayr, *Nuzha*, 202 & 202 fn. 1 and al-Maqrīzī, *Khiṭaṭ*, Vol. 2, 321).

1496 In *Nuzat* and *Khiṭaṭ*: "entered through Bāb al-Qanṭara to the palace." (Ibn al-Ṭuwayr, *Nuzha*, 202–203 and al-Maqrīzī, *Khiṭaṭ*, Vol. 2, 321).

1497 That is, in the usual processional protocol and company. (Ibn al-Ṭuwayr, *Nuzha*, 203).

described above, until he reached Bustān al-Dikka.[1498] The corridors (*dahālīz*) of this garden were decorated with ornaments for this occasion. The caliph entered alone and allowed his horse to drink water inside. The caliph then exited to stop by the protrusion (*ra'na*)[1499] that is called Khalīj al-Dār.[1500] He then entered through Bāb al-Qanṭara and marched to his palace.[1501]

THE SECOND KIND: BRIEF PROCESSIONS DURING THE YEAR

These were [the processions] held on four or five days between the beginning of the year and Ramadan, on Tuesdays and Saturdays only.[1502] If the caliph decided to ride on one of these days, the arms would be first distributed to the Equestrian Escorts (*rikābiyya*), as mentioned in the procession on occasion of the beginning of the year.[1503] The caliph mostly rode to Miṣr [on these processions], with the vizier behind him, in a smaller company and fewer arrangements than the grand processions. On these days, he wore golden-weaved white and coloured costumes, with a matching turban-cloth (*mindīl*) that was wrapped differently[1504] than other [people's turbans]. The tail of his turban (*dhu'āba*) fell close to the left side [of his face]. He was girded with his Arabian sword that was adorned with jewels, but he neither [put on] the *ḥanak* nor was he [accompanied by] the parasol.[1505] He crossed Cairo through the Great Street (al-Shāriʿ al-Aʿẓam), beyond Ibn Ṭūlūn's Mosque and [on] to the shrines (*mashāhid*),[1506] until he reached the Old Mosque (the Mosque of ʿAmr). When he reached the gate of the mosque,

1498 Al-Dikka Garden which was by the time of Ibn ʿAbd al-Ẓāhir a residential area. (Ibn ʿAbd al-Ẓāhir, *Khiṭaṭ*, 125).

1499 *Al-Ra'na* is "the protruding hill" or "mountain peak"; however, in Ibn ʿAbd al-Ẓāhir's account, the term employed is *al-tur'a*, which means a canal or channel and is the accurate meaning in this context. Ibn ʿAbd al-Ẓāhir explains that Bustān al-Dikka had a canal (*tur'a*) connected to the Nile, which provided the gardens with water. (Ibn ʿAbd al-Ẓāhir, *Khiṭaṭ*, 123 & 125 and http://www.baheth.info/all.jsp?term=رعن)

1500 Mistake, should be Khalīj al-Dhakar, which according to Ibn ʿAbd al-Ẓāhir, was the canal (*tur'a*) used to feed the gardens. (See Ibn ʿAbd al-Ẓāhir, *Khiṭaṭ*, 123 & fn. 484).

1501 See Ibn ʿAbd al-Ẓāhir's account in *Khiṭaṭ*, 125.

1502 See also Ibn al-Ṭuwayr's account. (Ibn al-Ṭuwayr, *Nuzha*, 168–171).

1503 Ibn al-Ṭuwayr explains that the distribution of the arms from the Treasury of Arms (*khizānat al-silāḥ*) only among Ṣibyān al-Rikāb (the Equestrian Guards) was the sign that the caliph intended to ride. (Ibn al-Ṭuwayr, *Nuzha*, 168).

1504 "*'Usr*" in text, which is meaningless in this context. The editor of Subḥ notes that it is probably "*ghayr*" (other than), which is in accordance with Ibn al-Ṭuwayr's account that states that the wrapping (*shadda*) was unique or unmatched (*mufrada*) compared to other people's turbans. (*Ṣubḥ*, Vol. 3, 521 fn. 1 and Ibn al-Ṭuwayr, *Nuzha*, 171).

1505 According to Ibn al-Ṭuwayr, he did not wear the Matchless jewel (*yatīma*) either, since these were the instruments used on specific days. (Ibn al-Ṭuwayr, *Nuzha*, 171).

1506 The shrines referred to here are the ones in today's al-Ashrafiyya Street, in between the mosque and Shrine of al-Sayyida Nafīsa and Ṣalība Street. (Ibn al-Ṭuwayir, Nuzha, 168–169 fn. 1).

he found the preacher (*khaṭīb*)[1507] standing on a platform (*maṣṭaba*) next to it. The platform had a mihrab, was furnished with rugs and a carpet was hung on it. The preacher would be holding the honourable Quran manuscript whose script is attributed to ʿAlī b. Abī Ṭālib, the Prince of the Faithful. He handed it to the caliph who kissed it and acquired its blessings,[1508] then ordered donations to be distributed to the people [serving] the mosque[1509].

1507 Ibn al-Ṭuwayr tells us that this preacher was a *sharīf* (honourable descendant). (Ibn al-Ṭuwayr, *Nuzha*, 168).

1508 Ibn al-Ṭuwayr continues: "several times." (Ibn al-Ṭuwayr, *Nuzha*, 169).

1509 Ibn al-Ṭuwayr gives further description of the donation and how it was distributed, see (Ibn al-Ṭuwayr, *Nuzha*, 169, also see his full account 168–171).

The Third Category
On the Caliph's Appearance

His Appearance in His Palaces

Ibn al-Ṭuwayr said: The caliph had costumes that he wore inside [his] residences, with sleeves half [the lengths] of the sleeves of his processional costumes. Typically, the caliph did not move from one place to the other inside the palace, whether day or night, except mounted.[1510] He did not only ride horses inside the palaces, but also rode mules and female donkeys as needed to pass through low roofed passages[1511] and to climb up ramps to the tops of the belvederes (*manāẓir*) and residential quarters.[1512] At night, women tenders were assigned for pulling[1513] what the caliph needed to ride of mules and donkeys. Each part of the palace had a fountain that was filled with water in fear of night fires.

Fifty horsemen spent every night outside the palace to guard it. When the last prayers of ʿishā'[1514] were called for inside Qaʿat al-Dhahab, the assigned imām led the prayers which were performed by the resident masters (*ustādhūn*) and the others. An amir with the title of Sinān al-Dawla,[1515] who had the same position as the present day *amīr jāndār* (Personal Guard),[1516] stood at the gate of the palace. When he knew that the prayers were over, the horn-players (*būqiyya*) played the drums, horns and the like nicely for an hour.[1517] Then a master who was assigned to this salutation protocol (*khidma*) came out and said: "The Prince of the Faithful salutes Sinān al-Dawla back with peace." Sinān al-Dawla then pinned a spear to the door then lifted it with his hand.[1518] When he lifted it, he closed the door, and then circled the palace seven times. When this was done,

1510 According to Ibn al-Ṭuwayr, no one other than the caliph was allowed to ride inside the palace. (Ibn al-Ṭuwayr, *Nuzha*, 210).

1511 *Sarādīb* (sing. *sirdāb*).

1512 *Masākin* (sing. *maskan*). In al-Maqrīzī's account: "*al-amākin*" (the places). (Al-Maqrīzī, *Khiṭaṭ*, Vol. 2, 112 and Ibn al-Ṭuwayr, *Nuzha*, 210).

1513 *Shaddādāt*.

1514 Night prayer; the last of the mandatory five daily prayers.

1515 Sinān al-Dawla b. al-Karkandī, which was probably a name and title of an amir who performed this job of guarding the caliph. (See Ibn al-Ṭuwayr , *Nuzha*, 210 & 210 fn. 4).

1516 One of the sultan's personal guarding amirs who were responsible of admitting the amirs to the sultan's *khidma*. (See Glossary).

1517 In Ibn al-Ṭuwayr's account: When Sinān al-Dawla knew that the prayers were over, he ordered the playing of shifts of drums, horns and their accompanying instruments. The instruments were many and they played pleasantly for an hour. Al-Maqrīzī replaces the "accompanying" instruments with the "suitable." (Ibn al-Ṭuwayr, *Nuzha*, 210–211 and al-Maqrīzī, *Khiṭaṭ*, Vol. 2, 281–282).

1518 In Ibn al-Ṭuwayr's and al-Maqrīzī's account, Sinān al-Dawla "cried out" before doing that. (Ibn al-Ṭuwayr, *Nuzha*, 211 and al-Maqrīzī, *Khiṭaṭ*, Vol. 2, 282).

he assigned the doorkeepers (*bawwābīn*)[1519] and the caretakers (*farrāshīn*) to the door, while the mu'azzins retired to their rooms (*khazā'in*) there. A chain[1520] was hung at the narrow passage (*maḍīq*), which was at the end of Bayn al-Qaṣrayn, at al-Suyūfiyyīn, to prevent passersby from this place until the horn-players played again just before dawn, when the chain was lifted and people passed.[1521]

1519 Sing. *bawwāb*. In Ibn al-Ṭuwayr's and al-Maqrīzī's accounts: "*bayyātīn*" (those who spend the nights). (Ibn al-Ṭuwayr, *Nuzha*, 211 and al-Maqrīzī, *Khiṭaṭ*, Vol. 2, 282).

1520 *Al-Silisla*, which was located at the intersection of today's Al-Mu'izz li Dīn Allah and Jawhar al-Qā'id streets of Fatimid Cairo.

1521 See Ibn al-Ṭuwayr's account in *Nuzha*, 210–211.

The Sixth Clause On their attention to their fleets and the defence of coastal cities (*thughūr*); their concern with jihad; their manner of ruling their subjects, and persuading the hearts of their opposers

Their attention to the fleets, guarding the coastal borders, and their concern with jihad were among their most important matters and greatest considerations. All their coastal cities had assigned fleets, such as Alexandria and Damietta in Egypt; Ascalon, Acre, Tyre and other cities of the Syrian coast, when they still had control over them, before they were seized by the Crusaders. [Each of] their generals (*quwwād*)[1522] had a regiment (*jarīda*)[1523] of more than 5000 registered[1524] fighters,[1525] whose salaries (*jawāmik*)[1526] ranged between twenty, fifteen, ten, eight and two dinars.[1527] A high-ranking amir, one of the notable and most courageous, headed the fleet. At the time, their fleet consisted of more than seventy-five[1528] *shīniyyāt,*[1529] ten *musaṭṭaḥāt*[1530] and ten *ḥammālāt.*[1531] Shipbuilding activity ran continuously in al-Ṣināʿa, without interruption. When

1522 Sing. *qā'id.*

1523 In this case, the term is used to refer to a navy regiment. *Jarīda* is generally used to denote a regiment of cavalry that does not include infantry. (Al-Baqli, *Ta'rīf*, 84).

1524 *Mudawwana*, which probably means: registered in the bureau (*dīwān*).

1525 In *Nuzha*: "Towards the end of their era, the regiment of [each of] the fleet commanders in chief had more than five-thousand registered [fighters], including ten dignitaries who were called the *quwwād* (commanders in chief), sing. *qā'id.*" (Ibn al-Ṭuwayr, *Nuzha*, 95).

1526 Also, *jāmakiyyāt* and *jamākī* (sing. *jāmakiyya* and *jāmik*): A Persian word which referred to the decreed salaries of state employees or men of the military. It generally refers to monthly pecuniary salaries or compensations. (M. Dahman, *Mu'jam*, 51 and H. Abbas, *Masālik* (2002), Vol. 3, 435 fn. 3 & 448 fn.1).

1527 In Ibn al-Ṭuwayr's account, these were the salaries of the commanders. See also the same account for the *iqṭā'āt* that they received. (Ibn al-Ṭuwayr, *Nuzha*, 95–96).

1528 In *Nuzha*: "around eighty." (Ibn al-Ṭuwayr, *Nuzha*, 96).

1529 Also, *shawānī*, sing. *shīnī* and *shīniyya*, a galley, a big military ship of Egyptian origin. One of its types was sailed using 140 oars carrying its sailors and fighters. The *shawānī* had towers or fortresses used for offense and defence and were equipped to attack the enemy with fire. At their front tips at the times of war was fixed a very long, pointed piece of iron called *al-lijām*, which was used to pierce the enemy ships to flood them with water and force them to surrender. The *shawānī* were huge enough to contain wheat granaries and cisterns of potable water. (A. Sayyid, *Tafsīr*, 744, Ibn al-Ṭuwayir, Nuzha, 95 fn. 2, andal-Baqli, *Ta'rīf*, 211).

1530 Sing. *musaṭṭaḥ*, which was a type of large military ships that carried 500 or more men. It was used by both Muslims and Crusaders in the Middle Ages. (A. Sayyid, *Tafsīr*, 744, Ibn al-Ṭuwayir, Nuzha, 95 fn. 4, and al-Baqli, *Ta'rīf*, 311).

1531 Sing. *ḥammāla*, which means a "carrier," and as the name suggests, was a military ship used for transportation, possibly of ammunition and other supplies.

the caliph wanted to equip[1532] [the ships in preparation] for invasion, he personally sat for the audience of expenditure until it was done.[1533]The caliph then went out[1534] with the vizier to the Nile bank at al-Maqsim where they sat in a belvedere (*manẓara*)[1535] at Bāb al-Baḥr Mosque for bidding [the fleet] farewell. The generals brought the ships beneath the belvedere, moving them back and forth, rowed by oars, in a combat drill. The ships were decorated with arms, while the catapults (*manjanīqāt*)[1536] and [small] mangonels (*lu'ab*)[1537] were set up in some of them. Then the commander (*muqaddam*) and the head (*rayyis*)[1538] presented themselves before the caliph[1539] who advised them and bid them a safe return. The ships then sailed down to Damietta then out to the sea; they were famous and reputable in the lands of the enemies. If they captured an enemy ship, the caliph selected the captive war prisoners, men, women or children, as well as the weaponry, for his possession. Whatever else of the the booty would be for those who captured it, and no one was allowed to share it with them.

1532 "*Tajhīzahā*," from the verb: "*jahhaza.*"

1533 The more elaborate account of Ibn al-Ṭuwayr, copied by al-Maqrīzī, explains that when the number of fleet ships required for a certain year was gathered in Cairo and they were fully equipped for invasion, the caliph sat for an audience to distribute the *nafaqa* (expenditure). The *nafaqa* were the payments given to the men of the fleet, which was done in a convened council that included the vizier and high state officials from Army Bureau (*dīwān al-jaysh*). Each man was paid five dinars, which were equal to thirty-six dirhams, based on the list of names registered in the Army Bureau. (See Ibn al-Ṭuwayr, *Nuzha*, 96–98 and al-Maqrīzī, *Khiṭaṭ*, Vol. 2, 330–331).

1534 "Rode." (Ibn al-Ṭuwayr, *Nuzha*, 97–98).

1535 The *manẓara* of al-Maqs, which was located to the north of the Mosque of al-Maqs built by Caliph al-Ḥākim in 393 AH/1003 AD (this is the mosque known in modern times as the Mosque of Awlād ʿAnān). The *manẓara* overlooked the Nile and was the place where the caliph sat to welcome the fleet and bid it farewell. Ibn al-Ma'mūn, the historian, informs us that Caliph al-Āmir sat in it in 517 AH/1123 AD to bid the fleet farewell before it sailed to fight the Crusaders. (Ibn al-Ṭuwayr , *Nuzha*, 98 & 98 fn. 2).

1536 Sing. *manjanīq*.

1537 Sing. *lu'ba*. Ibn al-Ṭuwayr says that the ships "had the catapults, and played to slide and take off with oars like was done upon facing the enemy at sea." He does not mention the *lu'ab*, but uses the verb "*tal'ab*" (to play) to describe the action of the ships. (Ibn al-Ṭuwayr, *Nuzha*, 98).

1538 "*Ra'īs*" in Ibn al-Ṭuwayr's account. (Ibn al-Ṭuwayr, *Nuzha*, 98).

1539 "*Yaḥḍir ilā bayna yaday al-khalīfa.*" (*Ṣubḥ*, Vol. 3, 523).

[The Fatimids] also had a fleet in ʿAydhāb,[1540] which received[1541] the spices (*kārim*)[1542] in between ʿAydhāb and Sawākin[1543] and its surroundings. This was out of fear for the ships of the spices (*kārim*) from some people who [inhabited] the islands of the Red Sea there, and attacked the ships. The fleet, which served to protect, comprised five ships that later became three, and the Governor of Qūṣ was the administrative governor (*mutawallī*) responsible for it. One of the amirs of the gate (*bāb*)[1544] may have also been assigned this responsibility, and enough weaponry from the Treasuries of Arms (*khazā'in al-silāḥ*) was transported to him.

As for how [the Fatimids] ruled their subjects and persuaded the hearts of their opposers, they were generous to whoever visited them from the people of the provinces, may they be high or low of status. They met everyone with the hospitability he deserved and reciprocated gifts with multiples of their values. They were friendly to Sunnis and allowed them the public [practice of] their rites, according to their different schools of interpretation (*madhāhib*).[1545] They did not prevent the *tarāwīḥ*[1546] prayers in congregational mosques (*jawāmiʿ*) and mosques (*masājid*), even though their doctrine disagreed with that . . .[1547]

1540 A port on the Red Sea coast of Egypt, which became an important trade centre during the Fatimid era. Nāṣirī Khusraw, the Persian traveller who visited Fatimid Egypt, reports that in 442 AH/1051 AD, when he visited the port, he witnessed the collection of taxes (*mukūs*) from ships arriving from lands like Yemen and Ethiopia. Ibn Jubayr, the Andalusian traveller who visited Egypt in the Fatimid era, reports that in 579 AH/1183 AD, Ships from Yemen and India arrived at and departed from the busy port of ʿAydhāb, in addition to the pilgrimage ships. By the beginning of the 9th century of the Hijra (late 14th century AD), ʿAydhāb started losing its status as a major port and trade centre. (A. Sayyid, *Tafsīr*, 192 fn. 2).

1541 "*Yutallaqā bihi*," also "met with."

1542 Also, spice merchants or spice trade: The linguistic origin of the term *kārim* (also, *kārimiyya* and *akārim*) is controversial; while some scholars agree that it refers to sea trade, others believe that the name is a distortion of "Kānim," in Sudan, from where the first group of the merchants of this trade came. The *kārim* trade was mainly concerned with spices, dyes and similar products, particularly with India, during the Fatimid era, when the name referred primarily to spice merchants. Ports like Eden, ʿAydhāb, Qūṣ, and Fustat, were all important centres of the *kārim* trade. The Fatimid state provided special protection for this trade using its fleet, which ensured its success. There is a possibility that this protection was only provided to wealthy merchants who paid for it. The Fatimid caliphs participated in this trade, to the extent that the Fatimid missionaries (*du'āt*) were not differentiated from the merchants. (A. Sayyid, *Tafsīr*, 496–500 and A. Maged, *Ẓuhūr*, 253).

1543 A port on the Red Sea coast of Sudan, which was near ʿAydhāb, and where the ships arriving from Jeddah docked. (Al-Ḥamawī, *Mu'jam*, Vol. 3, 276).

1544 That is, one of the high-ranking amirs of the court.

1545 Sing. *madhhab*, the Sunni schools of interpretation. (See Glossary).

1546 *Al-Tarāwīḥ* Prayers are special, non-mandatory prayers that Muslim Sunnis perform after *'Īshā'*(night) prayers during the month of Ramadan. They are mostly performed in units of two *rak'a*s to range from eight to twenty *rak'a*s, according to one's ability. They are preferably performed as group prayers.

1547 The editor of Subḥ remarks that the original text has an empty space equivalent to one word here. (*Ṣubḥ*, Vol. 3, 524 fn. 1). It can be deduced from the context that the Fatimids allowed the mention and honouring of the Companions. Some of the Prophet's companions who are most

with the mention of the Companions. The Sunni schools of Mālik, al-Shāfi'ī and Ibn Ḥanbal, but not Abū Ḥanīfa's, however, were publicly practiced under [the Fatimids]. They observed[1548] the Māliki School and if someone asked them to rule by it, they complied.

Typically, [their] caliphs only wrote: "Praise be to Allah, Lord of the worlds,"[1549] for their mark (*'alāma*). The caliph addressed no one in written correspondences except in the singular form,[1550] even a vizier who was a Man of the Sword. The correspondences written by the vizier; however, were the ones that [used] different levels [of respect].[1551] No one was addressed on their behalf except with his decreed designations and known prayers. [The Fatimids] were considerate to the descendants of those who died in their service, and if they received allowances (*murattab*), these were transferred to their descendants, men or women.

revered by Sunnis, are sometimes not shown the same respect by Shiites, which is a matter of huge controversy between the two main Muslim sects.

1548 "*Yurā'ūn*," which may mean "regard" or "consider," as well as "abide by."

1549 Quran: Sūrat al-Fātiḥa (The Opening Chapter), 1:2, and a very common expression of praise to Allah. Ibn al-Ṭuwayr reports that all the Fatimid caliphs used this phrase for their mark (*'alāma*). (Ibn al-Ṭuwayr, *Nuzha*, 89 and http://corpus.quran.com/translation.jsp?chapter=1&verse=2)

1550 Addressing with the "*kāf*" means using the singular form. Highest respect is indicated by using the plural form, rather than the singular, in addressing a single person.

1551 This means that the vizier addressed some people in a singular form, and others in a plural form.

The Seventh Clause On providing running salaries (*arzāq*) and grants for the Heads of Services (*arbāb al-khidam*) of their state, and the relevant banquets

As for providing running salaries and grants, [the part] on the Bureau of Armies (*dīwān al-juyūsh*) explained that it was divided into three sections:

- A section that had to do with parades, decoration of soldiers and the markings (*shiyyāt*) of their rides,
- A section that had to do with managing the *iqṭā'āt* allocated to soldiers (*ajnād*), and
- A section that had to do with identifying the allowance (*rātib*), running wage (*jārī*), and running ration (*jirāya*)[1552] of every state employee (*murtaziq*).[1553]

Each of the three sections had its own scribes, especially [assigned] for its service. Here [below] is [a description of] the third section, which gave out its allowances (*rawātib*) in army dinars (*al-danānīr al-jayshiyya*).[1554] This section included eight subsections:

The First: The allowance (*rātib*) of the vizier, his sons and his entourage:

The monthly allowance of the vizier was 5000 dinars. His sons and brothers received monthly allowances ranging from 300 to 200 dinars. No vizier's son was assigned

1552 Pl. *jirāyāt*, see Glossary.

1553 See also "*dīwān al-rawātib*" (Bureau of Allowances) and its detailed categories in *Nuzha*. It is notable that in his account, Ibn al-Ṭuwayr mentions that this bureau documented the names of all those receiving a salary from the state (*murtaziq*) and the *jārī* (running wage) and *jirāya* (running ration) of each. He only mentioned the term *rātib* (salary) in relevance to the vizier. Al-Qalqashandī entitles the first category "the *rātib* of the vizier, his sons, and his entourage." He does not name what the other categories receive monthly, but only mentions the amounts. (Ibn al-Ṭuwayr, *Nuzha*, 83–85).

1554 Sing. *al-dīnār al-jayshī*. Al-Qalqashandī explains the term as follows: "As for *al-dīnār al-jayshī*, it was a nominal rather than an actual value. It was used by the people of the Army Bureau to evaluate the *iqṭā'* lands by assigning a certain number of dinars for each land. Some lands may have not been assigned such equivalent value of dinars. This was, however, a useless practice for 100 dinars in one piece of an *iqṭā'* land might have yielded a profit of more than 200 dinars, or even more in another. The author of *Qawānīn al-Dawāwīn* (the Canons of Bureaus) mentioned *al-dīnār al-jayshī* in some *iqṭā'* areas with a value that fluctuates according to strata. He mentioned that *al-dīnār al-jayshī* of the Turkish, Kurdish and Turkoman military was a whole dinar, while that of the Kittāniyya (Kuttabiyya) and the 'Asāqila (the ones from Ascalon) was half a dinar. The Arab Bedouin dinar was probably 1/8th of a dinar and according to custom 13 and 1/3rds of a dirham. This was as if the same rules of the army's arrangement of the old times were followed. The value of gold in ancient times was similar to this; that is why blood money was calculated by jurists to be equivalent to 1000 dinars or 12,000 dirhams, which meant that each dinar was equal to 12 dirhams." Al-Qalqashandī uses the verb *'abbara* to denote the evaluation of *iqṭā'* lands with *al-dīnār al-jayshī*, which means "weighing gold dinar by dinar and not exaggerating the weight." (*Ṣubḥ*, Vol. 3, 442–443 and http://baheth.info/all.jsp?term=عبر; also see Glossary: *'abra*).

500 dinars except al-Kāmil, son of Shāwir.[1555] The vizier's entourage was assigned allowances ranging from 500, to 400 and 300 dinars, in addition to the *iqṭā'āt*.

The Second:The caliph's entourage:

At the top [of the hierarchy] of the entourage were the *muḥannakūn* masters according to their ranks, then: the Overseer of the Palace (*zimām al-qaṣr*); Head of the Public Treasury (*ṣāḥib bayt al-māl*); Messenger (*ḥāmil al-risāla*); Keeper of the Register (*ṣāḥib al-daftar*); Wrapper of the Crown (*shādd al-tāj*); Overseer of the Honourable Relatives (*zimām al-ashrāf al-aqārib*), and Master of the Audience Hall (*ṣāḥib al-majlis*), each assigned a monthly allowance of 100 dinars. The lesser [offices received allowances] that ranged from 90 to ten dinars, according to their ranks.[1556] These included the two private [royal] (*khāṣṣ*) physicians, each receiving 50 dinars monthly, while each of the lesser level resident physicians at the palace got ten dinars.[1557]

The Third: The Holders of Ranks (*arbāb al-rutab*) who serve in the caliph's capital (*ḥaḍra*)

The first [position] documented[1558] in this [subsection] was the Scribe of the Pedestal (*kātib al-dast*), who is now known as the Confidential Scribe (*kātib al-sirr*), and who received a monthly [allowance] of 150 dinars. Each of his scribes got 30 dinars. Following was: the Signer with the Fine Script (*al-muwwaqi' bi-l-qalam al-daqīq*), who received 100 dinars; the Master of the Gate (*ṣāḥib al-bāb*), who received 120 dinars; then the Sword-bearer (*ḥāmil al-sayf*) and the lance-bearer (*ḥāmil al-rumḥ*), each [entitled to] 70 dinars, and the rest of the overseers of the soldiers and the Sudanese troops (*azimmat al-'asākirwa-l-sūdān*) [whose allowances] ranged between 50, 40 and 30 dinars.

1555 Shujā' b. Shāwir, al-Kāmil, (d. 564 AH/1169 AD), son of Vizier Shāwir, who was appointed a deputy vizier by Caliph al-'Āḍid, in 559 AH/1164 AD, during the vizierate period of his father; an unprecedented assignment in the Fatimid era, which showed that Shāwir had become too weak. Shujā' was aware of the alarming Crusader threat in these last Fatimid years, and sought the help of Nūr al-Dīn Zankī of Damascus (see Glossary: "Zangids" and "Ayyubids"), for an alliance with a Muslim Sunni ruler was much more tolerable than a defeat by the Crusaders. Caliph al-'Āḍid, however, assassinated Shujā'; an action that al-Maqrīzī reports was frowned upon by Asad al-Dīn Shīrkūh (see Glossary: "Ayyubids"), the delegate army leader Nūr al-Dīn sent to Egypt. Shīrkūh, despite obeying the caliph's orders to kill Shāwir, appreciated that Shujā' prevented his father from attempting to kill him and his company. (A. Sayyid, *Tafsīr*, 295 & 340–341 and al-Maqrīzī, *Itti'āẓ*, Vol. 3, 287, 300–301 & 304). It may be concluded that Shujā' b. Shāwir received this exceptional salary, not for merely being a vizier's son, but for being a deputy vizier.

1556 According to Ibn al-Ṭuwayr, this category included more than one-thousand men. (Ibn al-Ṭuwayr, *Nuzha*, 84).

1557 Ibn al-Ṭuwayr says that these lesser physicians were the ones assigned to treat the palace residents, rather than referring to them as residents at the palace as in the above account. (Ibn al-Ṭuwayr, *Nuzha*, 84).

1558 *Masṭūr*: written.

The Fourth

Which included the Chief Judge and the Chief Missionary, who received a monthly allowance of 100 dinars each, and the Reciters in the Presence of the Caliph (*qurrā' al-ḥaḍra*), [whose allowances] ranged between twenty, fifteen and ten dinars.[1559]

The Fifth: Heads of the Bureaus (arbāb al-dawāwīn) and similar offices

The first was the Director of the Supervisory Bureau (*mutawallī*[1560] *dīwān al-naẓar*),who received a monthly [allowance of] 70 dinars, then: Director of the Bureau of Verification (*mutawallī dīwān al-taḥqīq*), 50 dinars; Director of the Bureau of the Council (*mutawallī dīwān al-majlis*), 40 dinars; Director of the Bureau of Armies (*mutawallī dīwān al-juyūsh*), 40 dinars; Keeper of the Council's Register (*ṣāḥib daftar al-majlis*), 35 dinars; the Signer with Dignified Script (*al-muwwaqi' bi-l-qalam al-jalīl*), who was equivalent to the present day Secretariat Scribe (*kātib al-darj*), 30 dinars, and for every assistant, ten, seven or five dinars.

The Sixth

This [subsection] encompassed the employees (*mustakhdamīn*) in Cairo and Miṣr, who were in service of their governors (*wulāt*) and were each assigned 50 dinars. The guardians(*ḥumāt*)[1561] at the granaries; the [camel] settlement areas (*munākhāt*); the [lands subject to] annual taxes on non-Muslims (*jawālī*); gardens; [land] properties (*amlāk*), and the like, were assigned [allowances] ranging between twenty, fifteen, ten and five dinars, according to their tasks.

The Seventh

This [subsection] encompassed the caretakers (*farrāshīn*) who were assigned to serve the caliph and attend to the palaces, clean their exteriors and interiors, hang the needed curtains and look after the belveders (*manāẓir*) outside the palace.

1559 To this category, Ibn al-Ṭuwayr adds the preachers (*khuṭabā'*, sing. *khaṭīb*) of the mosques, and the poets, who received from twenty to ten dinars. (Ibn al-Ṭuwayr, *Nuzha*, 84).

1560 *Mutawallī* may be translated as "the director," as well as "the administrative governor." The *mutawallī* of abureau (*dīwān*)was an important governmental position, hierarchically beneath the *nāẓir* (supervisor) and above the *mustawfī* (comptroller or financial administrator). (M. Ahmad, *Itti'āẓ*, Vol. 3, 126 fn. 4).

1561 Sing. *ḥāmī*: "protector" or "guard," who was an amir, for according to Ibn al-Ṭuwayr, the Fatimid camel settlement area (*munākh*), which comprised grain mills, warehouses and houses, had a guardian (*ḥāmī*), who was one of the amirs, along with a group of employees who managed it. Another possible meaning for *ḥāmī* is a black *ghulām* (slave-boy). (See Ibn al-Ṭuwayr, *Nuzha*, 141–142 and http://www.baheth.info/all.jsp?term=حام).

Each of them received a monthly allowance of or around 30 dinars.[1562] Beneath the caretakers (*farrāshīn*) were the sprinklers (*rashshāshīn*),[1563][who worked] inside and outside the palace, and were around 300 men [with allowances] varying between ten and five dinars.[1564]

The Eighth

This [subsection] encompassed the Equestrian Escorts (*rikābiyya*) and their commanders. Each commander received 50 dinars monthly, while each of the Equestrian Escorts received [anallowance] that varied between fifteen, ten and five dinars.[1565]

As for the banquets, they were of two categories:

THE FIRST CATEGORY: BANQUETS SPREAD IN RAMADAN AND THE TWO FEASTS[1566]

During the month of Ramadan, the caliph offered a nightly banquet that was held at Qāʿat al-Dhahabin the palace from the beginning of the fourth day to the end of the twenty-sixth.[1567] Each night, he sent for an alternate group of amirs to the banquet; thereby, a different group attended every night, so that none of them was deprived of breaking his fast at his home for the whole month. Out of respect, the Chief Judgewas only required to attend on Thursday nights.[1568] The caliph did not attend these banquets, but the vizier did. He sat at the head of the banquet, and if he was absent, his son or brother replaced him. If none of them was present, the Master of the Gate sat in substitution. This was one of the grandest

1562 According to Ibn al-Ṭuwayr, among the *farrāshīn*, was a group of private caretakers (*khāṣṣ*), who especially served the caliph. These were fifteen men, who included the Master of the Feast Table (*ṣāḥib al-mā'ida*) and the guardian (*ḥāmī*) of the kitchens, and who, in addition to their allowances, received special designated portions (*rusūm*)and were privileged with sitting near the caliph in banquets. The accound shows that these private caretakers were the ones who received allowances of or around thirty dinars. (Ibn al-Ṭuwayr, *Nuzha*, 85).

1563 Sing. *rashshāsh*: "The *rashshāshīn* were the ones who sprinkled water inside and outside the palace." (Al-Baqli, *Ta'rīf*, 159).

1564 Ibn al-Ṭuwayr explains that these sprinklers had superintendenants (*'urafā'*) and were supervised by a master from the caliph's private entourage (*khawāṣṣ*). (Ibn al-Ṭuwayr, *Nuzha*, 85).

1565 In Ibn al-Ṭuwayr's account, this category is called" *ṣibyān al-rikāb*" (Equestrian Guards), who were more than 2000 men and had twelve commanders. Each commander received 50 dinars monthly, while the the guards were divided into three groups: a group whose members receieved fifteen dinars each, a second whose members received ten, and a third whose members received five. (Ibn al-Ṭuwayr, *Nuzha*, 85).

1566 See also Ibn al-Ṭuwayr, *Nuzha*, 211–219 and al-Maqrīzī, *Khiṭaṭ*, Vol. 2, 112–115.

1567 Al-Qalqashandī's account suggests that the banquet was held from last meal before the fourth day of Ramadan, that is, on the third night. Ibn al-Ṭuwayr says that it was held starting the fourth day till the end of the twenty-sixth, while al-Maqrīzī says it was from the fourth to the twenty-sixth. (*Ṣubḥ*, Vol. 3, 527, Ibn al-Ṭuwayr, *Nuzha*, 211 and al-Maqrīzī, *Khiṭaṭ*, Vol. 2, 112).

1568 *Layālī al-juma'*, the nights of Fridays, which means the nights followed by Friday mornings.

and finest banquets, which was spread out from the centre of the main wall of the hall (*qā'a*) up to about its two-thirds with various types of magnificent foods. [The invitees] left one or two hours after the last ʿishā' prayers. The banquet's leftovers were distributed every night, and the Men of Designated Portions (*arbāb al-rusūm*) exchanged them as presents until they reached most people.[1569] If the vizier attended the banquet, the caliph would send him a meal from his own food to honour him, and might also especially grant him some of his *suḥūr*[1570].[1571]

As for the banquets on the two feasts, they were spread beneath the throne (*sarīr al-mulk*), on ʿĪd al-Fiṭr and ʿĪd al-Aḍḥā, in Qāʿat al-Dhahab, in front of the audience hall (*majlis*) where the caliph sat for public audience on procession days.[1572] A silver table, known as "*al-mudawwara*" (the Round One),[1573] was placed above the chair (*kursī*).[1574] Golden and China vessels[1575] containing magnificent foods, only worthy of kings, were placed on this table. The public banquet was extended beneath the throne.[1576] It was made of painted wood,[1577] ran along the whole length

1569 Neither Ibn al-Ṭuwayr nor al-Maqrīzī mention the term "*arbāb al-rusūm*" in their accounts. Ibn al-Ṭuwayr tells us that the banquet was plentiful enough for all the attendees to take shares with them. Consequently, much of it reached the people of Cairo, or some of it reached most of the people of Cairo, from one person to the other. A single man took what was enough for a group of people. Al-Maqrīzī's account seems to have missed out a sentence copying Ibn al-Ṭuwayr's; he says that some of the banquet reached the people of Cairo, from one person to another, and a single man took what was enough for him. (Ibn al-Ṭuwayr, *Nuzha*, 212 and al-Maqrīzī, *Khiṭaṭ*, Vol. 2, 113).

1570 The *suḥūr* is the last meal eaten at night before the fasting day begins. It has to be eaten before the first ray of dawn as indicated by the call for dawn prayers.

1571 Al-Maqrīzī, copying Ibn al-Ṭuwayr, misses a sentence and fails to refer to the vizier here, which results in his misinterpretation of what a single man took after the banquet was over. According to Ibn al-Ṭuwayr, if the vizier attended the banquet, some of the caliph's own food, which he ate with his own hands, was taken out especially for the vizier to honour him. The vizier might then take out for his own *suḥūr* an ample share of the meal designated for the caliph. (Ibn al-Ṭuwayr, *Nuzha*, 212 and al-Maqrīzī, *Khiṭaṭ*, Vol. 2, 113).

1572 Ibn al-Ṭuwayr explains that three banquets were offered on the feasts: two on ʿĪd al-Fiṭr and one on ʿĪd al-Aḍḥā. (Ibn al-Ṭuwayr, *Nuzha*, 212–213 and see full account 212–219).

1573 This table is also sometimes described as a wooden table that was smaller than the bigger table called "*sufra*." *Al-Mudawwara* is a term that also had other meanings in the Mamluk era, such as a kind of a round seat or chair; the centre of the main space or wall of the audience hall (*majlis*) where the sultan or the amir sits, or the sultan's *mudawwara*, which was one of his big tents that was pitched on travels and ceremonies. (Ibn al-Ṭuwayir, Nuzha, 213 fn. 3, M. Dahman, *Mu'jam*, 137, S. Ashour, *'Aṣr*, 469, and see Glossasry).

1574 That is, the royal chair. Probably another name of the throne or refers to one part of it, since Ibn al-Ṭuwayr mentions twice that *al-mudawwara* was placed above the throne (*sarīr al-mulk*). (Ibn al-Ṭuwayr, *Nuzha*, 213 & 215).

1575 In Ibn al-Ṭuwayr's account: silver, golden and China vessels. (Ibn al-Ṭuwayr, *Nuzha*, 213).

1576 In front of the throne and up to the gate of the audience hall (Bāb al-Majlis), which was opposite the throne. Bāb al-Majlis was the door to the *qā'a* that was reached through Bāb al-Baḥr of the palace. (Ibn al-Ṭuwayr, *Nuzha*, 213).

1577 Wooden benches, which probably means oblong, low tables. (Ibn al-Ṭuwayr, *Nuzha*, 214).

of the hall (*qā'a*) and was ten cubits wide. Fragrant flowers were spread on the banquet and bread, baked of pure flour, was stacked to its sides, each [triangular] heap (*shābūra*)[1578] weighing three pounds.[1579] The inner part of the banquet[1580] served 21 huge platters that covered its whole length. Each platter contained 21 grilled sheep and 350 birds of poultry, namely chicken, pullet and small pigeons.[1581] The platters were filled up until they were as high as a tall man and were surrounded with[1582] slices of dry sweets (*ḥalwā'*)[1583] of different colours. [The spaces] in between the platters on the banquet were completely covered with around 500 ceramic plates, brimful with excellent sorts, each containing seven chickens of melted[1584] sweets (*ḥalwā'*) and magnificent foods.[1585] Two castles of sweets (*ḥalwā*)[1586] were prepared at Dār al-Fiṭra, to be mentioned later, each weighing 17 kantars. They were of most beautiful shape and [decorated] with a variety of animals' images.[1587] They were carried to the hall and placed at the two ends of the banquet.[1588]

The caliph came [in] mounting his horse, dismounted on the throne upon which the silver table was installed and sat at the table with four of the high-ranking *muḥannakūn* masters standing to serve him.[1589] He then called only for the vizier, who came and sat to his right near the throne's door. [Next], he signalled to the Collared Amirs and the lesser ranking amirs, so, they sat at the banquet according

1578 Triangular-shaped heap or pile. (Ibn al-Ṭuwayir, Nuzha, 214 fn. 2).

1579 The upper sides of the bread were brushed with water while being baked to make them shiny and beautiful. (Ibn al-Ṭuwayr, *Nuzha*, 214).

1580 Probably, in between the two sides carrying the bread heaps.

1581 Ibn al-Ṭuwayr states that there was 350 of each of the three kinds of poultry. (Ibn al-Ṭuwayr, *Nuzha*, 214).

1582 *Yusawwar*, which means surrounded or bordered with. Ibn al-Ṭuwayr uses the verb "*yushawwar*," which means "decorated with." (Ibn al-Ṭuwayr, *Nuzha*, 214 and http://www.baheth.info/all.jsp?term=شور).

1583 *Ḥalwā'* is a term that refers to all sweet foods and is also used to denote fruits. (http://www.baheth.info/all.jsp?term=حلواء).

1584 "*Al-Mā'i'a*," which may be "liquid," "fluid" or "melted."

1585 Some words are missing from al-Qalqashandī's account if compared to Ibn al-Ṭuwayr's. Ibn al-Ṭuwayr more clearly explains that the spaces among the platters were filled with around 500 pottery plates, each containing seven chickens, and brimful of excellent colours of melted or liquid *ḥalwā'* and seasoned mutton. (Ibn al-Ṭuwayr, *Nuzha*, 214).

1586 *Ḥalwā*, which means sweets or desserts. Ibn al-Ṭuwayr uses the term *ḥalwā'*. (Ibn al-Ṭuwayr, *Nuzha*, 215).

1587 Ibn al-Ṭuwayr explains that both castles were "painted with gold leaves" and decorated with figurines (*shukhūṣ*), which were made using moulds. (Ibn al-Ṭuwayr, *Nuzha*, 215).

1588 According to Ibn al-Ṭuwayr, each castle was taken from Dār al-Fiṭra to the *qā'a* via a particular route. One was taken from Qaṣr al-Shawk, in the eastern facade of the palace, to Bāb al-'Īd Plaza, to al-Rukn al-Mukhallaq, and finally to Bāb al-Dhahab. The other castle was taken along Bayn al-Qaṣrayn. (Ibn al-Ṭuwayr , *Nuzha*, 215 & 215 fn. 1).

1589 As well as four of the caretakers (*farrāshīn*)from the private entourage (*khawāṣṣ*). (Ibn al-Ṭuwayr, *Nuzha*, 215).

to their ranks and ate.[1590] Meanwhile, the reciters in presence of the caliph (*qurrā' al-ḥaḍra*) recited Quran.[1591] The banquet remained spread until it was almost the time for *ẓuhr* prayers, when it was completely consumed, either by eating or by carrying away from it, as well as distributing among the Men of Designated Portions (*arbāb al-rusūm*).[1592]

THE SECOND CATEGORY: ON WHAT WAS DONE AT DĀR AL-FIṬRA ON ʿĪD AL-FIṬR[1593]

[The Fatimids] gave immense attention to Dār al-Fiṭra. Ibn ʿAbd al-Ẓāhir mentioned its kinds [of its contents] saying: They were 1000 loads[1594] of flour; 400[1595] kantars of sugar; six kantars of pistachio;[1596] 430 ardebs of raisins;[1597] fifteen kantars of honey; three kantars of vinegar; two ardebs of sesame; two ardebs of anise; 50 pounds of rosewater; five musk jars (*nawāfij*);[1598] ten *mathāqīl* of old camphor; 150[1599] dirhams of ground saffron; 30 kantars of oil designated for lighting,[1600] [and] other kinds [of components] that would take too long to describe.[1601] Ibn

1590 Their seating according to their ranks was in the same order they stood in the caliph's presence. Ibn al-Ṭuwayr also explains that eating at this banquet was not obligatory, since "some of the attendees did not believe in breaking their fast on that day." (Ibn al-Ṭuwayr, *Nuzha*, 216). This was most probably because some of the invitees were Sunni and at times the celebration of ʿĪd al-Fiṭr and other religious occasions differed a day from the celebration of Shiites.

1591 Ibn al-Ṭuwayr adds that a plentiful share was taken to the reciters. (Ibn al-Ṭuwayr, *Nuzha*, 216).

1592 According to Ibn al-Ṭuwayr, after this banquet was over almost around noon prayers, people left. He does not mention how the leftovers were distributed, but al-Qalqashandī seems to add the customary manner for that. After the people left the banquet, the vizier moved from the palace to his vizierial house (*dār*), served by the attendees, where he held a banquet for his relatives, entourage and the amirs dear to him. This banquet was most humble if compared to the caliph's. (Ibn al-Ṭuwayr, *Nuzha*, 216).

1593 See also Ibn al-Ṭuwayr's account of Dār al-Fiṭra. (Ibn al-Ṭuwar, *Nuzha*, 143–146)

1594 "*Ḥamla*," which means "load," and is identified by al-Maqrīzī in a later context, during the Mamluk era in 797 AH/1394 AD, as equivalent to six "*buṭaṭ*," a term that possibly either means a flattened or compressed sack, or a container with a neck shaped like a duck's. The earlier is the more probable description of what may have been used to transport loads of flour. (See al-Maqrīzī, *Sulūk*, Vol. 5, 366).

1595 Seven-hundred in Ibn ʿAbd al-Ẓāhir's account, copied by al-Maqrīzī. (Ibn ʿAbd al-Ẓāhir, *Khiṭaṭ*, 27 and al-Maqrīzī, *Khiṭaṭ*, Vol. 2, 202).

1596 "Pistachio hearts" in Ibn ʿAbd al-Ẓāhir's *Khiṭaṭ*, 27–28 and al-Maqrīzī's *Khiṭaṭ*, Vol. 2, 202.

1597 Three-hundred in Ibn ʿAbd al-Ẓāhir's *Khiṭaṭ*, 28 and al-Maqrīzī's *Khiṭaṭ*, Vol. 2, 202.

1598 Sing. *nāfija*, see http://www.baheth.info/all.jsp?term=نافجة.

1599 One-hundred and twenty in Ibn ʿAbd al-Ẓāhir's account and one-hundred and fifty in al-Maqrīzī's. (Ibn ʿAbd al-Ẓāhir, *Khiṭaṭ*, 28 and al-Maqrīzī, *Khiṭaṭ*, Vol. 2, 202).

1600 "*Zayt ṭayyib*," or "good oil" in Ibn ʿAbd al-Ẓāhir's account, which is a term used to refer to olive oil. (Ibn ʿAbd al-Ẓāhir, *Khiṭaṭ*, 28).

1601 The list given by Ibn ʿAbd al-Ẓāhir and copied by al-Maqrīzī includes several other items, such as almond hearts, hazelnut hearts, sesame oil, as well as containers and covers. (Ibn ʿAbd al-Ẓāhir, *Khiṭaṭ*, 27–29 and al-Maqrīzī, *Khiṭaṭ*, Vol. 2, 200–203).

al-Ṭuwayr said: One-hundred desert-makers were delegated to Dār al-Fiṭra, as well as one-hundred additional caretakers (*farrāshīn*) to those already appointed in it[1602] for distributing the trays (*ṭawāfīr*)[1603] to the Men of Designated Portions (*aṣḥāb al-rusūm*).[1604] The caliph visited Dār al-Fiṭra, accompanied by the vizier, in the second half of Ramadan.[1605] He sat on the throne (*sarīr*) that was inside it and the vizier sat on his chair. It was a time when its contents that were ready for consumption[1606] looked like firmly set mountains.[1607] Desserts varying from a quarter of a kantar, to ten pounds, to one pound and *khushkanān* varying from 100, to 75, to 33, to 25, to 20 pieces were distributed. The portions to be distributed among the Sudanese were handed to their commanders[1608] according to the individuals [they headed],[1609] whether composed of nine,[1610] seven, five, or three men, every group according to its number . . .[1611] . . .[1612] with the banquet of ʿĪd al-Fiṭr,[1613] what was spread at the Great Iwan before the banquet was spread at Qaʿat al-Dhahab. Ibn al- Ṭuwayr gave two contradicting accounts on this banquet in his book, for once he mentioned that it was held before the caliph rode for ʿĪd prayers, and later said that it was held after the caliph returned from prayers.[1614]

1602 The appointed ones were five, and they were responsible for keeping its contents. (Ibn al-Ṭuwayr, *Nuzha*, 144 and al-Maqrīzī, *Khiṭaṭ*, Vol. 2, 201).

1603 Also *ṭayāfīr*, sing. *ṭayfūr*, see Glossary.

1604 Same as *arbāb al-rusūm*. (See Ibn al-Ṭuwayr, *Nuzha*, 144).

1605 Ibn al-Ṭuwayr explains that of the caliph's visits to the treasuries, the vizier only accompanied him when he went to Dār al-Fiṭra, because it was the only treasury located outside the palace. (Ibn al-Ṭuwayr, *Nuzha*, 144).

1606 Al-Qalqashandī uses the term "*al-musta'malāt*," which refers to the contents of a treasury that are to be used. Ibn al-Ṭuwayr says "*al-ḥawāṣil al-ma'mūla*," that is the prepared contents, in this case, foods. (*Ṣubḥ*, Vol. 3, 529 and Ibn al-Ṭuwayr, *Nuzha*, 145).

1607 Firmly set mountains (*rawāsī*) is an expression borrowed from Quran, which refers to huge mountains standing fixed and immovable. It is employed here as an exaggeration that indicates the huge sizes of the heaps. (See *rawāsiya* in http://corpus.quran.com/search.jsp?q=root%3Aرسو).

1608 Al-Qalqashandī uses the word "*muqaddam*" (commander), while both Ibn al-Ṭuwayr and al-Maqrīzī use "'*urafā*'" (sing. *'arrīf*): supervisor or superintendent. (*Ṣubḥ*, Vol. 3, 529 and Ibn al-Ṭuwayr, *Nuzha*, 146 and al-Maqrīzī, *Khiṭaṭ*, Vol. 2, 201).

1609 In Ibn al-Ṭuwayr's account, copied by al-Maqrīzī, the portions given to the Sudanese slaves were not presented in trays (*ṭayāfīr*). Ibn al-Ṭuwayr says that they were put in "*afrād al-khūṣ*," which may be translated as "individual wicker baskets." Al-Maqrīzī adds a letter, which leads to the meaning that the supervisors of the Sudanese slave groups were "*afrād al-khawāṣṣ*," that is, "individuals from the private entourage." (Ibn al-Ṭuwayr, *Nuzha*, 146 and al-Maqrīzī, *Khiṭaṭ*, Vol. 2, 201).

1610 Ten in Ibn al-Ṭuwayr's account. (Ibn al-Ṭuwayr, *Nuzha*, 146).

1611 "*Kul ṭā'ifa 'alā miqdārihā*," which may also mean "every group according to its level."

1612 The editor of Subḥ notes that this is a blank space in the original copy. (*Ṣubḥ*, Vol. 3, 529, fn.1).

1613 "*Bi-simāṭ 'Īd al-Fiṭr*," which could also be "at the banquet of 'Īd al-Fiṭr." (*Ṣubḥ*, Vol. 3, 529).

1614 Ibn al-Ṭuwayr actually mentions that there were two banquets offered on occasion of 'Īd al-Fiṭr; one that was set on the night before the *'īd*, which people were allowed to eat at and take from after the caliph had prayed the dawn (*fajr*) prayers, and the other apparently after the caliph came back from the *'īd* prayers, which the one described above by al-Qalqashandī. (Ibn al-Ṭuwayr, *Nuzha*, 212–213).

The Eighth End[1615] On the vizier's sitting in audience for the grievances (maẓālim), if he was a man of the sword, and the arrangement of his council[1616]

The vizier sat at the centre of the main wall of the place,[1617] while the Chief Judge sat opposite him, with two esteemed witnesses to his sides, and the vizier's scribe of the fine script (*al-qalam al-daqīq*), followed by the Head of the Treasury Bureau (*ṣāḥib dīwān al-māl*)[1618].[1619] The Master of the Gate and the *isfihsalār* stood in his service, while [subsequently] having the deputies and the *ḥujjāb*, of different ranks, standing in their service.[1620] This council was held two days a week.

*****

ʿUmāra al-Yamanī[1621] had lamented the extinction of [the Fatimids] and the seizure of the kingdom by Ṣalāḥ al-Dīn b. Ayyūb in a poem in which he described their monarchy, listed their processions, and told their honourable qualities and their obvious, excellent [traits], . . .[1622]

I say: This ʿUmāra was not of Shiite conviction, but was a Shāfiʿī religious scholar. He came to Egypt carrying a message from al-Qāsim b. Hāshim b. Abī Fulayta,[1623] the amir of Mecca, to al-Fā'iz, one of their caliphs, in the year 550 AH/1155 AD, during the vizierate of al-Ṣāliḥ Ṭalā'iʿ b. Ruzayk. [The Fatimids] were kind and excessively generous to him, so he stayed [at their court] and became intimate with them. He [excelled] in praising them with mind-dazzling [poetry] and remained on his allegiance to them until their kingdom ceased to exist, and was seized by Sultan Ṣalaḥ al-Dīn Yūsuf b. Ayyūb, so he composed this poem in lamentation. This poem was the last reason for his demise, for he was crucified at Bayn al-Qaṣrayn, among the followers of the Fatimid state, who faced the same fate.

1615 The editor of Subḥ notes that this chapter was not divided into ends. (*Ṣubḥ*, Vol. 3, 529, fn. 2).

1616 See also Ibn al-Ṭuwayr's account. (Ibn al-Ṭuwayr, *Nuzha*, 120–121).

1617 A designated place at the palace. (Ibn al-Ṭuwayr, *Nuzha*, 120).

1618 Most probably the same as Head of the Public Treasury (*ṣāḥib bayt al-māl*).

1619 According to Ibn al-Ṭuwayr, the two witnesses sat to the sides of the Chief Judge. The signer with the fine script (*al-muwwaqi' bi-l-qalam al-*daqīq) sat to the side of the vizier, followed by the Head of the Treasury Bureau (*ṣāḥib dīwān al-māl*). (Ibn al-Ṭuwayr, *Nuzha*, 120–121).

1620 "Standing in service" here is the translation of "*bayna yadayhi*" and "*bayna aydīhimā*."

1621 Same poet mentioned above as ʿUmāra al-Tamīmī. See fn. 1221.

1622 The poem runs for 41 verses and starts with the words: "Oh Time, You have paralyzed the hand of glory", *Ṣubḥ*, Vol. 3, 530–532.

1623 Al-Qāsim b. Hāshim b. Abī Fulayta (or b. Fulayta) (d. 557 AH/1162 AD) succeeded his father in the rule of Mecca, which he became the amir of in 549 AH/1154 AD – al-Qalqashandī alternatively states that he started his rule in 527 AH/1133 AD. Al-Qāsim's uncle overtook his seat for a few years (553 AH/1158 AD to 557 AH/1162 AD, or about one year in al-Qalqashandī's account). Al-Qāsim's attempt to restore his dominion over Mecca failed and he was killed either by his uncle, or his uncle's supporters. (Al-Zurkalī, *A'lām*, Vol. 5, 186 and *Ṣubḥ*, Vol. 4, 271).

THE THIRD STATUS OF THE CONDITIONS OF THE KINGDOM

On the Regulation of the Kingdom from the Beginning of the Ayyubid State until Our Times The Ayyubids and Mamluks

You should know that when the Ayyubid state overcame the Fatimid and succeeded them in ruling Egypt, it altered much of the state regulation and changed most of its features. The Ayyubid state followed the Atabek[1624] State of ʿImād al-Dīn Zankī[1625] of Mosul[1626]then his son al-Malik al-ʿĀdil Nūr al-Dīn Maḥmūd[1627]

1624 *Atābek* is a Turkish term composed of two syllabi: *aṭā* (father) and *bek* (amir), which may be translated as "father-commander." It was a title given to the mamluk amirs appointed as guardians over "young Seljuq princes sent out as provincial governors." The *atābek*s were in charge of educating and mentoring these princes. They were appointed custodians or regents over minor sultans and princes, and in many instances they married the minors' mothers, so that their relationship with them became semi-parental. As time passed, the responsibilities and powers of the *atābek*s increased, which was one of the factors that resulted in the division of the Saljuq sultanate into smaller states, each governed by an Atābek who had his own hereditary line of rule. The Zangids (see Glossary) were one of these Atabek or Atabeg states. The title "*atābek*" was later employed in the Mamluk era to refer to the general commander of the army (*atābek al-ʿasākir*), since he was like a father to all the amirs and soldiers. (H. al-Basha, *Alqāb*, 122–124, al-Baqli, *Ta'rīf*, 14 and Clifford E Bosworth,*The New Islamic Dynasties: A Chronological and Genealogical Manual* (Edinburgh, 1996), 188).

1625 Zangid founder and ruler of dynasty from 521 AH/1127 AD to 541 AH/1146 AD. (See Glossary: "Zangids")

1626 Al-Mawṣil, city in northern Iraq, overlooking the Tigris.

1627 Zangid ruler of Aleppo and Damascus from 541 AH/1146 AD to 569 AH/1174 AD. (See Glossary: "Zangids" and "Ayyubids")

of Damascus and its affiliated [lands]. It was their custom to wear the yellow caps (*kalawtāt*)[1628] on their heads, exposed without turbans. They loosened their hairlocks (*dhawā'ib*)[1629] below the caps, whether they were mamluks, amirs or otherwise. It is even related that [among the practices of] al-Malik al-Mu'aẓẓam 'Īsā b. al-'Ādil Abū Bakr,[1630] the Ruler of Damascus, to renounce pretences was that he wore the yellow cap (*kalawta*) without muslin (*shāsh*)[1631] and walked through the markets with no one before him to clear the roads like other kings. When Sayf al-Dīn Ghāzī b. 'Imād al-Dīn Zankī[1632] ruled Mosul after his father, he introduced carrying the [small yellow] banner (*sanjaq*)[1633] above his head, so

1628 Or "*kullawtāt*" (sing. *kalawta* or *kullawta*): A small headgear worn separately or with a turban, also called "*kulfa*," "*kulaftāh*" or "*kulaftah.*" It is thought to have resembled the head cover worn by Mevlevi dervishes in modern times, and probably covered parts of the ears. The term is either thought to be of Latin origin or Arabized from Persian. The Ayyubid sultans introduced wearing the *kalawtāt* to Egypt. They used to wear the yellow broadcloth *kalawtāt* on their heads, without turbans, while loosening their forelocks or hair locks below the *kalawtāt*, as described above. "The sultans and soldiers continued to wear the yellow *kalawtāt* without turbans up to the mid Bahri Mamluk era." When Sultan al-Manṣūr Qalāwūn came to rule, he introduced muslin (*shāsh*) to the *kalawta*. "During the reign of his son, al-Ashraf Khalīl, all the amirs were ordered to ride among their mamluks in gold-brocaded caps (*kalawtāt zarkash*), while the yellow broadcloth ones were worn by those beneath the amirs in rank. When Sultan al-Nāṣir Muḥammad came to power, he introduced the *Nāṣiriyya* turbans, which were small. He shaved his head after pilgrimage, the amirs followed him, and they relinquished the hairlocks. The *Nāṣiriyya* turbans were later replaced with the *Yalbughāwiyya*, which were attributed to Amir Yalbughā al-Khāṣṣakī al-'Umarī." The *Yalbughāwiyya* remained in use until the reign of Sultan al-Ẓāhir Barqūq, "the first of the Circassian Mamluk sultans, who introduced the *Jarkasī* (Circassian) *kalawtāt*, which were bigger than the *Yalbughāwiyya* ones," and the turban cloths were wrapped around them in a bent fashion.(Al-Baqli, *Ta'rīf*, 288–289; al-Maqrīzī, *Khiṭaṭ*, Vol. 3, 73–74; M. Dahman, *Mu'jam*, 130–131; S. Ashour, *'Aṣr*, 466; K. al-Juburi, *Masālik* (2010), Vol. 3, 291 fn. 5, and H. Abbas, *Masālik* (2002), Vol. 3, 435 fn. 1).

1629 Sing. *dhu'āba*, which either means a hair lock, a forelock, a hair braid or the tail of a turban. In this context the author specifically mentions that it is the *dhu'āba* of the hair that was loosened beneath the turban.

1630 'Isa b. al-'Adil was the Ayyubid ruler of Damascus from 515 AH/1221 AD to 624 AH/1227 AD.

1631 A type of fine cloth that was used for wrapping around turbans as well as wounds. Women also used it, decorated with gold and pearls, to cover their heads. The term was used to denote this type of turban-cloth, as well as scarves. (M. Dahman, *Mu'jam*, 95,S. Ashour, *'Aṣr*, 449 and Yedida K. Stillman, *Arab Dress from the Dawn of Islam to Modern Times: A Short History*, ed. Norman A. Stillman (Leiden, 2003), 135 fn. 44).

1632 Zangid ruler of Mosul and its dependencies from 541 AH/1146 AD to 544 AH/1149 AD. (See Glossary: "Zangids").

1633 Pl. *sanājiq*: A Turkish term that originally means "lance." The *sanājiq* were small yellow banners carried by the Sanjaqdār (the bearer of the *sanjaq*). It seems that the sultan usually rode on processions during peace time only with the *sanājiq* along his side. However, at times of war, the sultanic procession was accompanied by flags that included the *sanājiq*, a great yellow silk banner, called "*'iṣāba*," embroidered with gold and carrying the sultan's name and titles, and another great banner with a hair lock at its top, called "*jālīsh*." All these banners were the responsibility of the Amīr 'Alam (Prince of the Banner or Prince of the Flag), who handled the the sultanic flags, standards and the *ṭablakhānāh*, and was normally an amir of ten. (Al-Baqli, *Ta'rīf*, 49 & 186).

other kings followed. He obliged the soldiers to tie their swords to their waists and place their maces (*dabābīs*) beneath their knees as they rode, which was reported by Sultan ʿImād al-Dīn, the Ruler of Hama, in his *Tārīkh*.[1634]

When Sultan Ṣalāḥ al-Dīn Yūsuf b. Ayyūb ascended to the throne of Egypt, he followed this course, or one that was similar. When the Turkish State reached power, the kingdom's [regulation] had already been refined and made orderly, so it continued to improve this regulation, organize the monarchy and establish its splendour. This state copied the best of every kingdom and followed the paths [of such excellent practices], imitating their patterns, until it became most refined and best regulated, and excelled over all other monarchies, making its kings the proudest of all.

The sultan and soldiers (*jund*) continued to wear the yellow cap without a turban until Sultan al-Malik al-Ashraf Khalīl b. Sultan Qalāwūn[1635] came to power. He introduced [wearing] muslin with it, which made it extremely beautiful.[1636] They started wearing [their headgears in this fashion] on top of their loosened hairlocks, as was the original custom. [This remained the practice] until Sultan al-Malik al-Nāṣir Muḥammad b. Qalāwūn went on pilgrimage in his third reign, so he shaved his head, which people followed by shaving their heads too.[1637] Shaving the heads and giving up the hairlocks remained [the practice since then] and until our present times.[1638]

And the [description of state regulation] will be described in [the following] ten purposes.

The First Purpose
On the protocols and instruments of royalty: Some common to kings, or most kings, and some particular to this kingdom.

The Throne (sarīr al-mulk) – also called "*takht al-mulk*" (the seat of sovereignty),[1639] which is one of the general items [used by] monarchs. As was

1634 Abū al-Fidā', *Tārīkh*, Vol. 3, 21.

1635 The text incorrectly mentions al-Ashraf Khalīl as the son of al-Nāṣir Muḥammad b. Qalāwūn. Khalīl was the elder brother of Muḥammad, who ruled from 689 AH/1290 AD to 692 AH/1293 AD.

1636 According to al-Maqrīzī, Khalīl introduced embroidered (*zarkash*) *kalawtāt*, as well as other ornamented costume items and equestrian attire that were all only worn by the amirs to differentiate them from others. (Al-Maqrīzī, *Khiṭaṭ*, Vol. 2, 590).

1637 Shaving or cutting some of the hair – only cutting some of it in the case of women – is one of the rituals marking the end of pilgrimage.

1638 See also Al-Maqrīzī, *Khiṭaṭ*, Vol. 2, 590–591.

1639 *Takht* is an elevated pedestal or seat that functions as a throne. It could have been a mobile unit or a fixed one called *takht al-mamlaka* (Kingdom Chair) or *kursī al-'arsh* (Throne Chair). *Takht* is also a Persian word used in Arabic to denote the clothes container, be it a box or a large cloth encasement. (M. Dahman, *Mu'jam*, 42, S. Ashour, *'Aṣr*, 422 andhttp://www.baheth.info/all.jsp?term=تخت).

mentioned earlier, the first Muslim [ruler] to use a mattress (*martaba*)[1640] to sit on was Muʿāwiya,[1641] after he had aged and weakened. After him, the caliphs and kings of the Islamic [world] competed over [the enhancement of] this [item] until they employed the thrones (*asirra*).[1642] The thrones of the Abbasid caliphs in Baghdad reached a height of about seven cubits. In this [Mamluk] kingdom, the thrones are marble pulpits (*manābir*) that are placed at the centre of the main wall of the sultan's iwan, where he sits. They have the shapes of mosque minbars, except that they stand with their backs to the walls. The sultan sits on this minbar on important days, such as receiving envoys and the like. On other days, he sits on a wooden chair covered with silk and if he let down his legs, they almost reach the floor. Inside his palaces, the sultan sits on a small iron chair that is carried along with him to wherever he sits.

The maqṣūra – For praying in the congregational mosque. It was mentioned previously, in the account on the caliphate's organization, that Muʿāwiya was the first Muslim ruler to use it. It later became a custom of Muslim kings that distinguished sultans from subjects. In this [Mamluk] kingdom, it is a *maqṣūra* at Mosque of the Citadel, which is placed near the minbar and made of compact iron grills.[1643] The sultan prays inside it on Fridays, along with his closest *khāṣṣakiyya.*

Inscribing the Sultan's Name (naqsh ism al-sulṭān) – On woven and inscribed garments and the *ṭuruz*[1644] made of silk or [embroidered with] gold. [The inscription is embroidered] with a colour different than that of the textiles or the *ṭuruz*, so that the sultanic clothes and *ṭuruz*are distinguishable from others; a distinction that shows the standard of the wearer, whether the sultan, a person the sultan honours by bestowing [such a gift] upon, on occasion of being appointed to a position or as a grant, or otherwise. A particular factory[1645] in Alexandria, called "Dār al-Ṭirāz" (the House of Ṭirāz), is allocated to [the manufacture of these textiles]. Both the Umayyad and Abbasid caliphs followed the same practice [of having such a royal factory], when the caliphate existed.

The Cover (al-ghāshiya) – This is the gold-embroidered[1646] leather cover of a saddle. It appears to the viewer as if it is all made of gold. It is carried immediately in front of[1647] the sultan in the crowded processions, such as the squares' (*mayādīn*)[1648] and feasts' processions and their likes. One of the Holders of the

1640 Also "pedestal," see Glossary: "*martaba*".

1641 Muʿāwiya b. Abī Sufyān, first Muslim monarch. (See Glossary: "Umayyads").

1642 Sing. *sarīr*.

1643 "*Min shibāk ḥadīd muḥkamat al-ṣunʿ.*" (*Ṣubḥ*, Vol. 4, 7).

1644 Sing. *ṭirāz*, see Glossary.

1645 *Dār* (house), which in this context means "factory" or "workshop."

1646 *Makhrūza bi-l-dhahab*, which means "embroidered with gold," since "*al-kharz*" means "the sewing of leather." (See http://www.baheth.info/all.jsp?term=خرز).

1647 "*Bayna yadayhi*".

1648 Sing. *maydān*: "square." See the author's description of square processions later.

Stirrups (*rikābdāriyya*)[1649] carries it, raises it on both hands and turns it to the right and left. This item is particular to this kingdom.[1650]

The Parasol (miẓalla) – Called "*al-jitr*,"[1651] is a yellow silk dome brocaded with gold[1652] that has a gold-plated silver bird at its apex. It is carried above the sultan's head during [the processions of] the two feasts. This item was carried over from the Fatimid era, and it was described in detail earlier, in the section on the regulation of the [Fatimid] kingdom.

The Neck-[cover] (al-raqaba) – A yellow satin (*aṭlas*)[1653] neck-[cover] (*raqaba*) that is brocaded with gold, so densely that the satin disappears beneath the gold. It is put on the horse's neck during the squares' and feasts' [processions] and it [extends] from beneath the horse's ears and up to the end of its mane. This item is particular to this kingdom.

Al-Jifta[1654] – These are two similarly aged stable boys (*ushāqiyya*)[1655] from the [sultan's] stable swearing two yellow silk coats (*aqbiya*),[1656] with a gold-brocaded[1657] *ṭirāz*, and two gold-brocaded hats. They ride two equipped whitish-gray[1658] horses, each with a neck-[cover] (*raqaba*). Their horses are identical to the sultan's horse, as if they are prepared for him to ride. The two [*ushāqiyya*] rode in front of the sultan on certain occasions, such as riding to play *kura* in the Great Square (al-Maydān al-Kabīr), and the like. They were particular to this kingdom.

The Flags (al-aʿlām) – These are several banners including: A huge yellow silk banner, called "*al-ʿiṣāba*,"[1659] that is embroidered with gold and bears the

1649 The *rikābdāriyya* were affiliated to the *rikābkhānāh* (the house of saddles, bridles and the like). (M. Dahman, *Mu'jam*, 83 and S. Ashour, *'Aṣr*, 442).

1650 Both the Ayyubid and Mamluk sultans went on processions with the "*ghāshiya*." (Al-Baqli, *Ta'rīf*, 254 and al-Maqrīzī, *Sulūk*, Vol. 1, 335, 349 & 378).

1651 Al-Qalqashandī details the pronunciation of the term: "*jīm maksūra, qad tubaddal shīnan mu'ajjama, wa tā' muthannāt fawq*." This may be translated as follows: "A *ji*, which may be transformed into a *chi*, and a *t*, the one with two dots above." The remark that the *tā'* (*t*) is the one with two dots above is used to distinguish between this letter and the ones similarly written, but differ according to the number of dots above or below the letter, such as the *bā'* (*b*) and *yā'* (*y*); a custom as old as the early undotted Arabic written texts.

1652 "*Muzarkash*" (gold-brocaded).

1653 A type of silk; satin.

1654 Also, "*al-jiftāh*." (Al-Baqli, *Ta'rīf*, 86).

1655 The *ushāqiyya* or *ujāqiyya* (sing. *ushāqī* or *ujāqī*), were stable boys or a troop of sultanic servants responsible for riding the horses for movement and sports, so as to keep them fit. (Al-Baqli, *Ta'rīf*, 57, and S. Ashour, *Aṣr*, 416).

1656 Sing. *qabā'*: An overgarment, like a caftan, that by the Mamluk era had tight sleeves and were either white or coloured with alternating red and blue stripes. (S. Ashour, *'Aṣr*, 460 and M. Dahman, *Mu'jam*, 121).

1657 *Zarkash*.

1658 *Ashhab*.

1659 Pl. *'aṣā'ib*, processional banners as described above. (S. Ashour, *'Aṣr*, 457).

names and titles of the sultan; a huge banner, called "*al-jālīsh*,"[1660] which has a hair lock at its top, and small yellow banners called "*al-sanājiq*."[1661]

Sultan ʿImād al-Din, the Ruler of Hama, mentioned in his *Tārīkh* that the first king to have the *sanjaq*carried above his head in his processions was Ghāzī b. Zankī, brother of Sultan Nūr al-Dīn Maḥmūd b. Zankī of Damascus.

Al-Ṭablakhānāh – Various drums, accompanied with horns and pipes[1662] of different sounds that play to a certain beat. They are played nightly at the Citadel after the *maghrib* prayers. They accompany the battalions (*ṭulb*)[1663]in travels and wars, and are among the general items used by all kings. It is related that Alexander was accompanied by forty loads of *ṭablakhānāh*.[1664] Aristotle wrote in *Kitāb al-Siyāsa* (the Book of Politics),[1665] which he authored for Alexander, that the secret behind this was to terrify the enemies at war. Some researchers have concluded that the secret behind it was that the sounds of the instruments fuel the enthusiasm and bravery of the forces, the same way *ḥidā'*[1666] urges the camels [to march], and the like.

The Cymbals (al-kūsāt) – Copper cymbals that resemble a small [round] shield (*turs*).[1667] One of them is banged against the other to a certain beat. They are accompanied by drums and a flute (*shabbāba*).[1668] [These instruments] are played twice a night at the Citadel, and circle its interior[1669] once after the last

1660 A Persian word that means "hair," and was used to refer to the advance guard or the front troops of an army or in a battlefield. *Al-Jālīsh* banner was raised above the *ṭablakhānāh* building or tent for forty days before setting out for war, and was particularly raised in war processions. (M. Dahman, *Mu'jam*, 50 and S. Ashour, *'Aṣr*, 425).

1661 Sing. *sanjaq*.

1662 Al-Qalqashandī uses the word (*zumur*) to denote the pipes. The editor of Subḥ notes that this is an uncommon plural that should have been "*zummārāt*," (sing. *zummāra*). (*Ṣubḥ*, Vol. 4, 8 and 8 fn. 1).

1663 Also, *ṭulab* (pl. *aṭlāb*):An originally Kurdish term, which means "the amir who leads two-hundred horsemen in the battlefield," and is also used for those who lead 100 or 70 horsemen. The term is used to refer to the Mamluk battalion that belonged to an amir and was formed of 70 to 200 horsemen. The term later came to mean an army battalion. M. Dahman states that the plural of *ṭulb* is *aṭlāb*; Sa'id Ashour also identifies the *aṭlāb* as the "private guards of the mamluk amirs," who bore arms like soldiers did. (S. Ashour, *'Aṣr*, 413 & 455 and M. Dahman, *Mu'jam*, 108).

1664 Load: *ḥiml*; that is, forty beasts of burden carrying these instruments.

1665 Aristotle's *Politics*.

1666 Special singing sung for the camels to urge them forward.

1667 *Turs* is a generic term which means "shield" and refers to various types of shields, some of which were circular and could have been made of iron, steel, wood or leather. In this context, the author is most probably particularly referring to circular shields. (A. Yasin, *Asliḥa*, 249–250 and http://www.baheth.info/all.jsp?term=ترس).

1668 Al-Qalqashandī defines the *shabbāba*as a musical instrument made of hollowed reed or cane, which may also be referred to as the "Iraqi pipe." (*Ṣubḥ*, Vol. 2, 144).

1669 "*Yudāru bihā fī jawānibihā*," which means "they are made to circle its sides," implying being inside the Citadel.

'ishā' prayers, and once before the *tasbīḥ*[1670] that is called from the minarets.[1671] This "round"[1672] is so called [as it marches] around the Citadel; also, when the sultan travels these [instruments] march around his tent.

The Tents and Pavilions (al-khiyām wa-l-fasāṭīṭ)[1673]– [Used] on travels. The [Mamluk] sultan has a large supply of tents and pavilions. Grand tents of various sizes and [quality of] manufacture, made of Damascene[1674] cotton, coloured with white, blue, red and otherwise, as well as diversely coloured broadcloth, were assigned to the sultan. These tents bedazzle the minds with their beauty and are used as substitute[royal] residences to the palaces.

Other royal instruments than the ones listed above will be mentioned later, separately, in their contexts.

The Second Purpose
On the sultan's warehouses,[1675] which are of four kinds[1676]

The First Kind: The Warehouses called "the houses" (*al-buyūt*)[1677]

They add to each name the word "*khānāh*," such as *al-ṭishtkhānāh* (the House of Basins), *al-sharābkhānāh* (the House of Beverages),[1678] and so on. *Khānāh* is a Persian word that means "house" (*bayt*). The meaning of each term then is: "The house of so and so." However, the syllabi are inverted [to mention the word "house" last, unlike the rules of Arabic,][1679] which follows custom of the Persians (*'Ajam*).[1680]

These are eight houses:

1670 Glorification and praise of Allah.

1671 Al-Qalqashandī uses the plural "*al-mawādin*" for "minarets." The editor of Subḥ notes that the correct plural is "*al-ma'ādhin*" and that the author frequently uses colloquial terms. (*Ṣubḥ*, Vol. 4, 9 & 9 fn. 1).

1672 Marching round of instruments.

1673 *Al-Khiyām* (sing. *al-khayma*: tent); *al-fasāṭīṭ* (sing. *al-fusṭāṭ*: tent or pavilion).

1674 Or Syrian: *Shāmī*.

1675 Or storehouses: *ḥawāṣil*.

1676 The editor of Subḥ comments that the classification into four kinds might have been a mistake made by the manuscript's copier, since it was not followed in the text, which lists eight warehouses without classification. (*Ṣubḥ*, Vol. 4, 9 fn. 2).

1677 Sing. *al-bayt*.

1678 See below.

1679 Linguistically, the Arabic term would be composed of two syllabi arranged, for example, as *bayt al-sharāb*: the House of Beverages, where the word *bayt* (house of) comes first.

1680 A term that is generally used to describe non-Arabs and sometimes particularly refers to Persians, which is the case here. (See http://www.baheth.info/all.jsp?term=عجم).

The First: *Al-Sharābkhānāh*, which means "the House of Beverages" (*bayt al-sharāb*)

This house includes the [various] kinds of drinks[1681] assigned to the sultan's private use (*khāṣṣ*), and the private sugar and *aqsima*[1682] drinks, and the like, as well as the sugar particularly used for these drinks. It also includes the precious vessels of exquisite Chinaware of lapis lazuli and otherwise,[1683] where one small bowl[1684] is worth around 1000 dirhams. The position of the inspector (*shādd*)[1685] of the *sharābkhānāh* is [assigned] to one of the high-ranking amirs of hundreds,[1686] of the trustworthy *khāṣṣakiyya*. It has a chief superintendent (*mihtār*)[1687] known as "*mihtār al-sharābkhānāh*," who is responsible for its contents.[1688] He holds a high status and supervises slave-boys (*ghilmān*) designated for service (*khidma*), each called a "*sharāb dār*" (holder of the drink).[1689] The addition of "*dār*"[1690] [to titles] and similar [terms] will be explained later in the Third Article.[1691]

The Second: *Al-Ṭishtkhānāh*, which means the House of the Basin (*bayt al-ṭisht*)

It is so called because it includes the basins used for washing hands and cloths. The more commonly used word is *ṭisht*, the correct form of which is

1681 Or syrups: *ashriba.*

1682 A drink made by soaking raisin in water, sometimes defined as the wine of raisin. For it to be *ḥalāl* (religiously approved or allowed), it has to be made without mixing the raisins with other components or allowing the mixture to stay for longer than three days, so that it does not become alcoholic. Otherwise, this drink would become alcoholic, which makes it *ḥarām* (religiously forbidden). In the Mamluk era, it was a type of sweetened and cooled drink. We are told that in 797 AH/1395 AD, during the reign of Sultan Barqūq, Amir Tamarbughā introduced a new drink, made by soaking ten pounds of raisin in forty pounds of water and leaving them for days. This drink, named *al-Tamarbaghāwī*, after the amir, was an alcoholic drink demanded by the sultan and his amirs, although Barqūq was not known for drinking before that. (Musṭafā al-Suyūṭī al-Ruḥaybānī and Ḥasan al-Shaṭṭī al-Ḥanbalī, *Maṭālib Ulī al-Nuhā fī SharḥGhāyat al-Muntahā* (Damascus, 1961), Vol. 6, 215; Aḥmad b. Taymiya, *Mawsū'at al-Ijmā' li-Shaykh al-Islām Ibn Taymiya*, ed. Abd Allah b. Mubarak al-Busi (Ta'if, 1999), 571; M. Dahman, *Mu'jam*, 21 and L. Nassar, *Tarfīh*, 120).

1683 "*Al-Ṣīnī al-fākhir min al-lāzawardī wa ghayrihi.*"

1684 "*Al-Sukurruja*," which is a kind of bowl. (http://www.baheth.info/all.jsp?term=سكرجة).

1685 The *shādd* of something was its inspector. (Al-Baqli, *Ta'rīf*, 193, S. Ashour, *'Aṣr*, 448–449, M. Dahman, *Mu'jam*, 95, and See Glossary: "*shādd*").

1686 See Glossary: "Amirs of Hundreds".

1687 *Mihtār* is an originally Persian word and is used to refer to the chief of something or the best at something. (Al-Baqli, *Ta'rīf*, 333, S. Ashour, *'Aṣr*, 478, and M. Dahman, *Mu'jam*, 146).

1688 *Ḥawāṣil*, sing. *ḥāṣil*, also "acquisitions." The term is also used to denote the warehouse itself. (See Glossary).

1689 This is the title given to the person who serves in the *sharābkhānāh* of the sultan or amir. (S. Ashour, *'Aṣr*, 450, and M. Dahman, *Mu'jam*, 97).

1690 A Persian term that means "holder of." (M. Dahman, *Mu'jam*, 72).

1691 A section of *Ṣubḥ* that is not translated in this work.

ṭast. The original word is *ṭass*, where the last *sīn*[1692] was replaced by a *tā'*[1693] for easier pronunciation. In the plural and diminutive forms, the *sīn* is used as in the original word, so the plural is: *ṭisās* or *ṭusūs*, and the diminutive form is: *ṭusais*. Al-Jawharī said that it is also called *ṭassa*, plural: *ṭassāt*, and people now call it *ṭāsa*, plural: *ṭāsāt*, and refer to a particular kind [of basins] with the term *ṭast* and to another with the term *ṭāsa*.

The *ṭishtkhānāh* also includes what the sultan wears, such as the caps (*kalawtāt),* the coats (*aqbiya*), and all other costumes, as well as the sword, the light shoes (*khuff*),[1694] the low shoes (*surmūza*),[1695] and other [items]. It comprises all that the sultan uses for sitting, such as seats, cushions, prayer rugs and similar [items]. It also has one of the high superintendents (*mihtāriyya*), known as "*mihtār al-ṭishtkhānāh*" (Superintendent of the House of Basins), who has several slave-boys (*ghilmān*) under his supervision, some known as the "*ṭisht dāriyya*" (Holders of the Basins),[1696] and some known as the "*rukhtuwāniyya*."[1697] He manages distributing meat from the House of Assorted Needs (*ḥawā'ijkhānāh*)[1698] to the Sultanic Mamluks and providing[1699] [assigned shares] to the recipients of meat [rations].[1700] Both the slave-boys of the *ṭishtkhānāh* and the distributors of meat are referred to as "*bābā*,"[1701] which is a Byzantine[1702] word that means "father." The term was

1692 The letter *sīn* in Arabic is equivalent to the "S."

1693 The letter *tā'* in Arabic is equivalent to the "T."

1694 Light shoes, shoes or sandals. (http://www.baheth.info/all.jsp?term=الخف).

1695 "A kind of low shoe (*na'l*) removed when entering a house." (Leo A. Mayer, *Mamluk Costume: A Survey* (Geneva, 1952), 72 & 74).

1696 Sing, *ṭisht dār*:holder of the *ṭisht*.

1697 "*Rukht*" is a Persian word that has several meanings, including decoration, expensive textiles, furniture, and amirial and sultanic clothes and textiles, as well as the decoration of the horse. The *rukhtuwān* (pl. *rukhtuwāniyya*) were, as described above, the servants of the *ṭishtkhānāh* who handled the textiles. The term was also used to refer to the servants who took care of the sultan's or the amir's belongings on their travels, and to the servants who minded the furniture in the Mamluk palaces. (Al-Baqli, *Ta'rīf*, 158, S. Ashour, *'Aṣr*, 441, and M. Dahman, *Mu'jam*, 82).

1698 See below.

1699 "*Iqāmat*," which linguistically means hosting or appointing. The term was also used to either mean providing the soldiers with the supplies they needed, such as food rations or fodder for their rides, or to refer to what is required to host a traveller, or for his residence, such as the equipped tents and all other needs. (S. Ashour, *'Aṣr*, 413).

1700 "*Qubbāḍ al-laḥm*" (sing. *qābiḍ al-laḥm*), which refers to those entitled to meat rations. (See al-Nuwayrī, *Nihāya*, Vol. 8, 223).

1701 Pl. *bābiyya*, an originally Roman word that means "Father of Fathers." This was a general title given to all the men working in the *ṭishtkhānāh*, who handled washing, polishing, and other duties. They were given this title because they were responsible for their masters' luxury, in terms of cleaning their clothes and improving their appearances, like a compassionate father, therefore, the title. The title was also used to refer to high-ranking Christian clergy. (Al-Baqli, *Ta'rīf*, 59, S. Ashour, *'Aṣr*, 416, and M. Dahman, *Mu'jam*, 28).

1702 "*Rūmiyya*."

[first] used to refer to the Superintendent of the House of Basins to honour him then it was extended to [the] others. The slave-boys serving in this house are well-trained on arranging the loads[1703] carried on the backs of mules for decoration during grand processions and similar [occasions]. They come up, for these [decorations], with all amazing [sorts of] marvellous craftsmanship and peculiar danglings. They take pride in this and compete in it with each other.

The Third: *Al-Firāshkhānāh*, which means the House of Furnishings (*bayt al-firāsh*)[1704]

It contains [all] kinds of furnishings [that are spread out], such as rugs and tents. It has a superintendent known as "*mihtār al-firāshkhānāh*" (Superintendent of the House of Furnishings), who supervises a large group of slave-boys assigned to serve in it, whether on travels or in cities and towns.[1705] These slave-boys are called the "*farrāshīn*" (caretakers), and they are among the most skilled and energetic of slave-boys. They are highly trained on pitching tents to the extent that one of them may be able to pitch a huge tent and erect it on his own, without an assistant. They have complete knowledge of tying the loads carried on the backs of mules on processions, where one load reaches around fifteen cubits of height.

The Fourth: *Al-Silāḥkhānāh*, which means the House of Arms (*bayt al-silāḥ*)

It may also be called "*al-zardkhānāh*," which means "the House of Chainmail" (*bayt al-zard*), because of the chainmail armour it comprises. It contains [all] kinds of weaponry, such as: swords; Arabian bows; arrows; lances; armour made of excellent chainmail (*zard*), and brigandines (*qarqalāt*) made of iron plates[1706] that are covered with red and yellow silk brocade (*dībāj*), as well as other [items], such as battle-axes (*aṭbār*)[1707] and all other kinds of arms. It has but a few of the crossbows (*qisiyy al-rijl wa-l-rikāb*),[1708] for they are not intended [for use]

1703 "*Aḥmāl*," see Glossary.

1704 The "*firāsh*" is anything that is spread out, such as a carpet or bedding.

1705 "*Ḥaḍar*:" cities and towns (http://www.baheth.info/all.jsp?term=حضر).

1706 Sing. *qarqal*, which was a brigandine made of iron plates that are attached or revited together. This was a common type of armour used in the Mamluk era, and its best fit was to be neither tight nor loose. Its sleeves had to be made of small units so as to allow easy movement. In a non-military context, the "*qarqal*" was sometimes used to refer to a kind of shirt worn by women, or a sleeveless shirt. (A. Yasin, *Asliḥa*, 127–128, *Ṣubḥ*, Vol. 2, 136 and L. Mayer, *Costume*, 40).

1707 Sing. *ṭabar*.

1708 Can be literally translated as "of the foot and stirrups." He is referring to a type of crossbow that had a foot strap which is a stirrup-like u-shaped metal piece fixed to its end to assist the archer when pulling the bowstring to load the bow. For excellent pictures and description see Byam, Michele, Eyewitness – Arms and Armor, DK Publishing, New York 2004, 18–21.

in Egypt, except in the coastal cities, like Alexandria and others, where they are common. Annually, the [arms and armour] manufactured in the Treasury of Arms (*khizānat al-silāḥ*) are carried to the *silāḥkhānāh*.[1709] They are carried on the heads of porters in a celebrative procession[1710] to the Citadel, on a day that [therefore,] becomes memorable. A large number of resident craftsmen [work] in the *silāḥkhānāh* to mend the gear and renew that which is used.[1711] Each of these craftsmen is called "*al-zardakāsh*,"[1712] which is a Persian[1713] word that seems to mean "the armour-maker." The *silāḥkhānāh* also has other slave-boys and caretakers (*farrāshīn*) to attend to the cloth and its supply.

The Fifth: *Al-Rikābkhānāh*, which means the House of Stirrups (*bayt al-rikāb*)

It contains the gear for [riding] horses, such as: saddles; bridles; caparisons (*kanābīsh*);[1714] the capes of rides;[1715] capes of stables;[1716] housings (*ajlāl*);[1717] sacks (*makhālī*)[1718] and other kinds [of items] that would take too long to describe. It includes saddles covered with gold and silver, either plated or plain; caparisons made of gold brocade and floriated, or not, with feathers; capes

1709 Also, the armour acquired by this treasury.

1710 "*Yuzaff*," see Glossary: "*zaffa*".

1711 "*Al-Musta'malāt*".

1712 The person responsible for making, mending and maintaining arms. (S. Ashour, *'Aṣr*, 445, and M. Dahman, *Mu'jam*, 86).

1713 "*'Ajamiyya*," see Glossary: "*'ajam*".

1714 Sing. *kunbūsh* (sometimes distorted to *kunfūsh*, pl. *kanāfīsh*). Al-Qalqashandī defines the *kunbūsh* as the cover of the back and croup of the horse, which is brocaded with gold or silver inlaid with gold (*makhāyish*), or made of inscribed wool. He adds that it is used for the rides of the judges and religious scholars. The term is defined by others as the pack (*bardha'a* or *barda'a*) placed beneath the horse's saddle. It also has other meanings including: a cover for the sword, and in Spain and North Africa: a small cotton bonnet for children, the baby's bib, and the face veil used to cover the chin and the nostrils for protection against cold and dampness of the morning air. (*Ṣubḥ*, Vol. 2, 129; al-Baqli, *Ta'rīf*, 289; S. Ashour, *'Aṣr*, 467, and M. Dahman, *Mu'jam*, 131).

1715 *'Ibiy al-marākīb* (*'ibiy*, sing. *'abā'a*: mantle, cape or robe, *al-marākīb*, sing. *al-markūb*: the ride). Al-Qalqashandī explains that the *'abā'a* (cape) was used to in place of the *kunbūsh* (caparison). (*Ṣubḥ*, Vol. 2, 129).

1716 *Al-'Ibiy al-iṣṭabliyyāt* (*'ibiy* are capes and*al-iṣṭabliyyāt* means "those belonging to the stables").

1717 Also *jilāl* (sing. *jull* or *jall*), which is what the animal is dressed in. It was a cloth cover made of wool or bristle, which was used for horses in the Mamluk era. The term is also defined as "saddle cloth." (Vernon J. Parry, *War, Technology and Society in the Middle East*, ed. Malcolm E. Yapp (London, 1975), 155, G. Qaddumi, *Gifts*, 86 and http://baheth.info/all.jsp?term=أجلال).

1718 Sing. *mikhlāt*. (http://www.baheth.info/all.jsp?term=مخلاة).

made of silk and the wool of *al-sahak*,[1719] as well as other valuable gear and amazing[1720] riding equipment that can only be afforded by great kings. It has a superintendent, called "*mihtār al-rikābkhānāh*". (Superintendent of the House of Stirrups), responsible for its contents (*ḥawāṣil*), who had subordinate men that aided him.

The Sixth: *Al-Ḥawā'ijkhānāh*, which means the House of [Assorted] Needs (*bayt al-ḥawā'ij*)

This warehouse is not like the previous ones, for it does not comprise a particular [kind of] content. However, it has a unit (*jiha*),[1721] under the control of the vizier, from which the assigned meat [portions] are distributed to the sultan's kitchen and houses,[1722] as well as the allowances (*rawātib*) of the amirs;the Sultanic Mamluks, the rest of the soldiers, the Men of the Turban (*muta'ammimīn*),[1723] and others who are entitled to allowances (*arbāb al-rawātib*), whose names fill the registers.[1724] The food spices for the sultan's kitchen and houses;[1725] and

1719 *Al-Sahak* has several meanings, including: the awful odour, such as that of rancidity or of fish, the rust of iron, and the slow running movement of an animal or the fast one of a horse. The editor of Subḥ comments that he found no animal with the name "*al-sahak*," and concludes that it might be a writing error of a word that should have been "*al-samand*," which is the grey horse. However, this is not a convincing explanation, since as mentioned above, it is an animal that produced a type of wool, or may be the name of a certain kind of wool. It is possible that this was a kind of animal that gave off a foul smell; a skunk. (See (*Ṣubḥ*, Vol. 4, 12, http://www.baheth.info/all.jsp?term=سهك and http://www.baheth.info/all.jsp?term=سمند).

1720 "That amaze the minds and surprise the eyes."

1721 *Jiha* (pl. *jihāt*) is direction or district. One of the meanings of the term is the resource units or properties that supplied the state payments in money and kind, such as the allowances (*rawātib*) or the salaries (*jāmakiyyāt*). These include, for example, a bureau or one of its sub-units, such as a branch or an administrative directorate; service units, such as the bakeries and the granaries; or lands and properties that generate revenue. The term is also used to refer to imposts; or the lands, districts or properties that are subject to taxes, or yield revenue for general state expenditures. In his account on the Supervision of Acquisitions (*naẓar al-ḥāṣilāt*), also Supervision of Imposts (*naẓar al-jihāt*), al-Qalqashanī explains that this office managed the money of vizierate's imposts, by collecting, spending or paying to the Public Treasury. (See *Ṣubḥ*, Vol. 3, 464, and al-Nuwayrī, *Nihāya*, Vol. 29, 465 & Vol. 30, 22).

1722 *Al-Dūr al-sulṭāniyya*.

1723 *Al-muta'ammimīn* or *ahl al-'imāma*, which means "those wearing turbans" or "people of the turbans," "who were the religious scholars, scientists, men of literature and writers, also referred to as 'the Men of the Pen'" in the Mamluk society. "These men worked in administrative, religious and educational jobs." The terms used to refer to these men are a little misleading for they seem to suggest that they were the only ones who wore turbans. In fact, Egyptian men of all levels wore some sort of head cover, but the *muta'ammimīn* wore large turbans that increased in size according to their statuses. Some of them exaggerated the sizes of their turbans that we find this mentioned in the sources. The *muta'ammimīn* was an important social stratum, who came next only to the ruling mamluk class. (H. al-Battawi, *'Imāma*, 3–4).

1724 *Al-Dafātir* (sing. *al-daftar*).

1725 *Al-Dūr al-sulṭāniyya*.

for the amirs who are assigned allowances of spices,[1726] and others; as well as oil for lighting, grains and other various types [of needs], are also [supplied by this house]. The *ḥawā'ijkhānāh* has managers (*mubāshirīn*) who are especially assigned to it and keep accurate records of the names of those deserving of rations[1727] and the sizes of portions they should be given. It is one of the largest [administrative] bodies for the distribution [of provisions][1728] to the extent that the cost of meat [it provides] daily mounts up to 30,000 dirhams or more, not to mention the cost of the rest of the items.

The Seventh: The Kitchen (*al-maṭbakh*)

It is [the house] where the assigned[1729] food for the sultan's lunch and supper is cooked, as well as other unexpected [meals] by day or night and the banquets held at the Great Iwan of the House of Justice (Dār al-ʿAdl)[1730] on procession days. It is supplied with [specific], known and assigned portions of meat, spices and all other kinds [of needs] from the House of Assorted Needs (*ḥawā'ijkhānāh*), mentioned above. The Kitchen consumes enormous quantities of meat, chicken, geese and other magnificent foods daily. It has an amir, called "*ustādār al-ṣuḥba*" (Master of the Kitchen and Banquets),[1731] who controls it and is aided by another called the "*mushrif*" (Overseer). It also has a head chef, who is recognizably skilled, called the "*asbāslār.*"[1732]

The Eighth: *Al-Ṭablakhānāh*, which is the House of Drums (*bayt al-ṭabl*)

It includes the drums, horns, and other accompanying [musical] instruments. An Amir of Ten,[1733] known as the "Amir of the Flag" (*amīr 'alam*),[1734] controls [the contents of this house]. He commands [the routine of] playing these instruments

1726 "*Tawābil murattaba*": assigned spices.

1727 *Arbāb al-mustaḥaqqāt.*

1728 "*Jihāt al-ṣarf*": resource units, or bodies, of expenditure.

1729 *Rātib.*

1730 See Glossary.

1731 See later.

1732 This term is a distortion of the Persian *isfihsalār* (or *asfahsilār*, see Glossary: "*isfihsalār*"). Commoners used the term *aspāslār* or *asbāslār* to call the aids or assistants (*a'wān*) who stood at the sultan's gate. It appears that this title was especially used by the *ṭablakhānāh* amirs, but it was abandoned by al-Qalqashandī's time, either because the amirs disapproved of it being used for the aids, or because its original meaning was forgotten or misunderstood. (*Ṣubḥ*, Vol. 6, 7–8).

1733 See Glossary.

1734 The *amīr 'alam* (Amir of the Flag) was normally an amir of ten who was responsible for the sultanic flags, banners, and standards, as well as for supervising the *ṭablakhānāh*. He had to be knowledgeable of the types of flags required for each kind of royal procession. (S. Ashour, *'Aṣr*, 415 and al-Baqli, *Ta'rīf*, 49).

nightly and handles their affairs on travels. The house has a superintendent, called "*mihtār al-ṭablakhānāh*" (Superintendent of the House of Drums), who is responsible for its contents. He is aided by the [musicians] he supervises, namely, the drummer (*dabandār*), who beats the drums; the horn player (*munaffir*), who plays the horns; the cymbals player (*kūsiy*), who bangs the copper cymbals against each other, as well as other such craftsmen.[1735]

1735 "*Ṣunnā'*," which is a general term that applies to all craftsmen and professionals, and in this context refers to musicians.

The Third Purpose
On the dignitaries of the kingdom and the holders of posts (*arbāb al-manāṣib*) on whom the kingdom's order and the establishment of sovereignty depend

Four Categories – The First Category

Men of the Sword, discussed from two aspects[1736]

The First Aspect: A [description] of their levels, in general, which are of two kinds

THE FIRST KIND: THE AMIRS, WHO ARE OF FOUR RANKS

The First Rank:
The Amirs of Hundreds, Commanders of Thousands (*umarā' al-mi'īn, muqaddamū al-ulūf*)[1737]

Each of these amirs has [a force of] one-hundred horsemen. The author of *Masālik al-Abṣār* said: Each of them may have an additional ten or twenty [horsemen to the one-hundred].[1738] Each amir also has the command over one-thousand horsemen of lower ranking amirs. Even though the amirs' ranks are comparable, this rank is the highest level and the high holders of offices and viceroys are chosen from it. The established [decreed administrative division] of the kingdom, according to the cadastral surveyof Muḥammad b. Qalāwūn (*al-rawk al-Nāṣirī*),[1739] was that twenty-four Commanders [of Thousands] were [employed] in Egypt. This continued to be the case until the end of the reign of Sultan al-Ashraf Sha'bān b.

1736 For a discussion of the Mamluk army and its organization, see T. Abdelhamid, *Jaysh*.

1737 See Glossary.

1738 See al-ʿUmarī, *Masālik*(2010), Vol. 3, 287.

1739 *Al-Rawk* is the Egyptian term used for the cadastral survey of the agricultural land that determined the land taxes (*kharāj*). In the early Islamic eras, these taxes were delivered to the Public Treasury (*bayt al-māl*) of the caliphate. The expected *kharāj* of Egypt fluctuated depending on the agricultural production and inhabitation of the villages, which is why the cadastral survey was conducted several times, two of which during the Mamluk era. This survey, which sometimes entailed changes in the geographical administrative divisions, also served to indicate the values of lands and subsequently, the distribution of land grants. The Fatimids had followed the Abbasid custom of occasional distribution of land grants, but the Ayyubids established an *iqṭā'*system, which divided the agricultural lands among the sultan, the amirs and the soldiers, using a particular ratio. This *iqṭā'*system was adopted by the Mamluks, who had their own divisions as well. The first *rawk* in the Mamluk era was conducted during the reign of Sultan Ḥusām al-Dīn Lājīn (r. 695 AH/1296 AD to 697 AH/1298 AD), hence called "*al-rawk al-Ḥusāmī*," and was probably done because the amirs had overtaken too many of the *iqṭā'āt*, leaving the soldiers with almost none. The second, "*al-rawk al-Nāṣirī*," was conducted during the reign of Sultan al-Nāṣir Muḥammad in 715 AH/1315 AD. (Al-Baqli, *Ta'rīf*, 165 and S. Ashour, *'Aṣr*, 443).

Ḥusayn.[1740] When the Separate Bureau (*al-dīwān al-mufrad*)[1741] was introduced for [serving] the private domain (*khāṣṣ*) of the sultan in the reign of al-Ẓāhir [Barqūq] and [the salaries and allowances of] a large number of the sultanic and employed (*mustakhdamīn*) mamluks[1742] were especially assigned to it, the number of the commanders decreased from what it used to be, and came to range from eighteen to twenty, including the viceroys of Alexandria and Upper and Lower Egypt.

The Second Rank:
Amirs entitled to drum bands (*umarā' al-ṭablakhānāh*)[1743]

Mostly, each of them has [a force of] forty horsemen. The author of *Masālik al-Abṣār* said: Some of them had bigger numbers of up to seventy horsemen,[1744] while he mentioned in *al-Ta'rīf*, in the latest correspondences,[1745] that each of them had eighty horsemen.[1746] He said in *Masālik al-Abṣār*: The *ṭablakhānāh* rank is not given to those who have [forces] of less than forty [horsemen].[1747] The number of the amirs of this rank is not controlled for it varies by increase or decrease, because whenever the *ṭablakhānāh* rank is divided, it results intwo amirial ranks of twenties or four of tens; or if groups of tens or the like were combined, they result in a *ṭablakhānāh* rank.[1748] The second rank of position holders, the Supervisors of

1740 Bahri Mamluk sultan who ruled from 764 AH/1363 AD to 778 AH/1376 AD.

1741 The "Separate Bureau" or the "Special Bureau" (*al-diwān al-mufrad)* was the term used to refer to a bureau that was newly introduced and had a specific assigned function. In the Fatimid era, Caliph al-Ḥākim established *al-diwān al-mufrad* in 400 AH/1009 AD, to collect the money confiscated from those whom the caliph was displeased with or those who ended up being killed. This was possibly the bureau called "the Bureau of Reclaims" (*dīwān al-murtaja'*), which was one of the importantbureausby the late Fatimid era. In the Mamluk era, *al-dīwān al-mufrad* was introduced by Sultan Barqūq and it was the bureau which managed the *iqṭā'* he used to have as an amir. Then more agricultural lands were allocated to the bureau, as well as rented properties in Egypt and Syria. The revenues and the produce collected by this bureau were used for the salaries (*jāmakiyyāt*), allowances (*rawātib*), fodder and clothing of the Sultanic Mamluks, paying the mamluks of Syria and providing the needs and expenditures of the sultanic warehouses. (*Ṣubḥ*, Vol. 3, 457; A. Sayyid, *Tafsīr*, 348 & 538; S. Ashour, *'Aṣr*, 439; T. Abdeldhamid, *Jaysh*, 91–92, and M. Dahman, *Mu'jam*, 79).

1742 These were the mamluks who were not bought by the sultan, but were mamluks of previous sultans or amirs, who have joined his service. (T. Abdelhamid, *Jaysh*, 49–50 and see Glossary: "*mustakhdamīn*").

1743 These were the amirs entitled to have a musical band during their processions; the amirs of forty to eighty horsemen. Needless to say, the higher rank of the Commanders of Thousands, as well as the sultan, had larger bands that announced their arrival and departure, located by the doors of their residences and on procession, travel and in wars. (T. Abdelhamid, *Jaysh*, 22–23 and see Glossary).

1744 See al-'Umarī, *Masālik* (2010), Vol. 3, 287.

1745 Sing. *mukātaba*, which, in this context, means "correspondence." *Al-Ta'rīf* is a book on the terminology, composition and protocol of writing correspondences.

1746 See al-'Umarī, *Ta'rīf*, 74.

1747 See al-'Umarī, *Masālik* (2010), Vol. 3, 287.

1748 The editor of Subḥ notes that text which says "and it was considered a *ṭablakhānāh*" probably has an extra "*wāw*" or "and" (*Ṣubḥ*, Vol. 4, 15, fn. 1).

Lands and Embankments (*kushshāf*)[1749] of the provincial divisions (*a'māl*), and the high governors (*wulāt*) are [chosen] from the amirs of the *ṭablakhānāh.*

The Third Rank:
Amirs of Tens (umarā' al-'asharāt)[1750]

Each of these amirs has [a force of] ten horsemen. The author of *Masālik al-Abṣār* said: Some of them may have had forces of twenty horsemen, but were still only considered amirs of tens.[1751]The number of amirs of this rank, too, is not controlled, for it increases and decreases like the amirs of the *ṭablakhānāh* mentioned above. The less important governors and similar position holders are [chosen] from this rank.

The Fourth Rank:
Amirs of Fives (*umarā' al-khamsāt*)[1752]

These are very few, especially in Egypt. The rank is mostly assigned to the sons of deceased amirs who are included, out of regard for their late fathers. In fact, they are like high-ranking soldiers.

THE SECOND KIND: THE SOLDIERS (*AJNĀD*), WHO ARE OF TWO RANKS[1753]

The First Rank
The Sultanic Mamluks (*al-mamālīk al-sulṭāniyya*)

These are the soldiers who are closest to the sultan, and are of greatest status and highest positions. They are given the most bountiful *iqṭā'āt* and the amirs of

1749 Sing. *kāshif*, who was a man of the sword responsible for supervising the conditions of the lands or the embankments, therefore sometimes referred to as *kāshif al-turāb* (Supervisor of Lands) or *kāshif al-jusūr* (Supervisor of Embankments). The *jusūr*, which the *kushshāf* supervised,were embankments of earth established on the river or canal banks to prevent the overflow of water in the flood season and reserve the water to be used for irrigation. Al-Qalqashandī lists two kinds of embankments; sultanic and civil. The sultanic embankments were the main ones used collectively for several villages, and equipped, financed and supervised by the sultanic bureau, while the civil embankments were individual ones in the villages, which were the responsibility of the *iqṭā'* owners, and were subject to taxes. Al-Qalqashandī gives further explanation on the number of *kushshāf* in Egypt and where they were appointed. (Al-Baqli, *Ta'rīf*, 283, M. al-Shistawi, *Mutanazzahāt*, 27 fn. 1, and *Ṣubḥ*, Vol. 4, 448–450).

1750 See Glossary.

1751 See al-'Umarī, *Masālik* (2010), Vol. 3, 287.

1752 See Glossary.

1753 The regular or the rank-and-file army of the Mamluks comprised several factions of soldiers, two of which were listed by al-Qalqashandī, namely, the sultanic mamluks and the soldiers of the *ḥalaqa*. The sultanic mamluks were either those bought by or for the sultan, housed at the sultanic barracks (*ṭibāq*) and educated, raised and trained under his supervision, to be eventually set free when their training is complete and are ready to enter active service; or the employed mamluks (*mustakhdamīn*) who were not bought by the sultan, but were mamluks of previous sultans or amirs, who have joined his service. The salaries and allowances of the sultanic mamluks were paid from the Separate Bureau (*dīwān al-mufrad*). The soldiers of the *ḥalaqa* were horsemen entitled to *īqṭā'āt* that were registered in the Army Bureau (*dīwān al-jaysh*). (See T. Abdelhamid, *Jaysh*, 44–76,al-Baqli, *Ta'rīf*, 15–16 and see Glossary: "*ajnād*").

different ranks are [chosen] from amongst them. Their number, whether large or small, is according to the sultan's preference. They were of numerous numbers and abundant supply during the days of both sultans al-Malik al-Nāṣir Muḥammad b. Qalāwūn and al-Malik al-Ẓāhir Barqūq, due to their long reigns and their care for bringing and buying mamluks.

The Second Rank

Soldiers of the *ḥalaqa* (*ajnād al-ḥalaqa*)[1754]

These are numerous and may include those not in the capacity of soldiers, such as the Men of the Turban (*muta'ammimīn*) and others, by means of relegating *iqṭā'āt* to them. It was customary for the Army Bureau (*dīwān al-jaysh*) to not count the total number of soldiers so as not to make it known. The author of *Masālik al-Abṣār* said: A commander from amongst them is assigned to every forty individual [soldiers]. He only has authority over them when soldiers set out for war, when he is the one who decides and manages their marching placement at their assigned positions [in army formations].[1755]

There is a third faction of soldiers called *al-Baḥariyya*,[1756] who spend the nights in the Citadel and around the sultan's tents (*dahālīz*)[1757]during his travels like guards. The first to so name and employ them was Sultan al-Malik al-Ṣāliḥ Najm al-Dīn Ayyūb b. al-Kāmil Muḥammad b. al-ʿAdil Abū Bakr b. Ayyūb.

1754 The *ḥalaqa* is the "ring," and *ajnād al-ḥalaqa* (soldiers of the ring) is a term generally used in the Mamluk era to denote a category of warrior horsemen of the army who were entitled to receive revenues from the *iqṭā'āt* "in return for their military service." These lands and their revenues were specifically documented in the Army Bureau, as explained by al-Qalqashandī. The original definition of the *ḥalaqa* is not very clear in the sources, for it may have been used to refer to the ring of soldiers who guarded the sultan, the Turkish strategy of combat in forming a ring around the enemy forces, the ring formed around the preys during the sultanic hunting expiditions, among other meanings. The conditions of the *ḥalaqa* and its soldiers changed throughout Mamluk history and the term should be examined in the context of the era of each historian. (See T. Abdelhamid, *Jaysh*, 56–64).

1755 "*Kān mawqifuhum ma'hu wa tartībuhum fī mawqifihim ilayhi.*" (Al-ʿUmarī, *Masālik* (2010), Vol. 3, 288 and *Ṣubḥ*, Vol. 4, 16).

1756 *Al-Ajnād al-baḥariyya* were a group of soldiers who were apparently only responsible for the night guard of "the citadels in major cities," as well as "the sultan's tent on travel." Originally, this group was formed under Sultan Qalāwūn, and included the sons of the Bahri mamluks of Sultan al-Ṣāliḥ Najm al-Dīn. Qalāwūn allocated allowances for them and assigned them to "guarding the Citadel's gate." "He called them al-Baḥariyya and they became one of the categories of soldiers." (T. Abdelhamid, *Jaysh*, 65–66).

1757 Sing. *dihlīz*, which is the sultan's royal tent. Al-Baqli explains that this term particularly applied to the tent that accompanied the sultan in times of war, which was different from others that were pitched for him on hunting or leisure expeditions. The *dihlīz* was different in that it was pitched independently, with no smaller tents next to it, like the ones usually set up to prepare the sultan's needs at the times of peace. According to M. Dahman, the term *dihlīz* was a generic one used for the royal tent that accompanied the sultan at times of war and on hunting and leisure expeditions. The term also has other meanings; "corridor" or "vestibule," as explained earlier. (Al-Baqli, *Ta'rīf*, 138 and M. Dahman, *Mu'jam*, 77).

The Second Aspect: On the holders of offices among the Men of the Sword mentioned above: Two Kinds

THE FIRST KIND

Those in the vicinity of the sultan's presence (*ḥaḍra*): Twenty-five Offices

The First: The Viceroyship (*al-niyāba*)

The holder of this position is called "*al-nā'ib al-kāfil*" (the Plenipotentiary Viceroy) and "*kāfil al-mamālik al-islāmiyya*" (the Plenipotentiary of the Islamic Kingdoms). The author of *al-Ta'rīf* said:[1758] He rules over what the sultan rules over, and puts his mark[1759] on the Diplomas of Investiture (*taqālīd*),[1760] Signed Decrees (*tawāqī'*),[1761] Decrees of Grants (*manāshīr*),[1762] and other [documents] of this kind that the sultan marks. The rest of the viceroys cannot mark except what relates to their own viceroyships. He added: This is clearly an exceptional rank. In *Masālik al-Abṣār*, he said: All the viceroys of the kingdom write to him about the same [issues] they correspond with the sultan on, and they review these [issues] with him like they review [them] with the sultan. He employed soldiers[1763] without having to consult[1764] the sultan, appointed the holders of grandoffices, such as the vizier and the confidential scribe (*kātib al-sirr*), and

1758 Al-'Umarī, *Ta'rīf*, 94.

1759 "*Yu'allim*:" puts his *'alāma*, see Glossary.

1760 Sing. *taqlīd*, which was the decree that the sultan signed to appoint someone in a high position, such as the viceroys and the judges. (S. Ashour, *'Aṣr*, 424 and M. Dahman, *Mu'jam*, 46–47).

1761 Sing. *tawqī'*, (see Glossary). In the Ayyubid era, the *tawāqī'* were the decrees of assigning the *iqṭā'āt*. In the Mamluk era, they were certain kind of official documents of investiture, like appointing governors and the like. (*Ṣubḥ*, Vol. 11, 114–115 and Vol. 13, 144).

1762 Sing. *manshūr*, which in the Mamluk era was a sultanic decree to allocate *iqṭā'āt*. There were four kinds of *manāshīr*, which differed in their types or cuts of paper according to the grade of the grant's recepient. Before the Mamluk era, the *manāshīr* were decrees or correspondences that may not have required stamps, unlike other official decrees, such as those of appointment of the governors (*wulāt*). (*Ṣubḥ*, Vol. 13, 157–158 and al-Baqli, *Ta'rīf*, 332).

1763 "*Yastakhdim al-jund.*"

1764 "*Mushāwara*," which means "consultation." It should be noted that the Mamluk sultans had a system of consultation through what was known as "*majlis al-mashūra*" (the Consultation Council). This council included the high-ranking amirs and grand state officials, whom the sultans consulted before taking any major decisions. The sultan headed this council and its members were the *atābek* of soldiers (*atābik al-'askar*), the Abbasid caliph, the vizier, the judges of the Four Sunni Schools, and the amirs of hundreds, who were twenty-four in number. If the sultan was a minor, his guardian (regent) or the Viceroy of the Sultanate (*nā'ib al-salṭana*) headed the council instead. Customarily, the sultan did not address the council himself so as to not to be contradicted in opinion or argued with, out of respect. *Al-Mushīr* (the Consultant), normally a high-ranking amir whose office was called "*al-ishāra*" (the Consultation), spoke on the sultan's behalf. The Consultation Council discussed several matters, such as wars and peace treaties, the appointments of viceroys and other grand offices. The sultan was, however, not obliged to consult this council for he was an absolute ruler who had the right to take independent decisions on all matters. (S. Ashour, *'Aṣr*, 364 & 412 and *Ṣubḥ*, Vol. 11, 153–156).

his appointees for such offices were rarely rejected [by the sultan]. He is a "reduced" sultan, or rather, a second sultan. It is customary for him to ride on procession days accompanied by the soldiers (*'askar*), while everyone marched in his service (*khidma*). When he arrives to the presence (*ḥaḍra*) of the sultan, he stands in the corner of the iwan. When the service [audience] (*khidma*) is over, he leaves with the amirs for the House of Viceroyship (Dār al-Niyāba) at the Citadel, where he sits for public audience. The holders of offices attend this audience and the *ḥujjāb*[1765] *stand in front of the viceroy. The petitions (qiṣaṣ)* are read to him during this audience then he offers a banquet for the amirs, as the sultan does, so they eat and leave. If the viceroyship [position] existed as such, the sultan did not sit for reading the petitions and hearing the complaints in person. He[1766] ordered what he saw fit concerning this, such as writing an *iqṭā'* allocation decree (*mithāl*)[1767] or the like, but he did not personally and solely dictate what was to be written by the Sultanic Court;[1768] he rather wrote his recommendation and noted so,[1769] then [the decrees] were signed with the Honourable Mark (*al-'alāma al-sharīfa*)[1770] afterwards.

As for the Army Bureau (*dīwān al-jaysh*),[1771] it only holds its audience (*khidma*) at his [place] and [its officials] only meet with him. They were not

1765 Sing. *ḥājib* (see Glossary).

1766 That is, the Viceroy, which is clearly understood from al-ʿUmarī's account and suits the rest of al-Qalqashandī's. (See *Masālik* (2010), Vol. 3, 307).

1767 A *mithāl* (pl. *mithālāt*) was a brief, preliminary decree issued from the Army Bureau to "grant, reallocate, return, or increase" an *iqṭā'*. It was signed by the sultan then the *ḥājib* delivered it to the mamluk granted the *iqṭā'*, who kissed the floor in gratitude. The *mithāl* was then returned to the Army Bureau to be kept there. The term also sometimes applied to written petitions (*qiṣaṣ*). (S. Ashour, *'Aṣr*, 361–362 & 468, M. Dahman, *Mu'jam*, 135 and *Ṣubḥ*, Vol. 13, 153).

1768 "*Al-Abwāb al-sulṭāniyya*" (also, "*al-abwāb al-sharīfa*"), which means the sultanic gates or doors, implying the royal court.

1769 "*Yaktub bi-ishāratihi wa-yunabbih 'alayhā.*" The "*ishāra*" was a brief recommendation or advice that the plenipotentiary viceroy, the vizier, or men of similar positions wrote on official documents or grievances. These recommendations were then eloquently expanded, according to the rules of the Chancery Bureau, by the secretariat scribes (*kuttāb al-darj*). Normally, a formula accompanied this *ishāra* to denote its origin. In case of the plenipotentiary viceroy, this formula was "by the high recommendation" (*bi-l-ishāra al-'āliya*). This formula is probably what al-Qalqashandī means by "noting to" the recommendation, since a brief look at the document would indicate who ordered its writing out. Al-ʿUmarī's account explains that the viceroy noted in what he wrote that this was his "*ishāra*" on the document. (*Ṣubḥ*, Vol. 1, 138, Vol. 7, 233, & Vol. 13, 161–162 and al-ʿUmarī, *Masālik* (2010), Vol. 3, 307).

1770 That is, the sultan's *'alāma*, which al-Qalqashandī tells us in his time, whether in sultanic or amirial documents, occupied a particular section at the top of the document called "*bayt al-'alāma*" (the house of the mark). The sultan's mark was either his name, his name and his father's or brother's, or a certain formula like: "Allah is my Hope," "Allah is sufficient for me," "Kingdom is Allah's," or the like, in ornamental calligraphic form. (*Ṣubḥ*, Vol. 6, 196 & 314, Vol. 13, 161–162, and Vol. 14, 103).

1771 Al-ʿUmarī notes that when this viceroyship was in place, the Bureau of *iqṭā'* was called "the Army Bureau." (*Masālik* (2010), Vol. 3, 454).

entitled to meet with the sultan for any matter. The viceroy either personally reported the problematic issues that had to be communicated to the sultan, or sent him a messenger. This is the end of the account of the author of *al-Masālik*.[1772]

However, this viceroy was sometimes appointed and at other times [the position] was suspended in the kingdom. This was the case during the reign of al-Nāṣir Muḥammad b. Qalāwūn and is true for our times as well, when this post is intermittent.[1773] If a viceroy is appointed, he has the authority to reallocate certain *iqṭā'āt*,[1774] but not others; the Manager of the Army Bureau (*ṣāḥib dīwān al-jaysh*) is the one who keeps to his constant company and the Supervisor of the Army (*nāẓir al-jaysh*)[1775] keeps to the sultan's.

The author of *al-Ta'rīf* said: As for the Viceroy in Absence (*nā'ib al-ghayba*), he is left [to rule][1776] when both the sultan and the plenipotentiary viceroy are absent. He is only to suppress revolutions and [resolve grievances to] deliver rights.[1777] The protocol of writing to him is the same as that applied with comparable amirs.[1778]

The Second: The Office of the Atabek (*al-atābikiyya*)

The holder of this position is referred to as "*atābik al-'asākir*" (the Atabek of Soldiers). Sultan 'Imād al-Dīn said in his *Tārīkh*: The original term is *aṭābik*, which means "the boy amir." The first to hold this title was Niẓām al-Dawla, Vizier of the Saljuq Malikshāh b. Alp Arslān,[1779] when Malikshāh authorized him to manage the kingdom in the year 465 AH/1072 AD, thereby giving him titles, including this one. It was also said that "*aṭābik*" means "the father amir," denoting "the father of amirs," who is the highest commander amir after the plenipotentiary viceroy. He does not have an office that entails ruling, ordering or prohibiting, for this office's sole purpose is [honourary], to elevate [its holder's] position and raise his status.

1772 In this instance, al-Qalqashandī specifically remarks that what he copies from *Masālik al-Abṣār* ends here. He does not always note the ends of the accounts he cites. See al-'Umarī's full account in *Masālik* (2010), Vol. 3, 306–307 and his account in *Ta'rīf*, 94–95.

1773 Al-'Umarī (d. 749 AH/1348 AD) remarks that the viceroyship at the capital (*ḥaḍra*) continued to deteriorate until it ceased to exit at his time. (*Masālik* (2010), Vol. 3, 307).

1774 *Ikhrāj al-iqṭā'āt*, which means confiscating an *iqṭā'* from a person to allocate it to another.

1775 See below.

1776 The editor of Subḥ notes that the intended meaning is: He is left to rule, independently or according to what he sees fit.(*Ṣubḥ*, Vol. 4, 17 fn. 1).

1777 "*Khalāṣ al-ḥuqūq*" (delivering rights), which can also mean delivering justice. This could also refer to executing the verdict on a grievance, such as the cases when the sultan sends his orders of execution to his provincial viceroys. (see *Ṣubḥ*, Vol. 7, 195–196).

1778 See al-'Umarī, *Ta'rīf*, 94–95.

1779 Niẓām al-Mulk, the Persian vizier of the Great Saljuk Sultan Malikshāh (r. 465 AH/1072 AD – 485 AH/1092 AD). (See Glossary: "Saljuqs").

The Third: The Office of the The Head of Watch (*ra's nawba*)

This position entails judging[1780] and punishment of[1781] the Sultanic Mamluks. The holders of this position are usually four amirs: one commander of one-thousand (*muqaddam alf*) and three *ṭablakhānāh* [amirs].

The Fourth: Office of the Amir of Council (*imrat majlis*)

The holder of this position . . .[1782] and he supervises the physicians, the ophthalmologists[1783] and their likes. Only one man is assigned to this position.[1784]

The Fifth: Office of the the Amir of Arms (*imrat silāḥ*)

This position originally entails the responsibility of holding the sultan's arms in large assemblies. The holder of this position is the commander of the *silāḥdariyya* (Bearers of Arms) [faction] of the Sultanic Mamluks and the supervisor of the sultanic arsenal (House of Arms: *silāḥkhānāh*), and what is requisitioned (*yusta'mal*) for it and presented to it. He can only be one of the commander amirs.[1785]

The Sixth: Office of the Amir of the Sultanic Stables (*imra ākhūriyya*)[1786]

This position entails the supervision of the sultanic stable and horses. The holder of this office, who handles its general supervision, is customarily a commander of one-thousand and is the one who resides in the sultanic stable.[1787]He heads three *ṭablakhānāh* amirs, in addition to innumerable amirs of tens and soldiers.

The Seventh: Office of the Bearer of the Inkwell [or Chancellor] (*al-dawādāriyya*)[1788]

The author of *Masālik al-Abṣār* said: This office entails delivering the sultan's messages, reporting all general issues, presenting petitions (*qiṣaṣ*) to the sultan, consulting[1789] him on who comes to the royal court,[1790] and presenting the mail,

1780 "*Al-Ḥukm 'alā*," which may also mean "controlling."

1781 "*Al-Akhdh 'alā aydīhim*," which may also mean "to restrain them."

1782 The editor of Subḥ notes that a phrase is missing from the original manuscript, and concludes that it might be that this position entailed managing the sultan's council, that is his court audience. (*Ṣubḥ*, Vol. 4, 18 fn. 1).

1783 "*Al-Kaḥḥālīn*" (sing. *al-kaḥḥāl*), which means the eye doctor or the ophthalmologist. (M. Dahman, *Mu'jam*, 129).

1784 He was also responsible for managing the sultan's or amir's council or court audience (*majlis*), concerning matters of arrangement and the like. (Al-Baqli, *Ta'rīf*, 50).

1785 Al-'Umarī says that he also supervises what is released from the Treasury of Arms and that the holder of this position can only be an Amir of Hundreds. (*Masālik* (2010), Vol. 3, 308).

1786 The holder of this position is called *amīr ākhūr*. It is a title similar to "Master of the Horse" in England and the "Grand Écuyer" ("Grand Squire") of France.

1787 *Iṣṭabl al-khāṣṣ*. See fn. 814.

1788 The Grand Secretary or the Chancellor, who is termed *"al-dawādār*."

1789 "*mushāwara*," see Glossary.

1790 *Al-Bāb al-sharīf* (The Honourable Gate), which is a term that refers to the sultan's court or audience.

along with the personal guard (*amīr jāndār*) and the confidential scribe (*kātib al-sirr*).[1791] He is responsible for securing the sultan's signature[1792] on all decrees of grants (*manāshīr*), signed decrees (*tawāqīʿ*), and correspondences (*kutub*). And if the sultan ordered him [to see to the] writing of a decree (*marsūm*), he carried his message (*risāla*), and so it was designated in the written [text].[1793] This will be explained later in the section on the letter-writing protocols, according to the rules of the Chancery Bureau.[1794]

Several amirs and soldiers are in this office. During the days of al-Nāṣir Muḥammad and later [reigns], no holder of this position was a commander of one-thousand amir. Eventually, the highest ranking of the [holders of this office] became a commander of one-thousand, with a *ṭablakhānāh* amir for his deputy. The first commander of one-thousand amir to be appointed in the office of bearing the inkwell (*dawādāriyya*) was Ṭughaytamur al-Najmī[1795] during the reign of al-Nāṣir Ḥasan.[1796] Later, the holders of this position were mostly commanders of thousands, or were sometimes *ṭablakhānāh* amirs.

1791 See Glossary.

1792 "*al-khaṭṭ*." (See M. Dahman, *Muʿjam*, 69).

1793 The sentence does not have diacritical marks and is a little difficult to decipher. It may also read: "And if the sultan ordered him to [see to] the writing of a decree, it bore his message and it was designated in what was written." We know from several accounts in *Ṣubḥ* that there was a long process that changed over time, by which a sultan's letter, message or official decree was transferred by the *dawādār* to the Chancery Bureau to be properly written out for sending or announcing, as well as archived. This process documented the accountability of each official and clerk at almost all stages. We also understand that the *dawādār* indicated at a certain space in the document and with a standard formula that this was issued under his supervision. Like the "*ishāra*" of the viceroy referred to above, the *dawādār*'s formula was termed a "*risāla*" (message), since it started with or included "*bi risālat*" (with the message from)." The *risāla* comprised the order of the sultan, as officially reported by the *dawādār*, to be written out by the chancery. The *taʿyyīn* (designation or appointment) was the assignment of writing to a certain scribe or in a particular kind or cut of paper. (See *Ṣubḥ*, Vol. 1, 114–116 & 138, Vol. 6, 209–212 and Vol. 7, 233 and see also al-ʿUmarī's account in *Masālik* (2010), Vol. 3, 309).

1794 A section of *Ṣubḥ* not translated in this work.

1795 According to Ibn Ḥajar al-ʿAsqalānī, Ṭughaytamur al-Najmī was one of the mamluks of Sultan al-Nāṣir Muḥammad. He was promoted, but did not reach the rank of amir until the reign of Sultan al-Ṣāliḥ Ismāʿīl (r. 743 AH/1342 AD – 746 AH/1345 AD). He was appointed a grand *dawādār*(chancellor) during the reign of Sultan al-Muẓaffar Ḥajjī (r. 747 AH/1346 AD – 748 AH/1347 AD), when he became quite powerful, until the sultan exiled him and ordered his assassination in 748 AH/1347 AD. He was known for his chivalry and philanthropy. He was the patron of the Dawādāriyya Khānqāh, known as the Najmiyya, outside Bāb al-Barqiyya. Al-Maqrīzī menions that Ṭughaytamur al-Najmī, the *dawādār*, had died in the same year, without referring to an assassination, and that his khanqah was outside Bāb al-Maḥrūq. Both reports indicate that Ṭughaytamur died before Sultan Ḥasan came to rule. (Al-ʿAsqalānī, *Durar*, Vol. 2, 385 and al-Maqrīzī, *Sulūk*, Vol. 4, 67).

1796 Bahri Mamluk sultan who ruled from 748 AH/1347AD to 762 AH/1361 AD, with an interregnum from 752 AH/1351 to 755 AH/1354 AD.

The Eighth: Office of the *ḥājib* (*al-ḥujūbiyya*)

The author of *Masālik al-Abṣār* said: This office entails arbitrating between the amirs and the soldiers, sometimes in person and other times after consulting with the viceroy, if there is one.[1797] The *ḥājib* is responsible for presenting [and announcing] those who pass by or arrive at [the sultan's court], as well as parading soldiers and what goes with it. Customarily, this position is assigned to five men, two of them commanders of thousands, who are the chief *ḥājib* (*ḥājib al-ḥujjāb*); the one referred to[1798] by the Honourable Sultanic Court (*al-bāb al-sharīf*), who [also] deputises for the viceroy in many issues.[1799] You should know that the Umayyads were the first to introduce this title,[1800] during the reign of Caliph ʿAbd al-Malik b. Marwān.[1801] The holder of this position at that time was responsible for screening[1802] the sovereign from the public, and closing and opening a door in between them, according to [need],[1803] at [certain] times. The Abbasids followed this Umayyad [practice]. Sultan ʿImād al-Dīn, the Ruler of Hama, mentioned that Caliph al-Muqtadir[1804] had 700 *ḥujjāb*. This was when the caliphate was becoming weak, and [the nature of the position] was different than nowadays. This position entails other functions in the kingdoms of the Maghrib, which will be explained in the [section] covering them.[1805]

1797 Al-ʿUmarī says that the *ḥājib* sometimes arbitrated among them himself, and other times after consultation (*mushāwara*) with the sultan or the viceroy, if there was one. (*Masālik* (2010), Vol. 3, 307).

1798 "*Al-Mushār ilayhi min al-bāb* . . ." which could also mean "the one consulted" or "the one signalled at."

1799 *Al-Bāb al-sharīf* (the Honourable Gate), that is the sultan or his court. The editor of Subḥ notes that some words are missing from the original manuscript; al-Qalqashandī does not mention the second commander of thousands, who might have been the deputy of the chief *ḥājib*. Al-ʿUmarī states that when there is no viceroy, the chief *ḥājib* is the one referred to, or signaled at, at the gate (*al-mushār ilayhifī al-bāb*), which probably denotes that he was consulted by the sultan. Al-ʿUmarī' adds that he also substitutes for the viceroys in many issues. (*Ṣubḥ*, Vol. 4, 19 fn. 1 and *Masālik* (2010), Vol. 3, 307).

1800 In another section of the book, al-Qalqashandī, citing al-Qaḍāʿī, mentions that this position was as old as the Islamic caliphate. It entailed reporting the subjects' news to the ruler and asking his permission to allow visitors in. (*Ṣubḥ*, Vol. 5, 449).

1801 Umayyad Caliph from 65 AH/685 to 86 AH/705 AD.

1802 "*Ḥajb*," also veiling or concealing; hence *ḥājib* (the one who veils or screens).

1803 "*'Alā qadrihi*," which may also be translated as "according to his rank," if it is meant to refer to the chief *ḥājib*, or "up to its width," if it is meant to refer to the door.

1804 Abbasid Caliph from 295 AH/908 AD to 320 AH/932 AD with interims in 296 AH/909 AD and 317 AH/929 AD.

1805 A section of *Ṣubḥ* that is not translated in this work.

The Ninth: Office of the Personal Guard (*imrat jāndār*)[1806]

This office entails that its holder requests permission for the amirs to enter for service (*khidma*) and precedes them into the [sultan's] court hall (*dīwān*). The author of *Masālik al-Abṣār* said: He presents the mail [to the sultan], along with the Chancellor (*dawādār*) and the Confidential Scribe (*kātib al-sirr*). He added: The holder of this office is like a keeper of the [sultan's] court (*bāb*), who manages a group of aides (*bardadāriyya*),[1807] and factions of the Equestrian Escorts (*rikābiyya*) and the treasuries' staff (*khāzindāriyya*)[1808] at it.[1809] If the sultan wants to punish or kill someone, the holder of this office is the one responsible for executing this job. He supervises the Armory (*zardkhānāh*),[1810] which is the highest level [place of] detainment,[1811] where detainees do not stay for long, since they are swiftly either released or killed. The holder of this office is also responsible for going around the sultan with the announcement procession (*zaffa*)[1812] on his travels.[1813] Usually, two amirs hold this position: a commander of one-thousand and a *ṭablakhānāh*. The [above description] refers to [the job of] the commander [of one-thousand].

1806 The office occupied by the *amīr jāndār*. Al-Qalqashandī explains that *jāndār* is a term composed of two syllabi: "*jān*," which means "soul" in Persian and Turkish, and "*dār*," which means "holder of" in Persian. He concludes that *amīr jāndār* (the Amir who holds the soul) is so called because he guards the sultan's life and only allows trusted people to meet the sultan. (*Ṣubḥ*, Vol. 5, 461).

1807 Sing. *bardadār*, who was in service of the managers (*mubāshirūn*) of the bureaus and supervised their staffs. The original term for the name of this position is the Persian "*fardādār*," which is composed of two syllabi: "*fardā*," which means "curtain" and "*dār*," which means "holder of," therefore the term means "holder of the curtain." It seems that originally, the *bardadār* used to stand by Bāb al-Sitāra (the Curtain Door), then was transferred to serve in the bureaus. (*Ṣubḥ*, Vol. 5, 468–469 and al-Baqlī, *Ta'rīf*, 62).

1808 Those who work in the sultanic treasuries.

1809 Al-ʿUmarī's account rather mentions "the *bardadāriyya*, as well as factions of the *rikābiyya*, the *ḥarīsāniyya* and the *jāndāriyya*," where the *ḥārīsāniyya* seem to have been some faction of guards, while the *jāndāriyya* were either the assistants of the *jāndār* or lesser ranking guards who served a similar function. (Al-ʿUmarī & H. Abbas, *Masālik* (2002), Vol. 3, 455 and 455 fn. 1 and *Masālik* (2010), Vol. 3, 308).

1810 House of Chainmail, where "*zard*," or chainmail, is manufactured. (See also *silḥkhānāh*).

1811 Al-ʿUmarī notes that it is the higher place of detainment than prison. (*Masālik* (2010), Vol. 3, 308).

1812 The *zaffa* (announcement procession) was the round of playing musical instruments that accompanied the sultan on some occasions, such as on his travels.

1813 Al-ʿUmarī adds: "at night and in the morning." (*Masālik* (2010), Vol. 3, 308).

The Tenth: Office of the Master Supervisor of Warehouses (*al-ustadāriyya*)[1814]

The author of *Masālik al-Abṣār* said that this position entails the supervision of all the sultanic warehouses (*buyūt*), such as the kitchens and the House of Beverages (*sharābkhānāh*), as well as the entourage and the boy-slaves (*ghilmān*). He is the one responsible for implementing the sultan's demands, and managing his boy-slaves and his doorkeeper (*bāb dār*).[1815] He supervises the food tasters (*jāshankīriyya*),[1816] even though their commander is of the same rank as his, an amir of hundreds. He has absolute authority and complete free hand over obtaining whatever is needed by those who are at the sultan's house, such as [provisions for] expenditures and clothes, as well as the same needs for the mamluks and others.[1817] Usually, the holders of this position are four: one commander of one-thousand and three *ṭablakhānāh* amirs. They may also be less than four.

The Eleventh: Office of the Food Taster (*al-jāshankīriyya*)[1818]

This office entails the supervision of the banquet, along with the *ustādār*, as mentioned above. The Food Taster (*jāshankīr*) stands overseeing the banquet with the Master of the Kitchen and Banquets (*ustādār al-ṣuḥba*). The highest ranking Food Taster (*jāshankīr*) is a commander amir.

The Twelfth: Office of the Treasurer (*al-khāzindāriyya*)[1819]

This office entails the supervision of the sultanic monetary treasuries of coins,[1820] cloth and others. The office was usually assigned to a *ṭablakhānāh* amir then came to be assigned to a commander of one-thousand. He is accountable to the Supervisor of the Private [Sultanic] Bureau (*nāẓir al-khāṣṣ*), who will be mentioned below.

1814 Office of the *ustadār* (or *istaddār*, according to al-Qalqashandī), which was a position in the sultan's and the high-ranking amirs' entourage. He also managed the monetary dealings of the sultan or amir, such as receiving and spending. The originally Persian term is composed of two syllabi: "*istidh*," which means "taking," and "*dār*," which means "holder of." The intended meaning is "the one responsible for receiving," which refers to his job as the recipient and manager of money. (*Ṣubḥ*, Vol. 5, 457 and Al-Baqli, *Ta'rīf*, 28).

1815 H. Abbas, *Masālik* (2002), Vol. 3, 455 fn. 5.

1816 See Glossary: "*jāshankīr*".

1817 See account in *Masālik*, Vol. 3, 308.

1818 Office of the *jāshankīr* (the food taster), who was responsible for tasting the foods and drinks instead of the sultan of the amir, out of fear they may be poisoned. The term is composed of two Persian syllabi: "*jāshnā*," which means "the tasting," and "*kīr*," which means "the one who handles," therefore the term means: "the one who handles tasting." (*Ṣubḥ*, Vol. 5, 460, M. Dahman, *Mu'jam*, 50 and S. Ashour, *'Aṣr*, 425).

1819 The holder of the office is called the "*khāzindār*."

1820 *Naqd*, which means golden or silver coins. (http://www.baheth.info/all.jsp?term=نقد and http://www.almaany.com/home.php?language=arabic&lang_name=عربي&word=نقد&type_word=0).

The Thirteenth: Office of the Inspector of the House of Beverages (*shadd al-sharābkhānāh*)[1821]

This office entails the supervision of the sultanic House of Beverages (*sharābkhānāh*) and what is prepared for it, such as sugar, drinks, fruits and other [items]. Sometimes the holder of this position is a commander [of one-thousand] and other times he is a *ṭablakhānāh* amir.

The Fourteenth: Office of the Master of the Kitchen and Banquets (*ustādāriyyat al-ṣuḥba*)[1822]

This office entails supervising the sultanic kitchen, overseeing the food, walking ahead [of the offered food] and standing in charge of the banquet. Usually, the holder of this position is an amir of ten.

The Fifteenth: Office of the Commander of Mamluks (*taqdimat al-mamālīk*)[1823]

This office entails supervising and controlling the sultanic mamluks. The holder of this position must be one of the eunuch servants (*khuddām*)[1824] and he is usually a *ṭablakhānāh* amir, with a deputy amir of ten.

The Sixteenth: Office of the Overseer of the Sultanic Residences (*zimāmiyyat al-dūr al-sulṭāniyya*)[1825]

The holder of this office is one of the highest-ranking eunuch servants (*khuddām*), who is termed "the Overseer" (*zimām*). He is usually a *ṭablakhānāh* amir.

The Seventh: Office of the Captain of the Armies (*niqābat al-juyūsh*)[1826]

The author of *Masālik al-Abṣār* said: This officeis for decorating[1827] the soldiers on their parades. The captains (*nuqabā'*)[1828] march along the holder of this office. If the sultan, the viceroy, or the *ḥājib* demand the presence of an amir or

1821 Office of *shādd al-sharābkhānāh*.

1822 The office of *ustādār al-ṣuḥba*.

1823 The office of "Muqaddam al-Mamālīk." (See Glossary).

1824 Sing. *khādim*, see Glossary.

1825 The office of *zimām al-dūr al-sulṭāniyya*. Al-Qalqashandī explains that *al-zinān dār*, which was distorted by the commoners to *al-zimām dār*, is an originally Persian term, where "*zinān*" means "the women," and "*dār*" means "the holder of," which in this context means "the keeper of." In Arabic *al-zimām* is "the reins," and is used to mean "the leader," while *dār* is "house," which would justify the distortion of the term, according to al-Qalqashandī. *Al-Zinān dār*, *zimām al-dār* or *zimām al-dūr*was the eunuch-servant who kept and guarded the Curtain Door or Gate of the Curtain (*bābal-sitāra*) of the amir or the sultan, that is, the women. *Al-Sitāra* (from Ar. *satr*: covering or veiling) was the term used to refer to the door of the women's quarters. (Ṣubḥ, Vol. 5, 459–460 and al-Baqli, *Ta'rīf*, 172).

1826 The office of *naqīb al-juyūsh*.

1827 *Taḥliya*; the *ḥilya* is the soldeir's decoration.

1828 Sing. *naqīb*, which means "captain" or "corporal" and refers to a job or providing minor services to the sultan or amir (S. Ashour, *'Aṣr*, 481 and M. Dahman, *Mu'jam*, 152).

some other person, the holder of this office is responsible for fetching them. He added: he is like a junior *ḥājib* who is [also] responsible for requesting guards for processions and travel.[1829]

The Eighteenth: Office of the Visitors' Host (Chief of Protocol; *al-mihmandāriyya*)[1830]

This position entails receiving the arriving messengers, Arab Bedouin amirs and others who come travelling from the people of the kingdom, as well as other peoples.

The Nineteenth: Office of the Inspector of the Bureaus (*shadd al-dawāwīn*)[1831]

The holder of this office accompanies the vizier to be in charge of collecting money and similar tasks. The rank of this position is usually amir of ten.

The Twentieth: Office of the Amir of the Battle Axe (*imrat ṭabar*)[1832]

This office entails carrying the battle axe (*ṭabar*) in processions. The holder of this officesupervises the bearers of the battle axes (*ṭabardāriyya*) beneath him in rank and is usually an amir of ten as well.

The Twenty-first: Office of the Amir of the Flag (*imrat 'alam*)[1833]

This office entails supervising and managing the sultanic House of Drums (*ṭablakhānāh*) and its staff. The rank of this position is usually amir of ten.

The Twenty-second: Office of the Amir of Hunting (the Game Keeper; *imrat shikār*)[1834]

This office entails supervising the sultanic birds and animals of prey, as well as the sultanic hunted animals and birds, the birds' enclosures and the like. The rank of this position is amir of ten.

1829 Al-Qalqashandī's account states that he is responsible for "requesting guards" on processions and travel, while al-'Umarī's account may mean that he was responsible for the contents of the warehouses while on processions or travel. (*Ṣubḥ*, Vol. 4, 22 and *Māsālik* (2010), Vol. 3, 309).

1830 The office of the *mihmandār*. Al-Qalqashandī explains that this term was divided into two Persian syllabi: "*mihman*," which means "visitor" and "*dār*," which means "holder of"; that is the official who managers matter of visitors. (*Ṣubḥ*, Vol. 5, 459).

1831 The office of *shādd al-dawāwīn*.

1832 The office of the *amīr ṭabar*.

1833 The office of *amīr 'alam*.

1834 Also, the Bird Master. This is the office of the *amīr shikār*, where "*shikār*" is a Persian word that means "hunting," therefore the term means "the Amir of Hunting." (*Ṣubḥ*, Vol. 5, 461).

The Twenty-third: Office of the Bird Keeper (*ḥirāsat al-ṭayr*)[1835]
This office entails supervising the keeping of birds, such as the cranes allocated for the sultan to hunt, at the places where these birds land, like plantations and and the like. The rank of this position is amir of ten.

The Twenty-fourth: Office of the Inspector of Construction (*shadd al-'amā'ir*)[1836]
This office entails supervising the sultanic establishments that the sultan chooses to build or renew, such as palaces, houses and walls. The rank of this position is amir of ten.

The Twenty-fifth: The Governorship (*al-wilāya*)[1837]
The governors in the capital are of two types:

The First Type:
The Chiefs of Police (*wulāt al-shurṭa*), known in Egypt as the "Chiefs of War" (*wulāt al-ḥarb*), who are three: one in Cairo, one in al-Fustat, which is known as Miṣr, and one in the Qarafa (al-Qarāfa: the cemetery).

As for the Wālīof Cairo, he rules over Cairo and its suburbs, and is the highest-ranking of the three, usually a *ṭablakhānāh* amir.

As for the Wālī of Fustat, he rules over Miṣr, in the same manner as the Wālī of Cairo rules and is usually an amir of ten.

And as for the Wālī of the Qarafa, he rules over the *qarāfa*, which is the cemetery of these two cities, and is under the supervision of the Wālī of Miṣr. He is usually an amir of ten. Currently, the Qarāfa is added to Miṣr and the governorship of both is now a single office of the *ṭablakhānāh* amirial rank; nevertheless, it remains a lesser position than the Wālī of Cairo.

The Second Type: Chiefs of the Citadel (*wulāt al-qal'a*), who are two
One is the Wālī of the Citadel (*wālī al-qal'ā*), who is a *ṭablakhānāh* amir. He supervises the Great Gate of the Citadel, from which the ordinary soldiers enter and exit, by controlling its opening, closing and so forth.

The second is the Master of Bāb al-Qulla (*wālī* Bāb al-Qulla), who is an amir of ten. He supervises this gate and those who use it in same way the Wālī of the Citadel supervises the Great Gate, mentioned above.

1835 The office of *ḥāris al-ḥayr*.

1836 The office of *shādd al-'amā'ir*.

1837 The office of the *wālī* (ruler or governor).

THE SECOND KIND

OUTSIDE THE SULTANIC CAPITAL(*ḤAḌRA*) – THREE GRADES

The First Grade

The Viceroys of the Sultanate

Currently Egypt has three viceroyships, all recently introduced.

The First: The Viceroyship of Alexandria

It is a grand viceroyship that is equivalent to those of Tripoli,[1838] Hama,[1839] and Safad,[1840] of the Syrian Kingdom, which will be mentioned later. It has [the viceregal insignia of] a sultanic chair (*kursī*) and dagger (*nimjāh*),[1841] which is placed on the chair. The Viceroy of Alexandria is one of the commander amirs, who rides in processions accompanied by the sultanic flute (*shabbāba*), as well as the Soldiers of the *ḥalaqa* who are appointed in Alexandria. He goes on his procession to the exterior of the city, outside Bāb al-Baḥr (The Gate of the Sea),[1842] where the amirs appointed to Alexandria meet him. He then returns with them to the House of Viceroyship (Dār al-Niyāba) and offers the sultanic banquet, where the amirs and the soldiers eat. The judges [also] attend this banquet and the petitions are read, according to the customs of viceroyship, then everyone leaves.

This office was first introduced in 767 AH/1366 AD during the reign of al-Ashraf Shaʿbān b. Ḥusayn, when the forsaken Frankish enemies entered Alexandria, attacked its people, killed a great number of them and plundered huge amounts of money. Before that, the position was only a governorship (*wilāya*) among the othergovernorships, and its governor (*wālī*) was of a dignified rank and high status among the high-ranking amirs of the *ṭablakhānāh*.

The Second: The Viceroyship of Upper Egypt

This office was among the ones introduced during the reign of al-Ẓāhir Barqūq and its holder is of the same rank as the Viceroy of Lower Egypt, however, of a

1838 Tripoli in present day Lebanon.

1839 Hama in present day Syria.

1840 Safad, one of the major cities of medieval Palestine.

1841 Also, *nimshāh* or *nimsha*, which isan Arabized Persian word that is used to refer to "a curved dagger that resembles a small sword," or a small or elegant sword that the sultan or the viceroy keeps next to him for protection against assassination attempts. It is considered to be one of the instruments of sovereignity and rule. (Al-Baqli, *Ta'rīf*, 352 and M. Dahman, *Mu'jam*, 152).

1842 The northern gate of the walls built in the Abbasid era to enclose the inhabited areas of Alexandria. These walls were restored and reconstructed again during the Ayyubid and Mamluk eras. (Mohamed Abdelaziz and Tarek Torky, "Alexandria: Gateway to the West," in *Mamluk Art: The Splendour and Magic of the Sultans* (Cairo, 2001), 189–190).

higher authority. The city of Asiūṭ,[1843] mentioned before, is the seat of this office and the viceroy rules over all the villages (*bilād*) of Upper Egypt. The level of this office compared to that of Lower Egypt is mentioned above. Previously, this position was occupied by a Supervisor of Lands and Embankments (*kāshif*) who was called the Chief Governor (*wālī al-wulāt*), which was also the case in Lower Egypt.

The Third: The Viceroyship of Lower Egypt

This office was also introduced during the reign of al-Ẓāhir Barqūq. The Viceroy of Lower Egypt is a Commander Amir, who is of the same rank of the Commander of Soldiers (*muqaddam al-'askar*)[1844] of Gaza, which will be mentioned later.[1845]Damanhūr,[1846] the capital of al-Buḥayra, mentioned above, is the seat of this viceroyship. This office is not of the same level as the viceroyships (*niyābāt*), rather, it is actually a high Governorship of War (*wilāyat ḥarb*). Previously, the holder of this office was a Supervisor of Lands and Embankments (*kāshif*) called the Chief Governor (*wālī al-wulāt*), who did not have a particular seat of rule.

The Second Grade The Supervisors of Lands and Embankments (*kushshāf*)

It was mentioned above that before introducing the viceroyship (*niyāba*) in both Upper and Lower Egypt, their rulers were Supervisors of Lands and Embankments. When the viceroyship was established in both, a supervisor (*kāshif*) from the *ṭablakhānāh* amirs was made to rule over the villages (*bilād*) of Lower Egypt, as was the original custom, except for the provincial division (*'amal*) of al-Buḥayra, for it was close to the Viceroy of Lower Egypt. Another supervisor (*kāshif*) of the same rank was appointed to rule the provincial division (*'amal*) of al-Fayyūm[1847] and the office of its governor (*wālī*) was cancelled. The provincial division (*'amal*) of al-Bahnasā[1848] was added [to al-Fayyūm] as well, while the rest of Upper Egypt was under the authority of its viceroy, mentioned above.

The Third Grade The Governors (*wulāt*) of Upper and Lower Egypt:

The provincial divisions (*a'māl*) of both were mentioned earlier,[1849] and the ranks of their governors are limited to two.

1843 Capital of the present day governorate bearing the same name, Asiūṭ, in Upper Egypt.

1844 The Commander of Soldiers of Gaza, which is another term used to refer to the viceroyship (*niyāba*) of Gaza. The Viceroy of Gaza was sometimes promoted to the office of the Viceroy of the Sultanate (*nā'ib al-salṭana*), and he could only be a commander of one-thousand. (*Ṣubḥ*, Vol. 4, 198).

1845 In a section of *Ṣubḥ* that is not translated in this work.

1846 Present day capital city of al-Buḥayra Governorate, in northwest Egypt.

1847 City and governorate in present day northern Upper Egypt.

1848 Village in present day al-Minyā Governorate in Upper Egypt.

1849 In a section that is not translated in this work.

The First Rank
Governors from the *ṭablakhānāh* amirs:Seven[1850]governorships (*wilāyāt*) in Upper and Lower Egypt

As for Upper Egypt, it has four governors of this rank:

The First – The Wālīof al-Bahnasa, which is now the closest among the *ṭablakhānāh* governors in Upper Egypt to the rank of the Wālī of Cairo.

The Second – The Wālīof al-Ushmūnīn.

The Third –The WālīofQūṣ and Ikhmīm,[1851] who is the highest ranking among of the governors of Upper Egypt, to the extent that he rides on processions with the sultanic flute (*shabbāba*), like the viceroys of the kingdoms.

The Fourth – The Wālīof Aswān:[1852] This [office] was introduced during the reign of al-Ẓāhir Barqūq. Before that, Aswan was additionally [included under the authority of] the Wālī of Qūṣ, while the governorship of al-Fayyūm was a *ṭablakhānāh* that later became established as a Supervision of Lands and Embankments (*kashf*),[1853] as mentioned above.

As for Asiūṭ, it did not have a governorship (*wilāya*) position, since it was the seat of the Viceroy of Upper Egypt, and was formerly the seat of the Chief Governor (*wālī al-wulāt*) of Upper Egypt.

An account will be given below of the offices that were governorships of *ṭablakhānāh* [amirs] then were transferred to the level of a governorship [of amirs] of tens.

As for Lower Egypt, it has four governors of this rank:

The First – The Wālīof al-Sharqiyya, whose seat is the city of Bilbais.

The Second – The Wālīof Munūf.

The Third – The Wālīof al-Gharbiyya, whose seat is in the city ofal-Maḥalla and whose rank is equivalent in sublime status to that of the Wālī of Qūṣ in Upper Egypt.

The Fourth – The Wālī of al-Buḥayra, whose seat is the city of Damanhūr.

1850 The editor of Subḥ notes that actually eight are mentioned. (*Ṣubḥ*, Vol. 4, 26).

1851 Town in present day Sūhāj Governorate in Upper Egypt, to the east of Sūhāj city, on the eastern bank of the Nile.

1852 The capital city of the southern-most governorate of present day Upper Egypt, also bearing the same name.

1853 Office of a *kāshif.*

It was mentioned above that Alexandria, before becoming a seat for a viceroyship, had a governor from the *ṭablakhānāh* amirs.

The Second Rank

Of the Governors who are Amirs of Tens – Seven Governors in Upper and Lower Egypt.

As for Upper Egypt, it has three governors

The First – The Wālī of Giza, who was of the *ṭablakhānāh* rank, then was transferred to the level of [amirs of] tens.

The Second – The Wālī of Iṭfīḥ,[1854] who remains to be [an amir of] ten.

The Third – The Wālī of Manfalūṭ,[1855] who is currently an amir of twenty, but, as mentioned earlier, any amir having [a force of] less than forty, was considered an aimr of ten. To add, this governoship was previously one of the *ṭablakhānāh* rank then it was demoted.

During the reign of al-Nāṣir [Muḥammad], ʿAydhāb had a governor who was an amir of ten. He was appointed by the sultan and turned to the Wālī of Qūṣ concerning important matters.

1854 One of the administrative divisions and city in present day governorate of Ḥilwān.

1855 The Governorate (*wilāya*) of Manfalūṭ, previously "*al-a'māl al-Manfalūṭiyya*" (provincial division of Manfalūṭ), was an administrative division in Upper Egypt, whose base was the ancient city of Manfalūṭ, in present day Governorate of Asiūṭ. (M. Ramzy, *Qāmūs*, Vol. 4, 78).

As for Lower Egypt, it has four governors of this rank

The First – The Wālī of Qalyūb,[1856] who remains to be an amir of ten.

The Second – The Wālī of Ushmūm, who also remains to bean amir of ten.

The Third – The Wālī of Damietta.

The Fourth – The Wālī of Qaṭyā,[1857] who was previously of the *ṭablakhānāh* rank.

1856 City in present day governorate of al-Qaliyūbiyya, south of the Egyptian Delta.

1857 An Egyptian village that was located near al-Faramā and close to the sea. (Al-Ḥamawī, *Mu'jam*, Vol. 4, 378).

The Second Category Of the kingdom dignitaries and position holders who are Men of the Pen – Two Kinds

The First Kind Holders of offices at the bureaus (al-waẓā'if al-dīwāniyya): These offices are too many to account for, but the most significant nine, which [the account] should be limited to, are detailed below:[1858]

The First: The Vizierate (*al-wizāra*)[1859]

This is actually the greatest and highest-ranking position, if not made to diverge from its nature and deviate from its norm. The author of *Masālik al-Abṣār* said: The holder of this position should be second only to the sultan, if treated fairly and if his rights were recognized. However, when the viceroyship (*niyāba*) was introduced, the vizierate retreated and its status remained in place, to the extent that the vizier became like the Supervisor of the Treasury (*nāẓir al-māl*),[1860] who had no authority beyond supervising the finances and was not allowed any [freedom of] action. He did not have the power to appoint or dismiss, for the sultan sought to be thoroughly aware of the details of all issues.[1861] He added: The vizierate had

1858 The editor of Subḥ notes that al-Qalqashandī listed twenty-six positions, therefore, he meant that the most important were nine, but he described more. (*Ṣubḥ*, Vol. 4, 28 fn. 1).

1859 During the Mamluk era, this was the most esteemed position for a "Man of the Pen". The Mamluks inherited the administrative system of the Ayyubids, who stipulated that a vizier must possess certain qualities that included being the most superior of the "Men of the Turban" (*muta'ammimūn*), incorruptible, noble, and most respectable and honest. However, the position of the vizier suffered a setback in the Mamluk era, since Men of the Sword started competing with Men of the Pen for it, and particularly after the position of the viceroy of the sultanate (*nā'ib al-salṭana*) was introduced. "If the vizier was a Man of the Pen, he was given the title of"*al-ṣāḥib*" (the companion), and if he was a Man of the Sword, then he had to be an amir." The vizier who was from the Men of the Turban was chosen from the Men of the Pen who reached the high position of Inspector of the Bureaus (*shādd al-dawāwīn*), to which he was promoted from smaller administrative jobs such as the scribe (*kātib*) and the manager (*mubāshir*). The Mamluks first employed religious scholars (*'ulamā'*) for the vizierate then they allowed employing Copts and other Christians. In 713 AH/1313 AD, Sultan al-Nāṣir Muḥammad introduced the position of the Supervisor of the Private Bureau (*nāẓir al-khāṣṣ*), which overtook much of the responsibilities of the vizierate. Similar gradual steps led to the diminishing of the authorities of the vizier, until in 740 AH/1340 AD, the first Man of the Sword was employed in this position, which was the start of the stage where more Men of the Sword than Men of the Pen became viziers. (H. al-Battawi, *'Imāma*, 15–17).

1860 Also, Supervisor of the Public Treasury (*nāẓir bayt al-māl*), who was one of the Men of the Turban (*muta'ammimūn*). He supervised the revenue from Egypt and Syria that was submitted to the Public Treasury (Bayt al-Māl) at the Citadel, the treasury's expenditures and all its financial matters. He was one of the most dignified state employees and he headed a number of tellers, witnesses and clerks. Only a man of piety and knowledge was appointed in this post. The treasury disappeared by the beginning of the 15th century, after the major economic problems that occurred then. (Al-Baqli, *Ta'rīf*, 341 and H. al-Battawi, *'Imāma*, 30–31).

1861 "*Li-taṭallu' al-sulṭān ilā al-iḥāṭa bi-juz'iyyāt al-aḥwāl.*" (*Ṣubḥ*, Vol. 4, 28 and *Masālik* (2010), Vol. 3, 309).

become an office of both men of the sword and the pen, with pays that matched the expenditure,[1862] and its [duties] are too well known to be mentioned.[1863]

He added: This sultan – namely, al-Nāṣir Muḥammad b. Qalāwūn – had cancelled this office and divided its responsibilities among three offices: the Supervisor of the Treasury (*nāẓir al-māl*), aided by the Inspector of Bureaus (*shādd al-dawāwīn*) to collect money and pay expenditures; the Supervisor of the Private [Sultanic] Bureau (*nāẓir al-khāṣṣ*) to handle general issues and appoint the managers (*mubāshirīn*), and the Confidential Scribe (*kātib al-sirr*) to sign what the vizier had the authority to sign at the House of Justice (Dār al-ʿAdl), after consultation [with the sultan][1864] as well as at his own authority.[1865]

I say: When the vizierate was reinstated after that, it reverted back to being confined to supervising monetary [issues], while the office of the Confidential Scribecontinued to [handle] signing (*tawqīʿ*) the petitions (*qiṣaṣ*) at the House of Justice, and the like. If the vizier was a Man of the Pen, he independently managed the office's [tasks by] supervision, execution and accounting for money. If he was a Man of the Sword, his [responsibilities] were limited to supervision and execution, while the accounting for money was up tothe Supervisor of the State (*nāẓir al-dawla*)[1866] together with him.

1862 Probably means that the paywas not standard. The sentence is copied from al-ʿUmarī's account. (*Masālik* (2010), Vol. 3, 302 & 309).

1863 Al-Qalqashandī's text actually states that this office's "*qaṭīʿa*" was too famous to be mentioned. However, the statement in al-ʿUmarī's account, which he copies, is: "*wa-waẓīfat al-wizāra ash-har min ʿan yudhkar waḍʿ mubāshirihā*," that is: "the office of the vizierate is too famous to mention the status of its holder." It appears that the word was miscopied in *Ṣubḥ* to become "*qaṭīʿa*" rather than "position." (*Ṣubḥ*, Vol. 4, 28 and *Masālik*(2010), Vol. 3, 309).

1864 "*Mushāwara*," see Glossary.

1865 Al-ʿUmarī adds that none of these officials was to act independently without turning to the sultan concerning all issues. See al-ʿUmarī's full account in *Masālik* (2010), Vol. 3, 309–310.

1866 *Naẓir al-dawla* was one of the Men of the Turban (*mutaʿammimīn*) whose post was also termed "*al-ṣuḥba al-sharīfa*" (the Honourable Companionship) and "*nāẓir al-nuẓẓār*" (Supervisor of Supervisors, meaning the Chief Supervisor). He shared the authority of the vizier and his power of signature, for he signed the documents after the vizier's signature. If the vizier was a man of the sword, *nāẓir al-dawla* managed the financial matters, and the vizier was responsible for supervision and implementation. If the vizier was absent or his position was void, *nāẓir al-dawla* performed his tasks, such as collecting money from the inspector of bureaus (*shādd al-dawāwīn*) and allocating it to the proper channels of expenditures and costs. *Nāẓir al-dawla* had assistants, headed by the high comptroller (*mustawfī al-ṣuḥba*), who participated in all the job tasks of concern in both Egypt and Syria and wrote decrees for the sultan to sign. Next in hierarchy to *mustawfī al-ṣuḥba* was the state comptroller (*mustawfī al-dawla*), who also participated in locating money assets and expenditures. The post of *nāẓir al-dawla* was important because it was one of the higher stages of the administrative hierarchy of the Men of the Turban on the way to the vizierate post. *Nāẓir al-dawla* was no different from the vizier who was also a Man of the Pen, the Supervisor of the Private Sultanic Bureau (*nāẓir al-khāṣṣ*) or the Supervisor of the Army (*nāẓir al-jaysh*), for all of them worked in the financial state administration and many Copts or other Christians were appointed in these offices. *Nāẓir al-dawla* was a high-ranking and lucrative office, which sometimes also led to deposition, confiscation and punishment that occasionally reached the death penalty. However, this position's rank deteriorated in the late Mamluk era and it was held by ordinary men. (H. al-Battawi, *'Imāma*, 29).

The vizierate has several subordinate offices, the grandest of which are: the Supervision of State (*naẓar al-dawla*), Office of the High Comptroller (*istīfā' al-ṣuḥba*) and Office of the State Comptroller (*istīfā' al-dawla*).[1867]

As for the Supervision of State, which is also termed "the Honourable Companionship" (*al-ṣuḥba al-sharīfa*)[1868] in the Bureaus of Dense Employment (*al-dawāwīn al-ma'mūra*),[1869] it entails sharing the authority of the vizier over all tasks, participating in writing all that the vizier writes, and signing following the vizier's signature, on all that the latter signs. If the vizier was a man of the sword, the Supervisor of State (*nāẓir al-dawla*) would be responsible for the accounting mattersand what was relevant to them, while the vizier's responsibility was restricted to supervision and implementation.

As for the Office of the High Comptroller (*istīfā' al-ṣuḥba*), it is a grand office of high status. The author of *Masālik al-Abṣār* said: The holder of this office has authority over the whole the kingdom; Egypt and Syria. He writes the decrees (*marāsīm*) that the sultan marks, which sometimes dictated: what to be done with [the lands] of the villages,[1870] the granted tax-free lands (*iṭlāqāt*),[1871] assigning high [officials] to small provincial divisions,[1872] and similar issues. He added: This bureau is the highest financial bureau, where the sultanic signed decrees (*tawāqī'*) and [royal] decrees (*marāsīm*) are documented. All other financial bureaus branch from this one; they are accountable to it and it is where their businesses culminate.[1873]

As for the Office of the State Comptroller (*istīfā' al-dawla*), it was a principal office, whose holder manages the control, documentation and knowledge of

1867 See below.

1868 The *ṣuḥba* (also, *ṣaḥāba*: accompaniment, companionship or fellowship; office of a *ṣāḥib*) denoted other meanings in different contexts, for it sometimes refers to the vizier, the ruler of one of the kingdom's or caliphate's provinces, the head of a bureau or its manager/deputy supervisor. (See Glossary: "*ṣāḥib*").

1869 "*Al-Dawāwīn al-ma'mūra*" is an expression that describes the bureaus as being "inhabited," "populated" or "full." The adjective "*al-ma'mūr*" (the inhabited) was used to describe the bureaus, among other entities, to draw good omen that these bureaus remain inhabited with their scribes, or efficiently running because of the power of the sultan and the stability of his state. (*Ṣubḥ*, Vol. 6, 185).

1870 *Bilād* (sing. *balad*), which means "lands" and may refer to villages or the kingdom's lands at large.

1871 Sing. *iṭlāq*: This was a type of decree that either amended a decision or a declaration made by an earlier monarch, introduced a new act of goodness, or added to an earlier decree of generosity. The *iṭlāq* is a term that was also used to mean a piece of land that was granted and exempted from all taxes. (Al-Baqli, *Ta'rīf*, 36).

1872 "*Istikhdāmāt kibār fī ṣighār al-a'māl*," which may also mean employing high officials for minor tasks (*a'māl*, sing. *'amal*). Al-'Umarī's sentence reads: "*istikhdāmāt kuttāb fī ṣighār al-a'māl*," which means employing scribes at the small provincial divisions. (See *Masālik*, Vol. 3, 311).

1873 In his account that al-Qalqashandī copies parts of, al-'Umarī describes the Army Supervision or the Army Bureau. He mentions that the *mustawfī al-ṣuḥba* (the High Comptroller) was the head of the financial administrators under the Supervisor of the Army (*nāẓir al-jaysh*). (See al-'Umarī, *Masālik* (2010), Vol. 3, 310–311).

the monetary assets and their channels of expenditure. Two or more [men] are assigned to this position of a Comptroller (*mustawfī*).

The Second: Office of the Confidential Scribe (*kitābat al-sirr*)

The author of *Masālik al-Abṣār* said: This office entails reading the letters sent to the sultan, writing their replies, obtaining the sultan's signature on these [replies], and sending them [by mail]. It also involves managing the [royal] decrees (*marāsīm*); receiving them and issuing them out, sitting in audience at the House of Justicefor reading petitions (*qiṣaṣ*) and issuing them with the Signature (*tawqī'*). It was mentioned above in the account of vizierate that the holder of this officehad come to sign [documents] with the authority of the vizier, after reviewing matters with the sultan as needed;[1874] [he also handled] other matters,[1875] such as supervising the mail and managing the postmen and messengers,[1876] as well as participating with the Chancellor (*dawādār*) on most sultanic affairs, as mentioned above in detail. His bureau (*dīwān*)[1877] includes: Scribes of the Pedestal (*kuttāb al-dast*), who sit with him at the House of Justice, read the petitions (*qiṣaṣ*) to the sultan, and issue them with the signature (*tawqī'*) according to the sultan's orders; and the Secretariat Scribes (*kuttāb al-darj*) who write the decrees of inverstitute of governors (*wilāyāt*), the correspondences (*mukātabāt*) and similar documents issued by the Honourable Sultanic Court (*al-abwāb al-sharīfa*); [tasks] which the Scribes of the Pedestal may join them in performing.

The Third: Supervision of the Private [SultanicBureau] (*naẓar al-khāṣṣ*)

This office was newly introduced; Sultan al-Malik al-Nāṣir Muḥammad b. Qalāwūn introduced it when he cancelled the office of the vizier as mentioned above. It orignally entailed supervising what is especially [relevant] to the sultan's money. The author of *Masālik al-Abṣār* said: The holder of this office became like a vizier due to his closeness to the sultan and his management [of matters]. Hebecame responsible for handling all issues and appointing managers (*mubāshirūn*); he meant,[1878] at the times when the vizierate's office was suspended. He added: The holder of this office cannot take any independent decisions without getting back to the sultan.[1879] He had too many assistants to count, from the scribes of the Private [Sultanic] Bureau (*dīwān al-khāṣṣ*), such as the Private [Sultanic] Comptroller (*mustawfī al-khāṣṣ*), Supervisor of the Private [Sultanic] Treasury (*nāẓir khizānat al-khāṣṣ*), and the like.

1874 See al-'Umarī's account in *Masālik* (2010), Vol. 3, 310.

1875 "On other matters."

1876 "*Quṣṣād*," which means messengers or ambassadors.

1877 Also, his office or office hall (*dīwān*).

1878 That is, the author of *Masālik al-Abṣār*.

1879 See al-'Umarī's account in *Masālik* (2010), Vol. 3, 306 & 310.

The Fourth: Supervision of the Army (*naẓar al-jaysh*)[1880]

This office entails supervising all matters of the *iqṭā'āt* in Egypt and Syria, sending correspondences with orders to inspect these lands,[1881] consulting[1882]the sultan concerning them, and obtaining his hand signature (*khaṭṭ*) [as needed]. It is a grand, highly-esteemed position and its bureau (*dīwān*) was the first to be established in Islam, after the Prophet [died], during the caliphate of 'Umar. Al-Zuhrī[1883] said: Sa'īd b. al-Musayyīb[1884]said this[1885] was in the year 20 AH/641 AD. Further description will be given in the account on writing the Decrees of Grants (*manāshīr*) in the Sixth Article.[1886]The Supervisor of the Army (*naẓir al-jaysh*) has subordinates in his bureau (*dīwān*)[1887] who are appointed by the sultan, such as: The Manager of the Army Bureau (*ṣāḥib dīwān al-jaysh*),[1888] its scribes and witnesses; Manager of the Bureau of Mamluks (*ṣāḥib dīwān al-mamālīk*), the scribe of the mamluks and their witnesses, because the Sultanic Mamluks are a branch of the army and their supervision falls under the Supervisor of the Army (*nāẓir al-jaysh*).

1880 The office of *nāẓir al-jaysh* (Overseer of the Army Bureau): This was one of the positions of the Men of the Turban (*muta'ammimūn*) in the Mamluk state, which was inherited from the Ayyubid administrative system, and entailed handling the *iqṭā'āt* allocated to soldiers. During the Mamluk era, the Overseer of the Army Bureau became responsible for all the *iqṭā'āt* of Egypt and Syria; he consulted the sultan on their matters, managed the military salaries, and kept count of the number of soldiers for purposes of knowing their wages or their capacity for war. A group of clerks assisted him, such as the Manager of the Army Bureau (*ṣāḥib dīwān al-jaysh*) and the Manager of the Bureau of Mamluks (*ṣāḥib dīwān al-mamālīk*), and their scribes and witnesses. *Nāẓir al-jaysh* had to have certain qualities, such as knowledge, honesty and good management of soldiers. He had to be respected by the sultan and be notable and esteemed. If a man of strong character, he enjoyed a lofty statusand an absolute authorityduring the Mamluk era. Many of the Men of the Turban sought this office, even with bribery, and several of them held it in addition to other posts, especially posts like Overseer of the Private Sultanic Bureau (*naẓar al-khāṣṣ*) and the Vizierate. This multitasking was not odd, since these posts were of a similar nature. Holders of such posts were known for their power and cunning. *Nāẓir al-jaysh* was wealthy, as was customary for other financial officers of the state throughout the Mamluk era. (H. al-Battawi, *'Imāma*, 26–27).

1881 "*Wa-l-kitāba bi-l-kashf 'anhā*" (and writing correspondences with orders to perform *kashf* over them; that is, the lands). "*Kashf*" is inspecting lands and embankments.

1882 "*Mushāwara*," which may also refer to obtaining the sultan's "*ishāra*." (See Glossary).

1883 Muḥammad b. Muslim b. 'Ubayd Allah b. Shihāb al-Zuhrī (d. 124 AH/742 AD), one of the followers (*tābi'ūn*) and narrators of the Prophet's traditions.

1884 Sa'īd b. Al-Musayyib, Abū Muḥammad al-Qurashī al-Makhzūmī (d. 94 AH/715 AD), one of the followers (*tābi'ūn*) and narrators of the Prophet's traditions.

1885 The establishment of the *dīwān*.

1886 Sixth Article of *Ṣubḥ*; not translated in this book.

1887 Also, his office or office hall.

1888 Manager of Dīwān al-Jaysh. The *ṣāḥib* of a *dīwān*is its manager, second in administrative authority after its *nāẓir*. (M. Dahman, *Mu'jam*, 101).

The Fifth: Supervision of the Bureaus of Dense Employment and the Honourable Companionship (*naẓar al-dawāwīn al-ma'mūra wa-l-ṣuḥba al-sharīfa*)

The holder of this office is termed "The Supervisor of State" (*nāẓir al-dawla*). This office entails managing all that the vizier manages. The holder of this office [participates] in writing all that the vizier writes; writing [to affirm what is] decreed by the vizier.

The Sixth: Supervision of the Treasury (*naẓar al-khizāna*)[1889]

The author of *Masālik al-Abṣār* said: This was originally an office of high status, for it was the depository of the kingdom's wealth, but when the private [sultanic] office (*waẓīfat al-khāṣṣ*) was introduced, its [level] was demoted and it was termed the Great Treasury (*al-khizāna al-kubrā*), which is an exaggerated title. He added: Now, it only comprises robes of honour that are bestowed from it, and whatever was brought to it, was directly dispensed. Its supervisor is mostly one of the judges, or those associated with them.[1890]The Supervisor of the Treasury (*nāẓir al-khizāna*) has subordinates whom the sultan appoints, such as the Manager of the Treasury Bureau (*ṣāḥib dīwān al-khizāna*).

The Seventh: Supervision of the Warehouses and Entourage (*naẓar al-buyūt wa-l-ḥāshiya*)[1891]

This is a grand supervisory office, whose holder is entitled to participate with the Master Supervisor of Warehouses (*ustādār*) on all the latter's supervisory [decisions]. The office of the *ustādār* was described previously.

The Eighth: Supervision of the Public Treasury (*naẓar bayt al-māl*)

This office entails bringing in the kingdom's revenues (*ḥumūl*)[1892] to the Public Treasury (Bayt al-Māl) and managing it sometimes through receipt and expenditure, and sometimes through permission (*taswīgh*) [for] collection and

1889 The holder of this office was one of the Men of the Turban (*muta'ammimūn*). (H. al-Battawi, *'Imāma*, 30).

1890 See al-'Umarī's account in *Masālik* (2010), Vol. 3, 311.

1891 Also, Supervision of Warehouses (*nāẓar al-buyūt*): One of the administrative posts usually taken up by Men of the Pen or the Men of the Turban (*muta'ammimūn*). The holder of this office participated with the Master Supervisor of the Warehouses (*ustādār*), who was a Man of the Sword, in managing all the sultanic warehouses, such as the kitchen, the House of Drinks (*sharāb khānāh*), the entourage, and the slave-boys (*ghilmān*). Like the other supervisors (*nuẓẓār*) of the bureaus, he was aided by several clerks, such as: the manager of the bureau (*ṣāḥib al-dīwān*); the witness (*shāhid*); the comptroller (*mustawfī*); the teller or cashier (*ṣayrafī*), and others. (Al-Baqli, *Ta'rīf*, 342, H. al-Battawi, *'Imāma*, 31, and M. Dahman, *Mu'jam*, 103).

1892 Sing. *ḥiml*: Whatever is brought to the sultan from the produce of the provinces; either the produce itself or its monetary equivalent. It sometimes also means what a convicted person is sentenced to pay and is brought forward to the sultanic the treasury, whether justly or not. (S. Ashour, *'Aṣr*, 431).

expenditure. The author of *Masālik al-Abṣār* said: Only notably equitable men of knowledge and piety were assigned to this office.[1893]

The Ninth: Supervision of Sultanic Stables (*naẓar al-iṣṭablāt al-sulṭāniyya*)[1894]
This position entails managing the sultanic stables and supervising the kinds of sultanic horses, mules, camels and beasts of burden,[1895] as well as the animals' fodder and equipment. He also manages what is allocated of requisitions (*isti'mālāt*) and grants (*iṭlāqāt*) for these stables; all that is bought for and sold from the stables; the allowances (*arzāq*) of the employees (*mustakhdamīn*) [working] in them, and the like.[1896]

The Tenth: Supervision of the Guest House and the Markets (*naẓar dār al-ḍiyāfa wa al-aswāq*)
This office entails managing the acquired [income]from the horses' and slaves' markets, and their likes, and spending these revenues on hosting those who come tovisit the sultanic court, such as the ambassadors of kings and similar visitors, as well as the monthly allowances that are assigned to some people. The decisions concerning the appointment, dismissal and execution of this office are up to the Chancellor (*dawādār*). The vizier is entitled to share the revenue with him, according to a specific ratio.[1897]

The Eleventh: Supervision of the Treasuries of Arms (*naẓar khazā'in al-silāḥ*)
This office entails managing all the requisitions (*yusta'mal*) of the sultanic arms. Customarily, the holder of this office collects all the annually requisitioned and acquired [armour], which is then prepared[1898] [for procession] on a certain day.[1899] The armour is carried above the heads of porters to the arms treasuries at the Protected Citadel.[1900] He and the managers (*mubāshirūn*) who accompany him are [then] bestowed upon with robes of honour.

1893 See al-'Umarī's account in *Masālik* (2010), Vol. 3, 311.

1894 See al-'Umarī's account in *Masālik* (2010), Vol. 3, 311.

1895 "*Dawāb*," also livestock or rides.

1896 For example, the scribes (*kuttāb*) of the stables, who registered the names and dates of entry of the horses to the stables in specific logs. (H. al-Battawi, *'Imāma*, 31).

1897 "*Al-Mushāraka ma'hu fī al-mutaḥaṣṣil fī shay' makhṣūṣ*," (to share with him the revenue; with a specific share."

1898 "*Yujahhaz*," that is "equipped for travel."

1899 In another account in this book, the author explains that the holder of this office manages what is used and bought, of all kinds of weaponry, for the arms treasuries. Therefore, the collection activity, also mentioned above, was either of manufactured, bought, or possibly otherwise acquired weapons. (See *Ṣubḥ*, Vol. 11, 345).

1900 "*Al-Qal'a al-maḥrūsa*," where "the protected" (m. *al-maḥrūs*, f. *al-maḥrūsa*) is a title used for cities and coastal cities to draw good omen that they remain protected. Al-Qalqashandī explains that when the term is used for citadels or fortresses, it has an obvious meaning, for they are fortifications protected by their walls. In all cases, he is inclined to believe it is a wish in good faith, rather than a mere statement of a fact. (*Ṣubḥ*, Vol. 6, 184).

The Twelfth: Supervision of the Sultanic Properties (*naẓar al-amlāk al-sulṭāniyya*)[1901]

This office entails the management of the sultan's properties, such as the plantations,[1902] the *ribā'*,[1903] and the like.

The Thirteenth: Supervision of the Spices and Spice Trade (*naẓar al-bahār wa al-kārimī*)[1904]

This office entails managing the types of spices and kinds of merchandisethat the spice merchants (*kārimiyya*) bring from Yemen. This is a grand office that is sometimes added and affiliated to the vizierate, other times to the private [sultanic bureau] (*khāṣṣ*), or made independent according to what the sultan sees fit.

The Fourteenth: Supervision of the Granaries at Miṣr, in the Shipyard (*naẓar al-ahrā' bi-Miṣr bi-l-ṣinā'a*)

This is the sultanic granary, which the vizier supervises. Its supervision entails managing what arrives to the granary from the districts (*nawāḥī*),[1905] such as grains and the like, and what is allocated from it to the Honourable [Sultanic] Stables, the sultanic [camel] settlement areas (*munākhāt*), and the like.

The Fifteenth: Supervision of the Estates Left by the Heirless (*naẓar al-mawārīth al-ḥashriyya*)

This office entails managing the Bureau of the Estates Left by the Hierless (*dīwān al-mawārīth al-ḥashriyya*), [which handles] the inheritance of those who die leaving no one entitled to inheriting them, or leaving an heir who does not have

1901 The Bureau of Properties (*dīwān al-amlāk*) was a bureau introduced by Sultan al-Ẓāhir Barqūq, to which he allocated villages that he called "*amlāk*" (properties) so as to finance it. These properties were managed by specifically assigned employees. This bureau was a private sultanic one that was not responsible for other expenditures. (*Ṣubḥ*, Vol. 3, 457).

1902 *Ḍiyā'*, sing. *ḍay'a*.

1903 Sing. *rab'*.(See Glossary: "*ribā'*").

1904 The editor of Subḥ explains that in the author's *Ḍaw' al-Ṣubḥ al-Musfir* (summary of *Ṣubḥ*), the term used is "*al-kānimī*," which refers to *al-kānim* – A Sudanese sect, some of whom resided in Egypt, that were merchants of spices such as pepper, cloves and the like, which are brought from India and Yemen. (*Ṣubḥ*, Vol. 4, 32, fn. 1).

1905 Sing. *nāḥiya*. The *nāḥiya*, *qarya* and *balad* (also, *bilda*) were terms that were used interchangeably in Egypt after the Islamic conquest to refer to the administrative and fiscal divisions that mean "village." A Coptic historical source (483 AH/1090 AD) that surveyed the villages of Egypt used the term "*nāḥiya*" to mean village (*bilda*), while *kafr* was used to denote a hamlet that was affiliated to the village. The cadastral survey that was carried out in 697 AH/1298 AD, in the reign of Sultan Ḥusām al-Dīn Lājīn (r. 695 AH/1296 AD – 697 AH/1298 AD), which is known as *al-rawk al-Ḥusāmī*, showed that these hamlets had by the time developed into fiscal districts (*nawāḥī*), which means that they came to have affiliated agricultural lands. (M. Ramzi, *Qāmūs*, Vol. 1, 5, 12 &19–22).

the right to the whole inheritance. This office also supervises the grants (*iṭlāq*) for all the deceased,[1906] Muslims and non-Muslims.

The Sixteenth: Supervision of the Sultanic Mills (*naẓar al-ṭawāḥīn al-sulṭāniyya*)

These mills were also located at Miṣr, in al-Ṣināʿa. This was [at] a huge yard (*maghlaq*) that comprised ten millstones, which produced about fifty [large] sacks (*tillīs*)[1907] per day.

The Seventeenth: Supervision of Acquisitions (*naẓar al-ḥāṣilāt*)[1908]

Also termed "*naẓar al-jihāt*" (the Supervision of Imposts). This office entails managing the money [generated by the] imposts of the vizierate, whether acquired, spent, [deposited as] revenue (*ḥiml*) at the Public Treasury (Bayt al-Māl), or the like.

The Eighteenth: Supervision of Reclaims (*naẓar al-murtaja'āt*)

This office entails managing what is recovered after the death of an amir or similar cases. It was rejected and was mostly unoccupied. The reclaims became the responsibility of the Comptroller of Reclaims (*mustawfī al-murtaja'*), who rules over the cases of the bureaus and arbitrates[1909] them according to the protocol of bureaus, which is called "the Sultan's Bureau" (*dīwān al-sulṭān*).

The Nineteenth: Supervision of Giza (*naẓar al-Jīza*)

This office entails managing the acquired [revenues] from the provincial division (*'amāl*) of al-Jīziyya,[1910] which is the sultan's private (*khāṣṣ*) [property]. It is one of the branches of the bureaus (*furū' al-dawāwīn*).

The Twentieth: Supervision of Upper Egypt (*naẓar al-wajh al-qiblī*)

This office entails managing all the acquired [revenues] from all the lands of Upper Egypt, such as inheritance and the like.

1906 The "*iṭlāq al-mawtā*" appears to have been a grant given by the state to ensure the proper washing (*ghusl*) and burial of the dead bodies according to Islamic law. (See Ibn Taghrī Birdī, *Nujūm*, Vol. 10, 161).

1907 The sack used for packing agricultural produce and straw. (M. Dahman, *Mu'jam*, 48).

1908 Also, Supervision of Receipts.

1909 "*Yafṣilhā*" (arbitrate or segregate them). (See later when the term is used for arbitrating grievances).

1910 *Al-Jīziyya* was an administrative geographical division first established in the Fatimid era to comprise the subdivisions of Awsīm and Manf. Both were ancient cities in Giza; the first still carries its name and is located to the south of the city of Giza, on the western bank of the Nile, and the second, called Memphis by the Greeks, was located near Mīt Rihīna village. Al-Jīziyya division remained the same under the Ayyubids and Mamluks, and was called "*al-a'māl al-Jīziyya.*" (M. Ramzy, *Qāmūs*, Part 1, 422 & Vol. 3, 6, 48–49, 57–58).

The Twenty-first: Supervision of Lower Egypt (*naẓar al-wajh al-baḥarī*)
The office has the same functions as the Supervision of Upper Egypt mentioned above, [but concerning Lower Egypt].

The Twenty-second: Deputy Supervision of the Army Bureau (*ṣaḥābat dīwān al-jaysh*)
This office entails managing all issues of the*iqṭā'āt*that the Supervisor of the Army (*nāẓir al-jaysh*) manages.

The Twenty-third: Deputy Supervision of the Hospital Bureau (*ṣaḥābat dīwān al-bīmāristān*)
This office entails managing all that the Supervisor of the Hospital (*nāẓir al-bīmāristān*) manages.

The Twenty-fourth: Deputy Supervision of the Endowments Bureau (*ṣaḥābat dīwān al-aḥbās*)
This office entails [participating] with the Supervisor of Endowments (nāẓir al-aḥbās) in all that he writes,[1911] but it is abolished [now].

The Twenty-fifth: High Financial [Bureau] (*istīfā' al-ṣuḥba*)
State Financial [Bureau] (*istīfā' al-dawla*)[1912]

1911 "*Yaktub*" (to write) in this context probably refers to having the authority of writing.

1912 The editor of Subḥ notes that both *istīfā' al-ṣuḥba*and *istīfā'al-dawla* were explained before, that is why the author felt no necessity reiterate them. (*Ṣubḥ*, Vol. 4, 34). It is notable that *istīfā' al-dawla* is just listed and not counted as position number twenty-six.

The Second Kind
Holders of Religious Offices: Two Types

The First Type Those who have the right to attend in the sultanic audience (*ḥaḍra*) at the Honourable House of Justice (Dār al-ʿAdl), which are limited to five offices:

The First Office: Office of The Chief Judge (*qaḍā' al-quḍāt*)
This office entails supervising the religious legislative rulings (*al-aḥkām al-shar'iyya*) and executing their cases, applying religious doctrines, arbitrating between opponents, and appointing deputies to handle what would be difficult for him to pursue in person. This is the most sublime and greatest ranking religious post, which is of the highest status.

You should know that in earlier times, this position was limited to one judge (*qaḍī*) in Egypt, whatever his School of Interpretation (*madhhab*) was. During the Fatimid era, there was a single judge for Egypt, Syria,[1913] and the Maghrib. He was additionally responsible for ruling over issues regarding prayers, minting houses, and other matters that will be explained later in the section detailing the Diplomas of Investiture (*taqālīd*) of some of their judges, in the part on the Diplomas of Investiture (*taqālīd*) of the judges.[1914] In the year 663 AH/1265 AD, during the reign of al-Ẓāhir Baybars, the situation settled on four judges from the Schools of Interpretation of the four imams: al-Shāfiʿī, Mālik, Abū Ḥanīfa, and Aḥmad b. Ḥanbal. The author of *Nihāyat al-Arab* mentioned the reason for this, which was that the only Chief Judge of Egypt at the time was Judge Tāj al-Dīn ʿAbd al-Wahhāb b. Bint al-Aʿazz,[1915] who was opposed on his matters by Amir Jamāl al-Dīn Aydughdī,[1916] one of the amirs of Sultan al-Malik al-Ẓāhir [Baybars] mentioned above. The amir dispraised the judge [in the eyes of] the sultan because of the judge's rigidity with issues and his suspension (*tawwaquf*)[1917] of rulings.One day, when the sultan was sitting for audience at the House of Justice (Dār al-ʿAdl),

1913 "*Ajnād al-Shām*".

1914 Section of *Ṣubḥ* that is not translated in this work.

1915 Shāfiʿī Chief Judge from 660/1261–62 to 665/1266–67. He died while he was still in office. Similar to many religious scholars of his time, he held several positions at once, including: Chief Judge; the preacher (*khaṭīb*) of al-Azhar; Supervisor of the Treasury (*nāẓir al-khizāna*); Supervisor of Endowments (*nāẓir al-aḥbās*); Shaykh of the Khanqah of Saʿīd al-Suʿadā'; Supervisor (*nāẓir*) of the inheritance of Sultan Baybars; teaching the Shāfiʿī School of Interpretation, and teaching at the Ṣāliḥiyya Madrasa. (H. al-Battawi, *'Imāma*, 81 & 173).

1916 Amir Jamāl al-Dīn Aydughdī al-ʿAzīzī (d. 664 AH/1266 AD), who was one of the prominent amirs during the reigns of sultans Aybak and Quṭuz, and one of the high-ranking amirs of Sultan Baybars. (See al-Maqrīzī, *Sulūk*, Vol. 1, 468 & Vol. 2, 39 and Ibn Taghrī Bardī, *Nujūm*, Vol. 7, 109–110 & 665).

1917 *Tawwaquf* (halting, suspending or pausing) is a jurisprudence term that refers to abstaining from issuing a verdict due to the obscurity of the case, for example, use of vague words or actions by the opponents, which requires further investigation of the incidents. This term is not employed by al-Nuwayrī; however, he says that Ibn Bint al-Aʿazz was rigid, slow and careful with his rulings. (See al-Nuwayrī, *Nihāya*, Vol. 30, 117).

he received a petition concerning a place[1918] that Judge Badr al-Dīn al-Sanjārī[1919] had sold, and after his death, his heirs claimed that it was an endowment. Amir Aydughdī then kept dispraising the judges in the presence (*ḥaḍra*) of the sultan and the sultan kept silent. He[1920] then asked Judge Tāj al-Dīn: "What is the ruling for this case?" He replied: "If the endowment is proven, then the price should be paid back from the seller's inheritance." He asked: "What if the inheritance was not enough to cover this?" The judge replied: "Then the place should remain endowed." The sultan was not happy with this [ruling], but he kept silent. Then other issues were discussed at this council (*majlis*) that the judge [also] ruled should be suspended [and] did not pass. It the end, Amir Aydughdī convinced the sultan with appointing four judges from the four Schools of Interpretation, so he did. He appointed Judge Tāj al-Dīn b. Bint al-Aʿazz for the Shāfiʿī School; Shaykh Shihāb al-Dīn Abū Ḥafṣ ʿUmar b. ʿAbd Allah b. Ṣāliḥ al-Subkī[1921] for the Mālikī; Judge Badr al-Dīn b. Salmān[1922] for the Ḥanafī, and Judge Shams al-Dīn Muḥammad b. al-Shaykh ʿImād al-Dīn Ibrāhīm al-Qudsī[1923] for the Ḥanbalī. The sultan gave the four of them the authority to appoint deputies in all the provincial divisions (*a'māl*) of Egypt. Judge Tāj al-Dīn was solely assigned to supervise the endowments and the orphans' monies. To that effect, Judge Muḥyi al-Dīn b. ʿAbd al-Ẓāhir[1924] composed a Diploma of Investiture (*taqlīd*) that started with: "Praise be to Allah, the One who draws the sword of Truth upon the aggressors."[1925] Each of the four judges ruled over what his School of Interpretation necessitated in Cairo and Fustat, appointed deputies and assigned the seating of witnesses. The Shāfiʿī judge was the only one who had the right to appoint deputies in the districts (*nawāḥī*) of Upper and Lower Egypt, solely, without anyone else's [authority].

1918 "*Makān*," which is a general term that may be used for any kind of establishment or building property. In al-Nuwayrī's account "*dār*" (house).(See al-Nuwayrī, *Nihāya*, Vol. 30, 117).

1919 Yūsuf b. al-Ḥasan b. ʿAbd Allah al-Zirzārī al-Kurdī, known as Badr al-Dīn Abū al-Maḥāsin al-Sinjārī (d. 663 AH/1265 AD), was a Shāfiʿī judge, who was as elegant as the grand viziers. He was very close to the Ayyubid Sultan al-Ṣāliḥ Najm al-Dīn, who appointed him the judge of Miṣr in 639 AH/1242 AD, and later he became the judge of both Cairo and Miṣr. Although suspected of bribery, he was appointed vizier in addition to his tasks as a judge in 655 AH/1257 AD. He was arrested in 659 AH/1261 AD, after al-Ẓāhir Baybars became sultan, then released, and he stayed at his home until he died. (Al-ʿAsqalānī, *Quḍāt*, 474–475).

1920 That is, the sultan, according to al-Nuwayrī's account. (Al-Nuwayrī, *Nihāya*, Vol. 30, 117).

1921 In al-Nuwayrī's account: "Sharaf al-Dīn," who was the Mālikī Chief Judge from 663/1264–65 to 667/1268–69. He died while he was still in office. (H. al-Battawi, *'Imāma*, 182 and al-Nuwayrī, *Nihāya*, Vol. 30, 118).

1922 In al-Nuwayrī's account: Ṣadr al-Dīn Sulaymān, who was the H.anafī chief judgefrom 663/1264–65 to 678/1269–70. He was deposed. (H. al-Battawi, *'Imāma*, 179 and al-Nuwayrī, *Nihāya*, Vol. 30, 118).

1923 In al-Nuwayrī's account: "al-Maqdisī," who was the H.anbalī chief judge from 663/1264–65 to 670/1271–72. He was deposed. (H. al-Battawi, *'Imāma*, 185 and al-Nuwayrī, *Nihāya*, Vol. 30, 118).

1924 Al-Nuwayrī does not seem to mention the name of Ibn ʿAbd al-Ẓāhir in this account. (See al-Nuwayrī, *Nihāya*, Vol. 30, 119).

1925 See al-Nuwayrī's full account in *Nihāyat*, Vol. 30, 117–122.

The Second Office: Office of the Military Judge (*qaḍā' al-'askar*)[1926]

This is an old and grand office that was found during the era of Sultan Ṣalāḥ al-Dīn Yūsuf b. Ayyūb, whose Military Judge (*qāḍī al-'askar*) was Bahā' al-Dīn b.....[1927] The position entails attending [the sessions] at the House of Justice (Dār al-ʿAdl) with the judges mentioned above, and travelling with the sultan if he travels. Only three judges are appointed in this position: a Shāfiʿī, a Ḥanafī and a Mālikī, but the Ḥanbalī School has no share in this office. Their [status of] seating at the House of Justice is inferior to the four judges mentioned above, as will be explained later.

The Third Office: Office of the muftī of the House of Justice (*iftā' dār al-'adl*)[1928]

This office entails similar functions to those of the Office of the Military Judge and four men are appointed to it, one from each school. Their [status of] seating isinferior to the Military Judges, as will be mentioned later.

1926 Office of *qāḍī al-'askar*: The holder of this position was one of the Men of the Turban (*muta'ammimūn*) who specialized in the matters of military personnel and only had authority over them. He arbitrated the cases of conflicts between the military personnel and civilians. The Military Judge (*qāḍī al-'askar*) had a clerk to assist him, especially in finding equitable witnesses to assign from the soldiers, which was not an easy task according to some sources. The office of the Military Judge was an old and supreme one, which held a higher status in the Ayyubid era than it did under the Mamluks. There was a Military Judge for the Shāfiʿī, the Ḥanafī, and the Mālikī schools, while the Ḥanbalis had a judge only occasionally. The holders of this position attended the councils of the House of Justice along with the chief judges of the four schools, but their order of seating indicated their lesser rank than the chief judges. They normally accompanied the sultan in his travels. (H. al-Battawi, *'Imāma*, 71–72).

1927 The editor of Subḥ comments that a part is missing from the text in the original manuscript. (*Ṣubḥ* , Vol. 4, 36 fn. 1). The intended name is Abū al-Maḥāsin Bahā' al-Dīn Yūsuf b. Rāfiʿ b. Shaddād (d. 632 AH/1234 AD); a historian and judge who was close to Sultan Ṣalāḥ al-Dīn and wrote his biography. (Al-Zarkalī, *A'lām*, Vol. 8, 230).

1928 Office of *muftī dār al-'adl*: The *muftī* (mufti) was a sort of a secondary post or additional task held by religious scholars who worked in several offices such as the judiciary, teaching, being the shaykhs of khanqas, etc. The *iftā'* (job of the mufti) entailed guiding learners, giving religious opinions and advice on how to deal with certain situations, as well as conveying their knowledge to the seekers. There was an independent post of *iftā'*, however, which was *muftī dār al-'adl*. The sultan appointed a *muftī* for each of the four Sunni schools to attend sessions and councils of the House of Justice, when the sultan sat in audience to look into grievances and see to arbitrations. They were to provide religious opinions (*iftā'*) concerning the verdicts if needed. To show their rank in the order of seating, they sat following the *muḥtasib*. (H. al-Battawi, *'Imāma*, 72 and *Ṣubḥ*, Vol. 11, 207).

The Fourth Office: Office of the Agent of the Public Treasury (*wakālat bayt al-māl*)[1929]

This is a highly regarded office of great statusthat entails managing all that is relevant to the sales and purchases of the Public Treasury (Bayt al-Māl), which includes lands, houses, and other [properties], and ratifying the contracts of such [transactions], and similar tasks. The author of *Masālik al-Abṣār* said: This position is only given to men of knowledge and piety.[1930] The [status of] seating of the holder of this position at the House of Justiceis sometimes superior and other times inferior to the *muḥtasib*, depending on the individual status of each of them.

The Fifth Office: Office of the *muḥtasib* (*al-ḥisba*)

This is a grand and highly regarded office[1931] that entails the authority of ordering and prohibiting, supervising livelihoods and crafts, and restraining those who

1929 Office of *wakīl bayt al-māl*: In the Mamluk era, the holder of this office supervised the wills that he was responsible for enforcing, the money deposits, and the properties of Bayt al-Māl, as well as following its interests through selling, purchasing, etc. *Wakīl bayt al-māl* also worked in several other offices, such as those of the Deputy Judge (*nā'ib al-qāḍī*), the Teacher (*mudarris*), Supervisor of Endowments (*nāẓir al-aḥbās*) and others. (H. al-Battawi, *'Imāma*, 72).

1930 Probably referring to the above account on the Supervision of the Public Treasury (*naẓar bayt al-māl*), where he copies the intended meaning of al-ʿUmarī's description.

1931 This office appeared in the late Umayyad era, during the reign of Caliph Hishām b. ʿAbd al-Malik (r. 105 AH/724 AD – 125 AH/743 AD). Although many secondary sources translated this office using terms that associate it with inspecting and regulating markets, it entailed a wider job description of "commanding good and preventing vice." The *muḥtasib* was a controller of many aspects of civil life through an authority that placed him somewhere between a judge and a chief of police, with overlaps with the authorities and tasks of both offices. In Islamic history, he was sometimes respected and influential enough to punish the rulers themselves, and in other instances his authority was restricted to verbally criticizing them while minding a polite tone in his critique. The *muḥtasib* was one of the most important officials from the Men of the Turban. The conditions for being appointed in this post included that he had to be learned in jurisprudence and knowledgeable of the rules of *sharī'a*, as well as a diligent follower of the traditions of the Prophet. He was responsible for controlling and regulating the roads, markets, and several other aspects of civil life, according to religious law. The *muḥtasib* was a sort of a junior judge who executed minor verdicts over general matters that the judge should be spared from indulging in. However, occasionally the positions of both the judge and the *muḥtasib* were given to one man, for the *muḥtasib* was but a quicker judge who decided on violations and executed punishments rapidly. Due to the wide range of responsibilities of the *ḥisba* during the Mamluk era, it was divided based on areas or specializations. For example, some areas had their *muḥtasib*, such as al-Ḥusayniyya and the Citadel, while some professions had their *muḥtasib* too, such as bread-bakers, tobacco traders, cooks, etc. The general or grand *muḥtasib* most probably supervised all the other *muḥtasib*s or deputies. This position was occupied by men of religion until Sultan al-Mu'ayyad Shaykh (r. 815 AH/1412 AD – 824 AH/1421 AD) appointed one of his amirs in this office in 816 AH/1413 AD and gave him the title of *faqīh* (jurist), to provide him with an undeserved quailification for the job. Since then, the mamluks competed with the Men of the Turbanfor the *ḥisba*. "The *muḥtasib* was one of the most important state officials of the era of the Mamluk sultans, for he was a mediator between rulers and subjects, due to his direct relation with both the sultan and the people." In addition to al-Qalqashandī's explanation of the job and what it entails, al-Maqrīzī, who himself held this position for some time, gave a detailed account of the office, listing some of its conditions and duties. He mentioned that only a

deviate from the right path in their means of living and professions. There are two *muḥtasib*s in the sultan's capital (*ḥaḍra*): one in Cairo, who is of grander status and higher level, and who has the authority of regulation, and appointing [deputies] over all of Lower Egypt except for Alexandria, which had its own *muḥtasib*. The second is in Fustat and his rank is lower than that of the first. He has the authority to supervise and appoint [deputies] over all of Upper Egypt. Only the *muḥtasib* of Cairo, and not that of Fustat, sits at the House of Justice on procession days, and his seating position is inferior to that of the Agent of the Public Treasury (*wakīl bayt al-māl*). He may sit at a superior position to the agent if he was of higher knowledge, or the like.

The Second Type Of the Holders of Religious Offices: Those who have no seat at the sultanic audience (ḥaḍra)

These offices are too numerous to detail and there is no way to fully mention all of them and their various levels; therefore, only the important ones will be mentioned. Some of these offices are assigned to one person, and some are common offices held by a number of people.

As for the offices assigned to one person, they include:

The Chieftain of Honourable Descendants (*niqābat al-ashrāf*)[1932]

This is an honourable office of noble level that entails managing [the affairs of] the descendants of ʿAlī b. Abī Ṭālib and Fāṭima, the daughter of the Prophet;those termed "The Honourable Ones" (*al-ashrāf*). The holder of this position investigates their lineages, manages [the matters of] their relatives, restrains the aggressors among them and the like. During the caliphate era [mentioned] before,[1933] this position was termed Chieftain of the Ṭālibiyyīn (*niqābat al-Ṭālibiyyīn*).

dignitary Muslim and a notable equitable would be appointed in this office, since it is a religious service. The *muḥtasib* sits on alternate days at the two main mosques of Cairo and Fustat and is entitled to appointing deputies in Cairo, Fustat and other Egyptian provinces. His deputies go around supervising craftsmen, inspecting food-sellers, such as meat and inquiring who the butcher is, as well as inspecting cooks. They check roads and make sure that no one is harassing people or illegally occupying road sections. They ensure the commitment of boat owners not to overload their boats for safety concerns and they make sure that porters do not over-burden the beasts that carry loads. They order water-sellers to cover water pots with cloths to prevent its pollution, and prohibit them from exceeding their assigned water loads or wearing indiscrete clothing. The *muḥtasib*'s deputies also warned the teachers of the *katātīb* (sing. *kuttāb* or *maktab*, school for little children) not to beat the boys violently or where it might cause fatal injury, and the swimming trainers not to seduce people's children. They were responsible for setting straight whoever cheated in dealings and supervising weights and balances. Chiefs of police and governors were sometimes assigned to help the *muḥtasib* as needed. (Siham Abu Zayd, *Al-Ḥisbafī Miṣr al-Islāmiyya* (Cairo, 1986), 41, 43, 142–143, 186, 221, &237–238, Al-Baqli, *Ta'rīf*, 302–303, and H. al-Battawi, *'Imāma*, 75–76).

1932 Office of *naqīb al-ashrāf.*

1933 The Fatimid Caliphate.

Office of the Grand Shaykh (*mashyakhat al-shuyūkh*)[1934]

This is the office of the shaykh of the khanqah that al-Malik al-Nāṣir Muḥammad b. Qalāwūn built in Siryāqūs,[1935] in the outskirts of Cairo.

The office of the shaykh (*mashyakha*) of the khanqah of Ṣalāḥ al-Dīn, known as the Khanqah of Sa'īd al-Su'adā', is inferior to that of Siryāqūs, despite its old age and high grandeur.

Office of Supervision of the Charitable Endowments (*naẓar al-aḥbās al-mabrūra*)[1936]

This is an office of lofty status that entails managing the incomes (*rizaq*)[1937] [collected from] specifically [endowed] lands, particularly in the Egyptian districts (*nawāḥī*), to [be spent over] congregational mosques, mosques, ribats, zawiyas, and madrasas. It also entails spending parts of this income on charity and alms for certain people. The origin of this position was that al-Layth b. Sa'd

1934 Office of *shaykh al-shuyūkh* (the Shaykh of Shaykhs or the Grand Shaykh): "Customarliy, each khanqah had one or more shaykh, who was a man of knowledge and religion." The first to be termed *shaykh al-shuyūkh* (Grand Shaykh) was the shaykh of the Khanqah of Sa'īd al-Su'adā', and when al-Nāṣir Muḥammad built the Khanqah of Siryāqūs in 725 AH/1325 AD, he gave its head the same title. Then all subsequent shaykhs appointed for this khanqah were called "*shaykh al-shuyūkh*," until 806 AH/1404 AD, when Egypt faced a lot of tribulations, and the shaykh of every khanqah was given that same title. The holder of this position "had to have reached a high stage according to the conditions of Sufi orders." He had to be presentable and knowledgeable of jurisprudence and other religious sciences, including all four Sunni schools, while specializing in his own. "*Shaykh al-shuyūkh* of the khanqah supervised the Sufi practices, and many times taught, according to the stipulations indicated by the endower." Some endowers dictated that the *shaykh al-shuyūkh* should have a deputy. (H. al-Battawi, *'Imāma*, 80–81).

1935 This is the khanqah that al-Nāṣir Muḥmmad built in Siryāqūs in present day Governorate of al-Qalyūbiyya, north of Cairo, in 723 AH/1325 AD. Al-Maqrīzī mentions that the sultan chose this location after finding himself suddenly very sick while on a hunting expedition, and thus vowing to build a place of worship there, if he was saved. Having healed from this illness, the sultan rode along with a company of architects to that site, where they set the plan for the khanqah that included 100 individual cells for Sufis, a bath, and a kitchen. A Friday mosque was built next to it and the establishment was inaugurated in a celebration which the sultan attended himself along with the amirs, the judges, and the shaykhs of the khanqahs. The sultan appointed a shaykh for this khanqah, whom he gave the title *shaykh al-shuyūkh* (the Grand Shaykh), which until then, was kept solely for the shaykh of the khanqahof Sa'īd al-Su'adā'. The site of the khanqah became inhabited with people who wanted to live around it, and who built houses, shops and caravanserais. It developed into a large town that housed several baths in addition to that of the khanqah, which indicates its big population. The town remained as populated by al-Maqrīzī's time, where a big Friday market was held. The town's trade dealings were all exempted from taxes out of respect for the khanqah. (Al-Maqrīzī, *Khiṭaṭ*, Vol. 3, 587–589).

1936 Office of *nāẓir al-aḥbās al-mabrūra*.

1937 The *rizaq* were the incomes generated from endowed lands to be distributed over specifically assigned chartibale purposes. The *rizqa* was the endowed or granted land. (M. Dahman, *Mu'jam*, 82 and S Ashour, *'Aṣr*, 441).

had bought lands that were in the outskirts of some villages[1938] from the Public Treasury (Bayt al-Māl) and endowed them for charitable purposes,[1939] which are called "*wujūh al-'ayn*" (channels of endowment expenditure)[1940]in the Bureau of Endowments (*dīwān al-aḥbās*). Then [other establishments] were added to that, such as the known ribā'[1941] and houses in Fustat and elsewhere. Then the incomes allocated to sermons[1942] were added to [the expenditures]. Later, the incomes generated from [endowed] lands increased in the reign of al-Ẓāhir Baybars, by means of [the efforts of] al-Ṣāḥib[1943] Bahā' al-Dīn b. Ḥanna[1944] and they continued to rise until our days. These generated incomes were sometimes managed by the sultan personally, or the viceroy, but mostly by the Grand Chancellor (al-dawādār al-kabīr), which is the current arrangement of matters.

Supervision of the Hospital (*naẓar al-bīmāristān*)

The hospital meant here is al-Manṣūr's Hospital (*al-bimāristān al-Manṣūrī*), which al-Manṣūr Qalāwūn built at Bayn al-Qaṣrayn. It used to be a house owned by Sitt al-Mulk, the sister of the Fatimid [Caliph] al-Ḥākim, which Qalāwūn altered the features of and added to.[1945] Its charity and favour are unmatched any where in the world. The supervision of this hospital is one of the grandest and

1938 "*Fī nawāḥī min al-buldān*"; the *naḥiya* (pl. *nawāḥī*) and the *bilda* (also, *balad*, pl. *buldān*) were both terms that meant "village." Al-Qalqashandī, in the above context, probably means that these lands were in the outskirts of villages.

1939 "*Wujūh al-birr*," also "pious purposes." (See Adam Sabra, *Poverty and Charity in Medieval Islam: Mamluk Egypt, 1250–1517*, (Cambridge, 2000), 50).

1940 "*Wujūh*" (sing. "*wajh*") has several meanings including: "aspects," "directions," "intentions" and "reasons." The way the word is employed in a sentence determines its meaning. Al-Qalqashandī, for example, uses it to refer to both the sources of collected revenues and the channels of expenditure (*Ṣubḥ*, Vol. 1, 39). "*Al-'Ayn*"is a term that refers to the endowed property that is the source which produces the profit to be spent in the channels dictated in the endowment deed; for example, a land that is endowed and produces crops, which are sold for profit. Naturally, the rules of *waqf* (endowment) necessitate that the *'ayn* itself is never sold or dissolved in any way, and it has to conform to certain stipulations before it is endowed, such as being free of debts. The term "*wujūh al-'ayn*" may, therefore, be translated as "channels of endowment expenditure."

1941 Sing. *rab'*, see Glossary: "*ribā'*".

1942 "*Rizaq al-khaṭābāt*," which were the incomes generated from endowed lands to be assigned to the mosque preachers (*khuṭabā'*, sing. *khaṭīb*). (See A. Sabra, *Poverty*, 71–72).

1943 The vizier, see Glossary.

1944 'Alī b. Muḥammad b. Salīm, Abū al-Ḥasan, al-Ṣāḥib Bahā' al-Dīn b. Ḥanna al-Miṣrī (the Egyptian) (d. 677 AH/1279 AD) was one of the smartest, firmest, most experienced and strongest-willed men of his time. Sultan al-Ẓāhir Baybars appointed him vizier, gave him full authority, and highly respected him. Bahā' al-Dīn was known for his honesty, tolerance and charity. Although several people tried to slander and get rid of him, they did not manage to find enough reason to defame him. He built a madrasa and allocated an endowment. He died at the age of 74after serving as vizier to al-Ẓāhir's son, Sultan Baraka Khān (r. 676 AH/1277 AD – 678 AH/1279 AD). (Al-Ṣafadī, *Wafayāt*, Vol. 22, 21–23 and al-Maqrīzī, *Sulūk*, Vol. 2, 114–115).

1945 That is, changed and renovated.

highest offices, usually given to the high-ranking amirs of Egypt who are men of the sword.

As for the general offices assigned to a number of people, [they include]: Office of the Preachers (*al-khaṭāba*)[1946]

This is actually the grandest and highest-ranking office, for the Prophet used to carry it out himself then the four Rightly-guided Caliphs followed him, then their successors. The holders of this office are as many as the numerous mosques of Egypt, and are, therefore, enumerable. Only a few and rare ones are appointed by the sultan, such as at the Mosque of the Citadel, unless it was separated from the office of the Chief Judge (*qaḍā'*), and similar [cases] that do not have a special supervisor (*nāẓir*).[1947]

Offices of the Teachers (*al-tadārīs*)[1948]

This entails teaching all the various [sciences], such as Jurisprudence (*fiqh*); the Prophet's Traditions (*ḥadīth*); Interpretation (*tafsīr*);[1949] Grammar (*naḥw*), Language (*lugha*) and the like. The sultan only appoints the holders of this office at highly-esteemed and critical places that do not have a special supervisor (*nāẓir*), such as the Ṣalāḥiyya Madrasa next to the tomb of al-Imām al-Shāfi'ī;

1946 Office of the *khaṭīb*, the Sermon Giver or the Preacher: This was the man responsible for delivering sermons on Fridays, 'Īd al-Fiṭr, 'Īd al-Aḍḥā, and on occasions of solar and lunar eclipses. The *khaṭīb*, like the imām, had to be known for his piety and have a great knowledge of religion and rituals, for he held one of the most respected posts. He had to memorize the Quran and be excellent in its recitation, as well as have a good voice. The *khaṭīb* had to know the rules of sermon-giving and be good at it. The sultan only appointed sermon-givers at the major mosques, such as the Citadel mosque, where mostly the Shāfi'ī Chief Judgewas made the *khaṭīb*, for it was the mosque where the sultan prayed. Sometimes if the sultan heard a particular *khaṭīb* and liked him, he appointed him at the mosque of the Citadel. (H. al-Battawi, *'Imāma*, 79–80). In this translation, the term *khaṭīb* is translated as "preacher" for simplification. The more accurate term would be sermon-deliverer, since the preacher is the translation of "*wā'iẓ*."

1947 The intended meaning is probably that the sultan appointed the *khaṭīb* of the Mosque of the Citadel, in case this office was separated from the office of the Chief Judge (*qaḍā'*), therefore not automatically occupied by the Chief Judge himself. The relevant supervisors were the ones normally responsible for appointing preachers and teachers, as apparent from the author's accounts.

1948 Office of *al-mudarris*, the Teacher: Teaching establishments spread throughout Egypt, and they were not restricted to madrasas, for the mosques and the Sufi establishments were also learning centres. The sultan appointed the senior teachers at major madrasas, such as the ones listed above. The rest of the teachers were appointed according to the stipulations of the endower of each establishment. Brilliant students assisted their teachers either through repeating and facilitating the lessons to the learners (*al-mu'īd*, the repeater), or through conducting further research for more benefit (*al-mufīd*, the beneficial or the helpful). The schools had their jurists; reciters responsible for teaching the proper recitations; shaykhs who taught the Prophet's traditions (*ḥadīth*); Quranic reciters; religious singers of the Prophet's praise; librarians, and other officials. Both men and women attended these lessons at the religious establishments and assemblies, although in separate sections and using separate exits. (H. al-Battawi, *'Imāma*, 78–79).

1949 Interpretation or explanation, is the science of exegesis of the Quran.

the Ṣalāḥiyya Zawiya at the Old Mosque [of ʿAmr] in Fustat, which is known as al-Khashshābiyya;[1950] the Manṣūriyya Madrasa in the above mentioned Manṣūrī Hospital at Bayn al-Qaṣrayn; the lesson (*dars*) at the Mosque of Ibn Ṭūlūn, and the like.

1950 Al-Maqrīzī does not mention a zawiya with this name in his listing of the several zawiyas at the Mosque of ʿAmr in the account of the *Khiṭaṭ*,but refers to it in *Sulūk*. The first zawiya he mentions in the *Khiṭaṭ* is the one attributed to al-Imām al-Shāfiʿī and built by Sultan Ṣalāḥ al-Dīn's son, Sultan al-ʿAzīz ʿUthmān, which was probably the most prominent zawiya. Another zawiya, al-Tājiyya, was located in front of the wooden mihrab (*al-miḥrāb al-khashab*). It is difficult to judge whether the zawiya called al-Khashshābiyya at the Mosque of ʿAmr was of any relevance to either the one built by Ṣalāḥ al-Dīn's son or al-Tājiyya. (Al-Maqrīzī, *Khiṭaṭ*, Vol. 3, 169–170 and *Sulūk*, Vol. 3, 150, Vol. 4, 94, & Vol. 5, 357).

The Fourth Purpose
On the attire of the kingdom dignitaries who hold sultanic posts (*arbāb al-manāṣib al-sulṭāniyya*) in Egypt

Their costumes and equestrian attire

Four Categories

The First Category
Men of the Sword, whose attire is divided into two divisions:

First: Their Costumes

Their costumes differ depending on which part of the body they cover. As for the headgear, it was explained earlier that the Ayyubids used to wear yellow caps (*kalawtāt*) without turbans and that they hadhair locks (*dhawā'ib sha'r*) that they loosened behind their backs. In his reign, al-Ashraf Khalīl b. Qalāwūn changed the colour of the caps to red instead of yellow, and ordered wearing turbans upon them. This remained the case until al-Malik al-Nāṣir Muḥammad b. Qalāwūn went on pilgrimage towards the end of his reign and shaved his head, so everyone shaved theirs, and they continue to do so until now. Their turbans used to be small, until they were enlarged in the reign of al-Ashraf Shaʿbān b. Ḥusayn, which resulted in a more beautiful and finer shape [of turbans] that remains [the case] up to our times.

As for their clothes, they wear Tartar Coats(*al-aqbiya al-tatariyya*),[1951] above which they put on the *taklāwāt*,[1952]then the Islamic Coat (*al-qabā' al-Islāmī*)[1953] above all. They gird their swords above that on the left side, while the leather sack

1951 *Al-aqbiya al-tatariyya* were coats worn by Mamluk amirs;their hems crossed the chest in a diagonal from left to right, unlike the old form of traditional straight cut that was used by the Fatimids. This garment was made of wool, silk or cotton and was white or adorned with alternating blue and red bands, which was called "*al-mushahhar*." It also had tight sleeves. (Y. Stillman, *Dress* , 63, K. al-Juburi, *Masālik*(2010), Vol. 3, 291 fn. 1 and see Glossary: "*qabā*"").

1952 Some sources define the word as the plural form of an unidentified type of garment that the Mamluk amirs used to wear. Another definition of the word is that it is the plural of *taklāt*, which is a horned hat of Mongol origin that resembles an animal horn. This second definition, however, provides an unlikely meaning to the word in the context above, since it refers to an overall body garment worn in between the two coats (*aqbiya*). (S. Ashour, *'Aṣr*, 424 and al-ʿUmarī, *Masālik* (2002),Vol. 3, 434).

1953 It appears that there is no exact definition for this coat, except that it had distinctive tailoring. Al-Qalqashandī mentions in another context that *al-aqbiya al-islāmiyya* may have tight sleeves. (K. al-Juburi, *Masālik* (2010), Vol. 3, 291 fn. 3 and *Ṣubḥ*, Vol. 4, 381).

(*ṣawlaq*)[1954] and the dagger (*kizlik*)[1955] are [tied] on the right. Sultan ʿImād al-Dīn, the Ruler of Hama, said in his *Tārīkh* that: The first to order this was Ghāzī b. Zankī, brother of al-ʿĀdil Nūr al-Dīn al-Shahīd,[1956] when he reigned over Mosul after his father.[1957]As for the amirs, the commanders (*muqaddamūn*) and the elite soldiers (*a'yān al-jund*), they wear coats (*aqbiya*) with short sleeves above that, which are shorter than the sleeves of the under-coat (*al-qabā' al-taḥtānī*), without much difference in the lengths of the sleeves. The short sleeves are wide, while the long sleeves are tight.

In summertime, all cloths [used] for top coats (*fawqānī*)[1958] or otherwise were white, of the *naṣāfī*[1959] *[cloth] and the like. A waist belt* (*minṭaqa*),[1960] which is the strap (*ḥiyāṣa*),[1961] is tied above the Islamic Coat. Most of their waist belts (*manāṭiq*) are made of gold-plated silver, or may be gold, and possibly inlaid

1954 Pl. *ṣawāliq*: A leather sack or bag that the mamluk tied to the right side of his waist strap (*ḥiyāṣa*). The *ṣawlaq* was used to keep the food rations required on travel. (Al-Baqli, *Ta'rīf*, 224 and S. Ashour, *'Aṣr*, 452).

1955 A Persian word that means a knife or "the curved point of a sword or dagger." (F. Steingass, "A Comprehensive Persian-English Dictionary,"http://dsal.uchicago.edu/cgi-bin/philologic/search3dsal?dbname=steingass&query=kizlik&matchtype=exact&display=utf8). It is used to refer to a kind of a dagger.

1956 Al-Shahīd, "the Witness," was one of the early Zangid titles that was acquired by al-ʿĀdil Nūr al-Dīn. In reference to the Quranic verse Sūrat al-Baqara – Chapter of the Cow, 2:143 (See http://corpus.quran.com/translation.jsp?chapter=2&verse=143), the word is used to mean witnessing the actions and deeds of people. If this title is associated with the name of a deceased man, it means "the martyr." (H. al-Basha, *Alqāb*, 363–364).

1957 It seems that this is the same account that al-Qalqashāndī referred to earlier, which mentions that Sultan Ghāzī was the first to order soldiers to ride only with the swords tied to their waists and the maces beneath their knees. (See Abū al-Fidā', *Tārīkh*, Vol. 3, 21).

1958 Also *fawqāniyya* (pl. *fawqāniyyāt*), which is defined as the robe worn above the clothes, or the overgarment, as opposed to the *taḥtāniyya* (the undergarment). Men used to wear the *fawqāniyya* above the *jubba* (buttoned robe, opened from the neck to below the chest). In older times, the *fawqāniyya* was confined to the judges. One secondary source reports that this type of robe was made of broadcloth (*jūkh*), but another notes that broadcloth was not worn by the Men of the Turban, since it was considered of a lower grade, and was only worn at times of severe economic crises by distinguished people, including the vizier and the chief judge, when people could not afford otherwise. (S. Ashour, *'Aṣr*, 460, S. Abu Zayd, *Ḥisba*, 117 fn. 25, and H. al-Battawi, *'Imāma*, 135–136).

1959 Sing. *niṣfiyya*, which was a kind of fine cloth made of silk or linen. The term was also used to a type of garment made of rough cotton. (S. Ashour, *'Aṣr*, 481 and Al-Baqli, *Ta'rīf*, 347).

1960 Also *minṭaq*, is a kind of a waist belt or strap, mostly made of gold or silver and sometimes made of cloth or leather. (S. Ashour, *'Aṣr*, 478).

1961 The *ḥiyāṣa* was the waistbelt, strap, or whatever that was used to tie the waist. The term was originally used for the girdle used to tie the horse's saddle. Al-Qalqashandī defined it as one of the old instruments, for it is related that Caliph ʿAlī b. Abī Ṭālib used to wear a waist belt (*minṭaqa*). The Mamluk sultans did not regularly wear a waist belt, but they granted their amirs with this item as a part of the costumes of honour. The *ḥiyāṣa* differed according to the amir's rank, sometimes golden and inlaid with gemstones, or made of and decorated with other materials. (Al-Baqli, *Ta'rīf*, 112).

with jade (*yashm*).[1962] The author of *Masālik al-Abṣār* said: It was not inlaid with jewels unless it was among the costumes of honour that the sultan was to bestow on the high-ranking amirs of hundreds.[1963]

In wintertime, their top coats (*fawqāniyyāt*) are colourful and made of precious wool and excellent silk. Beneath them, they wear furs of young squirrels. The high-ranking amirs wearthe furs of sable, lynx, ermine and fennec, and they hang a small kerchief (*mindīl*) from the waist belt to cover the leather sack. Most of them wear embroidery of gold brocade (*zarkash*) or inscribed black silk on the two sleeves. The author of *Masālik al-Abṣār* said: Only one who had an *iqṭā'* in the *ḥalaqa* was entitled to wear embroidered clothes, but those who were still at the level of [only receiving] a salary (*jāmukiyya*) were not entitled to that.[1964]

As for their feet, in summer, they wear the *'Alawiyya*[1965] *white shoes (khifāf)*[1966] and in winter they wear the yellow ones made of *Ṭā'ifī*[1967] *leather. They tie silver inlaid*[1968] *spurs (mahāmīz)*[1969] to their feet, above the shoes. The author of *Masālik al-Abṣār* said: Only one who had an *iqṭā'* in the *ḥalaqa* was allowed to have gold inlaid spurs,[1970] as mentioned above regarding wearing embroidery.

Second: Their Rides

Their rides, especially those of the amirs and men of similar level, are well-bred, marked (*musawwama*) and highlypriced horses. They never ride mules, but their slave-boys (*ghilmān*) ride mules behind them in precious cloths, fine appearance, and silver adorned horseshoes.[1971] The horseshoes may be completely covered with silver, even perhaps gold for [the rides of] the sultan and the dignitaries among the amirs, along with long, colourful capes (*'ibiy*) of excellent wool, or may be silk for the dignitaries' [rides]. The caparisons (*kanābīsh*) contours that

1962 Persian for a fine kind of jade; A particular type of jasper or agate that was believed to come from India or China, and to have protective power against lightening by diverting it from the place where it is kept or the person who wears it. (F. Steingass, "A Comprehensive Persian-English Dictionary,"http://dsal.uchicago.edu/cgi-bin/philologic/search3dsal?dbname=steingass&query=yashm&matchtype=exact&display=utf8).

1963 Al-'Umarī, *Masālik* (2010), Vol. 3, 292.

1964 Al-'Umarī, *Masālik* (2010), Vol. 3, 292.

1965 Probably the name of this particular type of shoes.

1966 Sing. *khuff*: also light shoes or sandals (see http://www.baheth.info/all.jsp?term=الخف and Glossary).

1967 A special kind of leather, probably attributed to al-Ṭā'if, city in present day Saudi Arabia, to the south east of Mecca.

1968 *Al-Musaqqaṭa bi-l-fiḍḍa*, which is understood to mean "inlaid with silver," given the later reference to the golden inlaid spurs in the same sentence.

1969 Sing. *mihmāz*.

1970 Al-'Umarī, *Masālik* (2010), Vol. 3, 292.

1971 *Qawālib* (sing. *qālab* or *qālib*), which has several meanings, one of which is shoe or wooden shoe, and in the above context refers to horseshoes. (http://www.baheth.info/all.jsp?term=قالب).

are brocaded [with silver inlaid with gold][1972] are sometimes used instead. The [capes] may also be gold-brocaded (*zarkash*) for the sultan and the amirs. The bridles are adorned and inlaid with silver,[1973] according to the owner's choice. The riders [fastened] the mace (*dabbūs*) in a ring attached to the saddle below their right knees. The Ruler of Hama said: The first to order them to do that was Ghāzī b. Zankī, when he also commanded them to gird the swords to their waists,[1974] as mentioned above. The author of *Masālik al-Abṣār* said: On the whole, their attire is elegant[1975] and their equipment is excellent and precious.[1976]

The Second Category Holders of religious offices, such as the judges and the rest of religious scholars, whose attire is also divided into two categories:

First: Their Costumes

Their costumes differ based on their levels. The judges and religious scholars among the [the holders of religious offices] wear turbans made of enormous muslin [cloths] (*shāshāt*). Some of them release a turban tail (*dhu'āba*) that runs between their shoulders and up to the pommels (*qarabūs*)[1977] of their saddles as they ride. Others replace this turban tail with an excellent turban cover (*ṭaylasān*) and wear a wide and long-sleeved robe (*dilq*)[1978] over their shoulders, that is opened, without a vent,[1979] and falls straight on their feet.[1980] The chief judges of the Shāfi'ī and Ḥanafī schools are distinguished by wearing a headscarf (*ṭarḥa*) that covers their turbans and falls on their backs, which was originally specific

1972 "*Al-Kanābīsh bi-l-ḥawāshī al-makhāyish*," that is: "the caparisons with brocaded contours." Al-Qalqashandī explains that the "*makhāyish*" are the caparisons brocaded with silver inlaid with gold. (*Ṣubḥ*, Vol. 2, 129).

1973 "*Tussaqaṭ-bi-l-fiḍḍa*".

1974 Abū al-Fidā', *Tārīkh*, Vol. 3, 21.

1975 "*Ẓarīf*," which may also mean "adorned," since the verb *ẓarrafa* also means "to embellish" or "to adorn."

1976 Al-'Umarī, *Masālik* (2010), Vol. 3, 292, also see the account for other types of cloths they used.

1977 Pl. *qarābīs*, pommel of the saddle: A small piece of wood at the frontal and the rear parts of the saddle. (L. Mayer, *Costume*, 50, A. Maged, *Nuẓum*, Vol. 1, 176 and S. Abu Zayd, *Ḥisba*, 116 fn. 19).

1978 Also, *daliq*: A robe worn by religious figures that was composed of several pieces of cloth of different colours. It is also thought to have been made of fur or leather. Many religious scholars exaggerated the sizes and widths of such robes to the extent that a single sleeve was big enough to tailor a whole other robe. These huge sleeves were left to drag on the ground for they were too heavy to carry. This exaggeration, like the sizes of turbans, was a sign of higher social status and professional rank. Some Sufi shaykhs imitated the judges in wearing the *dilq*, but theirs was not to be too long to drag behind them or be long-sleeved. (S. Ashour, *'Aṣr*, 438, S. Abu Zayd, *Ḥisba*, 116 fn. 22,H. al-Battawi, *'Imāma*, 135, andL. Mayer, *Costume*, 50).

1979 "*Bi-ghayr tafrīj*," that is, without a too wide an opening or vent. (S. Abu Zayd, *Ḥisba*, 116 fn. 23 and L. Mayer, *Costume*, 50).

1980 L. Mayer, *Costume*, 50.

to the Shāfi'ī judge. Those beneath that [level of headgear] among them wear smaller turbans and instead of the *dilq*, another robe (*farjiyya*)[1981] that is opened at the front from top to bottom and buttoned up with buttons. None of them wear silk or garments that are majorly made of silk.[1982] In winter, the top coats (*fawqānī*) of their clothes are made of white Maltese wool and they only wear the coloured [ones] in their homes. Some of them may wear woollen ones on the streets. They wear *Ṭā'ifī* leather shoes (*khifāf*), without spurs.[1983]

Second: Their Rides

The dignitaries of this category, such as judges and the like, ride highlypriced mules that are of equivalent prices to well-bred, marked horses (*musawwama*). Their mules have heavy bridles and coloured saddles that are not adorned with silver. They put broadcloth (*jūkh*) covers (*qarqashīn*)[1984] around their saddles. The author of *Masālik al-Abṣār* said: This is similar to a saddle dress, only smaller.[1985] Instead of the capes (*'ibiy*) [of rides], they use woollen inscribed caparisons (*kanābīsh*) [to cover] the mules up to the croup. The rides of the chief judges are distinguished by using the broadcloth cover (*zunnārī*)[1986] instead, which is similar to a cape (*'abā'a*); it runs circular behind the croup and is not topped by a *birdanab*[1987] *or a qūsh.*[1988] They sometimes ride with the caparisons (*kanābīsh*), while those within this category who are inferior to them [in level] may ride horses with caparisonsand capes [of rides].[1989]

The Third Category Sufi Shaykhs

Like the religious scholars, they wear a robe (*dilq*), except that it does not fall down [to their feet], nor is it long-sleeved. They send a little turban tail (*dhu'āba*)

1981 The *farjiyya* was a long-sleeved robe similar to the *jubba* or the *qabā'* (coat). It was open at the front from top to bottom and had buttons, as described above. (H. al-Battawi, *'Imāma*, 135 and S. Ashour, *'Aṣr*, 460).

1982 Based on a Prophet's tradition, wearing silk and gold is religiously forbidden for men.

1983 See also al-'Umarī's account in *Masālik* (2010), Vol. 3, 303–304.

1984 The *qarqashīn* was a sort of a robe for the saddle, used to cover it. In al-'Umarī's account: "*'arqashīn*." (H. al-Battawi, *'Imāma*, 136 and al-'Umarī, *Masālik* (2010), Vol. 3, 303).

1985 Al-'Umarī, *Masālik*, Vol. 3, 303.

1986 A kind of housing (*ajlāl*): A cover of the horse's body that is open at its chest and cast on its rump to cover its tail. The *zunnārī* was granted instead of the caparison (*kunbūsh*) to those favoured and appreciated by the sultan. It was usually made of red satin (*aṭlas*) or broadcloth. (Al-Baqli, *Ta'rīf*, 173 and S. Ashour, *'Aṣr*, 446).

1987 This is an assumed pronunciation since no diacritics are provided. The word probably refers to something that covered the croup or hind legs.

1988 Possibly a particular piece of cloth that covered the croup or rump, since "posterior" is one of the meanings of the word (http://www.baheth.info/all.jsp?term=قوش).

1989 See also al-'Umarī's account in *Masālik* (2010), Vol. 3, 303–304.

on their left ears that hardly reaches their shoulders. They ride their mules with caparisons (*kanābīsh*), as mentioned above.

The Fourth Category Holders of Offices at the Bureaus (*arbāb al-waẓā'if al-dīwāniyya*)

Their dignitaries, such as the viziers and their likes, wear buttoned robes (*farājī*)[1990] that are similar to the above-mentioned ones worn by the religious scholars. They might wear robes (*jibāb*)[1991] that have vents at the back. The author of *Masālik al-Abṣār* said: The notables among them wore sleeves with open vents (*bādhanjāt*),[1992] which is now limited to their costumes of honour (*tashārīf*).[1993] Those of inferior [levels] wear the buttoned robes (*farjiyyāt*) with vents at the back, mentioned above.

As for their rides, these are similar or close to the rides of soldiers. The author of *Masālik al-Abṣār* said: The attire and costumes of this category is better decorated in Egypt than it is in Syria,[1994]except for the stories told about the Copts of Egypt regarding the luxury of status and [generous] spending in their homes, to the extent that, in their offices (*dawāwīn*), they may be wearing the cheapest clothes, eating the most modest food and riding donkeys, until they reach their homes, where they transfer to another state, [as if] from nothingness to existence.[1995] He added: People may exaggerate in the stories they tell about them in that concern.[1996]

1990 Also, *farjiyyāt*, sing. *farjiyya*.

1991 Sing. *jubba*, a robe similar to the *farjiyya*.

1992 Sing. *badhahanj*, *bādāhanj*, or *bādhanj*: A Persian architectural term that means a wind catcher, a ventilation opening, or a skylight. The term also refers to the openings in a sleeve. (M. Dahman, *Mu'jam*, 29, and S. Ashour, *'Aṣr*, 417).

1993 Costumes that the sultan bestows on the high-ranking amirs on special occasions, especially upon appointments to high ranking positions. (S. Ashour, *'Aṣr*, 423).

1994 In fact, al-'Umarī says the opposite, which better suits the use of "except" in the next sentence in his account and in that copied by al-Qalqashandī. (*Masālik* (2010), Vol. 3, 304).

1995 An expression that denotes a complete change of situation.

1996 Al-'Umarī adds that this exaggeration may be due to "the remoteness of their affairs and the variance in their conditions." See his full account in *Masālik* (2010), Vol. 3, 304.

The Fifth Purpose
On the Sultan's Appearance in Royal Protocol
– [Seven Modes of Appearance][1997]

The First Mode of Appearance

His Appearance at his Audience Council at the House of Justice (Dār al-ʿAdl) to Resolve Grievances[1998]

If the sultan is at the Citadel, except for the month of Ramadan, he usually sits for audience on early Monday mornings at his Great Iwanthat is called "the House of Justice," which was mentioned earlier in the account on the Citadel, in the [section] on the Egyptian capital. The sultan sits on the chair (*kursī*) that is placed beneath the throne (*sarīr al-mulk*).[1999] The author of *Masālik al-Absḥār* said: The chief judges of the Four Schools [of Interpretation] sit to the sultan's right, followed by the Agent of the Public Treasury (*wakīl bayt al-māl*),then the Supervisor of the *ḥisba* (*al-nāẓir fī al-ḥisba*). The Confidential Scribe (*kātib al-sirr*) sits to the sultan's left, while the Supervisor of the Army (*nāẓir al-jaysh*) and the group of signers (*muwaqqi'ūn*) sit opposite him, which completes a circular ring.[2000] He said: If the vizier is a man of the pen, he sits between the sultan and the confidential scribe. If he is a man of the sword, he stands at a distance with the other Holders of Offices. Similarly, if thereis a viceroy, he stands with the holders of offices. Young mamluks[2001] of the Bearers of Arms (*silāḥdāriyya*), the Keepers of Robes (*jamadāriyya*)[2002] and the *khāṣṣakiyya* stand behind the sultan, to his right and left. Elderly, high-ranking amirs of hundreds, who are the Amirs of Consultation (*umarā' al-mashūra*),[2003] sit at an estimated distance of fifteen cubits, also to the right and left of the sultan. The high-ranking amirs sit following and beneath them, while the Holders of Offices [remain] standing and the rest of the amirs stand behind the Amirs of Consultation. The *ḥujjāb* and the Bearers of Inkwells (*dawādāriyya*) stand behind this ring that surrounds the sultan to bring in the petitions (*qiṣaṣ*) of those in need and bring in

1997 The original text reads "three". The The editor of Subḥ comments that the author details seven modes of appearance, just as stated in his other manuscript, *al-Ḍaw'*. (*Ṣubḥ*, Vol. 4, 44). The text uses the term "*hay'a*," which can be translated as mode, manner or form of appearance. "Mode of Appearance" will be used for translating this term henceforth.

1998 "*Khalāṣ al-maẓālim*".

1999 In al-ʿUmarī's account, the chair is placed next to the throne (*takht al-mulk*). (*Masālik* (2010), Vol. 3, 292).

2000 "*Ḥalaqa dā'ira*" (circular ring).

2001 "*Mamālīk ṣighār*" (young mamluks); in *Masālik*: "*mamālīk saffān . . .*" (two rows of mamluks). (*Masālik* (2010), Vol. 3, 293).

2002 The *jamadār* or the *jāmādār* was the wardrobe master, who was responsible for dressing the sultan or the amir. The term is Persian, composed of two syllabi: *jāmā*, meaning "robe," and *dār*, meaning "the holder of." The *jamadāriyya* were the group or faction of mamluks responsible for the sultanic wardrobe.(Al-Baqli, *Ta'rīf*, 90 and *Ṣubḥ*, Vol. 5, 459).

2003 See Glossary: "*mushāwara*".

the needy.[2004] The petitions are read to the sultan, whoturns to the judges for their advice as needed. Where it concerns the military (*'askar*), he discusses with the *ḥājib* and the Supervisor of the Army (*nāẓir al-jaysh*).[2005] He orders what he sees fit concerning the remaining matters.

I say: The present and established [seating order]is that two judges of the Four sit to the sultan's right, namely, the Shāfiʿī and the Mālikī, and the other two, namely, the Ḥanafīthen the Ḥanbalī, sit to his left. After the Mālikī Judge, to the right side, sit the three Military Judges (*quḍāt al-'askar*) mentioned before, namely, the Shāfiʿī, the Ḥanafī, then theMālikī. The muftis[2006] of the House of Justice sit following the Military Judges in that same order. They are followed by the Agent of the Public Treasury then the Supervisor of the *ḥisba* of Cairo. The *muḥtasib* may sit in a superior position to the Agent of the Public Treasury if he is of a higher level of knowledge or leadership.[2007] All these [officials sit] in one row to the right of the sultan with their backs to the iwan's main wall, while facing its door. The two judges, the Ḥanafī and the Ḥanbalī, [sit] similarly to the sultan's left. If the vizier is a man of the pen, he [sits] by the sultan's chair, at an angle to the left side, followed by the Confidential Scribe. The ring closes so that [some of] them sit with their backs to the iwan's door, as mentioned in the account of *Masālik al-Abṣār* above.[2008]

The Second Mode of Appearance

On [Other] Days

On weekdays, other than Mondays and Thursdays, the sultan customarily came out of his interior palaces[2009] mentioned above, to his big palace[2010] that overlooks his stables. Sometimes he sits on the throne (*takht al-mulk*) at the centre of of the iwan's main wall, and sometimes he sits on the floor.[2011] The amirs stand around him in the order mentioned above in the account on sitting at the iwan, except for the Amirs of Consultation and those who are strangers to him,[2012] for they do

2004 "*Masākīn*" (sing. *miskīn*), also the poor, destitute, or miserable.

2005 "*Kātib al-jaysh*" (the Army Scribe or the Army Secretary) in al-ʿUmarī's account. (*Masālik* (2010), Vol. 3, 293).

2006 See Glossary.

2007 "*Riyāsa*" (leadership) is a general term that applies to those of higher levels or ranks in many fields. In the Mamluk era, the title "*al-ra'īs*" (the leader or the head) was mainly used for Men of the Pen, whether religious scholars or official clerks. It was also used to denote the head of the Jewish population. (H. al-Basha, *Alqāb*, 308–309).

2008 For discussion of the Audience at the House of Justice, see Nasser Rabbat, *Citadel*.

2009 *Al-Quṣūr al-jawwāniyya*.

2010 *Al-Qaṣr al-kabīr* or al-Ablaq Palace.

2011 In al-ʿUmarī's account: "sits beneath it, on the floor." (*Masālik* (2010), Vol. 3, 294). The intended meaning is that the sultan either sat on the throne, which is a pulpit, or on a chair directly on the floor, not at such an elevated level.

2012 "*Al-Ghurabā' minhu*," in al-Qalqashandī's account, which may be translated as "those who are strangers to him," which is linguistically inaccurate and does not fit the context. In al-ʿUmarī's

not usually attend this council unless needed. He leaves at the third hour of the day[2013]and enters his interior palaces to [attend to] the interests of his kingdom. The Holders of Offices among his Private [sultanic] Retinue (*khāṣṣ*), such as the vizier, the Confidential Scribe,the Supervisor of the Private [sultanic] Bureau (*nāẓir al-khāṣṣ*) and the Supervisor of the Army, pass by him for work issues that are relevant to him, as need calls.[2014]

The Third Mode of Appearance

His Appearance on Friday Prayers and [Prayers of] the two Feasts

As for Friday prayers,[2015] the sultan usually exits his palace to the mosque near it that was mentioned before, accompanied by the amirs of his Private Retinue (*khāṣṣ*) and enters the mosque from the nearest of its doors to the palace.[2016] He prays inside a private *maqṣūra* in the mosque, which is to the right of the mihrab. The high-ranking amirs of his Private Retinue pray with him inside this *maqṣūra*. The rest of the amirsof the Private Retinue, as well as the ordinary ones, come and pray outside the *maqṣūra*, to its right and left, according to their ranks. When the sultan finishes prayers, he enters his women quarters and the amirs leave, each to his place.[2017]

As for the prayers of the Feasts, the sultan customarily rides from his palace's gate and descends from an exit in the stable to the square (*maydān*) right next to it, where the [royal] tent (*dihlīz*) is pitched for him in the best possible form. The preacher (*khaṭīb*) of the Citadel's Mosque comes to the square to lead the sultan in the [congregational] prayer and deliver the sermon. When the sultan is done listening to the sermon, he rides and exits the gate of the square, surrounded by the walking amirs and mamluks. The sultanic processional banners (*al-'āṣā'ib al-sulṭāniyya*), are held above his head, while the saddle cover (*ghāshiya*) is carried in front of him. The parasol (*jitr*), which is the *miẓalla*, is carried above his head by one of the high Commander Amirs who rides a horse next to the sultan. The two Royal Stable Boys (*al-ushāqīyyān al-jifta*), mentioned earlier, ride in front of the sultan, while the side rides (*janā'ib*) march behind him, as the sultanic processional banners are above his head,[2018] and the Holders of Offices among the Bearers of Arms (*silāḥdāriyya*) all ride behind him. The Bearers of the Battle-axes (*ṭabardāriyya*) march on foot

account, which al-Qalqashandī copies in part, the phrase is "*al-qurabā' minhu*," which gives the opposite meaning of "those close to him." (*Ṣubḥ*, Vol. 4, 45, and al-'Umarī, *Masālik* (2010), Vol. 3, 294).

2013 The third hour of the day, or *al-ḍuḥā*, is around 9 a.m.

2014 See al-'Umarī's account in *Masālik* (2010), Vol. 3, 293–294.

2015 See also al-'Umarī's account in *Masālik* (2010), Vol. 3, 296–297.

2016 Al-'Umarī adds that the rest of the amirs enter from one of the other mosque's doors. (*Masālik* (2010), Vol. 3, 296).

2017 "*Makān*," which most probably means "house".

2018 The editor of Subḥ notes that this is a repetition; mentioned above. (*Ṣubḥ*, Vol. 4, 46 fn. 1).

holding their battle-axes in front of the sultan. He exits the stable's gate and ascends to the Great Iwan mentioned earlier. A banquet is stretched out and the sultan bestows costumes of honour on the Bearer of the Parasol (*ḥāmil al-jitr*); the Amir of Arms (*amir silāḥ*); the Master Supervisor of Warehouses (*ustādār*); the Food Taster (*jāshankīr*) and a group of the Holders of Offices who provide service[2019] to [execute] important tasks of the *'īd*, such as the deputies of the Master Supervisorof Warehouses, the lesser Food Tasters (*jāshankīriyya*), the Supervisor of Warehouses (*nāẓir al-buyūt*), and their likes.

The Fourth Mode of Appearance

His appearance for playing *kura*at the Great Square (al-Maydān al-Akbar)

The sultan customarily rides on three consecutive processions for this, every Saturday, after the Fulfillment of the Nile. He descends from his palace in the early morning and exits the stable's gate, riding in the [above-]mentioned appearance for the *'īd*, except for the parasol (*jitr*), which is not carried above his head. The saddle cover (*ghāshiya*) is carried in front of him, at the beginning and end of the road. He reaches the Square and stays at its palaces, while the amirs stay at their [designated] places according to their ranks. He then rides with the amirs to play *kura* after *ẓuhr* prayers. He then goes down[2020] to rest, while the amirs continue to play*kura* until the call for *'aṣr* prayers. The sultan then prays *'aṣr* and rides in the same appearance of the early morning, up to his palace.

The Fifth Mode of Appearance

His appearance for riding to break the Khalījat the Fulfillment of the Nile (*wafā' al-Nīl*)

You should know that the sultan may ride to break the Khalīj and it is not the custom for him to ride for this procession with a parasol (*miẓalla*), a neck cover (*raqaba*) for the horse, a saddle cover (*ghāshiya*), or similar [instruments] that were mentioned above in the processions of the Square and the two Feasts. He only rides with the small yellow banners (*sanājiq*), [accompanied by] the Bearers of the Battle-axes, the Ushers (*jāwīshiyya*),[2021] and the like. He rides from the Citadel after the Overseer of the Nilometer (*ṣāḥib al-miqyās*)[2022] goes up to inform him of the

2019 Or attend the service protocol (*khidma*).

2020 Or "dismounts" (*yanzil*).

2021 Sing. *jāwīsh*, also *shāwīsh*, which is a Turkish word. The *jāwīshiyya* in the Mamluk state in Egypt were four of the Soldiers of the *ḥalaqa*, whose job was to march in front of the sultan or the viceroy in processions, to call out and point the attention of the passersby. The *jāwīsh* was also a low-ranking soldier whose master assigned with small tasks, such as delivering messages. (Al-Baqli, *Ta'rīf*, 82).

2022 This was the official responsible for monitoring the rise of the water level at the Nilometer during the flood season. He measured the rise every afternoon and reported the reading in written form to the notables of the state officials among the Men of the Sword and the Men of the Pen.

Fulfillment of the Nile, whatever the time is. He then heads to the Nilometer and enters it through its door. He offers a banquet there for his company of amirs and mamluks to eat. Saffron is then dissolved in a bowl that is handed to the Overseer of the Nilometer, who swims in the Nilometer's well until he reaches the [measuring] column, with the bowl of saffron in his hand, and perfumes the column then goes back to perfume the corners of the well. The sultan's boat (*ḥirrāqa*) will have been decorated with [various] kinds of ornaments, and so would be the amirial boats (*ḥarārīq*). The Nilometer's window, which overlooks the Nile from the direction of Fustat, will have been opened and covered with a curtain. The sultan's boat (*ḥirrāqa*) is brought to this window, from which he descends [onto the boat] and sails, surrounded with the amirial boats (*ḥarārīq*). The Nile would be filled with boats carrying spectators that sail behind the *ḥarārīq* until the sultanenters Fumm al-Khalīj. The great sultanic *ḥirrāqa*, known as the Golden One (al-Dhahabiyya), and theamirial *ḥarārīq* [fire their *nafṭ* canons[2023]] from their bows.[2024] The sultan sails in his small *ḥirrāqa* until he reaches the dam, which is then broken in his presence. He then rides and leaves for the Citadel.

The Sixth Mode of Appearance

His Appearance on His Travels

It is not customary on travels to show the decorations mentioned before, for the processions of the Feast and the Square. Instead, the sultan rides among a large number of amirs: High and low-ranking ones; the Private [sultanic] Retinue (*khawāṣṣ*); the foreigners[2025] and his private (*khawāṣṣ*) mamluks. He does not ride, along the way, with the neck cover (*raqaba*) or the processional banners (*'aṣā'ib*) and is not followed by side rides (*janā'ib*). Mostly, travel is intentionally postponed until nighttime. When night falls, many lanterns (*fawānīs*) and torches (*mashā'il*)[2026] are carried in front of the sultan. As he approaches his camp, he is

He reported the incremental increases in fingers, then in arms (cubits), noting the date in both Hijri and Coptic calendars and comparing the rise to the same time of the previous year. The situation was not announced to the public until the rise reached the critical sixteen cubits of the Nilometer column, indicating the Fulfillment of the Nile. A public daily announcement was then made of the further increase in fingers and in cubits. (*Ṣubḥ*, Vol. 3, 297).

2023 There is some ambiguity in the term "*nafṭ*", which can either mean gunpowder or a flamable mixture. So the canon mentioned can either be using gunpowder to fire missiles or else it can be a form of syphon that ejects the flammable mixture, like a modern day flamethrower. (See Glossary).

2024 "*Yul'ab bihā fī wasaṭ imtidādihā*," where "*yul'ab*," is understood as "being fired from." The whole passage may also mean that the ships sail throughout the length of the Fumm al-Khalij varying their path and while firing their canons till they reached the location of the dam.

2025 "*Al-Ghurabā'*". In this instance, the same word is employed in al-ʿUmarī's account. (*Masālik*, Vol. 3 (2010), 294).

2026 *Fawānīs* (lanterns, sing. *fānūs*) and *mashā'il* (torches, sing. *mash'al*): Al-Qalqashandī defines the *fānūs* as a spherical instrument with iron sides, covered with light white linen. It is used for lighting by fixing a candle inside it, at its bottom. As for the *mash'al*, it was an iron instrument,

received with candles fitted in inlaid candlesticks, while the Ushers (*jāwīshiyya*) immediately in front of him hail and everyone dismounts, except for the Bearers of Arms and the Royal Stable Boys (*ūshāqiyya*) riding behind him. The Bearers of the Battle-axes march around him until he enters the first tent (*dihlīz*) of his camp, where he descends and enters the *shuqqa*,[2027] which is a wide, circular tent and from it into a smaller *shuqqa*, then into a *lājūq*.[2028] A wooden *kharkāh*[2029] wall runs inside each tent, around all its sides. A small wooden house is erected at the center of the main side of the lājūq [for ths sultan] to sleep in. A bath is erected opposite the *shuqqa*, which is equipped with lead pots[2030] and a basin (*ḥawḍ*), in the same fashion as city baths, only that it is smaller. When the sultan goes to sleep, the mamluks go around him in a circle, while the guards go around everyone. The announcement procession (*zaffa*) circulates around the royal tent(*dihlīz*) twice every night; once when he goes to sleep and once when he wakes up. A high-ranking amir[2031] goes around with the *zaffa*, surrounded by lanternsand torches. The Holders of Offices, such as the captains (*nuqabā'*)[2032] and others,[2033] spend the night at the door of the royal tent (*dihlīz*). When the sultan enters the city, he rides in the appearance of the *'īd* prayer processions, with the parasol (*jitr*) and other [elements]. This [above description] is concerned with what is particular to the sultan.

like a cage with an opened top and a small opening in its bottom, in which dry wood was burnt for lighting. Both instruments were carried in front of the sultans or the amirs at night on their travels. (*Ṣubḥ*, Vol. 2, 130–131).

2027 Pl. *shiqāq* or *ashqāq*: Al-Qalqashandī defines it as a kind of tent made of linen, with leather handles used to pitch it with wedges. It was round and included several compartments (*akhbiya*, sing. *khabā'*) and partitions made of hair (*buyūt al-sha'r*, that is hair-lined cloths). This *shuqqa* had four doors or entrances in each direction, and is called "*al-ḥawsh*" (the court) in Egypt. Other definitions of the term include a woolen textile lined with fine, thin hair and a piece of linen or goat-hair, one of which, or more, were put on a tent or its entrance to distinguish it from the rest of the tents. (*Ṣubḥ*, Vol. 5, 209, al-Baqli, *Ta'rīf*, 203–204 and M. Dahman, *Mu'jam*, 99).

2028 *Lājūq* is a Persian word that means tent, or "an osier tent covered with felt." It was probably a tent or a partition of the bigger tent that was for the sultan's private stay, since the account above shows it was his last place of rest. (See F. Steingass, "A Comprehensive Persian-English Dictionary": http://dsal.uchicago.edu/cgi-bin/philologic/getobject.pl?c.5:1:6361.steingass).

2029 Pl. *kharkawāt*: Wooden huts made of special shapes and covered with broadcloth or a similar textile. They were carried along on travels to be put inside the tent to protect the dwellers from the cold. (Al-Baqli, *Ta'rīf*, 117 and*Ṣubḥ*, Vol. 2, 131).

2030 "*Qudūr*" (sing. *qidr*), which were among the travel instruments that al-Qalqshandī lists; however, being cooking pots, usually made of copper and sometimes of earthenware. Kings boasted of the number and sizes of these pots, for they showed a king's generosity and the number of his men. (*Ṣubḥ*, Vol. 2, 131).

2031 Al-'Umarī notes that each *zaffa* is led by an Amir Jāndār (the Personal Guard). (*Masālik* (2010), Vol. 3, 295).

2032 Sing. *naqīb*, see Glossary.

2033 According to al-'Umarī, the chiefs and those responsible for the shifts from among the servants (*arbāb al-nuwab min al-khadam*) were the ones who spent the nights at the door of the royal tent. (*Masālik* (2010), Vol. 3, 295).

As for sultan's procession where the multitude of his mamluks marches, it is marked with the Commander of Mamluks (*muqaddam al-mamālīk*) and the Master Supervisor of Warehouses (*ustādār*) who accompany them. They are preceded by the treasuries (*khazā'in*), the side rides (*janā'ib*) and the camels. All that need calls for of physicians, ophthalmologists, surgeons, as well as kinds of medicines, syrups, drugs, and the like, travel in his company. All of these[2034] are given to anyone who falls sick en route.[2035]

The Seventh Mode of Appearance

Sleep

It is customary that the sultan's Private Retinue (*khawāṣṣ*) mamluks from the amirs and the Holders of Offices, such as the Keepers of Robes (*jamadāriyya*) and others, spend their nights next to him; staying up in shifts divided among them using sandglasses.[2036] When the shift of a group ends, they wake up the group that is [to guard] the shift after them. Each of them finds means to distract him from sleep; some of them read from Quran manuscripts, some play chess, some eat, or otherwise.[2037]

2034 That is, the medicines, syrups, drugs, and the like. According to al-ʿUmarī, anyone who fell sick was visited by one of the physicians, who prescribed what the patient needed and prescription was issued from the relevant treasuries that were carried along on travel. (*Masālik* (2010), Vol. 3, 295).

2035 See al-ʿUmarī's account in *Masālik* (2010), Vol. 3, 294–295.

2036 Or hourglasses: *banākīm* (also *binkāmāt*, sing. *binkām*).

2037 See also al-ʿUmarī's account in *Masālik* (2010), Vol. 3, 296 and *Masālik* (2002), Vol. 3, 441.

The Sixth Purpose
On the sultan's custom of providing running salaries (*arzāq*) – Two Categories

The First Category – The Running and Continuous: Two Kinds

The First Kind: The *iqṭā'āt*[2038]

The *iqṭā'āt* in this [Mamluk] kingdom are distributed among the amirs and soldiers (*jund*). The majority of their *iqṭā'āt* are villages (*bilād*) and lands that are exploited[2039] and dealt with by their owners (*muqṭa'ūn*)[2040] in any way they wish. Sometimes, the *iqṭā'āt* included money that the owner (*muqṭa'*) received from imposts (*jihāt*), which was little. They varied depending on the different situations of their lords.

As for the amirs of Egypt, the author of *Masālik al-Abṣār* mentioned that the *iqṭā'* of each of the high-ranking amirs amounts to 200,000 army (*jayshī*) dinars, and may be more. This [amount] decreases, considering the degradation in rank, to 80,000 dinars, or around. The *iqṭā'* of each of the *ṭablakhāna* amirs amounts to 30,000 dinars or more, and may go down to 23,000 dinars. The *iqṭā'* of each of the amirs of tens amounts to 9,000 dinars or less. The *iqṭā'* of each of the commanders of the *ḥalaqa* amounts to 1,500 dinars, and similarly, that of [each of]the elite of the soldiers of the *ḥalaqa* (*a'yān jund al-ḥalaqa*), [then it decreases for the rest to] 250 dinars.[2041]

The *iqṭā'āt* of Syria do not come close to these amounts, but only amount to two-thirds of all that is mentioned above. This is except for the high Commander Amirs of Egypt, who have no match in Syria, but for the Viceroy of Syria, who comes close to them in this [level].[2042] The author of *Masālik al-Abṣār* said: The viceroys of the kingdoms[2043] have no authority to assign an amir to the amirial rank (*ta'mīr*) of another,[2044] but if an amir dies, whether he was high or low [-ranking], the sultan is notified [of his death], so as to appoint in his place whom he wants from those in his service and send him to the location of service. As for those who

2038 Land grants, see Glossary.

2039 "*Yastaghilluhā*," in reference to "*iqṭā' al-istighlāl*." (See Glossary: "*iqṭā'*").

2040 Sing. *muqṭa'*: the recipient of the*iqṭā'* and its temporary owner based on the terms of the grant.

2041 Al-'Umarī's account is a little different; he states that the Amirs of Tens receive up to 7000 dinars and the Soldiers of the *ḥalaqa* receive up to 1500 dinars. This level of 1500 dinars, or around, is the amount allocated to the elites of the Soldiers of the *ḥalaqa*, who are appointed as their commanders (*a'yān al-ḥalaqa al-muqaddamīn 'alayhim*). Then those who are inferior to this rank receive amounts that decrease until they reach 250 dinars. Al-'Umarī adds that the *iqṭā'āt* allocated to the soldiers of the amirs are up to the amirs who decide their amounts. (*Masālik* (2010), Vol. 3, 288 and *Ṣubḥ*, Vol. 4, 50).

2042 It may be understood from al-'Umarī's account that there were *iqṭā'āt* of the level received by the high Commander Amirs of Hundreds that were allocated in Syria, except that this was too rare and he knew no one of that level except the Viceroy of Syria. (*Masālik* (2010), Vol. 3, 288)

2043 That is, in Syria. (See al-'Umarī, *Masālik* (2010), Vol. 3, 301).

2044 In al-'Umarī's account: "another who had died." (*Masālik* (2010), Vol. 3, 301).

were in the [same] locations of service, or those transferred to them from another province, this was up to the sultan's decision.[2045]

As for the Soldiers of the *ḥalaqa*, if one of them dies, the viceroy employs another in his replacement.[2046] He writes a *ruq'a* [documenting this] at the Army Bureau of this kingdom. A mailman (*barīdī*) is equipped to travel with it[2047] to the sultan's court, where he receives an approval of the *ruq'a*[2048] from the Army Bureau of the capital. Then, if the sultan approves it, he writes "to be written" (*yuktab*) on it. It is then written in a murabba'a[2049] from the Army Bureau, and a Decree of Grant (*manshūr*) is written for it.[2050]

All the amirs in the sultan's capital (*ḥaḍra*) receive daily running allowances of meat, spices, bread, fodder and oil. The dignitaries among them also receive clothes and candles. The Sultanic Mamluks and the position holders among the soldiers (*jund*) also [receive allowances] that vary in quantities depending on their ranks and their special preference by and closeness to the sultan. The author of *Masālik al-Abṣār* said: If an amir's son grows up, he is granted dinars, bread, meat and fodder, until he qualifies [to receive] an *iqṭā'* from the total of the *ḥalaqa*. Then some of them are transferred to [the rank of the] Amirs of Ten or *ṭablakhānāh*, according to their luck and fortune.

The Second Kind: Salaries of the Men of the Pen

These are sums of money that are paid to them on a monthly basis. The author of *Masālik al-Abṣār* said: The grandest among them, such as the vizier, receives 250 army (*jayshī*) dinars monthly, in addition to the allowances (*rawātib*) and grains[2051] that if expanded[2052] and evaluated, would have the same [value as the

2045 See al-'Umarī, *Masālik* (2010), Vol. 3, 301.

2046 "*Istakhdam al-nā'ib 'awaḍahu.*"

2047 "He is equippd to travel with a mailman . . .," while al-'Umarī more plausibly mentions the official document travels by mail. (*Masālik* (2010), Vol. 3, 301).

2048 "*Yuqābal 'alayhā.*"

2049 The *murabba'a* (pl. *murabba'āt*, the square-shaped) was a particular type of document, square in shape and made into two opposite sheets, mostly written in a certain format and used to document matters such as the grants (*iṭlāqāt*) and the *iqṭā'āt*. Al-Qalqashandī refers to the *murabba'a*in his account of the documents of allocating the *iqṭā'āt* that were written in the Army Bureau before being submitted to the Chancery Bureau; this particular document was called: "*al- murabba'aal-jayshiyya*" (the army *murabba'a*). In another instance, al-Qalqashandī refers to the *murabba'āt* that may be written from the Vizierate Bureau (*dīwān al-wizāra*) to document the *iṭlāqāt* in the hand of the High Comptroller (*mustawfī al-ṣuḥba*). Al-Baqli, citing one case mentioned by al-Qalqashandī, defines the *murabba'a* as square decrees written on Damascene paper – a kind of paper used at the time – by the managers (*mubāshirūn*) of the Private Sultanic Bureau (*dīwān al-khāṣṣ*), to document the *iṭlāqāt*. (Al-Baqli, *Ta'rīf*, 307–308, *Ṣubḥ*, Vol. 6, 200–202 & Vol. 13, 153–155 and K. al-Juburi, *Masālik* (2010), Vol. 3, 301 fn. 1).

2050 See also al-'Umarī's account. (*Masālik* (2010), Vol. 3, 301).

2051 Or crops (*ghalla*).

2052 "*Busiṭa*," which means "explained" or "stretched out." In al-'Umarī's account, "*tasattar*," which means "written down." (Al-'Umarī, *Masalik* (2010), Vol. 3, 302).

allowance]; then lesser and lesser values [of allowances were given according to ranks].[2053] The dignitaries among them receive running allowances of meat, bread, fodder, wax, sugar, clothing and the like. This is in addition to the running [allotments] for the religious scholars (*'ulamā'*) and the men of piety, such as the allowances and eternally endowed lands,[2054] as well as similar items that are inheritable, from ancestor to successor, that are not to be found in any of the kingdoms or cities.[2055]

The Second Category Bestowals and similar items that are offered at certain times and not others, which are of five kinds:

The First Kind: Robes of Bestowal and Costumes of Honour (*al-khila' wa-l-tashārīf*)

The author of *Masālik* [*al-Abṣār*] said: The sovereign of Egypt has the upper hand over this [practice], to the extent that his court remains to be a market where every importation[2056] is expended, and people sought it from every country, until this almost exhausted the kingdom and was about to completely deplete its acquisitions (*mutaḥaṣṣilāt*). He added: This was mostly decreed by this sultan,[2057] who has burdened those succeeding him because of his immense kindness.[2058]

This [kind] is divided into three types:

The First Type: Costumes of Honour (*tashārīf*) for Men of the Sword

These are of [different] levels, the highest being the costumes especially [allocated] to the Commander Amirs, such as the viceroys and others: A red satin (*aṭlas*) top coat (*fawqānī*) with golden brocaded bands (*ṭuruz zarkash*) that is adorned with squirrel fur and contoured by an external drapery with beaver skin; with a yellow satin coat (*qabā'*) beneath it. In addition to a golden brocaded cap (*kalawta*) with golden clasps (*kalālīb*)[2059] and thin muslin (*shāsh*), to which two white silk ends[2060] are attached.[2061] These silk ends are inscribed with the titles of the sultan along with amazing designs (*nuqūsh*) of coloured silk. A golden waist belt (*minṭaqa*) fixed to a silk lining is used to gird the waist; the grades of these waist

2053 See al-'Umarī's account in *Masālik*(2010), Vol. 3, 302.

2054 "*Al-Arāḍī al-mu'abbada*," which were eternally endowed lands, not to be sold or inherited. (http://www.baheth.info/all.jsp?term=مؤبد).

2055 "*Miṣr*," city or country. (http://www.baheth.info/all.jsp?term=مصر).

2056 "*Majlūb*," which may also mean exotic importations.

2057 The sultan at the time of al-'Umarī, who is al-Nāṣir Muḥammad b. Qalāwūn.

2058 See al-'Umarī, *Masālik* (2010), Vol. 3, 321.

2059 Sing. *kallāb*: A pin or hook that is used to adorn the cap (*kalawta*). (S. Ashour, *'Aṣr*, 466).

2060 "*Ṭarafān*" (sing. *ṭaraf*), which means "end" and may refer to two tails that were sewn to the muslin (*shāsh*).

2061 That is, sewn to it.

belts (*manāṭiq*) vary according to rank. In their highest [grades], the columns[2062] are made of bawākīr[2063] at the centre and two clamps that are inlaid with spinel, emerald and pearls.[2064] Then there is the [lesser] one with a single inlaid *bīkāriyya*, then the [least] one with a single *bīkāriyya*, without inlay. If the costume of honour (*tashrīf*) was for an investiture (*taqlīd*) for a grand governorship (*wilāya*), a gold-ornamented sword and a saddled, bridled horse with a golden brocaded caparison (*kunbūsh*) were added. The high viceroys, like the Viceroy of Damascus, may be given an additional golden brocaded border (*tarkība*)[2065] [to be worn] above the top coat (*fawqānī*) and an Alexandrian silk muslin [turban-cloth] (*shāsh*), undulated with gold that is called "*al-mutammar*"[2066]; this was the muslin [turban-cloth] of the Ruler of Hama, who was given a [horse] cover (*zunnārī*) of red satin, instead of a caparison. The lesser costumes of honour include the coats of hunting

2062 "*'Umadihā*," also "its supports." (See http://www.baheth.info/all.jsp?term=عمد).

2063 Also, *bīyākīr* and *bawākīr* (sing. *bīkāriyya*):The editor of Subḥ notes that this word is not in the original manuscript, but was borrowed from *Ḍaw' al-Ṣubḥ* by al-Qalqashandī, which is his summary of *Ṣubḥ al-A'shā*. The *bīkāriyya* was an ornament that is sometimes described as two thin, oblong metal sheets that bore the inscribed name of the amir for whom the adorned item was made. The *bīkāriyya* is also defined as "a roundel," and the term has several other meanings including: "compass" (Ar. *al-firjār*, *al-birkār*, *al-barjal*), that is, the geometric instrument; "opening" and "a round piece of cloth." It should also be noted that the *bīkār* is a musical symbol, namely "natural" (♮). The Persian word *bīkār* means "war," in the general sense of the word. It is possible that the *bīkāriyya* was composed of a circle, which encompassed a shape that was either two metal sheets, as described above, or another one similar to the musical symbol. (*Ṣubḥ*, Vol. 4, 52; M. Dahman, *Mu'jam*, 41; S. Ashour, *'Aṣr*, 421; H. Abbas, *Masālik* (2002),Vol. 3, 395 fn. 1, 467 fn. 1, & 468 fn. 5; K.al-Juburi, *Masālik* (2010), Vol. 3, 318 fn. 4 and David G. Alexander, *The Arts of War: Arms and Armour of the 7th to 19th Centuries* (New York, 1992), 17 and al-Qalqashandī, *Ḍaw' al-Ṣubḥ al-Musfir*, ed. Mahmud Salama (Cairo, 1906), 260).

2064 Al-'Umarī's account describes the most precious waist belts (*manāṭiq*) saying that the *bawākir* are inserted in between the columns (*'umadihā*), one in the centre and two to the sides; rather than the above statement which leads one to conclude that the *bawākīr* themselves formed the supports, which were placed at the centre, in addition to two side clasps. (Al-'Umarī, *Masālik* (2002), Vol. 3, 318).

2065 "Fitting," which Mayer translates to "border," indicating that it was "placed right round the top coat (*fawqānī*)." Y. Stillman translates it as "trimming." (L. Mayer, *Costume*, 59 and Y. Stillman, *Dress*, 135).

2066 An unidentified kind of valuable cloth. Al-Qalqashandī's account says: "*mumawwaj bi-l-dhahab wa yu'raf dhalik bi-l-mutammar*," (undulated with gold, that is, according to Mayer, "with a pattern of wavy lines," which is known as *al-mutammar*). Mayer notes that only al-'Umarī and the sources copying him, like al-Qalqashandī, use the term "*al-mutammar*." Other sources mention another term, namely, "*al-muthmin*," which may be translated as "the precious." In the absence of diacritics, "*al-muthmin*" may also be read "*al-muthamman*," which may be translated as "the highly evaluated" or "the highly valued." Another form of the term is "*al-muthammar*," which is another unidentified term. (L. Mayer, *Costume*, 15 & 58; al-'Umarī, *Masālik* (2002), Vol. 3, 467 and K. al-Juburi, *Masālik* (2010), Vol. 3, 318 fn. 8; Jamāl al-Dīn Abū al-Ḥasan al-Qifṭī, *Akhbār al-'Ulamā' bi-Akhyār al-Ḥukamā'*, ed. Ibrahim Shams al-Din (Beirut, 2005), 257; Muhammad A. Marzuq, *History of Textile Industry in Alexandria: 331 B.C. – 1517 A.D.* (Alexandria, 1955), 59; http://www.baheth.info/all.jsp?term=مثمر, and http://www.baheth.info/all.jsp?term=مثمن).

scenes (*aqbiyaṭard waḥsh*)[2067] that are manufactured in Alexandria, Egypt and Damascus;[2068] decorated with bands (*mujawwakh*): Inscribed bands (*jākhāt*)[2069] with the sultan's titles, [figural] bands with the images of beasts or small birds, and coloured bands that are undulated with golden brocade. These coats' bands are separated by [decorative] motifs. A golden brocaded *ṭirāz* is fittedabove the coat, with the squirrel fur and beaver skin above it, as described earlier. Beneath it is a coat, which is made of a fine Alexandrian fabric;[2070] in addition to a golden-brocaded cap with clasps and muslin, as mentioned above, and a golden waist strap (*ḥiyāṣa*) that is sometimes adorned with *bīkāriyya* and sometimes not. This waist strapis for the lesser amirs of hundreds and those similar to them, as well as the holders of offices who are especially [relevant] to this,[2071] such as the Polo Master (*jūkandār*),[2072] the governors, and those who are comparable to them.[2073]

Moreover, the Costumes of Honour were bestowed on certain occasions:

> One of which is when an amir or a holder of a post is assigned to an office, then he wears a Costume of Honour that suits his assignment, depending on what the rank dictated, whether ascent or descent.

Another is ʿĪd al-Fiṭr, when all the Holders of Offices are bestowed upon. These include: Amirs; Men of the Pen, such as the Master Supervisor of Warehouses (*ustādār*); the Chancellor (*dawādār*); the Amir of Arms; the Vizier; the Confidential Scribe; the Supervisor of the Private [Sultanic] Bureau; the Supervisor of the Army, and their likes,whoeach received a suitable bestowal.

The author of *Masālik al-Abṣār* said: Customarily, a robe of bestowal (*khil'a*)[2074] was prepared for the sultan for each *'īd*), as if for him to wear, of the type of the

2067 *Ṭard*: chasing, *waḥsh*: wild beast – A type of silk cloth that was decorated with hunting and chasing scenes, and was sometimes used to make costumes of honour to be bestowed by the sultan. (S. Ashour, *'Aṣr*, 454).

2068 "Al-Shām," may also be Syria.

2069 Sing *jākha*: a band. (Y. Stillman, *Dress*, 134).

2070 According to Y. Stillman, this fine fabric was most probably a kind of linen. It is termed "*ṭarḥ sakandarī mufarraj*" in the text, where the *ṭarḥ* is defined as one of the "quality fabrics that still await more precise identification." (Y. Stillman, *Dress*, 57 & 72). *Sakandari* means "Alexandrian," and M. Marzuq defines the *mufarraj* as a kind of precious cloth that may have been decorated (M. Marzuq, *Textile*, 95).

2071 "*Aṣḥāb al-waẓā'if al-mukhtaṣṣa bi-dhalik*": The relevance of the position holders is not clear.

2072 Title of the amir who held the *jūkān* (polo stick) for the sultan for playing *kura*. The *jūkān* is a Persian word that refers to the polostick, while "*dār*" is Persian for "holder of." Therefore, the title translates to "Holder of the Polostick." (*Ṣubḥ*, Vol. 5, 485).

2073 The The editor of Subḥ remarks that the author has not mentioned the robes of honour of the viziers, the scribes, the judges and the religious scholars (*ulama*), which are detailed in *Ḍaw' al-Ṣubḥ*. (*Ṣubḥ*, Vol. 4, 53 fn. 1). See al-ʿUmarī's account in *Masālik* (2010), Vol. 3, 317–320 and al-Qalqashandī's in *al-Ḍaw'*, 260.

2074 Pl. *khila'*: Throughout Islamic history, bestowing a *khil'a* was customary as a sign of approval, appreciation and honouring from a soverign.

robes of bestowal (*khila'*) for the high-ranking Amirs of Hundreds.[2075] He does not, however, wear these, but specially bestows them on some of the high-ranking Amirs of Hundreds.[2076]

Another [occasion] is the [processions] of the squares, where the high-ranking amirs are bestowed upon. Each square is specifically used for one or more amir to wear a robe of bestowal of gold-adroned *mufarraj*.

Another is the Procession of the Kaʿba's Covering (*dawarān al-maḥmil*)[2077] in the month of Shawwāl, when the Holders of Offices of the *maḥmil*,[2078] such as the Judge (*qāḍī*); the Supervisor (*nāẓir*); the *muḥtasib*; the Witness; the Commanders; the Guides (*adilla*)[2079]; the Supervisor of the Kaʿba's Covering (*nāẓir al-kiswa*) and its managers (*mubāshirūn*),[2080] and the like, are bestowed upon [with robes].

The Second Kind: The Horses

The sovereign of Egypthas the habit of bestowing horses on his amirs twice every year: The first occasion is when he leaves for the places where his horses are tied up, by the trefoil [fields], towards their late spring.[2081] The sultan then bestows the horses he chooses upon his distinguished (*akhiṣṣā'*) amirs, according to their

2075 "*Min nisbat khila' akābir al-mi'yn*": The expression "*min nisbat*" may also be understood as "from among." Al-ʿUmarī uses this expression several times with the meanings: "of the type," "similar to," and "of relevance" to indicate affiliation or association, or "from among" to indicate inclusion. (See Al-ʿUmarī, *Masālik* (2002), Vol. 3, 367, 371, 469, 471, Vol. 4, 73, 180, Vol. 9, 595 and http://www.baheth.info/all.jsp?term=نسبة)

2076 *Masālik* (2010), Vol. 3, 321.

2077 Also, *dawarān al-maḥmal* (The Circulation of the Camel's Load): *Al-Maḥmil* was the howdah that contained the lavishly decorated and most precious cloth cover (*kiswa*) of the Kaʿba, which was sent annually from Cairo to Mecca. *Dawarān al-maḥmil* was the festivity that took place twice a year to announce the start of the journey of this honoured cover (*kiswa*). (See Glossary and M. Dahman, *Mu'jam*, 136).

2078 "*Bi-l-maḥmil*," which probably refers to the Holders of Positions involved in the preparation of the Kaʿba's cover, its procession and its journey to Mecca.

2079 Sing. *dalīl*, guide: These were possibly the travel guides who accompanied the *maḥmil* on its journey. The term is also applicable to the guides who escorted and helped the pilgrims (*al-muṭawwifūn*, sing. *al-muṭawwif*).

2080 Al-Qalqashandī explains later that the Cover of the Kaʿba (*kiswa*) had its own supervisor, who is referred to above. It is not clear who the other supervisor, who is mentioned after the Judge, is.

2081 "*Ilā marābiṭ khuyūlihi 'alā al-qurṭ fī awākhir rabī'ihā*": *marābiṭ al-khuyūl* may be translated as "the places where his horses are tied up." *Al-Qurṭ* is the trefoil, and apparently the statement means that the horses were tied at the trefoil fields. "*Fī awākhir rabī'ihā*" means "towards its late spring," that is at the time when the trefoil fields reached full growth and were due for pasturing. Al-ʿUmarī's sentence is: "*ilā marābiṭ khaylihi fī al-rabī' 'inda iktimāl tarbī'ihā*." The "*tarbī'*" most probably refers to the fodder of the rides and beasts of burden in springtime. Another meaning of the word is the fourth irrigation run of a crop. Al-ʿUmarī's sentence, therefore, means that this was when the sultan goes out to the places where his horses are tied up, in spring, after their spring fodder is fully ready. (Al-ʿUmarī & H. Abbas, *Masālik* (2002), Vol. 3, 431 fn. 3 & 432 and see http://www.baheth.info/all.jsp?term=قرط,http://www.baheth.info/all.jsp?term=ربيع, and http://www.baheth.info/all.jsp?term=تربيع).

ranks. The horses [bestowed on] the commanders among them are saddled and bridled, with golden brocaded caparisons (*kanābīsh*), while those bestowed on the *ṭablakhānāh* amirs are uncovered, without cloth. The second occasion is when he plays *kura* in the Maydān, when the horses [bestowed on] both the commanders and the *ṭablakhānāh* amirs are saddled and bridled, with little silver [ornamentation] and no caparisons. He also sends [bestowals] to the viceroys of Syrian kingdoms, each according to his rank. The Amirs of Tens have no luck with this, except for what he [bestows on them] upon inspecting them,[2082] as a grant.[2083]

Al-Maqarr al-Shihābī ibn Faḍl Allah[2084]said: The close and distinguished among the commander and the *ṭablakhānāh* amirs receive many additional [bestowals] that sometimes reach 100 horses annually for some of them. The sultan has other occasions when he distributes horses among his mamluks, and perhaps grants some of the commanders of the *ḥalaqa*. When any of his mamluks' horses dies, he provides them with [another], in compensation. He may also grant horses to the elderly among the high-ranking amirs when he goes out to hunt and the like.[2085]

Annually, the horses of the amirs are assigned granted lands (*iṭlaqāt*) in the provincial divisions (*a'māl*) of Jīza to plant trefoil (*qurṭ*) for their horses, without land-tax (*kharāj*). The Sultanic Mamluks are assigned planted clover (*barsīm*),[2086] according to their ranks. What is provided for them of trefoil is instead of the barley fodder assigned to them at times other than springtime. Each fodder lot is compensated by half a feddan of trefoil standing on its roots for a period of three months.[2087]

The Third Kind: The Garments (*kiswa*) and the Straps *(ḥawā'iṣ)*

It is the sultan's custom to annually bestow garments in winter and garments in summer on his mamluks and the distinguished (*khawāṣṣ*) holders of posts among the pen-bearers,[2088] depending on their ranks. It is also one of his customs to distribute golden waist straps (*ḥawā'iṣ*) among some of the Commander Amirs when he rides

2082 "*Mā yatfaqqadhum bihi*"; "*yataffaqad*" means "to inspect."

2083 See al-'Umarī's account in *Masālik* (2002), Vol. 3, 432.

2084 Ibn Faḍl Allah al-'Umarī, author of *Masālik al-Abṣār.Al-Maqarr*, is linguistically derived from "*istiqrār*," which means "settlement," and was used as an honourary reference to a person's authority over a place. This title was given to sultans, apparently only rarely, until Qalāwūn's investiture in 678 AH/1279 AD, and was most probably also used for the high-ranking amirs. Later, it was only adopted by the Men of the Sword, amirs and viziers, until it was extended to civilians, high-ranking officials of the bureaus, and religious scholars and men of piety by the time of al-Qalqashandī. (H. al-Basha, *Alqāb*, 489–494 and Al-Baqli, *Ta'rīf*, 322). Al-Shihābī is a title in reference to one of the author's names or titles: Shihāb al-Dīn.

2085 See more details in al-'Umarī's account, *Masālik* (2002), Vol. 3, 432–433.

2086 May also mean "lands of planted clover," (See http://www.baheth.info/all.jsp?term=مزدرع and http://www.baheth.info/all.jsp?term=ازدرع).

2087 "*Al-Qurṭ al-qā'im 'alā aṣlihifī muddat thalāthat ashhur*," which probably means trefoil that was planted, or has grown out of its roots, three months earlier.

2088 "*Ḥamalat al-aqlām*," also "Men of the Pen."

to play *kura* in the Maydān. The sultan grants two amirs in turn, on every square procession, until all of them are bestowed upon over three or four years, depending on whose turn it is in that. The author of *Masālik* [*al-Abṣār*] said: As for the amirs of Syria, they do not have luck with [such] grants other than a single coat (*qabā'*) to be worn in wintertime, except for those who come to seek the sultan, then the sultan bestows on them according to what their situations dictate.[2089]

The Fourth Kind: The Grants and Endowments

Most of the time, there are no restraints to the sultan's grants, for they depend on the closeness of the bestowed upon and his privilege with the sultan. The author of *Masālik al-Abṣār* said: The distinguished (*khāṣṣa*) of the Commander Amirs receive a variety of grants, such as properties (*'aqār*) and large buildings, on some of which more than 100,000 dinars may be spent; in addition to costumes made of a variety of cloths, and fodder and money on their travels, when they go out hunting and the like.[2090]

The Fifth Kind: Food and Drinks

This[2091] sultan [offers] his greatest banquets at the Great Iwan on procession days. When the judges and the rest of the Men of the Pen leave the circle,[2092] the banquet is spread out in the Great Iwan, from its beginning to its end, with a variety of magnificent foods. The sultan sits at the head of the table (*khiwān*),[2093] while the amirs sit to his right and left, in order of their levels of closeness to the sultan. They eat light food then leave, and the lesser ranking amirs sit [at the table], one group after the other, then the table is removed. As for the rest of days, the table is stretched out at the two ends of the day[2094] for the amirs in general, except the *Barrāniyyūn* of whom only few and hardly any are present at this table.

2089 See more details in al-'Umarī's account, *Masālik* (2002), Vol. 3, 432.

2090 See al-'Umarī, *Masālik* (2002), Vol. 3, 432.

2091 Probably influenced by al-'Umarī's constant use of "this sultan" to refer to al-Nāṣir Muḥammad b. Qalāwūn.

2092 "*Min al-khadama*," where *al-khadama* is the circle, ring, or group of people: The diacritics show that the word is *al-khadama* rather than *al-khidma* (service), which denotes that the banquet was offered after the judges and the rest of the Men of the Pen retired from the meeting circle at the Great Iwan, while the rest remained. However, the diacritics may have been arbitrarily inserted, while the intended word was "*al-khidma*." (See http://www.baheth.info/all.jsp?term=خدمة).

2093 "*Khiwān*" is an originally Persian word, which means "the table" or what is used to eat on. (M. Dahman, *Mu'jam*, 70 and http://dsal.uchicago.edu/cgi-bin/philologic/getobject.pl?c.5:1:4945.steingass).

2094 "*Ṭarafay al-nahār*," which is an expression borrowed from Quran to mean dawn or morning and noon or afternoon, or may be dawn and evening (See Sūrat Hūd – Chapter of Hūd 11:114 – http://corpus.quran.com/translation.jsp?chapter=11&verse=114). The context below suggests that the two ends intended here are the morning and the afternoon.

In the beginning of the day, a first banquet is spread out that the sultan does not eat anything from then a second one[2095] [is offered] after it, from which the sultan may or may not eat. A third one, called The Incidental (*al-ṭāri'*), [is set] after that, from which the sultan eats.

Towards the ends of the day, two banquets, a first one and a second,which is called the Private One (*al-khāṣṣ*), are spread out. Then, if an incidental one (*ṭāri'*) is requested, it is brought in; otherwise, all depends on the given orders. In all these banquets, drinks of sugary *aqsimā* are served after eating. As for the night, platters of different kinds of food and excellent drinks are kept near where the sultan sleeps, so that those on [guard] shifts distract themselves from sleep by food and drinks. The author of *Masālik al-Abṣār* said: The sultan is required to provide each of the amirs of Egypt, from his Private Retinue (*khawāṣṣ*), with sugar and sweets in the month of Ramadan, in addition to the sacrificial animal [for 'Īd al-Aḍḥā], according to their ranks.[2096]

2095 In al-'Umarī's account, this second banquet is called "*al-khāṣṣ*" (the Private One). (*Masālik* (2010), Vol. 3, 296).

2096 See al-'Umarī's account in *Masālik* (2010), Vol. 3, 296 and *Masālik* (2002), Vol. 3, 431 & 440–441.

The Seventh Purpose
On the privilege the sovereign of this kingdom has, owing to the special territories within its domain; those that distinguish him from Muslim and non-Muslim monarchs of the earth.

These include: The Glorified Kaʿba,[2097] which falls within the domain of this kingdom; and he is especially responsible for [the preparation of] its covering (*kiswa*) and for the covering's procession (*dawarān al-maḥmil*), annually.

As for the Covering of the Kaʿba (*kiswat al-Ka'ba*),[2098] it was a special responsibility of the caliphs in the early times. The Abbasid caliphs used to annually prepare it for travel[2099] from Baghdad. Later, it became the responsibility of the monarchs of Egypt, who prepared it yearly for travel, and remains to be until now. The incidence of the seizure of this [privilege] in some years by some of the kings of Yemen in certain eras,should not be considered.[2100] This covering is woven in Cairo, the Protected City (al-Qāhira al-Maḥrūsa), at the Shrine of al-Ḥusayn, from black silk that is embroidered with white inscriptions in the woven [textile] itself, which include: "Indeed, the first House [of worship] established for mankind was that at Bakka," – to the end of the verse.[2101] Then, by the end of the reign of al- Ẓāhir Barqūq, the inscription settled on being yellow and threaded with gold.[2102] This covering has its own independent supervisor (*nāẓir*) and an

2097 The Ka'ba, in Mecca, according to Islam, is the first House of Allah, which was built by Prophet Ibrāhīm (Abraham) and his son, Prophet Ismā'īl (Ishmael). The five daily Muslim prayers are performed in the direction of the Ka'ba (the *qibla*), and pilgrimage, which includes visiting it, among other rituals, is one of the five pillars of the Islamic faith.

2098 Providing a precious *kiswa* (covering) for the Ka'ba was an honour and a privilege prior to and after Islam. A none too extravagant *kiswa* covered the Ka'ba at the time of the Prophet and the Rightly-guided caliphs, which gradually became an extremely valuable item. The keepers of the Ka'ba customarily took the older covering, after replacing it with the newer one, and gave parts of it as presents to kings and dignitaries. Another silk, inscribed cover was kept inside the Ka'ba, though this one required changing only after some years, since it was not exposed to the environmental factors, such as the sun, nor to the touching or grabbing by people's hands. (Al-Baqli, *Ta'rīf*, 287 and see *Ṣubḥ*, Vol. 4, 277–284).

2099 "*Yujahhizūnahā*," from the verb *jahhaza*.

2100 Al-Qalqashandī is referring to the years when the Rasulids of Yemen (626 AH/1229 AD – 858 AH/1454 AD), who were one of the autonomous Islamic dynasties that ruled under the nominal authority of the Abbasid caliph at the time, managed to declare their "sovereignty over Mecca by sending and draping the *kiswa* over the Ka'ba." This was during the reign of the Rasulid Sultan al-Malik al-Muẓaffar Yūsuf (r. 647 AH/1249 AD – 694 AH/1295 AD), in the years 662 AH/1262 AD, 666 AH/1268 AD and 671 AH/1273 AD. (Francis E. Peters, *Mecca: A Literary History of the Muslim Holy Land* (Princeton, 1994), 149).

2101 Sūrat Āl 'Imrān – Chapter of The Family of 'Imrān, 3:96: "Indeed, the first House (of worship) established for mankind was that at Bakka – blessed and a guidance for the worlds." Bakka is one of the names of Mecca. (See http://corpus.quran.com/translation.jsp?chapter=3&verse=96).

2102 "*Musha''ara bi-l-dhahab*," which means that the yellow inscription was woven with golden "hairs" or fine threads.

endowment (*waqf*) that is the land of Bīsūs[2103] in the outskirts of Cairo, which is used to pay for its manufacture (*isti'mālihā*).

As for the Procession of the Covering of the Kaʿba (*dawarān al-maḥmil*), it is customary that it circulates twice a year: The first time after the mid of the month of Rajab, when it is carried [around]; and three days before that, the owners of the shops on the roads where it circulates are called upon to decorate their shops. The circulation takes place on either a Monday or a Thursday and not on any other day. The howdah (*maḥmil*) is carried by a camel, in a pleasant appearance of a [wooden] hut (*kharkāh*) that is covered with a yellow silk satin (*aṭlas*) cover, and atop it is a silver-gilded[2104] dome. The night before its circulation, the *maḥmil* is kept inside Bāb al-Naṣr, near the door of the Mosque of al-Ḥākim. It is carried after morning rise on the mentioned camel and marched to [the Square] Below the Citadel. The vizier, the four judges, the *muḥtasib*, the witnesses, the Supervisor of the Kaʿba's Covering (*nāẓir al-kiswa*), and others then ride in front of it. A group of the Sultanic Mamluk Lancers (al-Rammāḥa)[2105] also ride, dressed in iron shields (*maṣaffāt*)[2106] that are covered with coloured silk. Their horses are dressed in [body] armour (*birkistiwānāt*)[2107] and steel face-[masks], as if in combat. They hold lances that bear the sultanic emblems (*shaṭfāt*)[2108] in their hands and play below the Citadel, as if in a situation of war. Each one of a young group of them holds two lances in his hands, which he rotates, while standing on the horse's back. He may also stand in wooden shoes (*na'l*) on two sword tips from each side, while he similarly [rotates the lances]. They prepare a huge number of large

2103 One of the old villages that later came to be called Bāsūs, which is its modern and current name. It was a pleasant, populated village, which alternated in affiliation between the administrative divisions of al-Qalyūbiyya and al-Sharqiyya. It is presently a village in al-Qalyūbiyya Governorate. (M. Ramzy, *Qāmūs*, Vol. 1, 55).

2104 "*Maṭliyya*," which means painted or coated.

2105 Al-Rammāḥa, "the lancers," was a group of forty mamluks headed by an amir, who was their trainer and who was helped by four assistants. They used to wear red costumes that distinguished them. They paraded in front of the sultan, showing their amazing skills in playing with the lances, and the sultan usually bestowed magnificent costumes of honour on them. These mamluks invented new ways of playing with the lances every year and mastered this skill superbly. Their performance was an important act in the *dawarān al-maḥmil* celebration, which although halted for thirty-five years during the reign of Sultan Qaitbāy (r. 872 AH/1468 AD – 901 AH/1496 AD), was resumed under Sultan al-Ghawrī (r. 906 AH/1501 – 922 AH/1516 AD), and went on to the end of the Mamluk era.(M. Al-Shishtawi, *Mayādīn*, 45–48).

2106 Sing. *maṣaffa*, is most probably derived from *al-ṣafaf*, which is what is worn beneath the shield. (http://www.baheth.info/all.jsp?term=صفف).

2107 Sing. *birkistiwān* (also, *birkiṣṭawān*), which was a kind of body armour for horses. It is also defined as the embroidered cover used for the horses' bodies, as well as for other animals, such as elephants; as well as a caparison. (Al-Baqli, *Ta'rīf*, 63 and S. Ashour, *'Aṣr*, 418).

2108 Sing. *shaṭfa*, which was a royal logo that was carried like a flag. The term is also used to refer to the division of the circular blazon or emblem (see Glossary: "*rank*"), as well as the bevelling or chamfering (*mashṭūf*). (M. Dahman, *Mu'jam*, 98 and Leo A. Mayer, *Saracenic Heraldry: A Survey* (Oxford, 1933), 26).

jars[2109] of naphtha (*nafṭ*)[2110] and other [containers of flammable materials], which are fired below the Citadel during this [performance]. The *maḥmil* then goes to Fustat, and crosses through its centre, then returns to [the Square] Below the Citadel for similar [festivities] to the first ones, only lesser. After that, it is carried from[2111] the Mosque of al- Ḥākim, where it is kept at a place there until Shawwāl. Throughout all this [procession], the sultanic music bands (*ṭablakhānāt*) and cymbals (*kūsāt*)[2112] are played behind it. A numerous group of people are bestowed upon with costumes of honour during this [procession], which is repeated on the mid of Shawwāl, only this time the *maḥmil* returns from [the Square] Below the Citadel to Bāb al-Naṣr, then leaves for al-Raydāniyya[2113] to travel [to Mecca], and does not head to Fustat.

2109 "*Azyār*," sing. *zīr*.

2110 *Nafṭ* is the Arabic term for either naphtha, that is Greek fire, or gunpowder. (See Robert Irwin, "Gunpowder and Firearms in the Mamluk Sultanate Reconsidered," in *The Mamluks in Egyptian and Syrian Politics and Society*, ed. Michael Winter and Amalia Levanoni (Leiden, 2004), 120–121).

2111 The editor of Subḥ comments that the author means "to" (*ilā*) rather than from (*min*). (*Ṣubḥ*, Vol. 4, 58 fn. 1).

2112 May also mean large kettledrums.

2113 An area to the north of Cairo, east of al-Ḥusayniyya, which is now taken up by al-ʿAbbāsiyya district and some of its surroundings in Heliopolis, al-Waylī al-Ṣaghīr, and Manshiyyat al-Bakrī. (M. Al-Shishtawi, *Mutanazzahāt*, 238–239).

The Eighth Purpose
On how news reaches the Sultan[2114] – Three Kinds

The First Kind

News of kings that reach him through their correspondences

The custom was that if a messenger sent by one of the kings arrives in the peripheries of his kingdom, the viceroy of that province (*jiha*) writes to the sultan to inform him of the messenger's arrival, and asks his permission to send[2115] the messenger to him. The sultanic decrees (*marāsīm*) are then issued for him to come [to the court], and then he comes. When his arrival is detected,[2116] and if his sender was of a great status among kings, such as one of the khans (*qānāt*)[2117] from monarchs of the East, some high-ranking amirs like the viceroy, the Chief *ḥājib*, and their likes, go out to meet him. He is hosted in the sultan's palaces at the Square, where he plays the *kura*, which is the highest residence for messengers. If he is lesser than this [status], heis received by the Chief of Protocol (*mihmandār*), who asks the permission of the Chancellor (*dawādār*) to allow him in, and hosts him at the Guest House (Dār al-Ḍiyāfa) or some other place, depending on his rank. Then a procession day is awaited, when the sultan sits in his iwan, and the kingdom dignitaries entitled to attend from the Men of the Sword and the Men of the Pen are present. This messenger is then brought with the letter that arrived with him and kisses the ground. The Chancellor takes the letter from him and wipes it on the face of the messenger, then hands it over to the sultan who opens[2118] it and passes it to the Confidential Scribe who reads it to the sultan then [writes down] his orders concerning it.[2119]

The Second Kind

The news he receives from his viceroys

It is the custom of this[2120] sultan that the viceroys of his kingdom inform him of all their new important and semi important matters. His orders are taken [by the

2114 See also al-ʿUmarī's account of how the news reached the sultan in *Masālik* (2010), Vol. 3, 297.

2115 "*Ishkhāṣihi*," which means sending him from one place to another. (http://www.baheth.info/all.jsp?term=إشخاص).

2116 "*Waqaʿa al-shuʿūr bi-ḥuḍūrihi*," which probably means "when there is a notification of his arrival."

2117 Sing. *qān* (also *khāqān*), which is "the chief" or "the master" in the Tartar culture. *Al-Qān* was a royal title used for the king of China and was minted on the Mongol coins as title of their kings. (M. Dahman, *Muʿjam*, 120 and H. al-Basha, *Alqāb*, 423).

2118 *Faḍḍa*, which also means to unfold or unwrap, and most probably refers to breaking the seal of the letter. (http://www.baheth.info/all.jsp?term=فضض) .

2119 "*Ya'mur fīhi amrahu*," which denotes that conveyed the sultan's orders.

2120 The use of "this sultan" is because this sentence is copied from al-ʿUmarī's account. (See *Masālik* (2010), Vol. 3, 297).

concerned officials], and his responseswith what he sees on these [matters]reach his viceroys from the Chancery Bureau; or he may initiate [a correspondence] with what his opinion dictates. [The correspondences] are either sent with the mailmen[2121] or on the wings of carrier pigeons, which will be mentioned in the Third Article of the book.[2122]

It is the custom that if a mail arrives from one of the kingdom's provinces or if the [mailman]equipped for travel, who was sent from the Honourable Sultanic Court (*al-abwāb al-sharīfa*), arrives with a reply, the Personal Guard (*amīr jāndār*), the Chancellor and the Confidetial Scribe bring him to the sultan, where he kisses the ground. The Chancellor then takes the letter, wipes it on the face of the mailman, and hands it over to the sultan, who opens[2123] it, and the Confidential Scribe sits to read it to the sultan then [writes down] his orders concerning it.

As for the written messages (*baṭā'iq*)[2124] carried by pigeons, if a flying carrier pigeon alights with a written message, the keeper of the dovecot (*barrāj*)[2125] takes it and brings it to the Chancellor, who cuts the message from the pigeon with his hand. He then carries the message to the sultan and the Confidential Scribe comes and reads it as mentioned above.

The Third Kind

The news of his capital (*ḥāḍira*)

The custom is that the Chief of Police (*wālī al-shurṭa*) enquires daily about the new happenings within his governorship,[2126] such as killings, big fires, or the like, from his deputies. A comprehensive report[2127] is written on this and taken every morning to the sultan to be informed of it. The author of *Masālik al-Abṣār* said: As for what happens to the people in their personal affairs, it is not [included in the report].[2128]

2121 "*Al-Burud*" (sing. *al-barīd*), which means the mail messengers who travel on horses. (http://www.baheth.info/all.jsp?term=بـرد).

2122 The Third Article of *Ṣubḥ*, which is not translated in this work.

2123 "*Yafuḍḍuhu*".

2124 Sing. *biṭāqa*, which means the written message or letter. (M. Dahman, *Ta'rīf*, 35).

2125 "The Tower-man" or "the man of the tower," which in this context means the one responsible for the dovecot, called a pigeon-tower in Arabic. The mail system of the Mamluks was run by a special bureau that managed mail and pigeon focal stations, which employed mailmen and pigeon-keepers. The pigeon stations included dovecots, which in an important station like the Cairo's Citadel, housed 1900 pigeons in the year 687 AH/1288 AD. The pigeon station at the Citadel was kept by several commanders, each responsible for a certain section. (K. Azab, *Qal'a*, 187–209).

2126 "*Wilāyāt*" (governorships). Al-'Umarī explains that the governors in charge (or the governors of matters; *wulāt umūr*) of a city, who are its chiefs of police, enquire daily about the happenings within their governorships. (Al-'Umarī (2010), *Masālik*, Vol. 3, 297).

2127 "*Muṭala'a*," which means something to be read, from the verb *ṭāla'a*, which means to view, know, or read. (http://www.baheth.info/all.jsp?term=طالع).

2128 Al-'Umarī (2010), *Masālik*, Vol. 3, 297.

The Ninth Purpose On the Appearance of the Amirs of Egypt and the Order of their Emirate.

You should know that each of the Amirs of Hundreds or the *ṭablakhānāh* amirs is a lesser sultan in most of his conditions. Each of them has houses of service[2129] like those of the sultan, such as the House of Basins (*ṭishtkhānāh*); the House of Furnishings (*firāshkhānāh*); the House of Saddles (*rikābkhānāh*); the House of Chainmail (*zardkhānāh*); the Kitchen and the House of Drums (*ṭablakhānāh*); except for House of Assorted Needs (*ḥawā'ijkhānāh*), which is particular to the sultan. Each of these houses has a superintendent (*mihtār*) responsible for its contents (*ḥāṣil*), under whose supervision are men and slave-boys (*ghilmān*), each having a specific job. Moreover, each of these [amirs] has warehouses (*ḥawāṣil*), such as horse stables, settlement areas (*munākhāt*) for camels and granaries. Each also has a Master Supervisor of Warehouses (*ustādār*); a Head of Guard (*ra's nawba*); a Chancellor (*dawādār*); an Amir of Council (*amīr majlis*); Keepers of Robes (*jamadāriyya*); an Equerry (*amīr ākhūr*); a Supervisor of Kitchen and Banquets (*ustādār suḥba*); and an Overseer (*mushrif*); all from his soldiers (*ajnād*). The houses are termed "The Noble" (*al-karīma*) in the amirial bureaus (*dawāwīn*); therefore the expression used is "The Noble Houses" (*al-buyūt al-karīma*), same as the sultanic houses are called "The Honourable Houses" (*al-buyūt al-sharīfa*).[2130] This is [applicable] to each one of them; so, the expressions used are: "The Noble House of Basins" (*al-ṭishtkhānāh al-karīma*), "The Noble House of Furnishings" (*al-firāshkhānāh al-karīma*), and similarly for the rest. The stable is termed "The Fortunate" (*al-sa'īd*); hence [the expression used] is: The Fortunate Stable (*al-iṣṭabl al-sa'īd*), and so termed is the settlement area (*munākh*). The granaries are termed "The Full" (*al-ma'mūra*); therefore a granary is called "The Full."

The author of *Masālik al-Abṣār* said: The protocol of amirs [dictates] that when an amir rides, wherever that may be, he is followed by a saddled, bridled[2131] side ride (*junayb*). The high among their[2132] amirs may ride with two side rides (*junayb*), whether inside or outside[2133] the capital. He added: Each of them has abattalion (*ṭulb*) that includes most of his mamluks; for the [amirs of the]

2129 "*Buyūt khadama*," which in this context would mean "Houses of Service"; however, the diacritics are problematic.

2130 It should be noted that, linguistically, *al-karīma* and *al-sharīfa* convey quite similar meanings and connotations, with the first additionally implying generosity and the second mostly reflecting honour and dignity. (See http://www.baheth.info/all.jsp?term=كريم and http://www.baheth.info/all.jsp?term=شريف).

2131 Al-ʿUmarī does not specify that they were saddled and bridled in this instance. See also the end of the account. (*Masālik* (2010), Vol. 3, 290).

2132 That is, the Mamluks.

2133 "*Al-Barr*," which generally means " on land," and refers to outside the capital in this context. In al-ʿUmarī's account, he says that this is in the cities, the capital and on land (*al-barr*). (*Masālik* (2010), Vol. 3, 290 and see http://www.baheth.info/all.jsp?term=البر).

ṭablakhānāh, they are preceded by a treasury that is carried on one camel, which is pulled by a rider on another camel; while the [amirs of] thousand are accompanied by two camels or, in case of some of them, more.[2134] In front of this treasury are several side rides pulled by mamluks who are riders of horses and camels, as well as Arab riders on camels; preceded by camels with their saddles (*akwār*)[2135] on the sides. *Ṭablakhānāh* amirs are [preceded by] one train of four [camels], in addition to the ride of the camel master (*hajjān*). The [amirs of] thousand are accompanied by two trains, or may be more for some of them.[2136] He added: The number of side rides, whether many or a few, is up to the opinion and wealth[2137] of the amir. Some of the mentioned side rides are saddled and bridled, while others are only [covered with] a [ride's] cape (*'abā'a*)[2138] – end of his words.[2139]

It is also their custom that when an amir rides, he is preceded by the high-ranking among his soldiers (*ajnād*), who are holders of offices, such as the Head of Guard, the Chancellor, the Amir of the Council, and the marchers in service (*mushāt al-kidma*); the highest-ranking being closest to the amir. The Keepers of Robes from his young mamluks move behind him, while his Equerry moves behind the whole lot; he is accompanied by the side rides and the Stable Boys (*ūshāqiyya*), in the same manner of the sultan in this [processional arrangement].

It is the custom of [the] dignitaries[2140] in the councils (*majālis*) of their houses to raise a backrest (*bushtmīkh*)[2141] of red broadcloth that is floriated with coloured

2134 Al-'Umarī's does not specifically mention the Amirs of Thousand, but states that "the money" (*māl*) was carried on two camels. (*Masālik* (2010), Vol. 3, 290).

2135 Sing. *kūr*, which is what the rider of a camel sits on, like a saddle, also called "*raḥl*." Its fore and back parts are sometimes covered with gold or silver. (Al-Bqalī, *Ta'rīf*, 290, *Ṣubḥ*, Vol. 2, 129, and http://www.baheth.info/all.jsp?term=الكور).

2136 Again, al-'Umarī's account does not specify the Amirs of Thousand, but states that the money (*māl*) was carried on two trains of camels. (*Masālik* (2010), Vol. 3, 290).

2137 "*Si'at nafsihi*," which refers to one's generosity and may also mean wealth.

2138 In al-'Umarī's account: "while some of them are only with their rein (*'inān*)." (*Masālik* (2010), Vol. 3, 290).

2139 That is, end of al-'Umarī's account. See *Masālik* (2010), Vol. 3, 290.

2140 Al-Qalqashandī's sentence starts with: "*wa min 'ādat akābir majālis buyūtihim* . . ." (And it is the custom of the dignitaries in the councilsof their houses . . .). The editor of Subḥ notes that the more probable intended meaning is: "*wa min 'ādat al-akābir fī majālis* . . .," (And it is the custom of the dignitaries in the councils . . .). (*Ṣubḥ*, Vol. 4, 61 fn. 1)

2141 Al-'Irainy defines this term as "backrest." It is originally Persian, and is understood to be composed of two syllabi: "*pusht*"and "*mīkh*." *Pusht* has several meanings, among which is "back" and "support," while *mīkh* means "nail"; therefore, *pusht mīkh* may be translated as "back-nail" (Hallaq & Sabbagh, 40). It may also be possible that *mīkh* is a distortion of the Persian *mūkh*, which means "a standard" or "an ensign." Al-Jazīrī (d. circa 977 AH/1570 AD), the historian, mentions the *bushtmīkh* among the elite furnishings known in the "old times." He refers to it as the "yellow, sultanic *bushtmīkh*," which indicates that, it was at times also a royal, not only an amirial, item. Yellow is known to have been a colour of Mamluk sultanic banners and insignia. Al-Jazīrī does not specifically define the *bushtmīkh*, but his account suggests that it usually had accessories, namely "*mushalshalāt al-ḥarīr*," which were probably silk cushions or small mattresses. (Al-Sayyid al-Baz al-'Irainy, *al-Mamālīk* (Beirut, 1999), 226; Hassan Hallaq

broad cloth behind the amir's back. It bears the blazon (*rank*)[2142] of the amir and a band (*ṭirāz*) with his titles. The amir sits on a seat (*maq'ad*), resting his back to the *bushtmīkh*. The dignitaries among them may sit on a leather round seat (*mudawwara*),[2143] with their feet touching the floor. People sit in the amir's council (*majlis*) in an order of proximity to him according to their ranks.

It is the custom of each amir, whether high or low ranking, to have a blazon (*rank*) that is particular to him, such as a goblet (*hannāb*);[2144] a penbox (*dawāt*);[2145] a lozenge (*buqja*);[2146] a fleur-de-lys (*faransīsiyya*),[2147] and the like; with one or two divisions (*shaṭfa*),[2148] with different colours, according to each amir's choice and preference in this. This [blazon] was painted on the doors of their houses and the places attributed to them; such as the sugar kitchens, the granaries, the properties, the boats, and the like; as well as on the cloths [covering] their horses, [made] using cut, coloured broadcloth, and on the cloth [covers] of their camels, [made] using coloured woollen threads that were woven on capes [of rides] (*'ibiy*), capes

and Abbas Sabbagh, *al-Mu'jam al-Jāmi' fī al-Muṣṭalaḥāt* (Beirut, 1999), 40; ʿAbd al-Qādir b. Muḥammad al-Anṣārī al-Jazīrī, *Al-Durar al-Farā'id al-Munaẓẓama fī Akhbār al-Ḥājj wa Ṭarīq Makka al-Mu'aẓẓama*, ed. Muhammad Hasan Ismail (Beirut, 2002), Vol. 1, 208; and F. Steingass, "*mūkh*" (p. 1342) and "*pusht*" (p. 251) in "A Comprehensive Persian English Dictionary," http://dsalsrv02.uchicago.edu/cgi-bin/philologic/getobject.pl?c.6:1:7958.steingass and http://dsalsrv02.uchicago.edu/cgi-bin/philologic/getobject.pl?c.1:1:3576.steingass).

2142 Pl. *runūk*: Arabized word from the Persian *ranq* or *ranj*, meaning colour. It is used to refer to the official blazons used by mamluk sultans and amirs to display their signs of office. These emblematic symbols existed before the Mamluks, probably since the time of the Zangids. The amirial blazons of the Mamluk era include, for example: the cup or goblet (*hannāb*), the symbol of the *sāqī* (the Cupbearer of the sultan); the penbox (*dawāt*), the symbol of the *dawādār* (Chancellor); the lozenge (*buqja*), the symbol of the *jamādār* (Wardrobe Master) and the *jūkān* (polo sticks), symbol of the *jūkāndār* (Polo Master).Originally, the amirial blazons incorporated single symbols each referring to a particular office. Later, high-ranking amirs of the sultan started using similar blazons with composite symbols of office. The blazon of the sultan was normally all epigraphic and it developed in complexity and calligraphic finesse over the Mamluk era. The *rank* was commonly circular, with divisions (*shaṭfāt*) that included the symbols or inscriptions. (See al-Baqli, *Ta'rīf*, 163, T. Abdelhamid, *Jaysh*, 33–37 and L. Mayer, *Heraldry*, 26).

2143 "The Round," which in this context refers to a kind of a round seat or chair. The word is also used to refer to the centre of the main space or wall of the audience hall (*majlis*) where the sultan or the amir sits. The sultan's *mudawwara* is his big tent, which is pitched on travels and ceremonies. (See Glossary, M. Dahman, *Mu'jam*, 137, and S. Ashour, *'Aṣr*, 469).

2144 Drinking goblet. (S. Ashour, *'Aṣr*, 483).

2145 Also, inkwell or ink-box, see Glossary.

2146 Pl. *buqaj*, which is an originally Turkish word that was distorted to refer to a lozenge-shaped piece of cloth or napkin. It was used as a bundle to wrap clothes or papers by tying its four ends together. (M. Dahman, *Mu'jam*, 36 and L. Mayer, *Heraldry*, 14).

2147 "The Franksih," which is the fleur-de-lys. The Mamluk fleur-de-lys differed in design from the one "used by the kings of France," although still comprising three petals. (Maria Pia Pedani, "Mamluk Lions and Venetian Lions 1260–1261,"*EJOS*, VII, no. 21 (2004), p.5 fn. 7).

2148 The divisions in the circular blazon (*rank*).

[of rides that are made of hair] (*balāsāt*),[2149] and the like. The [blazons] may also be put on swords, bows, the body armours (*birkiṣṭiwānāt*) of horses, and other [items].

The customs of the amirs of soldiers at the sultanic capital (*ḥaḍra*) include their riding for procession on Mondays and Thursdays, joining the Plenipotentiary Viceroyof the sultanate, if there is one, or else they join the Chief *ḥājib*. They parade several times below the Citadel then stop at the horses' market where the auctioned horses (*khuyūl al-munādāt*) are displayed for them. Many riding equipment, tents, huts (*kharkāwāt*), and arms may also be auctioned. The author of *Masālik al-Abṣār* said: Many buildings may also be auctioned. Then they go up [to the Citadel] for the sultanic audience (*khidma*), as mentioned before.[2150]

The rules of this kingdom include parading all the amirial soldiers (*ajnād al-umarā'*) at the Bureau of Sultanic Armies (*dīwān al-juyūsh al-sulṭāniyya*),[2151] where their detailed names are registered.Previously, they showed up personally [to enlist] in the bureau, but now this [practice] is abandoned and it is enough for the amirial bureaus to send papers [detailing] the names of their soldiers, which are kept at the Bureau of Armies. Whenever a soldier dies or is expelled from service, another one is presented in his place at the Army Bureau, after the registration of [his name] is sent from the amir's bureau.[2152]

It is their custom that if an amir or a soldier dies before finishing his year of service, he receives the deserved payment (*mustaḥaqq*) of his *iqṭā'* only for the period served. [A calculation of] this account (*muḥāsaba*)[2153] is sent to him from the Bureau of Armies. The gathered yield is shared by the person settled [in the land] (*mustaqirr*) and the deceased or the withdrawn [from service], depending on the deserved payment (*istiḥqāq*) as calculated in carats (*qarārīṭ*),[2154] with every month of the year calculated as two carats.

It is customary for the amirs that if the sultan passes by the *iqṭā'* of a high-ranking amir while on a hunting trip, the amir offers him what a man of his [stature] can afford of geese, chicken, sugarcane and barley, which the sultan accepts, then bestows a full attire (*khil'a*) on the amir to wear. He may also order granting some of such amirs some money, which they receive.

2149 Sing. *balās*, which is one of the names given to the cloth or rug made of animal hair, a type of sackcloth. (See http://www.baheth.info/all.jsp?term=بلاس and http://www.baheth.info/all.jsp?term=حلس).

2150 See also al-'Umarī's account in *Masālik* (2010), Vol. 3, 298.

2151 Same as the Army Bureau (*Dīwān al-Jaysh*).

2152 "*Wāḥid makānuhu ya'bur fīhi 'arḍ min dīwān dhalik al-amīr*," which may be understood, given the explanation before it, that the replacement's name is first registered in the amirial bureau, then sent to the sultanic one.

2153 The *muḥāsaba* was the calculation, auditing and adjustment of accounts.

2154 Singular: *qīrāṭ*, which in this case refers to a unit of measuring areas, with each 24 carats equaling one Feddan (4200 square meters). (See Glossary: "*qīrāṭ*")

The Tenth Purpose On the governors in charge (*wulāt al-umūr*)of the provincial divisions (*a'māl*) of the Egypt, who are from the Men of the Sword

These are divided into four levels

The First Level The Viceroys – Three stable viceroyships

The First – The Viceroyship of Alexandria

This is a grand viceroyship, whose viceroy is a Commander Amir, equivalent in rank to the Viceroy of Tripoli[2155] and similar or comparable viceroyships. It has a *ḥājib* who is an Amir of Ten; a *ḥājib* who is a soldier (*jundī*); a chief [of police] (*wālī*) for the city;[2156] Soldiers of the *ḥalaqa*, who are 200 in number, and are called Soldiers of the Two-hundred (*ajnād al-mā'atayn*); a Chief Judge of the Mālikī school; a Ḥanafī Judge, which is a newly introduced [post], and a Shāfi'ī Judge may be appointed for it [too]. The Mālikī Judge is the greatest of all there, and he supervises the orphans' funds (*amwāl*) and the endowments. However, in previous times, its appointed Chief Judge may have been a Shāfi'ī. This viceroyship also includes a Singer that is referred to in [this city] as the Confidential Scribe,and a Supervisor (*nāẓir*) who supervises the monies (*amwāl*) of the bureaus, who is aided by a Comptroller (*mustawfī*), and under whose authority are scribes and witnesses. It has a *muḥtasib* but does not have Military Judges or *muftī*s for the House of Justice. Its Agent of the Public Treasury (*wakīl bayt al-māl*) is a deputy of the Deputy of the Public Treasury (*nā'ib bayt al-māl*) of Cairo. The commander and *ṭablakhānāh* amirs are stationed at the [city] at the times when the might of winds does not prevent the sailing of war ships from it. A Chief of Stationing (*wālī al-tarkīz*), called the "*ḥājib*" [is similarly based there]. The dealings (*mu'āmala*)[2157] and conditions of this viceroyship were mentioned before in the account of the stable bases of the Egyptian Lands; therefore, there is no need to repeat them here.

Despite the grand status and eminent situation of this viceroyship, it does not have a provincial division (*'amal*), to be ruled over by its viceroy, judge or *muḥtasib*. Their rule is confined to the city and its outskirts, no more, unlike the rest of the kingdom's viceroyships. It has a sultanic chair (*kursī*) at the House of Viceroyship; and the custom of the sultanic audience (*khidma*) there on processional days is that the Sultanic Viceroy (*nā'ib al-salṭana*) rides from the House of Viceroyship, with his mamluks and the above-mentioned Soldiers of Two-hundred, in his

2155 Tripoli of the Levant.

2156 The *wālī al-madīna* is a city's chief of police. (Al-'Umarī, *Masālik* (2010), Vol. 3, 279).

2157 The *mu'āmala* (pl. *mu'āmalāt*) are the financial dealings for which al-Qalqashandī dedicates one of the sections of the Second Article of *Ṣubḥ*. This section includes explanations of the various kinds of coinage, measurements and prices. (*Ṣubḥ*, Vol. 3, 440–447).

[processional] service (*khidma*). He exits the House of Viceroyship at sunrise and moves in his procession, with the sultanic flute (*shabbāba*) immediately in front of him, until he goes out of Bāb al-Baḥr. The stationed amirs leave [their residences] separately too, meet at the procession,march outside Bāb al-Baḥr for an hour, then return. The Viceroy then heads to the House of Viceroy ship among his mamluks and the Soldiers of Two-hundred, after the stationed amirs leave him each heading to his house. When he arrives at the House of Viceroy ship, and if this procession includes a banquet, the chair, covered with yellow satin (*aṭlas*), is placed at the centre of the main wall of the iwan. A sultanic dagger (*nimjāh*) sword is put on it, while the banquet is spread out below it and the viceroy's mamluks and the Soldiers of Two-hundred [sit to] eat. The viceroy sits at a side of the iwan, while the window overlooks the city's port. The Mālikī Judge sits to his right; the Ḥanafī Judge to his left; the Supervisor (*nāẓir*) inferior to him; the Signer (*muwaqqiʿ*) immediately in front of him, and the Heads of the City (*ru'ūs al-balad*) [sit] according to their statuses. The petitions (*qiṣaṣ*) are submitted and the Signer (*muwaqqiʿ*) reads them for the Viceroy, who arbitrates them[2158] in the presence of the judges, then the procession leaves.

I say: This is a new viceroyship that was first introduced in 767 AH/1366 AD, during the reign of al-Ashraf Shaʿbān b. Ḥusayn, when the Franks invaded [the city], attacked its people, killed, pillaged and took war prisoners. Prior to that, it was a governorship (*wilāya*) among the governorships (*wilāyāt*) of the *ṭablakhānāh* [rank]. Its governor (*wālī*) was of one of grand rank and lofty status.

The Second – Viceroyship of Lower Egypt

This was among the introductions in the reign of al-Ẓāhir Barqūq. The Viceroy is a Commander Amir who is of the same rank as the Commander of Soldiers (*muqaddam al-'askar*) of Gaza, who will be mentioned later in the account on the Syrian Kingdoms.[2159]Its seat of the viceroyship is the city of Damanhūr in al-Buḥayra and this viceroy rules over all the villages (*bilād*) of Lower Egypt that were mentioned earlier in the account on the stable provincial divisions (*a'māl*) of the Egyptian Lands,[2160] except for Alexandria. This viceroyship does not follow the same rules of the viceroyships in riding processions and the like, for its viceroy is actually a high Land Supervisor (*kāshif*). The only viceregal protocols this position has are wearing the costumes of honour (*tashrīf*), writing the diplomas of investiture (*taqlīd*), and the use of the letter-writing [protocol] [that is appropriate] for such as its viceroy, [considering his level] among viceroys.[2161] The holder of

2158 "*Yafṣilhā.*"

2159 A section of *Ṣubḥ* that is not translated in this work.

2160 The author means his account of the stable *nawāḥī* (villages) and *a'māl* (provincial divisions) of Egypt, which is not translated in this work. The term *bilād* may also have the general meaning of "provinces." (*Ṣubḥ*, Vol. 3, 396–410).

2161 "*Wa-l-mukātaba bimā yukātab bihi nā'ibuhā min al-nuwwāb*," which may also mean: "being written to, from the other viceorys, with the protocol [appropriate] to such as its viceroy."

this position in the early times, before it stably became a viceroyship, was referred to as "the Chief Governor" (*wālī al-wulāt*).

The Third – Viceroyship of Upper Egypt

This was also among the introductions of the reign of al-Ẓāhir Barqūq. The seat of this viceroy was the City of Asiūṭ and he rules over all the villages (*bilād*) of Upper Egypt. In level and rank, this office is the same as the Viceroyship of Lower Egypt mentioned above, except that it is more critical.[2162] The holder of this office used to also be termed "Chief Governor," as mentioned above for Lower Egypt.

The Second Level Supervisors of Lands and Embankments (kushshāf)

It was mentioned before that prior to the introduction of the viceroyships in Upper and Lower Egypt, they had two Supervisors of Lands and Embankments (*kushshāf*), each called "Chief Governor" (*wālī al-wulāt*). When both became stable viceroyships, a Supervior of Lands (*kāshif*) who was a *ṭablakhānāh* amir, according to the earlier custom, was appointed for Lower Egypt. In reality, he was under the authority of the Viceroy of Lower Egypt and his seat [of rule] was Munyat Ghamr[2163] in al-Sharqiyya. Another Supervisor of Lands was appointed for al-Bahnasāwiyya[2164] and al-Fayyūm. The office of the Governor (*wālī*) of al-Fayyūm was cancelled, while the rest of Upper Egypt fell under the authority of its Viceroy. Al-Jīziyya had a Supervisor of Lands who supervised its embankments and all that is relevant to it, and his authority did not extend [outside it] to the other districts (*nawāḥī*).

The Third Level The Governors (wulāt) of Upper and Lower Egypt

The provincial divisions (*a'māl*)of both [Upper and Lower Egypt] were mentioned before. The ranks of their governors (*wulāt*) are either of two:

The First Rank: The governors who are ṭablakhānāh amirs, over seven[2165] governorships (wilāyāt) in Upper and Lower Egypt, according to the [current] established situation

As for Upper Egypt, it has four of the governorships (*wilāyāt*) of this rank, namely: The Governorship of al-Bahnasā; the Governorship of al-Ushmūnīn, the Governoship of Qūṣ, which is the greatest, to the extent that its governor

2162 "*A'ẓam khaṭaran fī al-nufūs*," which may be translated as "perceived more gravely in the hearts and minds," implying that it was a more critical office.

2163 Called Mīt Ghamr and affiliated to al-Daqahliyya Governorate in modern times, it was one of the old villages that had a market and shops. (M. Ramzy, *Qāmūs*, Vol. 1, 263).

2164 Al-Bahnasā or Al-Bahnasāwiyya Province: an ancient administrative geographical division whose capital was the city of al-Bahnasā. It was replaced in modern times by the governorates of Minya and Banī Swaif in Upper Egypt. (M. Ramzy, *Qāmūs*, Vol. 3, 16).

2165 The editor of Subḥ notes that the author lists eight. (*Ṣubḥ*, Vol. 4, 66 fn. 1).

rode with the flute (*shabbāba*), like the viceroys of the kingdoms, and the Governorship of Aswan, which was introduced in the reign of al-Ẓāhir Barqūq. Before that, the Governorship of Aswan used to be added to the Wālī of Qūṣ, who appointed a deputy for it under his authority. The Governorship of al-Fayyūm used to be a *ṭablakhānāh* [rank], then it settled as a Supervision of Land (*kāshf*), as mentioned earlier.

As for Asiūṭ, it did not have a governor because it was the seat of the viceroy of Upper Egypt, and prior to [this office],it was the seat of the Chief Governor. The governorships of Upper Egypt that were a *ṭablakhānāh* [rank] then changed will be mentioned below.

As for Lower Egypt, it has four governorships of this rank, namely: The Governorship of al-Sharqiyya, the seat of whose *wālī* is Bilbais; the Governorship of al-Munūfiyya, the seat of whose *wālī* is the City of Munūf; the Governorship of al-Gharbiyya, the seat of whose *wālī* is al-Maḥalla al-Kubrā, and which is equivalent to the Governorship of Qūṣ, except that its *wālī* never rode with the flute (*shabbāba*), and the Governorship of al-Buḥayra, the base of whose *wālī* is the City of Damanhūr. The governorship office of al-Buḥayra may be cancelled, since it is the seat of the viceroy. It was mentioned earlier that the governorship [rank] of the Viceroy [of Lower Egypt], before becoming a viceroyship, was a governorship [rank] of a *ṭablakhānāh*.

The Second Rank: The governors who are Amirs of Tens, over seven governorships in both Upper and Lower Egypt

As for Upper Egypt, it has three governorships of this rank: The Governorship of Giza, which was a *ṭablakhānāh* before; the Governorship of Iṭfīḥ, which remains to be a governorship of [the rank of an Amir of] Ten, and Manfalūṭ, which is a governorship of [the rank of an Amir of] Twenty and was a *ṭablakhānāh* before. In the reign of al-Nāṣir Muḥammad b. Qalāwūn and later, a *wālī* was appointed to ʿAydhāb, who was an Amir of Ten assigned by the sultan, and who turned to the Wālī of Qūṣ for important matters.

As for Lower Egypt, it includes four governorships of this rank: The Governorship of Munūf; the Governorship of Ushmūm, the Governorship of Damietta, and the Governorship of Qaṭya, which was a *ṭablakhānāh* before that.

The Fourth Level The Arab Bedouin Amirs of the Districts (nawāḥī) of the Egypt

The origins of the Arab lineages were mentioned earlier in the First Article, within the account of what a scribe needs.[2166] This included their division into al-Qaḥṭāniyya,[2167]

2166 First Article of *Ṣubḥ*, which is not translated in this work.

2167 Sons of Qaḥṭān, the great grandfather of the original Arabs Yemen, who expanded into many tribes. (A. Hammuda, *Tārīkh*, 39).

who are the [original] Arabs,[2168] and al-ʿAdnāniyya,[2169] who are the Arabized;[2170] an explanation of the origins of each of the clans (*buṭūn*)[2171] of the Arabs, now present in the Egyptian Lands and elsewhere, back to the tribes they are attributed to, and an account of the tribes which now inhabit Upper and Lower Egypt, and the sub-clans (*afkhādh*)[2172] branching from each tribe. What I mean to do here is to list the Arab Bedouin Amirs in Upper and Lower Egypt, in the old and new times.

As for Upper Egypt, al-Ḥamadānī[2173] mentioned that the emirate of Upper Egypt was established in three provincial divisions (*a'māl*):

The First Division (*'amal*) – The Division of Qūṣ, where the emirate was from two houses of [the tribe of] Baliy[2174] of Quḍāʿa b. Ḥimyar b. Saba',[2175] of al-Qaḥṭāniyya:

> The First [House]: Banū Shādd, known as Banū Shādī, who resided at the ruined palace known as Qaṣr Banī Shādī in the Divisions of Qūṣ (*al-a'māl al-Qūṣiyya*).[2176] It was mentioned earlier there that it was said they were from the Banū Umayya b. ʿAbd Shams of Quraysh.[2177]

2168 "*Al-'Āriba*:" The primary and original Arabs, who were the first to speak the Arabic Language and were situated in Yemen, then migrated northwards. (A. Hammuda, *Tārīkh*, 39).

2169 Sons of ʿAdnān, a descendant of Prophet Ismāʿīl, who expanded into many tribes. (A. Hammuda, *Tārīkh*, 39).

2170 "*Al-Musta'riba*": Those of non-Arab origins, also known as the Arabs of the North, the Arabs of Hijaz, or the Ismāʿīliyya Arabs. These were situated in the middle of the Jazira, and from the Hijaz to the desert of the Levant. The differences between the original Arabs (*al-'Āriba*) and the Arabized (*al-musta'riba*) were due to the natural environment, the social norms, the languages, the religions, as well as other factors. (A. Hammuda, *Tārīkh*, 39–40).

2171 Sing. baṭn, which means "abdomen, belly or stomach," is a hereditary social division that is smaller than the qabīla (tribe, pl. qabā'il) and bigger than the sub-clan (fakhdh, pl. afkhādh). The English terms do not exactly describe these divisions, which are culturally specific and sometimes fluid or changeable when used by different historians to refer to the hereditary grouping or social division of a particular tribe or clan. (Ṣubḥ, Vol. 1, 309, A. Hammuda, Tārīkh, 176 and Gianluca Paolo Parolin, Citizenship in the Arab World: Kin, Religion and Nation-state (Amesterdam, 2009), 30–31).

2172 Sing. *fakhdh*,which means "thigh," is a social division that is smaller than the *baṭn* (clan). (*Ṣubḥ*, Vol. 1, 309 and A. Hammuda, *Tārīkh*, 176).

2173 Yūsūf b. Sayf al-Dawla b. Zammākh b. Abū al-Maʿālī b. Ḥamadān al-Taghlibī (died c. 700 AH/1300 AD), Badr al-Dīn, known as Ibn Mihmandār al-ʿArab, was an Egyptian poet and historian whose works included a book on lineages. (Al-Ṣafadi, *A'yān*, Vol. 5, 637–642 and al-ʿAsqalānī, *Durar*, Vol. 6, 227).

2174 Baliy b. ʿAmr b. al-Ḥāfī b. Quḍāʿa, a subdivision of the Quḍāʿa tribe of Qaḥṭānī origin, whose remnants were found in Upper Egypt, Hijaz, and other places. Some of them were amirs in Upper Egypt. (*Ṣubḥ*, Vol. 1, 316 and Mahmud al-Sayyid, *Tārīkh al-Qabā'il al-'Arabiyya fī 'Aṣr al-Dawlatayn al-Ayyūbiyya wa-l-Mamlūkiyya* (Alexandria, 1998), 34).

2175 Quḍāʿa was one of the main clans (*buṭūn*) of Ḥimyar, a chief tribe of al-Qaḥṭāniyya. (A. Hammuda, *Tārīkh*, 39 & 41).

2176 *Al-A'māl al-Qūṣiyya* was the province whose base was the City of Qūṣ from the Fatimid to the end of the Mamluk era. (M. Ramzy, *Qāmūs*, Part 2, Vol. 4, 189).

2177 The tribe of the Umayyad House, which originated from al-ʿAdnāniyya. (A.Hammuda, *Tārīkh*, 46 and M. al-Sayyid, *Qabā'il*, 39).

The Second [House]: Al-ʿAjāla, who are Banū al-ʿUjayl b. Al-Dhi'b, also from [Banū Umayya] and were there with them.

The Second Division (*'amal*) – Al-Ushmūnayn, where the emirate was from the house of Banū Thaʿlab of al-Salaṭina, who are the sons of Abū Juḥaysh of the Ḥayadira,[2178] who are the descendants of Ismāʿīl b. Jaʿfar al-Ṣādiq, who descends from al-Ḥusayn al-Sibṭ,[2179] son of the Prince of the Faithful, ʿAlī b. Abī Ṭālib. They resided in Darwat Sarabām,[2180]which was taken over by al-Sharīf Ḥiṣn al-Dīn b. Thaʿlab,[2181] and so became known as Darwat al-Sharīf since then. He captured it, along with the villages (*bilād*) of Upper Egypt, and it was mentioned earlier that he existed towards the end of the Ayyubid era. When al-Muʿizz Aybak al-Turkumānī, the first Turkish sultan of the Egypt, ascended to the sultanate, al-Sharīf disdained his rule and aspired to become sultan himself. Al-Muʿizz equipped and sent armies [to confront] him and they fought him but were not able to capture him. This remained the case until the reign of al-Ẓāhir Baybars, who set tricky traps for al-Sharīf, captured him using them, and hung him in Alexandria.

The Third Division (*'amal*) – Al-Bahnasā, where the emirate was from two houses:

The First [House] – Awlād Zuʿāziʿ (Children of Zuʿāziʿ)[2182] of Banū Jadīdī of Banū Balār, of Luwātha[2183] of the Berbers or of Qays ʿAylān, which is the controversy mentioned before in the account of their lineage in the First Article.[2184] Al-Ḥamadānī said: They are the most famous of those in Upper Egypt.

2178 Of the several origins and branches of the Quraysh tribe of the ʿAdnāniyya, from whom Prophet Muḥammad descends, al-Qalqashandī lists the origin of ʿAbd al-Muṭṭalib b. Hāshim, the Prophet's grandfather. Among the descendants of this origin are al-Ḥasan and al-Ḥusayn, the Prophet's grandchildren through his daughter Fāṭima who married his paternal cousin, ʿAlī b. Abī Ṭālib. Al-Qalqashandī lists al-Ḥayādira and al-Salāṭina as two of the clans (*buṭūn*) of the many descendants of al-Ḥasan and al-Ḥusayn; however, he combines them here, mentioning one as descending from the other. (*Ṣubḥ*, Vol. 1, 359).

2179 "Al-Sibṭ," which means "the grandchild," is a title given to al-Ḥasan and al-Ḥusayn being the grandchildren of the Prophet. (http://www.baheth.info/all.jsp?term=سبط).

2180 Darwat Sarabām is the old Coptic name of the present day village of Dayrūṭ al-Sharīf in Asiūṭ Governorate. It was a village of "many gardens and palmtrees," where al-Sharīf Ḥiṣn al-Dīn b. Thaʿlab al-Jaʿdī built palaces and a mosque overlooking Baḥr Yusūf (Sea of Joseph; the canal running from the Nile at Dayrūṭ and up to Fayyum). The village's name is attributed to Ṣarbāmūn, an eminent monk of the early Coptic era. (Al-Ḥamawī, *Mu'jam*, Vol. 2, 453 and M. Ramzy, *Qāmūs*, Part 2, Vol. 4, 47).

2181 "Al-Sharīf" is "the Honourable," indicating descent from the line of the Prophet. Al-Qalqashandī refers to him earlier as al-Sharīf Ḥiṣn al-Dīn b. Taghlib, the governor of Darwat Sarabām. (*Ṣubḥ*, Vol. 1, 359).

2182 "*Awlād*" means "Children of."

2183 The editor of Subḥ mentions that another source states the pronunciation of this name as "Luwāta." (*Ṣubḥ*, Vol. 4, 68, fn. 2).

2184 See *Ṣubḥ*, Vol. 1, 364–365. Qays ʿAylān is one of the branch tribes of Muḍur, a major tribe of al-ʿAdnāniyya. (A. Hammuda, *Tārīkh*, 42–43).

> The Second [House] – Awlād Quraysh.[2185] Al-Ḥamadānī said: They are the amirs of Banū Zayd[2186] and they reside in Nuwayrat Dalāṣ.[2187] He added: This Quraysh[2188] was a good servant [of Allah], who made a lot of charitable donations (*ṣadaqa*). His sons include Sa'd al-Mulk, whose sons are famous there.

Al-Maqarr al-Shihābī Ibn Faḍl Allah mentioned in *al-Ta'rīf*that the emirate of Upper Egypt in his time – that is the sultanate of al-Nāṣir Muḥammad b. Qalāwūn and the regins after it – was given to Nāṣir al-Dīn 'Umar b. Faḍl,[2189] but neither mentioned his seat of governance nor from which Arab [origins] he was. He also mentioned that the emirate in the area beyond Aswan was in an Arab [house] called al-Ḥidāriyya;[2190] given to Samīra b. Mālik.[2191] He said: He had numerous [forces] and the power to vanquish [his enemies].[2192] He used to invade Ethiopia and the Sudanese peoples and came back with booties and prisoners of war. He was a man of praiseworthy memory and remembered virtue. He arrived visiting the sultan, who lodged him hospitably. A banner (*liwā'*) was assigned to him,[2193] and he was honoured with a costume of honour (*tashrīf*) and given an investiture (*taqlīd*). Letters were sent to all the governors (*wulāt*) of Upper Egypt and all of its Bedouin Arabs to help and support him, and ride for raids with him whenever he wanted. A decree of grant (*manshūr*) was written for him, [encompassing] the places he conquered; and he was given a diploma of investiture (*taqlīd*) to become the amir of the Bedouin Arabs

2185 One of the branches of a clan (*baṭn*) of Luwāta, the Arabized Berbers, along with Awlād Zu'āzi'. (*Ṣubḥ*, Vol. 1, 364–365 and M. al-Sayyid, *Qabā'il*, 40).

2186 Banū Zayd were also one of the branches of a clan (*baṭn*) of Luwāta. (*Ṣubḥ*, Vol. 1, 365).

2187 In al-Bahnasā, presently in Banī Suwaif Governorate: Al-Qalqashandī refers to it in the First Article as al-Nuwayra. M. Ramzy lists two separate, old villages in al-Bahnasā, one named al-Nuwayra and the other named Dalāṣ. Dalāṣ was described historically as a great, inhabited small city, famous for the manufacture of iron products, especially bridles, which were attributed to it (named *al-Dalāṣiyya*). It is also mentions that it was governed by the Luwāta Berbers, which suggests that it is more probably the village referred to above. (*Ṣubḥ*, Vol. 1, 365 and M. Ramzy, *Qāmūs*, Vol. 3, 153 & 159–160).

2188 The great grandfather of the Berber Awlād Quraysh, whose name should not be confused with Quraysh, the major 'Adnāniyya tribe, from which Prophet Muḥammad descends.

2189 Al-Qalqashandī mentions Nāṣir al-Dīn 'Umar b. Faḍl in the Fourth Article of *Ṣubḥ*, citing *Ta'rīf*, as one of the two Arab amirs of Upper Egypt, the other being Samura or Samīra b. Mālik. (*Ṣubḥ*, Vol. 7, 162 and al-'Umarī, *Ta'rīf*, 77).

2190 One of the houses that belonged to Judhām tribe. (*Ṣubḥ*, Vol. 1, 332).

2191 This name is written differently in the Fourth Article – Samura b. Mālik – and the description given above is repeated. (*Ṣubḥ*, Vol. 7, 162).

2192 "*Shawka munkiya*," which means "a vanqushing thorn," denotes the power to overcome one's enemies.

2193 Assigning a *liwā'* (*'aqd al-liwā'*) is the expression used to show that this man was given the leadership of an army or a fighting force. (See http://www.baheth.info/all.jsp?term=لواء).

of Upper Egypt,[2194] beyond Qūṣ and up to wherever his limit reached and his flag was planted.[2195]

I say: as for our times, since the Arabs of Hawwāra[2196] changed their targeted [quarters] from the division (*'amal*) of al-Buḥayra to Upper Egypt and resided there, they spread all over it like locusts.[2197] They established their control over [the area] from the division (*a'māl*) of al-Bahnasā up to the borders of Upper Egypt, at Aswan and what is beyond it. All the other Bedouin Arabs of Upper Egypt submitted to them, sided with them, and followed their leadership.

The emirate now is from two of their houses:

> The First [House] – Banū ʿUmar: Muḥammad and his brothers, who reside in Jarjā[2198] and Munsha'at Ikhmīm,[2199] and who dominate [the region] up to Aswan southwards, and as far as the end of the villages (*bilād*) of al-Ushmunīn northwards.
>
> The Second [House] – Awlād Gharīb, who control the villages of al-Bahnasā and reside in Dahrūṭ[2200] and its environs.

2194 The term used here is *'urbān al-qibla*. The account in the Fourth Article of *Ṣubḥ*, as well as the account in *Ta'rīf*, refer to them as "*al-'urbān al-qibliyya*." *Al-Qibla* is the name given to the region encompassing parts of Sinai and some of the Red Sea western and eastern coastal cities, that is, in Egypt and the Hijaz. (See *Ṣubḥ*, Vol. 3, 391–391 & Vol. 7, 162 and al-ʿUmarī, *Ta'rīf*, 77).

2195 See al-ʿUmarī's account in *Ta'rīf*, 77.

2196 An Arabized Berber tribe believed to have originally been from the Arabs of Yemen. They resided and controlled the area of al-Buḥayra and the west of Alexandria since they arrived in Egypt from the Maghrib prior to the Ayyubid era. This remained the case until they moved to Upper Egypt. This either happened towards the end of the reign of al-Ẓāhir Barqūq, when they were defeated by other Arab tribes of al-Buḥayra, and settled, gathered and expanded in Upper Egypt, where they powerfully controlled the region beyond Qūṣ to the west of al-Bahnasā; or during the reign of al-Manṣūr ʿAlī b. Shaʿbān, in 782 AH/1380 AD, after which, since 815 AH/1412 AD, they controlled Upper Egypt and became the leaders of all its Arab tribes. Hawwāra worked in agriculture and the manufacture of sugar, which increased their wealth. They were among the Arab tribes that joined the Mamluk armies; however, they revolted in 882 AH/1477 AD, and in other years, against the unfair policies of the Mamluks, but were subdued and continued to control Upper Egypt. (M. al-Sayyid, *Qabā'il*, 43 & 51–52 and *Ṣubḥ*, Vol. 1, 363–364).

2197 "To spread like locusts" is a common Arabic expression indicating vast and dense expansion over an area of land.

2198 Also Dijarjā, one of the old villages or cities of Upper Egypt, presently in Sūhāj Governorate. (See M. Ramzy, *Qāmūs*, Vol. 4, 113–114).

2199 Also Al-Minsha'a and Abshāya, along with several other names; it was one of the oldest Egyptian cities. In modern times, it became one of the administrative divisions of Sūhāj Governorate. (See M. Ramzy, *Qāmūs*, Vol. 4, 109–111).

2200 One of the old villages of Upper Egypt, presently in al-Minyā Governorate. Its people claim descent from Abū Bakr al-Ṣiddīq, the Prophet's companion and the first of the Rightly-guided

As for Lower Egypt, al-Ḥamadānī mentioned that the emirate was over five of its provoncial divisions (*a'māl*):

The First Division (*'amal*)- Al-Sharqiyya.[2201] He said: Its emirate was from two tribes:

The First [Tribe] – Tha'laba;[2202]and he mentioned that the amirs who belonged to them were Shuqyar b. Jurjī of al-Maṣāfiḥa of Banū Zurayq[2203] and 'Umar b. Nufayla of al-'Ulaymiyyīn.[2204]

The Second [Tribe] – Judhām;[2205]of which he mentioned five houses had amirs:

The First [House] – The house of Abū Rushd b. Ḥabashī, b. Najm, b. Ibrāhīm of al-'Uqaliyyīn: Banū 'Uqayl b. Qurra, b. Mawhūb, b. 'Ubayd,[2206] b. Mālik, b. Suwayd,[2207]of Banū Yazīd b. Ḥarām, b. Judhām;[2208] who was appointed an amir with the horn and the flag.[2209]

Caliphs, which al-Qalqashandī mentions in the First Article. (M. Ramzy, *Qāmūs*, Vol. 3, 247–248 and *Ṣubḥ*, Vol. 1, 354).

2201 "*'Amal al-Sharqiyya*" or "*a'māl al-Sharqiyya*" was the name given to the provincial division of al-Sharqiyya in 715 AH/1315 AD, which is roughly the same Governorate of al-Sharqiyya in modern times. (M. Ramzy, *Qāmūs*, Part 2, Vol. 1, 22).

2202 A tribe of origins going back to al-Qaḥṭāniyya, which arrived in Egypt during the reign of Sultan Ṣalāḥ al-Dīn, after having fought against the Crusaders in Syria. Sultan Ṣalāḥ al-Dīn ordered them to stay in al-Sharqiyya. Al-Ḥamadānī mentions that this tribe included prominent men, who gave considerable support to kings and states, and were appointed amirs. (M. al-Sayyid, *Qabā'il*, 41–42 and *Ṣubḥ*, Vol. 1, 322–323).

2203 Banū Zurayq is a sub-tribe of Tha'laba, while al-Maṣāfiḥa is one of the houses that branched from a clan (*baṭn*) of Banū Zurayq. (*Ṣubḥ*, Vol. 1, 323).

2204 Al-'Ulaymiyyīn is one of the houses that branched from another clan (*baṭn*) of Banū Zurayq. (*Ṣubḥ*, Vol. 1, 323).

2205 Judhām is a Yemeni tribe which is controversially believed to have 'Adnānī origins. They came to Egypt with 'Amr b. al-'Āṣ and were given villages that remained their *iqṭā'* until al-Qalqashandī's time. This tribe settled in al-Sharqiyya at the beginning of the Ayyubid era, until Ṣalāḥ al-Dīn ordered them to move to al-Buḥayra in 565 AH/1169 AD, because he objected to their trading activities with the Crusaders. However, some of them remained in al-Sharqiyya. In al-Qalqashandī's time, they had several clans (*buṭūn*) spread over many places in Egypt. (M. al-Sayyid, *Qabā'il*, 40–41 and *Ṣubḥ*, Vol. 1, 330–331).

2206 Al-'Uqaliyyīn, the sons of 'Uqayl b. Qurra b. Mawhūb b. 'Ubayd, are one of the subdivisions of a clan (*baṭn*) of the many clans (*buṭūn*) of Judhām, namely, Halbā Suwayd. (*Ṣubḥ*, Vol. 1, 331–332).

2207 Mālik b. Suwayd was one of the men of Halbā Suwayd, whose sons, Banū Mālik b. Suwayd, formed one of the branches of Halbā Suwayd, namely, Halbā Mālik. (*Ṣubḥ*, Vol. 1, 331–332).

2208 One of the clans (*buṭūn*) of Judhām. (*Ṣubḥ*, Vol. 1, 331).

2209 "*Ummira bi-l-būq wa-l-'alam*," which means "he was appointed an amir with the horn and the flag." The *ta'mīr* (the investiture of a mamluk amir) was a process that involved several steps: A celebration; a bestowal of attire (as well as a particular headgear in the Bahri Mamluk period); riding on procession, allocating the *iqṭā'*, and assigning a position and the blazon

The Second [House] – Ṭarīf b. Maknūn,[2210] of Banū al-Walīd, of Suwayd, mentioned earlier.[2211] Banū Ṭarīf of al-Sharqiyya villages (*bilād*) are attributed to this Ṭarīf. Al-Ḥamadānī said: He was one of the most generous Arabs, whose guesthouse [hosted] 12,000 people to eat during the days of soaring prices, and who used to smash sop (*tharīd*)[2212] in boats.[2213] He added: Among his descendants are Faḍl b. Samḥ b. Kammūna and Ibrāhīm b. ʿĀlī, who were both appointed amirs with the horn and the flag.

The Third [House] – The house of Awlad Manāzil,[2214] who were among the descendants of al-Walīd [b. Suwayd] mentioned above, and of whom was Maʿbad b. Mubārak, who was appointed an amir with the horn and the flag.

The Fourth [House] – The house of Namiy b. Khathʿam[2215] of Banū Mālik, b. Halbā b. Mālik b. Suwayd. Khathʿam, the son of the aforementioned Namiy was given an *iqṭā'* and was appointed an amir. He owned a number of Turkish, *Rūm* and other mamluks. He reached a status [of closeness] to al-Malik al-Ṣāliḥ [Najm al-Dīn] Ayyūb, then acquired a lofty grade under al-Malik al-Muʿizz Aybak al-Turkumānī, who made him the Commander of

(*rank*). According to T. Abdelhamid, apart from the celebration, wearing the headgear then the procession, there is no conclusive evidence of the order of these steps in the primary sources for the Bahri Mamluk period. W. Leaf and S. Purcell conclude from al-Qalqashandī's statement that the investiture of an amir in the Mamluk era necessitated the presentation of the flag and the horn to him, being "the visible sign that a mamluk has been made an amir." However, it seems that al-Qalqashandī and al-ʿUmarī mention "the horn and the flag" in such context and with this composition only in relation to the investiture of Bedouin Arab (*'urbān*) amirs in particular. In *Itti'āẓ*, al-Maqrīzī defines the *ṭulb* (battalion), in the language of the Ghuzz, as the Commander Amir who has "an assigned flag and a blown horn" (*'alam ma'qūd wa būq maḍrūb*), and a force of two-hundred, one-hundred, or seventy soldiers. (See T. Abdelhamid, *Jaysh*, 24–30 & 24 fn. 75; William Leaf and Sally Purcell, *Heraldic Symbols: Islamic Insignia and Western Heraldry* (London, 1986), 76; *Ṣubḥ*, Vol. 1, 323 & 332, Vol. 4, 70–71; al-ʿUmarī, *Masālik* (2002), Vol. 4, 378, 379, 386, and al-Maqrīzī, *Itti'āẓ*, Vol. 3, 327).

2210 The editor of Subḥ notes that the author states this name as "Ṭarīf b. Baktūt" in the first volume. Ṭarīf bore the title "Zayn al-Dawla." (*Ṣubḥ*, Vol. 4, 70, fn. 1 and Vol. 1, 332).

2211 Banū al-Walīd b. Suwayd (Sons of al-Walīd b. Suwayd) is one of the branches of Halbā Suwayd. (*Ṣubḥ*, Vol. 1, 332).

2212 Sop: Bread smashed or broken into pieces and soaked in soup, usually with meat, which is a typical Arab dish. The preparation of *tharīd* and offering it to one's guests is a sign of generosity. (See http://www.baheth.info/all.jsp?term=ثريد).

2213 That is, sending the meals of smashed bread in soup using boats that salied along canals to feed other areas as well. (Amr Abd al-Aziz Munir, *al-Sharqiyya bayn al-Tārīkh wa al-Folklore*, (Cairo, 2004), 177).

2214 The Children of Manāzil, who are not listed among the descendant branches of al-Walīd b. Suwayd in the First Article, possibly due to being a smaller subdivision than the ones mentioned. (See *Ṣubḥ*, Vol. 1, 332).

2215 Not listed among the descendant branches of Mālik b. Suwayd in the First Article, possibly due to being a smaller subdivision than the ones mentioned. (See *Ṣubḥ*, Vol. 1, 332).

the Arabs of the Egypt, which he remained to be until his slave-boys (*ghilmān*) killed him. Al-Muʿizz then appointed his two sons: Salamā and Daghash in his place and they proved to be the best successors. Then Daghash went to Damascus, where the [Ayyubud] al-Malik al-Nāṣir, who ruled Damascus at the time, appointed him an amir with a horn and a flag. Al-Malik Aybak also appointed his brother, Salamā, similarly.

The Fifth [House] – The house of Mufarrij b. Sālim of Halbā Baʿja, b. Zayd, b. Suwayd, b. Baʿja, of Banū Zayd b. Ḥarām b. Judhām,[2216] whom al-Muʿizz also appointed an amir with the horn and the flag; for when he wanted to appoint Salamā b. Khathʿam, mentioned above, he refused to assume the appointment until Mufarrij b. Ghānim[2217] was appointed, so he was.[2218]

The Second Division (*'amal*): Al-Manūfiyya[2219]

Its emirate is from the house of Awlād Naṣīr al-Dīn of Lawāta;[2220] however, it corresponds to a Chieftain of Arabs (*mashyakhat 'Arab*).[2221]

The Third Division (*'amal*): Al-Gharbiyya[2222]

Its emirate is from the house of Awlād Yūsuf of Al-Khazaʿila, of Sinbis of Ṭayyi' of Kahlān, of al-Qaḥṭāniyya,[2223] whose seat [of emirate] is the city of Sakhā[2224] in al-Gharbiyya.

2216 Banū Baʿja, like Banū Suwayd, were among the branches of Banū Zayd b. Ḥarām, one of the clans (*buṭūn*) of Judhām in al-Sharqiyya. Halbā Baʿja were among the branches of Banū Baʿja. (*Ṣubḥ*, Vol. 1, 331–332).

2217 The editor of Subḥ comments that the author probably means "Sālim." (*Ṣubḥ*, Vol. 4, 70, fn. 2).

2218 Al-Qalqashandī mentions in the First Article that Mufarrij's son, Ḥassān, inherited his father's amirial rank. (*Ṣubḥ*, Vol. 1, 333).

2219 "*'Amal al-Manūfiyya*" or "*a'māl al-Manūfiyya*" is the name given to this province in 715 AH/1315 AD, whose borders have changed over time until it became the modern day Governorate of al-Munūfiyya. (M. Ramzy, *Qāmūs*, Part 2, Vol. 2, 15).

2220 Children of Naṣīr al-Dīn, who are not listed among the subdivisions of Luwāta in al-Manūfiyya in the First Article, possibly due to being a smaller subdivision than the ones mentioned. (See *Ṣubḥ*, Vol. 1, 365).

2221 Rank of Shaykh al-ʿArab, who was the grand leader of all the Arab tribes or houses in a particular province, although not as high in rank as an amir, as indicated above.

2222 "*'Amal al-Gharbiyya*" or "*al-a'māl al-Gharbiyya*" is the name given to this province in 715 AH/1315 AD, which later developed into the Governorate of al-Gharbiyya. (M. Ramzy, *Qāmūs*, Part 2, Vol. 2, 8).

2223 Kahlān is a Yemeni tribe and one of the main tribes of al-Qaḥṭāniyya which came to Egypt. Ṭayyi' is one of the divisions of Kahlān, and Sinbis is one of the many clans (*buṭūn*) of Ṭayyi', while al-Khazāʿila is one of the clans (*buṭūn*) of Sinbis, which incorporates the house of Banū Yūsuf. (*Ṣubḥ*, Vol. 1, 318, 320–322).

2224 Today in Kafr al-Shaykh Governorate, Sakhā was one of the old big cities and an important provincial centre of Lower Egypt, which had markets, baths, agriculture, particularly of grains, and a manufacturing activity of linen. (M. Ramzy, *Qāmūs*, Vol. 2, 141).

The Fourth Division (*'amal*): Al-Buḥayra

The author of *al-Ta'rīf* mentioned that its emirate during the reign of al-Naṣir Muḥammad b. Qalāwūn was assigned to: Khālid b. Abī Sulaymān and Fā'id b. Muqaddim.[2225] In *Masālik al-Abṣar*, he said: They were two respectful amirs, who were [honourable] masters (*sāda*),[2226]generous, charitable, brave, daring and resolute.[2227]

The Fifth Division (*'amal*): Barqa[2228]

The author of *al-Ta'rīf* said: There were no remaining Arab amirs in Barqa, that is, at his time, except Ja'far b. 'Umar,[2229] who continued to alternate between obedience and defiance; roughness and flexibility. Armies were sent to [subdue] him all the time, but were rarely able to accomplish victory over him, or come back with booty, even if he was stricken by one of Time's calamities. He added: The last heard about him is that he took the oasis road until he left al-Fayyūm and came to the sultan's court asking for his forgiveness. He arrived with no prior announcement and the sultan did not know of [his visit] until someone asked permission for him to meet the sultan, while he stood among those at the sultan's door. He was honoured most generously and bestowed upon with the most respectful costumes of honour (*tashārīf*). He stayed for a while enjoying the [sultan's] hospitality, while his people did not know what had happened, where he headed, or to which place he aimed [his travel], until the happy news reached them from him. The sultan asked him: "Why have you not informed your people that you had set out seeking us?" He answered: "I feared they would say the sultan will kill you, which would have discouraged me." The sultan liked his answer and generously bestowed upon him. He was then sent back to his people, where his life turned upside down with the grace and favour of Allah, so that no friend pitied him, nor did an enemy gloat over him.[2230]

2225 Al-Qalqashandī mentions in the Fourth Article that the author of *al-Ta'rīf* does not give accounts on either men; the first of whom he alternatively names Muḥammad b. Abī Sulaymān and the second, Fā'id b. Muqaddam. He concludes that both must have been quite reputable that their were enough a statement. In al-'Umarī's account the names are: Muḥammad b. Abī Sulaymān and Qā'id b. Muqaddam. Al-'Umarī adds that they followed the Arab tradition of frequent travel, for they used to travel to Qairawān and Qābis, in present day Tunisia, then come to the Mamluk capital. (*Ṣubḥ*, Vol. 7, 160 and al-'Umarī, *Ta'rīf*, 76).

2226 Sing. *sayyid*; of descent that goes back to the Prophet.

2227 Al-'Umarī adds that last he knew, possibly meaning when he was still in official position, was that these men were the amirs of al-Buḥayra. (Al-'Umarī, *Masālik* (2002), Vol. 4, 389).

2228 In eastern Libya today.

2229 Al-Qalqashandī mentions him in a very similar account in the Fourth Article, although he does not provide more details about him or his lineage there either. He only additionally mentions, after *Ta'rīf*, that the Arabs of al-Buḥayrakept trying to change the sultan's heart against Ja'far. (*Ṣubḥ*, Vol. 7, 163 and al-'Umarī, *Ta'rīf*, 77).

2230 Al-'Umarī, *Ta'rīf*, 77–78.

I say: Today's amir of Barqa is ʿUmar b. ʿArrīf, who is a religious man. His father, [ʿArrīf, was a man of firm religiosity, whom I saw][2231] in Alexandria after the year 780 AH/1378 AD; and I met with him and found that the signs of goodness showed on him.

***

2231 The editor of Subḥ notes that the phrase between brackets was missing from the original text, and he copied it from *al-Ḍaw'* by al-Qalqashandī. (*Ḍaw'*, 268).

GLOSSARY

A

Abbasids

The Abbasids were descended from the Prophet's uncle, al-ʿAbbās b. ʿAbd al-Muttalib. They formed the second dynastic Islamic caliphate which ruled from AH 133 / AD 750 to AH 656 / AD 1258. Rising against the ruling dynasty, the Umayyads, the Abbasids started an armed revolt from Khurasan (in present day Iran), and, after a series of battles, they eventually captured and killed the Umayyad caliph in AH 133 / AD 750, then eliminated all the males of the Umayyad house except one Umayyad prince, who escaped and founded an independent Umayyad Caliphate in Andalusia. The history of the Abbasid Caliphate may be divided into three main periods: the first Abbasid period or the "Abbasid Golden Age" (AH 132–232 / AD 750–847), the second Abbasid period, or the "Age of Fragmentation and Autonomous States" (AH 232–656 / AD 847–1258) which ended with the Mongol sack of Baghdad and the murder of the caliph, and the third Abbasid period with the "Revival of the Abbasid Caliphate in Cairo" (AH 658–923 / AD 1261–1517) that ended with the conquest of Egypt by the Ottoman Sultan Selim I who took the Abbasid caliph with him to Istanbul, and the caliphate was transferred to the Ottoman dynasty (Bosworth, *Islamic Dynasties*, 9; ʿAbdelhamid, Jaish, 55–7; al-Qalqashandī, *Ṣubḥ*, Vol. 3, 258–67, 270–76).

ʿabīd al-shirāʾ

ʿAbīd al-shirāʾ (the "Bought Slaves"), were first introduced to the Fatimid army by Caliph al-Ḥākim. They multiplied in number under Caliph al-Mustanṣir, when they formed a huge brigade of 50,000 warriors. Al-Mustanṣir's mother was herself originally a black slave, which explains why she bought, and induced her son to buy, numerous black slaves to serve in the army, so as to combat the power and influence of the Turkish factions. *ʿAbīd al-shirāʾ* seem to have not been the only black forces of the Fatimid army, for the account by the Persian traveller, Nāṣirī Khusraw, who visited Cairo around AH 440 / AD 1049, specifies two black factions: the *zunūj* (the Negros), who fought with their swords only, and *ʿabīd al-shirāʾ* (Gamal al-Din, *Dawla*, 190–91; Sayyed, *Tafsīr*, 668–90).

'abra

The fixed monetary tax imposed on every piece of land that is allocated as an *iqṭā'* (Sayyid, *Nuzha*, 86 n. 3).

adhān

The call to prayer which is chanted from mosques. The Sunni and Shi'ite formulae for *adhān* are slightly different.

adilla *(sing.* dalīl*)*

"Guides": these were possibly the travel guides who accompanied the *maḥmil* on its journey. The term is also applicable to the guides who escorted and helped the pilgrims (*al-muṭawwifūn*, sing. *al-muṭawwif*).

'adl *(pl.* 'udūl*)*

The *'adl* ("the equitable one") is the man known for his honesty, especially when reporting on something or someone. The *'udūl* witnesses were chosen by the *qāḍī* (judge) to help him with his duties. They sat to his right and left in the Council of Judgement (*majlis al-ḥukm*) in order of their seniority of *ta'dīl* (being deemed *'adl*). Some of them were appointed to high offices in the Fatimid era, such as the *ḥisba* and the Agent of the Public Treasury (*wakālat bayt al-māl*).

In the Mamluk era, the witnesses were clerks from the Men of the Turban (*muta'ammimūn*). They provided arbitration testimonies and documented the rights, properties, debts and dealings of people in registers. They studied the cases presented to the judges and assisted them with the verdicts. A witness had to be known for being equitable and had to be learned in jurisprudence, which was required for documenting cases and contracts. The witness was a lesser judiciary office that advanced in promotion to higher ones.

The witnesses also did some work for other administrations than the judiciary. Some of them helped in the bureaus, for example, by testifying to the rights of those deserving of income or payment from a bureau. The witnesses did not enjoy the same economic prosperity that their peers in the judicial system had (al-Baqli, *Ta'rīf*, 242; al-Battawi, *'Imāma*, 67–8).

afkhādh *(sing.* fakdh*)*

"Sub-clans": *fakhdh*, which means "thigh", is a social division that is smaller than the *baṭn* ("clan") (al-Qalqashandī, *Ṣubḥ*, Vol. 1, 309; Hammuda, *Tārīkh*, 176).

Agent of the Public Treasury

See *wakīl bayt al-māl*.

ahl al-bayt *(also* āl al-bayt*)*

A term used to refer to the family of the Prophet and his descendants, with different interpretations in the Sunni and Shi'ite doctrines. The Sunni interpretation encompasses all the Prophet's wives and descendants, sometimes extending to his clan and their descendants, while the Shi'ite one generally restricts the term to descendants from the line of Fāṭima and ʿAlī (El Sandouby, "The Ahl al-bayt in Cairo and Damascus", 28–39).

aḥmāl *(sing.* ḥiml*)*

A term that could refer to any loads carried on mounts, including howdahs. Al-Qalqashandī uses the word either to refer to loads carried on mules in grand processions, for decoration and other uses, such as musical instruments, or loads of ice transferred on the backs of camels (see al-Qalqashandī, *Ṣubḥ*, Vol. 4, 11; Vol. 5, 97; Vol. 14, 397; Ibn al-Ṭuwayr, *Nuzha*, 194–5; http://www.baheth.info/all.jsp?term=أحمال).

al-ajall

This was a most sublime title that was restricted to the Fatimid wazirs and other high officials of their status. When Badr al-Jamālī, the first powerful Fatimid Wazir of Delegation came to power in Cairo, he terminated the use of the title *al-wazīr al-ajall* (the "Most Dignified Wazir") and started the use of the new title of the wazirs: *al-sayyid al-ajall* (the "Most Dignified Master"), which was replaced by the title *al-malik* (the "King") with Wazir al-Ṣāliḥ Ṭalā'iʿ (al-Baqli, *Ta'rīf*, 15; Sayyid, *Nuzha*, 48°).

'ajam

A term that is generally used to describe non-Arabs and sometimes particularly refers to Persians (see http://www.baheth.info/all.jsp?term=عجم).

ajlāl *(also* jilāl,sing. jull *or* jall*)*

"Housings": what the animal is dressed in. It was a cloth cover made of wool or other material which was used for horses in the Mamluk era. The term is also defined as "saddle cloth" (Parry, *War*, 155; Qaddumi, *Gifts*, 86; http://baheth.info/all.jsp?term=أجلال).

ajnād *(also,* jund; sing. jundī*)*

"Soldiers": in the Mamluk era, the regular or the rank-and-file army comprised two categories: the amirs and the soldiers (*ajnād*), who were divided into factions.

Some of these soldiers were appointed in low-ranking official positions, lesser ranking governorships, as commanders of small forts and in similar positions that did not require the amirial rank. Al-Qalqashandī mentions two of the factions of soldiers, namely, the sultan's Mamluks and the soldiers of the *ḥalaqa*. The sultan's Mamluks were either those bought by or for the sultan, housed at the sultan's barracks (*ṭibāq*) and educated, raised and trained under his supervision, to later be set free, or the employed Mamluks (*mustakhdamīn*) who were not bought by the sultan, but were Mamluks of previous sultans or amirs, who have joined his service. The salaries and allowances of the sultan's Mamluks were paid from the Separate Bureau (*dīwān al-mufrad*). The soldiers of the *ḥalaqa* were horsemen entitled to *iqṭā'āt* that were registered in the Army Bureau (*dīwān al-jaysh*) (Abdelhamid, *Jaysh*, 18, 44–76; al-Baqli, *Ta'rīf*, 15–16).

ajnād al-ḥalaqa

See *ḥalaqa*.

akhlāṭ al-'askar

Akhlāṭ means a mixed group of people. P. Sanders refers to *akhlāṭ al-'askar* as the "mixed groups of elite soldiers", while A. Gamal al-Din remarks that these were irregular soldiers. The term denotes that they were of various racial and tribal origins, which could mean that they were the same as "factions of soldiers" (*ṭawā'if al-ajnād*). In Ibn al-Ṭuwayr's account, the phrase used is *akhlāṭ min al-'askar*, which changes the meaning to "a mixture of soldiers". In the Mamluk context, al-'Umarī uses the term *mukhtalaṭ* (also "mixed" or "mingled") to describe soldiers whom he goes on to mention the various races of (Sanders, *Ritual*, 92; Gamal al-Din, *Dawla*, 270; Ibn al-Ṭuwayr, *Nuzha*, 163; al-'Umarī, *Masālik* (ed. Abbas), Vol. 3, 429; http://www.baheth.info/all.jsp?term=أخلاط).

akwār (sing. kūr)

"Saddles": what the rider of a camel sits on, also called *raḥl*. Its fore and back parts were sometimes covered with gold or silver (al-Baqlī, *Ta'rīf*, 290; al-Qalqashandī, *Ṣubḥ*, Vol. 2, 129; http://www.baheth.info/all.jsp?term=الكور).

āl al-bayt

See *ahl al-bayt*.

'alāma

Literally "the mark", meaning signature. The *'alāma* was an individual, unique hand-signature phrase that the caliph, the sultan and the wazir used. In the Fatimid era, some prominent women of the court, such as the caliph's mother or sisters, had to write on any document that they issued, such as letters, decrees, *tawqīʿāt* (sing. *tawqīʿ*). The *ʿalāma* was normally placed under the first line of the text. Ibn al-Ṭuwayr and other primary sources state that all Fatimid caliphs had the same *ʿalāma*: "Praise be to Allah, the Lord of the worlds". Other primary sources and surviving documents testify to the signature formulae of other rulers and statesmen. Al-Qalqashandī tells us that in his time, whether in sultanic or amirial documents, the *ʿalāma* occupied a particular section at the top of the document called *bayt al-ʿalāma* (the "house of the mark"). The sultan's mark was either his name, his name and his father's or brother's, or a certain formula like "Allah is my Hope", "Allah is sufficient for me", "the kingdom is Allah's", or the like, in ornamental calligraphic form (Sayyid, *Nuzha*, 89 n. 1; al-Baqli, *Taʿrīf*, 253; al-Qalqashandī, *Ṣubḥ*, Vol. 6, 196, 314; Vol. 13, 161–2, Vol. 14, 103).

aʿmāl *(also* ʿamal*)*

After the cadastral survey of AH 715 / AD 1315, in the reign of the Mamluk Sultan al-Nāṣir Muḥammad, known as *al-rawk al-Nāṣirī*, the term *aʿmāl* was used to refer to provincial divisions that were equivalent to present-day governorates (Ramzy, *Qāmūs*, Pt 2, Vol. 1, 22).

amir (amīr)

Loosely "prince": the person who has the authority to order, rule, command and dominate. In early Islam, the term was used to denote rulers in general as well as high military leaders. Later, it came to denote the rulers of the provinces under the Islamic caliphate. In the Umayyad and Abbasid eras, it also referred to those who were next in line to become caliphs. In the Fatimid era, this title was used by the caliph's sons, and was given to some statesmen, caliph's Mamluks and provincial rulers. Members of the Ayyubid ruling family used this title. Generally, the term denoted belonging to a certain category or was employed as a military rank or an honourific title. By the Mamluk era, the term was used to refer mainly to military leaders, who were categorized according to the numbers of the forces they commanded (al-Basha, *Alqāb*, 179–85; Abdelhamid, *Jaysh*, 21).

amīr al-muʾminīn

Prince of the Faithful: A title given to Muslim caliphs. It started being used with Caliph ʿUmar b. al-Khaṭṭāb (al-Basha, *Alqāb*, 194).

amīr ʿalam

"Amir of the Flag", who was normally an Amir of Ten who was responsible for the sultan's flags, banners and standards, as well as for supervising the *ṭablakhānāh*.

He had to be knowledgeable of the types of flags required for each kind of royal procession (Ashour, *'Aṣr*, 415;al-Baqli, *Ta'rīf*, 49).

amīr jāndār

"Personal guard": al-Qalqashandī explains that *jāndār* is a term composed of two syllabi: *jān*, which means "soul" in Persian and Turkish, and *dār*, which means "holder of" in Persian. He concludes that *amīr jāndār* (the "amir who holds the soul") is so called because he guards the sultan's life and only allows trusted people to meet the sultan (al-Qalqashandī, *Ṣubḥ*, Vol. 5, 461).

Amir of the Flag

See *amīr 'alam*.

amir shikār

"Amir of Hunting": game keeper or bird master. *Shikār* is a Persian word that means "hunting" (al-Qalqashandī, *Ṣubḥ*, Vol. 5, 461).

*Amirs of Five (***umarā' al-khamsāt,** *sing. amīr* **khamsa***)*

These were the lowest-ranking of the Mamluk amirs, who were considered high-grade soldiers. The Amirs of Five each had a force of less than ten Mamluks. Most of these amirs were sons of Mamluk amirs, who were thus assigned in appreciation of the services of their deceased fathers and were ranked in the army so as to be entitled to an *iqṭā'*. The number of the amirs in this category reached 30 (al-Baqli, *Ta'rīf*, 43; Ashour, *'Aṣr*, 414; Abdelhamid, *Jaysh*, 24).

Amirs of One Hundred, Commanders of Thousands (umarā' al-mi'īn, muqaddamū al-ulūf,sing. amīr mi'a, muaqaddam alf)

Also called commander amirs and Amirs of Thousands, this was the highest rank of Mamluk amir, who each had a force of 100 horsemen. They are also defined as the amirs who were entitled to buy at least 100 Mamluks and were responsible for the command of 1,000 army soldiers of the *ḥalaqa* in times of war, and they had the right to lead a thousand horsemen of Mamluks and lesser-ranking amirs. The important viceroyships and positions were assigned to the amirs of this rank. A particular number of drums, pipes and horns played for the amirs of this rank to announce their processions, which indicated their status, as customary at the time. The number of these amirs varied throughout the Mamluk era: there were 24 at the beginning of the reign of Sultan al-Nāṣir Muḥammad, 25 at its end; numbers ranged from 18 to 20 in the Circassian Mamluk era and reached 26 in the reign of Sultan Qānṣūh al-Ghūrī in AH 922 / AD 1516. The head of this category of amirs was called *ra's muqaddamī al-ulūf* ("Head of the Commanders of Thousands") (Abdelhamid, *Jaysh*, 22; Ashour, *'Aṣr*, 415; al-Baqli, *Ta'rīf*, 319).

Amirs of Ten (umarā' al-'asharāt, sing. amīr 'ashara)

Amirs of Ten each had a force of ten horsemen under their command, which may have increased to twenty. Most of these amirs, like the Amirs of Twenty and the Amirs of Five were the sons of commander or *ṭablakhānāh* amirs. Al-Qalqashandī does not list the Amirs of Twenty as a separate category, but considers them in the rank of the Amirs of Ten. Although al-Qalqashandī mentions that, like the *ṭablakhānāh* amirs, the number of the Amirs of Ten was variable, probably since he includes the Amirs of Twenty in the same category, al-Maqrīzī counts seven Amirs of Ten in Egypt. They were appointed in lower-ranking positions, such as the lesser governors (al-Baqli, *Ta'rīf*, 44; Ashour, *'Aṣr*, 415; Abdelhamid, *Jaysh*, 23).

'ammāriyyāt (sing. 'ammāriyya)

"Howdah" (Sayyid, *Nuzha*, 149 n. 7).

al-aqbiya al-tatariyya

"Tartar coats": these were coats worn by Mamluk amirs. Their hems crossed the chest in a diagonal from left to right, unlike the old form of traditional straight cut that was used by the Fatimids. This garment was made of wool, silk or cotton and was white or adorned with blue and red bands, which was called *al-mushahhar*. It also had tight sleeves (Stillman, *Dress*, 63;al-ʿUmarī, *Masālik* (ed.al-Juburi), Vol. 3, 291 n. 1).

'aqd al-liwā'

"Assigning the banner": *'aqd al-liwā'* was the expression used to show that a man was given the leadership of an army or a fighting force (see http://www.baheth.info/all.jsp?term=لواء).

aqsima

A drink made by soaking raisins in water, sometimes defined as wine of raisins. For it to be *ḥalāl* (religiously approved or allowed), it has to be made without mixing the raisins with other components or allowing the mixture to stay for longer than three days, so that it does not become alcoholic, which would make it *ḥarām* (religiously forbidden). In the Mamluk era, it was a type of sweetened and cooled drink. We are told that in AH 797 / AD 1395, during the reign of Sultan Barqūq, Amir Tamarbughā introduced a new drink, made by soaking ten pounds of raisin in forty pounds of water and leaving them for days. This drink, named *al-tamarbaghāwī*, after the amir, was an alcoholic drink demanded by the sultan and his amirs, although Barqūq was not known for drinking before that (al-Ruḥaybānī and al-Ḥanbalī, *Maṭālib*, Vol. 6, 215; Ibn Taymiya, *Mawsū'at al-Ijmā'*, 571; Dahman, *Mu'jam*, 21; Nassar, *Tarfīh*, 120).

Arabian bows

Wooden bows that shot several arrows in various directions simultaneously (Maged, *Nuẓum*, Vol. 1; Sayyid, *Tafsīr*, 702).

'arāḍī (sing. 'araḍī)

A term used many times by historians to refer to more than one cloth item: a piece of clothing like a scarf, a textile cover used for plates and vessels, a type of textile belt, or a kind of head cover (Sayyid, *Nuzha*, 130 n. 1).

al-arāḍī al-mu'abbada

Eternally endowed lands, which could not be sold or inherited (see http://www.baheth.info/all.jsp?term=مؤبد).

'arānīs *(sing.* 'irnās*)*

The *'irnās* is "the post that carries the bed canopy" or "the distaff". These posts were made of turned, light wood that were attached or embedded in both sides of the door of the pavilion (*bayt*). They were painted and had fitting curtains (Ibn al-Ṭuwayr and Sayyid, *Nuzha*, 193, 198, 198 n. 1; al-Maqrīzī, *Khiṭaṭ*, Vol. 2, 315).

arbāb al-khidam

Arbāb al-khidam may be translated as "heads of services" or "lords of services", which means "providers of services". A. Sayyid cites ibn al-Ṭuwayr's *Nuzha* and al-Maqrīzī's *Khiṭaṭ* to show that the Collared Amirs (*al-umarā' al-muṭawwaqūn*), who were Men of the Sword, were also called *arbāb al-khidam al-jalīla* ("heads of dignified services", meaning royal services). The reference in the primary sources may also suggest that certain category of the collared amirs was called *arbāb al-khidam al-jalīla*. P. Sanders separates the two categories, since she refers to *arbāb al-khidam* as "other high dignitaries" (Ibn al-Ṭuwayr, *Nuzha*, 208; Sanders, *Ritual*, 33).

arbāb al-rawātib

"Those entitled to allowances": state officials, administrative and military, who received specific allowances, as well as other officially listed recipients, for example, al-Ashrāf al-Ṭālibiyyīn. The *rātib* (allowance) was not only given in the form of money but normally also included rations of food, clothes, fodder and so on (Sanders, *Ritual*, 105, 187; Ibn al-Ṭuwayr, *Nuzha*, 75, 77, 83–5, 113; Sayyid, *Tafsīr*, 350, 363, 395, 722–3).

arbāb al-rusūm

Also *aṣḥāb al-rusūm*. P. Sanders translates *arbāb al-rusūm* as "men of designated portions". The *rusūm* or "designated portions" in this context refer to the bestowals given in kind, probably food, on ceremonial occasions by the caliph to state officials, as well as those patronized by the state: for example, a visiting physician from Andalusia that al-Maqrīzī mentions in *Itti'āẓ*. Historical accounts indicate that *arbāb al-rusūm* also "sponsored their own networks of patronage" (Sanders, *Ritual*, 66). The term also applied to those who received rations indirectly, since they were entitled fractions from a bestowal granted by the caliph to some dignitary. Among its meanings, *rusūm* was also used to refer to the pensions given to high-ranking officials (Sanders, *Ritual*, 66, 84; al-Maqrīzī, *Khiṭaṭ*, Vol. 2, 115, 201, 217; al-Maqrīzī, *Itti'aẓ*, Vol. 3, 78–80, 94, 95, 105, 341; Ibn al-Ṭuwayr, *Nuzha*, 145, 184–5, 195, 216).

arbāb al-rutab

"Holders of ranks", which P. Sanders translates as "highest ranking officials". These were actually of variable ranks, for Ibn al-Ṭuwayr refers to *arbāb al-rutab 'alā ikhtilāf al-ṭabaqāt*, "those of ranks of different levels", as well as one rank of state officials, which he terms *arbāb al-rutab bi-ḥaḍrat al-khalīfa*, "officials at the capital" (Sanders, *Ritual*, 105, 187; Ibn al-Ṭuwayr, *Nuzha*, 75, 77, 83–5, 113; Sayyid, *Tafsīr*, 350, 363, 395, 722–3).

arbāb al-ṣadaqāt

Those deserving of or receiving *ṣadaqa*. The *ṣadaqa* was a charitable, recommended donation in Islam, which is optional but most encouraged, while the *zakat* (alms) is mandatory and its percentage is precisely calculated, whether monetary or in kind.

ardeb

Ardeb is the English word for *al-irdabb*, which was a unit of volume used to measure grains, such as wheat. The values of this unit fluctuated according to place and time, but on average the old *irdabb* called *al-irdabb al-Miṣrī* or *al-irdabb al-'Arabī* (the Egyptian or Arab ardeb) was equivalent to 66 litres. The modern *irdabb* is 198 litres.

Al-'Āriba

The primary and original Arabs, who were the first to speak the Arabic language and were situated in Yemen, then migrated northwards (Hammuda, *Tārīkh*, 39).

asbāslār

"Head", "chief", "leader": this term is a distortion of the Persian *isfihsalār* (or *asfahsilār*). Commoners used the term *aspāslār* or *asbāslār* to call the aids or assistants (*a'wān*) who stood at the sultan's gate. It appears that this title was especially used by the *ṭablakhānāh* amirs, but it was abandoned by al-Qalqashandī's time, either because the amirs disapproved of it being used for the aids, or because its original meaning was forgotten or misunderstood (al-Qalqashandī, *Ṣubḥ*, Vol. 6, 7–8).

aṣḥāb al-quḍub

Al-Qalqashandī uses the term *aṣḥāb al-quḍub*, which means "holders of the staffs", while Ibn al-Ṭuwayr uses the term *arbāb al-qaṣab*, which means "holders of *al-qaṣab*". *Al-qaṣab*were lances "dressed with silver tubes inlaid with gold", except for an upper section that was adorned with decorated multicoloured *sharb* cloths. The heads of these lances were silver bosses (*ramāmīn*) inlaid with gold as well as hollow crescents. They had bells which rang when they moved. There were around onehundred of these lances which were takenout of the treasury in honour of the wazir, high-ranking amirs and "the commanders of troops and of the regiments of cavalry and infantry" (Sanders, *Ritual*, 178; Ibn al-Ṭuwayr, *Nuzha*, 149).

aṣḥāb al-tawqī'āt

Aṣḥāb al-tawqī'āt means "the Holders of the Signatures" and refers to those state officials who held a signing authority. Al-Qalqashandī lists the state officials, from both categories: Men of the Pen and Men of the Sword, who had this authority in his time during the Mamluk era, along with a detailed description of the protocols, prologues and language of correspondence (al-Qalqashandī, *Ṣubḥ*, Vol. 11, 114–33).

'āshir

The person who collects *al-'ushr* alms (*zakāt al-'ushr*), which were alms on agricultural produce that amounted to 10 or 5 per cent of the yield. The fraction depended upon whether the land was naturally irrigated, which entailed no extra cost on the cultivator, who should then hand out 10 per cent of his yield, or required the aid of machines, therefore more cost to receive water, whereby the cultivator gives away only 5 per cent of the produce.

ashrāf

"The *ashrāf* (pl. of *sharīf*) – the 'nobles' – or the *sāda* (pl. of *sayyid*) – the 'masters' – were usually considered to be the descendants of the Prophet Muḥammad by the marriage of his daughter Fāṭima to 'Alī b. Abī Ṭālib. More precisely, the *ashrāf* are descendants of 'Alī's elder son, Ḥasan, and the *sāda*, of his younger son, Ḥusayn. During the Abbasid period, the term *ashrāf* was applied to all *ahl al-bayt* (the Prophet's family, including for example, the descendants of Muḥammad ibn al-Ḥanafiyya, ʿAlī's second wife and the Hashimites), but the Fatimid rulers of Egypt (358 AH/969 AD – 566 AH/1171 AD) restricted its use to the descendants of Ḥasan and Ḥusayn. This restriction remained in force even after the government of Egypt became Sunni again" (Winter, *Egyptian Society*, 179).

ashriba

Drinks or syrups.

asinna *(sing.* sinān*)*

Spearhead, lance-head or similar.

asmiṭa *(sing.* simāṭ*)*

The cloth or table spread to serve food on, and the term is used to mean banquet.

ʿaṣr

"Afternoon", afternoon and third mandatory daily prayer.

Atabek (atābek)

Atābek is a Turkish term composed of two syllabi: *aṭā* (father) and *bek* (amir), which may be translated as "father-commander". It was a title given to the Mamluk amirs appointed as guardians over "young Seljuq princes sent out as provincial governors". The *atābeks* were in charge of educating and mentoring these princes. They were appointed custodians or regents over minor sultans and princes, and in many instances they married the minors' mothers, so that their relationship with them became semi-parental. As time passed, the responsibilities and powers of the *atābeks* increased, which was one of the factors that resulted in the division of the Saljuq sultanate into smaller states, each governed by an *atābek* who had his own hereditary line of rule. The Zangids were one of these *atābek* or *atabeg* states. The title *atābek* was later employed in the Mamluk era to refer to the general commander of the army (*atābek al-ʿasākir*), since he was like a father to all the amirs and soldiers (al-Basha, *Alqāb*, 122–4; al-Baqli, *Taʿrīf*, 14; Bosworth, *Islamic Dynasties*, 188).

aṭlas

A type of silk, satin.

Awlā

"Children of".

al-'ayn

A term that refers to the endowed property that is the source which produces the profit to be spent in the channels dictated in the endowment deed: for example, a land that is endowed and produces crops, which are sold for profit. Naturally, the rules of *waqf* (endowment) necessitate that the *'ayn* itself is never sold or dissolved in any way, and it has to conform to certain stipulations before it is endowed, such as being free of debts.

Ayyubids

The Sunni dynasty that ruled over Egypt, Syria, Diyar Bakr and Yemen in the mid sixth to eighth century AH / twelfth to fifteenth century AD. Ṣalāḥ al-Dīn Yūsuf b. Ayyūb ruled Egypt after ending the Fatimid Caliphate in AH 567 / AD 1171, then started expanding into Syria eventually uniting both countries. His main achievement was the destruction of the Crusader Kingdom of Jerusalem and recapturing most of the Syrian coast from the Crusaders. He successfully repelled the Third Crusade which succeed in capturing Acre after a three year siege but failed in recapturing Jerusalem. His line of successors, the Ayyubids, embarked upon several architectural projects to serve their purpose of propagating Sunni Islam, including madrasas, mosques and shrines. They fought the Crusaders throughout their reign, as well as the Mongols, towards the end of their era. They established a system for owning and training Mamluks as their army, and eventually the Bahri Mamluks managed to succeed them in sovereignty over Egypt and Syria. Several Ayubid dynasties ruled in different parts of Syria, the most memorable was the Ayyubid house of Aleppo, which was ended by the conquest of the city by the Mongols in AH 658 / AD 1260 then the subsequent killing of the last Ayyubid Sultan of Aleppo, al-Nāṣir Yūsuf (II) after the battle of ʿAyn Jālūt (see Q. Qasim, *Tārīkh*, 5–49).

azyār *(sing.* zīr*)*

Large jars.

B

b.

Short for *ibn*: "son of".

bābā *(pl.* bābiyya*)*

An originally Roman word that means "father of fathers". This was a general title given to all the men working in the *ṭishtkhānāh*, who handled washing, polishing and other duties. They were given this title because they were responsible for their masters' luxury, in terms of cleaning their clothes and improving their appearances, like a compassionate father.The title was also used to refer to high-ranking Christian clergy (al-Baqli, *Ta'rīf*, 59; Ashour, *'Aṣr*, 416; Dahman, *Mu'jam*, 28).

badana

"A silk, golden, and inscribed robe that the Fatimid caliph wore on the procession day to open the Khalīj." It was manufactured at Tinnīs and almost all woven in golden threads so skillfully that it required no tailoring or sewing. It cost 1,000 dinars (al-Baqli, *Ta'rīf*, 61; Ibn al-Ṭuwayr and Sayyid, *Nuzha*, 124 n. 4, 198).

badhanjāt *(sing.* badhahanj, bādāhanj, *or* bādhanj*)*

"Vents": a Persian architectural term that means a wind-catcher, a ventilation opening or a skylight. The term also refers to the openings in a sleeve (Dahman, *Mu'jam*, 29; Ashour, *'Aṣr*, 417).

badla

This was a costume for men that consisted of a number of pieces, probably ranging between three and five, and had different accessories that went with it, such as turban-cloths (*manādīl*) and sleeves. The materials from which the costume was made varied, for example, the sources mention silk and gold embroidery. It was worn by the caliphs, bestowed as a costume of honour, was sometimes specified as processional, and/or of a particular colour. The number of pieces, the accessories and the material form which the costume was made or with which it was adorned, all determined the rank of the man allowed to wear this outfit. The processional *badla* of the Fatimid caliphs consisted of eleven pieces (Ibn al-Ma'mūn and Sayyid, *Nuṣūṣ*, 41, 48–9, 50–55, 151 nn. 1, 2; Gamal al-Din, *Dawla*, 221; Sayyid, *Tafsīr*, 390).

Bahari Mamluks

The term Bahari (or Bahri) Mamluks (*al-mamālīk al-baḥariyya*) was first used to refer to the Mamluks which the Ayyubid Sultan al-Ṣāliḥ Najm al-Dīn (r. AH 638–47 / AD 1240–49) bought and barracked at the citadel he built in al-Rawḍa Island overlooking the Nile (*baḥr* or *baḥr al-Nīl*, hence the name). Al-Ṣāliḥ's Mamluks were of various ethnicities, including: Turkish, Mongolian, Slav (*Ṣaqāliba*), Spanish, German, Circassian and others, but their majority was Kipchak (or Qïpchaq: a Turkic tribal confederation of Central Asian origin, which expanded over the Eurasian steppe) and Caucasian. These Mamluks were subjected to rigorous military and religious training and were taught allegiance to their master (*ustādhiyya*) and loyalty to their colleagues of the same faction or their comradeship (*khushdāshiyya*).

The Bahari Mamluks came to power, following several incidents, as the first Mamluk rulers of Egypt and Syria, which the primary sources refer to as the reign of the Turkish Mamluks, the second being that of the Circassian Mamluks. In AH 647 / AD 1250, the Bahari Mamluks of Sultan al-Ṣāliḥ Najm al-Dīn confronted and defeated the Crusaders in northeastern Egypt, even after the death of the sultan of chronic illness at his military camp in al-Manṣūra. Al-Ṣāliḥ's wife, Shajarr al-Durr, kept the sad news from the army so as not to affect their spirits and protected the throne until the arrival of its rightful heir, her stepson, Tūrān Shāh, then a governor in the peripheries of Iraq. The news became known despite her efforts, but one of the exceptional military amirs of his time, Baybars al-Bunduqdārī, later Sultan al-Ẓāhir Baybars, got her approval, since she was the figure in actual authority, for a battle plan by which the army and the Egyptians of al-Manṣūra fought and defeated the Crusaders. Tūrān Shāh arrived and continued the victory of the Ayyubids over the Crusaders, ending the Seventh Crusade with the capture of King Loius IX of France.However, Tūrān Shāh was not fond of his father's Mamluks and declared his animosity to the Baharis and Shajarr al-Durr, who conspired to kill him. The Mamluks chose to appoint Shajarr al-Durr as their woman sultan, herself originally a Turkish or Armenia slave whom al-Ṣāliḥ Najm al-Dīn bought, set free and married. Being a woman, this choice was frowned upon by the Islamic world, the Egyptian public and the Abbasid caliph, who refused to acknowledge her appointment, a matter that could only be resolved by her marrying one of the high amirs. She married ʿIzz al-Dīn Aybak, in whose favour she abdicated, and who carried the title al-Malik al-Muʿizz (r. AH 648–65 / AD 1250–57).The new Mamluk state witnessed unrest and assassinations until in AH 658 /AD 1260, despite being a dynasty of slave origins, they managed to triumph over the mighty, then undefeated Mongols in Palestine, under the leadership of the new Sultan al-Muẓaffar Quṭuz (r. AH 657–8 / AD 1259–60), with the help of Baybars al-Bunduqdārī. It is related that Baybars was denied the governance of Aleppo that he had aspired for, even after his major role in the victory. This, in addition to the inherent rivalry between the two Mamluk factions that Quṭuz and Baybars belonged to, Baybars participated in killing the sultan. The early Bahari Mamluk sultans undertook several measures to consolidate their rule, but their state did not assume its complete and unrivalled authority over Egypt and most of Syria until the reign of this powerful true builder of the dynasty, Sultan al-Ẓāhir Baybars (r. AH 658–76 / AD 1260–77) (Qasim, *Salāṭīn*, 7–10; Tārīkh, 107–11, 128–9, 141–2).

al-baḥariyya

Al-ajnād al-baḥariyya was a group of soldiers who were apparently only responsible for the night guard of "the citadels in major cities" and "the sultan's tent on travel". Originally, this group was formed under Sultan Qalāwūn, and included the sons of the Bahri Mamluks of Sultan al-Ṣāliḥ Najm al-Dīn. Qalāwūn allocated allowances for them and assigned them to "guard the Citadel gate". "He called them *al-Baḥariyya* and they became one of the categories of soldiers" (Abdelhamid, *Jaysh*, 65–6).

baḥr

Any body of water: a sea or a river.

balad *(also* bilda; *pl.* bilād*)*

Balad may mean "village" or "country". In plural form, *bilād* may be used to refer to a province, for example, al-Qalqashandī refers to the western oases of Egypt as*bilād al-wāḥ* (al-Qalqashandī, *Ṣubḥ*, Vol. 3, 393).

balāsāt *(sing.* balās*)*

Riding cape made of hair. One of the names given to the cloth or rug made of animal hair, a type of sackcloth (see http://www.baheth.info/all.jsp?term=بلاس; http://www.baheth.info/all.jsp?term=مسح).

banākīm *(also* binkāmāt, *sing.* binkām*)*

"Hourglasses" or "sandglasses".

banū *(also* banī*)*

"Sons of".

bardadāriyya *(sing.* bardadār*)*

A man serving the manager (*mubāshirūn*) of a bureau and supervisingthe staff. The original term for the name of this position is the Persian *fardādār*, which is composed of two parts: *fardā*, which means "curtain" and *dār*, which means "holder of". Therefore the term means "holder of the curtain". It seems that originally, the *bardadār* used to stand by Bāb al-Sitāra (the Curtain Door), then was transferred to serve in the bureaus (al-Qalqashandī, *Ṣubḥ*, Vol. 5, 468–9; al-Baqlī, *Ta'rīf*, 62).

barrāj

Keeper of the dovecot: *barrāj* means "the tower-man" or "the man of the tower", which in this context means the one responsible for the dovecot, called a pigeon-tower in Arabic. The mail system of the Mamluks was run by a special bureau that managed mail and pigeon stations, which employed mailmen and pigeon-keepers. The pigeon stations included dovecots, which in an important station like the Cairo Citadel, housed 1,900 pigeons in AH 687 / AD 1288.The pigeon station at the Citadel was kept by several commanders, each responsible for a certain section (Azab, *Qal'a*, 187–209).

Barrāniyyūn

Al-Barrāniyyūn, also *al-Barrāniyya* and *al-Kharjiyya*, "the outer" or "exterior" Mamluks as opposed to *al-Juwwāniyyūn* or *al-Juwwāniyya*, the "inner" or "insider" mamliks, which was another name for the *Khāṣṣakiyya*. *Al-Barrāniyyūn* were the amirs and Mamluks who did not belong to the *Khāṣṣakiyya*, which means that they were not close to the sultan, might not have been bought by him, and were not among his special and private retinue (Shams, *Nujūm*, Vol. 11, 47 n. 3, 51 n. 1; Ashour, *'Aṣr*, 417).

barrāqa *(pl.* barrāqāt*)*

"Hat which shines", from the verb *baraqa*, "to shine". Ibn al-Ṭuwayr uses the term *bazzāqa*, meaning "snail" or "slug", from the verb *bazaqa*, "to spit", or "to dawn" for the sun. Both *barrāqa* and *bazzāqa* are used to refer to the glass cups or little lamps that are installed in a metal chandelier (Ibn al-Ṭuwayr, *Nuzha*, 222; Baer, *Metalwork*, 313; http://www.baheth.info/all.jsp?term=بزاقة).

bāshūra

A bent entrance, with possibly several turns, for military defense purposes.

basnadūd

A Persian dessert or delicacy made of flour and dates (Shams, *Nujūm*, Vol. 4, 100 n. 7).

baṭā'iq *(sing.* biṭāqa*)*

Written messages or letters (Dahman, *Ta'rīf*, 35).

bawākīr *(also* bīyākīr *and* bawākir; *sing.* bīkāriyya*)*

The *bīkāriyya* was an ornament sometimes described as two thin, oblong metal sheets that bore the inscribed name of the amir for whom the adorned item was made. The *bīkāriyya* is also defined as "a roundel", and the term has several other meanings including a "pair of compasses" (*al-firjār*, *al-birkār*, *al-barjal*); "opening" and "a round piece of cloth". It should also be noted that the *bīkār* is a musical symbol, namely "natural" (♮). The Persian word *bīkār* means "war", in the general sense of the word. It is possible that the *bīkāriyya* was composed of a circle, which encompassed a shape that was either two metal sheets or another one similar to the musical symbol (al-Qalqashandī, *Ṣubḥ*, Vol. 4, 52; Dahman, *Mu'jam*, 41; Ashour, *'Aṣr*, 421; al-'Umarī, *Masālik* (ed. Abbas), Vol. 3, 395 n. 1, 467 n. 1, 468 n. 5; al-'Umarī, *Masālik* (ed. al-Juburi), Vol. 3, 318 n. 4; Alexander, *Arts of War*, 17; al-Qalqashandī, *Ḍaw'*, 260).

bawwābīn *(sing.* bawwāb*)*

"Doorkeepers" or "gatekeepers".

bearers of small weaponry

See *al-ḥāmilūn li-l-silāḥ al-ṣaghīr*.

belvedere

See *manẓara*

bīmāristān *(pl.* bīmāristānāt*)*

Originally Persian term that means "hospital".

birdanab

This is an assumed pronunciation since no diacritics are provided. The word probably refers to something that covered the croup or hind legs of a rider's mount.

birkistiwānāt *(sing.* birkistiwān; *also,* birkiṣṭawān*)*

Armour for the limbs of the horse. It is also defined as the embroidered cover used for the horses' bodies, as well as for other animals, such as elephants; as well as a caparison (al-Baqli, *Ta'rīf*, 63; Ashour, *'Aṣr*, 418).

buqja *(pl.* buqaj*)*

"Lozenge": originally a Turkish word that was distorted to refer to a lozenge-shaped piece of cloth or napkin. It was used as a bundle to wrap clothes or papers by tying its four ends together (Dahman, *Mu'jam*, 36; Mayer, *Heraldry*, 14).

Bureau of Correspondence

See *dīwān al-rasā'il*.

***Bureau of* Iqta'**

See *dīwān al-iqṭā'*.

Bureau of Properties

See *dīwān al-amlāk*.

burud *(sing.* barīd*)*

Mail messengers who travel on horseback (http://www.baheth.info/all.jsp?term=بريد).

bushtmīkh

This term is defined as a "backrest" (al-ʿIrainy,*Al-Mamālīk*, 226). It is originally Persian and is understood to be composed of two syllables: *pusht* and *mīkh*. *Pusht* has several meanings, among which is "back" and "support", while *mīkh* means "nail"; therefore, *pusht mīkh* may be translated as "back-nail" (Hallaq and Sabbagh, *Jāmiʿ*, 40). It may also be possible that *mīkh* is a distortion of the Persian *mūkh*, which means "a standard" or "an ensign". Al-Jazīrī, the historian (d. *c.* AH 977 / AD 1570), mentions the *bushtmīkh* among the elite furnishings known in the "old times". He refers to it as the "yellow, sultanic *bushtmīkh*", which indicates that, it was at times also a royal, not only an amirial, item. Yellow is known to have been a colour of Mamluk sultanic banners and insignia. Al-Jazīrī does not specifically define the *bushtmīkh*, but his account suggests that it usually had accessories, namely *mushalshalāt al-ḥarīr*, which were probably silk cushions or small mattresses (al-ʿIrainy, *Al-Mamālīk*, 226; Hallaq and Sabbagh, *Jāmiʿ*, 40; al-Jazīrī, *al-Durar*, Vol. 1, 208; Steingass, *Persian–English Dictionary*, 1342, http://dsalsrv02.uchicago.edu/cgi-bin/philologic/getobject.pl?c.6:1:7958.steingass; Steingass, *Persian–English Dictionary*, 251; http://dsalsrv02.uchicago.edu/cgi-bin/philologic/getobject.pl?c.1:1:3576.steingass).

buṭūn *(sing.* baṭn*)*

"Clans": *baṭn*, which means "abdomen, belly or stomach", is a hereditary social division that is smaller than the *qabīla* (pl. *qabāʾil*: "tribes") and bigger than the sub-clan (*fakhdh*, pl. *afkhādh*). The English terms do not exactly describe these divisions, which are culturally specific and sometimes fluid or changeable when used by different historians to refer to the hereditary grouping or social division of a particular tribe or clan (al-Qalqashandī, *Ṣubḥ*, Vol. 1, 309; Hammuda, *Tārīkh*, 176; Parolin, *Citizenship*, 30–31).

Buwayhids

A Shi'ite dynasty that ruled vast areas of northern, western and southern Persia and Iraq from AH 321–461 / AD 933–1069. They were one of the semi-autonomous states that emerged as the Abbasids weakened (Bosworth, *Islamic Dynasties*, 154–5).

C

Caparison

See *kunbūsh*.

carat

See *qīrāṭ*.

Chancery Bureau

See *dīwān al-inshā'*.

chief judge

See *qāḍī al-quḍāt*.

Circassian Mamluks

The Circassian (*al-Jarākisa/al-Sharākisa*) or Burjī Mamluks (*al-Burjiyya*) were the sovereigns of the second Mamluk dynasty (AH 784–923 / AD 1382–1517). The Bahri Mamluk Sultan Qalāwūn (AH 679–89 /AD 1279–90) bought a large number of young Circassian Mamluks, who came from the areas to the north of the Caspian Sea and east of the Dead Sea. Qalāwūn quartered these Mamluks in the towers (*burūj*) of the Cairo Citadel,which was also called Qalʿat al-Burj: hence the title, *al-burjiyya*. Historical sources inform us that the number of these Mamluks reached 3,000 and that Qalāwūn was most generous to them and separated them from the rest of the Mamluk factions. The sons of Qalāwūn kept the tradition of buying Circassian Mamluks and depending on them. Their power increased gradually and the Bahri Mamluks tried to control them and eliminate their privileges; however, they remained to play an important role in state control. They became more influential politically, possibly especially after their courage in defeating the Mongols near Damascus in AH 702 / AD 1302. The Circassians managed to briefly reach the throne in AH 708–9 / AD 1308–9, when Baybars al-Jāshankīr, one of their amirs, became sultan, but they were firmly under the control of Sultan al-Nāṣir Muḥammad b. Qalāwūn during his third and longest reign (AH 709–41 / AD 1310–41). Al-Nāṣir's descendants were mostly not as powerful, and the Circassians managed to establish their state when one of their high amirs, Barqūq, seized the throne in AH 784 / AD 138, and to remain in power until the advent of the Ottomans in AH 923 / AD 1517.

The Circassian era witnessed the deterioration of the rigid Mamluk system which ensured loyalty to the master and respect for comradeship.Circassian Mamluk sultans and amirs started buying and employing older Mamluks, who were already beyond puberty.This inevitably led to the inability of the sultan and amirs to fully control their Mamluks, which resulted in riots, disorders and fights in Cairo and other Egyptian cities, particularly towards the end of the era (Qasim, *Salāṭīn*, 17, 203–5; Bosworth, *Islamic Dynasties*, 78).

Commander of Mamluks

See *muqaddam al-mamālīk*.

comptroller

See *mustawfī.*

covering of the Ka'ba

See *kiswat al-Ka'ba.*

crossbows of the foot and stirrups

See *qisiy al-rijl wa-l-rikāb.*

crown

See *tāj.*

cubit (dhirā')

Dhirā' al-'amal (the "working arm" or "cubit") or *al-dhirā' al-Hāshimī* (the "Hashimite arm" or "cubit") was equivalent to 0.656 m (Sayyid, *Khiṭaṭ*, 20 n. 2). There are other types of cubit.

cymbals

See *ṣunūj.*

D

dabandār

"Drummer".

dabbūs *(pl.* dabābīs*)*

According to al-Qalqashandī, this was also called *'āmūd* ("pole"), which was a type of mace that was made of iron and had sides (*aḍlā'*). It was used to fight warriors wearing iron headpieces (al-Qalqashandī, *Ṣubḥ*, Vol. 2, 135).

dabīqī

A type of cloth that was embroidered with golden and silk threads or embroidered silk cloth, which was attributed to Dabīq (also Dibīq and Dibqū), a no-longer extant town of present day Damietta that overlooked al-Manzala Lake.Dabīq's site is today taken up by another town called Tall Dabīq (Hill of Dabīq), to the north-east of Ṣān al-Ḥajar Village in al-Sharqiyya Governorate (al-Baqli, *Ta'rīf*, 133).

daftar al-majlis

A register composed of plain papers used to record data like gifts, bestowals, *rusūm* ("designated portions", "pensions" and other similar expenses), presents sent to other kings and several other similar royal expenses (Ibn al-Ṭuwayr, *Nuzha*, 75; Sayyid, *Tafsīr*, 383; Sanders, *Ritual*, 66, 84).

dā'ī al-du'āt

The "Missionary of Missionaries", meaning the chief missionary. In the Shi'ite Ismā'īlī doctrine adopted by the Fatimids, *dā'ī al-du'āt* held a sublime status, second only to the imām (the rightful caliph) in the hierarchy of *da'wa* (organized missionary work). Primary sources do not provide enough information about this position. Ibn al-Ṭuwayr details some of the Grand Missionary's duties, stating that he had twelve assistants as well as deputies in all lands and giving some description of the locations where he performed his job and the rituals of pledging. Ibn al-Ṭuwayr says that the *dā'ī* recited the *daftar* ("register") called *majlis al-ḥikma* (the "council of wisdom"), which was written by the state's religious scholars then delivered to the *dā'ī* who got the caliph's signature on it at *al-Iwān al-Kabīr* for men and at *majlis al-dā'ī* (the missionary's audience) for women. This account shows that the *dā'ī*'s audiences were not only held at Dār al-'Ilm. *Dā'ī al-du'āt* was also responsible for collecting a special kind of alms that the Ismā'īlis dictated be paid to the members of the House of the Prophet and was therefore received by the caliph (the *najwā*). Although *dā'ī al-du'āt* was in religious status second only to the caliph, the Fatimid court protocol (*rusūm*) deemed him second to *qāḍī al-quḍāt*, who many times held the position of *dā'ī al-du'āt* in addition to his own position, while the opposite never occurred. In the age of powerful wazirs, which started with Badr al-Jamālī, the wazirs held the positions of wazir, army supreme leader, *qāḍī al-quḍāt*, and *dā'ī al-du'āt*; however, a deputy *qāḍī* and a deputy *dā'ī* performed the duties of these two positions, which means that the wazir held the two posts only nominally.The system of the *da'wa* successfully propagated Fatimid influence to far lands such as India and Yemen. Al-Maqrīzī provides a description of the audience of *dā'ī al-du'āt*, copies a document that details how the *da'wa* worked and its nine levels of advancement, gives an account of how it started, and states part of the wording of the pledge that had to be taken by the new members of the sect (Sayyed, *Tafsīr*, 369–72; Ibn al-Ṭuwayr, *Nuzha*, 110–12; al-Maqrīzī, *Khiṭaṭ*, Vol. 2, 121–36).

ḍamān

The *ḍamān* ("guarantee", "tax farm") was a tax system that did not comply with religious legislation. This system "often involved putting up for auction of the right to collect the taxes of a given area, usually annually" (Lambton, "Reflections", 365). A *ḍāmin* ("tax farmer") guaranteed the annual payment of the taxes required from a village, for example, by paying them in advance to the government.In the Fatimid era, this system was apparently applied to lands, caravanserais, baths, *ribā'* and other establishments. The actual taxes expected from the guaranteed area or establishment was normally more than the amount of money the tax farmer paid, and this is how he made profit. If, however, the guaranteed area or establishment did not achieve the expected annual revenue, which was a rare occurrence, the tax farmer was not to be compensated, unless the government decided to pardon him. The Fatimids used this *ḍamān* system since the early years of their rule in Egypt, which provided a guarantee for all the state's money and ensured the availability of liquidity for paying salaries. The system also continued under the Ayyubids. The main tax farmer usually had secondary tax farmers who collected the taxes in certain areas. Most tax farmers were wealthy investors who could afford such huge commitments and even compete for them, since in return they made enormous profits. Many times the tax farmers made outdated, therefore crooked, contracts; exploited the taxpayers by imposing higher taxes; and failed to pay the whole amounts of money he owed the government (Lambton, "Reflections", 365; Sayyed, *Tafsīr*, 514–16; Sayyid, *Nuzha*, 80–81 n. 1; al-Qalqashandī, *Ṣubḥ*, Vol. 3, 470).

dār

"House", "quarters", "factory" or "workshop": also Persian for "holder of" (Dahman, *Mu'jam*, 72). Used as a suffix for many Mamluk titles to compose a composite word, meaning "holder of . . .".

Dār al-'Adl

The "House of Justice": The Ayyubid Sultan al-Kāmil built the first Dār al-ʿAdl at the Citadel, somewhere between Bāb al-Qulla and Bāb al-Mudarraj, in the Citadel's southern section, within the area that comprised the administrative buildings. Sultan al-Ẓāhir Baybars built another Dār al-ʿAdl at the Citadel in AH 662 / AD 1263, within the area of the sultan's stables, probably with an open facade overlooking the square next to the Citadel and the horse market. Baybars did not only use this Dār al-ʿAdl for the reviewing grievances: he also sat there on the days of military parades to watch them march from the square and by the Citadel walls. Sultan Qalāwūn built a new Dār al-ʿAdl in the southern section of the Citadel, but he did not sit in its councils because his Arabic language was weak (he was an *aghtam*) and assigned one of his high amirs in his place, Lājīn al-Manṣūrī, who was fluent in Arabic and later to become sultan himself (r. AH 695–7 / AD 1296–99). When Qalāwūn's son, al-Ashraf Khalīl, came to power, he destroyed his father's dome, or iwan, for the two words were interchangeably used in the sources to refer to the same building. Instead, he built al-Ashrafī Iwan (*al-Īwān al-Ashrafī*) in its place, which remained in use as Dār al-ʿAdl until Sultan al-Nāṣir Muḥammad tore it down and rebuilt it. K. Azab believes that this series of demolishing and rebuilding the same establishment within the brief period of half a century indicates the extent to which the sultans were concerned with one of their most important official institutions, and the closest institution to their subjects. During the Circassian Mamluk era, the area of the Citadel known as al-Ḥawsh (the courtyard) and the sultanic stables there alternated in hosting the council presided by the sultan to look into grievances, possibly changing locations to suit the seasonal weather changes. The first sultan to use the stables for such function was Barqūq then they were not employed for this purpose again until the reign of sultan Khusqadam (r. AH 864–71 / AD 1460–67).

The Mamluk Dār al-ʿAdl at the Citadel was used to hold the councils where grievances were presented to the sultan. The chancellor (*dawādār*) brought these grievances to the council, which the head of the Chancery Bureau (*dīwān al-inshā'*) and "scribes of the pedestal" (*kuttāb al-dast*) – who were also the "signers" (*muwaqqi'ūn*) – attended with the sultan or his deputy. If no verdict was made in the presence of the sultan or his deputy, the grievances were taken to the Chancery Bureau for investigation, then signed by the head of the bureau and sent to the concerned authorities for implementation (Azab, *Qal'a*, 74, 107–8, 146–7; al-Baqli, *Ta'rīf*, 130; Maged, *Nuẓum al-Mamālīk*, Pt 1, 66).

Dār al-Ḍarb

This was the minting house that was initially a Fatimid establishment built by al-Ma'mūn b. al-Baṭā'iḥī, the wazir of Caliph al-Āmir, in AH 315–16 / AD 927–8 in Khaṭṭ al-Qashshāshīn in Cairo. It was called al-Dār al-Āmiriyya, in reference to al-Āmir. Al-Ma'mūn also built other minting houses in Alexandria, Qūṣ and Ascalon. Dār al-Ḍarb of Cairo remained in this location until the time of al-Maqrīzī, who mentions in his *Khiṭaṭ* that Dār al-Ḍarb was in place of a part of the Fatimid palace. After the time of al-Maqrīzī, Dār al-Ḍarb was moved to the sultan'scourt (*al-ḥawsh al-sulṭānī*) of the Citadel at an unidentified date, an action caused by probably one of two reasons: the unrest the purchased Mamluks (*jilbān*) caused in the Circassian era, which required securing the Minting House, or as a measure taken to control the fluctuation in the monetary value during the same era. The present day Dār al-Ḍarb building might be occupying the same place it was moved to in the Mamluk era, where it stands close to the Mountain Gate (Bāb al-Jabal) of the Cairo Citadel, which facilitated the movement of those who dealt with it (al-Baqli, *Ta'rīf*, 129; Azab, *Qal'a*, 152–3).

Dār al-Fiṭra

This was the house built in the Fatimid era to bake the sweet pastries and delicacies in preparation for ʿĪd al-Fiṭr (the feast on occasion of breaking the fast of the month of Ramadan), which were given away to people, along with other bestowals. Dār al-Fiṭra was located near the present day Green Gate (*al-bāb al-akhḍar*) of the mosque of al-Ḥusayn (al-Baqli, *Ta'rīf*, 130–31).

Dār al-'Ilm

The "House of Knowledge": the Fatimid chief missionary (*dā'ī al-du'āt*) functioned at this house, where he taught learners the religious interpretation schools (*madhāhib*) of the Members of the House of the Prophet (*ahl al-bayt*) according to the Fatimid conviction. It was also probably there that the missionary pledged whoever decided to convert to the Fatimid Isma'īlī Shi'ite doctrine (al-Baqli, *Ta'rīf*, 130).

Dār al-Niyāba

"House of Viceroyship": it is thought that Sultan Qalāwūn established Dār al-Niyāba in AH 687 / AD 1288 for his viceroy; however, it was originally built by Sultan Baybars for his viceroy, on the southeast side of the *durkāh* of Bāb al-Qulla, "overlooking the Citadel's plaza (Raḥbat al-Qal'a)", within the Citadel's northern enclosure. "The Dār al-Niyāba was the organizational focus of the administrative area with other structures intended to house state functions." Qalāwūn most likely renovated it, adding a second floor and opening a window on the ground floor for the viceroy to sit "when he presided over official proceedings", meet with the people who presented grievances, and stand during the sultan's processions to convey the needs of the public. Dār al-Niyāba's floors and structural components served audience and ceremonial functions, the latter most probably being introduced during the reign of Qalāwūn. Although thought to have been destroyed by Sultan al-Nāṣir Muḥammad in AH 737 / AD 1337, when he cancelled the office of the viceroy, Dār al-Niyāba must have survived, at least in part, for it was reused in AH 744 / AD 1343, when it became "the real center of government", hosting the powerful viceroys of the time.Another building by the name Dār al-Niyāba was built in the northeast of Alexandria (Rabbat, *Citadel*, 114, 140–41, 151, 244; al-Baqli, *Ta'rīf*, 131).

Dār al-Wizāra

The "House of the Wazir" was built by Badr al-Jamālī near Bāb al-Naṣr, on the site of the current Khānqāh of Baybars al-Jāshankīr. This house remained a residence for some Fatimids and was the residence of Ṣalāḥ al-Dīn when he was appointed wazir by the Fatimid Caliph al-Āḍid until the caliph died, when Ṣalāḥ al-Dīn moved to the Fatimid palace.When the Ayyubid Sultan al-'Ādil resided at Dār al-Wizāra, it became known as Dār al-Sulṭān ("House of the Sultan"), for after being the residence of the wazir, it became the residence of the sultan. Many sovereignty functions were undertaken at this *dār*, for example, the famous Ayyubid wazir, Qarāqūsh, sat for reviewing grievances at this *dār*, during the reign of the Ayyubid Sultan al-'Azīz 'Uthmān. The Ayyubid Sultan al-Kāmil changed the place to host royal visitors and ambassadors coming to Egypt, after he moved the seat of rule to the Citadel when it was completed. The *dār* continued to serve this purpose for a long time.It was at this *dār* that the Mamluk Sultan

Quṭuz hosted amir Rukn al-Dīn Baybars al-Bunduqdārī, when he invited him to Egypt in AH 657 /AD 1258 to help him conquer the Mongols (al-Baqli, *Ta'rīf*, 131; Azab, *Qal'a*, 70–71).

daraqa *(pl.* daraq*)*

The *daraqa* was a shield made wholly of leather. It was circular with a domed centre and was held by a handle on its inner side (Yasin, *Asliḥa*, 257).

darārī' *(also* durrā'āt; *sing.* durrā'a*)*

Same as the *jubba* or the *farjiyya*, which was a robe that was open from the lower neck to below the chest, with buttons and button-holes. It was worn by Men of the Turban (*arbāb al-'imāma*) in the later eras. It was also a term used to refer to a vest worn by girls (al-Maqdisī, *Taqāsīm*, 44; Sayyid, *Nuzha*, 106 n. 1; al-Baqli, *Ta'rīf*, 133).

dawāb

Beasts of burden, livestock or riding animals.

dawādār

"Holder of the Inkwell", chancellor: this title is composed of two syllables: the first, Arabic, *dawāt* (inkwell), and the second, Perisan, *dār*, which means "holder of". The *dawādār* carried the inkwell for the sultan, the amir or other high statesmen.He also undertook other tasks, such as delivering messages, mail and grievances to the sultan as well as notifying him of the visitors to the royal court (*al-bāb al-sharīf*). Sultan Qalāwūn authorized the royal *dawādār* to use the sultanic *'alāma* (mark) (al-Baqli, *Ta'rīf*, 139).

dawarān al-maḥmil *(also* dawarān al-maḥmal*)*

The "circulation of the camel's load", which refers to the procession of the Ka'ba's covering: *Al-maḥmil* was the howdah that contained the lavishly decorated and most precious cloth cover (*kiswa*) of the Ka'ba, which was sent annually from Cairo to Mecca. *Dawarān al-maḥmil* was the festivity that took place twice a year to announce the start of the journey of this honoured cover (*kiswa*) (Dahman, *Mu'jam*, 136).

dawāt

Al-dawāt was the inkwell or pen-box. Al-Qalqashandī lists 17 writing tools, which were incorporated in a pen-box.Pen-boxes of al-Qalqashandī's time were made of metal, such as brass or steel, or fine wood, such as ebony and sandalwood, and were adorned with inlay and ornamentation.The *miḥbara* ("inkwell") was one of the main components of the *dawāt*, but it could also sometimes be carried separately.The terms *dawāt* and *miḥbara* were sometimes synonymously used to mean inkwell. In addition to the surviving Fatimid rock-crystal inkwells, it seems that there were many precious pen-boxes kept in the Fatimid treasuries (al-Qalqashandī, *Ṣubḥ*, Vol. 2, 430–72; Baer, *Metalwork*, 66–7).

ḍawwī

May be translated as "the one who lights": *arbāb al-ḍaw'* ("masters of light") in Ibn al-Ṭuwayr's *Nuzha*, whom al-Maqrīzī explains were the torch bearers (*mashā'iliyya*). They were the ones were responsible for lighting duties, such as lighting street lanterns (Ibn al-Ṭuwayr, *Nuzha*, 76: al-Maqrīzī, *Khiṭaṭ*, Vol. 2, 348; Dahman, *Mu'jam*, 13).

Daylam

The race and region to the southwest of the Caspian Sea.

dhu'āba *(also* ʿadhba*)*

The *dhu'āba* is either the tail of a turban, a hair braid, a forelock or hairlock (Sanders, *Ritual*, 90; al-Shayyal, *Itti'āẓ*, Vol. 1, 294 n. 2; http://www.baheth.info/all.jsp?term=ذؤابة; http://www.baheth.info/all.jsp?term=عذبة).

dhubābī

The *dhubābī* was a particular grade of emerald that was all green, without any traces of other colours, such as yellow or black. It was very glittery and was called *dhubābī* because its colour resembled that of big, green spring flies (*dhubāb*, sing. *dhubāba*). The *dhubābī* was the rarest and finest grade of emerald, which was believed to blind serpents if they looked at it, cure human sight defects if looked at for a long time and terminate epilepsy seizures if worn as a seal (al-Qalqashandī, *Ṣubḥ*, Vol. 2, 104–5).

dībāj

Dībāj is a kind of silk that is defined as both pure silk and silk brocade. The term is derived from *dabj* ("carving" or "ornamenting"), which is an Arabized, originally Persian, word.Since the term implies embroidery and the definition indicates purity, it may be understood that it is a type of pure silk, which is embroidered with silk alone. Al-Maqrīzī simply mentions that *dībāj* is silk, while there are sources that define the term as a textile that is brocaded with silk or golden threads (see http://

www.baheth.info/all.jsp?term=ديباج; Sanders, *Ritual*, 47, 244; Ibn Mājah, *Sunan*, Vol. 3, *Ḥadīth* no. 3589; al-Maqrīzī, *Khiṭaṭ*, Vol. 2, 604; Sayyid, *Nuzha*, 129 n. 3).

the dignified script

See *al-qalam al-jalīl.*

dihlīz *(pl.* dahālīz*)*

"Corridor", "vestibule" and the sultan's royal tent. Al-Baqli explains that in denoting the royal tent, the term *dihlīz* particularly applied to the tent that accompanied the sultan in times of war, which was different from others that were pitched for him on hunting or leisure expeditions. The *dihlīz* was different in that it was pitched independently, with no smaller tents next to it, like the ones usually set up to prepare the sultan's needs at the times of peace. According to Dahman, the term *dihlīz* was a generic one used for the royal tent that accompanied the sultan at times of war and on hunting and leisure expeditions (al-Baqli, *Ta'rīf*, 138; Dahman, *Mu'jam*, 77).

dilq *(also* daliq*)*

A robe worn by religious figures composed of several pieces of cloth of different colours. It is also thought to have been made of fur or leather. Many religious scholars exaggerated the sizes and widths of such robes to the extent that a single sleeve was big enough to tailor a whole other robe. These huge sleeves were left to drag on the ground for they were too heavy to carry. This exaggeration, like the sizes of turbans, was a sign of higher social status and professional rank. Some Sufi sheikhs imitated *quḍāt* ("judges") in wearing the *dilq*, but theirs was not to be too long to drag behind them or be long-sleeved (Ashour, *'Aṣr*, 438; Abu Zayd, *Ḥisba*, 116 n. 22; al-Battawi, *'Imāma*, 135; Mayer, *Costume*, 50).

al-dīnār al-jayshī *(pl.* al-danānīr al-jayshiyyya*)*

Al-Qalqashandī explains the term as follows: "As for *al-dīnār al-jayshī*, it was a nominal rather than an actual value. It was used by the people of the Army Bureau to evaluate the *iqṭā'* lands by assigning a certain number of dinars for each land. Some lands may have not been assigned such equivalent value of dinars. This was, however, a useless practice for 100 dinars in one piece of *iqṭā'* land might have yielded a profit of more than 200 dinars, or even more in another. The author of *Qawānīn al-Dawāwīn* (*The Canons of Bureaus*) mentioned *al-dīnār al-jayshī* in some *iqṭā'* areas with a value that fluctuates according to strata. He mentioned that *al-dīnār al-jayshī* of the Turkish, Kurdish and Turkoman military was a whole dinar, while that of the Kittāniyya (Kitābiyya) and the 'Asāqila (the ones from Ascalon) was half a dinar. The Arab Bedouin dinar was probably ⅛ of a dinar and according to custom 13⅓ dirhams. This was as if the same rules of the army's arrangement of the ancient times were followed. The value of gold in ancient times was similar to this: that is why blood money was calculated by jurists to be equivalent to 1,000 dinars or 12,000 dirhams, which meant that each dinar was equal to 12 dirhams." Al-Qalqashandī used the verb *'abbara* to denote the evaluation of *iqṭā'* lands with *al-dīnār al-jayshī*, which means "weighing gold dinar by dinar and not exaggerating the weight" (al-QalqashandīṢubḥ, Vol. 3, 442–3; http://baheth.info/all.jsp?term=عبر; see also *'abra*).

dirham

The dirham was both a weight unit and a monetary coin. The exact measure of the dirham in the Mamluk era, which al-Qalqashandī would have used, was not constant. Evidence suggests that it fluctuated around the approximate value of 3 grams of weight, which was close to the value of the dirham according to Islamic law: 2.97 grams. Al-Qalqashandī states that one dirham weight unit equals the weight of 16 kernels of carob. As an officially minted coin, he describes it as mainly an alloy of two-thirds silver and one-third copper, which was produced as wholes and fractions that varied in types and value (see al-Qalqashandī, *Ṣubḥ*, Vol. 3, 440–43).

dīwān *(pl.* dawāwīn*)*

May be translated as "bureau" and refers to administrative departments that are comparable to present day ministries. Caliph 'Umar b. al-Khaṭṭāb was the first Muslim ruler to found this system of administration, due to the vast expansion of the Islamic empire and the need for state regulation. *Dīwān* may also be used to refer to an office, office hall or court hall.

dīwān al-aḥbās

Dīwān al-aḥbās, the "Bureau of Endowments" was first established in the Umayyad era in Egypt in AH 115 /AD 733 to regulate the matters of endowments, and it was headed by a *qāḍī* (judge). In the Fatimid era, some of the endowments revenue was assigned to the Public Treasury (*bayt al-māl*), while *dīwān al-aḥbās* managed the endowed lands and properties, such as caravanserais (*qayāsir*) and residential buildings (*ribā'*). The revenues of these endowments were used to pay the salaries of men, such as muezzins, Qur'an reciters (*qurrā'*), religious jurists (*fuqahā'*), as well as for the upkeep of establishments, such as hospitals and the salaries of their staffs, in addition to other charitable channels, like paying for the shrouds required for burying the deceased. The senior state servants at the Fatimid *dīwān al-aḥbās* could only be equitable witnesses, since its management required religious knowledge.They were aided by a scribe and two assistants.

"By the early ninth/fifteenth century" the endowments in the Mamluk era were managed by three entities: *dīwān al-aḥbās*; *al-awqāf al-ḥukmiyya*, which were "under judicial (*ḥukmī*) supervision"; and *al-awqāf al-ahliyya*, which were endowed by individuals, rather than the state. *Dīwān al-aḥbās* managed the lands and properties that were endowed for maintaining the mosques, zawiyas and similar establishments, as well as support the salaries of their staffs, such as imams and preachers. The incomes (*rizaq*) generated by these *aḥbās* were controlled by the sultan, his viceroy or, more probably, the Grand Chancellor (*al-dawādār al-kabīr*). The bureau had a supervisor called *nāẓir al-aḥbās*, who was aided by several scribes from the men of the turban. He had to be known for his piety and religious knowledge. He managed the salaries of the religious scholars (*'ulamā'*), the jurists, the Qur'an reciters; scholars of the Prophet's traditions (*arbāb al-ḥadīth*), the imams of mosques and the teachers at the endowed schools. He was the only supervisor who, as a religious authority, was able to issue decrees and allocate or increase salaries without the need for a sultanic official decree or approval.

As for *al-awqāf al-ḥukmiyya*, these included the revenues of the endowed *ribā'* that were allocated for maintaining the sanctuaries at Mecca and Madina, paying alms and supporting students and the poor in Cairo and Fustat, as well as the prisoners of war.The chief Shāfi'ī judge used to appoint one of his deputies as a supervisor for these endowments, who was called *nāẓir al-awqāf*, until AH 785 / AD 1383, when the sultan started appointing the supervisor of endowments.The Bureau of Endowments employed a number of Men of the Turban who worked as scribes and revenue collectors.Alexandria's endowments were managed by the Mālikī judge, since this was the prevailing school of interpretation there; he was later joined by the Ḥanafī judge.

Al-Awqāf al-ahliyya were the endowments allocated by people for mosques, schools, khanqahs and similar establishments. The supervisors of such an endowment were "stipulated by the founders" and were usually the founders themselves, followed by their children after their death or by supervisors that the sultan appointed, who were normally Men of the Turban (Sabra, *Poverty*, 72; al-Battawi, *'Imāma*, 72–4, Sayyid, *Tafsīr*, 543–7; al-Baqli, *Ta'rīf*, 140–41).

dīwān al-amlāk

The "Bureau of Properties": a bureau that was introduced by Sultan al-Ẓāhir Barqūq, to which he allocated villages that he called *amlāk* ("properties") so as to finance it. These properties were managed by specifically assigned employees. This bureau was a private sultanic one that was not responsible for other expenditures (al-Qalqashandī, *Ṣubḥ*, Vol. 3, 457).

dīwān al-inshā'

The "Chancery Bureau" was responsible for looking into grievances, translating foreign correspondence and books, composing and writing correspondence, decrees, contracts and various similar documents. It was an essential part of Islamic administration and rule in all eras and dynasties, with the basic systems maturing during the Abbasid era. It was further developed in Egypt during the Fatimid era, with the same traditions continuing throughout the Ayyubid and Mamluk eras, when it seems to have developed further in the latter, due to the frequent correspondences between the Mamluk sultans and their Crusader and Mongol counterparts. Al-Maqrīzī informs us that there was a hall (*qā'a*) at the Citadel, located next to *qā'at al-ṣāḥib* (the "Wazir's Hall"), which served as *dīwān al-inshā'*. The *kātib al-sirr* (the "Scribe of the Secret"), the secretarial scribes (*kuttāb al-darj*) and the "scribes of the pedestal" (*kuttāb al-dast*) sat there, for the whole day on procession days, and they were served food from the sultan's kitchen. The incoming correspondence and the prepared responses from the sultan's court were kept at this hall. Al-Maqrīzī adds that he used to sit at this hall, when he worked with Judge Badr al-Dīn Muḥammad b. Faḍl Allah al-ʿUmarī, managing the sultan'ssignature (*tawqī'*), until about AH 770/AD 1369. In the second reign of Sultan Barqūq (AH 792–801/AD 1390–99), this hall was abandoned and the paper documents that were in it were sold in *kantar*s, according to al-Maqrīzī.

Dīwān al-inshā' followed a strict bureaucratic system and was headed by a Man of the Pen in the Ayyubid and Mamluk eras, who was usually Egyptian and held the title Master of the Chancery Bureau (*ṣāḥib dīwān al-inshā'*). He had to have excellent language and writing skills and be exceptionally eloquent. Some of the bureau's heads were learned in foreign languages, such as Turkish, and other languages used by the Crusaders, for example, to be qualified to read, translate and write responses to the correspondence (al-Baqli, *Ta'rīf*, 143–4; al-Maqrīzī, *Khiṭaṭ*, Vol. 3, 95–6).

dīwān al-iqṭā'

"Bureau of *Iqta'*": the Egyptian army in the Islamic era was given salaries, and in the Fatimid period, lands were granted to the army only very rarely. This became more common an approach; however, during the time of the Wazirs of Delegation (*wuzarā' al-tafwīḍ*), which led to founding *dīwān al-iqṭā'*. The Ayyubid Sultan Ṣalāḥ al-Dīn applied this land grant system, which continued into the Mamluk era, when *dīwān al-iqṭā'* and *dīwān al-jaysh* (the "Army Bureau") came to be the same thing.

The Mamluk allocation of land grants involved special ceremonial protocols. The sultan sat in audience, with the amirs sitting to his right and left, and the Supervisor of the Army Bureau (*nāẓir dīwān al-jaysh*) read out the decrees of allocation. The sultan signed the grants he approved to the amirs, while the soldiers mostly received their grants from the amirs; however, if an amir wanted to deprive a soldier of his grant, he had to get the approval of the sultan or his viceroy. The amirs normally got one third of the grants given to the soldiers. The *iqṭā'* system and its rules and decrees were often subjects of complaints, to the extent that at one point in time, the authorities threatened to imprison and confiscate the lands of the complainers. Some amirs benefited from acting as mediators to ensure the sultan's approval of a grant: a practice that was forbidden by an official decree.

Amirs were granted lands according to their rank.Some amirs had ten villages (*bilād*) of fertile land, while others had one. As for the soldiers, sometimes two of them shared one village (al-Baqli, *Ta'rīf*, 143; Maged, *Nuẓum al-Mamālīk*, Pt 1, 140–41).

dīwān al-jaysh

The "Army Bureau", also known as *dīwān al-jaysh wa-l-rawātib* (the "Bureau of the Army and Allowances"): al-Qalqashandī mentions that the Army Bureau was the first to be founded in the Islamic caliphate, in the era of Caliph ʿUmar. It was one of the important bureaus that were established in Egypt during the Fatimid era and it handled all military affairs. According to al-Qalqshandī, it was divided into three sections in the Fatimid era: the Army Bureau, the Bureau of Allowances and the Bureau of *Iqta'*. Only a Muslim was allowed to head the Army Bureau: he was highlyranked and most esteemed and had a *ḥājib* to serve him. This bureau documented the numbers and kinds of soldiers and their horses.The decrees to change the soldiers' salaries and allocate the *iqṭā'āt*, which were approved by the caliph, went through the head of this bureau. The Bureau of Allowances documented the names of all the employees of the state and their salaries and rations. The Bureau of *Iqta'* managed the land and grant revenues bestowed on soldiers.Ibn al-Ṭuwayr, however, gives an account ofthe Bureau of the Armyand Allowances, which he mentions was divided into the Army Bureau and the Bureau of Allowances, while he lists the Bureau of *Iqta'* as a separate bureau.In the Mamluk era, this bureau was headed by the Supervisor of the Army (*nāẓir al-jaysh*) and it managed the *iqṭā'āt* and all that was relevant to them (al-Baqli, *Ta'rīf*, 143–5; Ibn al-Ṭuwayr, 82–6).

dīwān al-mufrad

The "Separate Bureau" or "Special Bureau": *diwān al-mufrad* was the term used to refer to a bureau that was newly introduced and had a separate functionin the Fatimid era. Caliph al-Ḥākim established *diwān al-mufrad* in AH 400 /AD 1009, to collect the money confiscated from those whom the caliph was displeased with or those who ended up being killed.This was possibly the bureau called the Bureauof Reclamations (*dīwān al-murtaja'*), towards the late Fatimid era, which was one of the high bureaus. In the Mamluk era, *dīwān al-mufrad* was introduced by Sultan Barqūq and it was the bureau which managed the *iqṭā'* he used to have as an amir. Then more agricultural lands were allocated to the bureau, as well as rented properties in Egypt and Syria. The revenues and the produce collected by this bureau were used for the salaries (*jāmakiyyāt*), allowances (*rawātib*), fodder and clothing of the sultanic Mamluks, paying the Mamluks of Syria and providing the needs and expenditures of the sultan's warehouses (al-Qalqashandī, *Ṣubḥ*, Vol. 3, 457; Sayyid, *Tafsīr*, 348, 538; Ashour, *'Aṣr*, 439; Abdeldhamid, *Jaysh*, 91–2; Dahman, *Mu'jam*, 79).

dīwān al-rasā'il *(also* dīwān al-mukātabāt*)*

"Bureau of Correspondence" or "Bureau of Letters": this was one of the names of *dīwān al-inshā'* (the Chancery Bureau) in the early Fatimid era. The term *dīwān al-rasā'il* disappeared by the fourth century AH / twelfth century AD to be substituted with *dīwān al-inshā'*. Ibn Munjib al-Ṣayrafī was the head of the bureau during the reign of Caliph al-Āmir, a post that he occupied for forty years. He wrote a book called *Qānūn Dīwān al-Rasā'il* (*The Laws of Dīwān al-Rasā'il*), to be used as a guide for later heads of this bureau (Sayyid, *Nuzha*, 65°; al-Baqli, *Ta'rīf*, 146).

ḍiyā' *(sing.* ḍay'a*)*

"Plantation".

durkāh

"Canopied entrance or vestibule" (Rabbat, *Citadel*, 79).

E

equestrian escorts

See *rikābiyya*.

F

faransīsiyya

"The Frankish", which is the fleur-de-lys. The Mamluk fleur-de-lys differed in design from the one "used by the kings of France", although still having three petals (Pedani, "Mamluk Lions and Venetian Lions", 5 n. 7).

farjiyya *(pl.* farjiyyāt *or* farājī*)*

A long-sleeved robe similar to the *jubba* or the *qabā'* ("coat"). It was open at the front from top to bottom and had buttons (al-Battawi, *'Imāma*, 135; Ashour, *'Aṣr*, 460).

farrāsh *(pl.* farrāshūn *or* farrāshīn*)*

The *farrāsh* was a caretaker of the caliph and his palaces in the Fatimid era. He was responsible for cleaning the palaces, interior and exterior; hanging curtains; cleaning and maintaining the belvederes (*manāẓir*); and guarding the palace gates after their closure at night. Each *farrāsh* received a monthly salary of about 10 dinars. He also provided minor services in the bureaus: a sort of a messenger boy. Al-Qalqashandī uses the term in the Mamluk era to refer to a category of caretakers who worked in the warehouses (al-Baqli, *Ta'rīf*, 261).

faṣīl

A little camel, and more rarely, a little cow (http://www.baheth.info/all.jsp?term=فصيل).

Fatimids

An Ismāʿīli Shi'ite dynasty that ruled Egypt from AH 358 / AD 969 to AH 567 / AD 1171. They claimed descent from the line of ʿAlī b. Abī Ṭālib, the fourth of the *rāshidūn* (the "rightly guided caliphs") and his wife, Fāṭima, the Prophet's daughter. Before conquering Egypt, they had established themselves in North Africa and Sicily, and, with Egypt under their control, they managed to expand into Syria. The Fatimids were in rivalry with the Abbasids, the caliphs of the Muslim Sunni realm at the time, and Baghdad, in AH 450 / AD 1058, was briefly declared to be under the control of the Fatimid Caliph al-Mustanṣir (r. AH 427–487 /AD 1036–1094). The First Crusade marked the Fatimids' loss of most of their Syrian dominions, including Jerusalem. Their rule began to weaken by the mid sixth century AH / twelfth century AD, and Egypt became a fighting ground between the Crusaders and Nūr al-Dīn b. Zankī, resulting in the appointment of Ṣalāḥ al-Dīn Yūsuf b. Ayyūb al-Ayyubi as Fatimid Grand Wazir and eventually ending the Fatimid caliphate. The majority of the subjects of the Fatimids remained Sunni under "their generally tolerant rule". The Fatimid era was also mostly characterized by tolerance to Christians and Jews, some of whom "occupied high offices in the state up to the level of the vizierate", as well as remarkable "economic prosperity and cultural vitality". It was also an era of flourishing Islamic arts and architecture (see Bosworth, *Islamic Dynasties*, 63–5).

fawānīs *(sing.* fānūs*)*

"Lanterns": al-Qalqashandī defines the *fānūs* as a spherical instrument with iron sides, covered with light white linen. It is used for lighting by fixing a candle inside it at the bottom. It was carried in front of the sultans or the amirs at night on their travels (al-Qalqashandī, *Ṣubḥ*, Vol. 2, 130–31).

fawqānī *(also* fawqāniyya, *pl.* fawqāniyyāt*)*

"Top coat": the robe worn above the clothes, the overgarment, as opposed to the *taḥtāniyya* (the undergarment). Men used to wear the *fawqāniyya* above the *jubba* (buttoned robe, opened from the neck to below the chest). In older times, the *fawqāniyya* was confined to the *quḍāt* (judges). One secondary source reports that this type of robe was made of broadcloth (*jūkh*), but another notes that broadcloth was not worn by the Men of the Turban, since it was considered of a lower grade and was only worn at times of severe economic crises by distinguished people, including the wazir and the chief judge, when people could not afford otherwise (Ashour, *'Aṣr*, 460; Abu Zayd, *Ḥisba*, 117 n. 25; al-Battawi, *'Imāma*, 135–6).

firāsh

Anything that is spread out, such as a carpet or bedding.

fusṭāṭ *(pl.* fasāṭīṭ*)*

"Pavilion", "tent".

G

ghulām *(pl.* ghilmān, aghlām*)*

A term that literally means "young boys" and is used to denote slave-boys or Mamluks.

ghurfa

"Chamber" or "hall".

ghurra

Ghurra means "the beginning of" or "forehead" or "forelock". It is used to refer to the gifts that the Fatimid caliph distributed on the occasion of the beginning of the year.

Ghuzz

Turcoman or Turkish tribes (Dahman, *Mu'jam*, 115).

ground-renting

Istiḥkār (transforming into a *ḥikr*) (see *ḥikr*).

H

ḥājib *(pl.* ḥujjāb*)*

The *ḥājib*, sometimes translated as "chamberlain", was originally used to refer to the man who kept the ruler's door, asking for permission to allow in visitors. The verb *ḥajaba* means to veil, conceal or screen; hence the *ḥājib* is the one who veils or screens the ruler from the public. The office of the *ḥājib* was called the *ḥujubiyya*. According to al-Qalqashandī this position was as old as the Islamic caliphate. It entailed reporting the subjects' news to the ruler and asking his permission to allow visitors in. He also mentions that the Umayyads were the first to introduce the title of *ḥājib*, during the reign of Caliph ʿAbd al-Malik b. Marwān (AH 65–86 / AD 685–705). In the Mamluk era, the holder of this office arbitrated between amirs and soldiers, presented the visitors to the sultanic court and paraded soldiers. The chief *ḥājib* (*ḥājib al-ḥūjjāb*) sometimes substituted for the sultan's viceroy in several issues (al-Baqli, *Taʿrīf*, 101; al-Qalqashandī, *Ṣubḥ*, Vol. 5, 449; al-ʿUmarī, *Masālik* (ed. al-Juburi), Vol. 3, 307).

ḥalaqa

Literally "ring": the usual sitting arrangement for lessons. *Ajnād al-ḥalaqa* ("soldiers of the ring") is a term generally used in the Mamluk era to denote a category of warrior horsemen of the army who were entitled to receive revenues from the *iqṭāʿāt* "in return for their military service". These lands and their revenues were specifically documented in the Army Bureau, as explained by al-Qalqashandī. The original definition of the *ḥalaqa* is not very clear in the sources, for it may have been used to refer to the ring of soldiers who guarded the sultan, the Turkish strategy of combat in forming a ring around the enemy forces, the ring formed around the prey during the sultan's hunting expeditions, among other meanings.The conditions of the *ḥalaqa* and its soldierschanged throughout Mamluk history and the term should be examined in the context of the era of each historian (see Abdelhamid, *Jaysh*, 56–64).

ḥalwā'

Any sweet food, also used to denote fruit (http://www.baheth.info/all.jsp?term=حلواء).

al-ḥāmilūn li-l-silāḥ al-ṣaghīr

In Ibn al-Ṭuwayr's account: *arbāb al-silāḥ al-ṣaghīr*, or "the bearers of small arms", which refers to 300 black slaves, who each carried two spears and a shield (Ibn al-Ṭuwayr, *Nuzha*, 148–9, 165).

ḥamla

"Load", which is identified by al-Maqrīzī, in an account of AH 797 / AD 1394, as equivalent to six, *buṭaṭ*, a term that possibly either means a flattened or compressed sack or a container with a neck shaped like a duck's. The earlier is the more probable description of what may have been used to transport loads of flour (see al-Maqrīzī, *Sulūk*, Vol. 5, 366).

ḥammālāt *(sing.* ḥammāla*)*

Ḥammāla means "carrier", and, as the name suggests, was a military ship used for transportation, possibly of ammunition and other supplies.

ḥanak *(pl.* aḥnāk*)*

Ḥanak has more than one meaning including: "what is under the chin", "the mouth" and the "interior of the upper jaw". The act of wearing a *ḥanak* (*al-taḥannuk*) means wrapping the tail of the turban under the chin, like a beard (http://www.baheth.info/all.jsp?term=حنك; P. Sanders, *Ritual*, 89–90).

hannāb

"Drinking goblet" (Ashour, *'Aṣr*, 483).

ḥāra *(pl.* ḥārāt*)*

This term used to denote a residential quarter, unlike the present-day meaning of an alley. The *ḥāra* was originally mainly allocated for the residence of a particular group of people united by some common factor or attribute.Their houses would be grouped together in the quarter withtheir own mosque, madrasa and market, depending on the size of the quarter. In the early Fatimid era, each *ḥāra* housed a particular army faction or regiment, which were categorized according to the tribal affiliations (Gamal al-Din, *Dawla*, 197–8; Raymond, *Cairo*, 385).

ḥarba

A spear like a lance (*rumḥ*) only shorter (Gamal al-Din, *Dawla*, 259).

ḥawāṣil *(sing.* ḥāṣil*)*

Warehouses, storehouses, storerooms, containers or granaries; also contents, products or acquisitions, possibly in stacks or packs.

ḥawḍ

A water basin or trough for animals to drink from.

ḥawsh

"Courtyard".

ḥidā'

Special song to urge camels forward.

ḥikr

A *ḥikr* was a piece of empty land that was originally part of a *waqf* (endowment) and was allocated to a renter who paid a sum of money, equivalent to the land's value, as rent. This agreement entitledthe renter to the ownership rights of the land, even if he was not legally the owner. The renter paida minimal annual rental fee and may sell the lease or pass it on to his descendants. This lease is a long-term rental lease, which allows the renter to use the land, in case the owner cannot invest in it.

ḥirrāqa *(pl.* ḥarārīq *or* ḥarāriq*)*

There were two types of ships referred to by this term. One was a military ship which carried fire weapons, such as Greek fire, and equipped to throw fireballs. The other was a non-military type which sailed the Nile carrying amirs and statesmen in navy parades and official celebrations.When the Mamluk Sultan al-Ẓāhir Baybars wanted to revive the Egyptian fleet, after it had been neglected during the previous Mamluk reigns, he summoned the Men of the Fleets, whom the amirs employed in their non-military *ḥarārīq* and other ships (al-Baqli, *Ta'rīf*, 104).

ḥisba

Office of the *muḥtasib.*

ḥiyāṣa *(pl.* ḥawā'iṣ*)*

The waist belt or strap that was used to tie the waist. The term was originally used for the girdle used to fasten the horse's saddle. Al-Qalqashandī defined it as one of the old instruments, for it is related that Caliph ʿAlī b. Abī Ṭālib used to wear a waist belt (*minṭaqa*). The Mamluk sultans did not regularly wear a waist belt, but they granted their amirs this item as a part of the costumes of honour. The *ḥiyāṣa* differed according to the amir's rank, sometimes golden and inlaid with gemstones, or made of and decorated with other materials (al-Baqli, *Ta'rīf*, 112).

horse blanket

See *'ibiy al-iṣṭabliyyāt.*

housings

See *ajlāl.*

ḥumāt *(sing.* ḥāmī*)*

Guardian, protector or guard, of the rank of amir. According to Ibn al-Ṭuwayr, the Fatimid camel settlement area (*munākh*), which included grain mills, warehouses and houses, had a guardian (*ḥāmī*), who was one of the amirs, along with a group of employees who managed it. Another possible meaning for *ḥāmī* is a black *ghulām* ("slave-boy"). Ibn al-Ṭuwayr, copied by al-Qalqashandī, lists the *ḥumāt* at the granaries, the camel settlement areas (*munākhāt*), the lands subject to annual taxes on non-Muslims (*jawālī*), gardens, properties (*amlāk*) and the like, among the employees of the Fatimid state (see Ibn al-Ṭuwayr, *Nuzha*, 141–2; http://www.baheth.info/all.jsp?term=حام).

ḥumūl *(sing.* ḥiml*)*

"Revenues": whatever was brought to the sultan from the produce of the provinces, either the produce itself or its monetary equivalent. It sometimes also meant what a convicted person was sentenced to pay and was deposited in the sultan's treasury, whether justly or not (Ashour, *'Aṣr*, 431).

I

'ibiy al-iṣṭabliyyā

"Horse blanket": *'ibiy*are capes and*al-iṣṭabliyyāt* means "belonging to the stables".

'ibiy al-marākīb

"Riding capes": *'ibiy al-marākīb* (*'ibiy*, sing. *'abā'a*: "mantle", "cape" or "robe"; *al-marākīb*, sing. *al-markūb*: "riding animal"). Al-Qalqashandī explains that the *'abā'a* (cape) was used to in place of the *kunbūsh* ("caparison") (al-Qalqashandī, *Ṣubḥ*, Vol. 2, 129).

'Īd

All Muslims celebrate two annual religious feasts: ʿĪd al-Fiṭr, on occasion of breaking the fasting of the month of Ramaḍān (Ramadan), the ninth month of the Hijri calendar, and ʿĪd al-Aḍḥā, the sacrificial feast that celebrates Allah's sparing of the Prophet Ismaʿīl, son of the Prophet Ibrāhīm (Abraham) from slaughter. ʿĪd al-Aḍḥā is celebrated on 10 Dhū al-Ḥijja, the twelfth and last month of the Hijri calendar, one day after the most important ritual of pilgrimage, Waqfat ʿArafa (Standing on the Mount of ʿArafa). Both feasts have their morning congregational prayers.

'Īd al-Ghadīr (also 'Īd Ghadīr Khumm)

A Shi'ite festival that is celebrated on the occasion of the incident at Ghadīr Khumm (the Khumm Brook), which is located in between Mecca and Madina. On his way back from his last pilgrimage journey in the year AH 10 / AD 632, the Prophet stopped at there with his company. He gave a speech and emphasized his brotherly bond with his cousin, ʿAlī b. Abī Ṭālib, which was later interpreted by Shi'ite Muslims to be a declaration of ʿAlī's right to be the first caliph after the

Prophet. This occasion was first celebrated in Egypt in AH 362 / AD 973 (Sayyid, *Tafsīr*, 460–61).

Ikhshidids

Muḥammad b. Ṭughj, known as Abū Bakr al-Ikhshīd (r. AH 323–35 / AD 935–46), was the founder of the Ikhshīdid dynasty that ruled Egypt from AH 323 / AD 935 to AH 358 / AD 969. He "came of a Turkish military family", which was in the service of the Abbasids and was governor of Egypt. *Al-Ikhshīd* was the title that the Abbasid Caliph al-Rāḍī (r. AH 322–9 / AD 934–40) granted Ibn Ṭughj, which is an "Iranian title meaning 'prince, ruler'". Ibn Ṭughj was succeeded by his two sons, who were "mere puppets". The regent Ibn Ṭughj appointed for his sons, a Nubian slave by the name of Kāfūr (Camphor: regent AH 334–55 / AD 946–66; ruler AH 355–7 / AD 966–8), was the real authority over the state, who managed to protect it from the Fatimid attempts to conquer Egypt. Kāfūr was a "patron of literature and the arts", and his court hosted the most renowned Arab poet of his time al-Mutanabbī, who composed famous poems both in praise and slander of Kāfūr (Bosworth, *Islamic Dynasties*, 62).

imam (*imām*)

The term has the general meaning of "leader". It is mostly used to refer to the leader of the five mandatory daily prayers, as well as additional prayers, such as the *tarāwīḥ* prayers performed after the *'ishā'* prayers during Ramadan. He had to be known for his piety and have excellent knowledge of religion and rituals. He had to have a good voice, memorize the Qur'an and be most learned of its rules of recitation (al-Battawi, *'Imāma*, 79).

inkwell

See *dawāt*.

iqama

Literally "hosting" or "appointing": the term was also used to either mean providing the soldiers with the supplies they needed, such as food rations or fodder for their animals, or to refer to what is required to host a traveller, or for his residence, such as the tents and all other equipment (Ashour, *'Aṣr*, 413).

iqṭā' *(pl.* iqṭā'āt*)*

The *iqṭā'* was the system of allocating and exploiting lands in the Islamic world that is comparable to feudalism, although quite different. The *iqṭā'* in the Islamic world in general was not subject to rigid, formal laws, nor ownership rights or inheritance rules. There were two main types of *iqṭā'*: the first was *iqṭā' al-tamlīk* (the *iqṭā'* of ownership), which was "a concession of land designated for agricultural reclamation; in return the recipient was allowed tax reductions and the right to pass the property on to heirs". The second type was *iqṭā' al-istighlāl* (the *iqṭā'* of exploitation), which "allowed the recipient to pay a fixed rate to the treasury in return for a portion of peasants' crops that was greater in value". Al-Qalqashandī includes a section on the *iqṭā'* in *Ṣubḥ al-A'shā*, where he provides an account of the system's history in Islam, its legislative rules and its application in his time. He explains that the *iqṭā'* of the sultan is that which he had the right to use and allocate as he saw fit. This necessitated that the piece of land had no original rightful owner or proprietor. In the Mamluk era, the owner of the *iqṭā'* was like a sultan over his land and had the right to all its yield and income. The land granted was completely restored to the sultan's ownership as soon as the grant was over; the owner was dead – in cases where this was a lifetime only ownership; the owner broke one of the conditions of the grant; he fell out of favour; or at the will of the sultan. Al-Qalqashandī details the two types of *iqṭā'*, explaining that the *iqṭā'* of ownershipa applied to a piece of land allocated by the sultan, whether usable and inhabited or not. As for the *iqṭā'* of exploitation, he explains that it was the allocation of the land tax revenue, such as the *kharāj*. This type was either for a specific period of time, for example, ten years; for the recipient's lifetime and his heirs after him; or for the recipient's lifetime only. He goes on to explain that in his time, the *iqṭā'āt* (lands and revenues granted as *iqṭā'*) did not follow the laws of religious legislation (Esposito, "Iqta", 140; al-Qalqashandī, *Ṣubḥ*, Vol. 13, 104–17; al-Baqli, *Ta'rīf*, 37).

iron poles

See *'umad al-ḥadīd.*

'iṣāba *(pl.* 'aṣā'ib*)*

Huge yellow silk processional banners (Ashour, *'Aṣr*, 457).

isfihsalār

The person who holds the office of *isfihlāriyya* or *isfihsalāriyya*. The *isfihsalār* is a half-Persian, half-Turkish word meaning "commander of the soldiers or the army", who was also sometimes referred to as the *sbāslār*. The high commander of the Fatimid army, to whom the *isfihsalār* reported, during the first century of the era, became the caliph, until Badr al-Jamālī's appointment as wazir in AH 466 / AD 1074, which marked the beginning of an era of military wazirs who bore the title *amīr al-juyūsh*, the Amir of the Armies, meaning the high commander of the army. The title was also used by the Atabeks of Syria and by the Ayyubids (see Gamal al-Din, *Dawla*, 223; Sayyid, *Tafsīr*, 689–90).

'ishā'

"Evening", the evening and last mandatory prayer of the day.

ishāra

A brief recommendation or advice that the plenipotentiary viceroy, the wazir, or men of similar positions wrote on official documents or grievances. These recommendations were then eloquently expanded, according to the rules of the chancery, by the secretarialscribes (*kuttāb al-darj*). Normally, a formula accompanied this *ishāra* to denote its origin.In case of the plenipotentiary viceroy, this formula was "by the high recommendation" (*bi-l-ishāra al-'āliya*). This formula is probably what al-Qalqashandī means by "noting to" the recommendation, since a brief look at the document would indicate who ordered it. Al-ʿUmarī's account explains that the viceroy noted in what he wrote that this was his *ishāra* on the document (al-Qalqashandī, *Ṣubḥ*, Vol. 1, 138; Vol. 7, 233; Vol. 13, 161–2; al-ʿUmarī, *Masālik* (ed. Al-Juburi), Vol. 3, 307; see also *mushāwara*).

istifāḍa

A type of testimony that is used when a case cannot be proven by a witness who has directly seen or heard what he is testifying for. It relies on common, widespread knowledge and may be accepted when it is difficult to prove something without it.

istīmār ***(pl.*** **istīmārāt*)***

Istīmār or *istīmāra* is a Persian word that is still in use in Egypt to refer to the official forms used by the state administrations. The Fatimid *istīmār* was an official governmental record of budget, which included the allowances, wages and so on, monetary or in kind, to which the state servants were entitled, no matter what their ranks or levels were. Al-Qalqashandī summarizes Ibn al-Ṭuwayr's account on *istīmār* in his description of the record of allowances (*istīmār al-rawātib*). Ibn al-Ṭuwayr does not specifically describe the *daftar al-majlis* as an *istīmār*; however, he lists its contents in an account that al-Qalqashandī summarizes. Both historians apply the term *istīmār* generically to mean official records of budget in the bureaus (Ibn al-Ṭuwayr and Sayyid, *Nuzha*, 75–9, 76 n. 1; Ibn al-Ma'mūn, *Nuṣūṣ*, 59, 70–71; Sayyid, *Tafsīr*, 350–51; al-Baqli, *Ta'rīf*, 30).

istirfā'

The *istirfā'* was apparently a financial investigation and collection process of the bureausthat was usually coupled with auditing (*taftīsh*). Ibn Ḥajar mentioned the term in his narrative of an incident that happened in the late fourth century AH /

early eleventh century AD, where a state bureau owed a sum of money to a group of people.A scribe (*kātib*) was in charge of the *istirfā'* and the auditing of the accounts of the state officials who caused this deficit by acquiring the sums of money as loans. The description by al-Qalqashandī, copied from ibn al-Ṭuwayr, shows that the memoranda (*tadhākir*) were probably the financial accounting and documentation part of the audit, while the *istirfā'* was the money collection part. The term *istirfā'* is probably also related to another term: *irtifā'*, which meant the return of the state revenue or its income from agriculture, sometimes specifically translated as "gross receipts" (Murphy, *Agrarian Bureau*, 101). Linguistically *istirfā'* suggests collection by raising the money from those legally bound to pay (Ibn Ḥajar, *Quḍāt*, 141; Sayyid, *Tafsīr*, 467; Ibn al-Ṭuwayr, *Nuzha*, 91; Murphy, *Agrarian Bureau*, 101).

iṭlāq al-mawtā

"Grant of the deceased": this appears to have been a grant given by the state to ensure the proper washing (*ghusl*) and burial of the dead bodies according to Islamic law (see Ibn Taghrī Birdī, *Nujūm*, Vol. 10, 161).

iṭlāqāt *(sing.* iṭlāq *)*

Granted tax-free lands: the *iṭlāq* was a type of decree that either amended a decision or a declaration made by an earlier monarch, introduced a new act of goodness or added to an earlier decree of generosity. The *iṭlāq* was a term that was also used to mean a piece of land that was granted and exempted from all taxes.A l-Qalqashandī also employs the term in the Fatimid context to refer to designated rations, such as those allocated from the granaries (see al-Baqli, *Ta'rīf*, 36).

*iwan (*iwān*)*

The iwan is an Islamic architectural term of Persian origin that refers to a square or rectangular room with one side opening unto a court or a roofed hall. It is always a step or more higher than the court and may be flat-roofed or vaulted.

J

jākhāt *(sing.* jākha*)*

Bands, such as inscribed ornamental bands on clothes (Stillman, *Dress*, 134).

jālīsh

A Persian word that means "hair" and was used to refer to the advance guard or the front troops of an army or in a battlefield. Al-Qalqashandī describes it as one of the Mamluk banners, which was huge and had a lock of hair at its top. This banner was raised above the *ṭablakhānāh* building or tent for 40 days before setting out for war and was particularly raised in war processions (Dahman, *Mu'jam*, 50; Ashour, *'Aṣr*, 425).

jamadar

The *jamadār* or the *jāmādār* was the wardrobe master, who was responsible for dressing the sultan or the amir. The term is Persian, composed of two syllables: *jāmā*, meaning "robe", and *dār*, meaning "holder of". The *jamadāriyya* were the group or faction of Mamluks responsible for the sultanic wardrobe (al-Baqli, *Ta'rīf*, 90; al-Qalqashandī *Ṣubḥ*, Vol. 5, 459).

jāmakiyya *(also* jāmik, *pl.* jāmakiyyāt *and* jamākī*)*

A Persian word which referred to the decreed salaries of state employees or men of the military. It generally refers to monthly pecuniary salaries or compensations (Dahman, *Mu'jam*, 51; al-'Umarī, *Masālik* (ed. Abbas), Vol. 3, 435 n. 3, 448 n.1).

jāmi' *(pl.* jawāmi'*)*

See *masjid*.

janā'ib *(sing.* junayb *or* janab*)*

"The side ones", which were the spare horses that marched with the caliph or sultan in wars, travels and on other occasions, in case they were needed. The term was also used to refer to the escorting guards (al-Baqli, *Ta'rīf*, 92; Dahman, *Mu'jam*, 55; Ashour, *'Aṣr*, 428).

jarīda

"Regiment": the term is generally used to refer to a regiment of cavalry that does not include infantry (al-Baqli, *Ta'rīf*, 84). Al-Qalqashandī also uses it in reference to a Fatimid navy regiment.

jāshankīr

The food-taster, who was responsible for tasting the foods and drinks instead of the sultan of the amir, out of fear they may be poisoned. The term is composed of two Persian syllables: *jāshnā*, which means "tasting", and *kīr*, which means "the one who handles", therefore the term means: "the one who handles the tasting" (al-Qalqashandī, *Ṣubḥ*, Vol. 5, 460; Dahman, *Mu'jam*, 50; Ashour, *'Aṣr*, 425)

jawālī *(sing.* jāliya*)*

More commonly known as the *jizya*, *al-jawālī* was one of the early terms given to the annual poll tax paid by non-Muslims. The *jizya* was mandatory on free, adult men, while women, children, men of religion, slaves, the insane, and controversially also those without income, were exempted from it. Al-Qalqashandī divides the management of this tax into two sections in his time, one for the capital, that is Cairo and Fustat, and one for all that is outside it. The capital's section had a supervisor who was appointed by a sultanic official decree (*tawqī'*). He was aided by witnesses and collectors and had two subordinates, each called a *ḥāshir*, for counting the numbers of men: one for Jews and one for Christians. Each *ḥāshir* knew the names of his respective population registered in the bureau, including the boys when they reached adulthood, the men who moved to the capital, as well as those who died or converted to Islam: all being data that they reported to the scribes of the bureau for updating the records.As for the taxes outside the capital, they were paid to the owner of the *iqṭā'* (the *muqṭa'*) in each village. If the village belonged to an *iqṭā'* managed by a sultanic bureau, its tax was accordingly delivered to that bureau (Sayyid, *Nuzha*, 92 n. 2; al-Qalqashandī, *Ṣubḥ*, Vol. 3, 462–3; Ahmad, *Itti'āẓ*, Vol. 3, 341 n. 3).

jawāshin *(sing.* jawshan*)*

Mail or chainmail that covers the chest only and is backless. The *jawshan* is described in one primary source to have been made of "small iron platelets, animal horns, or leather" and covered with cloth. Another opinion informs us that the difference between the *zardiyya* or *zard* and the *jawshan* is that the first is composed of one type of metal ring, while the second is made of alternating rings that are inlaid or connected together with thin tin platelets (Yasin, *Asliḥa*, 51–2: al-Baqli, *Ta'rīf*, 93–4; Gamal al-Din, *Dawla*, 262).

jāwīshiyya *(sing.* jāwīsh, *also* shāwīsh*)*

"Ushers": a Turkish word.The *jāwīshiyya* in the Mamluk state in Egypt were four of the soldiers of the *ḥalaqa*, whose job was to march in front of the sultan or the viceroy in processions, to call out and point the attention of the passers-by. The *jāwīsh* was also a low-ranking soldier whose master assigned with small tasks, such as delivering messages (al-Baqli, *Ta'rīf*, 82).

jibāb *(sing.* jubba*)*

A robe similar to the *farjiyya*.

jiha *(pl.* jihāt*)*

"Direction", "district" or "impost": one of the meanings of the term is the resource units or properties that supplied the state payments in money and kind, such as the allowances (*rawātib*) or the salaries (*jāmakiyyāt*). These included, for example, a bureau or one of its sub-units, such as a branch or an administrative directorate; service units, such as the bakeries and the granaries; or lands and properties that generate revenue. The term was also used to refer to imposts; or the lands, districts or properties that are subject to taxes or yielded revenue for general state expenditures. In his account on the "supervision of acquisitions" (*naẓar al-ḥāṣilāt*), also "supervision of imposts" (*naẓar al-jihāt*), al-Qalqashanī explains that this office managed the money of wazirate's imposts, by collecting, spending or paying to the public treasury (see al-QalqashandīṢubḥ, Vol. 3, 464; al-Nuwayrī, *Nihāya*, Vol. 29, 465; Vol. 30, 22).

jihad (**jihād**)

May be translated as "struggling" or "fighting" and is a wide concept in Islam that ranges from fighting non-Muslim enemies to maintaining self-control.

jilbān *(also* **ajlāb***)*

Newly purchased Mamluks (Abdelhamid, *Jaysh*, 12, 29; Dahman, *Mu'jam*, 53).

jirāya *(pl.* **jirāyāt***)*

This was a salary given in kind rather than in money. A *jirāya* could be given in bread, wheat or barley (which was called *qaḍīm* rather than *jirāya* by some historians). The portions of the *jirayāt* were standard quantities, but soldiers received different quantities since some of them were entitled to two portions or one and a half portionsand so on. A portion was called a *waẓīfa* ("ration"), while the number of portions per individual was called *qadr al-jirāya* (size or amount of the *jirāya*) (Sayyid, *Tafsīr*, 722).

judge

See *qāḍī*.

jūkandār

"Polo Master": the title of the amir who held the *jūkān* (polostick) for the sultan for playing *kura*. *Jūkān* is a Persian word that refers to the polostick, while *dār* is Persian for "holder of": therefore, the title translates as "Holder of the Polostick" (al-Qalqashandī, *Ṣubḥ*, Vol. 5, 485).

jūkh

Broadcloth.

julab *(sing.* julba*)*

A piece of silver or other material used to attach the head of the lance to its body (Shams, *Nujūm*, Vol. 4, 83 n. 7).

jundī

See *ajnād.*

K

Ka'ba

The Ka'ba in Mecca, according to Islam, is the first House of Allah, which was built by Prophet Ibrāhīm (Abraham) and his son, Prophet Ismā'īl (Ishmael). The five daily Muslim prayers are performed in the direction of the Ka'ba (the *qibla*), and pilgrimage, which includes visiting it, among other rituals, is one of the five pillars of the Islamic faith.

kāghada

Kāghad is an Arabized word that means a paper or a paper cone (see al-Qalqashandī, *Ṣubḥ*, Vol. 2, 465; http://baheth.info/all.jsp?term=كاغد).

al-kaḥḥālīn *(sing.* al-kaḥḥāl*)*

"Eye doctor" or "ophthalmologist" (Dahman, *Mu'jam*, 129).

kalālīb *(sing.* kallāb*)*

"Clasps": pins or hooks used to adorn acap (*kalawta*) (Ashour, *'Aṣr*, 466).

kalawta *(also* kullawta, *pl.* kalawtāt *or* kullawtāt*)*

A small piece of headgear worn separately or with a turban, also called *kulfa, kulaftāh* or *kulaftah.* It is thought to have resembled the head cover worn by Mevlevi dervishes in modern times and probably covered parts of the ears. The term is either thought to be of either Latin origin or an Arabized from Persian. The Ayyubid sultans introduced wearing the *kalawtāt* to Egypt. They used to wear the yellow broadcloth *kalawtāt* on their heads, without turbans, while loosening their forelocks or hair locks below the *kalawtāt*. "The sultans and soldiers continued to wear the yellow *kalawtāt* without turbans up to the mid Bahri Mamluk era." When Sultan al-Manṣūr Qalāwūn came to rule, he introduced muslin (*shāsh*) to the *kalawta*. "During the reign of his son, al-Ashraf Khalīl, all the amirs were ordered to ride among their Mamluks in gold-brocaded caps (*kalawtāt zarkash*), while the yellow broadcloth ones were worn by those beneath the amirs in rank. When Sultan al-Nāṣir Muḥammad came to power, he introduced the *Nāṣiriyya* turbans, which were small. He shaved his head after pilgrimage, the amirs followed him, and they relinquished the hairlocks. The *Nāṣiriyya* turbans were later replaced with the *Yalbughāwiyya*, which were attributed to Amir Yalbughā al-Khāṣṣakī al-ʿUmarī." The *Yalbughāwiyya* remained in use until the reign of Sultan al-Ẓāhir Barqūq, "the first of the Circassian Mamluk sultans, who introduced the *Jarkasī* (Circassian) *kalawtāt*, which were bigger than the *Yalbughāwiyya* ones", and the turban cloths were wrapped around them in a bent fashion (al-Baqli, *Ta'rīf*, 288–9; al-Maqrīzī, *Khiṭaṭ*, Vol. 3, 73–4; Dahman, *Mu'jam*, 130–31; Ashour, *'Aṣr*, 466; al-ʿUmarī, *Masālik* (ed. al-Juburi), Vol. 3, 291 n. 5; al-ʿUmarī, *Masālik* (ed. Abbas), Vol. 3, 435 n. 1).

kanābīsh ***(sing.*** **kunbūsh,** ***sometimes distorted to*** **kunfūsh,** ***pl.*** **kanāfīsh*)***

"Caparison": al-Qalqashandī defines the *kunbūsh* as the cover of the back and croup of the horse, which is brocaded with gold or silver inlaid with gold (*makhāyish*) or made of inscribed wool. He adds that it is used for the mounts of judges and religious scholars.The term is defined by others as the pack (*bardha'a* or *barda'a*) placed beneath the horse's saddle. It also has other meanings including a cover for the sword and, in Spain and North Africa, a small cotton bonnet for children, a baby's bib, and a veil used to cover the chin and the nostrils as protection against the cold and dampness of the morning air (al-Qalqashandī, *Ṣubḥ*, Vol. 2, 129; al-Baqli, *Ta'rīf*, 289; Ashour, *'Aṣr*, 467; Dahman, *Mu'jam*, 131).

al-Kānimī

Used to refer to *al-Kānim*, a Sudanese sect, some of whom resided in Egypt, that were merchants of spices such as pepper, cloves and the like, which are brought from India and Yemen (al-Qalqashandī, *Ṣubḥ*, Vol. 4, 32, n. 1).

kanjawāt

Kajāwāt or *nuzha*, both words, of Persian origin, were used to refer to the same thing, which is a seated conveyance similar to the howdah (Sayyid, *Nuzha*, 149 n. 8; Shams, *Nujūm*, Vol. 4, 84 n. 6).

kantar

Al-Qalqashandī informs us that the Egyptian *kantar* (*qinṭār*) was equal to 100 pounds (*arṭāl*) (45.36 kg). The Egyptian Roman *kantar* was equal to 45.31 kg, while the Cairo *kantar* was 44.75 kg (al-Qalqashandī, *Ṣubḥ*, Vol. 3, 445; http://uqu.edu.sa/page/ar/76218).

kārim ***(also*** **kārimiyya** ***or*** **akārim*)***

"Spices", spice merchants or the spice trade. The linguistic origin of the term *kārim* is controversial: while some scholars agree that it refers to sea trade, others believe that the name is a distortion of Kānim, in Sudan, from where the first group of the merchants of this trade came. The *kārim* trade was mainly concerned with spices, dyes and similar products, particularly with India, during the Fatimid era, when the name referred primarily to spice merchants. Ports like Eden, ʿAydhāb, Qūṣ, and Fustat, were all important centres of the *kārim* trade. The Fatimid state provided special protection for this trade using its fleet, which ensured its success. There is a possibility that this protection was only provided to wealthy merchants who paid for it. The Fatimid caliphs participated in this trade, to the extent that the Fatimid missionaries (*du'āt*) were not differentiated from the merchants (Sayyid, *Tafsīr*, 496–500; Maged, *Ẓuhūr*, 253).

kāshif ***(pl.*** **kushshāf*)***

A Man of the Sword responsible for supervising the conditions of the lands or the embankments, therefore sometimes referred to as *kāshif al-turāb* ("Supervisor of Lands") or *kāshif al-jusūr* ("Supervisor of Embankments"). The *jusūr*, which the *kushshāf* supervised,were embankments of earth established on the river or canal banks to prevent the overflow of water in the flood season and reserve the water for irrigation. Al-Qalqashandī lists two kinds of embankments: sultanic and civil. The sultanic embankments were the main ones used collectively for several villages, and equipped, financed and supervised by the sultanic bureau, while the civil embankments were individual ones in the villages, which were the responsibility of the *iqṭā'* owners and were subject to taxes. Al-Qalqashandī gives further explanations on the number of *kushshāf* in Egypt and where they were appointed (al-Baqli, *Ta'rīf*, 283; al-Shistawi, *Mutanazzahāt*, 27 n. 1; al-Qalqashandī, *Ṣubḥ*, Vol. 4, 448–50).

kātib al-darj ***(pl.*** **kuttāb al-darj*)***

"Secretarial scribe": the *darj* was a large rectangular sheet of paper formed of several smaller ones, usually 20in number, which were attached together so that the sheet was easily folded. *Kuttāb al-darj* used to write on this particular type of paper. *Kuttāb al-darj* comprised the second, lesser category of the clerks of the Chancery Bureau, the first being the scribes of the pedestal (*kuttāb al-dast*). *Kuttāb al-darj* wrote down the documents that the Scribe of the Secret (*kātib al-sirr*) or the scribe of the pedestal (*kātib al-dast*) signed, which included decrees, announcements, orders and declarations. They were also called *kuttāb al-inshā'* (chancery scribes) because they wrote down the correspondence and other documents; however, they were not called *muwaqqi'ūn* ("signers"), for *tawqī'* ("signature") was a different task that entailed writing on the margins of grievances and the like. Al-Qalqashandī reports that by his time, the proficiency of *kuttāb al-darj* had deteriorated and *kuttāb al-dast* were the ones who wrote the royal and other important official documents, while *kuttāb al-darj* wrote the less important documents (al-Qalqashandī, *Ṣubḥ*, Vol. 1, 138; al-Baqli, *Ta'rīf*, 281).

kātib al-dast *(pl.* kuttāb al-dast*)*

"Scribe of the pedestal": the *dast* was the pedestal on which the sultan or caliph sat. *Kuttāb al-dast* were the higher category of the scribes or clerks of the Chancery Bureau, who sat in the caliph's or sultan's audience, as the subordinates of the Scribe of the Secret (*kātib al-sirr*). The other category were the secretarial scribes (*kuttābal-darj*). *Kuttāb al-dast* sat in order of their seniority and read the grievances to the sultan and wrote down his verdicts on them, adorned with his signature.They were the most deserving of the clerks of the Chancery Bureau of the title "signers" (*muwaqqi'ūn*), since, unlike the others, they signed in the margins of the grievances (al-Qalqashandī, *Ṣubḥ*, Vol. 1, 137).

kātib al-sirr *(pl.* kuttāb al-sirr*)*

The term means "Scribe of the Secret" and was used to refer to the royal confidential scribe who headed the Chancery Bureau, and who was sometimes called *kātim al-sirr* (the "Keeper of the Secret") by the public. During the Mamluk era, this office was occupied by one of the Men of the Turban and was also referred to as the Master of the Chancery Bureau (*ṣāḥib dīwān al-inshā'*) and the Supervisor of the Chancery Bureau (*nāẓir dīwān al-inshā'*). *Kātib al-sirr* had the privilege of the frequent and close company of the sultan, since he was the sultan's confident who was exposed to the same classified issues that were only known to the sultan's closest entourage, such as his wazir and family.

The tasks of *kātib al-sirr* included reading the sultan's mail, writing replies, getting the sultan's signature on them and sending them, and sometimes general supervision of the mail; conveying the news of other kingdoms to the sultan and communicating the royal orders to the viceroys; handling the issuance of official decrees, and reading grievances at the House of Justice (Dār al-ʿAdl), where he sat to the left of the sultan, and signing them with the *tawqī'*; keeping a log of salaries and other financial accounts; in addition to overseeing other state employees, such as the supervisors of lands and embankments (*kushshāf*) and the administrative supervisors (*nuẓẓār*), as well as supplementary services, such as the dovecotes.He was to only employ qualified scribes in his bureau and, like other royal officials, was bestowed with costumes of honour. To his assistance were the scribes of the pedestal (*kuttāb al-dast*), who also sat at the House of Justice to read the grievances to the sultan and sign them with his orders, and the secretarial scribes (*kuttāb al-darj*) who wrote the official decrees, correspondences, etc, for the sultan.

Holders of the office of *kātib al-sirr* reached this office via several routes. One was inheriting the office from their father or other family member, after being well-educated through memorizing the Qur'an, learning some *Ḥadith* and jurisprudence, as well as language and calligraphy, and having work experience at the Chancery Bureau.Another was through career advancement at the Chancery Bureau, where the exceptional among its high clerks were chosen for this office. Other means to reach this position included personal relations, where friendship with an amir could secure such a post, excellent linguistic and composition skills, or knowledge of foreign languages. When Sultan al-Nāṣir Muḥammad cancelled the office of wazir, the wazir's authority of signature was given to *kātib al-sirr*, who, in addition to his normal tasks, was responsible for the foreign ambassadors or messengers, and participated with the chancellor (*dawādār*) on many royal matters.

Kātib al-sirr was a high-ranking, lucrative post. The powerful among its holders had great authority over several state activities, either secretly or publicly. Most of the holders of this office came to Egypt, the seat of the Mamluk throne, from Syria, possibly because of their excellent language skills, or their knowledge of foreign languages. However, many of the confidential scribes ended up being subjected to confiscation of property, dismissed or even killed (al-Battawi, *'Imāma*, 32–6; al-Baqli, *Ta'rīf*, 282).

kawābij

Kawābij is a plural term for a word derived from the Turkish word *göbek*, which means "navel", indicating a convex or concave ornament in the centre of the shield. In another context, *kawābij* is explained to be the plural of a term derived from another Turkish word: *kopça*, which means a "clasp", "buckle" or "shoe clasp" (Sayyid, *Nuzha*, 148 n. 6; Iybish, *Dimashq*, 230 n. 1).

kaymakht

A type of tanned leather used for making shields (Sayyid, *Nuzha*, 148 n. 3).

khādim *(pl.* khuddām*)*

The term means "servant" and denotes eunuchs who were normally responsible for the palaces or the households.

Khalīj

The Khalīj was the canal of Fustat connecting the Nile with the Red Sea. The Ancient Egyptians originally dug the canal. It was redug after the Islamic conquest in AH 23 / AD 644 upon Caliph ʿUmar b. al-Khaṭṭāb's order to ʿAmr b. al-ʿĀṣ, providing a direct channel of transportation between the newly founded capital and the Arabian Peninsula.It then became known as Khalīj Amīr al-Mu'minīn (the "Canal of the Prince of the Faithful"), and later bore other names, such as Khalīj al-Qāhira ("Canal of Cairo"), al-Khalīj al-Ḥākimī ("al-Ḥākim's Canal"), after the Fatimid Caliph al-Ḥākim, and al-Khalīj al-Miṣrī ("Canal of Miṣr") (see Abouseif, *Architecture*, 3; Ibn ʿAbd al-Ẓāhir, *Khiṭaṭ*, 115; Ibn al-Ṭuwayr, *Nuzha*, 40, 201–3).

khan

See *qaysāriyya.*

khānqāh *(pl.* khānqāwāt, khanqah*)*

The *khānqāh* (khanqah), the *zāwiya* (zawiya), and the *ribāṭ* (ribat) are three types of Islamic Sufi religious, educational and residential establishments that proliferated throughout Egypt during the Mamluk era.The three terms were sometimes used interchangeably in the Mamluk sources, with little differentiation among their functions. These establishments were charitable, pious foundations funded by endowments documented in deeds (*waqfiyya*, pl. *waqfiyyāt*) that stipulated all the rules and conditions of running the institution and housing its residents.The *zāwiya* (pl. *zawāya*: "corners") was originally a term given to any small mosque, usually with no minaret or minbar, where a man known for his piety and asceticism preached or taught. *Khānqāh* (pl. *khānqāwāt* or *khawāniq*) is a word of Persian origin. The khanqah was a larger establishment than the zawiya, and was mostly, at least in the early Mamluk era, built by royal patrons or members of the royal entourage, while the zawiya had a wider range of patrons including the Sufi figures. The ribat (from the verb *rabaṭa*, "to tie") was originally the name given to the fortifications built for Muslim warriors on the borders or frontiers of Islamic lands (the *murābiṭūn*). It later came to also refer to establishments that sometimes hosted the poor and the needy, and some of them were dedicated solely for women; however, the ribats mostly functioned more as secluded Sufi residences (see Ashour, *'Aṣr*, 443–4; Ashour, *Mujtama'*, 187; Dahman, *Mu'jam*, 85; Homerin, "Saving Muslim Souls", 67, 75).

kharājī *(also* māl al-kharājī*)*

Kharājī was the annual tax taken from the agricultural lands that produced grains, palm trees, grapes and fruits, as well as what was taken from peasants as gifts of kind, such as sheep and poultry. *Al-māl al-hilālī*, on the other hand, was a religiously illegal tax imposed on a monthly basis on pastures, fishing, presses and other activities. It started being imposed in Egypt after AH 205 / AD 821 and was stopped by Aḥmad b. Ṭūlūn to be resumed under the Fatimids, when it became known as *al-mukūs* (sing. *al-maks*: "tax"). Sultan Ṣalāḥ al-Dīn cancelled this tax but it was imposed again after his death.It was imposed and cancelled several times during the Ayyubid and Mamluk eras (Dahman, *Mu'jam*, 67, 153; al-Maqrīzī, *Khiṭaṭ*, Vol. 1, 296–308).

kharīṭa

"Leather case": the term was also used to refer to the caliphal treasury, whereby *ṣāḥib al-kharīṭa* was the same as *ṣāḥib bayt al-māl* ("Master of the Public Treasury") (al-Baqli, *Ta'rīf*, 117).

kharkāh *(pl.* kharkawāt*)*

A wooden hut of a special shape and covered with broadcloth or a similar textile. The *kharkawāt* were carried on journeys to be put inside the tent to protect its occupants from the cold (al-Baqli, *Ta'rīf*, 117; al-Qalqashandī, *Ṣubḥ*, Vol. 2, 131).

khāṣṣa

See *khawāṣṣ*.

Khāṣṣakiyya

The sultan's private Mamluks, hence their name (*khāṣṣ*: "private"). The *Khāṣṣakiyya* were normally chosen by the sultan from the Mamluks he bought at a young age, so as to make sure that they grew up in loyalty and obedience to their master and that they were deserving of becoming his personal guards. This group of Mamluks was rather privileged, for they were closest to the sultan in his seclusion and travels, entered into his presence unannounced, and were assigned with honourable missions, such as the procession and travel of the covering of the Ka'ba (*maḥmil*). They received the most generous grants and gifts, and were known for their elegance and grace in costumes and riding. They attended the royal audience of service (*khidma*) carrying their swords and wearing their embroidered clothes. The number of Mamluks in this category was not defined, and was rather a matter of the sultan's preference (Ibn Taghrī Birdī, *Nujūm*, Vol. 7, 179–80; al-Baqli, *Ta'rīf*, 114; Abdelhamid, *Jaysh*, 37–41; Ashour, *'Aṣr*, 432–3; Dahman, *Mu'jam*, 66).

khatam

"Completion": recitation of the whole Qur'an.

khaṭīb *(pl.* khuṭabā'*)*

The "sermon-giver" or "preacher": the man responsible for delivering sermons on Fridays, 'Īd al-Fiṭr, 'Īd al-Aḍḥā, and on occasions of solar and lunar eclipses. The *khaṭīb*, like the *imām*, had to be known for his piety and have a great knowledge of religion and rituals, for he held one of the most respectful posts. He had to memorize the Qur'an and be excellent in its recitation, as well as have a good voice. The *khaṭīb* had to know the rules of sermon-giving and be good at it. The Mamluk sultan only appointed sermon-givers at the major mosques, such as the Citadel mosque, where mostly the chief Shāfiʿī judge was made the *khaṭīb*, for it was the mosque where the sultan prayed.Sometimes if the sultan heard a particular *khaṭīb* and liked him, he appointed him at the mosque of the Citadel (al-Battawi, *'Imāma*, 79–80).

khaṭṭ

"Hand signature".

khawāṣṣ *(also* khāṣṣa*)*

The close, private or special elite entourage. The *khawāṣṣ* were "the privileged class composed of caliph or sultan's kin, amirs, high officials, and wealthy merchants". *Khāṣṣa* is also used to denote "the private domains owned by caliphs, sultans or amirs" (Tsugitaka, *State*, 248).

khawkha *(also* khūkha, *pl.* khuwakh*)*

The small door in a city gate or a gate of a big building, which facilitated daily use instead of having to open and close the huge gates. The term was also applied to small doors in the city walls or the corners of streets and alleys.

khayma *(pl.* khiyām*)*

"Tent".

khāzindār

The *khāzindār* in the Mamluk era "was the person responsible for the sultanic, amirial, or other treasuries and their contents, such as money and grains" (al-Baqli, *Ta'rīf*, 113).

khidma

Khidma means "service" and referred to being in the caliph's or sultan's audience (the *ḥaḍra*), and therefore in his service. The term *khidma* was also used to mean saluting the caliph or sultan upon being in his presence, using certain gestures, such as kissing the floor, kissing his hand or feet or bowing or by mere salutation (*salām*). This protocol of salutation and gestures changed in details over time, depending on who was more favoured, since some gestures seem to have been regarded as a higher privilege than others and apparently according to what the sovereign deemed suitable. These gestures were signs of obedience and compliance, salutation and homage, and refusing to perform them was a declaration of insubordination. Being in the *khidma* also entailed specific codes of behaviour, such as standing inparticular places according to position and status and not talking to others to show complete attention to the sovereign. The *khidma* was not only a presence in the sovereign's court but was also a meeting between the amirs, the men of the state and the caliph or sultan, where they discussed the matters that needed to be presented to the him, and was therefore mainly a courtly meeting (Ashour, *Mujtama'*, 85–6; Sanders, *Ritual*, 15, 18–19, 143–5).

khilwa

The *khilwa* is "the place where a worshipper stays in secluded privacy for worship" (al-Baqli, *Ta'rīf*, 122). The word also refers to any secluded or isolated place or choice of stay.

khiṭṭa *(pl.* khiṭaṭ*)*

"Concession, block of land in a newly founded city" (Raymond, *Cairo*, 386). The term also means "neighbourhood" and "plan".

khiwān

"Table": an originally Persian word, which means "the table" or what is used to eat off (Dahman, *Mu'jam*, 70 Steingass, *Persian–English Dictionary*, 48, http://dsalsrv02.uchicago.edu/cgi-bin/philologic/getobject.pl?c.2:1:4784.steingass).

khizānat al-khāṣṣ

The "Private Treasury": this was the monetary treasury of the state, which later diminished into being the treasury for costumes of honour, called *al-khizāna al-kubrā* (the Great Treasury), to be granted by the Fatimid caliph. In the Mamluk era, the office of the Private Supervisor (*nāẓir al-khāṣṣ*) was introduced by Sultan al-Nāṣir Muḥammad in AH 713 / AD 1313, when he abolished the office of wazir and the term *al-khāṣṣ* (the "private", the "private domain") was used to refer to what was relevant to the money and finances of the sultan. Holders of this office were Men of the Pen who were responsible for the sultan's money and the sultan's treasury at the Citadel. With no wazir to serve the sultan, *nāẓir al-khāṣṣ* became as close to the sultan as his wazir, a proximity that gave him considerable power and authority, which sometimes exceeded those of the wazirs or the amirs. He managed matters and appointed the managers (*mubāshirūn*), and was aided by the Private Comptroller (*mustawfī al-khāṣṣ*) and the Supervisor of the Private Treasury (*nāẓir al-khizāna al-khāṣṣa*). However, *nāẓir al-khāṣṣ* could not take any decisions without going back to the sultan and he was aided by many assistants, who were clerks of the Private Bureau (*dīwān al-khāṣṣ*). Many of the holders of this post held additional major positions such as wazir, Supervisor of the State (*nāẓar al-dawla*) or Supervisor of the Army (*nāẓar al-jaysh*), and their authority encompassed most financial matters of the state. When the office of wazir deteriorated due to the sultans' dependence on them, the holders of this post advanced in status and became very wealthy. Most of the holders of this office in the Mamluk era were from the Men of the Truban (*muta'ammimūn*) of the Copts and the Copts who converted to Islam (*masālima*), who were known for their accounting skills and were particularly trusted by the Mamluk sultans and amirs to manage their financial matters (al-Baqli, *Ta'rīf*, 113–14; al-Qalqashandī, *Ṣubḥ*, Vol. 4, 30–31; al-Battawi, *'Imāma*, 23).

khizānat al-tajammul

The "Decoration Treasury": one of the literal meanings of *al-tajammul* is "beautification". P. Sanders translates *khizānat al-tajammul* as "treasury of parade equipment" and "treasury of parade arms". This treasury was a part of the Treasury of Arms (*khizānat al-silāḥ*), and it included many types of arms and precious instruments used on special occasions, such as boxes filled with gems, jewels, gold and silver pots; golden saddles, embroidered caparisons and clothes; ornamented waist straps; and other items. It had its own supervisor (*nāẓir*) (Sanders, *Ritual,* 177–8; Ibn al-Ṭuwayr, *Nuzha*, 135, 149; al-Baqli, *Ta'rīf*, 117–18).

khuff *(pl.* khifāf*)*

"Light shoes", "shoes" or "sandals" (http://www.baheth.info/all.jsp?term=الخف).

khushkanān *(also* khushkanānj*)*

Sometimes called *khushtanān* in Egypt, which is the originally Persian, Arabized name of a kind of pastry that is composed of two syllables: *khushk*, meaning "crusty" or "dry", and *nān*, meaning "bread". It was made of fine wheat flour kneaded with sesame oil. It was formed into rectangular pieces, in the middle of each almonds and ground sugar kneaded with rosewater were put, in an almond to sugar ratio of one to two. The dough was then baked in the oven. Another description of it is that it was a kind of a puff-paste shaped like a hollow ring, with almonds or pistachio in its middle (Sayyid, *Nuzha*, 144 n. 2; Shams, *Nujūm*, Vol. 4, 100 n. 6).

khuṭba

Any sermon given before or after prayers. A mandatory *khuṭba* has to be preached before Friday congregational prayers.

khuwadh *(sing.* khūdha*)*

Helmets made of the same materials used for making armour and worn fitting the heads beneath the cloth or leather head cover (*qalansuwa*) (Sayyid, *Tafsīr*, 702; Ashour, *'Aṣr*, 462).

kīmān *(sing.* kawm*)*

"Heaps": the resulting debris of the consecutive fires, famines and epidemics that Fustat faced. The major fire that started this phenomenon was in AH 564 / AD 1169 and was followed by several calamities that led to the formation of such heaps of wreckage (Azab, *Fustat*, 43, 49, 58–9).

kīs

"Pouch".

kiswat al-Ka'ba

Covering of the Ka'ba, providing a precious *kiswa* for the Ka'ba was an honour and a privilege prior to and after the arrival of Islam. A none too extravagant *kiswa* covered the Ka'ba at the time of the Prophet and *al-rāshidūn* (the "rightly guided caliphs"), which gradually became an extremely valuable item. The keepers of the Ka'ba customarily took the older covering, after replacing it with the newer one, and gave parts of it as presents to kings and dignitaries. Another inscribed silk cover was kept inside the Ka'ba, though this one required changing only after some years, since it was not exposed to the environmental factors, such as the sun, nor to the touching or grabbing by people's hands (al-Baqli, *Ta'rīf*, 287; see al-Qalqashandī, *Ṣubḥ*, Vol. 4, 277–84).

al-kittāniyya

This is a mistake or a misspelling, for the right term is either *al-kitābiyya* or *al-kuttābiyya*. *Al-kitābiyya* were the Mamluks of the sultan's barracks (*al-ṭibāq* or *al-aṭbāq*), who lived in there, received military training and learned how to write (*kataba* "to write", hence the name). Not all Mamluks were raised and educated in the barracks, for some directly joined the sultan's court and received private education and training with his sons. The *khāṣṣakiyya* were sometimes chosen from among these Mamluks who received such special treatment. Some sultans, however, like most of the amirs, sent their sons to the barracks (al-Baqli, *Ta'rīf*, 330; Shams, *Nujūm*, Vol. 11, 220 n. 1).

kizlik

A dagger: a Persian word that means a knife or "the curved point of a sword or dagger". It is used to refer to a kind of a dagger (Steingass, *Persian–English Dictionary*, 1027, http://dsalsrv02.uchicago.edu/cgi-bin/philologic/getobject.pl?c.5:1:2604.steingass).

kura *(also* akra*)*

A sport, similar to polo. *Al-kura* (the "ball") was big and made of light material and was thrown on the ground while the riding players, who formed two competing teams, tried to hit it, each using his *ṣawlajān* or *jūkān* ("sceptre", "mace" or "polostick"). A traveller during the Burji Mamluk era gave a description of the field, its division and how the game was played. The Arabs played it, and it was adopted by the Abbasids, who built special spacious courts for it, as well as a square (*maydān*) in Baghdad. Aḥmad b. Ṭūlūn was the first to establish a *maydān* for this sport in Islamic Egypt. The Fatimids, the Ayyubids and the Mamluks all practised this sport, which was as much of a military training as it was a pastime, for it required maximum control of the horse and excellent manoeuvring skills. The Mamluk sultans and amirs were particularly fond of this sport. Several squares around Cairo and Fustat were used for this sport, among other purposes. Historians also report that Sultan Baybars and other later Burji Mamluk sultans and amirs, played *kura* in the outskirts of Alexandria or by the sea. The sport was especially important for it had its recognized officials, tools, animals and processions. A banquet was offered following the game, usually by the defeated team if the sultan was not generous enough to offer it himself, even if he won. The sultan also normally bestowed costumes of honour on the participants, some of their followers, and other amirs and state officials after the game. Sultans were keen on hitting the first ball, announcing the beginning of the games season, as well as indicating the end of the season themselves too. A big audience of fans and players watched the games (Nassar, *Tarfīh*, 243–59).

kursī

"Chair".

kursī al-dawāt

"Chair of the inkwell".

kūsiy

"Cymbal player".

Kutāma

The Kutāma Berbers of the Maghrib were one of the important tribes that supported the rise of the Fatimids in the western Islamic lands. Some of them came with Jawhar and others arrived with Caliph al-Muʿizz (Gamal al-Din, *Dawla*, 201; Uthman, *'Imāra*, 190–1;Ahmad, , *Tārīkh*, 210).

kuwā *(also* kuwwāt, *sing.* kuwwa*)*

A small opening or a skylight that serves the purpose of a window.

L

labba

The middle of the lower neck (http://www.baheth.info/all.jsp?term=لبة).

lājūq

A Persian word that means "tent" or "an osier tent covered with felt". It was probably a tent or a partition of the bigger tent that was for the sultan's private use on his travels, since al-Qalqashandī's account shows that it was his last place of rest (see Steingass, *Persian–English Dictionary*, 1110, http://dsalsrv02.uchicago.edu/cgi-bin/philologic/getobject.pl?c.5:1:6361.steingass).

Layālī al-Wuqūd *(also* Layālī al-Waqīd*)*

The particular nights when mosques and streets are lit-up in celebration of occasions, such as *mawlid al-nabiy* (the Prophet's Birthday) or the *mawlid* ("birthday") of al-Ḥusayn and so on. Such festive occasions were introduced to Egypt by the Fatimids and among them were *Layālī al-Wuqūd al-Arba'*, which were the first and fourteenth nights of the months Rajab and Sha'bān of the Hijri calendar (al-Baqli, *Ta'rīf*, 293).

luʿab *(sing.* luʿba*)*

Small mangonels.

lutūt (sing. lutt*)*

A word of Persian origin meaning "the big axe" (al-Baqli, *Ta'rīf*, 292; Sayyid, *Nuzha*, 148 n. 4).

M

mace

See *dabbūs*.

madhhab *(madhāhib)*

School of religious interpretation, rite or doctrine.

Al-Madīna

Full name is Madīnat al-Nabī (the City of the Prophet) or al-Madīna al-Munawwara (the Illuminated City), originally Yathrib, to the north of Mecca.Prophet Muhammad was forced to immigrate from his hometown, Mecca, due to the rejection and hostility of its people towards him. His immigration (*hijra*) in AD 623 along with his closest friend and companion, and the first caliph of Muslims after him, Abū Bakr, marks the beginning of the Islamic calendar, or the Hijri calendar, which is a lunar calendar. He was welcomed by the people of Medina, later to be called *al-Anṣār* (the "Supporters"), then gradually joined by several of his companions (*al-Muhājirūn* or the immigrants). He only left his seat in Medina after he was able to conquer Mecca in the eighth year of the Hijra (AD 630).

*madrasa (***madrasa, *pl.* madāris***)*

An Islamic higher educational institution that mainly taught religious sciences, sometimes in addition to chosen secular sciences. A madrasa normally included residential quarters for students and functioned as a mosque as well. The running and upkeep of this institution, as well as the similar institutions that were of a Sufi nature, depended on charitable endowments that stipulated all relevant necessary conditions in detailed deeds called a *waqfiyya* (an endownment deed). Usually, a madrasa was established to teach one or more of the four Sunni doctrines of Islamic jurisprudence. The first madrasas in Egypt were built by the Ayyubids, and it later became an established institution usually with its founder's mausoleum attached to it. Founding a pious institution such as a madrasa with its mausoleum and a *waqfiyya* with sutiable assets for its upkeep became the goal of all sultans, amirs and other high ranking officials. Madrasas became a source of income to numerous factions, and became a necessary part of the educational system for the graduation of scholars and propagating the teachings of the four Sunni schools of jurisprudence. Those graduates were "men of the pen" who formed the bureaucracy necessary for the administration of the government (Al-Maqrīzī, *Khiṭaṭ*, Vol. 3, 455–8).

maghrib

"Sunset", sunset and third mandatory daily prayer.

Maghrib

The "Land of Sunset": a term that is generally given to the region currently comprising the North African Arab countries to the west of Egypt: Libya, Tunisia, Algeria and Morocco (Abun-Nasr, *Maghrib*, 1).

mahāmīz *(sing.* mihmāz*)*

"Spurs".

al-maḥmil

See *dawarān al-maḥmil.*

al-maḥrūsa *(m.* al-maḥrūs*)*

"The protected": a title used for cities and coastal cities to ensure that they remain protected. Al-Qalqashandī explains that when the term is used for citadels or fortresses, it has an obvious meaning, for they are fortifications protected by their walls. In all cases, he is inclined to believe it is a wish, rather than a mere statement of a fact (al-Qalqashandī, *Ṣubḥ*, Vol. 6, 184).

mā'ida

"The table spread with food", "the feast table" or "the feast" (Qur'an 5, "The Table Spread with Food": 114, http://corpus.quran.com/translation.jsp?chapter=5&verse=114).

makān

"Place": a general term that may be used for any kind of establishment or building property.

makhālī *(sing.* mikhlāt*)*

"Sacks".

makhāyish

Al-Qalqashandī explains that the *makhāyish* are caparisons brocaded with silver inlaid with gold (al-Qalqashandī, *Ṣubḥ*, Vol. 2, 129).

maks *(pl.* mukūs*)*

The *maks* was a tax imposed on products and commodities imported or ready to be exported in ports. During the Mamluk era, these taxes were imposed on houses, shops, *khāns* (caravanserais), baths, bakeries, mills, gardens, pastures, fisheries and presses, as well as on pilgrims, travellers, ships, fish, sheep, buffalos, cows, weddings and so on. This tax was actually unjust and illegal, since it was not derived from any of the religious legislations (*sharī'a*), therefore, some Mamluk sultans abolished it, in full or in part (al-Baqli, *Ta'rīf*, 324–5).

māl *(also* amwāl*)*

Māl is generally translated as "money", but means anything owned, such as money, goods, properties and so on, that constitute one's wealth

al-mamālīk al-sulṭāniyya

The "sultan's Mamluks": they were Mamluks who were bought and raised by the sultan to be set free or employed later. They were one of the categories of the rank-and-file Mamluk army and were divided into two main categories: the *jilbān* or *ajlāb*, who were purchased by the sultan and trained at the royal barracks (*ṭibāq*) at the Citadel, and the *mustakhdamīn*, who came to serve the sultan not through being purchased but acquired, since they were the forces of a previous sultan (*qarāniṣa*) or an amir (*sayfiyya*). The sultan's Mamluks also included elderly Mamluks and they were the highest-ranking, most respected, and closest to the sultan and received his most generous grants. Mamluk amirs of all ranks were usually chosen from among them. The sultan's Mamluks were led by a commander (*muqaddam*), who handled all their matters; arbitrated among them; rode behind them in processions; divided rations and grants among them; assigned their positions on processions; ensured travel and service protocols were followed; and supervised the commanders of the barracks and the *ṭawāshiyya*.The number of the sultan's Mamluks particularly increased under Sultans al-Nāṣir Muḥammad and Barqūq, due to their long reigns and their interest in buying and importing Mamluks. The sultan's Mamluks received their salaries and allowances from the Separate Bureau (*dīwān al-mufrad*) (Abdelhamdi, *Jaysh*, 44–51, 91–2; al-Baqli, *Ta'rīf*, 330; S. Ashour, *'Aṣr*, 477; Dahman, *Mu'jam*, 145).

*Mamluks (***mamlūk***)*

The term *mamlūk* means "the owned" and was used to refer to young boys who were bought or captured in war to be turned into slave soldiers. After rigorous training, the most prominent of these soldiers were emancipated and themselves turned into amirs. The tradition was initially introduced by the Abbasids, who started incorporating slave soldiers in their forces, particularly during the era of Caliph al-Muʿtaṣim (AH 218–27 / AD 833–42). This continued to be the case for centuries in several Islamic dynasties and the Ayyubids of Egypt and Syria were no exception. The Mamluk dynasty of Egypt and Syria (AH 658–923 / AD 1260–1517), when these slave warriors managed to reach power, is divided into two stages: the Bahri and the Burji.

Although it was supposedly a hereditary dynasty, Mamluk amirs competed vigorously for power and if a sultan was too young or weak, he was overthrown, killed or controlled as a puppet who only possessed nominal authority. Throughout the era, reaching the throne and keeping it was a privilege held only by the fittest and most powerful. The Mamluks remained for a good part of their history a dominant military force that controlled Egypt and Syria. They were great patrons of art and architecture whose buildings, metalwork, glass, calligraphy and epigraphy, and other forms of art remain to testify to their passion. In AH 923 / AD 1517, the Ottomans managed to defeat the last Mamluk sultan, Ṭūmān Bāy, in Cairo, thereby ending the era that mostly defines the Islamic architecture of Egypt (Bosworth, *Islamic Dynasties*, 78).

al-maʿmūra *(m.* al-maʿmūr*)*

"The inhabited": this adjective was used to describe the bureaus, among other entities, to ensure that these bureaus should remain inhabited with their scribes, or efficiently running because of the power of the sultan and the stability of his state (al-Qalqashandī, *Ṣubḥ*, Vol. 6, 185).

al-manḥar

"Slaughterground" or "sacrifice ground": "This was the location chosen by the caliphs to perform sacrificial slaughter on ʿĪd al-Aḍḥā and ʿĪd al-Ghadīr. This location was an empty piece of land in al-Darb al-Aṣfar that is now taken up by a group of buildings to the west of the mosque of Saʿīd al-Suʿadā', between al-Darb al-Aṣfar and al-Tumbukshiyya streets of al-Jamāliyya quarter" (al-Baqli, *Ta'rīf*, 332) (Sanders, *Ritual*, 79, 127; al-Baqli, *Ta'rīf*, 332; Ibn al-Ṭuwayr and Sayyid, *Nuzha*, 183–4 n. 2).

manjanīqāt *(sing.* manjanīq*)*

A catapult.

manshūr *(pl.* manāshīr*)*

"Decree of grant": in the Mamluk era, this was a sultanic decree to allocate *iqṭā'āt*. There were four kinds of *manāshīr*, which differed in their types or cuts of paper according to the grade of the grant's recipient. Before the Mamluk era, the *manāshīr* were decrees or correspondences that may not have required stamps, unlike other official decrees, such as those of appointment of the governors (*wulāt*) (al-Qalqashandī, *Ṣubḥ*, Vol. 13, 157–8; al-Baqli, *Ta'rīf*, 332).

al-mansūb

Al-khaṭṭ al-mansūb (the "proportioned script") was an Arabic calligraphic system developed by the Abbasid secretary and wazir, Ibn Muqla (d. AH 328 / AD 940). This system depended on the principles of geometric design, which were applied to letters. According to *al-mansūb* system, the sizes of letters were calculated "based on the rhombic dot formed when the nib of a reed pen is applied to the surface of the paper. Ibn Muqla calculated the height of an *alif*, the first letter of the Arabic alphabet, in terms of these dots and then calculated the size of all other letters in relation to the *alif*." *Al-mansūb* provided "a canon for each script" and "allowed a number of systematic methods or templates to be created for each of the six major scripts (*al-aqlām al-sitta*)": members of the rounded-hand family of cursive Arabic scripts (Bloom, "Calligraphy"; Tabaa, *Transformation*, 34; Gruber, *Manuscript Tradition*, 10–11).

manẓara *(pl.* manāẓir*)*

A term that originally denoted military watchtowers built on high ground overlooking the coasts to warn against enemy ships. The term then came to have a civil connotation during the Abbasid and Fatimid eras, when it meant a belvedere from which the royalty watched festivities and participated in them. Although the Fatimid belvederes disappeared, the idea remained during the Mamluk and Ottoman eras through using the same locations for leisure and festive purposes (al-Shishtawi, *Mutanazzahāt*, 227).

maqʿad *(pl.* maqāʿid*)*

"Sitting hall": the seating place or the place where one sits. "The word is usually translated as loggia, but in the Mamluk context it is a particular type of loggia with an arcaded opening" (Rabbat, *Citadel*, 212). The term also means seat, bench or stall for selling merchandise.

al-maqarr

A title that is linguistically derived from *istiqrār*, which means "settlement" and was used as an honourary reference to a person's authority over a place. This title was given to sultans, apparently only rarely, until Qalāwūn's investiture in AH 678 / AD 1279, and was most probably also used for the high amirs. Later, it was only adopted by the Men of the Sword, amirs and wazirs, until it was extended to civilians, high-ranking officials of the bureaus, and religious scholars and men of piety by the time of al-Qalqashandī (al-Basha, *Alqāb*, 489–94; al-Baqli, *Taʿrīf*, 322).

maqṣūra

This was an architectural element, mostly a wooden screen, partition or enclosure, which was inserted in the *qibla* area of a mosque, usually in front of the *mihrab* to separate the ruler (the caliph or governor) and his trusted retinue from the rest of the congregation. It was most probably introduced as a security measure after two Muslim caliphs were assassinated during their prayers at a mosque, namely, ʿUmar b. al-Khaṭṭāb and ʿAlī b. Abī Ṭālib. The oldest references we have is the *maqṣūra* added to the mosque of the Prophet in Madina by the fourth caliph, ʿUthman b. ʿAffan, built of mud-brick and rebuilt in wood during the reign of al-Walīd b. ʿAbd al-Malik. Other sources mention that the first ruler to use it was the first Umayyad caliph, Muʿāwiya b. Abī Sufyān, after he was wounded in an assassination attempt, while other sources put its use to a later date by the Umayyad Caliph Marawān b. al-Ḥakam also after an assassination attempt. Some later rulers, however, used the *maqṣūra* to distance themselves from their subjects, to boast and show their superiority. This latter development was a matter to which several religious scholars objected, for a security precaution was allowed in prayers, but not as an act of discrimination. We have a reference that the call for prayer were performed inside the *maqṣūra* in the mosque of ʿAmr in Fustat, however, the custom was annulled by the ʿAbbasid Caliph al-Muʿatasim (al-Maqrīzī, *Khiṭaṭ*, Vol. 4, 21; Azab, *Qal'a*, 103–4; Shafiʿai, *al-'Imara*, 649–50).

mark

See *'alāma*.

martaba

“Mattress”, from the Arabic verb *rattaba*, to “arrange”, “order”, or “grade”. Al-Qalqashandī explains the emergence of the early *martaba* as a throne, from which much grander structures evolved. Literally, *martaba* means a “level” or “grade”, which indicates that since its early use, it was elevated.According to al-Qalqashandī’s descriptions, as well as thoses of other historians, the *martaba* remained a mattress or a sofa-like piece of furniture, covered with embroidered or precious cloth, but was placed above the thrones and supported with cushions. As is clear from the al-Qalqashandī’s account, the *martaba* was not only used for the caliph’s throne, but also as a seat, probably above a pedestal or a platform, for the wazir and high state officials. The term was also employed to refer to a large bench or a pedestal used for sitting. In the early Fatimid era, the term was used to refer to the throne (*sarīr al-mulk*) (Sayyid, *Nuzha*, 206–7 n. 5; al-Maqrīzī, *Itti'āẓ*, Vol. 2, 4; Vol. 3, 88).

maṣaffāt *(sing.* maṣaffa*)*

“Under-shields”: most probably derived from *al-ṣafaf*, which is what is worn beneath the shield (http://www.baheth.info/all.jsp?term=صفف).

mashā'il *(sing.* mash'al*)*

“Torches”: al-Qalqashandī defines the *mash'al*, as an iron instrument, like a cage with an open top and a small opening in its bottom, in which dry wood was burnt for lighting. It was carried in front of the sultans or their likes at night on their travels (al-Qalqashandī, *Ṣubḥ*, Vol. 2, 131).

mashhad *(pl.* mashāhid*)*

“Shrine” or “memorial”.

mashhad ru'ya

A memorial built in a place associated with a vision.

mashyakhat 'arab

“Chief of Arabs”: rank of *shaykh al-'arab*, who was the grand leader of all the Arab tribes or houses in a particular province, although not as high in rank as an amir.

masjid *(pl.* masājid*)*

Masjid is the more generalterm applied to any place designated for prayers. Friday mosques were called *jawāmiʿ* (sing. *jāmiʿ*: "congregational mosque"), which is an abbreviation of the terms *masājid jāmiʿa* and *masājid al-jumʿa* (sing. *masjid jāmiʿ*: "Friday mosque"). They hosted the mandatory weekly mass prayer for Muslim men, which is performed on Friday at noon instead of *ẓuhr* prayer. Listening to the Friday sermon (*khuṭba*) is an essential component of this prayer. Friday mosques may also, of course, host the congregations performing any of the other daily prayers. Conducting mandatory prayers in groups is considered a better-rewarded observance than an individual prayer.

masnad *(pl.* masānid*)*

"Armrest" or "backrest".

maṣṭaba *(pl.* maṣāṭib*)*

Built, raised seats or platforms (see Rabbat, *Citadel*, 108, 112).

Master of the Feast Table

See *ṣāḥib al-mā'ida.*

al-mawārīth al-ḥashriyya

"Estate of the Heirless": according to Islamic law, inheritance is divided in specific fractions betweena deceased's relatives. Al-Qalqashandī explains that *al-mawārīth al-ḥashriyya* was the inheritance left when a person died and left no heir, whether through a blood relation (*qarāba*), marriage (*nikāḥ*) or having freed male slaves (*walā'*), which are the three categories entitled to inherit by Islamic law, as governed by its conditions. *Al-Mawārīth al-ḥashriyya* also included the inheritance that remained after the existing heirs had received their legitimate shares. Al-Maqrīzī explains that *al-mawārīth al-ḥashriyya* during the Fatimid era were handled differently, since their doctrine allowed the allocation ofall of the remaining money to blood relatives or to a single surviving daughter, for example. He adds that in the Ayyubid and Mamluk eras, however, such inheritance was assigned to the Public Treasury (*bayt al-māl*): this money was managed by the wazir's office, which was not necessarily done in a fair manner. Al-Qalqashandī mentions that the management of *al-mawārīth al-ḥashriyya* was divided into two sections: the capital, that is Cairo and Fustat, and all that is outside it. The capital's section was a directorate (*jiha*) under the wazir's office, whose supervisor (*nāẓir*) was appointed by an official sultanic decree (*tawqīʿ*). This supervisor was aided by a number of employees, such as managers (*mubāshirūn*), a scribe and witnesses. Normally, the scribe wrote a detailed account of the men, women and children, Muslim, Jew and Christian, in Cairo and Miṣr who died each day. Copies of these accounts were sent to the wazir'soffice, the Bureau of Supervision and the State Comptroller (*mustawfī al-dawla*). The revenue of the capital's section was taken to the Public Treasury and could be used to pay for regular state salaries or the like. As for the section of *al-mawārīth al-ḥashriyya* outside the capital, it had its own *mubāshirūn*, who collected the monies and delivered them to the sultanic bureau (al-Qalqashandī, *Ṣubḥ*, Vol. 3, 464; al-Maqrīzī, *Khiṭaṭ*, Vol. 1, 318; Sayyid, *Nuzha*, 92 n. 3; al-Baqli, *Ta'rīf*, 334–5).

mawrada

The place that the water reaches or the road to a water source. People used such places on the Nile and the canals to get water.

maydān *(pl.* mayādīn*)*

"Field", "square", "arena". Any stretch of open space used for the congregation or assembly of people or military units.

maẓālim *(sing.* maẓlamaor ẓalāma*)*

Maẓlama means "the violation of someone's rights and referred to grievances or petitions. Muslim jurisprudents use the term to mean an act of injustice or corruption of the state, which cannot be ruled on by ordinary judges and has to be raised to the highest authority" (al-Baqli, *Ta'rīf*, 314). The highest authority in this case means the caliph, the sultan or anyone acting in their place.

Men of the Turban

See *muta'ammimīn*.

miḍa'a

Ablution area: ablution is a washing ritual that is done before prayers. A *miḍa'a* is the washing area in a mosque which accommodates this ritual.

mihmandār

"Chief of Protocol": al-Qalqashandī explains that this term was derived from two Persian words: *mihman*, which means "visitor" and *dār*, which means "holder of"; that is the official who managers the visitors. In Mamluk times, the holder of this office received the ambassadors, messengers and the Arab Bedouins who arrived to meet the sultan, hosted them at Dār al-Ḍiyāfa ("House of Hospitality", the guest house) and supervised all matters pertaining to them (al-Qalqashandī, *Ṣubḥ*, Vol. 5, 459; al-Baqli, *Ta'rīf*, 334; Ashour, *'Aṣr*, 478).

*mihrab (*miḥrāb*)*

A niche or a flat carving on the wall or the columns of a mosque that indicates the direction of prayers (*qibla*), which is towards the Ka'ba in Mecca.

mihtār

"Superintendent": *mihtār* was originally a Persian word and is used to refer to the chief of something or the best at something (al-Baqli, *Ta'rīf*, 333;Ashour, *'Aṣr*, 478; Dahman, *Mu'jam*, 146).

minbar

The pulpit on which the sermon-giver stands or sits to address the congregation and be clearly heard and seen. It is normally placed next to the mihrab.

mindīl (pl. manādīl)

Mindīl means "kerchief" and is used to refer to turban-cloth, handkerchief, napkin or tablecloth. The *mindīl* was a piece of the royal or elite costume and was wrapped as a turban. Wazir al-Afḍal is said to have had 100 outfits (*badla*), each having a *mindīl* of matching colour (Sayyid, *Nuzha*, 155–6 n. 4; Qaddumi, *Gifts*, 261 n. 4).

minṭaqa *(also* minṭaq; *pl.* manāṭiq*)*

A kind of a waist belt or strap, usuallymade of gold or silver and sometimes made of cloth or leather (Ashour, *'Aṣr*, 478).

mīqāt

'Ilm al-mīqāt ("science of time keeping") was an established astronomical science in the medieval Islamic world. It was used to determine the times of the daily prayers, and the hours of day and night. For religious purposes, the muezzin (*mu'adhdhin*) may have confirmed the prayer times "with an astrolabe, or a professional astronomer called a *muwaqqit* could be hired. At the popular level, the hours of night could be determined by anybody who knew some astrology by looking at the lunar mansions; in daytime, by measuring the length of one's own shadow – and there were twenty or more methods of how to do this." Scholars developed "prayer-tables for each latitude", and the "muezzins were enjoined to use astronomical tables for determining prayer times and the astrolabe for finding the *qibla*" (Glick, "Islamic Technology", 34).

mithāl *(pl.* mithālāt*)*

A brief, preliminary decree issued from the Army Bureau to "grant, reallocate, return, or increase" an *iqṭā'*. It was signed by the sultan then the *ḥājib* delivered it to the Mamluk granted the *iqṭā'*, who kissed the floor in gratitude. The *mithāl* was then returned to the Army Bureau to be kept there. The term also sometimes applied to written petitions (*qiṣaṣ*) (Ashour, *'Aṣr*, 361–2, 468; Dahman, *Mu'jam*, 135; al-Qalqashandī, *Ṣubḥ*, Vol. 13, 153).

mithqāl *(pl.* mathāqīl*)*

The *mithqāl* was a term meaning "weight", whether big or small, but mostly applied to small weights. It was used to refer to the *dīnār* (a monetary coin), during the Umayyad era, when it was equivalent to one unit of gold (4.25 grams) (al-Baqli, *Ta'rīf*, 297).

mu'āmala *(pl.* mu'āmalāt*)*

Financial dealings of all kinds. This includes money, coinage, measurements (volumes, areas and weights), land, cloth, prices and anything related to monetary and financial transactions. Al-Qalqashandī dedicates one section of *Ṣubḥ al-A'shā* to a detailed description of all kinds of such transactions, dividing them into three main categories: coinage, measurements and prices (al-Qalqashandī, *Ṣubḥ*, Vol. 3, 440–47).

mubāshir *(pl.* mubāshirūn *or* mubāshirīn*)*

"Manager", "conductor" or "overseer": the *mubāshirīn* were administrative employees of the Mamluk state, who like the *kuttāb* ("scribes"), enjoyed a better social status than the rest of the public and many of them earned money illegally from the bureaus, in addition to their salaries. They were also occasionally subjected to confiscation of property and humiliation in the Mamluk era (al-Battawi, *'Imāma*, 31–2; Dahman, *Mu'jam*, 134; Ashour, *'Aṣr*, 468).

mudarris

"Teacher": teaching establishments spread throughout Egypt in the Mamluk era, and they were not restricted to madrasas, for the mosques and the Sufi establishments were also learning centres. The sultan appointed the senior teachers at major madrasas, whilethe rest of the teachers were appointed according to the stipulations of the endower of each establishment. Brilliant students assisted their teachers either through repeating and facilitating the lessons to the learners (*al-mu'īd*, "the repeater") or through conducting further research for more benefit (*al-mufīd*, "the beneficial" or "the helpful"). The schools had their jurists, reciters responsible for teaching the proper recitations; sheikhs, who taught the Prophet's traditions (*Ḥadith*); Qur'an reciters; religious singers of the Prophet's praise; librarians and other officials. Both men and women attended these lessons at the religious establishments and assemblies, although in separate sections and using separate exits (al-Battawi, *'Imāma*, 78–9).

al-mudawwara

"The round one": a table that is sometimes described as a wooden table, smaller than the bigger table called *sufra*. *Al-mudawwara* is a term that also had other meanings in the Mamluk era, such as a kind of a round seat or chair,the centre of the main space or wall of the audience hall (*majlis*) where the sultan or the amir sits, or the sultan's *mudawwara*, which was one of his big tents that was pitched on travels and ceremonies (Sayyid, *Nuzha*, 213 n. 3;Dahman, *Mu'jam*, 137; Ashour, *'Aṣr*, 469).

muezzin

The muezzin (*mu'adhdhin*) is the man who chants the *adhān* (the call to prayer) five times a day to mark the time for performing the daily prayers and summon the congregation who pray at mosques. He normally chants from the mosque's minaret, but sometimes from the rooftop. The *adhān* has a standard formula, but the Shi'ite formula is a little different from the Sunni one.

mufarraj

A kind of precious cloth that may have been decorated (Marzuq, *Textile*, 95).

muftī dār al-'adl

In the Mamluk era, the *muftī* ("mufti") was a sort of a secondary post or additional task held by religious scholars who worked in several offices such as the judiciary, teaching, being the sheikhs of khanqas and so on. The *iftā'* (the mufti's work) entailed guiding learners, giving religious opinions and advice on how to deal with certain situations, as well as conveying their knowledge to the seekers. There was an independent post of *iftā'*, however, which was *muftī dār al-'adl*. The sultan appointed a muftifor each of the four Sunni schools to attend sessions and councils of the House of Justice, when the sultan sat in audience to look into grievances and see to arbitrations. They were to provide *iftā'* concerning the verdicts if needed. To show their rank in the order of seating, they sat following the *muḥtasib* (al-Battawi, *'Imāma*, 72; al-Qalqashandī, *Ṣubḥ*, Vol. 11, 207).

muftī of the House of Justice

See *muftī dār al-'adl*.

muḥannakūn

See *al-ustādhūn al-muḥannakūn.*

muḥāsaba

The calculation, auditing and adjustment of accounts.

muḥtasib

This office appeared in the late Umayyad era, during the reign of Caliph Hishām b. ʿAbd al-Malik (r. AH 105–25 / AD 724–43). Although many secondary sources translate *muḥtasib* using terms that associate it with inspecting and regulating markets, it entailed thewider remit of "commanding good and preventing vice". The *muḥtasib* was a controller of many aspects of civil life through an authority that placed him somewhere between a judge and a chief of police, with overlaps with the authorities and tasks of both offices.In Islamic history, he was sometimes respected and influential enough to punish the rulers themselves; in other instances his authority was restricted to verbally criticizing them while minding a polite tone in his critique.

The *muḥtasib* was one of the most important officials from the Men of the Turban. The conditions for being appointed to thepost included being learned in jurisprudence, knowledgeable of the rules of *sharīʿa*, and a diligent follower of the traditions of the Prophet. The *muḥtasib* was responsible for controlling and regulating the roads, markets and several other aspects of civil life, according to religious law. He was a sort of a junior judge who passed minor verdicts over general matters that the judge (*qāḍī*) should be spared from having to be troubled with. However, occasionally the positions of both the judge and the *muḥtasib* were given to one man, for the *muḥtasib* was but a quicker judge who decided on violations and executed punishments rapidly.

Due to the wide range of responsibilities of the *ḥisba* during the Mamluk era, it was divided based on areas or specializations. For example, some areas had their *muḥtasib*, such as al-Ḥusayniyya and the Citadel, while some professions had their *muḥtasib* too, such as bread-bakers, tobacco traders and cooks. The general or grand *muḥtasib* most probably supervised all the other *muḥtasib*s or deputies. This position was occupied by men of religion until Sultan al-Mu'ayyad Shaykh (r. AH 815–24 / AD 1412–21) appointed one of his amirs tothis office in AH 816 / AD 1413 and gave him the title of *faqīh* (jurist), to provide him with an undeserved quailification for the job. Since then, the Mamluks competed with the Men of the Turban for the *ḥisba*.

"The *muḥtasib* was one of the most important state officials of the era of the Mamluk sultans, for he was a mediator between rulers and subjects, due to his direct relation with both the sultan and the people." In addition to al-Qalqashandī's explanation of the job and what it entails, al-Maqrīzī, who himself held this position for some time, gave a detailed account of the office, listing some of its conditions and duties. He mentioned that only a highly respected Muslim and a notable *'adl* ("equitable person") would be appointed in this office, since it was a religious service. The *muḥtasib* sat on alternate days at the two main mosques of Cairo and Fustat and was entitled to appointing deputies in Cairo, Fustat and other Egyptian provinces. His deputies went around supervising craftsmen, inspecting food-sellers, such as meat vendors and inquiring who the butcher was, as well as inspecting cooks. They checked roads and made sure that no one was harassing people or illegally occupying road sections. They ensured the commitment of boat owners not to overload their boats for safety concerns and they made sure that porters did not over-burden the beasts that carried loads. They ordered water-sellers to cover water pots with cloths to prevent its pollution and prohibited them from exceeding their assigned water loads or wearing indiscrete clothing. The *muḥtasib*'s deputies also warned the teachers of the *katātīb* (sing. *kuttāb* or *maktab*: "school for little children") not to beat the boys violently or where it might cause fatal injury, and the swimming trainers not to seduce people's children. They were responsible for setting straight whoever cheated in dealings and supervising weights and balances. Chiefs of police and governors were sometimes assigned to help the *muḥtasib* as needed (Abu Zayd, *Ḥisba*, 41, 43, 142–3, 186, 221, 237–8; al-Baqli, *Ta'rīf*, 302–3; al-Battawi, *'Imāma*, 75–6).

mujawwakh

"Decorated with bands" (*jākhāt*).

mujawwama

Jāma, in both Arabic and Persian, means "cup" or "goblet" and was also used to refer to a kind of a pot or vessel made of ceramic, glass or silver. The term also applied to circles as decorative motifs and was sometimes extended to other geometric motifs, such as hexagons. Commonly, the decorative bands of Fatimid textiles were composed of series of such motifs that framed floral or figural drawings (see *ṭirāz*). *Al-Mujawwama* in this context most probably refers to these bands (see Hasan, *Kunūz*, 121–2; Sayyid, *Nuzha*, 190 n. 3; http://www.baheth.info/all.jsp?term=جوم).

munaffir

"Horn player".

munākh *(pl.* munākhāt*)*

The term means "settlement area" and was used to refer to the settlement areas or barns, particularly for camels, as stables are for horses. The Mamluk sultan's *munākhāt* were affiliated to the sultan's stables. *Munākh* may also be used to mean the area where an army or a caravan arrives and camps.

According to Ibn al-Ṭuwayr, the site of *al-munākh al-sa'īd* (the "Fortunate Settlement Area") in the Fatimid era was in al-'Uṭūfiyya, behind the Eastern Palace and beyond the Great House of the Wazir (*dār al-wizāra al-kubrā*) and the barracks (*ḥujar*). This site is today taken up by the area behind the Khanqah of Baybars al-Jāshankīr in Bāb al-Naṣr Street and its extension northwards to al-'Uṭūfiyya Alley in al-Jamāliyya. The site was allocated for the wheat mills that supplied the palaces and included warehouses for wood, iron and other items. He added, in the account copied in part by al-Qalqashandī, that the *munākhāt* contained numerous warehouses or merchandise (*ḥawāṣil*): wood, iron, grain mills, fleet equipment manufactured by the Franks who resided there, flax (*qinnab*), linen, catapults and tar. These settlement areas included houses that were assigned to the Franks, who were numerous and worked in several professions, such as butchers, carpenters, bakers, tailors and kneaders and millers at the bakeries of rations (*jirāyāt*) and the mills. The *munākhāt* had a guardian (*ḥāmī*), who was one of the amirs, an equitable overseer, a witness of the expenses and two other workers who assisted with the tasks and the accounts. Wazir al-Ma'mūn b. al-Baṭā'iḥī added new mills at the *munākhāt* for providing allowances (*rawātib*). Ibn al-Ṭuwayr's account shows the importance of this place in the Fatimid era, since, in addition to wheat for the palaces, it supplied some of the rations, allowances and grants (*iṭlāqāt*) to most of the statesmen. Ibn al-Ṭuwayr also mentions that when the Ayyubids came to power, they made use of a lot of the items stored in that place (Ashour, *'Aṣr*, 477; Ibn al-Ṭuwayr and Sayyid, *Nuzha*, 141–2, 141 n. 2; al-Maqrīzī, *Khiṭaṭ*, Vol. 2, 242; al-Baqli, *Ta'rīf*, 331).

muqaddam *(pl.* muqaddamūn *or* muqaddamīn*)*

"Commander": officer commanding a group of soldiers.

muqaddam al-mamālīk

"Commander of Mamluks": this was the commander who managed the Mamluks for the sultan or the amir and who was normally a *ṭawāshī*. The royal commander of the sultan's Mamluks was usually an amir of the *ṭablakhānāh* rank and had a deputy Amir of Ten. When the sultan rode in procession, this commander rode behind his Mamluks, as if guarding them. The commanders of the sultan's training barracks (*ṭibāq*) at the Citadel were accountable to him, and he supervised all the teachers and trainers of these barracks. He was responsible for all matters of the sultan's Mamluks; supervising them and arbitrating among them; dividing rations, grants and clothing among them; and assigning their positions according to protocol on processions, travel and service (Abdelhamid, *Jaysh*, 49; al-Baqli, *Ta'rīf*, 322; Ashour, 474; Dahman, *Mu'jam*, 142).

muqṭa'ūn *(sing.* muqṭa'*)*

The recipient of the *iqṭā'* and its temporary owner based on the terms of the grant.

murabba'a *(pl.* murabba'āt*)*

"The square-shaped": this was a particular type of document, square in shape and made into two opposite sheets, mostly written in a certain format and used to document matters such as the grants (*iṭlāqāt*) and the *iqṭā'āt*. Al-Qalqashandī refers to the *murabba'a* in his account of the documents allocating the *iqṭā'āt* were written bythe Army Bureau before being submitted to the Chancery Bureau. This particular document was called *al-murabba'a al-jayshiyya* (the army *murabba'a*). In another instance, al-Qalqashandī refers to the *murabba'āt* that may be written from the Wizir's Bureau (*dīwān al-wizāra*) to document the *iṭlāqāt* in the hand of the High Comptroller (*mustawfī al-ṣuḥba*). Al-Baqli, citing one case mentioned by al-Qalqashandī, defines the *murabba'a* as square decrees written on Damascene paper – a kind of paper used at the time – by the managers (*mubāshirūn*) of the Private Bureau (*dīwān al-khāṣṣ*) to document the *iṭlāqāt* (al-Baqli, *Ta'rīf*, 307–8; al-Qalqashandī, *Ṣubḥ*, Vol. 6, 200–202; Vol. 13, 153–5; al-'Umarī, *Masālik* (ed. al-Juburi), Vol. 3, 301 n. 1).

murtaziq *(pl.* murtaziqīn*)*

Those who receive salaries or on-going payments from the state.

muṣallā

The term is derived from *ṣalāt*, which means "prayer" and generally denotes "a place for prayers". It is mostly used to refer to a wide, open area outside city walls, normally "uncovered and bordered by low walls", especially used for the prayers of the two Islamic feasts: 'Īd al-Fiṭr, on occasion of breaking the fasting of the month of Ramadan, and 'Īd al-Aḍḥā, on occasion of offering sacrifice (Sayyid, *Nuzha*, 178 n. 2).

musāmaḥa *(pl.* musāmaḥāt*)*

A term that meant pardoning the taxpayer from paying the amount remaining after the calculation of land taxes was changed from *al-hilālī* system to *al-kharājī* one (Sayyid, *Nuzha*, 90 n. 1).

musaṭṭaḥāt *(sing.* musaṭṭaḥ*)*

A large military ship that carried 500 or more men. It was used by both Muslims and Crusaders in the Middle Ages (Sayyid, *Tafsīr*, 744; Sayyid, *Nuzha*, 95 n. 4; al-Baqli, *Ta'rīf*, 311).

musawwama

Trained, well-bred and branded horses (see Qur'an 3, "The Family of Imrān", 14: http://corpus.quran.com/translation.jsp?chapter=3&verse=14;http://www.baheth.info/all.jsp?term=مسومة).

mushāwara

"Consultation": the Mamluk sultans had a system of consultation through what was known as *majlis al-mashūra* (the Consultation Council). This council included the high amirs and grand state officials, whom the sultans consulted before taking any major decisions. The sultan headed this council and its members were the *atābek* of soldiers (*atābik al-'askar*), the Abbasid caliph, the wazir, the judges of the four Sunni schools and the Amirs of One Hundred, Commanders of Thousands, who were 24 in number. If the sultan was a minor, his guardian (regent) or the Viceroy of the Sultanate (*nā'ib al-salṭana*) headed the council instead. Customarily, the sultan did not address the council himself so as to not to be contradicted in opinion or argued with, out of respect. *Al-Mushīr* (the "consultant"), normally a high amir whose office was called *al-ishāra* (the "consultation"), spoke on the sultan's behalf. The Consultation Council discussed several matters, such as wars and peace treaties, the appointments of viceroys and other grand offices. The sultan was, however, not obliged to consult this council for he was an absolute ruler who had the right to take independent decisions on all matters (Ashour, *'Aṣr*, 364, 412; al-Qalqashandī, *Ṣubḥ*, Vol. 11, 153–6).

mustakhdamīn ***(sing.*** **mustakhdam*)***

"The employed": a general term that referred to the employees of the state. In the case of Mamluks, the *mustakhdamīn*, were those who came to serve the sultan not through being purchased but acquired, since they were the forces of a previous sultan (*qarāniṣa*) or an amir (*sayfiyya*) (Abdelhamid, *Jaysh*, 49–50).

al-musta'riba

"The Arabized": those of non-Arab origins, also known as the Arabs of the North, the Arabs of Hijaz, or the Ismā'īliyya Arabs. These were situated in the middle of the Jazira and from the Hijaz to the desert of the Levant. The differences between the original Arabs (*al-'āriba*) and the Arabized (*al-musta'riba*) were due to the natural environment, social norms, language, religion, as well as other factors (Hammuda, *Tārīkh*, 39–40).

al-mustaṣna'ūn ***(also*** **al-muṣṭana'ūn** ***or*** **al-muṣṭana'a*)***

Al-Mustaṣna'ūn were those under a particular system of patronage. The term is often translated as "protégés". The meanings of *iṣṭinā'* include "adopting", "taking up" or "employing", as well as bestowing charity. In the Fatimid era, "the institution of patronage was a powerful instrument linking masters and protégés among free-born people; master to their slaves and freedmen; individuals as well as groups. The conferring of patronage on an individual or a whole group was a public act, and those on whom it was bestowed were referred to as being under patronage" (Lev, *State and Society*, 87). When used to denote "whole groups of eunuchs", the term was uncertain, and Y. Lev concludes that it probably indicated that they were allowed to bear arms (Lev, *State and Society*, 88) (Lev, *State and Society*, 87–8; Sanders, *Ritual*, 91, 166; al-Maqrīzī, *Itti'āẓ*, Vol. 2, 10; al-Maqrīzī, *Khiṭaṭ*, Vol. 2, 254–5; Ibn Taghrī Birdī, *Nujūm*, Vol. 4, 94–5; http://www.baheth.info/all.jsp?term=اصطناع).

mustawfī

"Comptroller": one type of *mustawfī* performed an administrative financial function in the bureaus. In this case, the *mustawfī* managed the accounts of his bureau, ensuring their accuracy, and collected the monies due to the state. He was also responsible for communicating what was due for collection to the head of the bureau and drawing attention to new resources that could provide money for the benefit of the bureau. He was accountable for any delays or neglect in the collection of the moneies. "Due to the importance of this job, its holder was termed *quṭb al-dīwān* (the "bureau's pole") since he managed its daily tasks as well as monitored its employees." It also seems that there were holders of this title who were not directly concerned with financial tasks (al-Baqli, *Ta'rīf*, 210; Ashour, *'Aṣr*, 470).

mutaʿammimīn *(also* ahl al-ʿimāma*)*

Al-muta'ammimīn, which means "those wearing turbans" or "Men of the Turban", "were the religious scholars, scientists, men of literature and writers, also referred to as 'the Men of the Pen'" in Mamluk society. "These men worked in administrative, religious and educational jobs." The terms used to refer to these men are a little misleading for they seem to suggest that they were the only ones who wore turbans. In fact, Egyptian men of all levels wore some sort of head cover, but the *muta'ammimīn* wore large turbans that increased in size according to their status. Some of them exaggerated the sizes of their turbans so much that we find itmentioned in the sources.The *muta'ammimīn* was an important social stratum, who came secondonly to the ruling Mamluk class (al-Battawi, *'Imāma*, 3–4).

Al-mutammar

An unidentified kind of valuable cloth. Al-Qalqashandī's account says: "*mumawwaj bi-l-dhahab wa yu'raf dhalik bi-l-mutammar* (undulated with gold [that is, according to Mayer, "with a pattern of wavy lines"] which is known as *al-mutammar*)". Mayer notes that only al-ʿUmarī and the sources copying him, like al-Qalqashandī, use the term *al-mutammar*. Other sources mention another term, namely, *al-muthmin*, which may be translated as "the precious". In the absence of diacritics, *al-muthmin* may also be read *al-muthamman*, which may be translated as "the highly evaluated" or "the highly valued". Another form of the term is *al-muthammar*, which is also unidentified (Mayer, *Costume*, 15, 58; al-ʿUmarī, *Masālik* (ed. Abbas), Vol. 3, 467; al-ʿUmarī, *Masālik* (ed. al-Juburi), Vol. 3, 318 n. 8; al-Qifṭī, *Akhbār*, 257; Marzuq, *Textile*, 59;

http://www.baheth.info/all.jsp?term=مثمر; http://www.baheth.info/all.jsp?term=مثمن).

mutaṣaddirīn

Al-mutaṣaddirīn bi-l-jawāmiʿ ("presiders at the congregational mosques"): al-Qalqashandī lists the *taṣdīr* among the religious offices and explains that it entailed sitting at the centres of councils or assemblies (*ṣadr al-majlis*) of mosques or similar institutions to interpret verses of the Qur'an and provide further religious explanations (al-Qalqashandī, *Ṣubḥ*, Vol. 11, 251).

mutawallī

Mutawallī may be translated as "director" or "administrative governor". The *mutawallī* of a bureau was an important governmental position, hierarchically beneath the *nāẓir* ("supervisor") and above the *mustawfī* ("comptroller" or "financial administrator") (Ahmad, *Ittiʿāẓ*, Vol. 3, 126 n. 4).

muwashshaḥa

"Ornamented": the term bears the general meaning of ornamentation, but also possibly refers to adornment with two colours or with decorative bands. A *wishāḥ* is a sash or scarf and *muwashshaḥa* also has the meaning of being decorated with a sash. It is, therefore, possible that in this case, the ornamentation of the costume was with coloured bands (see Hasan, *Kunūz*, 121–2; Sanders, *Ritual*, 88; http://www.baheth.info/all.jsp?term=موشح)

muwwaqiʿ al-ḥukm

The *muwwaqiʿ al-ḥukm* ("verdict signer") or *kātib al-qāḍī* ("judge's scribe") was an assistant to the *qāḍī*. *Muwwaqiʿ al-ḥukm* attended the judge's council to copy the court verdicts so as to announce them to the public, record them and execute them. He had to have an excellent knowledge of the language and be well-informed of the meanings and significances of the colloquial and classical words and terms. Knowing colloquial terminologies and expressions was essential to ensure that the signer or scribe would express the exact meanings intended by the adversaries or witnesses. In the Mamluk era, the holders of the post of verdict signer were later entitled to be promoted to the office of *nāʾib al-qāḍī* ("deputy judge"), then to the office of chief judge, if they had the required qualifications. They also contributed to other work fields, such as education and Sufism (al-Battawi, *'Imāma*, 67).

N

nabl

The *nabl* were the arrows particularly used with Arabian bows (al-Qalqashandī, *Ṣubḥ*, Vol. 2, 135).

nadd muthallath

Nadd was a composite paste used as perfume or incense and made by mixing several ingredients in specific proportions, using certain preparation methods.The final product came out in a variety of shapes, sometimes as necklaces or rosaries. According to al-Nuwairī (d. AH 733 / AD 1333), whom al-Qalqashandī copies, in his time, the Egyptians referred to *nadd* as "amber", using "raw amber" to refer to the amber itself. *Al-nadd al-muthallath* (the "tripled incense") was the finest and strongest type of *nadd* made in Egypt. It was composed of three kinds of amber, oud and musk.It was a soft paste that was put in pockets, used for incense, and the like (al-Nuwayrī, *Nihāya*, Vol. 12, 60–69; al-Qalqashandī, *Ṣubḥ*, Vol. 2, 119; Sanders, *Ritual*, 71).

nafṭ

The Arabic term for either naphtha, Greek fire, or gunpowder (see Irwin, "Gunpowder", 120–21). The term carries some ambiguity and it can either mean gunpowderor a flamable mixture.

nāḥiya

See *nawāḥī*.

al-nā'ib al-kāfil

"Plenipotentiary viceroy": the holder of this position had a similar authority to the Mamluk sultan and frequently replaced the sultan after his demise or deposition. He had the power to sign all the official documents that the sultan normally signed and the kingdom's viceroys corresponded with him concerning the same issues that they needed to consult the sultan on. *Al-nā'ib al-kāfil* had the authority to employ soldiers without conferring with the sultan, as well as appoint high officials, such as the wazir and the Confidential Scribe (*kātib al-sirr*), and the sultan only rarely rejected his nominations (al-Baqli, *Ta'rīf*, 345; Dahman, *Mu'jam*, 149).

naqd

Gold or silver coins (http://www.baheth.info/all.jsp?term=نقد; http://www.almaany.com/home.php?language=arabic&lang_name=عربي&word=نقد&type_word=0).

naqib *(pl.* nuqabā'*)*

"Chief of a sect": captain or corporal. The Mamluk *nuqabā'* provided minor services to the sultan or amir (Ashour, *'Aṣr*, 481; Dahman, *Mu'jam*, 152).

naqqārāt *(sing.* naqqāra*)*

This was similar to a kettle-drum. It was particularly used in wars to announce permission to start combat (Ibn Taghrī Birdī and Shams, *Nujūm*, Vol. 4, 86, n. 1; Ibn al-Ṭuwayr, *Nuzha*, 151).

naṣāfī *(sing.* niṣfiyya*)*

A kind of fine cloth made of silk or linen. The term was also used to a type of clothes made of rough cotton (Ashour, *'Aṣr*, 481; al-Baqli, *Ta'rīf*, 347).

nawāfij (sing. nāfija*)*

"Musk jar" (http://www.baheth.info/all.jsp?term=نافجة).

nawāḥī *(sing.* nāḥiya*)*

"Districts": *nāḥiya*, *qarya* and *balad* (also *bilda*) were terms that were used interchangeably in Egypt after the Islamic conquest to refer to the administrative and fiscal division equivalent to a "village". A Coptic historical source (AH 483/AD 1090) that surveyed the villages of Egypt used the term *nāḥiya* to mean village (*bilda*), while *kafr* was used to denote a hamlet that was affiliated to the village. The cadastral survey that was carried out in AH 697 / AD 1298, in the reign of Sultan Ḥusām al-Dīn Lājīn (r. AH 695–7 / AD 1296–8), which is known as *al-rawk al-Ḥusāmī* showed that these hamlets had by the time developed into fiscal districts (*nawāḥī*), which means that they came to have affiliated agricultural lands (Ramzi, *Qāmūs*, Vol. 1, 5, 12, 19–22).

nāẓir

"Supervisor": *nāẓir* was a term used to denote a supervisory role, depending on the function it was associated with. This role may have entailed overseeing money and expenditures, reviewing accounts and similar tasks. The *nāẓir* was primarily responsible for all the tasks of the bureau and all its subordinates were accountable to him. His official signature was necessary on all the documents produced by the bureau; he was answerable for all its financial dealings and kept all its financial data (al-Baqli, *Ta'rīf*, 341).

naẓir al-buyūt wa-l-ḥāshiya

"Supervisor of the Warehouses and Entourage", also Supervisor of the Warehouses (*nāẓir al-buyūt*): one of the administrative posts usually taken up by Men of the Pen or Men of the Turban (*muta'ammimūn*) in the Mamluk era. The holder of this office participated with the Master Supervisor of the Warehouses (*ustādār*), who was a Man of the Sword, in managing all the sultan's "warehouses", which included the kitchen, the House of Drinks (*sharāb khānāh*), the entourage and the slave-boys (*ghilmān*). Like the other supervisors (*nuẓẓār*) of the bureaus, he was aided by several clerks, such as the deputy supervisor of the bureau (*ṣāḥib al-dīwān*); the witness (*shāhid*); the comptroller (*mustawfī*); the teller or cashier (*ṣayrafī*) (al-Baqli, *Ta'rīf*, 342; al-Battawi, *'Imāma*, 31; Dahman, *Mu'jam*, 103).

naẓir al-dawla

"Supervisor of the State": one of the Men of the Turban of the Mamluk era whose post was also termed *al-ṣuḥba al-sharīfa* (the "Honourable Assistant") and *nāẓir al-nuẓẓār* ("Supervisor of Supervisors", meaning chief supervisor). He shared the authority of the wazir and his power of signature, for he signed the documents after the wazir's signature. If the wazir was a Man of the Sword, *nāẓir al-dawla* managed the financial matters, and the wazir was responsible for supervision and implementation. If the wazir was absent or his position was void, *nāẓir al-dawla* performed his tasks, such as collecting money from the Inspector of Bureaus (*shādd al-dawāwīn*) and allocating it to the proper channels of expenditures and costs. *Nāẓir al-dawla* had assistants, headed by the High Comptroller (*mustawfī al-ṣuḥba*), who participated in all the tasks of concern in both Egypt and Syria and wrote decrees for the sultan to sign. Next in hierarchy to *mustawfī al-ṣuḥba* was the State Comptroller (*mustawfī al-dawla*), who also participated in locating money assets and expenditures. The post of *nāẓir al-dawla* was important because it was one of the higher stages of the administrative hierarchy of the Men of the Turban on the way to the post of wazir. *Nāẓir al-dawla* was no different from the wazir who was also a Man of the Pen, the Private Supervisor (*nāẓir al-khāṣṣ*) or the Supervisor of the Army (*nāẓir al-jaysh*), for all of them worked in the financial state administration and many men who were appointed in these offices from the Men of the Turban were Copts or other Christians. *Nāẓir al-dawla* was a high-ranking and lucrative office, which sometimes also led to deposition, confiscation of property and punishment that occasionally involved the death penalty. However, this position's rank deteriorated in the late Mamluk era and it was held by ordinary men (al-Battawi, *'Imāma*, 29).

nāẓir al-jaysh

"Supervisor of the Army Bureau": this was one of the positions of the Men of the Turban in the Mamluk state which was inherited from the Ayyubid administrative system and entailed handling the *iqṭā'āt* allocated to soldiers. During the Mamluk era, the Supervisor of the Army Bureau became responsible for all the *iqṭā'āt* of Egypt and Syria. He consulted the sultan on their matters, managed the military salaries, and kept count of the number of soldiers for purposes of knowing their wages or their capacity for war. A group of clerks assisted him, such as the deputy supervisor of the Army Bureau (*ṣāḥib dīwān al-jaysh*) and the deputy supervisor of the Bureau of Mamluks (*ṣāḥib dīwān al-mamālīk*) and their scribes and witnesses. *Nāẓir al-jaysh* had to have certain qualities, such as knowledge, honesty and good management of soldiers. He had to be respected by the sultan and be notable and esteemed. If he was of strong character, he enjoyed a lofty status and an absolute authority during the Mamluk era. Many of the Men of the Turban sought this office, even with bribery, and several of them held it in addition to other posts, especially posts like Superivisor of the Private Bureau (*naẓar al-khāṣṣ*) and wazir. This multi-tasking was not odd, since these posts were of a similar nature. Holders of such posts were known for their power and cunning. *Nāẓir al-jaysh* was wealthy, as was customary for other financial officers of the state throughout the Mamluk era (al-Battawi, *'Imāma*, 26–7).

nāẓir al-māl *(also* nāẓir bayt al-māl*)*

"Supervisor of the Public Treasury", who, in the Mamluk era, was one of the Men of the Turban. He supervised the revenue from Egypt and Syria that was submitted to the Public Treasury (*bayt al-māl*) at the Citadel, the treasury's expenditures and all its financial matters. He was one of the most dignified state employees and he headed a number of tellers, witnesses and clerks. Only a man of piety and knowledge was appointed in this post. The treasury disappeared by the beginning of the eight century AH / fifteenth century AD, after the major economic problems that occurred then (al-Baqli, *Ta'rīf*, 341; al-Battawi, *'Imāma*, 30–31).

nimjāh *(also* nimshāh *or* nimsha*)*

"Dagger": an Arabized Persian word that is used to refer to "a curved dagger that resembles a small sword" or a small or elegant sword that the sultan or the viceroy keeps next to him to for protection against assassination attempts (al-Baqli, *Ta'rīf*, 352; Dahman, *Mu'jam*, 152).

P

plenipotentiary viceroy

See *al-nā'ib al-kāfil*.

presiders

See *mutaṣaddirīn*.

private guards

See *ṣibyān al-khāṣṣ*.

Q

qā'a

"Hall".

qabā' *(pl.* aqbiya*)*

An overgarment, like a caftan, that by the Mamluk era had tight sleeves and were either white or coloured with alternating red and blue stripes (Ashour, *'Aṣr*, 460; Dahman, *Mu'jam*, 121).

al-qabā' al-islāmī

"Islamic coat": It appears that there is no exact definition for this coat, except that it had distinctive tailoring. Al-Qalqashandī mentions in another context that *al-aqbiya al-islāmiyya* may have tight sleeves (al-ʿUmarī, *Masālik* (ed. al-Juburi), Vol. 3, 291 n. 3; al-Qalqashandī, *Ṣubḥ*, Vol. 4, 381).

al-qabā' al-tatarī

See *al-aqbiya al-tatariyya*.

qāḍī (pl. quḍāt)

The *qāḍī* (judge) was the authority responsible for "resolving disputes among individuals and groups according to the stipulations of the Islamic *sharī'a* (religious law)" (al-Battawi, *'Imāma*, 46).

qāḍī al-'askar

"Military Judge": the holder of this position in the Mamluk era was one of the Men of the Turban who specialized in the matters of military personnel and only had authority over them. He arbitrated the cases of conflicts between the military personnel and civilians.The Military Judge had a clerk to assist him, especially in finding equitable witnesses to assign from the soldiers, which was not an easy task according to some sources. The office of the Military Judge was an old and supreme one, which held a higher status in the Ayyubid era than it did under the Mamluks. There was a Military Judge for the Shāfiʿī, the Ḥanafī, and the Mālikī schools, while the Ḥanbalis had a judge only occasionally. The holders of this position attended the councils of the House of Justice along with the chief judges of the four schools, but their order of seating indicated their lesser rank than the chief judges. They normally accompanied the sultan in his travels (al-Battawi, *'Imāma*, 71–2).

qāḍī al-quḍāt

"Judge of Judges", the chief judge: the office of *qāḍī al-quḍāt* was founded in the Fatimid era, during the reign of Caliph al-ʿAzīz; however, it existed before the Fatimids and fell under the authority of the Abbasid Caliphate in Baghdad. The Fatimid *qāḍī al-quḍāt* was an Ismāʿīlī Shi'ite to represent their religious sect, but during the wazirate of Aḥmad b. al-Afḍal, each religious school had its own *qāḍī al-quḍāt*, including Sunni schools, for there was one for the Shāfiʿīs and one for the Mālikis, in addition to two Shi'ite judges: an Imāmi and an Ismāʿīlī (Twelver and Sevener Shi'ites). During the Fatimid era, *qāḍī al-quḍāt* was initially appointed by the caliph, until the time of the powerful Wazirs of Delegation (*tafwīḍ*), when they were the ones who appointed the holders of this office.

In the Ayyubid and Mamluk eras, the sultans appointed the *qāḍī al-quḍāt* and the Mamluk sultans wrote a specific diploma of investiture, offered the judge his official costume of honour and held processions and celebrations on occasion of his appointment.

When Sultan Ṣalāḥ al-Dīn managed to abolish the Fatimid Caliphate and the Shiʿite doctrine in Egypt, he eliminated all Shiʿite systems, including the judiciary order. He had appointed a Sunni *qāḍī* of the Shāfiʿi School, who was termed *qāḍī al-quḍāt*, even when he was still the wazir of the last Fatimid Caliph, al-ʿĀḍid. The chief Shāfiʿī judge appointed deputies in all cities, which remained the case until the end of the Ayyubid era.

The office of *qāḍī al-quḍāt* was the highest judiciary post in the Mamluk era. The early Mamluk state followed the same system of one Shāfiʿi *qāḍī al-quḍāt*. When Sultan al-Ẓāhir Baybars came to power, he introduced a big change in the judiciary system in AH 663 / AD 1265, when he appointed four chief judges to independently represent each of the four Sunni schools of religious interpretation: the Shāfiʿī, the Mālikī, the Ḥanafī and the Ḥanbalī. The chief Shāfiʿi judge continued to have the privilege of supervising the orphans' funds and the trials concerning the Public Treasury.

The chief judge looked into criminal, civil and religious legislative cases. There was an organizational hierarchy that led to the final promotion to this office, which started at the base with the witness (*shāhid*), then the signer (*muwwaqiʿ* or *muwwaqiʿ al-ḥukm*), then the judge's deputy (*nuwwāb al-ḥukm*) in the capital and the provinces, then the office of *qāḍīal-quḍāt*. This hierarchy was not always mandatory, though. The sultan or the high and powerful amirs chose *qāḍī al-quḍāt*, depending on certain considerations and political conditions. He was chosen based on several factors, such as, his reputation as a man of religious knowledge and science, an inheritance of the post from father to son, or the friendly relations between the judge and the men of authority and power. Then the three remaining judges of the Sunnis schools were consulted on who can be their fourth. Some men also reached this position through bribery. The chief Shāfiʿī judge continued to have a higher status throughout the Mamluk era, for most of the population followed the Shāfiʿī school of interpretation (al-Baqli, *Ta'rīf*, 266; al-Battawi, *'Imāma*, 46–8, 51).

al-qalam al-jalīl

Al-qalam al-jalīl means "the dignified pen [script]" and it was considered the most supreme one used for writing documents. It was a term used to refer to a script called *qalam al-ṭūmār* (*ṭūmār* script). *Al-ṭūmār* was a most perfectly cut type of paper and this script was attributed to it. *Al-qalam al-jalīl* or *qalam al-ṭūmār* was an official enlarged type of the Thuluth script, one of the main cursive Arabic scripts (al-Qalqashandī, *Ṣubḥ*, Vol. 3, 53–5, 62; Vol. 6, 194–5).

qalam al-tawqī'

Qalam al-tawqī' was a particular script that the caliphs and wazirs used to sign the grievances. *Al-tawqi' bi-l-qalam al-daqīq*, means "signing with the fine pen", which is writing or signing in the fine or small font of the script (see al-Qalqashandī, *Ṣubḥ*, Vol. 3, 104).

qanā *(sing.* qanāt*)*

Qanāt which also means "canal", were lances that had hollow posts, like cylindrical tubes, ending in pointed teeth. Al-Qalqashandī, however, mentions that their bodies were made of canes or reeds, which have blocked interiors (i.e. not hollow) and which grew in India, then were exported to al-Khaṭṭ in Bahrain, from where they reached the rest of the Arab world. In another instance, A-Qalqashandī refers to the *qanā*, which is a plant that grows in Ethiopia, where the canes or reeds are either hollow or blocked.In this later instance, however, al-Qalqashandī makes no connection of the plant with lances (http://www.baheth.info/all.jsp?term=قنا; Gamal al-Din, *Dawla*, 262; Sayyid, *Tafsīr*, 702; al-Qalqashandī, *Ṣubḥ*, Vol. 2, 133–4; Vol. 5, 306).

qanādīl *(sing.* qindīl*)*

"Lanterns".

qānāt *(sing.* qān, *also* khāqān*)*

"Khans" the *qān* is the "chief" or the "master" in Tartar society. *Al-Qān* was a royal title used for the king of China and was stamped on the Mongol coins as title of their kings (Dahman, *Mu'jam*, 120; al-Basha, *Alqāb*, 423).

qanṭara *(pl.* qanāṭir*)*

A bridge that stands on an arched vault.

qarabūs *(pl.* qarābīs*)*

The pommel of the saddle: a small piece of wood at the front and the rear parts of the saddle (Mayer, *Costume*, 50; Maged, *Nuẓum*, Vol. 1, 176; Abu Zayd, *Ḥisba*, 116 n. 19).

qarāfa

"Cemetery": The name *al-Qarāfa* originally did not denote a cemetery, but the lesser and bigger cemeteries bearing this name got it from one of the clans of al-Maʿāfir tribe who were called Banū Qarāfa and had a neighbourhood (*khaṭṭ*) there.The present connotation of *qarāfa* with any burial ground was not found in the works of al-Maqrīzī and contemporaneous historians. Words such as *maqābir* or *madāfin* were rather used to generally mean a cemetery (Hamza, *Cemetery*, 20; al-Maqrīzī, *Khiṭaṭ*, Vol. 3, 642, 646–7).

Qarmatians

The Qarmatians (*c.* AH 272–471 / AD 886–1078) were a radical Shi'ite dynasty that emerged from the Ismaʿīlī sect. They started in the Syrian Desert and Iraq then moved to eastern Arabia.Although they were Ismaʿīlī Shi'ites, they did not follow the Fatimid caliphs. They are most remembered in Islamic history for seizing the Black Stone from the Ka'ba in Mecca in AH 317 / AD 930, in defiance of the reverence of an object. The Black Stone is an honoured object from the pre-Islamic era, believed to be traceable to Prophet Ibrāhīm (Abraham), and is located at the corner of the Ka'ba, where it marks the start and end of the circumambulation of it. Prior to the revelation of Islam, the Ka'ba was being restored after a fire, when a heated argument arose concerning who was to have the honour of replacing this stone. The judgement was left to Prophet Muhammad, who wisely suggested putting the stone on a piece of cloth, to be held by the all the representatives of the tribes, and carried over to the Ka'ba, where he held the stone and inserted it there. The Qarmatians only agreed to return the stone about 20 years later upon the pleading of the Fatimid Caliph al-Manṣūr (r. AH 334–41 / AD 946–53) of the Maghribi Fatimids.

The Qarmatians "grew more moderate in tone towards the end of the tenth century, and their principality evolved into something like a republic, with a council of elders" (Bosworth, *Islamic Dynasties*, 94–5).

qarqalāt *(sing.* qarqal*)*

A brigandine made of iron plates that were attached or riveted together. This was a common type of armour used in the Mamluk era, and its best fit was to be neither too tight nor too loose. Its sleeves had to be made of small units so as to allow easy movement. In a non-military context, *qarqal* was sometimes used to refer to a kind of shirt worn by women or a sleeveless shirt (Yasin, *Asliḥa*, 127–8; al-Qalqashandī, *Ṣubḥ*, Vol. 2, 136; Mayer, *Costume*, 40).

qarqashīn

A robe used to cover the saddle (al-Battawi, *'Imāma*, 136).

qaṣaba

Al-qaṣaba al-Ḥākimiyya was one of two measurement units used to calculate agricultural land area in Egypt, the other being *al-qaṣaba al-Sandafāwiyya*. The first and more commonly used unit was attributed to the the Fatimid Caliph al-Ḥākim, in whose reign it was introduced, while the second unit was attributed to the town of Ṣandafā, near al-Maḥalla al-Kubrā, and was only used in some of the Lower Egypt governorates. Four hundred *qaṣaba Ḥākimiyya* make one *feddan* (al-Baqli, *Ta'rīf*, 274). It was also the main axial avenue, an urban part or major section of a city. In western Islamic lands (Andalucia, Morocco and Tunisia), *qasaba* refers to the citadel of the city.

qaṭīʿa (pl. qaṭā'iʿ)

A segment of land, ward.

al-qātūl

Al-qātūl was the large tent also known as *khaymat al-faraj* (the "Tent of Wideness/ Comfort") or *khaymat al-faraḥ* (the "Tent of Happiness"). Some historians agree that it was first made at the time of Wazir al-Afḍal, while al-Maqrīzī mentions more than once that it was made for Caliph al-ʿAzīz. Ibn al-Ma'mūn informs us that when al-Afḍal first made this tent, he called it *khaymat al-faraj*, but it later came to be known as *al-qātūl* because two caretakers were killed while pitching it. In another instance, we are informed that whenever it was pitched, it killed one or two men. Consequently, servants and caretakers hated having to pitch it and the process was only executed in the presence of engineers. With time, only parts of it were pitched: these formed the large hall, passageways and a surrounding border (Ibn al-Ma'mūn and Sayyid, *Nuṣūṣ*, 55–6, 55 n. 1, 102–3; al-Maqrīzī, *Khiṭaṭ*, Vol. 2, 186–7; al-Maqrīzī, *Itti'āẓ*, Vol. 2, 287–8; al-Nuwayrī, *Nihāya*, Vol. 28, 285).

qawālib *(sing.* qālab *or* qālib*)*

Has several meanings, one of which is "shoe" or "wooden shoe", and is used by al-Qalqashandī to refer to horseshoes (http://www.baheth.info/all.jsp?term=قالب).

qawāwīr *(sing.* qawwāra*)*

A textile cover for food trays that was around the *shadda* (bundle) or was used itself as the *shadda* (Ibn al-Ṭuwayr and Sayyid, *Nuzha*, 129, 145–6 n.1, 170).

qaysāriyya *(pl.* qayāsir *and* qaysāriyyāt*)*

"Caravanserai", covered market. The terms *qaysāriyya*, *khān* and *wikāla* (also *wakāla*) were used to refer to caravanserais that housed merchants and their merchandise.The *qaysāriyya* originally denoted a closed or "covered market for trading luxury items" (al-Sayyad, *Cairo*, 143). The Mamluk *wikāla* comprised residential floors around a central courtyard, where the ground floor contained shops or storerooms for merchandise, as well as spaces for the beasts of burden (al-Sayyad, *Cairo*, 142–3; Raymond, *Cairo*, 387).

qibla

The direction of prayers, towards the Ka'ba in Mecca, is called the *qibla*, which, in Egypt, is to the southeast. To establish it accurately in a mosque, geographical calculations are required.

qīrāṭ *(pl.* qarārīṭ*)*

A unit of measurement that is a twenty-fourth of a whole. In measuring areas, each 24 carats equals one *feddan* (4,200 m^2). The term was also used to refer to a Fatimid coin.

qirṭās

Al-Qalqashandī explains that the *qirṭās* is the *kāghad* ("paper cone") and cites an earlier scholar who mentions that the *qirṭās* was a *kāghad* made of Egyptian papyri (al-Qalqashandī *Ṣubḥ*, Vol. 2, 474).

qisiy al-lawlab *(sing.* qaws al-lawlab*)*

"Winch-spanned crossbows": large crossbows "spanned [drawn back] with a windlass or winch". They had their own special arrows that were undetectable by the target until hit (Nicolle, *Crusader Warfare*, 91, 247; Maged, *Nuẓum*, Vol. 1; Sayyid, *Dawla*, 703).

qisiy al-rijl wa-l-rikāb

"Crossbows of the foot and stirrups": crossbows that were drawn backby pulling with the hand and supporting with one or both feet (*rijl*), or with the horse's stirrups (*rikāb*). They were mostly used in fleets and coastal forts, since the standard composite bows were not suitable for humid weather, given their need for glue in their manufacture (see Maged, *Nuẓum*, Vol. 1; al-Qalqashandī, *Ṣubḥ*, Vol. 2, 134–5).

qubbāḍ al-laḥm *(sing.* qābiḍ al-laḥm*)*

Recipients of meat rations, those entitled to meat rations (see al-Nuwayrī, *Nihāya*, Vol. 8, 223).

qudūr *(sing.* qidr*)*

"Pots": in his list of travel instruments, al-Qalqshandī defines the *qudūr* as a cooking pot, usually made of copper and sometimes of earthenware. Kings boasted of the number and sizes of these pots, for they showed a king's generosity and the number of his men. He also mentions lead pots that were used for equipping the Mamluk sultan's bath, along with a basin (*ḥawḍ*) on travels (al-Qalqshandī, *Ṣubḥ*, Vol. 2, 131; Vol. 4, 48).

qunṭariyya

Qunṭariyya is derived from a Greek word (*kontarion*). It was a type of short lance made with a beech wood body that ended in short, broad teeth, which looked like an axe (Sayyid, *Nuzha*, 151 n. 2).

qurqūbī *(also* al-furquby *or* al-thurqubī*)*

The *qurqūbī* textile was most probably attributed to Qurqūb, a town in the southwest of present-day Iran, near Ahvaz (al-Aḥwāz) in the Khuzistān region of western Iran. It was located between Basra and Wasit, in eastern Iraq, and Ahvaz, in western Iran.Qurqūb was a centre for textile manufacture that produced embroidered silk cloth and rugs. It hosted an official royal textile manufacture workshop. Arabic dictionaries also define *al-qurqūbī* as a white Egyptian linen cloth used to make robes (Lombard, *Golden Age*, 186; al-Ḥamawī, *Mu'jam*, Vol. 4, 328; http://www.baheth.info/all.jsp?term=قرقوب; http://www.baheth.info/all.jsp?term=فرقب).

qūsh

Possibly a particular piece of cloth that covered the croup or rump, since "posterior" is one of the meanings of the word (http://www.baheth.info/all.jsp?term=قوش).

quṣṣād *(sing.* qaṣid*)*

"Messengers" or "ambassadors".

R

raḥba *(pl.* riḥāb*)*

"Plaza": al-Maqrīzī defines the *raḥba* as "the large space" and adds that it might become occupied by buildings while retaining its name, although its character changed, or it might lose its name and character altogether. In other cases, some buildings might be demolished to leave a *raḥba* in their place. It is assumed that the *riḥāb* were like the squares we have in our modern cities, "and the *riḥāb* of Fustat might have been the meeting points of the streets and alleys of the city" Azab, Fustat, 78; also see Al-Maqrīzī, *Khiṭaṭ*, Vol. 2, 468.

rakʿa *(pl.* rakaʿāt*)*

From the verb *raka'a*, which means "kneel down" or "stoop". It is the repeated act of prayers that consists of standing for Qur'anic recitation, bowing, then prostrating twice, with a sitting between the two prostrations, each motion having particular prayers to be uttered in association with it. Every prayer, whether mandatory or not, has a specific number of *raka'āt*.

al-rammāḥa

"The Lancers": a group of 40 Mamluks headed by an amir, who was their trainer and who was helped by four assistants. They used to wear red costumes that distinguished them. They paraded in front of the sultan, showing their amazing skills with their lances, and the sultan usually bestowed magnificent costumes of honour on them. They invented new ways of performing with the lances every year and mastered this skill superbly. Their performance was an important act in the *dawarān al-maḥmil* celebration, which, although halted for 35 years during the reign of Sultan Qaitbāy (r. AH 872–901 / AD 1468–96), was resumed under Sultan al-Ghawrī (r. AH 906–22 / AD 1501–16), and went on to the end of the Mamluk era (al-Shishtawi, *Mayādīn*, 45–8).

rank *(pl.* runūk*)*

"Blazon": an Arabized word from the Persian *ranq* or *ranj*, meaning colour. It is used to refer to the official blazons used by Mamluk sultans and amirs to display their office. These emblematic symbols existed before the Mamluks, probably since the time of the Zangids. The amirial blazons of the Mamluk era include the cup or goblet (*hannāb*), the symbol of the *sāqī* (the sultan's cupbearer); the penbox (*dawāt*), the symbol of the *dawādār* (chancellor); the lozenge (*buqja*), the symbol of the *jamādār* (wardrobe master) and the *jūkān* (polosticks), symbol of the *jūkāndār* (polo master). Originally, the amirial blazons incorporated single symbols each referring to a particular office. Later, high-ranking amirs of the sultan started using similar blazons with composite symbols of office. The blazon of the sultan was normally all epigraphic and it developed in complexity and calligraphic finesse over the Mamluk era. The *rank* was commonly circular, with divisions (*shaṭfāt*) that included the symbols or inscriptions (see al-Baqli, *Ta'rīf*, 163; Abdelhamid, *Jaysh*, 33–7; Mayer, *Heraldry*, 26).

rashshāshīn *(pl.* rashshāsh*)*

"Sprinklers": "the *rashshāshīn* were the ones who sprinkled water inside and outside the palace" (al-Baqli, *Ta'rīf*, 159).

raṭl *(pl.* arṭāl*)*

Al-Qalqashandī informs us that the Egyptian *raṭl* was a unit of weight used in the capital, that is, Fustat, Cairo and the areas in their proximity. It was equal to 144 dirhams (al-Qalqashandī *Ṣubḥ*, Vol. 3, 445).

rawk

Al-rawk is the Egyptian term used for the cadastral survey of the agricultural land that determined the land taxes (*kharāj*). In the early Islamic eras, these taxes were delivered to the Public Treasury of the caliphate. The expected *kharāj* of Egypt fluctuated depending on the agricultural production and inhabitation of the villages, which is why the cadastral survey was conducted several times, two of them during the Mamluk era. This survey, which sometimes entailed changes in geographical administrative divisions, also served to indicate the value of land and subsequently, the distribution of land grants. The Fatimids had followed the Abbasid custom of occasional distribution of land grants, but the Ayyubids established an *iqṭā'* system, which divided the agricultural lands among the sultan, the amirs and the soldiers, using a particular ratio. This *iqṭā'*system was adopted by the Mamluks, who had their own divisions as well. The first *rawk* in the Mamluk era was conducted during the reign of Sultan Ḥusām al-Dīn Lājīn (r. AH 695–7 / AD 1296–8) and hence called *al-rawk al-Ḥusāmī*, and was probably done because the amirs had overtaken too many of the *iqṭāʿāt*, leaving the soldiers with almost none. The second, *al-rawk al-Nāṣirī*, was conducted during the reign of Sultan al-Nāṣir Muḥammad in AH 715 / AD 1315 (al-Baqli, *Taʿrīf*, 165; S. Ashour, *ʿAṣr*, 443).

ribāṭ *(pl.* ribṭ*)*

See *khānqāh*.

ribāʿ *(sing.* rabʿ*)*

Housing compounds containing rooms or small apartments that were rented to more than one dweller. A governmental official was appointed a guardian of the state's *ribāʿ*. He had to make sure they were wellprotected, ensure their continuous maintenance and upkeep, and collect their monthly rents. He was responsible for delivering the rest of the money remaining from the collected rents after the maintenance expenses were met to the state treasury (Sayyid, *Nuzha*, 93 n. 1).

riding cape

See *ʿibiy al-marākīb*.

the rightly guided caliphs

The term *khalīfa* ("caliph") means "successor [of the Prophet]". The rightly guided caliphs (*al-rāshidūn*) are the four caliphs who succeeded Prophet Muhammad in ruling the Muslim community and nation (*umma*). They are regarded, in Sunni context, as the exemplary pious rulers of Islam, who were chosen through an election system called *al-shūrā* (consultation), where the main Companions of the Prophet represented the Muslim community. All four caliphs were closely related to the Prophet: the first, Abū Bakr al-Ṣiddīq, who ruled from AH 11 / AD 632 to AH 13 / AD 634, was the first adult man to embrace Islam, the Prophet's closest companion and the father of one of his wives, ʿĀ'isha, herself an important and influential figure in Sunni Islam.The second caliph, ʿUmar b. al-Khaṭṭāb, was known for his strong character and the justness of his reign from AH 13 / AD 634 to AH 23 / AD 644. The Prophet prayed for ʿUmar to become a Muslim, which he did, turning into one of early Islam's most powerful figures. Umar's daughter, Ḥafṣa, was also married to the Prophet.ʿUmar was the first caliph to adopt the term *amīr al-mu'minīn* or Prince of the Faithful, meaning their leader or commander. The third caliph was ʿUthmān b. ʿAffān, who was married to two of the Prophet's daughters, for after the first one, Ruqayya, died, he married the second, Umm Kulthūm.ʿUthmān, who was known for his kindness and generosity, ruled from AH 24 / AD 644 to AH 35 / AD 656. The last of the four was ʿAlī b. Abī Ṭālib, the Prophet's cousin and husband of his daughter, Fāṭima, and father to his favoured grandsons, al-Ḥasan and al-Ḥusayn.ʿAlī was the first boy to embrace Islam and he joined the Muslim army at a young age. He was known for his valour, wisdom, and his most eloquent language skills. ʿAlī ruled from AH 35 / AD 656 to AH 40 / AD 661. Shi'ite Muslims believe that the caliphate should have been given to ʿAlī after the Prophet's demise and that it should have remained in his line of descent.

rikābiyya

"Equestrian escorts" or "mounted escorts" who rode alongside the caliph. *Rikāb* is the stirrups. In the same context, al-Qalqashandī uses the term *rikābiyya*, while Ibn al-Ṭuwayr uses *ṣibyān al-rikāb* ("equestrian guards"), also known as *ṣibyān al-rikāb al-khāṣṣ* ("private equestrian guards"), who were more than 1,000 or 2,000 men with 12 commanders (*muqaddamīn*). In the early Fatimid state, *ṣibyān al-rikāb* were called *al-sa'diyya* and were around 100 men responsible for joining the caliph as he rode on processions. They carried ornamented swords, and, in the time of Caliph al-Ḥākim, they started being responsible for executions ordered by the caliph (Sanders, *Ritual*, 228; Ibn al-Ṭuwayr and Sayyid, *Nuzha*, 124, 148, n. 1, 165 n. 1).

riwāq *(pl.* arwiqa*)*

"Corridor", "aisle" or "arcade": the term has more than one meaning in Islamic architecture. It is used to refer to one of the four hypostyle halls that form a courtyard mosque plan, a corridor of columns within a hypostyle plan, and a part of a mosque where a particular class of students receive their learning, which is named after the group.

riyāsa

"Leadership": a general term that applies to those of higher levels or ranks in many fields. In the Mamluk era, the title *al-ra'īs* ("the leader" or "the head") was mainly used for Men of the Pen, whether religious scholars or official clerks. It was also used to denote the leader of the Jewish population (al-Basha, *Alqāb*, 308–9).

rizaq

The salaries or on-going payments that the state allocated to people or the incomes generated from endowed lands to be distributed over specifically assigned chartibale purposes. The *rizqa* was the endowed or granted land (Dahman, *Mu'jam*, 82; Ashour, *'Aṣr*, 441).

rubā'iyya

A coin that the Fatimids especially minted on the occasion of the New Year and its procession. It weighed four times (*rubā'iyya* comes from *arba'a*, which means "four") another coin called the *qīrāṭ* (Ibn al-Ṭuwayr and Sayyid, *Nuzha*, 167,

n. 2; al-Maqrīzī, *Khiṭaṭ*, Vol. 2, 255; Ibn Taghrī Birdī and Shams, *Nujūm*, Vol. 4, 95, n. 2).

rukhtuwāniyya

Rukht is a Persian word that has several meanings, including "decoration", "expensive textiles", "furniture" and amirial and sultanic clothes and textiles, as well as the decoration of the horse. The *rukhtuwān* (pl. *rukhtuwāniyya*) were the servants of the *ṭishtkhānāh* who handled the textiles. The term was also used to refer to the servants who took care of the sultan's or the amir's belongings on their travels and to the servants who minded the furniture in the Mamluk palaces (al-Baqli, *Ta'rīf*, 158; Ashour, *'Aṣr*, 441; Dahman, *Mu'jam*, 82).

rumḥ *(pl.* rimāḥ*)*

A lance.

ruqʿa *(pl.* riqāʿ*)*

The *riqā'* were small papers used for brief correspondences, petitions, doctors' prescriptions and similar documents. The term was also used to refer to documents written by the chiefs of *ahl al-dhimma* (non-Muslim People of the Book) to record alphabetically the names of the members of their population who were obliged to pay the annual taxes on non-Muslims (*jawālī*). These record lists included the names of the population in their areas, as well as travellers and those passing through (al-Qalqashandī, *Ṣubḥ*, Vol. 3, 119; al-Baqli, *Ta'rīf*, 160).

ru'yā *(pl.* ru'ā*)*

"Vision": a prophetic vision seen in a dream. *Ru'yā* also means "sighting" and refers to validating the beginning of a new Hijrī month through seeing the crescent moon. In the case of Ramadan, the holy month of fasting, the *ru'yā* usually entails a celebration to welcome the month. Astronomical calculations are also used to determine the beginnings and ends of the months of the lunar calendar.

S

sabīl

A *sabīl* is a water reservoir used to distribute water for free, a recommended act of charity in Islam. Structurally, the *sabīl* is a building erected over an underground cistern, which is supplied with drinking water. The building overlooks the street through decoratively grilled windows and provides passers-by with water using small containers or basins.

sabkha

"Salt flat", marshy or salty land.

ṣadr

A term that literally means "chest" and indicates the person presiding over a council, sitting at its centre or occupying its most prominent position. In the early Islamic era, the title *al-ṣadr* was used for religious scholars. In the Mamluk era, it was used to refer to chief merchants, the heads or masters of a certain craft, or chief officials of the sultan's entourage, such as the chief architect or the Supervisor of the Warehouses (al-Basha, *Alqāb*, 377–8).

safaṭ

A basket woven of palm leaves, a casket or a chest. Historical accounts indicate that it was sometimes made of leather. The term is applied to different shapes that may be sealed or locked (see al-Nuwayrī and Higazy, *Nihāya*, Vol. 5, 105; Vol. 20, 477 n. 3; Vol. 22, 103; Qaddumi, *Gifts*, 248 n. 11; http://www.baheth.info/all.jsp?term=سفط).

ṣāḥib

"Master", "owner" or "companion": the term was used to refer to a ruler, wazir, head of a bureau or its manager, second in administrative authority after its supervisor (*nāẓir*). According to al-Maqrīzī, in the Mamluk era, the title *al-ṣāḥib* was used for wazirs only if they were Men of the Pen not Men of the Sword. In Syria, the chancery scribes (*kuttāb al-inshā'*) used this for the chief judges and religious scholars of similar status until the ninth century AH / fifteenth century AD (Dahman, *Mu'jam*, 101; al-Battawi, 31; al-Baqli, *Ta'rīf*, 212; al-Maqrīzī, *Khiṭaṭ*, Vol. 3, 89).

ṣāḥib al-daftar

"Master of the Register", also *ṣāḥib daftar al-majlis* ("Keeper of the Council's Register"): this position entailed supervising all the bureaus pertaining to caliphal matters. *Ṣāḥib al-daftar* was one of the caliph's entourage and he received a monthly salary of 100 dinars (al-Baqli, *Ta'rīf*, 213).

ṣāḥib al-mā'ida

"Master of the Feast Table": the Fatimid *ṣāḥib al-mā'ida* was one of the palace caretakers (*farrāshīn*) who directly served the caliph and was responsible for the banquets (Ibn al-Ṭuwayr, *Nuzha*, 85, 145, 170, 202, 224).

ṣāḥib al-miqyās

"Master of the Nilometer": this was the official responsible for monitoring the water level at the nilometer during the flood season. He measured the rise every afternoon and reported it in writing to the state officials among the Men of the Sword and the Men of the Pen. He reported the incremental increases in "fingers", then in "arms", noting the date in both Hijri and Coptic calendars and comparing the rise to the same time of the previous year. The situation was not announced to the public until the rise reached the critical 16 arms of the nilometer column, indicating the "faithfulness" of the Nile. A public daily announcement was then made of the further increase in fingers and in arms (al-Qalqashandī, *Ṣubḥ*, Vol. 3, 297).

ṣāḥib rikāb

"Master of the Stirups": responsible for saddling and bridling horses and escorting processions.

sā'is

"Groom" or "tender": the tamer and trainer of horses and similar animals (al-Baqli, *Ta'rīf*, 177).

Saljuqs

The Saljuqs were a tribe of Ghuzz Turks who lived in the east of the Islamic world during the Abbasid era, and who converted to Islam and followed the Sunni doctrine. They migrated to Transoxiana, then to the region of Khurasan (presently divided over northwest Iran, western and northern Afghanistan, and parts of Central Asia), and were finally able to establish the Great Saljuq state, in AH 429 / AD 1037, under their leader, Tughrul Bek (Tughrul Beg), in Nishapur, in present-day Iran. The Saljuqs grew to control Iran, Iraq, most of the Levant and Central Asia.They conquered Baghdad in AH 447 / AD 1055, terminating the Buwayhid dominance, and affirming their own over the eastern Islamic lands, under the Abbasid Caliphate. The Saljuqs proved themselves a world power during the reign of Alp Arslān (r. AH 455–65 / AD 1063–72), who expanded their territories and managed to defeat the Byzantines in the famous battle of Malazkird (Manzikart) in AH 463 / AD 1071. The Saljuq state reached its peak under Malik Shāh (r. AH 465–85 / AD 1072–92), son of Alp Arslān, when its widest dominion reached China to the east, Turkistan to the north, the Sea of Marmara to the west, and Yemen to the south. Malik Shāh was aided by a most able wazir, Niẓām al-Mulk, who was exceptionally skilled at the political and administrative levels. Niẓām al-Mulk is renowned for formally establishing the madrasa system in Baghdad and several other cities, a practice that quickly spread all over the Islamic world and contributed enormously to the continuous cultural and educational progress. The Saljuq state deteriorated after the death of Malik Shāh, which marked the end of the era of powerful sultans, the "Great Saljuqs". The sons of Malik Shāh competed for authority, which divided their kingdom into smaller ones, among which were the Saljuqs of al-Rūm (Byzantium) who reigned from AH 470 / AD 1077 to AH 696 / AD 1296, the Saljuqs of Iraq who reigned from AH 511 / AD 1117 to AH 573 / AD 1177, and the Saljuqs of Syria who reigned from AH 487 / AD 1094 to AH 508 / AD 1114 (Abu al-Nasr, *al-Salājiqa*, 7–9, 111 n. 5).

ṣamṣām *(pl.* ṣamāṣim*)*

"Unbending sword": strong, unbending and possibly straight swords that cut through the bones. Al-Qalqashandī explains that the word *ṣamṣāma* was used to describe a sword that has a blade on only one of its two sides (http://baheth.info/all.jsp?term=صمصم;al-Qalqashandī, *Ṣubḥ*, Vol. 2, 133; A. Sayyid, *Nuzha*, 148 n. 2).

sanjaq *(pl.* sanājiq*)*

A Turkish term that originally meant "lance". The *sanājiq* were small yellow banners carried by the Sanjaqdār (the "bearer of the *sanjaq*"). It seems that the sultan usually rode in processions during peace time with only the *sanājiq* at his side. However, in times of war, the sultan's procession was accompanied by flags that included the *sanājiq*, a great yellow silk banner, called *'iṣāba*, embroidered with gold and carrying the sultan's name and titles, and another great banner with a hair lock at its top, called *jālīsh*. All these banners were the responsibility of the *amīr 'alam* (Amir of the Flag), who handled the the sultanic flags, standards and the *ṭablakhānāh* and was normally an Amir of Ten (al-Baqli, *Ta'rīf*, 49, 186).

ṣaqāliba *(sing.* ṣaqlabī*)*

This is a term used to refer to slaves of Slavic and other, mostly eastern, European origin. This faction was markedly of fair complexion and sometimes red hair. They were commonly bought by the Umayyads of Andalusia and the Fatimids of North Africa and Egypt. They managed to reach high ranks, such as personal royal guards and military leaders, and of the caliph's guards in Umayyad Spain, some were "men of letters and culture". They were also sometimes employed as eunuchservants, which is why the term *ṣaqlabī* is occassionally synonymous with "Slavic eunuch" (Catlos, "Saqaliba", 22–3).

al-saqlāṭūn

Saqlāṭūn was a city or town within the Byzantine Empire that was known for textile manufacture. The term *al-saqlāṭūn* was used to refer to a type of refined silk or a kind of precious cloth that is thought to have been coloured scarlet, purple or blue, which was also manufactured in Baghdad and Tabriz (al-Baqli, *Ta'rīf*,

181; http://www.baheth.info/all.jsp?term=سقلاطون; Steingass, *Persian–English Dictionary*, 687, http://dsalsrv02.uchicago.edu/cgi-bin/philologic/getobject.pl?c.3:1:5484.steingass).

al-sarīriyya

The correct term is *al-sabarbariyya*, which is used by Ibn al-Ṭuwayr. *Al-Sabarbariyya* were the group armed with *al-sabarbarāt*, a non-Arabic term that means a type of lance 5 arms long with and long broad head (Ibn al-Ṭuwayr and Sayyid, *Nuzha*, 151, n. 1).

ṣawāmiʿ *(pl.* **ṣawāmiʿ***)*

Ṣawma'a, *manāra* (pl. *manārāt*) and *ma'dhana* (pl. *ma'ādhin*) were all used to mean "minaret".

ṣawlaq *(pl.* **ṣawāliq***)*

A leather sack or bag that Mamluks tied to the right side of their waist straps (*ḥawā'iṣ*). The *ṣawlaq* was used to keep the food rations required on travel (al-Baqli, *Ta'rīf*, 224; Ashour, *'Aṣr*, 452).

scribe of the pedestal

See *kātib al-dast*.

secretarial scribe

See *kātib al-darj*.

Separate Bureau

See *al-dīwān al-mufrad*.

service

See *khidma*.

shabbāba

A "flute": al-Qalqashandī defines the *shabbāba* as a musical instrument made of hollowed reed or cane, which may also be referred to as the "Iraqi pipe" (al-Qalqashandī, *Ṣubḥ*, Vol. 2, 144).

shābūra

Triangular-shaped heap or pile (Sayyid, *Nuzha*, 214 n. 2).

shādd

The *shādd* of something was its inspector, performing the job of *shadd* ("inspection"). For example, the *shādd* of the bureaus was responsible for auditing and reviewing their accounts and *shādd al-'amā'ir* ("Inspector of Buildings") was the one responsible for managing the construction, renovation and restoration processes of royal buildings, according to the sultan's orders (al-Baqli, *Ta'rīf*, 193; Ashour, *'Aṣr*, 448–9; Dahman, *Mu'jam*, 95).

shaddat al-waqār

"Wrapping of Veneration" or "Wrapping of Majesty", which was the particular wrapping method and shape of the royal turban on grand processions and special occasions.This wrapping fashion was indeed venerated, for when the caliph wore it, flags were fluttered and people avoided talking or making any sound (Sayyid, *Tafsīr*, 388; Ibn al-Ṭuwayr and Sayyid, *Nuzha*, 155–6, 155 n. 4; Sanders, *Ritual,* 25).

al-shahīd

Al-shahīd, "the Witness", was one of the early Zangid titles that was acquired by al-ʿĀdil Nūr al-Dīn. In the Qur'an the word is used to mean witnessing the actions and deeds of people (Qur'an, 2 "The Cow", 143: http://corpus.quran.com/translation.jsp?chapter=2&verse=143). If this title is associated with the name of a deceased man, it means "the martyr" (al-Basha, *Alqāb*, 363–4).

shāmiyyāt *(sing.* shāmiyya*)*

"Damascene": the more plausible term used by Ibn al-Ṭuwayr is *sāmān*, which is a kind of precious silk cloth that was manufactured in Sāmān, one of the villages of Isfahan, in present-day Iran (Ibn al-Ṭuwayr, *Nuzha*, 173; Shams, *Nujūm*, Vol. 4, 99 n.1).

sharāb dār

"Holder of the Drink": this is the title given to the person who serves in the *sharāb khānāh* ("House of Drinks") of the sultan or amir (Ashour, *'Aṣr*, 450; Dahman, *Mu'jam*, 97).

sharb

A type of textile that was rather thin and fine, sometimes very transparent. It could have been made of linen or silk, or may be a mixture of the two, and may have been adorned with golden threads (Sayyid, *Nuzha*, 129 n. 5; al-Baqli, *Ta'rīf*, 197; Dahmān, *Mu'jam*, 97).

shāri'

A large street.

shāsh *(pl.* shāshāt*)*

"Muslin": a type of fine cloth that was used for wrapping around turbans as well as wounds. Women also used it, decorated with gold and pearls, to cover their heads. The term was used to denote this type of turban-cloth, as well as scarves (Dahman, *Mu'jam*, 95; Ashour, *'Aṣr*, 449; Stillman, *Dress*, 135 n. 44).

shaṭfa *(pl.* shaṭfāt*)*

"Emblem": the *shaṭfa* was a royal logo that was carried like a flag. The term is also used to refer to the division of the circular blazon or emblem (see *rank*), as well as bevelling or chamfering (*mashṭūf*) (Dahman, *Mu'jam*, 98; Mayer, *Heraldry*, 26).

shawzak *(pl.* shawāzik*)*

The term used by Ibn al-Ṭuwayr, al-Qalqashandī and others to refer to the triangular parts or panels forming the parasol.

shaykh al-shuyūkh

"Sheikh of Sheikhs" or grand sheikh: "Customarliy, each khanqah had one or more shaykh, who was a man of knowledge and religion." The first to be termed *shaykh al-shuyūkh* was the sheikh of the khanqah of Sa'īd al-Su'adā', and when al-Nāṣir Muḥammad built the khanqah of Siryāqūs in AH 725 / AD 1325, he gave its head the same title. Then all subsequent sheikhs appointed for this khanqah were called *shaykh al-shuyūkh*, until AH 806 / AD 1404, when Egypt faced a lot of tribulations, and the sheikh of every khanqah was given that same title. The holder of this position "had to have reached a high stage according to the conditions of Sufi orders". He had to be presentable and knowledgeable of jurisprudence and other religious sciences, including all four Sunni schools, while specializing in his own. *Shaykh al-shuyūkh* of the khanqah supervised the Sufi practices and many times taught, according to the stipulations indicated by the endower. Some endowers dictated that the *shaykh al-shuyūkh* should have a deputy (al-Battawi, *'Imāma*, 80–81).

sheik *(*shaykh, *pl.* shuyūkh*)*

"Elderly man", also used to refer to religious scholars.

shīniyyāt *(also* shawānī; *sing.* shīnī *or* shīniyya*)*

A "galley", a big military ship of Egyptian origin. One of its types was sailed using 140 oars and carried sailors and fighters. The *shawānī* had towers or fortresses used for offence and defence and were equipped to attack the enemy with fire. In times of war, a very long, pointed piece of iron called *al-lijām* was fixed to the front and used to pierce enemy ships to flood them with water and force them to surrender. The *shawānī* were huge enough to contain wheat granaries and cisterns of potable water (Sayyid, *Tafsīr*, 744; Sayyid, *Nuzha*, 95 n. 2; al-Baqli, *Ta'rīf*, 211).

shiyya *(pl.* shiyyāt*)*

Any colour of a part of the horse's body that does not match its dominant colour, such as a white area on the forehead of a black horse (*adham*). Such colours, among other attributes, are indicators of the horse's grade of purity and quality of breed (see al-Qalqashandī, *Ṣubḥ*, Vol. 2, 19–21; al-Shawkānī and al-Sababti, *Nayl al-Awṭār*, Vol. 8, 101, n. 1).

shubbāk

The *shubbāk* was "a sort of fenced opening" or "iron-work grill" that was reached through Bāb al-ʿĪd ("Gate of the Feast") through long corridors and was situated roughly opposite the gate. It was located in Dihlīz Bāb al-Mulk, and there was either another *shubbāk* in the Great Iwan, or this single *shubbāk* was in between the iwan and the *sidillā*. The practice of sitting at the *shubbāk* was originally an Abbasid protocol that was adopted by the Fatimids. When al-Basāsīrī managed to take control of Baghdad in AH 450 / AD 1059, he sent the Abbasid *shubbāk*, among other items, to the Fatimid court. When Wazir al-Afḍal built Dār al-Wizāra (the "House of the Wazir") after AH 487 / AD 1094, he put the *shubbāk* in it "for the vizier to sit on and lean against". The *shubbāk* at Dār al-Wizāra was either golden or, according to al-Maqrīzī, made of iron. Al-Maqrīzī also reports that Baybars al-Jashankīr, the Mamluk Sultan (r. AH 708–9 / AD 1308–9), acquired the *shubbāk* from the ruins of Dār al-Wizāra and placed it in the mausoleum attached to his khanqah, which was built on the site of the house (Ettinghausen and Grabar, *Art and Architecture*, 172; Sayyid, *Nuzha*, 97–8°; Raymond, *Cairo*, 53; al-Maqrīzī, *Khiṭaṭ*, Vol. 2, 231; Sanders, *Ritual*, 213).

shuqqa *(pl.* shiqāq *or* ashqāq*)*

Al-Qalqashandī defines the *shuqqa* as a kind of tent made of linen, with leather handles used to pitch it with wedges. It was round and included several compartments (*akhbiya*, sing. *khabā'*) and partitions made of hair-lined cloths (*buyūt al-sha'r*). The *shuqqa* had four doors or entrances in each direction and was called *al-ḥawsh* ("the court") in Egypt. Other definitions of the term include a woolen textile lined with fine, thin hair and a piece of linen or goat-hair, one of which, or more, were put on a tent or its entrance to distinguish it from the rest of the tents (al-Qalqashandī, *Ṣubḥ*, Vol. 5, 209; al-Baqli, *Ta'rīf*, 203–4; Dahman, *Mu'jam*, 99).

Al-Sibṭ

"The Grandchild": a title given to al-Ḥasan and al-Ḥusayn being the grandchildren of the Prophet (http://www.baheth.info/all.jsp?term=سبط).

ṣibyān al-ḥujar

Al-ḥujar means "the chambers" and, in this context, "the barracks". Historians give several accounts on the origins of *ṣibyān al-ḥujar* or *al-ḥujariyya*. It seems that they were introduced by Fatimid Caliph al-Mui'zz, who built seven barracks for a regiment of the Fatimid army to be composed of boys and youths who were chosen from the sons of deceased soldiers, amirs and servants of the state, and who had the required moral qualities, like courage, manliness and good manners, as well as the physical qualities of a proper body build. When they grew to become competent youths, they received full arms that they had the right to keep. The exceptional among them were promoted to amirs or military commanders. At one point in time, this regiment reached 5,000 in number. The barracks of al-Mu'izz were located near Dār al-Wizāra and survived until AH 700 / AD 1301. During the era of al-Mu'izz, this regiment was under the supervision of the *ustādhūn* and each of its barracks had a certain name, such as al-Fatḥ (the Conquest), al-Manṣūra (the Triumphant) and al-Jadīda (the New). A stable was also built especially for this regiment, opposite their barracks and next to Bāb al-Futūḥ. Apparently, these barracks were abandoned and neglected after the era of al-Mu'izz, until the time of al-Afḍal who, most probably in AH 501 / AD 1107, recruited 300 sons of soldiers and reintroduced *ṣibyān al-ḥujar*, who were intended to be "a well-trained, easily mobilized regiment". Al-Afḍal divided them placing 100 in each barrack, to which he assigned a *zimām* ("overseer") and a *naqīb* ("captain"), and appointed an amir to be responsible for the whole regiment. The men of this regiment, who were supplied with all their needs, arms and otherwise, were al-Afḍal's private guards. *Ṣibyān al-ḥujar* were housed in separate barracks near Bāb al-Naṣr and taught the arts of combat and war. They were trained to be ready at all times and to respond immediately when called for duty, as they were responsible for serving and protecting the caliph and his premises. In the era of al-Zahir, in AH 427 / AD 1036, it is reported that *ṣibyān al-ḥujar* were taught all the arts of combat, as well as other sciences. Mamluk historians equated the term *al-ḥujar* with the Mamluk term *ṭibāq*, which were the barracks that housed the royal Mamluks at the Cairo Citadel. So, in a sense, this system of *ṣibyān al-ḥujar* may have been the direct precedent from which the Ayyubids, and consequently the Mamluks, took their system for training and upbringing Mamluks (Sanders, *Ritual*, 97–8; Gamal al-Din, *Dawla*, 218–19; Sayyid, *Tafsīr*, 275 n. 2, 689; Abdelhamid, *Jaysh*, 10–11; Maged, *Nuẓum*, 187–9; Ibn al-Ṭuwayr and Sayyid, *Nuzha*, 57–8, 158 n. 3).

ṣibyān al-khāṣṣ

"Private guards", also "elite guards": *ṣibyān* is the plural of *ṣabiy*, which means "boy" and *al-khāṣṣ* is "the private", that is royal, caliphal or sultanic. *Ṣibyānal-khāṣṣ* were a group of 500 who were among the special entourage of the caliph and could have been amirs or not. Al-Qalqashandī explains that they were like the Mamluk *khāṣṣakiyya*. *Ṣibyānal-khāṣṣ* are also described as the sons of soldiers, amirs and servants of the state, who were hosted by the state, after their fathers died, at certain places prepared especially for them, where they were taught the arts of war and horsemanship, which is a similar definition to *ṣibyān al-ḥujar* (Sanders, *Ritual*, 91, 98; Sayyid, *Dawal*, 689; Sayyid, *Nuzha*, 158 n. 3).

ṣibyān al-zard

"Chainmail guards": these were a group of riffraff or rabble (*awbāsh*) soldiers and commoners which al-Ḥasan, son of caliph al-Ḥāfiẓ (r. AH 525–45 / AD 1131–49), formed in AH 529 / AD 1135 during his conflict with his father. Al-Ḥasan distributed shields among this group and assigned them as his private forces (Ibn al-Ṭuwayr and Sayyid, *Nuzha*, 165, n. 3).

sidillā *or* sihdillā

Sidillā is an Arabized, originally Persian, term. A *sidillā* is described in the primary sources as "three houses in one", which means that it was a structure composed of a central room or iwan and two side rooms. The Fatimid *sidillā* was identified as a structure with three closed sides and one open one. The fourth open side contained the *shubbāk* ("window"). According to Nāṣirī Khusraw, the Persian traveller who visited Egypt during the Fatimid era, the *sidillā* was covered with three domes. The *sidillā* was probably located at the centre of the palace, in between Bāb al-ʿĪd and Bāb al-Baḥr. In another non-royal, but also Fatimid context, the *sidillā* is described as a built stone pedestal (*maṣṭaba*) that is covered with rests (*masānid*) and textile sheets on one end or on two opposite ends (Sayyid, *Nuzha*, 96–8°; Ettinghausen and Grabar, *Art and Architecture*, 172).

sijill *(pl.* sijillāt*)*

During the Fatimid era, the *sijillāt* were official documents that recorded administrative issues pertaining to state affairss or personnel, such as decrees of appointment or diplomas of investiture, rulings, declarations, announcements and so on. They were written in an eloquent style, usually by the highest scribe of the Chancery Bureau. Many examples of the Fatimid *sijillāt* are available in the primary sources (Sallam, *Adab*, 232). The term is also used to refer to a diploma of investiture.

slaughterground

See *al-manḥar*.

soldiers of the ḥalaqa

See *ḥalaqa*.

spare mounts

See *janā'ib*.

sufra

Al-Qalqashandī uses the term *sufra*, which means "dining table", while Ibn al-Ṭuwayr uses *ṣifriyya*, which also has the meaning "large tray" or "round table". The *ṣifriyya* was the term given to the round post head of huge tents. It was normally made of silver and other historical accounts also measure its width by that of the leather water container (*rāwiyat mā'*), particularly the one carried by camels (Ibn al-Ṭuwayr, *Nuzha*, 196; al-Maqrīzī, *Khiṭaṭ*, Vol. 2, 186–7, 313, 316; al-Maqrīzī, *Itti'aẓ*, Vol. 1, 242, 287)

ṣuḥba *(also* ṣaḥāba*)*

"Accompaniment", "companionship" or "fellowship": the office of a *ṣāḥib*, which denoted different meanings, for it sometimes referred to the wazir, the ruler of one of the kingdom's or caliphate's provinces, the head of a bureau or its deputy supervisor.

suḥūr

The last meal eaten at night before the fasting day begins. It has to be eaten before the first ray of dawn as indicated by the call to dawn prayers.

sukurruja

A kind of bowl (http://www.baheth.info/all.jsp?term=سكرجة).

the sultan's Mamluks

See *al-mamālīk al-sulṭāniyya*.

ṣunnā' *(sing.* ṣāni'*)*

A general term that applies to all craftsmen and professionals.

ṣunūj

"Cymbals": al-Qalqashandī mentions the *ṣunūj* in his description of the *duff*, as the small cymbals that were sometimes part of the instrument. In another instance, he mentions it among the processional musical instruments that accompanied the sovereign, in his account of the regulation of India, which means that in this case the *ṣunūj* were big cymbals unattached to a *duff* (al-Qalqashandī *Ṣubḥ*, Vol. 2, 144; Vol. 5, 97).

supervisor

See *nāẓir*.

Supervisor of the Army Bureau

See *nāẓir al-jaysh*.

Supervisor of the Public Treasury

See *nāẓir al-māl*.

Supervisor of the State

See *nāẓir al-dawla*.

Supervisor of the Warehouses and Entourage

See *nāẓir al-buyūt wa-l-ḥāshiya*.

surmūza

"Low shoes": "a kind of low shoe (*na'l*) removed when entering a house" (Mayer, *Costume*, 72, 74).

suwayqa

A small *sūq* or market.

suyūf al-Qaljūriyya

"Qaljūri swords": a type of sword. According to Ibn Saʿīd al-Maghribī, Qaljūr was a place in Africa near the Comoros, which was close to a site where an excellent metal was mined to make these swords. Al-Kindī, the famous Muslim philosopher and scientist of the ninth century, who also authored an important treatise on Islamic swords, however, says that the Qaljūri was a light sword attributed to an Andalusian city called al-Ṭurqūniyya. A. Sayyid refers to another opinion: that the word may be a derivative from the Turkish *qalj*, meaning "sword" (Ibn Saʿīd al-Maghribī, *Geography*, 2; al-Kindī, *Al-Suyūf*; Sayyid, *Nuzha*, 134 n. 1).

T

ṭabar (pl. aṭbār)

A battle-axe.

ṭabarī

The *ṭabarī* rugs or tapestry were originally made in Tabaristan, the region to the south of the Caspian Sea, now in the north of Iran, but they were also produced in the Palestinian city of Ramla (Ramleh). *Ṭabarī* is defined as "fabric for furnishings in the Ṭabarīstānī style.Ṭabarīstān was known for its woollen cloth and carpets" (Qaddumi, *Gifts*, 265) which were valuable items known by the Abbasid court, and probably earlier as well. Ibn al-Ṭuwayr's account mentions two types of these rugs or furnishing cloths: *ṭabarī* and "unparalleled golden-threaded Ṭabaristān" (Qaddumi, *Gifts*, 265; Raymond, *Cairo*, 61; Ibn al-Ṭuwayr, *Nuzha*, 207).

ṭablakhānāh

This is a Persian term that means "the House of Drums". *Ṭabl* means "drums" in both Arabic and Persian and *khānah* is Persian for "house". The *ṭablakhānāh* refers to the sultan's musical warehouse that included drums, horns and other instruments. This house was the responsibility of an Amir of Ten, known as the *amīr 'alam* ("Amir of the Flag"), who managed the sultan's musical band in its nightly shifts and on its travels. This warehouse, as typical of Mamluk sultan'swarehouses, had a superintendent (*mihtār*) who was responsible for its contents.He had a number of subordinate musicians who played the drums, horns, cymbals and other instruments.

Ṭablakhānākh is also used to refer to the drums or musical instruments in general that played for the sultan and the high amirs by their residences' doors, on processions, on travels or in wars. The number of loads (*aḥmāl*, sing. *ḥiml*) of *ṭablakhānāh* that were carried on the backs of beasts of burden to be played were indicative of status: for example, forty *ṭablakhānāh* (drum) loads, four *duhūl* drums (sing. *duhul*, which is a kind of drum), four pipes (*zumūr*, sing. *zummāra*) and twenty horns (*anfira*, sing. *nafīr*) were played for the sultan.The Amirs of One Hundred, Commanders of Thousands, had eight loads of *ṭablakhānāh*, two *duhul* drums, two pipes and four horns played for them.

The *ṭablakhānākh* rank of Mamluk amirs came second to the Amirs of One Hundred, Commanders of Thousands. The *ṭablakhānākh* amirs were also called Amirs of Forty, who were entitled to have a force of 40 to 80 horsemen and buy at least 40 Mamluks whom they may lead in the Mamluk army. Al-Qalqashandī states that the number of amirs in this rank was variable, for the amirial ranks of twenty or ten could be joined to form a *ṭablakhānākh* rank; however, al-Maqrīzī mentions that they were 14 amirs. The *ṭablakhānākh* amirs are defined as those who may have musical bands play for them during processions, even though the higher ranking Amirs of One Hundred, as well as the sultan, had larger bands play for them. Three *ṭablakhānākh* loads and two horns were played for these amirs, a band that lessened to two drums and two pipes. Al-Qalqshandī notes that the second grade of officials, the provincial supervisors of lands embankments (*kushshāf*) and the high governors were chosen from the amirs of this rank (al-Baqli, *Ta'rīf*, 228; Dahman, *Mu'jam*, 106; Ashour, *'Aṣr*, 414; Abdelhadmid, *Jaysh*, 22–3).

tadhākir *(sing.* tadhkira*)*

A memorandum issued by the sultan to his provincial deputies or viceroys or the men he sent on particular missions to remind them of the specific details of their assignments and provide official proof and documentation of their missions, if requested by the authorities they were to address or deal with. The term was also used to refer to a document which recorded the sums of money that a messenger travelled with so as to serve as a reminder and an official record (Sayyid, *Nuzha*, 91 n. 2; Dahman, *Mu'jam*, 43; al-Qalqashandī, *Ṣubḥ*, Vol. 13, 79; al-Baqli, *Ta'rīf*, 75). Alternatively, the term was also used to refer to medical treatise and the prescriptions given by physicians. The word is a derived from the Arabic root *dhakara*, "to remember".

ta'dīl

The step of *ta'dīl al-shāhid* (ruling that a witness is just and reasonable, therefore equitable) is one of the steps of Islamic legislation and court ruling.The criteria for a witness to be deemed *'adl* ("equitable") are normally five: Islam, adulthood, sanity, religious propriety and reputability.

taḥbīs

The decree to endow a piece of land or a building as a *waqf* so that its revenue is allocated for the running, maintenance and upkeeping of a religious or a social-service establishment (Sayyid, *Nuzha*, 90 n. 3).

tāj

The Fatimid crown was actually a royal turban decorated with precious stones. It was huge and had a specialist official responsible for wrapping it in a puffed and elongated shape around a *qalansuwa* or *qulunsuwa* (cloth or leather head cover). Historians of the early Fatimid era report various wrapping styles of the caliph's turban, depending on the material from which the turban's cloth was made, as well as the occasion. Later, the term the "Honourable Crown" (*al-tāj al-sharīf*) was used synonymously with the "Winding of Veneration" (*shaddat al-waqār*), which the caliph wore on grand occasions and processions (Sayyid, *Tafsīr*, 388; Ibn al-Ṭuwayr and Sayyid, *Nuzha*, 155–6, 155 n. 4).

tājir al-khāṣṣ

The merchant who bought Mamluks for the sultan (Abdelhamid, *Jaysh*, 4).

takbīrāt *(sing.* takbīr*)*

The *takbīr* is saying "Allahu Akbar" or "God is Great", which is essential in all prayers.In the regular mandatory five daily prayers, the *takbīr* marks the change of posture, from standing to bowing and so on. The number and function of the *takbīrāt* differs in the *'īd* and funerary prayers, for it they are uttered in specifics numbers, sometimes while standing without changing the posture. The *takbīrāt* of the *'īd* prayers also involve using a particular formula.

takhlīq

Khalūq and *khilāq* are two words that refer to a type of perfume that might have been saffron, to which other substances were added. It was reddish or yellowish in colour. One definition of it is that it was a perfume composed majorly of musk and saffron. *Al-takhlīq* means the process of applying this perfume to something, including the nilometer (http://baheth.info/all.jsp?term=خلوق; Shams, *Nujūm*, Vol. 4, 98 n. 1).

takht al-mulk

"Throne of Sovereignty": an elevated pedestal or seat that functioned as a throne. It could have been a mobile unit or a fixed one called *takht al-mamlaka* ("Throne of the Kingdom") or *kursī al-'arsh* ("Throne Chair"). *Takht* is also a Persian word used in Arabic to denote a clothes container, be it a box or a large cloth encasement (Dahman, *Mu'jam*, 42;Ashour, *'Aṣr*, 422; http://www.baheth.info/all.jsp?term=تخت).

taklāwāt

Some sources define the word as the plural form of an unidentified type of garment that the Mamluk amirs used to wear. Another definition of the word is that it is the plural of *taklāt*, which is a horned hat of Mongol origin that resembles an animal horn. This second definition, however, provides an unlikely meaning to the word in the context given by al-Qalqashandī, which refers to an overall body garment worn between two coats (*aqbiya*) (Ashour, *'Aṣr*, 424; al-ʿUmarī, *Masālik* (ed. Abbas), Vol. 3, 434).

tannūr

A chandelier.

taqlīd *(pl.* taqālīd*)*

"Diploma of investiture": this was the decree that the sultan signed to appoint someone in a high position, such as the viceroys and the judges (Ashour, *'Aṣr*, 424; Dahman, *Mu'jam*, 46–7).

tarāwīḥ

Al-tarāwīḥ prayers are special, non-mandatory prayers that Muslim Sunnis perform after *'īshā'* (night) prayers during the month of Ramadan. They are mostly performed in units of two *rak'a*s to range from eight to twenty *rak'a*s, according to one's ability. They are preferably performed as group prayers.

ṭard waḥsh

"Hunting scenes": from *ṭard* ("chasing") and *waḥsh* ("wild beast"). A type of silk cloth that was decorated with hunting and chase scenes, and was sometimes used to make costumes of honour to be bestowed by the sultan (Ashour, *'Aṣr*, 454).

ṭarḥ

"A fine Alexandrian fabric which was most likely a linen". It is one of the "quality fabrics that still await more precise identification" (Stillman, *Dress*, 57, 72).

ṭarḥa

A piece of cloth that covered the turban, wrapped around the neck and fell down one's back. It was characteristic of the office of the chief judge. In the Mamluk era, it was originally only worn by the holders of the office of chief Shāfiʿī judge, but those occupying the same post for the Ḥanafī school were granted their request to wear it on processions and special occasions like the Shāfiʿīs by the beginning of the ninth century AH / fifteenth century AD (al-Battawi, *'Imāma*, 134).

taʿrīfa *(pl.* taʿrīfāt*)*

Apparently an official document that contained all the required recorded data, itemized, detailed, and supported by numbers (Sayyid, *Tafsīr*, 534).

tarkība

"Fitting", which Mayer translates as "border", indicating that it was "placed right round the top coat (*fawqānī*)". Y. Stillman translates it as "trimming" (Mayer, *Costume*, 59; Stillman, *Dress*, 135).

ṭarrāḥa *(pl.* ṭarrāḥāt; *also* ṭurrāḥa, *pl.* ṭurrāḥāt*)*

A small, square mattress or a cushion to sit upon (al-Baqli, *Ta'rīf*, 229; Sanders, *Ritual*, 70; Ibn al-Ṭuwayr, *Nuzha*, 82, 88).

tashārīf

"Costumes of honour" bestowed by the sultan on high amirs on special occasions, especially upon appointment to high ranking positions (Ashour, *'Aṣr*, 423).

taswīgh *(pl.* taswīghāt*)*

The *taswīgh* is defined as either the permission to take deserved compensations or payments (*istiḥqāq*) directly from a certain land or entity (*jiha*) to facilitate the process or a form of land ownership that entails "complete immunity from taxation" (Tsugitaka, "Land Tenure", 447; Sayyid, *Nuzha*, 90 n. 2).

ṭawāriq

Ṭawāriq "were wooden shields, originally used by the Crusaders and the Byzantines". They were of elongated forms with circular tops and single points for ends, a form described as "kite-shaped". These shields were big enough to be used for defence by infantry and cavalry.They were sometimes decorated with gold enamel or paintedwith various dyes and drawings. Although some scholars define the *ṭawāriq* as other types of arms, such as swords or spears, the term most probably refers only to these shields. It seems not to have appeared in Arabic primary sources before those contemporaneous with the Crusader wars. Some manuscripts show Fatimid soldiers using such shields. The etymological origin of the word is suggestive of a Latin source and Italian and French derivatives that indicate its meaning and its Arabic derivative. Putting *ṭawāriq* on a gate was either for actual defense or as an announcement of some of the war trophies acquired by the sultan and his army (see Yasin, *Asliḥa*, 267–8, 276).

ṭawāshī *(pl.* ṭawāshiyya*)*

The *ṭawāshiyya* were originally "a special military formation" (Ayalon, "Studies", 464) that was an important faction during the Ayyubid era and disintegrated by the early Mamluk era. The *ṭawāshiyya* troops of Ṣalāḥ al-Dīn's time included "both *Mamluks* and freely recruited cavalrymen, each with his own horse, page or *Mamluk* follower, about ten animals to carry baggage, and a salary to purchase equipment. Organized into first-rate regiments which remained close to the ruler on campaign, each *ṭawāshī* was expected to serve in the army for a certain number of months every year" (Nicholson and Nicolle, *God's Warriors*, 28). Not enough information exists to know for sure whether they were Mamluks, but they were amirial troops in the Mamluk era. Sometime after the Mamluks came to power, the term was used to denote eunuch servants or slaves entrusted with guarding the women's quarters, as well as bringing up newly recruited young Mamluks who resided in the barracks (*ṭibāq*); however, the trainers of the new Mamluks were not always eunuchs, and many times high amirs were employed. The *ṭawāshiyya* were most respected and their chief was one of the dignitaries. Another relevant term used by historians is *khaṣiy*, "the emasculated", which al-Maqrīzī and Ibn Taghrī Birdī occasionally use to refer to Qarāqūsh (Nicholson and Nicolle, *God's Warriors*, 28, 120; Gibb, "Armies of Saladin", 76–7, 87; Abdelhamid, *Jaysh*, 6; Ayalon, "Studies", 464–7; Ashour, *'Aṣr*, 455; Dahman, *Mu'jam*, 109; al-Jazzar, "Al-Niẓām", 27).

tawqīʿ *(pl.* tawāqīʿ *or* tawāqīʿāt*)*

"Signature" or "diploma of investiture": al-Qalqashandī explains that the term was used by the administrative clerks of early times to refer to what was written in the margins of the grievances or petitions, that is, the verdicts or decisions taken concerning them, adorned with the caliph's or sultan's signature, which was replaced by that of the *kātib al-sirr* in al-Qalqashandī's time. Evidently, other administrative clerks of the Chancery Bureau also wrote these *tawāqīʿ* and were therefore termed *muwwaqi'ūn* (sing. *muwwaqi'*: "signer"), such as the scribes of the pedestal (*kuttāb al-dast*); however, the power of signature remained that of the sovereign's or the official in authority.

Al-Qalqashandī also informs us that in the Ayyubid era, the *tawāqī'* were the decrees assigning the *iqṭā'āt*. In the Mamluk era, they were certain kind of official documents of investiture, like appointing governors. The term *tawqī'* also referred to the formula that was written in such official decrees, such as: "An honourable *tawqī'* to whomever, with so and so", meaning a royal decision to assign something to a person. Al-Qalqashandī adds that the *tawāqī'* used to be the diplomas of investiture written for the Men of the Pen to appoint them as viceroys or the like, then were substituted by another type of official document. The *tawāqī'* were then used as decrees for assigning or appointing Men of the Turban, except for three supervision offices of religious establishments that were assigned to Men of the Sword (al-Qalqashandī, *Ṣubḥ*, Vol. 11, 114–15; Vol. 13, 144; al-Baqli, *Ta'rīf*, 78).

tawwaquf

"Halting", "suspending" or "pausing": this is a judicial term that refers to abstaining from issuing a verdict due to the obscurity of the case, for example, use of vague words or actions by the litigants, which requires further investigation of the incidents. This term is not employed by al-Nuwayrī; however, he says that Ibn Bint al-Aʿazz was rigid, slow and careful with his rulings (see al-Nuwayrī, *Nihāya*, Vol. 30, 117).

ṭayāfīr *(also* ṭawāfīr; *sing.* ṭayfūr*)*

A term employed in the Fatimid primary sources to refer to large vessels, deep plates, trays or tables that carried several vessels. Al-Maqrīzī reports that the largest *ṭayfūr* could carry three and one third *kantar*s of delicacies and the smallest held ten pieces (Sayyid, *Nuzha*, 131 n. 2; al-Maqrīzī, *Khiṭaṭ*, Vol. 2, 203; Sanders, *Ritual*, 110).

ṭaylasān

Ṭaylasān was a piece of cloth worn as a turban veil. There were two types of *ṭaylasān*: one that was wrapped around the turban and the neck until its ends almost met, covering the cheeks or most of the face and falling to the shoulders. The second type, namely, *al-ṭaylasān al-muqawwar* (the hollow *ṭaylasān*), apparently had an opening at the middle to pass one's face or head through. When religious scholars wore the *ṭaylasān* in the Mamluk era, they took care that one side was not longer than the other and used needles to attach it to the turban to prevent it from falling down on the chest. Al-Qalqashandī mentions that *al-ṭaylasān al-muqawwar* was similar to the *ṭarḥa* of his time, which was a veil that covered the turban, was wrapped around the neck and fell to the shoulders (al-Battawi, *'Imāma*, 134–5; al-Qalqashandī *Ṣubḥ*, Vol. 1, 428).

tharīd

Bread smashed or broken into pieces and soaked in soup, usually with meat, which is a typical Arab dish. The preparation of *tharīd* and offering it to one's guests is a sign of generosity (see http://www.baheth.info/all.jsp?term=ثريد).

thughūr *(sing.* thaghr*)*

Cities on the borders with enemies, including land borders, but generally used to mean coastal cities (see http://www.baheth.info/all.jsp?term=ثغر).

al-ṭibāq al-sulṭāniyya

The sultan's barracks: military barracks that hosted the Mamluks that the sultan bought. They formed floors or levels (*ṭibāq*) in the Citadel, where every level was occupied by Mamluks brought from the same country. At one point in time, there were 12 huge schools, each having several lodgings, which were big enough to host 1,000 Mamluks. It appears that there were other military schools inside and outside Cairo, which also hosted the amirs' Mamluks, in addition to the sultan's barracks of the Citadel (al-Baqli, *Ta'rīf*, 227–8; Ibn Shāhīn, *Zubdat al-Mamālik*, 27; Dahman, *Mu'jam*, 105).

tillīs

Sack used for packing agricultural produce and straw (Dahman, *Mu'jam*, 48).

ṭirāz *(pl.* ṭuruz*)*

Ṭirāz is an Arabized word of Persian origin that in the may refer to the inscription or decorative bands on textiles as well as on building walls. *Dūr al-ṭirāz* (sing. *dār al-ṭirāz*) were the textile factories of the state that manufactured products for the private use of the caliph and his family (*ṭirāzal-khāṣṣa*) and for more public use to be sold in markets (*ṭirāzal-'āmma*).

ṭisht dāriyya *(sing.* ṭisht dār*)*

"Holders of the Basins".

triple incense

See *nadd muthallath.*

ṭulb *(also* ṭulab, *pl.* aṭlāb*)*

An originally Kurdish term, which meant "the amir who leads two-hundred horsemen in the battlefield" and was also used for those who lead 70 or 100 horsemen. The term is used to refer to the Mamluk battalion that belonged to an amir and was formed of 70 to 200 horsemen. The term later came to mean an army battalion. M. Dahman states that the plural of *ṭulb* is *aṭlāb*. Saʿid Ashour also identifies the *aṭlāb* as the "private guards of the Mamluk amirs" who bore arms like soldiers did (Ashour, *'Aṣr*, 413, 455; Dahman, *Mu'jam*, 108).

Tulunids

The Tulunids (AH 254–91 / AD 868–904) were a semi-autonomous dynasty that reigned over Egypt and Syria under the realm of the Abbasid Caliphate. Aḥmad b. Ṭūlūn was a Turkish soldier whose father was in service of the Abbasids. He arrived in Egypt "as deputy of the Abbasid governor" but managed to gain total control of the state, becoming the governor himself and expanding into Syria. Aḥmad b. Ṭūlūn ruled from AH 254 / AD 868 to AH 270 / AD 884, followed by his son, Khumārawayh from AH 270 / AD 884 to AH 283 / AD 896, then three successors till the advent of the Ikhshidids (Bosworth, *Islamic Dynasties*, 60).

turba

"Burial ground" or "tomb".

turs *(also* tirs*)*

A generic term which means "shield" and refers to various types of shields, some of which were circular and could have been made of iron, steel, wood or leather (Yasin, *Asliḥa*, 249–50; http://www.baheth.info/all.jsp?term=ترس).

U

ʿumad al-ḥadīd

Ibn al-Ṭuwayr mentions a type of arms or instrument called *al-mustawfiyāt*, which were square-shaped iron poles of two arms length withrounded handles. These are probably the ones referred to by al-Qalqashandī as "iron poles" (see Ibn al-Ṭuwayr, *Nuzha*, 148).

Umayyads

This was the first dynastic caliphate in Islam, which followed the four *rāshidūn* (the "rightly guided caliphs"). The Umayyads ruled from AH 41 / AD 661 to AH 132 / AD 750 from their capital in Damascus, after their first caliph, Muʿāwiya, succeeded in securing the caliphate, following the assassination of ʿAlī b. Abī Ṭālib, the last of the *rāshidūn* by the Khawārij, a notoriously rebellious Muslim sect. Muʿāwiya had been in defiance to the authority of ʿAlī, maintaining his established office as the ruler of Damascus since the caliphate of ʿUmar b. al-Khaṭṭāb. In the reign of Muʿāwiya's son, Caliph Yazīd (r. AH 60–64 / AD 680–83), the grandson of the Prophet, al-Ḥusayn, along with other members of the Prophet's household, were killed in a battle after his revolt against the Umayyads: an incident that remains shocking to Muslims to this day. This incident marked the definite emergence of the Shi'ite sect, who believed in the mandatory rule of the descendants of the Prophet, through his paternal cousin and son in law, ʿAlī. Two Umayyad caliphs were of particularly important influence on the development of the Islamic world, namely, ʿAbd al-Malik b. Marwān (r. AH 65–86 / AD 685–705) and his son, al-Walīd b. ʿAbd al-Malik (r. AH 86–96 / AD 705–15), due to the reforms started by the first and completed under the second, which ensured the Arabization of the administrative bureaus of all the Islamic lands, as well as minting the first unified coin of the Islamic caliphate. Another important caliph, a descendant of Caliph ʿUmar b. al-Khaṭṭāb, was Caliph ʿUmar b. ʿAbd al-ʿAzīz (r. AH 99–101 / AD 717–20), who markedly followed his great grandfather's steps in just rule, piety and austerity.The Umayyads continued the Islamic conquests and reached Spain, the border of India, Bukhara and Samarqand. They suffered much turmoil and unrest, with many riots and revolts, which eventually led to their defeat by the Abbasids in AH 132 / AD 750. The Umayyads managed to revive a dynasty in Andalusia from AH 138 / AD 756 to AH 422 / AD 1031. Umayyad art and architecture is characterized by its eclecticism, being influenced by the Byzantine and Sassanian traditions, while adding new unique aspects and applying concepts dictated by the dogma that unified the Umayyad lands.

ummira bi-l-būq wa-l-'alam

"Appointed an amir with the horn and the flag." The *ta'mīr* (the investiture of a Mamluk amir) was a process that involved several steps: a celebration, a bestowal of attire (as well as particular headgear in the Bahri Mamluk period), riding in procession, allocating the *iqṭā'*, and assigning a position and blazon (*rank*). According to T. Abdelhamid, apart from the celebration, wearing the headgear then the procession, there is no conclusive evidence of the order of these steps in the primary sources for the Bahri Mamluk period. W. Leaf and S. Purcell conclude from al-Qalqashandī's statements that the investiture of an amir in the Mamluk era necessitated the presentation of the flag and the horn to him, being "the visible sign that a Mamluk has been made an amir". However, it seems that al-Qalqashandī and al-ʿUmarī mention "the horn and the flag" in such context and with this composition only in relation to the investiture of Bedouin Arab (*'urbān*) amirs in particular. In *Itti'āẓ*, al-Maqrīzī defines the *ṭulb* (battalion), in the language of the Ghuzz, as the commanding amir who has "an assigned flag and a blown horn" (*'alam ma'qūd wa būq maḍrūb*) and a force of 200, 100 or 70 soldiers (see Abdelhamid, *Jaysh*, 24–30, 24 n. 75; Leaf and Purcell, *Heraldic Symbols*, 76; al-Qalqashandī, *Ṣubḥ*, Vol. 1, 323, 332; Vol. 4, 70–71; al-ʿUmarī, *Masālik* (ed. Abbas), Vol. 4, 378, 379, 386; al-Maqrīzī, *Itti'āẓ*, Vol. 3, 327).

ʿUrūḍ *(sing.* ʿarḍ*)*

The categories of employees deserving of pay. Listed in detail by Ibn al-Ṭuwayr (Ibn al-Ṭuwayr, *Nuzha*, 83–5).

ushāqiyya *(also* ujāqiyya, *sing.* ushāqī *or* ujāqī*)*

Royal stable boys or a troop of sultanic servants responsible for riding the horses for movement and sports, so as to keep them fit (al-Baqli, *Ta'rīf*, 57; Ashour, *Aṣr*, 416).

ʿushārī *(also* ʿushāriyya, *pl.* ʿushāriyyāt*)*

'Ushārī is an Arabized term given to a type of small boat, which joined the fleets or larger ships and were used in the Red Sea, the Mediterranean and the Nile. These boats were used frequently in the Nile for several purposes, but mostly by caliphs, wazirs and governors. The *'ushārī* that sailed the Mediterranean had 20 oars and, unlike ships, wereable to approach the shore transporting men and cargo, like a ferry. They were also used for rescue when ships were at danger

during storms. In the Fatimid era, the *'ushārīyyāt* were used along the Nile to transport travellers, as well as the state's grain and other products. Some amirs had their own *'ushāriyyāt* that they used for their leisure sailingin the Nile, especially on the occasion celebrating the building of the Khalīj (Sayyid, *Tafsīr*, 746; al-Baqli, *Ta'rīf*, 245).

ustādhūn *(sing.* ustādh*)*

"Masters": *al-ustādhūn* were highly respected members of the Fatimid caliphal entourage. Some of them had positions in the caliph's private service, which are detailed by al-Qalqashandī. Abd Allah Gamal al-Din defines them as a faction of slaves, black and white, eunuch and not, mostly of foreign origin, who served the caliph. The title of *ustādh* was one of the general titles used since the Abbasid era, when it was applied to the eunuch slave-boys (*ghilmān*). Kafūr al-Ikhshīdī, the Ikhshidid ruler, bore this title before he came to power and kept it after the Abbasid Caliph, al-Muṭī' sent him his degree of investiture as ruler (*taqlīd*). The Fatimids continued to use this title, and, during the Mamluk era, it was used to refer to the master who bought, brought up and freed Mamluk soldiers. The term was also used to refer to craftsmen (al-Baqli, *Ta'rīf*, 29; al-Basha, *Alqāb*, 140; Gamal al-Din, *Dawla*, 220).

al-ustādhūn al-muḥannakūn

"The masters who covered beneath their chins": these were officials who wrapped the tails of their turbans beneath their chins or mouths and back around their heads during the Fatimid era and who held great positions, some of which were in the private service of the caliph. They were the caliph's confidants and also had the right to hold the title of amir. They received a montly salary of 100 dinars, and, as Ibn al-Ṭuwayr informs us, were more than 1,000 in number. It is highly unlikely that the caliph held 1,000 men close enough to be exposed to all his secrets and hidden matters of the state. One can, therefore, conclude that a small group of the *muḥannakūn* was chosen and trusted by the caliph. The *muḥannakūn* appear to have worn costumes that corresponded to their ranks or levels (al-Baqli, *Ta'rīf*, 31–2; Gamal al-Din, *Dawla*, 220–21).

W

wafā' al-nīl

The "faithfulness", "fulfilment", "sufficiency" or "loyalty" of the Nile: a celebration of the Nile inundation during the flood season reaching a certain measure to provide enough water for all purposes, indicating a prosperous year. The Nile annual flood season is from August/September to October/November.

wakāla

See *qaysāriyya*.

wakīl bayt al-māl

"Agent of the Public Treasury": in the Mamluk era, the holder of this office supervised wills, money deposits, and properties of the Public Treasury, as well as following its interests through selling, purchasing and so on. *Wakīl bayt al-māl* also worked in several other offices, such as those of the deputy judge (*nā'ib al-qāḍī*), the teacher (*mudarris*), and the supervisor of endowments (*nāẓir al-aḥbās*) (al-Battawi, *'Imāma*, 72).

wālī al-madīna

"Chief of the city": chief of police (al-ʿUmarī, *Masālik* (ed. al-Juburi), Vol. 3, 279).

waqf *(pl.* awqāf*)*

"Endowment": "the permanent dedication by a Muslim of any property, in such a way that the appropriator's right is extinguished, for charity or for religious objects or purposes, or for the founder of the *waqf* during his lifetime or after his death, for his descendants, and on their extinction, to a purpose defined by the founder". The deed itself is called a *waqfiyya.* There are three categories of *waqf*: a charity endowment (*waqf khairī*), a family endowment (*waqf ahlī*) and a mixed endowment (*waqf mukhtalaṭ*). The family endowment supported the family and descendants of the endower, according to the stipulations of the deed, while mixed endowment was used for both descendants and charity. Those deeds ascertained the protection of all assets covered by that deed for eternity, since sale, confiscation or dissolution of the *waqfiyya* was usually impossible under normal circumstances and Islamic law. The use of *waqf* thus became a tool for keeping wealth in the family of the endower, even after his death or confiscation or fall from favour, constant threats in turbulent and violent medieval times. Starting from the Ayyubid period, all state officials from the sultan down to even the least influential amirs established the custom of building their own mausoleum with a charitable institution (congregational mosque, madrasa, *khanqah*, *zawya*, etc.) attached to it, and endowed suitable assets covered by an endownment deed to ascertain the building's perpetual upkeep. The system became the cornerstone of building activities and religious education and a source of income and jobs for scholars and other factions (see Nasir, *Islamic Law*, 274).

wardrobe master

See *jamadār*.

warrāqūn *(sing.* warrāq*)*

"Papermakers": the *warrāqūn* were the transcribers (also *nassākhūn*, sing. *nāsikh*), binders, and traders of books. They were learned men: religious scientists, linguists and men of literature, who were also fine calligraphers and who often added their marginal editorial notes to the text. Their shops at the book markets were meeting places for cultured men to discuss and debate books and commentaries.

al-wasāṭa

"The Mediator": the holder of this office in the Fatimid era performed an intermediary role between the caliph and his officials and subjects, obeying the caliph's orders and making sure they were carried out and his prohibitions obeyed, while the caliph remained in full control over all state matters. Researchers disagree as to when this office was first introduced: some believe itwas in the reign of first Fatimid Caliph in Egypt, al-Muʿizz, others claim that Caliph al-Ḥākim created it to give himself absolute authoritative power over the wazirs (al-Baqli, *Ta'rīf*, 360; Sayyid, *Dawla*, 320; Daftary, *The Ismā'īlis*, 186–7).

wikāla

See *qaysāriyya*.

wilāya *(pl.* wilāyāt*)*

"Governorship": the *wilāya* was the office of the governor in any of the major provincial divisions, equivalent to modern day governorates. This office was sometimes promoted to the level of viceroyship in the case of Alexandria. The holder of the office was termed a *wālī* (pl. *wulāt*) and "the main duties of the *wulāt* were police work and keeping order". According to al-Maqrīzī, the *wilāya* was the term used to refer to what was called *shurṭa* (police) in older times (al-Baqli, *Ta'rīf*, 358; al-Maqrīzī, *Khiṭaṭ*, Vol. 3, 89).

winch-spanned crossbows

See *qisiy al-lawlab*.

al-wizāra

During the Mamluk era, the wazir was the most esteemed position for a Man of the Pen. The Mamluks inherited the administrative system of the Ayyubids, who stipulated that a wazir must possess certain qualities that included being the most superior of the Men of the Turban, the most just, incorruptible, noblest, respectable and honest. However, the position of the wazir suffered a set back in the

Mamluk era, since Men of the Sword started competing with Men of the Pen for it, particularly after the position of *nā'ib al-salṭana* (Viceroy of the Sultanate) was introduced. "If the vizier was a Man of the Pen, he was given the title of *al-ṣāḥib* (the companion), and if he was a Man of the Sword, then he had to be an amir." The wazir who was a Man of the Turban was chosen from those Men of the Pen who reached the high position of *shādd al-dawāwīn* ("Inspector of Bureaus"), to which they were promoted from smaller administrative jobs such as the *kātib* ("scribe") and the *mubāshir* ("managers").

The Mamluks first employed *'ulamā'* ("religious scholars") as wazirs, then later they started employing Copts who converted to Islam (Masalima). In AH 713 / AD 1313, Sultan al-Nāṣir Muḥammad introduced the position of *nāẓir al-khāṣṣ* ("Private Supervisor"), which overtook much of the responsibilities of the wazir. Similar gradual steps led to the diminishing of the authorities of the wazir, until in AH 740 / AD 1340, the first Man of the Sword was employed in this position, which was when more Men of the Sword than Men of the Pen became wazirs (al-Battawi, *'Imāma*, 15–17).

wizārat al-tafwīḍ

"Wazir of Delegation": as opposed to *wizārat al-tanfīdh* ("Wazir of Execution"), that is, one with limited powers), *wizārat al-tafwīḍ* was the wazirate that emerged in the second half of the Fatimid era, when the wazirs had the liberty of ruling the state and managing all its affairs independently, being the effective sovereigns. This position was introduced with Badr al-Jamālī, the Armenian, who was appointed by Caliph al-Mustanṣir to restore state order at a time of dire turmoil. The majority of the wazirs before Badr were Men of the Pen. Badr, a Man of the Sword, arrived from Acre, which he ruled, to become the both wazir and the commander of the Fatimid armies, holding the title of *amīr al-juyūsh* ("Amir of the Armies", commander). Badr and his successors – all Men of the Sword – strongly controlled and maintained all the military, administrative and religious aspects of the state, and had the same authority as the Mamluk sultans. *Amīr al-juyūsh* was originally the title given to the ruler of Damascus, but since the wazirate of Badr, it became the title of the caliph's wazir, although it is mostly used by historians to specifically refer to Badr. The last of the Wazirs of Delegation under the Fatimids was Ṣalāḥ al-Dīn, who held the title *sulṭān al-juyūsh* ("Sultan of the Armies"), which was adopted by his two predecessors, Shāwir and Shīrkūh. The wazirs of the Ayyubid and Mamluk eras never reached the level of authority allowed by *wizārat al-tafwīḍ*, until in the Mamluk period another position was created that held that authority, *al-nā'ib al-kāfil* (plenipotentiary viceroy) which was held by one of the leading amirs (Men of the Sword) (Sayyid, *Nuzha,* 43–5°, 52–3°; al-Baqli, *Ta'rīf*, 359).

Wrapping of Veneration

See *shaddat al-waqār*.

Y

yashm

Persian for a fine kind of jade, a particular type of jasper or agate that was believed to come from India or China and to have protective power against lightening by diverting it from the place where it is kept or the person who wears it (Steingass, *Persian–English Dictionary*, 1531, http://dsalsrv02.uchicago.edu/cgi-bin/philologic/getobject.pl?c.7:1:7611.steingass).

Z

zaffa

"Announcement procession": this was the round of playing musical instruments that accompanied the sultan on some occasions, such as on his travels.

Zangids

The Zangids were a Sunni dynasty that emerged from the realm of the Great Saljuqs. Originally, the Zangids were Turkish slave warriors who served the Saljuqs. Their founder, ʿImād al-Dīn Zankī, was governor of Mosul in Iraq. In AH 521 / AD 1127, the Zangids managed to form their principality in Mosul, which expanded into "Jazira, Syria, eastern Anatolia and Kurdistan". Zankī was able to survive his disputes with the Saljuqs as well as local disturbances. He defeated the Byzantines and the Crusaders, which "made him a hero of the Sunni world". After his death, the dynasty split into two lines, each led by one of his sons. The elder son, Sayf al-Dīn Ghāzī "inherited Mosul and its dependencies Sinjar, Irbil and Jazira". The younger son, Nūr al-Dīn Maḥmūd, usually referred to with the titles al-Malik al-ʿĀdil (the Just King) and al-Shahīd (the Witness), inherited the Syrian areas of the principality. Nūr al-Dīn is renowned for continuing his father's victories and defending Sunni Islam. His heir Ṣalāḥ al-Dīn Yūsuf b. Ayyūb (Saladin) is also most cherished in the history of Sunni Islam for his glorious confrontations with the Crusaders (Bosworth, *Islamic Dynasties*, 191).

zardakāsh

The person responsible for making, mending and maintaining arms (Ashour, *'Aṣr*, 445; Dahman, *Mu'jam*, 86).

zardiyyāt *(sing.* zardiyya*)*

"Chainmail": a shirt-like mail made of small iron rings that are tied or connected together in a web or linear arrangement. There were short and long chainmails of this type, where the long ones reached the ground to cover the whole body of a horseman (Yasin, *Asliḥa*, 75–6).

zāwiya *(pl.* zawāyā *or* zawiya*)*

See *khānqāh*.

zimām *(pl.* azimma*)*

"Overseer": in Arabic *al-zimām* is "the reins" and is used to denote a leader. Regarding the Mamluk *zimām* of the sultan's residences (*zimām al-dūr al-sulṭāniyya*), al-Qalqashandī explains that *al-zinān dār*, which was distorted by the commoners to *al-zimām dār*, is an originally Persian term, where *zinān* means "the women" and *dār* means "holder of", which in this context means "keeper of". Given the Arabic meaning of *zimām*, and that *dār* means "house", this would explain the distortion of the term, according to al-Qalqashandī. *Al-zinān dār*, *zimām al-dār* or *zimām al-dūr* was the eunuch servant who kept and guarded the curtain door or gate of the curtain (*bābal-sitāra*), that is, to the women's quarters of the amir or sultan. *Al-sitāra* (from *satr*,"covering" or "veil") was the term used to refer to the door of the women's quarters (al-Qalqashandī, *Ṣubḥ*, Vol. 5, 459–60; al-Baqli, *Ta'rīf*, 172).

ẓuhr

"Noon", noon and second mandatory daily prayer.

zunnārī

A kind of horse blanket (*ajlāl*): a cover for the horse's body that is open at its chest and hanging over its rump to cover its tail. The *zunnārī* was granted instead of the caparison (*kunbūsh*) to those whom the sultan favoured and appreciated. It was usually made of red satin (*aṭlas*) or broadcloth (al-Baqli, *Ta'rīf*, 173; Ashour, *'Aṣr*, 446).

zuqāq

"Narrow street" or "alleyway".

BIBLIOGRAPHY

Primary Sources

Abū al-Fidā' ('Imād al-Dīn Ismā'īl). *Al-Mukhtaṣar fī Akhbār al-Bashar*. Cairo: al-Matb'a al-Husayniyya, 1907.

Al-Bayrūnī, Abū al-Rayḥān Muḥammad b. Aḥmad. *Al-Qanūn al-Mas'ūdī* (*The Mas'ūdī Canon*). Haydarabad: Majlis Da'irat al-Ma'arif al-'Uthmaniyya, 1955.

Al-Ḥamawī (Shihāb al-Dīn Abū 'Abd Allah Yāqūt). *Mu'jam al-Buldān*. Beirut: Dar Sadir, 1977.

Al-Ḥimyarī, Abū 'Abd Allah b. 'Abd al-Mun'im. *Al-Rawḍ al-Mi'ṭār fī Khabar al-Aqṭār*. Edited by Ihsan Abbas. Beirut: Mu'assasat Nasir li-l-Thaqafa, 1980.

Ibn 'Abd al-Ẓāhir (Muḥyī al-Dīn Abū al-Faḍl 'Abd Allah). *Al-Rawḍa al-Bahiyya al-Zāhira fī khiṭaṭ al-Mu'iziyya al-Qāhira*. Edited by Ayman Fouad Sayyid. Cairo: Al-Dar al-Arabiyya li-l-Kitab, 1996.

Ibn Abī Usaybi'a (Muwaffaq al-Dīn Abū al-'Abbās Aḥmad b. al-Qāsim al-Sa'dī al-Khazrajī). *'Uyūn al-Anbā' fī Ṭabaqāt al-Aṭibbā'*. Edited by Imru' al-Qays b. al-Tahhan. Cairo: Al-Matba'a al-Wahbiyya, 1882.

Ibn al-Athīr (Majd al-Dīn Abū al-Sa'ādāt al-Mubarak b. Muḥammad). *Al-Nihāya fī Gharīb al-Ḥadīth wa-l-Athār*. Edited by Taher A. al-Zawy and Mahmoud M. al-Tanahy. Beirut: Al-Maktaba al-'Ilmiyya, 1979.

Ibn al-Ma'mūn (Jamāl al-Dīn Abū 'Alī Mūsā b. al-Ma'mūn al-Baṭā'iḥī, the Amir). *Nuṣūṣ min Akhbār Miṣr*. Edited by Ayman Fouad Sayyid. Cairo: Institut français d'Archeologie orientale du Caire, 1983.

Ibn al-Ṭuwayr (Abū Muḥammad al-Murtaḍā 'Abd al-Salām b. al-Ḥasan al-Qaysarānī). *Nuzhat al-Muqlatayn fī Akhbār al-Dawlatayn*. Edited by Ayman Fouad Sayyid. Beirut: Franz Steiner, 1992.

Ibn al-Zubayr (Aḥmad ibn al-Rashīd). *Book of Gifts and Rarities* (*Kitāb al-Hadāya wa-l-Tuḥaf*). Translated by Ghadah Hijjawi Qaddumi. Cambridge, MA: Harvard University Press, 1996.

Ibn Ḥajar (Shihāb al-Dīn Aḥmad b. 'Alī b. Muḥammad al-'Asqalānī). *Al-Durar al-Kāmina fī A'yān al-Mi'a al-Thāmina*. Edited by Muhammad Abd al-Mu'in Dan. Hyderabad: Majlis Da'irat al-Ma'arif al-'Uthmaniyya, 1972.

—— *Raf' al-Iṣr 'an Quḍāt Miṣr*. Edited by Ali Muhammad Umar. Cairo: Maktabat al-Khanji, 1998.

Ibn Ḥawqal (Abū al-Qāsim Muḥammad Ibn Ḥawqal al-Baghdādī al-Mawṣilī). *Ṣūrat al-Arḍ*. Beirut: Dar Sadir, 1938.

Ibn Kathīr (Ismāʿīl b. ʿUmar b. Kathīr al-Qurashī al-Dimashqī). *Asad al-Ghāba fī Maʿrifat al-Ṣaḥāba*. Beirut: Dar Ibn Hazm, 2012.

—— *Al-Bidāya wa-l-Nihāya*. Edited by Abd Allah b. Abd al-Muhsin al-Turki. Riyadh: Dar ʿAlam al-Kutub, 2003.

Ibn Khallikān (Abū al-ʿAbbās Shams al-Dīn Aḥmad). *Wafayāt al-Aʿyān wa-Anbāʾ Abnāʾ al-Zamān*. Edited by Ihsan Abbas. Beirut: Dar Sadir, 1994.

Ibn Mājah (Muḥammad b. Yazīd al-Qazwīnī). *Sunan*. Edited by Muhammad Fouad Abd al-Baqi and Mustafa Husayn al-Dhahabi. Cairo: Dar al-Hadith, 1998.

Ibn Nāṣir al-Dīn al-Dimashqī (Shams al-Dīn Muḥammad b. ʿAbd Allah b. Muḥammad b. Aḥmad b. Mujāhid). *Tawḍīḥ al-Mushtabah fī Ḍabt Asmāʾ al-Ruwāt wa-Ansābihim wa-Alqābihim wa-Kunāhim*. Edited by Muhammad Naim al-Irqisusi. Beirut: Mu'assasat al-Risala, 1993.

Ibn Qutayba (Abū Muḥammad ʿAbd Allah b. Muslim). *Gharīb al-Ḥadīth*. Edited by Abd Allah al-Jabury. Baghdad: Al-ʿAny Press, 1977.

Ibn Saʿīd al-Maghribī, Abū al-Ḥasan ʿAlī b. Mūsā. *Geography*. http://www.scribd.com/doc/3921002/الجغرافيا-ابن-سعيد (accessed 1 May 2012).

Ibn Shāhīn (Ghars al-Dīn Khalīl al-Ẓāhirī). *Zubdat Kashf al-Mamālik Bayān al-Ṭuruq wa-l-Masālik*. Edited by Paul Ravaisse. Paris: Imprimerie nationale, 1894.

Ibn Taghrī Birdī (Jamāl al-Dīn Abū al-Maḥāsin Yūsuf). *Al-Manhal al-Ṣāfī wa-l-Mustawfī baʿd al-Wāfī*. Edited by Muhammad Muhammad Amin. Cairo: General Egyptian Book Organization, 1984–93.

—— *Al-Nujūm al-Zāhira fī Mulūk Miṣr wa-l-Qāhira*. Edited by Muhammad Husayn Shams al-Din. Beirut: Dar al-Kutub al-ʿIlmiyya, 1992.

Ibn Taymiya (Abū al-ʿAbbās Taqiy al-Dīn Aḥmad). *Mawsūʿat al-Ijmāʿ li-Shaykh al-Islām Ibn Taymiya*. Edited by Abd Allah b. Mubarak al-Busi Al Sayf. Ta'if: Maktabat Dar al-Bayan al-Haditha, 1999.

Ibn Ẓuhayra (Jamāl al-Dīn Muḥammad b. Muḥammad). *Al-Faḍāʾil al-Bahira fī Maḥāsin Miṣr wa-l-Qāhira*. Edited by Kamil al-Muhandis and Mustafa al-Sakka. Cairo: Dar al-Kutub, 1969.

Al-Jawharī, Abū Naṣr. *Muntakhab min Ṣiḥāḥ al-Jawharī*. http://shamela.ws/index.php/book/28100 (accessed 1 Nov. 2013).

Al-Jazīrī, ʿAbd al-Qādir b. Muḥammad al-Anṣārī. *Al-Durar al-Farāʾid al-Munaẓẓama fī Akhbār al-Ḥājj wa-Ṭarīq Makka al-Muʿaẓẓama*. Edited by Muhammad Hasan Ismail. Beirut: Dar al-Kutub al-ʿIlmiyya, 2002.

Al-Kindī (Abū Yūsuf Yaʿqūb). *Al-Suyūf wa-Ajnāsuhā*. Edited by Abd al-Rahman Zaki. Cairo: Maktabat al-Thaqafa al-Diniyya, 2000.

Al-Maqdisī (Shams al-Dīn Abū ʿAbd Allah Muḥammad). *Aḥsan al-Taqāsīm fī Maʿrifat al-Aqālīm*. Edited by Michael Jan de Goeje. Leiden: E. J. Brill, 1906.

Al-Maqrīzī (Taqiy al-Dīn Aḥmad b. ʿAlī). *Imtāʿ al-Asmāʿbimā li-l-Nabiy min al-Ahwāl wa-l-Amwāl wa-l-Ḥafada wa-l-Matāʿ*. Edited by Muhammad Abd-al-Hamid al-Namisi. Beirut: Dar al-Kutub al-ʿIlmiyya, 1999. http://shamela.ws/index.php/main (accessed 1 Sept. 2013).

—— *Ittiʿāẓal-Ḥunafā bi-Akhbār al-Aʾimmā al-Fāṭimiyyīn al-Khulafā*. Vol. 1. Edited by Gamal al-Din al-Shayyal. Vols 2, 3. Edited by Muhammad Hilmi Ahmad. Cairo: The Supreme Council for Islamic Affairs, 1996.

—— *Al-Mawāʿiẓ wa-l-Iʿtibār bi-Dhikr al-Khiṭaṭ wa-l-Āthār*. Edited by Muhammad Zeinhom and Madiha al-Sharqawi. Cairo: Maktabat Madbuly, 1998.

—— *Al-Mawā'iẓ wa-l-I'tibār bi-Dhikr al-Khiṭaṭ wa-l-Āthār*. Edited by Ayman Fouad Sayyid. 6 Vols. London 2002.

—— *Al-Sulūk li-Ma'rifat Duwal al-Mulūk*. Edited by Muhammad Abd al-Qadir Ata. Beirut: Dar al-Kutub al-Ilmiyya, 1997.

Al-Nuwayrī (Shihāb al-Dīn Aḥmad b. ʿAbd al-Wahhāb). *Nihāyat al-Arab fī Funūn al-Adab*. Edited by Mustafa Higazy, revised by Muhammad Mustafa Ziyada. Cairo: Dar al-Kutub, 2002. http://shamela.ws/index.php/book/10283 (accessed 1 Sept. 2013).

Al-Qalqashandī, Abū al-ʿAbbās Shihāb al-Dīn Aḥmad. *Ḍaw' al-Ṣubḥ al-Musfir wa-Janiy al-Dawḥ al-Muthmir*. Edited by Mahmud Salama. Cairo: Matbaʿat al-Waʿiz, 1906.

—— *Kitab Ṣubḥ al-A'shā*. Cairo: Dar al-Kutub al-khidiwiyya, 1913–22.

—— *Kitab Ṣubḥ al-A'shā*. Edited by Fawzi Muhammad Amin, Cairo: Al-Hay'ah al'ama li-qusur al-thaqafa, 2004.

—— *Kitāb Ṣubḥ. al-A'shá fī ṣinā'at al-inshā*, ed. Musṭạfa Mūsa, Cairo: Al-Hay'ah al-Misṛīyah al-ʿĀmmah lil-Kitāb, 2006.

Al-Qifṭī (Jamāl al-Dīn Abū al-Ḥasan). *Akhbār al-'Ulamā' bi-Akhyār al-Ḥukamā'*. Edited by Ibrahim Shams al-Din. Beirut: Dar al-Kutub al-ʿImiyya, 2005.

Al-Ruḥaybānī (Musṭafā b. Saʿd b. ʿAbduh al-Suyūṭī) and Ḥasan b. ʿUmar b. Maʿrū al-Shaṭṭī al-Ḥanbalī. *Maṭālib Ulī al-Nuhā fī Sharḥ Ghāyat al-Muntahā*. Damascus: Al-Maktab al-Islami, 1961.

Al-Ṣadafī, Abū Saʿīd b. Yūnus. *Tārīkh Ibn Yūnus al-Miṣrī*. Beirut: Dar al-Kutub al-ʿIlmiyya, 2001.

Al-Ṣafadī (Ṣalāḥ al-Dīn Khalīl b. Aybak). *A'yān al-'Aṣr wa-A'wān al-Naṣr*. Edited by Ali Abu Zayd et al. Damascus: Dar al-Fikr, 1997.

—— *Al-Wāfī bi-l-Wafayāt*. Edited by Ahmad al-Arna'out and Tizki Mustafa. Beirut: Dar Ihya' al-Turath al-Arabi, 2000.

Al-Sakhāwī (Shams al-Dīn Muḥammad b. ʿAbd al-Raḥman). *Al-Ḍaw' al-Lāmi' li-Ahl al-Qarn al-Tāsi'*. Beirut: Dar al-Jil, 1992.

Al-Shawkanī (Muḥammad b. ʿAlī b. Muḥammad b. ʿAbd Allah). *Nayl al-Awṭār Sharḥ Muntaqā al-Akhbār*. Edited by Essam al-Din al-Sababti. Cairo: Dar al-Hadith, 1993.

Al-Subkī (Tāj al-Dīn b. ʿAlī). *Ṭabaqāt al-Shāfi'iyya al-Kubrā*. Edited by Mahmud al-Tanahi and Abd al-Fattah al-Helw. Cairo: Dar Hajr, 1992.

Al-Suyūṭī (Jalāl al-Dīn ʿAbd al-Raḥman). *Ḥusn al-Muḥāḍara fī Tārīkh Miṣr wa-l-Qāhira*. Edited by Muhammad Abu al-Fadl Ibrahim. Cairo: Dar Ihya' al-Kutub al-Arabiyya, 1967–68.

Al-ʿUmarī (Shihāb al-Dīn Aḥmad b. Yaḥyā b. Faḍl Allah). *Masālik al-Abṣār fī Mamālik al-Amṣār*. Edited by Hamza Ahmad Abbas. Abu Dhabi: Al-Majmaʿ al-Thaqafi, 2002.

—— *Masālik al-Abṣār fī Mamālik al-Amṣār*. Edited by Kamil Salman al-Juburi. Beirut: Dar al-Kotob Al-ilmiyah, 2010.

—— *Al-Ta'rīf bi-l-Muṣṭalaḥ al-Sharīf*. Cairo: Matbaʿat al-ʿAsima, 1895.

Al-Zamakhsharī, Abū al-Qāsim Maḥmūd b. ʿAmr, *Al-Fā'iq fī Gharīb al-Ḥadīth*. Edited by Ali al-Bajawy and Muhammad Abu al-Fadl Ibrāhīm. Second Edition. Beirut: Dar al-Maʿrifa, 2010.

Al-Zarkalī (Khayr al-Dīn b. Maḥmūd b. Muḥammad b. ʿAlī b. Fāris). *Al-A'lām: Qāmūs Tarājim li-Ashhar al-Rijāl wa-l-Nisā' min al-'Arab wa-l-Musta'ribīn wa-l-Mustashriqīn*. Beirut: Dar al-ʿIlm li-l-Malayin, 2002. http://shamela.ws/index.php/book/12286 (accessed 1 Oct. 2106).

Secondary Sources

Abd al-Karim, Ahmad Ezzat. "Wathā'iq al-Qalqashandī fī Ṣubḥ al-A'shā". In *Abū al-'Abbās al-Qalqashandī wa-Kitābuhu Ṣubḥ al-A'shā*. Edited by Ahmad Ezzat Abd al-Karim. Cairo: Al-Hay'ah al-Misṛīyah al-'Āmmah lil-Kitāb 1973.

Abdelaziz, Mohamed, and Tarek Torky, "Alexandria: Gateway to the West". In *Mamluk Art: The Splendour and Magic of the Sultans*, 187–97. Cairo: Al-Dar al-Masriah al-Lubnaniah, 2001.

Abdelhamid, Tarek Galal. "The Citadel of Cairo in the Ayyubid Period." In *Creswell Photographs Re-examined: New Perspectives on Islamic Architecture*, 1–41. Edited by Bernard O'Kane. Cairo: American University in Cairo Press, 2009.

—— "The Development of Pyrotechnics and Firearms in the Mamluk Period". *Proceedings of the Second International Conference on Egyptian Science through the Ages* (in press).

—— "The Impact of Firearms and Siege Weapons on Mamluk Military Architecture". *Proceedings of the Colloque "Guerre et paix dans le Proche-Orient médiéval" (IFAO-IFPO)* (in press).

—— *Al-Jaysh fī al-'Aṣr al-Mamlūkī*. Cairo: Dar Kitabat, 2012.

—— "Notes on Military Architecture of the Ayyubid Period." Unpublished MA thesis. The American University in Cairo, 2005.

Abu al-Nasr, Muhammad Abd al-Azim. *Al-Salājiqa: Tārīkhuhum al-Siyāsī w-al-'Askarī*. Cairo: Ein for Human and Social Studies, 2001.

Abu Zayd, Siham Mustafa. *Al-Ḥisba fī Miṣr al-Islāmiyya*. Cairo: General Egyptian Book Organization, 1986.

Abun-Nasr, Jamil M. *A History of the Maghrib in the Islamic Period*. Cambridge: Cambridge University Press, 1993.

Ahmad, Ahmad Abd al-Raziq. *Tārīkh wa-Athār Miṣr al-Islāmiyya Mundhu al-Fatḥ al-'Arabī Ḥattā Nihāyat al-'Aṣr al-Fāṭimī*. Cairo: Dar al-Fikr al-Arabi, 2006.

Alexander, David G. *The Arts of War: Arms and Armour of the 7th to 19th Centuries*. New York: Nour Foundation in association with Azimuth Editions and Oxford University Press, 1992.

Ashour, Sa'id Abd al-Fattah. *Al-'Aṣr al-Mamālīkī fī Miṣr wa-l-Shām*. Cairo: Dar al-Nahda al-'Arabiyya, 1976.

—— "Kitāb Ṣubḥ al-A'shā: Maṣdar li-Dirāsat Tārīkh Miṣr fī-l-'Uṣūr al-Wusṭā." In *Abū al-'Abbās al-Qalqashandī wa-Kitābuhu Ṣubḥ al-A'shā*, 50–70. Edited by Ahmad Ezzat Abd al-Karim. Cairo: General Egyptian Book Organization, 1973.

—— *Al-Mujtama' al-Miṣrī fī 'Aṣr Salāṭīn al-Mamālīk*. Cairo: Dar al-Nahda al-'Arabiyya, 1992.

Al-Ashqar, Muhammad Abd al-Ghany. *Al-Malḥama al-Miṣriyya: 'Aṣr al-Mamālīk al-Jarākisa wa-Radd al-I'tibār fī 'Ahd Bārsbāy*. Cairo: Maktabat Madbuli, 2002.

Ayalon, David. "Studies on the Structure of the Mamluk Army II". Bulletin of the School of Oriental and African Studies, Vol. 15 (1953): 448–76.

Azab, Khaled. *Aswār wa-Qal'at Ṣalāḥ al-Dīn*. Cairo: Maktabat Zahra' al-Sharq, 2006.

—— *Al-Fusṭāṭ: 'Āṣimat Miṣr al-Islāmiyya*. Cairo: Dar Kitab al-Yawm, 2008.

Baer, Eva. *Metalwork in Medieval Islamic Art*. Albany: State University of New York Press, 1983.

Al-Baqli, Muhammad Qandil. *Fahāris kitāb Ṣubḥ al-a'shá fī ṣinā'at al-inshā' lil-Qalqashandī*. Supervised by Ashur Sa'īd 'Abd al-Fattāḥ. Cairo: 'Ālam al-Kutub, 1972.

—— *Al-Ta'rīf bi-Muṣṭalaḥāt Ṣubḥ al-A'shā*. Cairo: General Egyptian Book Organization, 1984.

—— *Muṣṭalaḥāt Ṣubḥ al-A'shā*, Vol. 15. Cairo: Al-Hay'ah al'ama li-qusur al-thaqafa, 2006.

Al-Basha, Hasan. *Al-Alqāb al-Islāmiyya fī al-Tārīkh wa-l-Wathā'iq wa-l-Āthār*. Cairo: Al-Dar al-Fanniya li-l-Nashr wa-l-Tawzi', 1989.

Al-Battawi, Hasan Ahmad. *Ahl al-'Imāma fī Miṣr fī 'Aṣr Salāṭīn al-Mamālīk*. Cairo: Ein for Human and Social Studies, 2007.

Bauden, Frédéric, "Like Father, Like Son: The Chancery Manual (Qalā'id Al-Jumān) of Al-Qalqašandī's Son and its Value for the Study of Mamluk Diplomatics (Ninth/Fifteenth Century) (Studia Diplomatica Islamica, I)". *Eurasian Studies*, Vol. 11 (2013): 181–228.

Behrens-Abouseif, Dorris. *Islamic Architecture in Cairo: An Introduction*. Cairo: American University in Cairo Press, 1989.

Blair, Sheila S. *Islamic Calligraphy*. Cairo: American University in Cairo Press, 2006.

Bloom, Jonathan M. "Calligraphy". In *Medieval Islamic Civilization: An Encyclopedia*, 132–5. Edited by Josef W. Meri. New York: Routledge, 2006.

Bosworth, Clifford Edmund. "Al-Qalqashandī (756–821/1355–1418)". In *Encyclopedia of Arabic Literature*, 629. Edited by Julie Scott Meisami and Paul Starkey. London and New York: Taylor and Francis, 1998.

—— "Christian and Jewish Religious Dignitaries". *International Journal of Middle East Studies*, Vol. 3 (1972): 59–74, 199–216.

—— "A 'Maqāma' on Secretaryship: al-Qalqashandī's 'al-Kawākib al-durriyya fī'l-manāqib al-Badriyya'". *Bulletin of the School of Oriental and African Studies*, Vol. 27, no. 2 (1964), 291–8.

—— *The New Islamic Dynasties: A Chronological and Genealogical Manual*. Edinburgh: Edinburgh University Press, 1996.

—— "Some Historical Gleanings from the Section on Symbolic Actions in Qalqašandī's Ṣubḥ al-Aʿšā". *Arabica*, Vol. 10, no. 2 (June 1963): 148–53.

Byam, Michele, *Eyewitness: Arms and Armor*. New York: DK Publishing, 2004.

Calvo, Emilia. "Ibn Ḥawqal". In *Encyclopaedia of the History, Science, Technology and Medicine in Non-Western Cultures*, Vol. 1, 1103–4. Edited by Helaine Selin. Berlin: Springer, 2008.

Catlos, Brian. "Saqaliba". In *The Historical Encyclopedia of World Slavery*, 22–3. Edited by Junius P. Rodriguez. California: ABC-CLIO, 1997.

Daftary, Farhad. *The Ismā'īlis: Their History and Doctrines*. Cambridge: Cambridge University Press, 1999.

Dahman, Muhammad Ahmad. *Mu'jam al-Alfāẓ al-Tārīkhiyaa fī al-'Aṣr al-Mamlūkī*. Damascus: Dar al-Fikr, 1990.

D.S.M., "Subh al-A`asha, by Abu'l -`Abbas Ahmad al-Qalqashandi. Part xi. Cairo: Government Press, 1917". *Journal of the Royal Asiatic Society of Great Britain and Ireland*, Vol. 50, nos 3–4 (Oct. 1918), 558. https://www.cambridge.org/core/journals/journal-of-the-royal-asiatic-society/article/ub-al-asha-by-abul-al-qalqashandiabbas-ahmad-part-xi-cairo-government-press-1917/70A1D8EFF1F3C936915C1E11F7411 74B (accessed 9 Nov. 2016).

Espéronnier, Maryta, "Faste des costumes et insignes sous les Fatimides d'Egypte (Xè-XIIè ss.), d'après le Ṣubḥ al-ʿšā d'al-Qalqašandī". *Der Islam: Zeitschrift für Geschichte und Kultur des Islamischen Orients*, Vol. 70 (1993): 301.

—— "Les fêtes civiles et les cérémonies d'origine antique sous les Fatimides d'Egypte: *Extraits du tome III de Ṣubḥ al-A'ša d'al-Qalqašandī*". *Der Islam: Zeitschrift für Geschichte und Kultur des islamischen Orients*, Vol. 65 (1988): 1, 46–59.

Esposito, John L., "Iqta". In *The Oxford Dictionary of Islam*. Oxford: Oxford University Press, 2003. http://www.oxfordislamicstudies.com/article/opr/t125/e1061 (accessed 9 Nov. 2016).

Ettinghausen, Richard, and Oleg Grabar. *The Art and Architecture of Islam: 650–1250*. New Haven and London: Yale University Press, 1987.

Gamal al-Din, Abd Allah Muhammad. *Al-Dawla al-Fāṭimiyya: Qiyāmuhā bi-Bilād al-Maghrib wa-Intiqāluhā ilā Nihāyat al-Qarn al-Rābi' al-Hijrī ma' 'Ināya Khāṣṣa bi-l-Jaysh*. Cairo: Dar al-Thaqafa, 1991.

Gibb, Hamilton A.R. "The Armies of Saladin". In *Studies on the Civilization of Islam*, 74–90. Edited by Stanford J. Shaw and William R. Polk. London: Routledge & Kegan Paul, 1962.

Glick, Thomas F. "Islamic Technology". In *A Companion to the Philosophy of Technology*, 32–6. Edited by Jan Kyrre Berg Olsen, Stig Andur Pedersen and Vincent F. Hendricks. Chichester: Wiley-Blackwell, 2009.

Gordon, Matthew S. "Kindi, Al-". In *Medieval Islamic Civilization: An Encyclopedia*, Vol. 1, 440–41. Edited by Josef W. Meri and Jere Bacharach. New York: Routledge, 2006.

Gruber, Christiane J. "Introduction: Islamic Book Arts in Indiana University Collections." In *The Islamic Manuscript Tradition: Ten Centuries of Book Arts in Indiana University Collections*, 2–51. Edited by Christiane Gruber. Bloomington: Indiana University Press, 2010.

Gully, Adrian. "Epistles for Grammarians: Illustrations from the insha' Litearture". *British Journal of Middle Eastern Studies*, Vol. 23, no. 2 (Nov. 1966), 147–66.

Haji, Amin. "Institutions of Justice in Fatimid Egypt". In *Islamic Law: Social and Historical Contexts*, 198–214. Edited by Aziz Al-Azmeh. London: Routledge, 2013.

Hallaq, Hassan, and Abbas Sabbagh. *Al-Mu'jam al-Jāmi' fī al-Muṣṭalaḥāt al-Ayyūbiyya wa-l-Mamlūkiyya wa-l-'Uthmāniyya*. Beirut: Dar al-'Ilm li-l-Malayyin, 1999.

Hammuda, Abd al-Hamid Husayn. *Tārīkh al-'Arab Qabl al-Islām*. Cairo: Al-Dar al-Thaqafiyya li-l-Nashr, 2006.

Hamza, Abd al-Latif. *Al-Qalqashandī fī Kitābihi Ṣubḥ al-A'shā: 'Arḍ wa-Taḥlīl*. Cairo: Al-Hay'ah al-Misṛīyah al-'Āmmah lil-Kitāb, 1977.

Hamza, Hani. *The Northern Cemetery of Cairo*. Cairo: American University in Cairo Press, 2001.

Hasan, Hasan Ibrahim. *Tārīkh 'Amr b. al-'Āṣ*. Cairo: Maktabat Madbuli, 1996.

Hasan, Zaki Muhammad. *Kunūz al-Fāṭimiyyīn*. Cairo: Dar al-Athar al-'Arabiyya, 1937.

Haywood, John A. *Arabic Lexicography: Its History and its Place in the General History of Lexicography*. Leiden: E.J. Brill, 1965.

Holt, P.M. "Qalawin's Treaty with Acre in 1283". *English Historical Review*, Vol. 91, no. 361 (Oct. 1976): 802–12.

—— "The Treaties of the Early Mamluk Sultans with the Frankish States". *Bulletin of the School of Oriental and African Studies*, Vol. 43, no. 1 (1980): 67–76.

Homerin, Emil T. "Saving Muslim Souls: The *Khānqāh* and the Sufi Duty in Mamluk Lands". *Mamluk Studies Review*, Vol. 3 (1999): 59–82.

Houtsma, Martijn Theodor. "Babylon". In *E. J. Brill's First Encyclopaedia of Islam, 1913–36*. Vol. 2. Leiden: E. J. Brill, 1993 http://referenceworks.brillonline.com/browse/encyclopaedia-of-islam-1/alpha/b.

—— "Cairo." In *E. J. Brill's First Encyclopaedia of Islam, 1913–36*. Vol. 2. Leiden: E. J. Brill, 1993. http://referenceworks.brillonline.com/browse/encyclopaedia-of-islam-1/alpha/c.

Al-ʿIrainy, Al-Sayyid al-Baz. *Al-Mamālīk*. Beirut: Dar al-Nahda al-ʿArabiyya, 1999.

Irwin, Robert. "Gunpowder and Firearms in the Mamluk Sultanate Reconsidered." In *The Mamluks in Egyptian and Syrian Politics and Society*, 117–39. Edited by Michael Winter and Amalia Levanoni. Leiden: E. J. Brill, 2004.

Iybish, Ahmad. *Dimashq fī 'Aṣr Salāṭīn al-Mamālīk: Mshāhid wa-Aḥdāth min Nuṣūṣ Adab al-Riḥlāt al-'Arabiyya*. Damascus: Dar al-Sharq, 2005.

Jackson, Roy. *Fifty Key Figures in Islam*. Oxford: Routledge, 2006.

Hany Fakhry Attia al-Jazzar, "Al-Niẓām al-ʿAskarī fī Dawlat al-Mamālīk: 648–923 AH/1250–1517 AD". MA Thesis, Islamic University, Gaza, 2007.

El Kadi, Galila, and Alain Bonnamy. *Architecture for the Dead: Cairo's Medieval Necropolis*. Cairo: American University in Cairo Press, 2007.

Khan, Geoffrey, "The Historical Development of the Structure of Medieval Arabic Petitions". *Bulletin of the School of Oriental and African Studies*, Vol. 53, no. 1 (1990): 8–30.

Krenkow, Fritz, "Arabische Berichte über Goldgruben und Schlafsucht im Nigerlande." In *Texts and Studies on the Historical Geography and Topography of Africa*, 320–23. Collected and reprinted by Fuat Sezgin in collaboration with Mazen Amawi, Carl Ehrig-Eggert, Eckhard Neubauer. Institute for the History of Arab-Islamic Science: Frankfurt, 2009.

Kunitzsch, Paul. "Ibn Qutayba". In *Encyclopaedia of the History, Science, Technology and Medicine in Non-Western Cultures*, Vol. 1, 1114. Edited by Helaine Selin. Berlin: Springer, 2008.

Lambton, Ann K. S. "Reflections on the Iqṭāʿ". In *Arabic and Islamic Studies in Honour of Hamilton A. R. Gibb*, 358–76. Edited by George Makdisi. Leiden: E. J. Brill, 1965.

Lammens, H., SJ, "Correspondances diplomatiques entre les Sultans Mamlouks d'Egypte et les puissances chretiennes". *La Revue de L'Orient Chretien*, Vol. 9 (1904): 151–87, 359–92.

—— "Relations officielles entre la cour romaine et les Sultans Mamlouks d'Egypte". *La Revue de L'Orient Chretien*, Vol. 8 (1903): 101–10.

Lang, Christian, "Ḥisba and the Problem of Overlapping Jurisdictions: An Introduction to, and Translation of Ḥisba Diplomas in Qalqashandī's Ṣubḥ al-Aʿshā". *Harvard Middle Eastern and Islamic Review*, Vol. 7 (2006), 85–107.

Leaf, William, and Sally Purcell. *Heraldic Symbols: Islamic Insignia and Western Heraldry*. London: Victoria and Albert Museum, 1986.

Lev, Yaacov. *State and Society in Fatimid Egypt*. Leiden: E. J. Brill, 1991.

Lombard, Maurice. *The Golden Age of Islam*. Princeton: Markus Wiener Publishers, 2004.

Maged, Abd al-Mun'im. *'Nuẓum al-Fāṭimiyyīn wa-Rusūmuhum fī Miṣr*. Cairo: Anglo Egyptian Bookshop, 1985.

—— *Nuẓum Dawlat Salāṭīn al-Mamālīkwa-Rusūmihim fī Miṣr: Dīrāsa Shāmila li-l-Nuẓum al-Siyāsiyya*. Cairo: Anglo Egyptian Bookshop, 1982.

—— *Ẓuhūr al-Khilāfa al-Fāṭimiyya wa-Suqūṭuhā fī Miṣr: Al-Tārīkh al-Siyāsī*. Cairo: Dar al-Fikr al-ʿArabi, 1994.

Marzuq, Muhammad Abd al-Aziz. *History of Textile Industry in Alexandria: 331 B.C. – 1517 A.D.* Alexandria: Alexandria University Press, 1955.

Mayer, Leo Ary. *Mamluk Costume: A Survey*. Geneva: A. Kundig, 1952.
—— *Saracenic Heraldry: A Survey*. Oxford: Clarendon Press, 1933.
Michel, Bernard, "L'Organisation financière de l'Égypte sous les sultans mamelouks d'après Qalqachandi". *Bulletin de l'Institut égyptien*, Vol. 7 (1925): 127–47.
Muhammad, Suad Maher. *Masājid Miṣr wa-Awliyā'uhā al-Ṣāliḥūn*. 5 vols. Cairo: Supreme Council for Islamic Affairs, 1971–83.
Munir, Amr Abd al-Aziz. *Al-Sharqiyya bayn al-Tārīkh wa-l-Folklore*. Cairo: Dar al-Islam, 2004.
Murphy, Gladys-Franz. *The Agrarian Bureau of Egypt: From the Arabs to the Ottomans*. Cairo: IFAO, 1986.
Musa, Mustafa. *Kitāb Ṣubḥ al-A'shā fī Ṣinā'at al-Inshā Ta'līf al-Qalqashandī*. Cairo: General Egyptian Book Organization, 2006.
Al-Musawi, Muhsin Jassim. "Vindicating a Profession or a Personal Career? Al-Qalqashandī's Maqāmah in Context". *Mamlūk Studies Review*, Vol. 7 (2003): 111–35.
Nasir, Jamal J. *The Islamic Law of Personal Status*. London: Graham & Trotman Ltd, 1990.
Nassar, Lotfi Ahmad. *Wasā'il al-Tarfīh fī 'Aṣr Salāṭīn al-Mamālīk fī Miṣr*. Cairo: General Egyptian Book Organization, 1999.
Nicolle, David. *Crusader Warfare: Byzantium, Western Europe and the Struggle for the Holy Land: 1050–1300* AD. Hambeldon: Continuum, 2007.
Nicholson, Helen, and David Nicolle. *Gods Warriors: Crusaders, Saracens and the Battle for Jerusalem*. Oxford: Midland House, 2005.
Norris, Harry T. *Islam in the Balkans: Religion and Society between Europe and the Arab World*. Columbia: University of South Carolina Press, 1993.
O'Kane, Bernard. "The Ziyāda of the Mosque of al-Ḥākim and the Development of the Ziyāda in Islamic Architecture." In *L'Égypte fatimide: Son art et son histoire: actes du colloque organise à Paris les 28, 29 et 30 mai 1998*, 141–58. Edited by Marianne Barrucand. Paris: Presses de l'université de Paris-Sorbonne, 1999.
Parolin, Gianluca Paolo. *Citizenship in the Arab World: Kin, Religion and Nation-State*. Amsterdam: Amsterdam University Press, 2009.
Parry, Vernon J. *War, Technology and Society in the Middle East*. Edited by Malcolm E. Yapp. London and New York: Oxford University Press, 1975.
Pedani, Maria Pia. "Mamluk Lions and Venetian Lions 1260–1261". *Electronic Journal of Oriental Studies*, Vol. 7, no. 21 (2004): 1–17. https://iris.unive.it/retrieve/handle/10278/14215/17945/059_lions.pdf. (accessed 9 Nov. 2016).
Pellat, Charles, "Le 'Calendrier agricole' de Qalqašandī". *A*nnales Islamologiques, Vol. 15 (1979): 165–85
Peters, Francis E. *Mecca: A Literary History of the Muslim Holy Land*. Princeton: Princeton University Press, 1994.
Petersen, Andrew. *Dictionary of Islamic Architecture*. London: Routledge, 1996.
Petry, Carl, "Geographic Origins of Dīwān Officials in Cairo during the Fifteenth Century". *Journal of the Economic and Social History of the Orient*, Vol. 21, no. 2 (May 1978): 165–84.
Qasim, Qasim Abdo. *'Aṣr Salāṭīn al-Mamālīk*. Cairo: Dar al-Shorouk, 1994.
—— *Fī Tārīkh al-Ayyūbīn wa-l-Mamālīk*. Cairo: Ein for Human and Social Studies, 2005.
Qutb, Muhammad Ali. *Zawjāt al-Anbiyā' 'Alayhim al-Salām wa-Ummahāt al-Mu'minīn Raḍiya Allah 'Anhun*. Cairo: Al-Dar al-Thaqafiyya li-l-Nashr, 2004.

Rabbat, Nasser O. *The Citadel of Cairo: A New Interpretation of Royal Mamluk Architecture*. Leiden: E. J. Brill, 1995.

Ramzy, Muhammad. *Al-Qāmūs al-Jughrāphy li-l-bilād al-M\iṣriyya min 'Ahd Quadamā' al-Miṣriyyīn ilā Sanat 1945*. Cairo: General Egyptian Book Organization, 1994.

Raymond, André. *Cairo: City of History*. Translated by Willard Wood. Cairo: American University in Cairo Press, 2007.

Sabra, Adam. *Poverty and Charity in Medieval Islam: Mamluk Egypt, 1250–1517*. Cambridge: Cambridge University Press, 2000.

Sallam, Muhammad Zaghlul. *Al-Adab fī al-'Aṣr al-Fāṭimī: Al-Kitāba wa-l-Kuttāb*. Alexandria: Munsha'a al-Ma'arif, 1995.

—— *Al-Adab fī al-'Aṣr al-Fāṭimī: Al-Shi'r wa-l-Shu'arā'*. Alexandria: Munsha'a al-Ma'arif, 1988.

Sauvaire, Henri. Extraits de l'ouvrage d'el Qalqachandy intitulé Ṣubḥ al-aʿshā fī kitābat al-inshā'. Paris, 1887.

Al-Sayyad, Nezar. *Cairo: Histories of a City*. Harvard: Harvard University Press, 2011.

Sayyid, Ayman Fouad. *Al-Dawla al-Fāṭimiyyafī Miṣr: Tafsīr Jadīd*. Cairo: General Egyptian Book Organization, 2007.

—— *Al-Taṭawwur al-'Umrānī li-Madīnat al-Qāhira Mundhu Nash'atihā wa-Ḥattā al-Ān*. Cairo: Al-Dar al-Misriyya al-Lubnaniyya, 1997.

Al-Sayyid, Mahmud. *Tārīkh al-Qabā'il al-'Arabiyya fī 'Aṣr al-Dawlatayn al-Ayyūbiyya w-al- Mamlūkiyya*. Alexandria: Mu'assasat Shabab al-Jami'a, 1998.

Al-Shistawy, Muhammad. *Mutanazzahāt al-Qāhira fī al-'Aṣrayn al-Mamlūkī wa-l-'Uthmānī*. Cairo: Dar al-Afaq al-Arabiyya, 1999.

—— *Mayādīn al-Qāhira fī al-'Aṣr al-Mamlūkī*. Cairo: Dar al-Afaq al-'Arabiyya, 1999.

Al-Samarra'i, Zamya' Muhammad Abbas. *Al-Mahnaj al-Ta'rīkhī 'ind al-Qalqashandī: Dirāsa Taḥlīliyya*. Riyadh: King Faisal Center for Research and Islamic Studies, 2001.

Sanders, Paula. *Ritual, Politics and the City in Fatimid Cairo*. Albany: State University of New York, 1994.

El Sandouby, Aliaa. "The Ahl al-bayt in Cairo and Damascus: The Dynamics of Making Shrines for the Family of the Prophet". PhD Thesis, University of California, 2008.

Sauvaget, J. *La Poste aux chevaux dans l'empire des Mamelouks* (Paris: Librairie d'Amérique et d'Orient Adrien-Maissoneuve, 1941).

Sezgin, Fuat, *Two Studies on the Geography and Administration of Egypt according to al-Qalqašandī (d.1418)*, Frankfurt am Main: Institute for the History of Arabic-Islamic Science at the Johann Wolfgang Goethe University, 1992.

Shafi'I, Farid, *Al 'Imārah al-'Arabīyya fi Misr al-Islāmiyyah, 'Asr al-Wulah*, Vol. 1. Cairo: Al-Hay'ah al-Misṛīyah al-'Āmmah lil-Kitāb, 1994.

Silverstein, Adam, "Documentary Evidence for the Early History of the Barid". In *Papyrology and the History of Early Islamic Egypt*, 153–61. Edited by Petra M. Sijpesteijn and Lennart Sundelin. Leiden: E. J. Brill, 2004.

Spies, Otto, "An Arab Account of India in the 14th Century: Being a Translation of the Chapters on India from al-Qalqashandī's 'Ṣubḥ ul-aʿshā'". In *Texts and Studies on the Historical Geography and Topography of India and South East Asia* 2, 173–254. Edited by Fuat Sezgin et al. Stuttgart: Institute for the History of Arabic-Islamic Science at the Johann Wolfgang Goethe University, 1936.

Steingass, Francis Joseph. *Persian-English Dictionary*. http://dsal.uchicago.edu/dictionaries/steingass/ (accessed 27 Oct. 2016)

Stillman, Yedida Kalfon. *Arab Dress from the Dawn of Islam to Modern Times: A Short History*. Edited by Norman A. Stillman. Leiden: E. J. Brill, 2003.

Surur, Muhammad Gamal al-Din. *Tārīkh al-Dawla al-Fāṭimiyya*. Cairo: Dar al-Fikr al-ʿArabi, 1994.

Tabaa, Yasser. *The Transformation of Islamic Art during the Sunni Revival*. London: I. B. Tauris & Co. Ltd, 2002.

Tsugitaka, Sato. "Land Tenure and Ownership, or Iqṭāʿ". In *Medieval Islamic Civilization: An Encyclopedia*, Vol. 1, 447–9. Edited by Josef W. Meri. New York: Routledge, 2006.

—— *State and Rural Society in Medieval Islam: Sultans, Muqta's, and Fallahun*. Leiden: E. J. Brill, 1997.

Tulaymat, Abd al-Qadir Ahmad. "Wathā'iq al-Qalqashandī fī Ṣubḥ al-Aʿshā". In *Abū al-'Abbās al-Qalqashandī wa-Kitābuhu Ṣubḥ al-A'shā*, 117–44. Edited by Ahmad Ezzat Abd al-Karim. Cairo: General Egyptian Book Organization, 1973.

Uthman, Muhammad Abd al-Sattar. *Mawsū'at al-'Imāra al-Fāṭimiyya: Al-'Imāra al-Fāṭimiyya – Al-Ḥarbiyya, al-Madaniyya, wa-l-Dīniyya: Al-Kitāb al-Awwal*. Cairo: Dar al-Qahira, 2006.

—— *Mawsū'at al-'Imāra al-Fāṭimiyya: 'Imārat al-Mashāhid wa-l-Qibāb fī al-'Aṣr al-Fāṭimī – Al-Kitāb al-Thānī*. Cairo: Dar al-Qahira, 2006.

Van Berkel, Maaike. "Archives and Chanceries: Pre-1500, in Arabic". In *Encyclopaedia of Islam, Three*. Brill Online: Reference Works (2001–). http://referenceworks.brillonline.com/entries/encyclopaedia-of-islam-3/archives-and-chanceries-pre-1500-inarabic-COM_24390 (accessed 30 Sept. 2015).

—— "The Attitude towards Knowledge in Mamlūk Egypt: Organisation and Structure of the Ṣubḥ al-Aʿshā by al-Qalqashandī (1355–1418)." In *Pre-Modern Encyclopaedic Texts, Proceedings of the Second COMERS Congress*, 159–68. Edited by Peter Binkley.. Leiden: E. J. Brill, 1997.

—— "A Well-Mannered Man of Letters or a Cunning Accountant: Al-Qalqashandī and the Historical Position of the Kātib". *Al-Masāq* 13, (2001): 87–96.

Veselý, Rudolf. "Chancery Manuals" In *Encyclopaedia of Islam, Three*. Brill Online: Reference Works (2001–): http://referenceworks.brillonline.com/entries/encyclopaedia-of-islam-3/chancery-manuals-COM_25491

Wiet, Gaston, "Les Classiques du scribe Egyptien au xve siècle". *Studia Islamica*, Vol. 17 (1963): 41–80.

Williams, Caroline. *Islamic Monuments in Cairo: A Practical Guide*. Cairo: American University in Cairo Press, 1999.

Winter, Michael. *Egyptian Society under Ottoman Rule, 1517–1798*. London: Routledge, 2005.

Wüstenfeld, Ferdinand Heinrich, "Calcaschandi's Geographie und Verwaltung von Ägypten: Aus dem Arabischen". *Two Studies on the Geography and Administration of Egypt according to al-Qalqašandī (d.1418)*. Edited by Fuat Sezgin et al. Frankfurt am Main: Institute for the History of Arabic-Islamic Science at the Johann Wolfgang Goethe University, 1992.

—— "Calcaschandi's Geographie und Verwaltung von Ägypten: Aus dem Arabischen". In Fuat Sezgin et al. (eds), *Texts and Studies on the Historical Geography and Topography of India and South East Asia* 2, 320–23. Stuttgart: Institute for the History of Arabic-Islamic Science at the Johann Wolfgang Goethe University, 1936.

Yasin, Abd al-Nasir. *Al-Asliḥa 'Abr al-'Uṣūr al-Islāmiyya: Al-Kitāb al-Awwal*. Cairo: Dar al-Qahira, 2007.

Zaki, Abd al-Rahman. *Mawsū'at Madīnat al-Qāhira fī Alf 'Ām*. Cairo: Anglo Egyptian Bookshop, 1987.

Websites

ArchNet. www.archnet.org (accessed 27 Oct. 2016).

Al-Bāḥith al-'Arabī http://www.baheth.info/ (accessed 27 Oct. 2016).

"Al-Qinṭār". *Umm al-Qurā University*. http://uqu.edu.sa/page/ar/76218 (accessed 1 May 2012).

Almaany. http://www.almaany.com/ (accessed 27 Oct. 2016).

Dictionary.com http://www.dictionary.com (accessed 27 Oct. 2016).

The Quranic Arabic Corpus. http://corpus.quran.com/ (accessed 1 May 2012).

"Ziyada," *Islamic Art Network*. http://www.islamic-art.org/Glossary/NewGlossary.asp?DisplayedChar=26 (accessed 1 May 2012).

INDEX

A
Acre, 70, 159, 161, 222
Aḥmad b. Ṭūlūn, 35, 39, 40, 44, 51, 60, 118, 119, 125, 177
ajlāb, 93, 376, 392
ajnād al-ḥalaqa, 252
al-ʿalāma al-sharīfa, 254
al-ʿasharāt, 143, 251
al-Afram, 55, 56
al-aḥbās, 173, 278, 279, 281, 284, 285
al-Aqmar, 65, 98, 100, 188, 199
al-ashrāf, 152, 186, 207, 227, 283
al-Ashraf Khalīl, 53, 105, 112, 236, 237, 288
al-Azhar, 55, 65, 82, 83, 96, 100, 101, 104, 188, 190, 204, 279
al-Baḥariyya, 79, 252
al-Bahnasā, 265, 321, 325, 326
al-bīmāristān, 278, 285
al-Buḥayra, 36, 181, 265, 266, 320, 322, 326, 327, 330
al-darj, 8, 165, 166, 207, 228, 254, 272, 361, 372, 379, 380, 427
al-dast, 6, 8, 9, 163, 165, 166, 227, 272, 354, 361, 379, 380, 427, 440
al-Dhahabiyya, 298
Aleppo, 79, 95, 132, 235
Alexandria, 32, 34, 36, 40, 48, 52, 56, 80, 93, 100, 104, 109, 119, 135, 150, 155, 158, 160, 176, 179, 181, 186, 222, 238, 245, 250, 264, 267, 283, 304, 305, 319, 320, 323, 324, 326, 331
al-Fayyūm, 265, 266, 321, 322, 330
al-Firāshkhānāh, 244
al-Gharbiyya, 158, 181, 186, 266, 322, 329
al-Ḥabbāniyya, 92, 95, 104
al-Ḥāfiẓ, 94, 95, 146, 158, 170, 197
al-Ḥākim, 46, 55, 66, 71, 72, 74, 78, 81, 82, 85, 86, 87, 91, 93, 94, 95, 96, 97, 98, 101, 105, 130, 159, 160, 161, 162, 188, 189, 201, 204, 208, 223, 250, 285, 311
al-ḥawā'ijkhānāh, 246
al-Ikhshīd, 40, 63
al-jaysh, 96, 167, 172, 223, 251, 252, 254, 255, 270, 271, 273, 278, 294, 295
al-kāfil, 113, 148, 253
al-Kāmil Muḥammad, 70, 87, 101, 110, 252
al-khamsāt, 143, 251
al-khāṣṣ, 52, 107, 118, 127, 129, 130, 135, 145, 149, 162, 172, 177, 178, 202, 212, 260, 269, 270, 272, 273, 274, 296, 302, 309
al-khaṭṭ al-mansūb, 393
al-khizāna al-kubrā, 135, 274
al-kittāniyya, 387
al-maʿmūra, 271, 274, 315, 392
al-Maḥalla, 181, 208, 266, 322
al-maḥmil, 306, 310, 311, 356, 390, 419
al-Mahrānī, 45, 46, 76
al-maḥrūsa, 275, 391
al-mamālīk al-sulṭāniyya, 116, 146, 251, 391, 433
al-Ma'mūn, (Abbasid Caliph), 83
al-Ma'mūn al-Baṭā'iḥī, 68, 69, 93,94
al-Manūfiyya, 329
al-Maqs, 55, 58, 66, 74, 75, 76, 77, 90, 91, 98, 100, 107, 212, 213, 223
al-maṭbakh, 247
al-mawārīth al-ḥashriyya, 176, 276, 396, 397
al-Maydān al-Akbar, 297
al-miqyās, 297
al-Misbaḥī, 101
al-Muʿizz, 6, 40, 45, 58, 61, 63, 64, 66, 68, 69, 70, 71, 72, 73, 74, 75, 77, 78, 79, 81, 82, 83, 84, 88, 94, 96, 97, 98, 99, 104, 107, 118, 145, 324, 328, 329

al-Mu'izz (Fatimid Caliph), 63, 64, 87, 221, 324, 329
al-Mu'izz Aybak al-Turkumānī, 44, 58, 97, 99, 118, 324, 328
al-Muṣtanṣir, 6
al-muṭawwaqūn, 136, 143, 185, 216
al-Nāṣir Ḥasan, 81, 102, 257
al-Nāṣir Muḥammad b. Qalāwūn, 52, 56, 66, 70, 71,72, 77, 85, 87, 92, 96, 99, 102, 105, 107, 111, 112, 113, 114, 117, 118, 119, 150, 236, 237, 249, 257, 269, 270, 284, 303, 308, 336, 337, 353, 355, 378, 381, 385, 392, 421, 429, 448
al-Qaḍā'ī, 30, 44, 46, 48, 53, 60, 89
al-Qaḍī al-Faḍil, 7
al-Qāhira, 45, 46, 51, 53, 61, 62, 63, 74, 92, 150, 310
al-Qalqashandī, 2, 3, 4, 5, 6, 9, 10, 11, 13, 14, 15, 16, 19, 20, 21, 22, 23, 24, 30, 41, 43, 47, 48, 52, 63, 70, 76, 77, 78, 84, 85, 87, 90, 91, 100, 106, 108, 112, 114, 118, 127, 129, 130, 132, 133, 136, 137, 139, 140, 155, 156, 161, 165, 166, 168, 171, 178, 183, 187,뵀190, 191, 193, 197, 202, 204, 212, 214, 226, 229, 233, 239, 240, 241, 245, 251, 259, 261, 262, 270, 275, 285, 288, 289, 291, 298, 299, 302, 304, 306, 310, 316, 324, 325, 329, 330
al-Raṣad, 55
al-Rawḍa, 44, 45, 46, 58, 110, 120
al-Rawḍa, 44, 51, 53, 62
al-rawk al-Nāṣirī, 150, 249
al-Ṣāliḥ Najm al-Dīn Ayyūb, 45, 64, 93, 97, 110, 118, 119, 252
al-Ṣāliḥ Ṭalā'i' b. Ruzayk, 47, 80, 99, 103
al-saqlāṭūn, 135, 426
al-Sayyida Ruqayya, 62
al-sharābkhānāh, 241, 242, 261
al-Sharqiyya, 135, 181, 186, 266, 311, 321, 322, 327, 328, 329
al-silāḥkhānāh, 244
al-Ṣinā'a, 44, 45, 58, 142, 178, 211, 212, 222, 277
al-ṣuḥba, 152, 216, 247, 260, 261, 270, 271, 278, 302
al-ṭablakhānāh, 240, 247, 248, 250
al-ṭibāq al-sulṭāniyya, 146, 441
al-Ṭishtkhānāh, 242
al-Ushmūnīn, 266, 321
al-ustādhūn al-muḥannakūn, 401, 445
al-wasāṭa, 148, 447
al-wizāra, 148, 184, 269, 270, 302, 403, 404, 447
al-Yānisiyya, 94
al-Ẓāhir Barqūq, 51, 52, 98, 102, 103, 117, 236, 252, 264, 265, 266, 276, 320, 321, 322, 326, see also Barquq.
al-Ẓāhir Baybars, 43, 45, 46, 52, 53, 59, 64, 66, 71, 91, 92, 96, 110, 111, 113, 114, 119, 279, 280, 285, 324
'Alī b. Abī Ṭālib, 32, 36, 47, 50, 62, 68, 172, 191, 203, 219, 283, 289, 324
'Amr b. al-'Āṣ (also 'Amr), 31, 32, 33, 34, 35, 36, 37, 38, 42, 43, 46, 48, 49, 50, 51, 53, 55, 58, 59, 76, 120, 160, 189, 204, 214, 218, 287, 323, 327, 381
'Aydhāb, 224, 267, 322
A'māl, 150, 156, 181, 200, 251, 265, 267, 271, 277, 280, 307, 319, 320, 321, 323, 326, 327, 329
Amir of ten, 236, 247, 261, 262, 263, 267, 268
Amirs of Hundreds, 242, 249, 301, 306, 315
arms, 130, 131, 138, 150, 191, 197, 218, 224, 244, 245, 256, 275, 294, 296, 299, 304, 305
arzāq, 169, 170, 226, 275, 301
Ascalon, 69, 85, 99, 104, 158, 222, 226
Asiūṭ, 265, 266, 267, 321, 322, 324
Aswan, 266, 322, 325, 326
Aswān, 266
atabek, 235, 255
Aybak, 29, 45, 52, 55, 56, 58, 73, 97, 99, 101, 118, 279, 324, 328
Ayyūb, 57, 58, 69, 70, 71, 74, 80, 81, 85, 87, 92, 93, 108, 110, 118, 139, 148, 234, 237, 252, 281, 328

B

Bāb, 30, 58, 65, 66, 67, 68, 69, 70, 71, 72, 73, 74, 75, 76, 77, 78, 80, 82, 83, 84, 85, 86, 89, 90, 91, 92, 93, 94, 95, 97, 98, 99, 100, 102, 107, 110, 111, 112, 113, 114, 115, 118, 137, 142, 145, 146, 178, 187, 189, 191, 192, 199, 201, 202, 204, 205, 206, 208, 209, 211, 212, 213, 217, 218, 223, 230, 231, 256, 257, 258, 259, 263, 264, 311, 320
Bāb al-Naṣr, 72, 97, 145, 191, 199, 205, 312
Bāb Zuwayla, 69, 73, 94
Badr al-Dīn al-Sanjārī, 280
Badr al-Jamali, 6
Baghdad, 31, 32, 40, 44, 88, 89, 107, 119, 134, 135, 160, 179, 193, 238, 310

banquet, 119, 142, 208, 210, 211, 216, 229, 230, 232, 233, 254, 260, 261, 264, 297, 298, 308, 309, 320, 342, 388
Barqa, 64, 75, 84, 95, 330, 331
Barqūq, 11, 12, 98, 103, 117, 242, 250, 310, 338, 339, 350, 354, 360, 361, 362, 378, 392
Bayn al-Qaṣrayn, 64, 65, 66, 74, 75, 101, 103, 188, 191, 194, 199, 214, 221, 231, 234, 285, 287
bayt al-māl, 127, 152, 156, 185, 193, 201, 205, 213, 214, 227, 234, 249, 269, 274, 281, 282, 283, 294, 319
Birkat al-Fīl, 62, 74, 87, 92, 93, 94, 95, 104, 117

C
Cairo, 30, 31, 32, 36, 37, 38, 39, 40, 41, 42, 43, 44, 45, 46, 51, 52, 53, 55, 56, 57, 58, 61, 62, 63, 64, 66, 67, 68, 69, 70, 71, 72, 73, 74, 75, 76, 77, 78, 79, 80, 81, 82, 83, 84, 85, 86, 87, 88, 89, 90, 91, 92, 94, 95, 96, 97, 99, 100, 102, 103, 104, 106, 107, 108, 109, 110, 111, 112, 113, 115, 119, 120, 121, 133, 134, 135, 138, 139, 141, 142, 145, 150, 155, 156, 160, 162, 163, 168, 175, 183, 184, 187, 188, 189, 190, 191, 193, 197, 204, 205, 209, 210, 211, 213, 218, 221, 223, 228, 230, 263, 264, 266, 280, 282, 283, 284, 295, 304, 306, 310, 312, 314, 319, 328
Caliph, 32, 33, 36, 37, 38, 39, 40, 41, 43, 46, 47, 48, 49, 50, 55, 58, 61, 66, 68, 69, 70, 71, 72, 73, 74, 75, 78, 79, 80, 81, 82, 83, 84, 85, 86, 87, 88, 90, 91, 93, 95, 97, 100, 101, 105, 130, 133, 137, 140, 144, 145, 158, 159, 160, 162, 170, 178, 179, 183, 185, 189, 190, 193, 194, 197, 199, 201, 202, 204, 205, 206, 208, 209, 210, 211, 212, 215, 220, 223, 227, 228, 250, 258, 282, 285, 289
Chancery, 112, 113, 155, 160, 161, 163, 164, 165, 166, 169, 174, 203, 207, 210, 254, 257, 302, 314
Chancery Bureau, 1, 2, 3, 4, 5, 7, 8, 12, 163, 207
collared amirs, 136, 143, 185, 203, 231
costumes, 288, 291, 293, 303, 305

D
daftar, 152, 166, 171, 172, 190, 207, 227, 228, 246, 352, 372, 424
Damanhūr, 181, 265, 266, 320, 322
Damascus, 50, 52, 63, 67, 70, 72, 80, 83, 99, 105, 111, 121, 128, 160, 182, 227, 235, 236, 240, 242, 304, 329
Damietta, 135, 160, 173, 176, 181, 222, 268, 322
dār al-ʿAdl, 112, 210, 247, 270, 279, 281, 294
dār al-Fiṭra, 83, 142, 172, 190, 231, 232, 233
dār al-Mulk, 137, 212, 213
dār al-wizāra, 209, 215
dawādār, 256, 257, 259, 272, 275, 285, 305, 313, 315, 317
dawādāriyya, 256, 257, 294
dihlīz, 113, 212, 252, 296, 299
dinars, 53, 60, 64, 120, 133, 139, 144, 152, 164, 174, 182, 192, 200, 222, 223, 226, 227, 228, 229, 301, 302, 308
dīwān, 1, 2, 3, 4, 5, 6, 8, 10, 21, 33, 53, 105, 155, 159, 162, 163, 164, 165, 166, 167, 168, 169, 170, 171, 173, 174, 175, 176, 177, 178, 203, 210, 222, 223, 226, 228, 234, 250, 251, 252, 254, 255, 259, 272, 273, 274, 276, 277, 278, 285, 302, 318
dīwān al-inshā', 1, 2, 3, 5, 8
dīwān al-mufrad, 250, 335, 362, 392, 427
drums, 132, 216, 247, 248, 262, 315

E
Egypt, 30, 31, 32, 36, 37, 38, 39, 40, 42, 43, 44, 46, 47, 48, 49, 50, 51, 53, 55, 57, 58, 59, 61, 62, 63, 64, 68, 69, 70, 72, 73, 74, 77, 78, 80, 81, 82, 85, 87, 96, 99, 103, 105, 109, 110, 111, 112, 119, 120, 121, 135, 139, 146, 150, 153, 154, 157, 158, 159, 160, 165, 171, 173, 174, 175, 176, 177, 179, 180, 181, 182, 187, 192, 200, 208, 210, 211, 222, 224, 227, 234, 235, 236, 237, 245, 249, 250, 251, 263, 264, 265, 266, 267, 268, 269, 270, 271, 273, 276, 277, 278, 279, 283, 284, 285, 286, 288, 293, 297, 299, 301, 303, 305, 306, 309, 310, 315, 319, 320, 321, 322, 323, 324, 325, 326, 327, 329

F
farrāsh, 39, 85, 133, 165, 363
Fatimid Caliphate, 91, 283
Fatimids, 20, 39, 40, 47, 61, 68, 69, 70, 74, 78, 83, 96, 109, 115, 119, 126, 128,

133, 134, 140, 144, 146, 154, 155, 157, 158, 168, 171, 172, 173, 177, 179, 187, 191, 192, 205, 214, 224, 225, 232, 234, 249, 288, 338, 352, 353, 355, 364, 382, 388, 389, 413, 415, 420, 422, 426, 430, 445, 448
firāshkhānāh, 244, 315
Friday prayers, 55, 56, 57, 63, 96, 99, 114, 206, 296
Fustat, 29, 31, 32, 33, 34, 35, 37, 38, 39, 40, 41, 42, 43, 44, 45, 46, 47, 48, 53, 55, 57, 58, 59, 60, 61, 62, 63, 74, 75, 76, 77, 92, 93, 106, 107, 108, 112, 115, 118, 119, 120, 137, 139, 141, 150, 154, 155, 181, 189, 204, 205, 212, 215, 224, 263, 280, 282, 283, 285, 287, 298, 312

G

ghulām, 40, 64, 73, 82, 109, 228, 365, 369
governor, 34, 109, 159, 160, 161, 180, 191, 197, 224, 265, 266, 267, 321, 322

H

ḥaḍra, 114, 148, 153, 158, 185, 202, 211, 213, 216, 227, 228, 232, 253, 254, 255, 264, 279, 280, 283, 302, 318
ḥājib, 82, 149, 155, 164, 165, 167, 170, 171, 186, 187, 188, 214, 254, 258, 261, 295, 313, 318, 319
ḥalaqa, 80, 101, 169, 251, 252, 264, 290, 297, 301, 302, 307, 319
ḥalwā', 231, 366
ḥamla, 366
Ḥanafī, 52, 58, 64, 69, 79, 98, 105, 154, 280, 281, 291, 295, 319, 320
Ḥanbalī, 52, 64, 66, 142, 242, 280, 281, 295
ḥikr, 70, 85, 119, 365, 367
Hijaz, 30, 63, 87, 142, 323, 326
ḥirāsat al-ṭayr, 263
ḥirrāqa, 91, 212, 298
ḥisba, 21, 156, 160, 282, 294, 295, 333, 368, 401

I

Ibn ʿAbd al-Ẓāhir, 35, 53, 62, 66, 69, 70, 72, 73, 74, 75, 77, 78, 79, 82, 84, 85, 86, 87, 89, 90, 91, 92, 93, 94, 95, 96, 97, 98, 100, 104, 105, 107, 109, 110, 117, 118, 139, 188, 218, 232, 280
Ibn al-Ṭuwayr, 46, 68, 98, 100, 126, 129, 130, 131, 132, 133, 134, 135, 136, 137, 138, 139, 140, 141, 142, 143, 144, 145, 148, 149, 152, 153, 154, 155, 156, 157, 159, 160, 161, 162, 163, 164, 165, 166, 167, 168, 169, 170, 171, 172, 173, 174, 175, 176, 177, 178, 182, 183, 184, 185, 186, 187, 188, 189, 190, 191, 192, 193, 194, 195, 196, 197, 198, 199, 200, 201, 202, 203, 204, 205, 206, 207, 208, 209, 210, 211, 212, 213, 214, 215, 216, 217, 218, 219, 220, 221, 222, 223, 225, 226, 227, 228, 229, 230, 231, 232, 233, 234
Ibn Ṭūlūn, 39, 40, 41, 42, 44, 53, 54, 62, 63, 87, 92, 93, 97, 125, 189, 204, 211, 215, 218, 287
ʿĪd, 40, 65, 67, 68, 71, 83, 84, 85, 107, 117, 142, 172, 192, 193, 205, 206, 208, 209, 210, 213, 230, 231, 232, 233, 286, 305, 309
ʿĪd al-Aḍḥā, 40, 67, 142, 230, 286
ʿImād al-Dīn Zankī, 235
imam, 103, 104, 109, 203, 204
imrat jāndār, 259
ʿiṣāba, 236, 239, 371, 426
iqama, 370
iqṭāʿ, 118, 168, 169, 170, 250, 254, 255, 290, 301, 302, 327, 328, 333, 337, 348, 358, 359, 361, 362, 370, 371, 375, 399, 404, 444
iqṭāʿāt, 168, 169, 170, 171, 196, 222, 226, 227, 249, 251, 252, 253, 255, 273, 301, 302
isfihsalār, 149, 185, 197, 202, 206, 234, 247, 341, 371
ishāra, 253, 254, 257, 273, 372, 405
istīfā' al-dawla, 271, 278
istifāḍa, 60, 372
istīmār, 171, 173, 174, 372
iṭlāqāt, 101, 118, 141, 271, 275, 302
iwan, 66, 71, 101, 102, 111, 112, 114, 115, 118, 178, 183, 192, 208, 213, 233, 238, 247, 254, 295, 295, 297, 308, 313, 320, 353, 373, 430, 432
ʿIzz al-Dīn Aybak al-Afram. See Aybak

J

jālīsh, 236, 240, 373, 426
jamadār, 294, 374, 446
jāmakiyya, 222, 290, 374
janā'ib, 296, 298, 300, 374, 433
jarīda, 222, 374
jāshankīr, 260, 297, 374
jawālī, 173, 176, 228, 369, 375, 423

jawāshin, 138, 375
Jawhar al-Ṣaqalli (also Jawhar), 6, 40, 43, 58, 61, 63, 64, 66, 69, 71, 72, 73, 74, 75, 76, 77, 78, 80, 81, 82, 83, 84, 85, 86, 87, 88, 96, 100, 107, 151, 161, 162, 205, 221
jihad, 178, 222
jilbān, 93, 354, 376, 392
jirāya, 169, 226, 376
judge, 41, 52, 56, 69, 70, 73, 76, 79, 81, 82, 85, 88, 99, 104, 107, 109, 116, 118, 139, 153, 154, 155, 156, 164, 186, 188, 190, 195, 201, 202, 203, 206, 209, 217, 228, 229, 234, 279, 280, 281, 286, 295, 306, 319, 320
jūkandār, 305, 376

K

Ka'ba, 351, 356, 377, 383, 387, 398, 415, 417
kalawta, 236, 303, 377
kantar, 187, 208, 233, 378
kārim, 224, 379
kāshif, 251, 265, 266, 320, 321, 379
kātib al-sirr, 3, 4, 5, 7, 8, 9, 12, 53, 112, 163, 165, 166, 227, 253, 257, 259, 270, 294
khādim, 69, 80, 85, 95, 98, 103, 261
Khalīj, 45, 46, 58, 62, 74, 75, 76, 88, 89, 90, 91, 92, 99, 117, 141, 172, 182, 209, 212, 214, 215, 217, 218, 297, 298, 344, 381, 382, 445
khan, 382
Khān Masrūr, 100
khānqāh, 57, 59, 193, 382, 421, 450
khanqas, 59, 98, 103, 106, 281
kharkāh, 299, 311, 383
khāṣṣa, 111, 130, 144, 194, 308, 383, 384, 385, 442
khāṣṣakiyya, 116, 146, 347, 383
khaṭīb, 99, 109, 188, 202, 219, 228, 279, 285, 286, 296, 383, 384
khawāṣṣ, 111, 112, 115, 116, 117, 118, 144, 150, 164, 179, 186, 195, 213, 229, 231, 233, 298, 300, 307, 309, 383, 384
khawkha, 65, 83, 384
khazā'in al-silāḥ, 139, 191, 224, 275
khāzindār, 151, 152, 260, 384
khidma, 114, 115, 116, 118, 149, 157, 165, 173, 174, 175, 176, 177, 178, 186, 189, 194, 195, 196, 199, 200, 208, 209, 216, 220, 242, 254, 259, 297, 308, 318, 319, 320, 383, 384, 385, 427
khiṭaṭ (also khiṭṭa), 30, 32, 34, 35, 36, 40, 41, 42, 43, 45, 46, 47, 49, 51, 52, 53, 54, 55, 57, 58, 59, 62, 64, 65, 66, 68, 69, 70, 71, 72, 73, 74, 75, 77, 78, 79, 80, 81, 82, 83, 84, 85, 86, 87, 88, 89, 90, 91, 92, 93, 94, 95, 96, 97, 98, 99, 100, 101, 102, 104, 105, 107, 108, 109, 110, 117, 118, 120, 132, 133, 134, 135, 136, 137, 138, 139, 142, 146, 150, 156, 174, 177, 179, 184, 190, 191, 193, 195, 196, 197, 198, 199, 200, 204, 207, 210, 211, 212, 213, 214, 216, 217, 218, 220, 223, 229, 230, 232, 233, 236, 237, 284, 287, 390, 394
khiwān, 308, 385
khizānat al-khāṣṣ, 272, 385
khūdha, 138, 386
khushkanān, 208, 233, 386
khuṭba, 56, 57, 88, 96, 98, 99, 101, 103, 386, 396
khuwadh. See khūdha
kīmān, 44, 387
kitābiyya, 387
kura, 119, 239, 297, 305, 307, 308, 376, 387, 388
kushshāf, 251, 265, 321
kuttābiyya, 387

M

madrasa, 45, 51, 57, 58, 59, 64, 66, 69, 67, 68, 71, 80, 81, 85, 101, 102, 103, 105, 142, 158, 279, 285, 286, 367, 390, 425, 446
mā'ida, 216, 229, 391, 396, 424
mail, 51, 138, 256, 259, 272, 302, 314
majlis, 111, 151, 152, 154, 165, 166, 168, 171, 178, 183, 184, 186, 188, 190, 193, 195, 207, 216, 227, 228, 230, 253, 256, 280, 315, 317
maks, 90, 177, 382, 391
māl, 54, 90, 139, 150, 177, 181, 234, 271, 316, 319, 323, 333, 336, 359, 382, 383, 391, 396, 411, 434, 446
Mālikī, 52, 64, 81, 85, 158, 280, 281, 295, 319, 320
mamluk, 55, 60, 64, 72, 75, 76, 83, 99, 119, 129, 144, 207, 235, 240, 246, 254, 289, 317, 327
mamluks, 38, 40, 52, 73, 75, 79, 84, 93, 116, 118, 143, 145, 146, 156, 236, 250, 251, 252, 257, 260, 261, 273, 282, 294, 296, 298, 300, 307, 311, 315, 316, 319, 328

Manfalūṭ, 267, 322
manjanīq, 223, 393
manshūr, 253, 302, 325, 393
manẓara, 55, 68, 91, 119, 187, 212, 215, 216, 217, 223, 348, 393
maqṣūra, 50, 114, 155, 202, 204, 238, 296
martaba, 17, 114, 164, 170, 171, 184, 185, 193, 215, 238, 395
Masālik al-Abṣār (also Masālik), 42, 105, 106, 107, 108, 110, 115, 132, 169, 196, 222, 236, 249, 250, 251, 252, 253, 254, 255, 256, 257, 258, 259, 260, 269, 270, 271, 272, 274, 275, 282, 288, 290, 291, 292, 293, 294, 295, 296, 298, 299, 300, 301, 302, 303, 304, 305, 306, 307, 308, 309, 313, 314, 315, 316, 318, 319, 327, 330
maṣāṭib, 205, 212
mashhad, 62, 65, 69, 99, 189
masnad, 154, 164, 165, 170, 396
maydān, 40, 79, 117, 118, 119, 120, 200, 238, 296
Mecca, 32, 49, 50, 63, 68, 158, 234, 290, 306, 310, 312
Men of the Pen, 136, 153, 157, 159, 161, 162, 173, 194, 200, 246, 269, 274, 295, 297, 302, 305, 307, 308, 313
Men of the Sword, 6, 20, 136, 143, 148, 159, 161, 163, 194, 200, 203, 249, 253, 269, 270, 286, 288, 297, 303, 307, 313, 319
mihrab, 49, 50, 51, 52, 53, 54, 55, 66, 67, 97, 201, 203, 205, 206, 219, 287, 296
minbar, 49, 51, 59, 81, 114, 155, 188, 201, 202, 203, 205, 206, 207, 238
miqyās, 425
Miṣr, 29, 30, 31, 32, 40, 43, 46, 52, 56, 57, 58, 60, 75, 87, 106, 107, 109, 117, 119, 133, 137, 138, 150, 155, 156, 160, 178, 183, 189, 190, 204, 211, 212, 214, 215, 218, 228, 263, 276, 277, 280, 282, 303
miẓalla, 128, 149, 194, 196, 202, 206, 211, 215, 296, 297
mubāshir, 104, 169, 173, 269, 399, 448
muazzin (muezzin), 187, 53, 281, 398, 400
muftī, 281, 400
muḥannakūn, 68, 144, 151, 188, 191, 196, 197, 199, 203, 209, 213, 214, 215, 216, 227, 231, 401, 445
muḥtasib, 37, 155, 156, 281, 282, 283, 295, 306, 311, 319, 368, 400, 401, 402
Muḥyi al-Dīn b. ʿAbd al-Ẓāhir, 46, 70, 76, 73, 82, 88, 104, 107, 109, 116, 139, 280
mujawwama, 206, 402
munākh, 64, 115, 141, 142, 228, 315, 368, 402, 403
Munūf, 181, 266, 322
muqaddam, 80, 94, 114, 147, 149, 153, 223, 233, 256, 265, 300, 320, 350, 392, 403
muqṭaʿ, 301, 375, 404
murtaziq, 140, 169, 226, 404
muṣallā, 40, 205, 206, 208, 404
musaṭṭaḥ, 222, 404
musawwama, 290, 292, 405
mushāwara, 256, 258, 294, 372, 405
mustaʿriba, 37, 84, 323, 405
mustakhdam, 140, 405
mustakhdamīn, 140, 173, 175, 228, 250, 251, 275, 335, 392, 405
mustaṣnaʿūn, 405
mustawfī, 174, 178, 228, 270, 271, 272, 274, 277, 302, 319, 351, 385, 397, 404, 406, 407, 410
mutaʿammimīn, 246, 252, 270, 397, 406
muwashshaḥa, 206, 208, 407

N

nadd muthallath, 201, 408, 442
nafṭ, 298, 312, 408
naqd, 409
naqib, 409
nassākhūn, 86, 447
nawāḥī, 276, 280, 284, 285, 320, 321, 322, 408, 409
nāẓir, 3, 89, 101, 105, 131, 171, 228, 255, 260, 269, 270, 271, 272, 273, 274, 278, 279, 281, 284, 286, 294, 295, 296, 297, 306, 310, 311, 319, 320, 360, 361, 362, 380, 385, 386, 396, 407, 409, 410, 411, 424, 434, 446, 448
nāẓir al-dawla, 270, 271, 274
nāẓir al-jaysh, 255, 273, 295
nāẓir al-māl, 269, 270
Nile, 30, 42, 43, 44, 45, 46, 47, 51, 53, 55, 56, 58, 66, 76, 77, 90, 91, 92, 99, 106, 107, 115, 117, 118, 119, 135, 137, 141, 180, 181, 191, 200, 210, 211, 212, 213, 214, 215, 217, 218, 223, 266, 277, 297, 298, 324
Nilometer, 210, 211, 213, 214, 297
niyāba, 157, 253, 265, 269
Nubia, 49

P

parasol, 128, 129, 149, 194, 195, 202, 206, 208, 211, 215, 217, 218, 296, 297, 299
Prince of the Faithful, 46, 49, 120, 166, 179, 186, 188, 202, 207, 219, 220, 324
procession, 92, 112, 115, 116, 127, 128, 129, 131, 132, 150, 180, 182, 183, 187, 189, 191, 192, 194, 196, 197, 198, 199, 200, 202, 204, 205, 208, 211, 212, 213, 214, 215, 217, 218, 230, 236, 245, 247, 250, 254, 259, 264, 275, 283, 297, 299, 300, 306, 308, 310, 312, 313, 318, 320, 327
Prophet, 30, 31, 32, 33, 35, 36, 37, 39, 43, 46, 47, 48, 49, 50, 51, 52, 53, 54, 59, 65, 67, 68, 71, 73, 96, 101, 109, 121, 128, 129, 152, 155, 172, 187, 189, 190, 203, 206, 224, 273, 282, 283, 286, 292, 310, 323, 324, 325, 326, 330

Q

Qāʿat al-Dhahab, 178, 183, 184, 186, 195, 196, 210, 208, 220, 229, 230, 233
qāḍī al-ʿaskar, 281, 412
qāḍī al-quḍāt, 52, 56, 153, 186, 350, 352, 413, 414
Qalāwūn, 53, 64, 66, 79, 101, 102, 105, 110, 111, 112, 113, 119, 236, 237, 252, 285, 288, 303, 307, 308
Qalyūb, 181, 268
qanādīl, 59, 189, 414
qānāt, 313, 415
qanṭara, 62, 74, 92, 415
qarabūs, 291, 415
qarāfa, 120, 263, 415
qarāniṣa, 392, 405
Qarmatians, 74, 83, 87, 415, 416
qarqalāt, 244, 416
qaṣaba, 41, 416
Qaṭyā, 268
Qaysaba b. Kulthūm al-Tujībī, 48
qaysāriyya., 382, 446, 447
qibla, 49, 50, 51, 53, 97, 310, 326, 377, 394, 398, 417
qirṭās, 165, 417
qisiy al-lawlab, 139, 418, 447
qisiy al-rijl wa-l-rikāb, 138, 198, 351, 418
qudūr, 418
Qūṣ, 43, 96, 104, 158, 180, 181, 186, 224, 266, 267, 322, 323, 326

R

Ramadan, 40, 67, 96, 97, 142, 172, 200, 201, 202, 204, 205, 207, 218, 224, 229, 233, 294, 309
rank, 3, 38, 64, 105, 134, 141, 143, 145, 148, 150, 153, 155, 159, 163, 164, 167, 173, 181, 194, 236, 249, 250, 251, 253, 257, 258, 260, 262, 263, 264, 265, 266, 267, 268, 270, 281, 283, 289, 291, 301, 302, 304, 305, 307, 311, 313, 317, 319, 320, 321, 322, 327, 329, 334, 335, 336, 337, 338, 340, 344, 358, 362, 368, 378, 392, 395, 400, 403, 410, 413, 420, 429, 435, 436, 444
ra's nawba, 256, 315
Rāshida, 33, 55, 100
rashshāshīn, 229, 420
rawk, 150, 249, 276, 336, 409, 420, 421
ribats, 59, 103, 121, 284
rikābiyya, 130, 149, 191, 196, 197, 202, 218, 229, 259, 363, 422
riwāq, 51, 184, 185, 422
riyāsa, 422
Rūm, 30, 33, 34, 35, 41, 44, 82, 86, 146, 328

S

ṣāḥib, 3, 53, 85, 105, 127, 148, 151, 152, 164, 165, 166, 168, 184, 185, 192, 193, 195, 196, 201, 205, 207, 213, 216, 227, 228, 229, 234, 255, 269, 271, 273, 274, 297, 361, 380, 383, 396, 410, 411, 424, 425, 433, 448
saḥib al-barid, 6
ṣāḥib dīwān al-jaysh, 273
Ṣalāḥ al-Dīn, 39, 57, 58, 64, 67, 68, 69, 70, 72, 74, 75, 76, 79, 80, 85, 89, 95, 103, 104, 108, 109, 110, 112, 113, 115, 117, 118, 139, 148, 171, 176, 177, 179, 234, 237, 281, 284, 287, 327
Salaḥ al-Dīn al-Ayyubī, 7, 103, 104
Saljuqs, 88, 255, 425, 426, 449
ṣamṣām, 130, 426
sanjaq, 236, 240, 426
ṣaqāliba, 426
Sawākin, 224
sayfiyya, 392, 405
shabbāba, 240, 264, 266, 320, 322
shādd, 105, 227, 242, 261, 262, 263, 269, 270, 410, 428, 448
shadd al-ʿamā'ir, 263
shadd al-dawāwīn, 262

shaddat al-waqār, 126, 151, 428, 436, 448
Shāfi'ī, 47, 52, 54, 56, 58, 64, 85, 101, 108, 154, 225, 234, 279, 280, 281, 286, 287, 291, 295, 319
shāsh, 236, 303, 304, 377, 429
shaṭfa, 311, 317, 429
Shāwir al-Sa'dī, 43, 103
shikār, 262
shiyya, 168, 430
shubbāk, 192, 193, 208, 213, 430, 432
shurṭa, 150, 263, 314, 447
ṣibyān al-ḥujar, 145, 153, 431, 432
ṣibyān al-khāṣṣ, 412, 431
silāḥ, 130, 131, 138, 183, 197, 198, 218, 244, 245, 256, 297
Siryāqūs, 284, 429
slaughterground, 209
Sufis, 57, 68, 103, 284
Sultan al-Malik al-Ẓāhir, 52, 117, 279
Sultanic Mamluks, 116, 243, 246, 250, 251, 256, 273, 302, 307, 311
ṣunūj, 197, 198, 351, 433, 434
Syria, 31, 51, 58, 63, 72, 80, 110, 149, 181, 182, 250, 264, 269, 270, 271, 273, 279, 293, 301, 305, 308, 327

T

ṭabar, 244, 262, 435
ṭabardāriyya, 150, 262, 296
ṭablakhānāh, 116, 118, 143, 236, 240, 247, 250, 251, 256, 257, 259, 260, 261, 262, 263, 264, 265, 266, 267, 268, 302, 307, 315, 316, 319, 320, 321, 322, 336, 338, 341, 374, 403, 426, 435
Ṭablakhānākh, 435
ṭablkhānāh, 315
tadhākir, 174, 175, 182, 373, 436
tāj, 126, 151, 206, 227, 351, 436
Tāj al-Dīn 'Abd al-Wahhāb b. Bint al-A'azz, 279
tājir al-khāṣṣ, 437
takbīr, 206, 437
takht al-mulk, 114, 237, 294, 295, 437
taqālīd, 253, 279
Taqiy al-Dīn al-Subkī, 52, 53
taqlīd, 144, 253, 280, 304, 320, 325, 438, 445
ṭarrāḥa, 165, 169, 201, 205, 206, 216, 439
tashārīf, 135, 172, 293, 303, 330, 439
taswīgh, 167, 274, 439
ṭawāriq, 119, 120, 439
ṭawāshī, 74, 75, 78, 108, 144, 151, 403, 439
tawqī', 6, 7, 136, 164, 165, 166, 167, 253, 270, 272, 336, 361, 375, 379, 380, 396, 414, 440
ṭaylasān, 202, 213, 291, 441
thughūr, 176, 222, 441
ṭirāz, 81, 130, 135, 173, 206, 238, 239, 305, 317, 402, 442
ṭisht dāriyya, 243, 442
ṭishtkhānāh, 241, 243, 315
ṭulb, 240, 315, 327, 442, 444
Tulunid Mosque, 53, 93
Tulunids, 39, 54, 179, 442
turba, 442
Turkish, 43, 44, 58, 79, 86, 88, 99, 101, 128, 138, 149, 160, 161, 168, 226, 235, 236, 237, 252, 259, 297, 317, 324, 328
Tyre, 104, 182, 222

U

umad al-ḥadīd, 191, 371, 443
Umayyads, 4, 38, 47, 146, 238, 258, 365, 426, 443
Upper Egypt, 80, 175, 265, 266, 283, 321, 322, 323, 325, 326
Urūḍ, 169, 444
ushāqiyya, 239, 444
Ushmūm, 181, 268, 322
ustādār, 98, 152, 247, 260, 261, 274, 297, 300, 305, 315
ustādh, 63, 144, 164, 191, 216, 445

V

Viceroys, 180, 264, 319
Vizier (also wazir), 59, 100, 101, 113, 133, 151, 160, 163, 192, 193, 194, 197, 198, 199, 203, 206, 209, 227, 255, 305

W

wafā' al-Nīl, 200, 210, 297, 445
wakīl bayt al-māl, 333, 446
Wālī, 263, 266, 267, 268, 322
wālī al-madīna, 319, 446
waqf, 47, 55, 58, 70, 101, 104, 105, 167, 285, 311, 343, 367, 436, 446
warrāqūn, 86, 447
wilāya, 150, 181, 263, 264, 266, 267, 304, 320, 447
wizārat al-tafwīḍ, 448
wulāt, 150, 156, 180, 204, 228, 251, 253, 263, 265, 266, 314, 319, 321, 325

Y
Ya'qūb. Killis, 6
yashm, 290, 449

Z
zaffa, 245, 259, 299, 449
zard, 138, 197, 244, 259, 375, 432
zardakāsh, 245, 449
zardiyyāt, 138, 449
zardkhānāh, 244, 259, 315
zimām, 132, 145, 149, 151, 153, 185, 186, 193, 207, 227, 261
ziyyāda, 97, 154, 189
zunnārī, 292, 304, 450
zuqāq, 59, 72, 82, 84, 450
Zuwayla, 69, 71, 73, 74, 80, 81, 82, 83, 93, 94, 95, 98, 99, 211, 214